Multiculturalism:

A Critical Reader

For Gabriel, that the experience of his generation may
be more heterogeneous than the experience of mine

Multiculturalism:

A Critical Reader

David Theo Goldberg

BLACKWELL
Oxford UK & Cambridge USA

Copyright © Basil Blackwell Ltd 1994

First published 1994

Blackwell Publishers, the publishing imprint of Basil Blackwell Inc.
238 Main Street
Cambridge, Massachusetts 02142
USA

Basil Blackwell Ltd
108 Cowley Road
Oxford OX4 1JF
UK

Library of Congress Cataloging in Publication Data

Multiculturalsm: a critical reader / David Theo Goldberg.
    p.   cm.
Includes bibliographical references and index.
ISBN 0–631–18911–4 (alk. paper) — ISBN 0–631–18912–2 (pbk. : alk. paper)
  1. Multiculturalism — United States.   2. Pluralism (Social sciences) — United States. 3. United States — Ethnic relations.   4. United States — Race relations.
I. Goldberg, David Theo.
E184.A1M82 1994   94-34632
305.8'00973—dc20   CIP

British Library Cataloguing in Publication Data

A CIP catalogue record for this book is available from the British Library.

Typeset in 10 on 12 pt. Times Roman by Publication Assistance Center,
College of Public Programs, Arizona State University

Printed in Great Britain by Hartnolls Ltd, Bodmin

This book is printed on acid-free paper

Contents

89820

PART II: BREAKING THE BOUNDS OF DISCIPLINES

Preface

Multiculturalism: A Reader delineates the prevailing concerns and considerations, principles and practices, concepts and categories that fall under the rubric of "multiculturalism." Contributors spell out what they take multiculturalism to be committed to as much as against, what visions of education and knowledge and social relations form its fabric, what metaphors structure its representations in and across and beyond traditional definitions of the disciplines, what practices are encouraged by its articulations and expressions, and how these practices differ from and are opposed to and undertake to overthrow or go beyond those that are given and presumed that constitute the tradition and prevailing forms of common sense.

There are few societies in the world today not marked by multicultural heterogeneity of one kind and degree or another. Those who find themselves in one multicultural context might learn from or illuminate conditions in another. Contemporary South Africa, say, is often encouraged to benefit from attention to experiences in the United States; less emphasized is the fact that the United States now might well benefit from recent experiences in South Africa. Consider the success of the voter turnout campaign in South Africa's first free election in April 1994 and the implications for a democratic culture. Beyond these comparative possibilities, though, robust multicultural commitments would seem to suggest a specificity of multicultural conditions to a local social context. Contributors to this volume accordingly have focused our discussion primarily around the contemporary US experience, even as we note the importance of taking seriously multicultural conditions globally and their implications for the debates in the United States. This is not to say the book will not be useful to those in other societies struggling with multicultural issues; it is simply to own up explicitly to the primary social context framing the volume's contributors.

The debates around multiculturalism are also multi- and interdisciplinary. They necessarily involve politics and pedagogy, science and social science, the humanities and cultural studies, women's studies and ethnic studies, race, ethnicity, class, gender, nation, public administration, law, and political economy. Contributions to this volume weave across and between this traditional disciplinary architecture, collapsing the presumptive structures and running together objects of analysis all too readily disarticulated for the sake of simplicity.

The idea for this book developed out of a series of coffee-table conversations, bar-room banter, and telephone talk between Stephan Chambers and myself, joined occasionally by Andrew McNeillie. The book would not have materialized but for their insight, patience, and expertise, and the productive support of the Blackwell's bunch. Nor would it have materialized but for the incredible researching skills and tireless assistance of Barbara Jean Lammi, as well as the fabulous publishing facility of Janet Soper and her staff in the Publication Assistance Office, College of Public Programs, at Arizona State University. Janet courageously saw the book to completion despite life-threatening illness. As always, Kay Korman of the School of Justice Studies made my life administratively manageable throughout the process of production. I am grateful also to Anne Schneider, Dean of the College of Public Programs at ASU, for supporting in part the work that produced the reader. Pietro Toggia offered valuable research assistance along the way. In preparing the manuscript, I was lucky enough to benefit from a fine job of generous copyediting by Marian Buckley and from extensive conversations about multiculturalism and cultural studies with Shea McManus and Pat Lauderdale.

The timeliness of the book was supported by the enthusiasm of responses I received from those who found themselves unable to contribute and especially from the contributors whose gracious efforts transformed the chores of editing into a pleasurable experience. Kari Weil kindly made possible the inclusion of Barbara Christian's article.

In our own ways, Alena, Gabriel, and I form a micro-multicultural community. Lapsed Czech, South African, Protestant-Catholic, and Jew, living agnostic Americans all, critical dissidents to a fault. In the decade-long experiment, we have passed through exquisite pleasures and intense tensions, deep insights and deeper misunderstandings, difficult decisions and exhilarating changes. Given the choice, I can only say: I would do it all again.

GENERAL INTRODUCTION

Introduction:
Multicultural Conditions[1]

DAVID THEO GOLDBERG

"Oh, send him somewhere where they will teach him to think for himself!"

Mrs. Shelley answered: "Teach him to think for himself? Oh, my God, teach him rather to think like other people!"

Matthew Arnold, Essays in Criticism

Over the past decade or so, multiculturalism has been both championed and maligned. In the way proponents tend to talk past each other in debates about pedagogy and politics, multiculturalism has been idealized and dismissed as pedagogical instrument and political purpose. The praise is often uncritical, the condemnation distorted in ways bordering on the intentional. In the drive to characterize multiculturalism, to fix its meanings and delimit its possibilities by defining it in terms of necessary and sufficient conditions, it has been reduced to one or other of the competing components in a set of distorting contrasts: political doctrine or pervasive discourse, intellectual paradigm or philosophical episteme, pedagogical framework or ivory tower academic rhetoric, newly emergent institutional(ized) orthodoxy or radical critique.[2]

The multicultural condition, perhaps not unlike the condition of postmodernity, nevertheless cannot be reductively defined. Rather, it can be described phenomenologically; its conditions of possibility and transformation specified; its modes of expression characterized; its history periodized by delineating its forms of occurrence. Multiculturalism, as Peter Caws emphasizes ("Identity: Cultural, Transcultural, Multicultural"), stands for a wide range of social articulations, ideas, and practices that the "-ism" reduces to a formal singularity, fixing it into a cemented condition, the ideology of "political correctness."[3] Thus converted into the fundamentals of an "-ism," the heterogeneity characteristic of multicultural conditions is reduced to a pat and pedestrian doctrine, the dogma of presumptive correctness easily dismissed as politics hiding in an academic gown. The ghost of Socrates returns as Nietzsche to subvert the youth. The political trial no longer needs an apologetic court of law, only the mediated people's court of dismissive public opinion raising the specter of apocalyptic impropriety.

Proponents of multiculturalism, in many instances, are implicated in this reduction in terms of what they say and fail to and in relation to their expressed commitments and their lack. *Multiculturalism: A Critical Reader*, by contrast, is concerned primarily with the theoretical, philosophical, pedagogical, and political presuppositions and implications of multicultural commitments rather than with their superficial expressions, reactive responses to standard reductive criticisms, or facile charges of "political correctness." *Multiculturalism*, then, delineates the prevailing concerns and considerations, principles and practices, concepts and categories that now fall under the rubric of "multiculturalism." Contributors spell out critically the vision of knowledge and education as well as the social relations forming its fabric. Analytic focus is directed to a variety of related objects: to the metaphors structuring representations of the multicultural in and across and beyond traditional definitions of the disciplines; to the practices encouraged and represented by way of multicultural articulations and expressions; and to how these practices and their representations differ from, are opposed to, and undertake to overthrow or go beyond those that are given and presumed, those seemingly constitutive of the tradition and prevailing forms of common sense.

Thus, contributors to *Multiculturalism* interrogate the sets of relations between the principles and practices of multicultural expression, namely, between the theoretical claims constitutive of multiculturalisms and the praxis such theoretical claims evoke, and between the commitments to specific practices representative of multicultural conditions and the theoretical claims sustaining them. *Multiculturalism* explores the assertive foundations of disciplines, scrutinizing the boundaries of subjects, conceived as agents and disciplines. It pursues the interdisciplinary interpellation of (or calling to) subjectivity from within while transgressively challenging the confinements, the borders, of established institutional structures, subjects and subjectivities, and imposed disciplinary forms. Themes analyzed include the relations between Self and Other, selves and others, Subjects and subjects; between knowledge, power, pedagogy, politics, and empowerment. They also include relations between the states of national political formations and local and transnational capitals; between the institutionalized power of managed multiculturalism in the academy and the politics of insurgent, polyvalent, and critical multiculturalisms; between disciplinary definition and canonical confinement, inter- and trans- and postdisciplinarity. And they cover relations between the sciences, social sciences, and humanities; between meaning, ambiguity, and representation; between History and multiple, intersecting histories, Reason and rationalities; between culture, domination, resistance, and self-assertion; and, broadly conceived, between identities and differences, homogeneity and heterogeneity.

The reader is divided into two parts: "Thinking the Unthinkable: Setting Agendas" and "Breaking the Bounds of Disciplines." This partition should not be seen to reflect a proposed division between theory and practice. Rather, it reflects a rough distinction, points of emphasis, between the general and the particular: between the broad principles and practices articulating multicultural expression in any manifestation, and the ways these practical principles and principled practices prompt from within the confines of established institutional structures and imposed disciplinary forms the boundary transgression of inter- and transdisciplinarity. In this sense, the division into parts represents alternative points of approach to a common undertaking, though not to a predefined end. If the reader has a political purpose, then, it is to reflect the projected openness of multicultural projects, their pluralities rather than its pluralism, their antihegemonic thrusts rather than its univocity and singularity.

Most criticisms of multiculturalism disarticulate it, or the social expressions with which it is reductively identified, from the historical conditions of its emergence. But multiculturalism has a history. To begin to do justice to this history one needs to get clear about the monocultural commitments to which multiculturalism arose in response, what it is thus baldly against. In setting *the* self-understanding of the American academy, of what has defined it hegemonically for much of the twentieth century, monoculturalism is not uniquely determined by rational choice; it is not in this sense the *end* of historical progress. Monoculturalism, too, has a history: conditions of emergence, transformation, reification, resistance, and dissolution. To insist on monoculturalism's naturalism, on the presumption that it is the natural outcome of rational determination and thus universally ordained, is effectively to deny — to cover up — this history, to constitute it in this scheme of things as singularly rational. I turn first to a genealogy of monocultural conditions.

A History of Monoculturalism

While the institutional history of universities in the United States can be traced back to the inception of the Republic, monoculturalism as institutional ideology only emerged late in the nineteenth century to create the impression of an intellectual tradition where there was indeed none. The perceived need for tradition was fulfilled by the impression, a reconstructed reflection, of (and on) European cultural production, separate and unequal, represented in Arnoldian terms as "the best that has been said and thought in the world."[4] The universe of discourses that the idea of the university has been taken conceptually to signify[5] gave way immediately to (if it did not already conceptually presuppose) the discourse of universality, the insistence that the university stood for and on the unwavering and singular standard of universal truth. Local knowledge was effaced in the name of universalizing local standards as rationally required. By the middle of the twentieth century, this reflection of Europe had stiffened into the presumption of a given, the impression hardening into the Humean idea(l) of tradition. This idea(l) was then read back to fashion a history and an imagined academic community as exclusive and exclusionary as the political institutions and institutional politics it purported to represent but upon which it actually was impressed. In this sense, monoculturalism reflected, while it simultaneously reproduced, the lines of ethnoracialized demarcation initiated by US immigration policy accompanied by the encouragement of emigration. "Keeping America White" was as much an educational mandate of American culture as it was the eugenic end of American politics.[6]

By mid-century, this monocultural, ethnoracial Eurovision had become cemented in the United States as hegemonic intellectual ideology and institutional practice. It was virtually impossible without extreme marginalization to think and do other than in and through its terms. At the same time, the economy and technology of the world-system began to give way to US dominance, if not to outright domination. On the world stage, geopolitics got managed, indeed, (re)produced, in terms of the cold war formations of First and Second Worlds. The Third World was literally, and literarily, (re)created as a by-product and fodder for the commonly white ("Caucasian"?) Euro-American and Euro-Soviet (largely Russian) interests and appetites.[7] Knowledge production, sustained and constrained by monocultural presumptions, played a crucial role in perpetuating the cold war division between East and West and, thus, in covering over a certain confluence of colonizing interests vis-à-vis the "Third World." Area studies and applied social science (for which the Soviet sphere of influence had its counterparts) sprung forth to (in)form the instrumental geopolitical interests and strategies of dominant state powers. Of course, instrumentalities may have opened up possibilities for the emergence and development of intrinsic interests. The work of Placide Tempels on Bantu philosophy and Terence Ranger's inaugural lecture as Cecil John Rhodes Professor of Race Relations at Oxford University come to mind at opposite ends of this temporal spectrum. Nevertheless, these examples underline the fact that intrinsic interest guarantees neither the avoidance of insidious instrumental use nor, more pertinently, monocultural presuppositions and prescriptions in representing — speaking formally about *and* for — those deemed unable to represent themselves.[8]

Prompted and promoted by a variety of instrumental and intrinsic influences, then, the deeply ethnoracialized Eurovision centered at the heart of monoculturalism continued to dominate the "high culture" by which the US academy, like its European counterpart, took itself to be defined. As Peter McLaren indicates below ("White Terror and Oppositional Agency: Towards a Critical Multiculturalism"), this history of monoculturalism is contemporaneous with melting-pot assimilationism as the prevailing standard underlying policies concerning ethnoracial immigration and relations in the United States. The United States was taken in its dominant self-representation to have a core set of cultural and political values, and assimilation meant giving up all those "un-American" values to be able to assume those that would fashion one American subject to the warrant of monocultural interpretation. The core values were those of the class and racial culture that historically had become hegemonic. Blending into the mainstream melting pot meant renouncing — often in clearly public ways — one's subjectivity, who one literally was: in name, in culture, and, as far as possible, in color. The language of ethnoracial relations and harmony served the interests of those with power; those, that is, who continued to define what the acceptable core monocultural values were. It should be pointed out that prior to the 1940s, the model of assimilation, for the most part, did not apply to "Negroes," for *they* were considered inherently inassimilable. As late as the mid-sixties, those who were perceived to "act black" were treated thus: remember Goodman, Chaney, and Schwerner. Yet, once it became legally and politically viable to address institutional exclusions of black people in a sustained way from the 1940s onwards, the standard of equal treatment for blacks (still conceived as "Negroes") came to mirror the assimilationist melting-pot model for ethnic immigrants.[9]

Configured thus, monoculturalism as intellectual ideology and institutional practice effects another constriction. As its name subtly suggests, monoculturalism not only purports to universalize the presuppositions and terms of a single culture, it likewise denies *as culture* — as embodying and reflecting worthy value(s) — any expression that fails to fit its mold of "high culture." It is worth emphasizing accordingly that popular *culture* — television shows, movies especially, and then rock 'n roll — seemingly by contrast, emerged from mid-century on as a staple American export, along with US military-industrial personnel and products, automobiles, and jeans. The example of Elvis Presley reveals that popular culture and the culture of American products manufactured by capitalism's military-industrial complex went hand in hand. Both were configured to represent, indeed, to project the land of the free. Nevertheless, at least on the face of it, the monoculturalism of intellectual practice that the United States had made its own via mirrored importation was reconfigured in the popular wrap of exported cultural goods. The Voice of America — confident, perhaps even brash, uncritically unself-conscious, and overwhelmingly white — came to replace the equally white and homogeneous timbre of Her Majesty.

America's Eurovisioned drive to control global markets and global culture in the name of a universalism that effaced local culture at "home" and abroad also signaled the shift from empire and direct colonial bondage to less direct and hegemonic forms of postcolonial economic control. to the negligence of absentee (land-)lordship, oftentimes even to outright abandonment. Thus, as foreign investment in the former colonies by the G7 powers or multinationals has been rationalized in terms of "getting democracy off the ground" or "helping democracy to work," such investment is fashioned actually by the geopolitical and geoeconomic interests it is projected to serve. Capital's shadow follows the sunny lure of surplus value. At the same time, however, the repression — and sometime annihilation — of the Other in the assimilative imperative (those who could not be assimilated were wiped away, representationally, symbolically, and in many instances, physically) began to give way, globally and locally, to the self-assertion of the Other, politically and culturally. The majority of racialized others continued to be *economically* marginalized,[10] if not altogether ignored, even as they were *politically* and *culturally* acknowledged. In the 1960s, colonial and urban rule, commonly white dominated, typically gave in to majority *political* independence and metropolitan self-governance. Nevertheless, *economic* dependence tended to deepen if it did not result in wholescale abandonment and marginalization. In some ways, culture sustained political resistance, and cultural production enabled the economic advance of some who, hitherto, had been economically marginalized. Yet, as Tommy Lott argues ("Black Vernacular Representation and Cultural Malpractice"), the relation between culture and economic power is complex. Though the roots of rock 'n roll may have been recognized in jazz and blues and gospel, this made little difference to prevailing patterns of consumption and cultural profit in the 1950s and 1960s. "The savage mind," promoted academically as exhibiting some rationality, clearly wasn't engaged in self-interested maximization. In this imagined self-construction, those who *were* moved by rational self-interest, for the most part Euro-Americans, continued to maximize their egoistic advantage at the exploitative expense and in repetitive ignorance of the material conditions of the Other.

Nevertheless, and against the monocultural grain, the civil rights and countercultural movements of the 1960s signalled a shift from the prevailing assimilative standard to the new one of *integration*. Confronted by demographic shifts as well as by committed, vocal, and active social movements, the fragile grounds sustaining monoculturalism began to buckle. The new model of integration that emerged left cultural groups (including races) with effective control of their private autonomous cultural determinations and expressions at the sociocultural margins, while maintaining a supposedly separate and, thus, neutral set of common values (especially, but not only economic and legal ones) to mediate their relations at the center. In private, ethno-American, in public, American citizen; in private ethnic, in public American.[11] The common (re)public(an) culture was to furnish the grounds for cohesion, the conditions of Americanness. The dualism of this model is reflected in its pluralist allowances at the margins with its univocal core insistences at the center. The central values continued to be defined monoculturally. Where insurgent cultural expressions emerged, as in the racial self-representation "black," they either were quickly suppressed or diluted through the tokenism of economic and cultural appropriation. The integrative mode has focused primarily on alleviating intergroup conflict and tension, improving ethnoracial relations. It has stressed more or less genuine attempts to define and service improvements in conditions for those who continue to be identified as "minorities,"[12] all the while serving up good subjects for the monocultural model.

Multicultural Genealogies

Multiculturalism and commitments to cultural diversity emerged out of this conflictual history of resistance, accommodation, integration, and transformation. Accordingly, no sooner had multicultural demands and aspirations begun to be articulated than they were imparted multiple and conflicting interpretations, meanings, and implications. Broadly conceived, multiculturalism is critical of and resistant to the necessarily reductive imperatives of monocultural assimilation. But this critical realignment assumes multiple forms. As Peter Caws shows, multiculturalism may be used in descriptive fashion to reference the undeniable variety of cultures inter- and intranationally. By contrast, Charles Taylor ("The Politics of Recognition") identifies a normative conception: The discourse on multiculturalism here is about stipulating the procedural and substantive principles ordering a multicultural society (in the descriptive sense). In this latter regard, Peter McLaren distinguishes between various kinds of multicultural commitment: conservative, (left-)liberal, and critical. Cedric Robinson's vigorous critique of the social sciences ("Ota Benga's Flight Through Geronimo's Eyes: Tales of Science and Multiculturalism") adds historical depth to McLaren's distinctions. Robinson insists that the Western tradition of knowledge formation has always been marked by a multicultural constitution. In the past, however, this multicultural heritage has been represented by, for, and in the interests of those yielding ethnoracial power. Thus, what Robinson identifies as "premodern" and "modernist" multiculturalisms served dominant and exclusionary interests. Their prevailing and once hegemonic forms only now are being challenged by "anti(post)modernist multiculturalism."

At one end of the spectral range, then, are managed multiculturalisms — what the Chicago Cultural Studies Group ("Critical Multiculturalism") characterizes as "corporate multiculturalism" and what Terence Turner ("Anthropology and Multiculturalism: What is Anthropology That Multiculturalists Should be Mindful of It?") denominates "difference multiculturalism." These are the multiculturalisms of a centrist academy and multinational corporations that take themselves to be committed to the broad tenets of philosophical liberalism which are unconcerned, as Michele Wallace indicates ("The Search for the 'Good Enough' Mammy: Multiculturalism, Popular Culture, and Psychoanalysis"), with the redistribution of power or resources. Here, multiculturalisms assume the mantles of institutional logic, self-promotion, and ideological practice in one of two ways. They may be — they all too often are — glibly celebrated in the name of a standard pluralism that not only leaves groups constituted as givens but entrenches the boundaries fixing group demarcations as unalterable. Alternatively, if this indeed be an alternative, multiculturalism and cultural diversity are assumed as mantric administrative instruments that serve to contain and restrain resistance and transformation as they displace any appeal to economic difference by paying lip service to the celebration of cultural distinction. As the Chicago Cultural Studies Group reveals, this managed multiculturalism furnishes a society with more subtle local and international administrative abilities. The corporate culture of integration is defined through determinations by legal authority for what it takes to meet the letter of the law and thus avoid complaints of discrimination. This managed multicultural containment becomes especially pressing in light of the understanding of the university as a corporate entity that has come to prevail in the past decade. The university increasingly is understood, by administrators and students alike, as a provider of service (training), the product of which are graduates. Consumers of the product have to be generated. So consumers are no longer understood to be students (though internal to the institution their demands too have to be accommodated). Rather, increasingly important are corporations (including other universities), the employers of university graduates. Just as multiculturalism has become a profitable means of commodification (from "the united colors of Benetton" to "multicultural crayons" for kids), so it is being employed instrumentally by corporations to meet labor needs and maintain labor peace in an increasingly diversified society. It is in this context also that cultural diversity in the academy is invoked as a necessary recruiting mechanism at a time of decreasing enrollments, shrinking federal dollars, the reduction of affirmative action administratively to painting by numbers, and the increased pressures of globalized competition.[13]

The pluralist strains of these (lack of) commitments have enabled the institutionalization of the sorts of ethnic and women's studies programs sought more radically in the name of resistance and transformation, thereby appropriating the idea by undercutting the practice. As Ramon Gutierrez ("Ethnic Studies: Its Evolution in American Colleges and Universities") demonstrates in relation to ethnic studies, and Barbara Christian ("Diminishing Returns: Can Black Feminism(s) Survive the Academy?") in relation to the experience of black women in the academy, the administrative constraints circumscribed the possibilities promoted by the transformation of the commonplace. For the most part, programs or "minors" have been established rather than departments; faculty are borrowed from disciplinary duties rather than institutionalized as independent appointments; young professors are hired whose institutional duties are assumed to be primarily role models, advisors, and instructors of special — and largely marginalized — courses, their research contributions discounted or dismissed. Thus, faculty hired in the name of the multicultural or the demands of diversity are at once ghettoized and terrorized by traditional disciplinary determinations and considerations.[14] While the appeal of programs lies in their critical independence and transdisciplinarity, their vulnerability is revealed most immediately in times of economic retrenchment. Least institutionalized in the academy, they are most prone to deficit reduction; last created, first decimated.

Thus conceived and managed, modest and moderate monoculturalists — or those who conceive of themselves as representing standards, not just of rationality but of reasonableness — could probably tolerate multiculturalism as necessary to their general well-being (as the fly on Western civ's nose) or, perhaps more generously, as the natural progression in the playing out of the Enlightenment project. But the shifts from monoculturalist assimilation to pluralist integration are underpinned by migratory shifts (south to north, east to west) as well as by socioeconomic transformations (Fordist to flexible accumulation) and their attendant cultural articulations. Nevertheless, they are framed also by the monocultural requirement, identified by Derrick Bell, that social advances for all persons who are not white or male are promoted in universalist terms so that white-male support (and the attendant success of any policy) is predicated on the benefits to white males. This "universalist" commitment explains a good deal of the opposition to affirmative action as well as to ERA and support for anti-gay legislation in Colorado and elsewhere.[15]

Ironically, the shifts in the political economy and geoculture of the world-system have enabled the contours of a new standard to emerge, a new set of self-understandings, presuppositions, principles, and practices. This new way of thinking about the social and institutional, the intellectual and academic, is just beginning to appear in the struggles of cultural transformation. It is a way of thinking that is antiassimilationist and anti-integrationist (and for those reasons, ignorantly, though sometimes more insidiously dismissed, as separatist[16]). To contrast this with the standards of assimilation and integration, I refer to it as *incorporation*. The principle at issue here involves the dual transformations that take place in the dominant values and in those of the insurgent group as the latter insists on more complete incorporations into the body politic and the former grudgingly gives way. Incorporation, then, does not involve extension of established values and protections over the formerly excluded group, either a liberal bringing into or a Habermasian collectivist extension of the status quo. The continual renegotiation of sociocultural space is not fixed in and by a contract, a momentary communicative agreement that reifies relations. The body politic becomes a medium for transformative incorporation, a political arena of contestation, rather than a base from which exclusions can be more or less silently extended, managed, and manipulated.

The body of political relations is irreversibly altered as new parts attach themselves to and then work their own ways into its mechanisms of power and cultural expression. Incorporation undermines the grounds of integration and marginalization for it empowers those once marginalized in relation to the dominant and forceful of the body politic. It extends transformative power, not just to alter or end marginalization and not simply to appropriate cultural expressions of the Other into the canon while holding the Other at a nonthreatening distance. Rather, it seeks to undermine and alter from within the dominant, controlling, confining, and periphractic values of the cultural dominant. The central issue here, as Patricia Williams notes, "is precisely the canonized status of any one group's control."[17] Evidence that this incorporative ideal is now emergent may be found in a wide range of sociocultural domains: in the cultural struggles over the literary canon and the curriculum, as Henry Louis Gates Jr ("Goodbye Columbus? Notes on the Culture of Criticism") and Henry Giroux ("Insurgent Multiculturalism and the Promise of Pedagogy") indicate in their respective articles in this volume; in the stresses over defining and control of legal pedagogy, represented here by Anita Allen ("On Being a Role Model"); in (re)writing histories, as witnessed in the articles by Robert Stam and Ella Shohat ("Contested Histories: Eurocentrism, Multiculturalism, and the Media") and Cedric Robinson ("Ota Benga's Flight Through Geronimo's Eyes: Tales of Science and Multiculturalism") respectively; in the power of those so often institutionally silenced to (re)name, to represent themselves and to do so variously and not essentially or uniformly, as articulated and problematized in these pages by Michael Dyson ("Essentialism and the Complexities of Racial Identity") and Angie Chabram Dernersesian ("'Chicana! Rican? No, Chicana-Riqueña!' Refashioning the Transnational Connection"); in the transformative implications of science and social science for multiculturalism, and vice versa, as reflected upon by Sandra Harding ("Is Science Multicultural? Challenges, Resources, Opportunities, Uncertainties") and Terence Turner ("Anthropology and Multiculturalism"); in gangsta rap, as discussed by Tommy Lott ("Black Vernacular Representation and Cultural Malpractice"); and in the culture of hybrid and crossover fashion.[18]

The central value of this incorporative principle is "hybridity," a displacement of the histories that constitute its moment, thrusting forth, in Homi Bhabha's distinctive words, new "structures of authority, new political initiatives," promoting the emergence of "... a new area of negotiation of meaning and representation," that is incomprehensible and unrecognizable in terms of prevailing knowledge.[19] Hybridities are the modalities in and through which multicultural conditions get lived out, and renewed. In this sense, incorporative undertakings are transgressive, engaged by definition in infringing and exceeding the norms of the monocultural status quo and transforming the values and representations that have held racist culture together.

So, where assimilation previously had dominated America's prevailing ethnic self-image and presupposing a white face to go along with white culture,[20] pluralism represented the ideological and rhetorical outcomes of the liberatory struggles in the 1960s. And where the monocultural commitments of a common, singular, universal, canonical, liberal education — the Great Books, Western civilization,[21] European letters in spatial and racial senses — had dominated the academy without as much as having to register resistance, they now began to face the charged challenges from counter- to even anarchistic anticommitments. The exclusions matter-of-factly effected in the name of monoconceived Euro-American identity, culture, and material domination were confronted in ways that threw into question once and for all their apparent naturalism, revealing behind the seeming givenness of the monotonous voice the imposing force of a univocal institutional power. This universe of knowledge, and knowledge of the universe, imagined in and by the unicultural university, began to rupture under its self-imposed constrictions because it was unable to accommodate — unable to assimilate or placate — the insights, vision, and demands of those whose subjectivities it had acknowledged only as barbarian. Unable to speak, let alone write, the barbarians uttered unrecognizable sounds. Eventually, those sounds came to be named multiculturalism.

The emergence of contemporary multiculturalisms, then, is to be understood in relation to the twentieth-century dominance of monoculturalism. Monoculturalism was the more or less unchallenged ideological common sense of the first half of this century. Ahistorical circumscription of multicultural conditions to the terms of what they reject delimit their possibilities to the legitimacy of *given* terms. To speak a new language, so the insistence goes, one has to make it comprehensible to those whose terms of reference are nothing but the old. But this demand restricts the new perennially to the old, disabling the new from challenging the old by making the former literally — as well as politically — unthinkable. The new, where it is acknowledged at all, is conceived not just as a challenge to the truth of tradition but as a threat, not just to be critically engaged but to be resisted where it cannot be denied. It is cast (out) as nothing but politics dressed up as epistemology, the struggle for power played out over the putatively sacred neutrality of knowledge. But if the political charge against multiculturalism has meaning, then it implies that monocultural commitments are political also; indeed, that the struggle between them in the final analysis can be played out only on political terrain.

In this sense, universalizing monoculturalists cannot hide safely behind the charge that multiculturalists reduce pedagogy and culture to political struggles over power. For the arguments Stanley Fish has advanced in relation to the value of free speech may be generalized to pedagogy. Fish argues that free speech is not only partial but political. It is always the freedom to speak of those who possess power to proscribe the speech of others in favor of speech representing the values they prefer to the exclusion of the values of those lacking such power.[22] Similarly, as Henry Giroux points out in these pages, education and pedagogical values are instruments of political purpose, the use and meaning of which are to advance partisan political (and one might add economic) causes. Examples abound: the incursion of Whittle Communications into the educational *industry*; the politics of textbook production; the storming by fundamentalist Christians of school boards; or the politics of defunding threats faced by state universities from state legislatures because of the nature of some courses offered.[23]

The charge that multicultural critique is politically motivated may be at once embraced — it is true, and for good reason — yet redirected. Multicultural critique is indeed political in the sense of undertaking to redefine the public values constitutive of the polis, of the state in which we live, to make those values more open to incorporative transformation. But it is political insofar as the struggle over representative values has always been political. To date, the prevailing arguments in support of multiculturalism have been articulated in terms of identity and difference; nevertheless, it is the arguments so configured that have constricted the theoretical and practical possibilities available to proliferate and renew multicultural conditions. It is to this discussion I now turn.

Arguments from Identity/Difference

Identity and difference have framed the theoretical structure for the contests around multiculturalism. Vigorous attention has been given to defining identity; to analyzing why identities are important generally and academically; to the implications of proliferating identities and situated subjects for putatively universal concepts of value and rationality; and to notions of homogeneity that supposedly unite us all. Hegemonic or dominant identities and the exclusions they purport to license have been challenged in terms of difference, of local or particular identities. Claims to impartiality and appeals to "standard person" criteria have been confronted by plurality and difference, and by the varieties of (once silenced) Others speaking, if not striking back.

This conceptual framing in terms of identity and difference has proved theoretically, politically, and pedagogically valuable. But the frame has blurred some details just as it has sharpened the focus on others. Identity is generally conceived in this conceptual framework as a bond: as the affinity and affiliation that associates those so identified, that extends to them a common sense or space of unified sameness. It is a tie that holds members of the collective together. These at least are the elements that go into what might be deemed an affirmative conception of identity.[24]

This conception, however, can cut both ways. The bond, as Michael Dyson illustrates, can also be a bondage; the tie is something that may hold one in. It has been pointed out commonly that identity can be exclusionary of those who are outside its scope, those who are — or who are taken to be — in no way affiliated. You don't belong, you don't meet the conditions or criteria of belonging so we are going to keep you out. What is less observed is that identity can also be a bondage within. It can keep people in who don't want to be in. And it can do so by insisting on an essential racial character, or simply by requiring racial solidarity.

Similarly with the notion of difference. Difference can be straightforwardly exclusionary, indeed (as West points out), it can be deathly dangerous. There is a long history of racialized or gendered exclusion in the name of difference. Those deemed different are not part of the social formation, are not included under values of moral treatment, respect, and love. But difference also can be used as a mark of delineation to cut off — in organization, in interaction, in memory — those included as members of the group, of the same kind, in virtue of their differential heritage or biology. This (self-)imposed distinction may be cast as a mark of elevation or moral superiority, as being necessary to group survival or self-determination, or as a burden worth bearing, no matter one's desire or effort. Identity can sustain fascist social movements as readily as emancipatory ones, and difference may license genocide almost as easily as it does celebration.

On balance, the analysis of identity and difference may help theoretically to fashion multicultural formations. It may be objected that the metaphysical and abstract nature of much of the academic debate has tended to displace possibilities for political action. The conceptual pliability of identity and difference tends to reduce the politics of theory to an end in itself, to a politics that is nothing but theoretical. This objection may be too quick, however, for it too readily ignores the political dimensions of knowledge and the importance of representation to politics. Nevertheless, it does clear a space for a more nuanced set of critiques to be articulated.

The struggle over representation — over (self-)naming, and the language of articulation — is important in establishing the possibilities for self-direction. This political expression is what Charles Taylor below aptly calls "the politics of recognition." Nonetheless, the capacity to name oneself in the order of thought, while significant, does not guarantee on its own the material conditions and resources, the material power necessary for social flourishing and living freely. Identity politics reduce, in Henry Louis Gates' words, all too often to little more than "a politics of gesture," to political posing. The Hegelian drive to recognition may serve to delimit the possibilities of transformative power. Psychologic, while an important dimension in the transformation of political economy, often circumscribes sociologics. Hence the most visible political struggles are now around matters like "hate" speech and crimes and over the content of academic courses. This has tended recently to overshadow — indeed, to drown out — mobilization around material resources regarding education, employment conditions, and political power. At the same time, modest means for redistribution, like affirmative action, have come under significant attack. In any case, this elision of resource politics covers up, if it doesn't altogether wipe away, a range of emergent *local* sociopolitical movements which are at least equally necessary to living freely. Implicitly underlying the theoretical politics of identity, then, stands the standard of integration, of monovalent center and plural peripheries, even as identity formations and their attendant theoretical debates have helped to clear a space in which incorporative political movements could emerge more clearly. Yet presupposed as grounding this identity formation and the difference(s) it effects is the norm of whiteness to which Others will assimilate or with which they will integrate.[25]

This circumscription of the political has been reified by related theoretical reductions articulated in respect of identity and difference. First, the justified critical rejection of grand theoretical metanarratives advanced in the name of postmodernism has helped to fuel the multicultural drive. Nevertheless, this is accompanied too readily by theoretical oversimplification and impoverishment. Here, the call to a sustained antifoundationalist and antiessentialist theoretical practice, informed by and informing political praxis, is reduced in the academicist exercise of some to the nominalism of occasionally empty and sometimes politically naive theoretical sloganeering: "social construction," "strategic essentialism," "mobile subjectivities," "phallocentrism," "textuality," perhaps "difference" itself, and so on, literally ad nauseam.[26] Absent the demonstrated implication of these terms in a sustained antifoundational and antiessentializing theoretical praxis, and their implication in projects of emancipatory politics, little prevents their being taken up in behalf of a uniculturalist counterformation.[27]

This is tied to a further form of reduction. In the rush to avoid the Althusserian accusation of "economism," culturalism has taken charge. As Terence Turner insists below, political economy has disappeared almost altogether from contemporary cultural studies and, by implication, from much of the identity-driven analysis concerning multiculturalism. Politics is conceived in this scheme as "a signifying activity" through which identities are created[28] rather than as the mobilization of power(s) to effect ends in support of interests (in which identity formation may be more or less implicated). This romance with the cultural and the related ignorance of political economy has helped to promote the importance of cultural identification, especially for the racially marginalized but, as Peter Caws notes, it has served at once to cover (up) the political and economic roots of their marginalization.

Frederic Jameson's *Postmodernism, or the Cultural Logic of Late Capitalism* is the work in cultural studies that perhaps goes furthest to accommodate the intersection of political economy and culture. For Jameson, postmodernism is the cultural dominant of late capitalism. Citing Stuart Hall as authority, Jameson conceives of political struggle as being waged in the postmodern moment, not primarily in "activist" terms but over the legitimacy of concepts and ideologies. Jameson thinks legitimacy is fashioned presently in terms of concepts like *planning* and *the market* rather than on the basis of structural considerations. It is noteworthy, then, that he confines the chapter on Economics to the representations of market culture and the marketing of culture. Economics gets reduced to market representation, even as Jameson calls explicitly for (without ever engaging in) analysis of *real* markets. Completely absent from Jameson's considerable range of reference are relations of production, the mode of production, or power politico-economically (re)produced or resisted. Unlike Hall, Jameson has virtually nothing to say about cultural *production* or the culture of (re)production.

Over the past twenty-five years, manufacturing production has shifted increasingly from the dominant metropolitan centers in the world-system, first to submetropolitan peripheries, and then to peripheral offshore economies marked by disparately cheap labor costs. With these postmodernizing shifts, production has dissolved from theoretical focus. The market Jameson addresses is filled with goods that can be re-presented seemingly *ex nihilo.* Goods appear on the shelves of consumption — in the Benettons and Gaps and Nikes of contemporary cities and suburban malls — without trace, the cultural products of postmodern capital. (Since the Velvet Revolution, the colorful condom commercial uniting the bearers of the Benetton image has come to fill the Prague billboards previously adorned by the bust of Lenin.) Commercials for Benetton, Gap, or Nike fabricate a history of the goods' presence, of their present tense, that purport at once to evade (if not to erase) the goods' conditions of creation. These conditions are buried in Jameson's analysis, as they are in economic form in the age of electronic reproduction and circulation. Culturalism dissolves into an econocentrism dictated by — as its focus is restricted to — the cultural expressions of what Sassen calls the new global cities. These command centers of the world economy dictate what gets produced, and where in the world-system. They service capital's financial needs but serve at once as its primary consumer markets for products invisibly produced — elsewhere. The invisible man of modernity has become the invisible spaces and societies of late capital — and postmodern theory. These erasures accordingly explain Jameson's pregnant silences concerning race and gender as sites of oppression and marginalization — of superexploitation.[29]

There is a further way in which theorizing the multicultural in terms of identity/difference has been reductive. The paradigm of identity/difference has promoted a sustained critique of universalism, directed especially at liberalism's tendency to presume universal values in epistemology, ethics, aesthetics, and politics. Cultural studies and the associated expressions of multiculturalism standardly reiterate their commitment to the nonfoundational and nonessentialist implications of social construction. Nevertheless, they have failed completely to theorize a nuanced understanding of the *relativistic* implications of a nonfoundational and nonessentializing multicultural commitment, resorting, instead, mostly to simplistic assumptions of cultural relativism. This failure has enabled a more or less uncontested (re)emergence of dangerous claims to the truth (racialized representations of an underclass in terms of a purported poverty of culture, Holocaust denials, conspiratorial Jewish corporate and political power, Jews qua Jews as slave traders and slave owners, Muslim terrorism in Bosnia and beyond, ethnic bloodletting and tribal warfare as characteristic of any non-Western state too irrational to engage in politics, and so on). If the truth is relative simplistically to the group proclaiming it, then all claims to truth, no matter how much they lack substantiation, are on equal footing. Pat Lauderdale has noted recently that the critique of "objectivity" as veiling the imputation of Eurocentric value has buried justifiable concerns about accuracy.[30] A more robust and more robustly nuanced conception of relativism underpinning the multicultural project will enable distinctions to be drawn between more or less accurate truth claims and more or less justifiable values (in contrast to claims to *the* truth or *the* good).

These forms of reduction, together with the flippant dismissal of multiculturalism by its more extreme critics for resting necessarily upon an untenably simplistic relativistic epistemology, exemplify a common fallacy. They conflate the political epistemology of universality and particularity with the related epistemological politics of relativism and universalism.

The two sets of distinction, though obviously related, are usually collapsed. Thus critics of ("radical" or "strong") multiculturalism, dressed up as political correctness, presumptively insist that claims to the value of ethnic particularity necessarily rest on a simplistic epistemological and axiological relativism. (Here multiculturalism is reduced to the readily challenged Afrocentricity of Molefi Asante and Leonard Jeffries.)[31] Likewise the projected universality of the commonly human (in the name of which "divisive particularity" gets dismissed) is taken to rest upon epistemological and value universalism. Particularity is thought to stand or fall on the tenuous grounds of a simplistic relativism supposedly underlying it.

Critics are quick to show, in the standard philosophical way, that such relativism is inconsistent and incoherent (to use Hilary Putnam's prescient phrase, "if all is relative, the relative must be relative too"). As simpleminded relativism goes, so then are supposed to go the claims of ethnic-based value, and thus, too, of multiculturalism. More moderate monocultural critics, or at least monoculturalists in their more moderate moments, are willing to accommodate "weak multiculturalism." This consists in a strong set of common, universally endorsed, centrist values to which everyone — every reasonable person irrespective of the divisions of race, class, and gender — can agree. These universal principles are combined with a pluralism of ethnic insight and self-determination provided no particularistically promoted claim is inconsistent with the core values.[32]

This standard view rests in an only slightly revised fashion upon the traditional premise of philosophical liberalism. Particular identities (notably race and gender) are deemed axiologically irrelevant. They are considered partial characterizations of the human condition that human beings are not free, for the most part, to alter. Accordingly they cannot be the grounds of value or action for which individuals can be held responsible.

Even in this lightly revised version, contributors to the volume generally agree that the implicit monoculturalism dressed up as weak pluralistic multiculturalism presumes a fixed "we" or "us" at an unshifting center. It presupposes a foundational artifice necessary as universal crucible and grounded source of basic value. This imagined and imaginary Subject, pluralized as a matter of political accommodation into a "We," extends local values into universal ones. It ties together epistemological universalism with the political, ethical, and pedagogical axiology of universality, of the common and modern[33] Man of Reason (that one on the Clapham Bus — no acquaintance of mine), the product of Western civ and partial consumer of the Great Book(s).

There is no inherent necessity to run together universality with universalism, particularity with simplistically incoherent relativism. Axiological relativism is bound to deny neither some basic formal principles of thinking — call them universal, if necessary — nor generalizable value judgments concerning especially pernicious social conditions and practices.[34] So, owning up to formal principles of logical relation implies nothing about the assertive content of thought: consider the concept of logical validity. Logical formalism enables only that inconsistent and incoherent claims for the most part can be ruled out; it is thoroughly incapable of assertively promoting some coherent or consistent standard over another. It is equally incapable of fashioning rules for interpreting metaphors or of choosing one reasonable interpretation over another. Thus logical (in contrast, say, to conceptual) formalism must remain neutral between the significance of terms in the sense of competing meanings and a variety of values. (This is why logicians characterize as "informal" or "material" fallacies of reasoning that conflate meanings or values.) Matthew Arnold offers Hobson's choice in reducing the alternatives to thinking for oneself *or* thinking like other people. At most, a renewably critical multicultural commitment should be underpinned by a thin set of common rules of logic and basic inference so that people — individually and collectively, critically and self-critically — can think for themselves. Peter Caws may be read to suggest that being in a position to think for oneself entails having the widest range of reference reasonably possible in relation to an issue at hand, with the view to assessing alternatives and questioning dominant standards of assessment. It follows that a multicultural pedagogy will not be reduced to technique as it all too often is in its managed and market driven modes — to an obsession only with the instrumentalities of cooperative learning, say. Rather, it will be concerned as much with promoting an enthusiasm among students and teachers alike for always learning more (and more variously) about the subject matters at hand. And this entails that multicultural pedagogy be concerned also self-critically with questioning the grounds of the knowledge claims and truth values being advanced, and with challenging the dominant interpretation and underlying structures of institutional and ideological power represented in prevailing pedagogical narratives.

Moreover, Richard Rorty points out that human beings can and do make general value judgments — morally, about the unacceptability of racism and sexism, for instance, but more generally also about the desirability or aesthetic of some events or expressions. These judgments are made always from *within* the tradition of value notions of the society in which they stand. A tradition is highly likely to have emerged out of and be influenced by other traditions. This will be borne out by the arguments I offer shortly in behalf of heterogeneity, and it is a point reiterated by Peter Caws below. Axiological judgments are made not on the basis of appeal to some abstract, universal law (Kant's commands of reason), but on the basis of the prevailing yet contingent values, the traditions and principles of the society of which individuals take themselves to be members. The traditional historical commitment of philosophical liberalism to universal principles of reason and (moral) value presupposes universal ideas like intrinsic humanity, human dignity, and human rights — values, that is, that are thought to mark individuals in virtue of their very humanity. As Rorty insists, there is no transhistorical or supersocial Godly view on which such universal (moral) principles can be grounded or from which they can be derived. Axiological concepts and values are necessarily those of some historically specific community.[35] These concepts and values need not be taken as those of the dominant social class, though Rorty's bourgeois liberalism implies that they are. They may be produced out of contestation, and are always open to incorporative revision. Thus, any insistence on the universalism of values must be no more than the projected imposition of local values — those especially of some ethnoracial and gendered particularity — universalized. The supposed universalism of epistemological politics reduces to the political epistemology of an imposed universality.

I think it necessary to rupture more completely the connection insinuated by monoculturalist proponents between the epistemology of universalism and relativism on one hand, and the politics of universality and particularity on the other. It seems more accurate to reconceive the monoculturally-construed antithetical opposition between universality and particularity at the center of political epistemology as the contrastive relations between generality and specificity. *Universals* are laws or rules that purport to be valid in all instances, comprehensive and comprehensible to all persons irrespective of their point of view and particular identity. The fact that supposedly universal values tend to be the generalization of local and particular ones is revealed at least partially by recalling that the term "universal" etymologically pertains to being "of the Church" and includes "all Christians." By contrast, the *general* as a concept is more constrained concerning the possibilities of its comprehensive groundedness. Where it refers in common to all members of a class, it does so approximately or within implied limits. Like the universal, the general may be contrasted with the particular or partial, but it contrasts also to the local or sectional. And under some interpretations, it contrasts additionally with the universal, as in the claim to represent a variety of cases in its bulk of instances, though not without exception. Thus, where universalization purports to establish the necessity of natural or natural-like law, generalization inductively abstracts from particular instances to the probability of broad commonalities. The authoritative command of universal(ized) requirement gives way to the circumspection and self-conscious skepticism of general(ized) possibility.

The particular, moreover, is to be differentiated from the specific thus: The *particular* is at once an indistinguishable but separate instance of the universal. It is a representative member of the universal class whose representativeness nevertheless is achieved by dismissing or discounting its oddities, strangeness, and distinction; in short, its otherness. The *specific* represents a peculiar characteristic feature of the general, extending to the general a precision, definition, and exactitude, explicating the general by illustrating what it takes to fulfill the terms or conditions of generality.

It follows that the relativism upon which a sophisticated form of critical multiculturalism rests is not restricted to value particularism. Multicultural relativism is ready and able to fashion general judgments, that is, revisable inductive generalizations as the specificity of (particular) circumstances and relations warrant. These circumstances and relations will include often, though not necessarily always, racial, class, and gendered articulation. Thus multiculturalists are able to condemn a specific form of racism, say, apartheid, in terms of a general judgment that racist exclusions are unacceptable because they are unwarranted in a specifiable scheme of social value to which we do or should adhere for specifiable (and, perhaps, generalizable) reasons. But there is no transcendental proof or grounds, no universal foundation, for this scheme or any other. Cast in these terms, a critical multiculturalism will be able to offer a far more nuanced conception of racisms than the "understanding" generated by axiological universalism, namely, any race-based belief, action, practice, or program usually generated by axiological universalism. The critical, insurgent, and polyvalent multiculturalisms outlined in the following pages by the likes of the Chicago Cultural Studies Group, by Henry Giroux, and by Robert Stam and Ella Shohat, respectively, resort not to axiological universalism but to moral pragmatism. This antifoundational pragmatism is more readily able than monocultural traditionalists or differential pluralists to distinguish the warrant of flexible race-based distinctions now necessitated by sensitively administered affirmative action programs (see Anita Allen's article, "The Role Model Argument") from the fix of unwarranted racist practices, programs, and institutions afflicting this society, past and present.[36]

Against this background, Gerald Graff's exhortation to "teach the conflicts" would seem especially appealing. Rather than seek consensus, perhaps the best we can hope for is a form of coherence in which the various positions in the pressing conflicts — over methodology, principle, values, and so on — would exist uneasily but productively alongside each other. Nevertheless, Graff's suggestion presupposes that educators — even the humanists of Graff's address — occupy a neutral position, or at least can suspend their prejudices, in presenting the conflicts, and that the conflicts are fixed and immobile. One cannot teach the conflicts (or anything else, for that matter) by assuming this neutral "view from nowhere," for it is no view at all.[37] In other words, the Assumption of a View from Nowhere is the projection of local values as neutrally universal ones, the globalizing of ethnocentric values, as Stam and Shohat put it. Teaching the conflicts, then, necessitates also and always revealing the partialities and potentialities implicated in the undertaking — those as much of the educator and students as of the various sides.

In light of these considerations, I think it necessary to offer a different kind of argument for the multicultural project, to displace, in part, the way in which the debate is usually fashioned around identity and difference. I want to spell out a vigorous defense of multicultural commitments that are critical, insurgent, polyvocal, heteroglossial, and antifoundational. The central concept, then, is not identity/difference but heterogeneity. Forms of corporate and managed multiculturalism will be criticized accordingly because they necessarily reify homogeneity.

Arguing for and from Heterogeneity

The notion of *heterogeneity* has begun to emerge in the literature concerning multiculturalism but, for the most part, only obliquely and without sustained theorization. Iris Young has employed the concept usefully; and Edward Said notably suggests in the Introduction to his magisterial work *Culture and Imperialism* that the *de facto* heterogeneity of historical experience is deeply at odds with the narrowing theoretical insistence on social identity that must necessarily presuppose homogeneity.[38] By contrast, the primary unifying assumption of the motley crew who argue against multiculturalism — of William Bennett, that philosopher-educator turned drug czar and now guardian of the nation's virtues, of William Buckley, Linda Chavez and Lynne Cheney, Arthur Schlesinger in his analysis of the "disuniting of America," Saul Bellow, Allan Bloom, and the like — is one of the sociopolitical and cultural necessity of homogeneity.

The argument usually offered against a radically multicultural state is an argument very largely from the importance of homogeneity. Homogeneity is claimed as a necessary condition for community, for civility and perhaps even for civilization, and for the very possibility of knowledge and knowledge claims. The academy has to be defined by a community of scholars just as the nation-state rests upon the coherence of a national political community, and that community of scholars — like its national counterpart — requires a binding set of homogenizing values. The *fact* of great heterogeneity, where it is acknowledged at all (by Schlesinger, for instance), is taken to necessitate the *aspiration* to a set of unifying, homogenizing ideals.[39] Interpretation of these homogeneous ideals is assumed as given, in much the way mathematics may be assumed the unifying language of the natural sciences. At the extreme stands the English-only movement where projection of the associated moral and cultural values is explicit. But the extreme proves the rule. The kinds of text supposedly signifying standards of intellectual excellence as well as social and moral value remain overwhelmingly the canonical ones of the monocultural, Eurocentric tradition. They are elevated as best not in terms of a local scheme of value, but as best *tout court*. Thus, they are deemed valuable in the universal scheme of things because they are rationally definable and defensible and so universally extendable and applicable. The underlying presupposition, then, is either that homogeneity offers the traditional, historically prevalent condition of social life or it is the ideal to be pursued. In either case, homogeneity supposedly acquires value because it is presumed the proper application of Reason.

Two different arguments tend to be given for the common assumption of social homogeneity. The first kind might be called a naturalist argument: Homogeneity is considered a natural condition of human social existence. This is exemplified by the sociobiological claim that it is natural in the drive to survive for human beings to choose kin over nonkin. In choosing kin, one is choosing those of the same kind. From this apparently natural selectivity follows a commitment to homogeneity. It is in our make up, so to speak, if it is not straightforwardly in our genes.

The other argument is Humean. This is an historical argument, a commitment to the traditions and customs that are deemed worth preserving. Homogeneity is presumed the best means for their preservation. The values worth preserving are those identified, for instance, by and with Hume's interpretation of Englishness. The tradition of customs and virtues defined as Englishness in the eighteenth century were considered to have evolved since William conquered England in 1066. So, homogeneity becomes instrumentally necessary as a means to the preservation of values and virtues associated with Englishness and intrinsically valuable, as worthy of institutionalizing for its own sake.[40] This turns homogeneity into a common (and indeed national) condition, into what one would expect of and within a social formation. Homogeneity is to be expected for it is assumed (or ought to be) that members of a social tradition are introspective, closed off, and exclude others (or ought to) outside the prevailing (national or racial) group.

Now this cultural dominant, and the monocultural vision it at once assumes and projects, rests on a deeply inaccurate representation of the historical record. In broad strokes, the social condition of *Homo sapiens* is prevailingly migratory. It is not homogeneous in origin at all. It makes little sense to render homogeneity natural, in terms of social conditions or ideals and values. Homogeneity is an artifice. I am not claiming that migration is natural, but it is somehow part of our natural condition. It is, however (and in any number of ways), historically prevalent. People move and have moved since human inception. Vast migrations of hominids, of early and more recent human beings across large spaces, have been prompted by a variety of causes: by natural disasters, or to avoid them; because of warfare; because of climatological changes or the attractions of climate and resources; because of the push off the land or the pull of the urban; because of colonialism, enslavement, and labor supply; because of political repression or economic recession; and occasionally prompted simply by curiosity. It was not just in response to colonialism, for instance, that people moved; colonialism itself was a movement of population, for it sent people "out to" or between the colonies. Hegel argued in the early nineteenth century that a primary prompt of colonialism's expansionist drive was to find more space (and not only new raw materials and markets) for Europeans who were experiencing a sense of shrinking space in Europe. But colonialism also facilitated the movement of enslaved or indentured labor sources — from Africa and Asia to the Americas, or from Asia to Africa, and so on.

So the representative condition, the prevailing one historically — especially throughout modernity — has been movement and migration, heterogeneous mixing in ethnoracial and cultural terms. I don't deny there have been moments, even dominant ones, of homogeneity. Obviously, and especially in premodernity, there are. Yet the emphasis on the Same that is so deeply related to the logics of homogeneity has been dramatically overplayed. I do not mean to dismiss as implausible Ernest Gellner's distinction between the *relative* homogeneity characteristic of premodernity and the *relative* breakdown of homogeneous relations that accompanied the onslaught of the modern.[41] Nevertheless, Cedric Robinson identifies below a form of premodern multiculturalism. The distinction between premodernity and modernity likewise is a relative one and need not give in to the presumption that premodern space was completely or overwhelmingly homogeneous. Social homogeneity and heterogeneity accordingly may be specified in relation to local and global conditions. The more local the social conditions under analysis, the more plausibly social characteristics may be reduced analytically to a homogeneous Same, for the less dismissive of differentiated particularity will reductive abstraction likely need to be.

I have suggested that the underlying source of widespread human heterogeneity has been the overwhelming facts of movement and migration. Movement and migration, it could be said, are the defining sociohistorical conditions of humanity. Conceiving the prevailing state of the human social condition in terms of commodity flows and cultural traffic is tantamount to the shift in presupposition about the underlying state of matter from Aristotelian stasis to Galilean motion. So, Gabriel Josipovici's representation of Jewishness as a condition of going and resting might be generalized with some plausibility.[42] Israel, on Josipovici's argument, becomes one more place where Jews have rested. It does not make of Israel a permanent homeland; Jews are just another group of nomads. I wish to extend Josipovici's thematic as my motto here: Historically, the human condition is the condition of going and resting. Groups of people or subgroups — immigrants and migrants, colonialists and capitalist entrepreneurs, coolie labor and guestworkers, refugees and exiles, lingering tourists and travellers, students and intellectuals — move into new spaces or territory and become part of or integral to that space or society. Over a time, characterized perhaps by wars, cooperation and coexistence, integration, and social transformation, the groups in question may become identified with that social space. Thus the movement will tend to result in a more or less dramatic transformation of recipient space and society, whether or not they are already settled and well established.

The politics of the postcolonial condition have become increasingly diasporic. Diasporic politics, like their aesthetic counterparts, are not simply nostalgic. They only glance back longingly to a past condition to define themselves — their hopes and aspirations and struggles — in relation to what was left behind, but they are primarily prospective and are situated in the present contexts of their metropolitan experiences. Accordingly, diasporic politics fashion an interventionist, though oftentimes nationalistic, political substance and style — a body of representations in respect to significance and power — from the interface of conditions left and found, spatiotemporally distant and immediately present.[43]

The university has played a role, sometimes a central one, in these heterogenizing movements and migrations. The university may be thought of as a place for migrators, often from afar; the space that attracts people, to a center of sorts, for a variety of reasons and to various effects.

The modern university, in the European tradition, started in 1088 in Bologna. Nevertheless, higher education in the form of academies can be traced back at least to ancient Greece. The iconic figures of intellectual monoculturalism almost all experienced strong heterogeneous influences. Plato's academy attracted Aristotle, who was not Athenian but Macedonian. Aristotle was a member not just of the the people that conquered Athens, but actually a member of the ruling class of Alexander's court that controlled Athens when he went to study with Plato. Aristotle's biography may be likened accordingly not just to a Benjamin or Adorno of his day, but more readily to a Kipling or Tempels. Like the Sophists, Plato himself travelled around. When he died, he bequeathed his school not to Aristotle but to his nephew Theophrastus. Aristotle, in turn, started his own school in Athens, attracting people from the entire region as well.

Other major intellectual figures also come and go. St Augustine was born in Carthage, North Africa; a founding father of the Church, it must be insisted, was African. He studied in Rome, and returned to become Bishop of Hippo in North Africa. St Thomas Aquinas, born in the thirteenth century in Pisa, later studied in Paris and Cologne, and was deeply influenced by Aristotle, "The Philosopher" and Maimonides, the great Spanish Jew. The influence of Islamic learning and architecture, at the time, also was considerable. Aquinas taught in Paris, Rome, and finally in Naples. Tycho de Brahe, the Danish astronomer, ended up working for the court of Rudolf the Second in Prague. His assistant in Prague was Johannes Kepler who is usually characterized biographically as a German mathematician. Galileo started out in Pisa, moved to work in the Venetian Republic, a free state, and finished his life in Florence, under house arrest. The historical record is replete with other, even more dramatic examples, individual and collective. Bentham projected his panoptical prison as a result of his impressionable visit to Russia. Marx and Freud migrated across Europe to London and, certainly within the academy, the Vienna Circle and the Frankfurt school offer the most obvious examples of Europeans who found their way into universities throughout the world. Similarly, Du Bois and other black American modernists and musicians like Delaney and Wright and Lester Young and Baldwin settled, studied in, or made impressionable visits to Europe or Africa.[44] There has been a lively exchange for at least a century of African, African-American, Euro-American, and European academics and intellectuals, including scientists, writers, artists, musicians, missionaries, and entrepreneurs. These examples of major intellectual contributors carry with them the kind of heterogenizing implications I am driving at, even as in some notable cases their mandate may have been to impose repressive homogeneity. Nevertheless, they influence and at once are influenced by their new surroundings and interlocutors.

Starting out in small urban areas in the eleventh and twelfth centuries, the major European universities established over the next few centuries were either centered in important economic centers in Europe or became the basis for important economic centers. In this respect, universities worldwide followed a similar spatio-economic and cultural pattern. This is so whether the university was established directly as a result and in the service of colonial infiltration and administration (state run institutions, or those tied to the Catholic Church throughout Africa, Asia, and Latin America) or as an instrument of relatively independent state formations (for example, the emergence of big land-grant state institutions in the United States). So, universities became the media for disseminating dominant social, political, economic, and moral values, and for producing administrators, teachers, professionals, business persons, and state leaders. Heterogeneity has almost always given way to restrictive and repressive homogeneity; the conditions for the possible emergence of vigorous multiculturalisms have bowed to the comfort of some constrictive monocultural imperative. At the same time, however, universities became bases — at least potentially — around which urban centers could develop, renewing at least the possibility for the conditions of heterogeneity to reemerge.

The university has served accordingly as a grounds for urbanity, a barometer of changing styles of the urbane, a medium for refinement, the space in which the struggle between high culture and popular culture got to be played and replayed. Universities, in turn, became places of attraction, and not just in narrow economic terms as instruments of upward material mobility. People move, at least temporarily, to and through the universities and their urban environs. They are attracted to universities for they represent, as the Solomon Bros. put it, the place of recreation, of learning, of culture, of entertainment, of sport, of relaxation; in short, a microcosm of the social.[45] The university serves as an intersection of social mobilities. People come and go, bringing with them all kinds of energy, ideas, interests, backgrounds, aspirations, and projections.

It follows from this line of analysis that the notion of homogeneity intellectually and politically presupposes repression. To establish homogeneous social arrangements, even within the academy, it is necessary to repress heterogeneity, to shrink it, to exclude and silence it in various ways. At the extreme stand the variety of fundamentalisms. Motivations for migration are now largely political and economic. In some cases, as in famines, migration may be linked to natural events, but the appeal to nature more often takes the form of rationalization than it serves straightforwardly as migratory cause.[46] By contrast, underlying the presumption of homogeneity is a prevailing picture of community that is static:

fixed claims to a land, to a place or a space — whether a country, countryside, city, or neighborhood — and to their political, economic, and cultural expressions. These claims are usually couched in terms of origination or initiation: "We're starting from this common point and that's why we're homogeneous; this is what we've created and want to protect because it has value." Such claims are either completely ahistorical or only a partial representation of the historical record. In either case, the point of claimed initiation, of genesis, cuts off memory from what is conceived or conjectured as its prehistory. What went before is either wiped away entirely or put aside as the timelessness of the Primitive Other, at best the noble savage in the state of nature.

So human interaction and relations are promoted by as they effect heterogeneity, not insularity; fluidity, not fixedness. The conservative thrust of the appeal to community belies this. The currently fashionable communitarian adjustment to liberal hegemony is recourse to a homogeneous state. Population patterns are actually much more fluid as can be seen in terms of contemporary migratory trends. I do not mean this to deny the need and importance for some commonality or mutuality, some sort of communicability. The dialogic character of much social interaction, identified by Charles Taylor below, presupposes a common language as a medium of exchange, at the very least, mutually defined points of reference. But the admission of more or less prevalent heterogeneity places a very narrow limit on the desirability of fixity and closure, of the totalized boundedness and inward posture of the homogeneous and the common. Dialogic exchange presupposes neither a common style nor a common set of values. As a starting point, it requires only that people interact, which may range from the flash of a smile or scowl to a legal brief. The fact of heterogeneity, then, implies that homogeneity, communal or otherwise, is not natural but politically crafted, fabricated for purposes, however limited, of localizing power and its maintenance, and of guaranteeing control.

Throughout this past decade, representatives of what Stam and Shohat call "erudite culture" have insisted on the principle of homogeneity as the premise underlying dominant intellectual and sociocultural values. This insistence needs to be understood in the context of the radical individualization of civil society, public culture, and, indeed, of the academy. The edifice of homogeneity is necessitated precisely because of this stress on radical individualization. The greater the stress on individualism and the individualistic in a sociophilosophical tradition (rather than on the individual and individuality per se), the more socially repressive a society must be.[47] The philosophical commitment in the tradition of Western modernity is to radical and atomistic individualism — to rational (that is, self-interested), egoistic (self-maximizing), and self-providing individuals. On this model, any notion of the social or the collective is supposed to be a product of self-interested rationality. But atomism is inherently counter to social or collective formation. Rush Limbaugh, and libertarians generally, have recognized this with a vengeance. It follows that any introduction of the social is repressive, for it is seen to constrain and restrict the freedom of individuals, to produce uniformity. Rationality serves to rationalize such repression as necessary to the satisfaction of individual freedoms. In fact, the repression need be neither physical nor political. In a philosophical, legal, or constitutional tradition that purports to protect the individual from the social, repression is likely to be entrenched psychically, discursively. This, after all, is the space in and over and through which hegemony operates. Consider the case of an unrepressed or irrepressible five-year-old who starts school. In a radically individualistic society, socialization by definition is predicated on a restriction. It is a circumscription of the individual ideally promoted and effectuated by the individual him- or herself. So self-determination or autonomy becomes a condition of controlling oneself in order to fit (into) the space of the social.

By contrast, liberalism's primary response to heterogeneity within social formations is in terms of tolerating the different, thus presupposing the moral and political primacy of the homogeneous. Jameson is right, then, that much of what passes for a defense of difference is liberal tolerance, and so feeds institutionally into the model of managed or corporate multiculturalism. As Jameson indicates, tolerance turns accordingly on the assumption of social standardization, thus obliterating social heterogeneity by presupposing a denial of difference. But having said this, Jameson's Marxism moves him to dismiss "neoethnicity" as "yuppie" celebration absent any sustained analysis of raciation or engendering.[48]

Between the homogenizing, assimilative thrust of conservative (or weak) multiculturalism and the condescending tolerant pluralism of liberalism's managed multiculturalism (which, Michele Wallace points out, lumps together as homogeneous "people of color"), it should be evident that certain kinds of heterogeneity are experienced socially and academically as dangerous. And indeed they are. Heterogeneity may be dangerous, as Judith Stiehm illustrates ("Diversity's Diversity"), because it places distinct limits on the comfort and easiness of the established and already ordered, of the familiar and the controlled. It threatens the safe confines of disciplinarity with transgressive disruption, shifting the balance of power, and occasionally challenges prevailing forms of power altogether. It may be dangerous, again, because it confronts the projects of (racialized) purity and determinism with the distinct limits of their fabricated possibilities. Heterogeneity challenges the mythical inward obsessiveness of purity with the generative energy of impurity, the projection of "natural" normativity with abnormal transgression, the limit of the Same with the transformative renewability of the possible and the novel.

Heterogeneity, as Ellen Rooney notes in passing, is dangerous more generally also.[49] Heterogeneity is fragile and tenuous, in fact and as ideal. Just as the appeal to identity or difference can legitimate exclusionary or inclusionary social conditions, so heterogeneity can just as easily give way to fascist social movements as to emancipatory ones; and it can be open or promote closure as a response to manifold possibilities. It must include within its conditions of being the violent as much as the pacific, the vicious as much as the virtuous, the disciplinary as much as the inter- and transdisciplinary, those committed to the restriction and effacement of heterogeneity as much as those committed to its flourishing. Thus heterogeneity always includes within the possibility of its moment the forces that might render its moment impossible. Nevertheless, the former terms of these contrasts are in tension (and perhaps straightforwardly in contradiction) with heterogeneous flourishing. Heterogeneity necessitates incessant reiteration, the conscious and active and repeated renewal of the conditions of its possibility. This is a possibility that seems to be under challenge as much from within as from without. So some circumscription of conditions or expressions restrictive or repressive of heterogeneity may be in order, a circumscription the degree of which is to be commensurate with the danger posed to heterogeneous possibilities.

The academy, itself a site of conflicting heterogeneous interests and energies and reflecting the social more widely, has usually moved to appropriate transgressive interventions — especially those that strike a possibly transformative chord. Universities impute to transgressive interventions their own interpretations and self-understandings, their own discursive limits and horizons. In this way, the desirable is figured in terms of the familiar, delimited in terms of the constraints of what is consumable. The potentially subversive nature of transgressive intellectual interventions is cut off via this reconfiguration. The heterogeneity of the desirable (what may be valued and deemed valuable) is reinterpreted to fit preconceived assumptions — politically, morally, and epistemologically — about what ought to be desired and so pursued. Disciplinary boundaries are to desiring subjects what borders are to the migrant and the exiled.

As nations acquire borders, so disciplines acquire boundaries, and for much the same reasons: for policing and self-policing what can be said and done, for ordering the unacceptable and the foreign, and for licensing membership and citizenship. I do not mean to deny that the costs and deadly dangers of crossing states' borders are significantly greater than those associated with cutting across disciplinary boundaries; I intend the analogy to suggest that disciplinary boundaries are hardly natural, and their transgression also carries costs. By extension, normative commitment to transdisciplinarity, advanced in the name and for the sake of the multicultural, can be made analogous to the commitment to transnationality, the breaking down of national borders. But just as transnationality may be prompted and harnessed in the interests of global capital and flexible accumulation, so multi- and transdisciplinarity may be licensed and muzzled by an academy seeking to rationalize costs, minimize operational expenses, and control labor conditions.

Disciplines appear, as contemporary nations do, more or less with modernity. Prior to the seventeenth century, roughly, knowledge was pursued formally and legitimated in the name of Philosophy. Distinctions were drawn within Philosophy. It is worth recalling that until the nineteenth century the chair of

Physics in the European university was known as the chair of Natural Philosophy. Psychology, Sociology, Economics, Linguistics, and Anthropology were all carried out under the rubric of Philosophy, and by philosophers.

The introduction of disciplines with modernity, then, constituted an opening up and a circumscription of possibilities. The univocity and generality of Philosophy perhaps produced a different sort of circumscription and ordering prior to 1500, especially in the hands of church doctrinaire domination. Nevertheless, as the disciplinary imperative enabled specialization and the fine focus effected via structuration, its censorious introspection and confined fascination with the grounds of its own limits prompted the division of scientific labor and the dismissal of any object or claim falling outside its structure of interpretability. If, for modernity, the relation to (a fixed understanding of) nature was one of conquest, the medium was divide and rule. Initially, interdisciplinary (or transdisciplinary) studies were inconceivable and, once their possibility could be thought, they were derisively dismissed. However, as Barbara Christian and Angie Chabram Dernersesian point out, the confinement of disciplines is inadequate to the task of representing and comprehending intersectional identities, the nodal points (as Shea McManus puts it) marking the confluence of ethnorace, class, gender, ability, and age. Indeed, disciplines are inadequate, more generally, for their necessary partiality will fail to comprehend the complexity of nature and social life.

Irrepressible traces of heterogeneity, however tenuous, dot any mapping of human histories.[50] And if there is a functional point to the narrative I have woven, it is that I project (self-)critical multicultural conditions as ways of cultivating those improvizational expressions that have survived the repressive thrust of homogeneous and unicultural imposition. Even within the parameters of a culture — Dyson makes the point about African-American culture, but it can be generalized for Jewishness, or Islam, or Christianity, say — heterogeneity is the norm, and homogeneity (as in fundamentalisms) is achieved only at the cost of censorious restriction. Even in the face of the most extremely repressive forms of imposed homogeneity, the inevitable cultural hybridity that heterogeneity licenses promotes the renewable possibilities of playing novel expression. Witness jazz and gospel blues and rap in the United States, kwela music and sculpture parks in South Africa, religious animism throughout Africa, reggae in the Caribbean and beyond, cubism in Europe, tea drinking in England, pasta in Italy, and so on. This entails (perhaps as an inductive generalization) a commitment to expand and extend possible spaces for articulating heterogeneous multiplication and mixing, and to proliferate multiplicity because of the value of heterogeneity. In this sense, heterogeneity is the condition *and* outcome, the value *and* challenge, the danger *and* cost of living freely.

So multiculturalism is a political commitment. But it is no more political than monoculturalism, and for similar reasons. There has been a very careful micromanagement of the drive to diversify academically and corporatively.

Corporate and managed multiculturalisms have proved themselves effective tools for managing and maintaining a constriction of diversity that otherwise might be unmanageable and overwhelming from the standpoint of bureaucratic and administrative technologies. Heterogeneity threatens incorporatively to transform the rationalities of the technobureaucratic mode, even within the university. As Henry Louis Gates argues, a renewably common culture may emerge from the free exploration of the hybrid complexities inherent in heterogeneous expression. Judith Stiehm argues, however, that the appropriation of diversity has been used to legitimize the status quo and has resulted in token attempts to include representative members of the otherwise marginalized while leaving presuppositions, values, and the modes of control untouched. Despite the critical rhetoric around political correctness, then, corporate and managed multiculturalisms go hand in glove with monoculturalism. Their respective differences are no greater than those currently between the Democratic and Republican parties.

This constriction of multicultural possibilities to some variant of its corporate management is at one with the reduction of the political to questions about symbolic representation identified earlier. But it is crucial to recognize that political concerns run considerably deeper and wider. Generically, it may be useful to think of politics as a contestational (co)defining of the common conditions of a human collective (or set of collectives). This definition may assume three interrelated forms (the Chicago Cultural Studies Group identifies the initial two). The first (though not necessarily in order of priority) concerns the politics of cultural contestation, the media and symbols by which conditions and concerns, interests and idea(l)s are articulated. This is the politics of representation that has come to dominate postmodernism's self-understanding of the academy and the culture of late capitalism. The second concerns the politics of the state apparatus, the struggle over the distribution of institutionalized power and its material effects. The third form of the political concerns local issues of mobilization and social movements around material resources, powers, and opportunities outside — or beneath and beyond the reach — of the state apparatus. Taken together, politics here may be understood as the variety of contestations concerning power — about who expresses and represents power, about how power is configured, about what people invested with power are able to effect, and in what ways being so invested affects people's lives.

Contributors to the volume generally agree with Michael Walzer that critical multiculturalism is not simply a "product of ... greater social *and economic* equality," but that it represents more basically "a program for" greater equality. It cannot be the product of greater economic equality in any simple sense because throughout the "multicultural decade" of the 1980s in the United States, economic distribution grew more *unequal* and in racially defined ways (even as the size of the black middle class, for instance, grew).[51] At the very least, critical multiculturalism may be understood, in the way Tommy Lott puts it, as a form of resisting monoculturalism and cultural hegemony as well as socioeconomic exploitation and hardship. This raises new sites of possibility for the intersection of cultural studies and the social sciences and for the renewal of critical and insurgent multicultural conditions. Cultural theorizing in the name of multiculturalism, as I argued earlier, has suffered the poverty of avoiding, if not effacing, political economy. As Terence Turner suggests, this is an absence social science can serve to address by identifying the material conditions of institutional power, the prevailing "structure of opportunities," as Andrew Hacker expresses it.[52] But this positivity that defines so much of social science threatens it always with the incipient pull of positivism, those fixed and universalizing norms regulating meaning, reference, truth, and value that purport to be neutral but generalize local commitments. Multicultural theorizing in the critical vein, then, must be made constantly to confront social science positivity with laying bare the assumptions of its assertions, the grounds of its projections, the interests served by its representations. In short, critical multiculturalism must be made to serve social science with the limits of the latter's assertive positivity.

Read in this context, the various forms of multiculturalism identified in these pages are deeply implicated in the contest over power, over who mobilizes and expresses power, over how power is conceived and exercised, over who benefits from or suffers the effects of power and its institutionalization. As the Chicago Cultural Studies Group concludes, multiculturalism, accordingly, is not a postconflictual state. Where power is centralized, multiculturalism will either be suffered poorly or denied completely.[53] Here multicultural conditions and possibilities will be reduced at least to the managed mode of its corporate instrumentality. It is acceptable so long as it serves to produce the goods, to deliver the racialized up for further exploitation, to keep the peace, to entertain. Liberal multiculturalism is willing to share power — on the terms of those already holding it. But dancing with the devil has a habit of turning the devil into me. The aims of (self-)critical multiculturalisms, of promoting multicultural conditions, are to undo the effects of repressive and constraining power. Polyvocal and insurgent multiculturalisms undertake to transform power and its values to commonly emancipatory ends and effects. So the point of instituting renewable multicultural conditions is to facilitate and promote incorporative heterogeneity through hybrid interaction and the production of hybrid effect.

Iris Young offers an idealization of the heterogeneous public in the city as the normative aim and condition of a civic democracy. In support of this idealization, she articulates four virtues of such a normative ideal. I think it possible to refashion (and add to) them as multicultural virtues for the academy, horizons to be pursued, and pragmatic principles to be instituted.

Accordingly, multicultural heterogeneity (of the self-critical variety) first encourages and enables interactive and intersecting multiplicities in social and subject positions. It thus gives voice to, and works to clear an institutional space for, that which might otherwise be eclipsed or effaced. Second, it makes possible the living out of variety, imparting contextualized nuance and specificity to the general and the various. Third, it is committed critically to satisfying the excitement and desirability of the new, of multiple and diffuse possibilities. (Young calls this virtue "eroticism.") In this sense, multicultural heterogeneity is a generator of other (hybrid and novel) possibilities alongside the old, established, and familiar. It thus serves to limit the entrenchment of canonical values and establishment power. Fourth, multicultural heterogeneity must not only exist (silently), it must be seen to exist (publicly), for only then will its example furnish evidence of its rewards.[54] To these may be added two further virtues. Fifth, the inter- and transdisciplinarity to which multicultural heterogeneity is committed offers nonreductionistic complexity in social analysis (where and when sociocultural conditions warrant it) rather than the reductionistic simplism mandated by the homogeneous positivism of disciplinarity. Positivistic reductionism produced by disciplinary homogeneity turns on a presumption of truth as discrete, singular, simple, and self-contained rather than as relatively complex, nuanced, overdetermined, and multifaceted. As Ramon Gutierrez points out, this is as much a growing recognition among the physical and life sciences as it is among the humanities and social sciences. And finally, multicultural heterogeneity is committed to the renewable value of incorporative politics, to the continuous transformation of values as the university body politic (faculty, regents, administrators, staff, and students) becomes increasingly diverse and polyvocal — less white, male, and (upper) middle class. Consider, for example, the critical transformation in use — in speaking and writing — of English as the medium of instruction, transaction, and relation on the college campus (and the politics of bemoaning its impoverishment as the college campus becomes increasingly diverse). This has been accompanied by the metamorphosis of English qua discipline to cultural studies as the formative, if tentative, intersection of humanities and social science.

The academy accordingly offers multiple fora for expressing a wide variety of ideas and arguments: lecture course and seminar, curricular and extracurricular discussion groups and workshops, conferences and colloquia, student organizations and societies, student and faculty-staff newspapers, networks and bulletin boards, radio and television, libraries and laboratories, performance and music and film clubs. Perhaps the only limit on this heterogeneity should be whether an expression advances an idea, argument, or interpretation, or whether the expression harmfully disables the satisfaction of the university missions of learning and service opportunities and benefits fairly available to all its constituents. In this sense, Iris Young's two political principles of a heterogeneous public seem especially adaptable to the multicultural university: No person's actions or aspects of a person's life should be forced into privacy; and no social institutions or practices should be excluded a priori from being a proper subject for public discussion and expression.[55] Here, the only qualification may be that some fora made available within the space of the university may be more or less relevant and appropriate for some specific discussion and expression. Physics 101 may not be the time and place to discuss whether Khalid Abdul Mohammad[56] should be extended an invitation to speak on campus, though in the face of an otherwise prevailing silence — and consistent with the commitment to "multicultural science" promoted by Sandra Harding — it may be; and, as Harding implies ("Is Science Multicultural?"), Physics 101 emphatically may be the forum occasionally to introduce a discussion on the political economy of physics, or on the relative absence from physics faculties of those persons not white and not male.

White, middle-class, middle-aged, nonhandicapped, and heterosexual men assume institutional authority in the academy more, and more readily, than anyone else (although it is not quite so stark now as it once was). Men are brought up and socialized into such positions of authority, assuming authority's institutional positionality, voice, and tone. They are more practiced at social articulation and persuasion, tend materially to be more privileged, more confident, and have a history of institutional backing.[57] Against this background, multicultural heterogeneity is committed to making the transvaluational conditions of incorporation more amenable and accessible to all. It undertakes to promote procedural fairness in defining and instituting the mission and mandate of the academy in general and of a university specifically, for it problematizes univocity and multiplies not only quantities but kinds of inputs. It promotes airing the needs and interests of all constituents related to the pedagogy and political economy of the academy. These include concerns pertaining within and to the relation of science and social science, humanities and the arts, professional and pre- or nonprofessional programs, theory and practice, research, teaching, and service, as well as administrative governance and investment. Thus, multicultural heterogeneity politicizes explicitly what is otherwise political only silently and in the absence of acknowledgment (that is, what gets denied as political in the name of universal value). It renders explicit the contestation over values and entitlements making overtly political what in any case is implicitly so and, thus, reduces the possibility of manipulation and control as well as maintenance of the status quo. Finally, multicultural heterogeneity multiplies in number and quality the available nature and range of knowledge and practical wisdom.[58] And given that heterogeneity applies equally within and between groups, it likewise sets a limit on intragroup tyranny as it delimits intergroup oppression.

The university is an intersection of local and (more or less) general — even global — interests and concerns. It is a site — or better yet, a collection of radically contextual sites — for contesting exclusions, exploitation, and oppressions initiated or extended by the force of capital. Institutionally, the university offers a range of highly specific sites for addressing concerns about the work conditions for faculty, staff, and students; about principles and procedures of administration and (self-)governance (especially in the case of public institutions — and virtually every accredited institution of higher learning in the

United States receives public money); about investment decisions locally and globally; about who the university is servicing in its pedagogical and public functions; about what is taught and how; about the nature of the research conducted in the institution's name and whose interests it serves; and about the political commitments of the institution locally and more generally.

A university offers a wide range of expertise, but also conflicting interests and commitments. These interests may be more or less insular, and too often a university insulates domains of power. In contrast to the instrumentality of corporately-managed multiculturalism that serves to wrap up and project exclusionary power in currently fashionable but questionable terms, multicultural heterogeneity is concerned with contesting oppressive power, marginality, and exclusion in its local contexts. It seeks to transform the academy — the knowledge authorized in the academy's name and the institutions of which it is comprised and that do its bidding — to incorporative ends. It seeks to do this, however, in the more or less local contexts of specific historical and institutional circumstances confronting the parties at any moment. Those who work for the university may cross paths and engage with a wide variety of individuals and groups, ranging from the most marginal to the most powerful people throughout the world. It follows that "local contexts" similarly acquire significance from the specificity of the levels of intervention possible. So "local contexts" may range from departmental politics to international fora like UNESCO, from student representation to state transformation (as in South Africa), from mobilizing an urban "community" to offer housing for the homeless or mobilizing the homeless to demand decent housing for themselves to mobilizing the international "community" to intervene in Bosnia or Rwanda.

Thus I conclude this introduction to *Multiculturalism: A Critical Reader* with an opening, with questions related to that raised by Lauren Berlant and Michael Warner ("Introduction to 'Critical Multiculturalism'"): What sorts of critical normative generalizations can multicultural heterogeneity project from the specificity of local contexts to contest the imposition of more or less global homogeneous norms? And how might the heterogeneously multicultural guide relational comparisons across differentiated contexts and promote incorporative politics and pedagogies? It is to possible answers to these questions that contributors variously address themselves, testifying in the process to the heterogeneous vigor and openness of multicultural commitments.

Notes

1 This paper was completed with the partial assistance of a Dean's Incentive Grant from the College of Public Programs, Arizona State University. A discussion with members of the Brown Bag Discussion Forum in the School of Justice Studies, Arizona State University, helped to clarify some of the central ideas. I remain

indebted to Shea McManus, Pat Lauderdale, Lauren Berlant, and Stephan Chambers for their especially revealing readings of earlier drafts. Responsibility for any shortcomings should be directed to Gabriel's dog, Ego.

2 The back cover advertizing the paperback edition of *Debating P.C.*, the widely circulated collection edited by Paul Berman, sets up just these sorts of fixed dual oppositions: "White-male Eurocentrism ... or an essential cultural heritage?"; "Open-minded ... or politically correct?"; "Cultural diversity ... or gutting academic standards?" The front cover questions whether "P.C." is "Preparing Americans for a Wider World ... or Narrowing Academic Freedom?" Paul Berman, ed., *Debating P.C.: The Controversy over Political Correctness on College Campuses* (New York: Laurel Paperbacks, 1992).

3 Capitalism is the only "-ism" not considered irrational by its proponents, precisely because it is *the* economic system purportedly produced by a reductive rational choice, thus maximizing self-interest by allowing individual preference to flourish. It is notable, then, that capitalisms do not turn into "-isms" the politico-cultural formations they consider expressive of self-interest, but construe them under the rubric of democracy. Peter McLaren makes a similar remark in his exchange with Kelly Estrada, "A Dialogue on Multiculturalism and Democratic Culture," *Educational Researcher*, 22, 3 (April 1993), p. 27. Socialism or communism, or primitivism or postmodernism, for that matter, are deemed *not* rational either because they conflate economics with politics and culture, ideologically constraining rationality economically determined, or because they ignore economic self-interest altogether.

4 Matthew Arnold, *Culture and Anarchy* (Cambridge: The University Press, 1937), p. 6. On the history of mono- and multiculturalism, see the useful article by Michael Geyer, "Multiculturalism and the Politics of General Education," *Critical Inquiry* 19 (Spring 1993), esp. pp. 500–503.

5 Montefiore lists these as neutrality, indifference, and detachment; objectivity, impartiality, and openmindedness; disinterestedness, independence, and lack of bias; the political; and the academic. Alan Montefiore, ed. *Neutrality and Impartiality: The University and Political Commitment* (Cambridge: Cambridge University Press, 1975), pp. 4–46. Cf. Jaroslav Pelikan, *The Idea of the University —A Reexamination* (New Haven, CT: Yale University Press, 1992).

6 On black emigration, cf. Derrick Bell's parable about Atlantis in *Faces at the Bottom of the Well: The Permanence of Racism* (New York: BasicBooks, 1992), pp. 32–46. Edward Said has argued at length that the colonial project was borne in good part by its cultural reproduction in the minds of colonizing and colonized people, forced and imposed upon, as it was resisted by, the colonized. The same line of argument is tellingly appropriate in accounting for the terrible "success" of ethnoracial domination within the United States though this need not commit one to the thesis of "internal colonialism." See Edward Said, *Culture and Imperialism* (London: Chatto and Windus, 1993).

7 Dostoevsky and Tolstoy, and perhaps Lenin, Sholokhov, Pasternak, and Solzhenitsyn were considered part of the Euro-American tradition, perhaps even of the Euro-American canon, in ways that Cabral and Césaire, Nyerere and Fanon were not. Moreover, to criticize multiculturalism by pointing out that the likes of the latter were educated in European institutions and influenced by European philosophical

and social theories, as Steven Yates among others does, is to remain bound by the terms of monoculturalism. It is not simply that this line of criticism is irrelevant because it is aimed at a nonexistent object, nor just that it continues implicitly to elevate the supposed desirability of Eurocentered culture and values. It continues to promote the silence of those who will no longer be, and it does so by refusing to recognize even the possibility of speaking in a voice different from the magisterial monocultural one of America or Her Majesty. Steven Yates, "Multiculturalism and Epistemology," *Public Affairs Quarterly* 6, 4 (October 1992), esp. pp. 440–8. Andrew Apter has offered a very interesting analysis of a debate about which Yates and others like him are clearly altogether ignorant. Andrew Apter, *"Que Faire?* Reconsidering Inventions of Africa," *Critical Inquiry* 19 (Autumn 1992), pp. 87–104.

8 Placide Tempels, *Bantu Philosophy* (Paris: Presence Africaine, 1949); Terence Ranger, *Rhodes, Oxford, and the Study of Race Relations* (Oxford: Clarendon Press, 1989). For an analysis of Ranger's lecture, see the chapter on "Racial Knowledge" in my *Racist Culture: Philosophy and the Politics of Meaning* (Oxford: Basil Blackwell, 1993), esp. pp. 175–7.

9 I do not mean thus to deny or downplay the importance of black resistance to oppression and subjugation prior to the 1940s.

10 Where racialized others were too powerful or desirable to be economically ignored or marginalized, they were rearticulated either in ethnic (rather than racial terms), or implicitly — and sometimes explicitly — reclassified as "honorary whites" (or, depending on point of view and positionality, as "acting white.")

11 Lauren Berlant has pointed out to me that I mean "public" and "private" in narrower senses than those now imparted to them in the debates about "public culture" and the "public sphere." Obviously, an ethnic parade on Fifth Avenue is public in this broader sense. I mean the distinction I am drawing here to reflect the one discrimination law is made to turn on. Application of the Equal Protection Clause is circumscribed by this interpretation of the public/private distinction in cases, for example, regarding hate speech but also employment opportunity. This interpretation of the distinction is reflected also in the public and private economic sector, public and private universities, private clubs, and public and private corporations.

12 Besides the demographic inaccuracy that this identification often implies — in many of the larger urban centers in the United States it is plainly false, "minority" also carries with it the implication of being childlike, of requiring guardianship rather than meriting autonomy. Cf. Harry C. Triandis, "The Future of Pluralism Revisited," in *Eliminating Racism: Profiles in Controversy,* eds P. A. Katz and D. A. Taylor (New York: Plenum Press, 1988), p. 31. On the genealogy of monoculturalism and challenges to it, see Cornel West, "The New Cultural Politics of Difference," in *Out There: Marginalization and Contemporary Cultures,* eds R. Ferguson, M. Geyer, T. T. Minh-ha, and C. West (New York: New Museum of Contemporary Art and MIT Press, 1992); and Stuart Hall, "What's the 'Black' in Black Popular Culture?" in *Black Popular Culture,* ed. Gina Dent (Seattle: Bay Press, 1992), pp. 231–3.

13 The UNESCO report on universal multiculturalism offers a telling example of assuming relatively fixed and discrete cultural groupings. Cf. Ervin Laszlo, *The Multicultural Planet: The Report of a UNESCO International Expert Group* (Oxford: Oneworld, 1993). Henry Giroux has written revealingly of the

corporatizing of American education in "School for Scandal: Cultural Politics and the Pedagogy of Commercialization," *Transition* 59 (1993), pp. 88–103. Cf. John F. Coffey, "Race Training in the United States: An Overview," in *Strategies for Improving Race Relations: The Anglo-American Experience*, eds John W. Shaw, Peter G. Nordlie, and Richard M. Shapiro (Manchester: Manchester University Press,1987), p. 123; Homi Bhabha, "The Third Space: Interview" in *Identity: Community, Culture, Difference*, ed. Jonathan Rutherford (London: Lawrence and Wishart, 1990), pp. 207–8.

14 Ellen Rooney, "Discipline and Vanish: Feminism, the Resistance to Theory, and the Politics of Cultural Studies," *differences: A Journal of Feminist Cultural Studies* 2, 3 (1990), pp. 14–28.

15 Derrick Bell, *Race, Racism and American Law*, 3rd ed. (Boston: Little Brown, 1992), pp. 2, 38–9. The insistence Bell identifies runs clear from Daniel Patrick Moynihan in the mid-1960s to William Julius Wilson at the end of the 1980s. See Daniel Patrick Moynihan, *Daedalus* (Winter 1966), pp. 288–9; William Julius Wilson, *The Truly Disadvantaged* (Chicago: University of Chicago Press, 1987), esp. ch. 7. Stephen Steinberg usefully surveys this history in "The Liberal Retreat from Race," *New Politics* (Summer 1994), pp. 30–51. On economic and cultural transformations in the world economy, see David Harvey, *The Condition of Postmodernity* (Oxford: Basil Blackwell, 1989); and Immanuel Wallerstein, *Geopolitics and Geoculture: Essays on the Changing World-System* (Cambridge: Cambridge University Press, 1991).

16 To avoid misconception, perhaps this should be reconfigured as post- and transassimilationist; as post- and transintegrationist. Those strains of cultural separatism that do pertain are *mis*construed as part of multicultural self-understanding. Strains of cultural separatism, while in some ways understandable, are more properly to be conceived in terms of the logic of monoculturalism.

17 Patricia Williams, *The Alchemy of Race and Rights: The Diary of a Law Professor* (Cambridge: Harvard University Press, 1991), p. 121. See also Hazel Carby, "The Multicultural Wars," in *Black Popular Culture*, ed. Gina Dent (Seattle: Bay Press, 1992), pp. 189–90.

18 Concerning historical representation, perhaps the readiest indication of this rewriting may be found in Ronald Takaki's monumental if integrationist work, *A Different Mirror: A History of Multicultural America* (Boston: Little Brown, 1993). For a critique of the integrationist thrust of Takaki's commitments as evidenced in his earlier reader *From Different Shores* (Oxford: Oxford University Press, 1987), see E. San Juan Jr, *Racial Formations/Critical Transformations* (New Jersey: Humanities Press, 1992), pp. 98–102. Nevertheless, that this historical rewriting is more than an academic exercise with profound political and pedagogical (not to mention economic effects) is evidenced by considerations as diverse as the school textbook market from New York to California, and Michigan to Texas, as well as by the struggle to control not only the meanings and values, but also the empirical details and economic resources, for instance, surrounding the Alamo. Thus Daughters (and no doubt sons) of the Republic of Texas find their authority to control meanings, details, and value (normative and economic) strongly challenged by oppositional "revisionists." Cf. "For Defenders of the Alamo, Assault is Joined Anew," *The New*

York Times (March 29, 1994), pp. A1, 10. Fashion-wise, witness the long baggy street shorts extended broad cultural credentials via the creative brilliance of Michigan's Fab Five college basketball team from 1991 on. The day I write this, Arizona's state newspaper, *The Arizona Republic* (referred to by my colleague Manuel Pino as "The Repulsive"), ran a headline characterizing these shorts as "hideous." Racialized culture strikes again! *The Arizona Republic* (March 29, 1994), p. A1. On rap, see Tricia Rose, *Black Noise: Rap Music and Black Culture in Contemporary America* (Middletown, CT: Wesleyan University Press, 1994); and Houston A. Baker Jr, *Black Studies, Rap, and the Academy* (Chicago: Chicago University Press, 1993).

19 Homi Bhabha, "The Third Space: Interview," p. 211. Cf. David Theo Goldberg, "Made in the USA: Racial Mixing 'n Matching," in *Microidentities*, ed. Naomi Zack. Forthcoming.

20 There are attempts at hand to extend that dominant image by adapting it to the projected reconfigurations of managed multiculturalism. *Time Magazine*, for instance, issued a Special Fall Issue in 1993 devoted to "The New Face of America: How Immigrants are Shaping the World's First Multicultural Society." This "new" hybrid "face" of "multicultural America" is reconstituted, in *Time*ly fashion, as a whiter shade of pale. In an article entitled "The Art of Diversity: Hyphenated Americans can be found along the cutting edge of all the arts," *Time* includes in its list of exemplary hyphenated-American artists only those who are presumed as ethnoracially marked: Gloria Estefan, Derek Walcott, Amy Tan, Rosie Perez, and Black 47 ("the ... Irish-American group ... which mixes rap, reggae, and traditional Irish melodies"). Thus, the hybrid of ethnoracially-defined Americans remain, in this order of things, the exception to the supposed norm of ethnoracially neutral, nonhyphenated, authentic Americans — namely, northern European white Protestants. *Time Magazine* (Special Issue, Fall 1993), pp. 23–5.

21 Geyer, "Multiculturalism and the Politics of General Education," p. 509.

22 Stanley Fish, *There's No Such Thing as Free Speech, and It's a Good Thing Too* (Oxford: Oxford University Press, 1993).

23 In a slip of the keyboard, I first transposed "causes" for "courses." In 1994, as Arizona State University was fighting the possibility of further legislative budget cuts, President Lattie Coor was hauled before legislators to answer questions from irate Republicans, under explicit threat of cuts, about a course on lesbianism offered at the university and nudity in an American Playhouse production that aired on the state public television station, KAET, which is run by the university. On Whittle and the political economy of contemporary schooling in the United States, see also Henry A. Giroux, "School for Scandal: Cultural Politics and the Pedagogy of Commercialization," pp. 88–103.

24 See Cornel West, "Identity: A Matter of Life and Death," in *Prophetic Reflections: Notes on Race and Power in America* (Monro, ME: Common Courage Press, 1993), pp. 163–8.

25 David Theo Goldberg, "Hate or Power?," *APA Newsletter on Philosophy and the Black Experience* 93, 2 (Fall 1994); Carby, "The Multicultural Wars," p. 193.

26 Similarly, reference to "silenced subalterns" seems to have become a kind of mantra of cultural studies erudition. The Chicago Cultural Studies Group point out in "Critical Multiculturalism" below that cultural studies has assumed "the subaltern" as its primary object of knowledge. This appropriation, virtually without exception,

excludes any sustained analysis of the transformations in political economy or in the constitution of legality that have produced, or reproduce, the conditions of subalternality for those so referenced. In a romantic extension of exoticism, "the subaltern" is indiscriminately expanded to cover any and all who suffer exploitation, exclusion, domination, and subjugation with little or no contextualization of differentiated conditions of subalternation. Michael Keith, in his subtle analysis of the political economy and culture of the "street" in contemporary London's East End, offers some telling examples. Michael Keith, "Street Sensibility? Negotiating the Political by Articulating the Spatial," paper presented at the conference on Social Justice and Fin de Siecle Urbanism, School of Geography, University of Oxford, March 1994.

27 Kobena Mercer has shown how the civil rights rhetoric of the left was appropriated and emptied out in the 1980s by a resurrected conservativism trading on an essentialized identity politics defined in terms of a "fixed hierarchy of racial, sexual, or gendered oppressions." Kobena Mercer, "Welcome to the Jungle: Identity and Diversity in Postmodern Politics," in *Identity: Community, Culture, Difference*, ed. Jonathan Rutherford (London: Lawrence and Wishart, 1990), pp. 46–7. Two examples will suffice: First, *Diversity and Division: A Critical Journal of Race and Culture* is a new glossy magazine that appropriates the style and look — in design and representation — of critical race and cultural studies. (A number of friends and colleagues to whom I showed the magazine commented that its logo emulates — if not caricatures — the cover of my book, *Anatomy of Racism*.) Yet, in the name of a reconstructed liberalism claiming to represent "the voices of a new generation" (read: the "Young Conservatives"), the magazine seeks to forward "ideas that know no color." The articles are uniformly dismissive of what it reductively derides as the academic politics of political correctness, and its criticism is overwhelmingly directed at African-Americans, lumping together the likes of Tony Martin, Maya Angelou, Jocelyn Elders, Houston Baker, and Cornel West (whose identity with each other is clearly racially prefigured in the minds of the contributors). Guilt by associated identity. Second, and along somewhat the same lines, in the run-up to the first free and universal elections in South Africa in April 1994, F. W. de Klerk's ruling National(ist) Party, creator and executioner of apartheid, managed to recast itself as the representative of political moderation boxed between the extreme right of Buthelezi's Inkatha or the various white conservatives and neofascists, on one hand, and the leftist likes of the ANC, PAC, and so on, on the other. This electorally defined reconstruction was designed not only to appeal to whites but to those characterized as "Coloured" in the language and logic of apartheid. It worked with devastating effect in the Cape Province: on the strength of the Coloured vote, the National(ist) Party retained provincial power in the south. According to Steinberg, Moynihan has advocated this sort of "semantic infiltration" as effective political tactic for at least a decade. Steinberg, "The Liberal Retreat from Race," p. 36.

28 Rosemary Coombs, "Tactics of Appropriation and the Politics of Recognition in Late Modern Democracies," *Political Theory* 21, 3 (August 1993), p. 412.

29 Frederic Jameson, *Postmodernism, or the Cultural Logic of Late Capitalism* (New York: Verso, 1990), pp. 261–4, 272; Saskia Sassen, *The Global City* (Princeton: Princeton University Press, 1992); cf. Arjun Appadurai's compelling body of work, including "Disjuncture and Difference in the Global Cultural Economy," *Theory,*

Culture and Society 7 (1990), pp. 306 ff., "The Heart of Whiteness," *Callaloo* 16, 4 (1993), pp. 796–807, and "Consumption, Duration, and History," *Stanford Literature Review* 10 (1993), pp. 11 33; and Henry A. Giroux, *Disturbing Pleasures. Learning Popular Culture* (New York: Routledge, 1994), esp. "Consuming Social Change: The United Colors of Benetton," pp. 13–16. Steven Connor's book, *Theory and Cultural Value*, exemplifies the general issue. Connor usefully casts his discussion in terms of a critical account of the philosophical history of cultural evaluation and the commitment to value-neutrality. He notes, correctly, that any sharp distinction between economic and noneconomic value has become virtually impossible to sustain. Questions about goods are, at once, questions about evaluating what counts as (a) good. Yet in attempting to expand an understanding of economic value into the general question of evaluation and value-judgments, Connor skirts the question of the commodified (re)production of value altogether by displacing the discussion simply to textual products and evaluation. Economy comes to be understood in strictly psychoanalytic and literary terms. Raising the question of extratextual economic value does not fall back into a totalizing assumption of the "homogeneity of value"; quite the contrary. It is to insist that value is heterogeneous, but also that it is *produced* in a variety of ways. Steven Connor, *Theory and Cultural Value* (Oxford: Basil Blackwell, 1992), esp. ch. 4. It is noteworthy that of all the contributors to *Social Text*'s "Symposium on Popular Culture and Political Correctness," only Robert Stam and Ella Shohat engage the interrelated importance of culture and political economy. *Social Text* 36 (Fall 1993), pp. 3–40. By contrast, compare David Harvey's important work, most notably *The Condition of Postmodernity* (Oxford: Basil Blackwell, 1989).

30 Pat Lauderdale, "Frank Justice or Frankenstein Justice: Homogeneous Development as Deviance in a Diverse World," in *The Underdevelopment of Development*, eds S. Chew and R. Denemark (London: Sage), forthcoming, 1995.

31 Cf. Steven Yates, "Multiculturalism and Epistemology," *Public Affairs Quarterly* 6, 4 (October 1992), esp. pp. 48–52. It may be helpful to displace Afrocentricity by self-critical Afromodalities, the heterogeneous modes of African seeing, knowing, and doing that serve notice on the parochialism of Euromotivated vision, epistemologies, and practices.

32 Ibid. Arthur Schlesinger, Diane Ravitch, and Paul Berman, among others, I think, would concur with Yates.

33 On ABC'S "Nightline" (Tuesday, March 27, 1994), Cokie Roberts interviewed noted South African journalist Allister Sparks concerning the political violence leading up to the landmark elections enabling, for the first time, all adult South Africans to vote. In the ten minute or so exchange, Roberts repeatedly asked Sparks whether, given the violence, South Africa would be able to shed its past and "enter the modern world." It is a deep presumption that violence is absent from the politics of modernity. But where, if not in the modern world, and what, if not created by this modern world, is South Africa? Violence is as constitutive a feature of modernity's social life as racism and nationalism. Cf. Zygmunt Bauman, *Modernity and the Holocaust* (Oxford: Polity Press, 1989), and Appadurai, "The Heart of Whiteness," p. 798.

34 Contra Yates, "Multiculturalism and Epistemology," esp. pp. 440–8. But cf. Amy Gutmann's "The Challenge of Multiculturalism in Political Ethics," especially the

discussion of what Gutmann characterizes as "Deliberative Universalism." *Philosophy and Public Affairs* 22, 3 (Summer 1993), pp. 171–206.

35 Richard Rorty, "Postmodernist Bourgeois Liberalism," *The Journal of Philosophy* (1983). Cf. Joseph Margolis, *The Truth About Relativism* (Oxford: Basil Blackwell, 1991). Michael Walzer properly insists that multicultural relations are played out necessarily in terms of a local and specific set of social conditions and value tradition. Michael Walzer, "Multiculturalism and Individualism," *Dissent* (Spring 1994), p. 186.

36 Cf. Goldberg, *Racist Culture,* Chapter 9.

37 Gerald Graff, "'Teach the Conflicts': An Alternative to Educational Fundamentalism," in *Literature, Language, and Politics,* ed. Betty Jean Craige (Athens: The University of Georgia Press, 1988), pp. 99–109. Cf. Thomas Nagel, *The View from Nowhere* (New York: Oxford University Press, 1986); and Stephen L. Darwall, "How Nowhere Can You Get (and Do Ethics)?," *Ethics* 98, 1 (October 1987), pp. 137–57.

38 Edward Said, *Culture and Imperialism* (London: Chatto and Windus, 1993), pp. xxvii–ix; Iris Marion Young, *Justice and the Politics of Difference* (Princeton: Princeton University Press, 1990); Stuart Hall, "What is this 'Black' in Black Popular Culture?," p. 28. See also the helpful work of Arjun Appadurai, "Disjuncture and Difference in the Global Cultural Economy," pp. 295–310; and Walzer, "Multiculturalism and Individualism," esp. pp. 185–6. Walzer nevertheless interprets this heterogeneity in terms of the American pluralist tradition and understanding. Daniel Patrick Moynihan acknowledges interethnic heterogeneity, indeed, as a principle of history (just as he is silent about intraethnic differentiation), though he urges that the political insistence upon such heterogeneity must lead inevitably to "pandaemonium." Daniel Patrick Moynihan, *Pandaemonium: Ethnicity in International Politics* (New York: Oxford University Press, 1993).

39 Arthur M. Schlesinger Jr, *The Disuniting of America* (New York: W. W. Norton, 1992), 9–17. General Constand Viljoen, the presidential candidate for Freedom Forum, the far right-wing party in South Africa's first universal elections, couples Schlesinger's appeal to homogeneity to Verwoerd's logic of apartheid. He argued in his stump speech that because of the dangers to the body politic by South Africa's *de facto* heterogeneity, the only solution is to insist upon a separate homogeneous state for white Afrikaners.

40 For a contemporary US version of this, see the recent book edited by William Bennett, *The Book of Virtues* (New York: Simon and Schuster, 1993).

41 Ernest Gellner, *Nations and Nationalism* (Oxford: Basil Blackwell, 1983), esp. Chs. 2 and 3.

42 Gabriel Josipovici, "Going and Resting," in *Jewish Identity*, eds David Theo Goldberg and Michael Krausz (Philadelphia: Temple University Press, 1993), pp. 309–21. On the importance of movements and migrations to world-systems generally, see Andre Gunder Frank, "Bronze Age World-System Cycles" and respondents, *Current Anthropology* 34, 4 (August–October 1993), pp. 383–429. On the relations between commodity flows and cultural traffic, see Appadurai, "Disjuncture and Difference in the Global Cultural Economy."

43 Cf. Appadurai, "The Heart of Whiteness," p. 798.

44 See Paul Gilroy's *The Black Atlantic: Modernity and Double Consciousness* (Cambridge: Harvard University Press, 1993).

45 Robert and Jon Solomon, *Up the University: Recreating Higher Education in America* (Reading, Mass.: Addison and Wesley, 1993).

46 Droughts are natural events. Famines, as Amartya Sen so convincingly argues, are political-economic events. Famines usually follow from the likes of a civil war or administrative ineptitude and international disinterest. Amartya Sen, *Poverty and Famines: An Essay on Entitlement and Deprivation* (Oxford: The Clarendon Press, 1981).

47 Young, *Justice and the Politics of Difference*, p. 37.

48 Jameson, *Postmodernism, or the Cultural Logic of Late Capitalism*, pp. 341–2.

49 Rooney, "Discipline and Vanish: Feminism, the Resistance to Theory, and the Politics of Cultural Studies," p. 22.

50 There is growing evidence that diversity underpins evolutionary and ecological success too. "The more species an ecosystem has, the better it can withstand stress." William K. Stevens, "Study Bolsters Value of Species Diversity," *The New York Times* (February 1, 1994) p. B7.

51 Walzer, "Multiculturalism and Individualism," p. 191. Cf. Andrew Hacker, *Two Nations: Black and White, Separate, Hostile, Unequal* (New York: Charles Scribner, 1992), esp. ch. 3, "Being Black in America," pp. 31–49.

52 Ibid., p. 11.

53 I am grateful to Pat Lauderdale for raising the issue.

54 Young, *Justice and the Politics of Difference*, pp. 238–40.

55 Ibid., p. 120.

56 Khalil Abdul Mohammad was the spokesman for the Nation of Islam whom Louis Farrakhan suspended as a result of the furor caused by the racist remarks he repeatedly made in public. Mohammad continued to be invited to speak on college campuses despite his suspension and (perhaps in part because of his) remarks.

57 Young, *Justice and the Politics of Difference*, p. 184.

58 Ibid., pp. 185–6.

PART I:
THINKING THE UNTHINKABLE:
SETTING AGENDAS

1

White Terror and Oppositional Agency: Towards a Critical Multiculturalism

Peter McLaren[1]

Nothing can be denounced if the denouncing is done within the system that belongs to the thing denounced.

Julio Cortázar
Hopscotch, Chapter 99.

As we approach the year 2000, we increasingly are living simulated identities that help us adjust our dreams and desires according to the terms of our imprisonment as schizo-subjects in an artificially-generated world. These facsimile or imitative identities are negotiated for us by financial planners, corporate sponsors, and marketing strategists through the initiatives of transnational corporations, enabling a privileged elite of white Euro-Americans to control the information banks and terrorize the majority of the population into a state of intellectual and material impoverishment. With few, if any, ethically convincing prospects for transformation — or even survival — we have become cybernomads whose temporary homes become whatever electronic circuitry is available to us. In our hyperfragmented and postmodern culture, democracy is secured through the power to control consciousness and to semioticize and discipline bodies by mapping and manipulating sounds, images, and information, and forcing identity to take refuge in forms of subjectivity increasingly experienced as isolated and separate from larger social contexts. The idea of democratic citizenship has now become synonymous with the private, consuming citizen and the increasing subalternization of the "other." The representation of reality through corporate sponsorship and promotional culture has impeded the struggle to establish democratic public spheres and furthered the dissolution of historical solidarities and forms of community, accelerating the experience of circular narrative time and the postindustrial disintegration of public space. The proliferation and phantasmagoria of the image has hastened the death of modernist identity structures and has interpellated individuals and groups into a world of cyborg citizenry in which "other" individuals are reconstituted through market imperatives as a collective assemblage of "them" read against our "us."

The Debate over Multiculturalism

It is no secret, especially after the Los Angeles uprising — or what Mike Davis calls the "LA Intifada"[2] — that the white-controlled media (often backed by victim-blaming white social scientists) have ignored the economic and social conditions responsible for bringing about in African-American communities what Cornel West has called a *"walking nihilism* of pervasive drug addiction, pervasive alcoholism, pervasive homicide, and an exponential rise in suicide."[3] They have additionally ignored or sensationalized social conditions in Latin and Asian communities, polemicizing against their value systems and representing them as teleologically poised to explode into a swelter of rioting and destruction. Such communities have been described as being full of individuals who lash out at the dominant culture in an anarcho-voluntaristic frenzy in a country where there are more legalized gun dealers than gas stations. In this view, agency seems to operate outside of forces and structures of oppression and policing discourses of domination and social practices. Subalternized individuals appear politically constituted outside of discursive formations and are essentialized as the products of their pathological "nature" as drug or alcohol users and as participants in crime.

Furthermore, the white media has generated the racially pornographic term "wilding" to account for recent acts of violence in urban centers by groups of young African-Americans.[4] Apparently the term "wilding," first reported by New York City newspapers in relation to the Central Park rapists, was relevant only to violence committed by black male youth since the term was conspicuously absent in press reports of the attack by white male youths on Yusef Hawkins in Bensonhurst.[5] Thus the postmodern image which many white people now entertain in relation to the African-American underclass is one constructed upon violence and grotesquerie — a population spawning mutant youths with steel pipes who, in the throes of bloodlust, roam the perimeter of the urban landscape high on angel dust, randomly hunting whites. In addition to helping to justify police "attitude adjustments" inflicted upon black people in places such as LA, Detroit, and Hemphill in Sabine County, Texas, this image of minorities has engendered hostility to their efforts to articulate their own understanding of race relations and to advancing a conception of democracy in a way that is compatible with a critical multiculturalism.

Forms of Multiculturalism

This paper attempts to advance a conception of "critical multiculturalism" by exploring various positions held within the debate over multiculturalism which I have termed conservative or corporate multiculturalism, liberal multiculturalism and left-liberal multiculturalism. These are, to be sure, ideal-typical labels meant to serve only as a "heuristic" device. In reality the characteristics of each position tend to blend into each other within the general horizon of our social lifeworld. As with all typologies and criteriologies, one must risk monolithically projecting them onto all spheres of cultural production and instantiating an overly abstract totality that dangerously reduces the complexity of the issues at stake. My effort should be understood only as an initial attempt at transcoding and mapping the cultural field of race and ethnicity so as to formulate a tentative theoretical grid that can help discern the multiple ways in which difference is constructed and engaged.

Conservative Multiculturalism

Conservative multiculturalism can be traced to colonial views of African-Americans as slaves, servants, and entertainers, views which were embedded in the self-serving congratulatory and profoundly imperialist attitude of Europe and North America. Such an attitude depicted Africa as a savage and barbaric continent populated by the most lowly of creatures who were deprived of the saving graces of Western civilization.[6] It can also be located in evolutionary theories which supported United States Manifest Destiny, imperial largesse, and Christian imperialism. And it can further be seen as a direct result of the legacy of doctrines of white supremacy which biologized Africans as "creatures" by equating them with the earliest stages of human development. Africans were likened by whites to savage beasts or merry-hearted singing and dancing children. The former stereotype led a ten-year-old black boy — Josef Moller — to be exhibited at the Antwerp Zoo at the turn of the century. Closer to home and less remote in time is the case of Ota Benga, a "pygmy" boy exhibited in 1906 at the Monkey House in the Bronx Zoo as an "African homunculus" and as the "missing link" and was encouraged by zoo keepers to charge the bars of his cage with his mouth open and teeth bared.[7] In less sensational guise, this attitude continues right up to the present time. For instance, in 1992 the Secretary of Health and Human Services in the Bush Administration appointed Frederick A. Goodwin, a research psychiatrist and career federal scientist, as Director of the National Institute for Mental Health. Goodwin used animal research findings to compare youth gangs to groups of "hyperaggressive" and "hypersexual" monkeys and commented that "maybe it isn't just the careless use of word when people call certain areas of certain cities, 'jungles'."[8]

Whether conceived as the return of the repressed of Victorian Puritanism, a leftover from Aristotelian hierarchical discourse or colonial and imperialist ideology, it remains the terrible truth of history that Africans have been forcibly placed at the foot of the human ladder of civilization.[9] As Jan Nederveen Pieterse notes, America historically has been the "white man's country" in which "institutional and ideological patterns of the supremacy of white over black, and of men over women, supplemented and reinforced one another."[10]

While I do not wish to lapse into either an essentialized nativism which sees non-Western indigenous cultures as homogeneous or a view of the West that sees it as all of one piece — a monolithic block — and unaffected by its colonized subjects or solely as an engine of imperialism, I need to affirm the fact that many conservative multiculturalists have scarcely removed themselves from the colonialist legacy of white supremacy. Although they would like officially to distance themselves from racist ideologies, conservative multiculturalists pay only lip service to the cognitive equality of all races and charge unsuccessful minorities with having "culturally deprived backgrounds" and a "lack of strong family-oriented values." This "environmentalist" position still accepts black cognitive inferiority to whites as a general premise and provides conservative multiculturalists with a means of rationalizing why some minority groups are successful while other groups are not. This also gives the white cultural elite the excuse they need for unreflectively and disproportionately occupying positions of power. They are not unlike the *inscripti* of the right-wing Roman Catholic organization, *Opus Dei,* that attempts intellectually and culturally to sequester or barricade its members from the tools for critical analyses of social life in order to shore up its own power to manipulate and propagandize.

One particularly invidious project of conservative or corporate multiculturalism is to construct a common culture — a seamless web of textuality — bent on annulling the concept of "the border" through the delegitimization of foreign languages and regional and ethnic dialects, a persistent attack on nonstandard English, and the undermining of bilingual education.[11] Gramsci's understanding of this process is instructive and is cogently articulated by Michael Gardiner:

> For Gramsci, the political character of language was made apparent in the attempt by the dominant class to create a common cultural "climate" and to "transform the popular mentality" through the imposition of a national language. Therefore, he felt that linguistic hegemony involved the articulation of signs and symbols which tended to codify and reinforce the dominant viewpoint. Thus, Gramsci argued that there existed a close relationship between linguistic stratification and social hierarchization, in that the various dialects and accents found within a given society are always rank-ordered as to their perceived legitimacy, appropriateness, and so on. Accordingly, concrete language usage reflects underlying asymmetrical power

relations and it registers profound changes which occur in the cultural, moral, and political worlds. Such changes were primarily expressed through what Gramsci termed "normative grammar"; roughly, the system of norms whereby particular utterances could be evaluated and mutually understood ... which was an important aspect of the state's attempt to establish linguistic conformity. Gramsci also felt that the maintenance of regional dialects helped peasants and workers partially to resist the forces of political and cultural hegemony.[12]

In addition to its position on common culture and bilingual education, there are further reasons why corporate multiculturalism needs to be rejected. First, conservative or corporate multiculturalism refuses to treat whiteness as a form of ethnicity and in doing so posits whiteness as an invisible norm by which other ethnicities are judged. Second, conservative multiculturalism — as in the positions taken by Diane Ravitch, Arthur Schlesinger Jr, Lynne V. Cheney, Chester Finn, and others — uses the term "diversity" to cover up the ideology of assimilation that undergirds its position. In this view, ethnic groups are reduced to "add-ons" to the dominant culture. Before you can be "added on" to the dominant United States culture you must first adopt a consensual view of culture and learn to accept the essentially Euro-American patriarchal norms of the "host" country. Third, as I mentioned earlier, conservative multiculturalism is essentially monolingual and adopts the position that English should be the only official language. It often is virulently opposed to bilingual education programs. Fourth, conservative multiculturalists posit standards of achievement for all youth that are premised on the cultural capital of the Anglo middle class. Fifth, conservative multiculturalism fails to interrogate the high status knowledge — knowledge that is deemed of most value in the white, middle-class United States — to which the educational system is geared. That is, it fails to question the interests that such knowledge serves. It fails, in other words, to interrogate dominant regimes of discourse and social and cultural practices that are implicated in global dominance and are inscribed in racist, classist, sexist and homophobic assumptions. Conservative multiculturalism wants to assimilate students to an unjust social order by arguing that every member of every ethnic group can reap the economic benefits of neocolonialist ideologies and corresponding social and economic practices. But a prerequisite to "joining the club" is to become denuded, deracinated and culturally stripped.

Recent popular conservative texts set firmly against liberal, left-liberal, and critical strands of multiculturalism include Richard Brookhiser's *The Way of the Wasp: How It Made America and How It Can Save It, So to Speak*, Arthur Schlesinger Jr's *The Disuniting of America: Reflections on A Multicultural Society*, and Laurence Auster's *The Path to National Suicide: An Essay On Immigration and Multiculturalism*. According to Stanley Fish,[13] these texts, which appeal to national unity and a harmonious citizenry, can readily be traced to earlier currents of Christianity (which proclaimed that it was God's wish that the future of civilization be secured in the United States) and social Darwinism (United States Anglo-Saxon stock is used to confirm the theory of natural selection). Reflecting and enforcing the assumptions made by the authors (whom Fish describes as racist, not in the sense that they actively seek the subjugation of groups but who perpetuate racial stereotypes and the institutions that promote them) is the SAT test used in high school for college admission. Fish notes that one of the authors of this test, Carl Campbell Brigham, championed in his *A Study of American Intelligence* a classification of races which identified the Nordic as the superior race and, in descending order, located the less superior races as Alpine, Mediterranean, Eastern, New Eastern, and Negro. This hierarchy was first expounded by Madison Grant in *The Passing of the Great Race* and reflected in earlier European works such as *Essai sur l'inégalité des races humaines*, a four-volume testament to the racial superiority of the Germanic race by Joseph Arthur (Comte de Gobineau) and Edward Gibbon's *Decline and Fall of the Roman Empire*, a work which blamed miscegenation for the decline of civilization.[14] Not surprisingly, this hierarchy is confirmed in Brigham's later comparative analysis of intelligence. The library at the Educational Testing Service compound still bears Brigham's name. Also problematic, as Mike Dyson points out, are theories linking white racism to biological determinism, such as recent discussions of "melanin theory" in which black researchers view whiteness as a genetic deficiency state that leads whites to act violently against blacks because of white feelings of color inferiority.[15]

When we contrast Brookhiser's key WASP virtues with non-WASP virtues (those of the Asians, or African-Americans or Latinos) we see the Western virtues of the former — Conscience, Antisensuality, Industry, Use, Success, and Civic Mindedness — being distinguished as more American than the lesser virtues of the latter — Self, Creativity, Ambition, Diffidence, Gratification and Group Mindedness. This also reflects a privileging of Western languages (English, French, German, and ancient Greek) over non-Western languages.[16] Supposedly, Western European languages are the only ones sophisticated enough to grasp truth as an "essence." The search for the "truth" of the Western canon of "Great Works" is actually based on an epistemological error that presumes there exists a language of primordial Being and Truth. This error is linked to the phenomenalist reduction of linguistic meaning which endows language (through analogy) with sense perceptions and thereby reduces the act of interpretation to uncovering the "true understanding" that reciprocally binds the truth of the text to the preunderstanding, tacit knowledge, or foreknowledge of the reader. From this view of the mimetic transparency of language, aesthetic judgments are seen as linked directly to ethics or politics through a type of direct correspondence.[17] Language therefore becomes elevated to a "truth-telling status" which remains exempt from its ethico-political situatedness or embeddedness. It is this epistemological error that permits conservatives to denounce totalitarianism in the name of its own truth and serves as a ruse for expanding present forms of domination. It is not hard to see how racism can become a precondition for this form of conservative multiculturalism insofar as Western virtues (which can be traced back as far as Aristotle's Great Chain of Being) become the national-aestheticist ground for the conservative multiculturalist's view of civilization and citizenship. The power of conservative multiculturalism lays claim to its constituents by conferring a space for the reception of its discourses that is safe and sovereignly secure. It does this by sanctioning empiricism as the fulcrum for weighing the "truth" of culture. What discursively thrives in this perspective is an epistemology which privileges the logic of cause-and-effect narrative construction.[18] In this case, intelligence quotients and test scores become the primary repository of authoritative exegesis in what constitutes successful school citizenship. Fortunately, as Foucault points out, subjectivity is not simply constituted through discourses and social practices of subjugation. Liberal, left-liberal, and critical forms of multiculturalism envisage a different "practice of the self" and new forms of self-fashioning and subjectivity based on more progressive conceptions of freedom and justice.

Liberal Multiculturalism

Liberal multiculturalism argues that a natural equality exists among whites, African-Americans, Latinos, Asians, and other racial populations. This perspective is based on the intellectual "sameness" among the races, on their cognitive equivalence or the rationality imminent in all races that permits them to compete equally in a capitalist society. However, from the point of view of liberal multiculturalism, equality is absent in United States society, not because of black or Latino cultural deprivation, but because social and educational opportunities do not exist that permit everyone to compete equally in the capitalist marketplace. Unlike their critical counterparts, they believe that existing cultural, social, and economic constraints can be modified or "reformed" in order for relative equality to be realized. This view often collapses into an ethnocentric and oppressively universalistic humanism in which the legitimating norms which govern the substance of citizenship are identified most strongly with Anglo-American cultural-political communities.

Left-Liberal Multiculturalism

Left-liberal multiculturalism emphasizes cultural differences and suggests that the stress on the equality of races smothers those important cultural differences between races that are responsible for different behaviors, values, attitudes, cognitive styles, and social practices. Left-liberal multiculturalists feel that mainstream approaches to multiculturalism occlude characteristics and differences related to race, class, gender, and sexuality. The left-liberal position tends to exoticize "otherness" in a nativistic retreat that locates difference in a primeval past of cultural authenticity. We can identify this position with the male erotic iconography used by Baudelaire to describe his black mistress, Jeanne Duval, that transformed her into a mediating sign for male desire.[19] Those who work within this perspective have a tendency to essentialize cultural differences, however, and ignore the historical and cultural "situatedness" of difference. Difference is understood as a form of signification removed from social and historical constraints. That is, there is a tendency to ignore difference as a social and historical construction that is constitutive of the power to represent meanings. It is often assumed that there exists an authentic "female" or "African-American" or "Latino" experience or way of being-in-the-world. Left-liberal multiculturalism treats difference as an "essence" that exists independently of history, culture, and power. Often one is asked to show one's identity papers before dialogue can begin.

This perspective often locates meaning through the conduit of "authentic" experience in what I feel to be the mistaken belief that one's own politics of location somehow guarantees one's "political correctness" in advance. Either a person's physical proximity to the oppressed or one's own location as an oppressed person is supposed to offer a special authority from which to speak. What often happens is that a populist elitism gets constructed as inner-city teachers or trade unionists or those engaged in activist politics establish a pedigree of voice based on personal history, class, race, gender, and experience. Here the political is often reduced only to the personal where theory is dismissed in favor of one's own personal and cultural identity. Of course, one's lived experience, race, class, gender, and history are important in the formation of one's political identity, but one must be willing to examine personal experience and one's speaking voice in terms of the ideological and discursive complexity of its formation.

Of course, when a person speaks it is always from somewhere,[20] but this process of meaning production needs to be interrogated in order to understand how one's identity is constantly being produced through a play of difference linked to and reflected by shifting and conflicting discursive and ideological relations, formations, and articulations.[21] Experience needs to be recognized as a site of ideological production and the mobilization of affect and can be examined largely through its imbrication in our universal and local knowledges and modes of intelligibility and its relationship to language, desire, and the body.[22] As Joan Scott notes, "experience is a subject's history. Language is the site of history's enactment."[23] Of course, I am not arguing against the importance of experience in the formation of political identity, but rather pointing out that it has become the new imprimatur for legitimating the political currency and incontestable validity of one's arguments. This has often resulted in a reverse form of academic elitism. Not only is the authority of the academic under assault (and rightly so, in many cases), but it has been replaced by a populist elitism based on one's own identity papers.

Critical and Resistance Multiculturalism

Multiculturalism without a transformative political agenda can be just another form of accommodation to the larger social order. I believe that, because they are immersed in the discourse of "reform," liberal and left-liberal positions on multiculturalism do not go nearly far enough in advancing projects of social transformation. With this concern in mind, I am developing the idea of critical multiculturalism from the perspective of a resistance, poststructuralist approach to meaning, and emphasizing the role that language and representation play in the construction of meaning and identity. The poststructuralist insight that I am relying on is located within the larger context of postmodern theory — that disciplinary archipelago that is scattered through the sea of social theory — and asserts that signs and significations are essentially unstable and shifting and can only be temporarily fixed, depending on how they are articulated within particular discursive and historical struggles. From the perspective of what I am calling "critical multiculturalism," representations of race, class, and gender are understood as the result of larger social struggles over signs and meanings and in this way emphasizes not simply textual play or metaphorical displacement as a form of resistance (as in the case of left-liberal multiculturalism), but stresses the central task of transforming the social, cultural, and institutional relations in which meanings are generated.

From the perspective of critical multiculturalism, the conservative and liberal stress on sameness and the left-liberal emphasis on difference is really a false opposition. Identity based on "sameness" and identity based on "difference" are forms of essentialist logic: in both, individual identities are presumed to be autonomous, self-contained, and self-directed. Resistance multiculturalism also refuses to see culture as nonconflictual, harmonious, and consensual. Democracy is understood from this perspective as busy — it's not seamless, smooth, or always a harmonious political and cultural state of affairs.[24] Resistance multiculturalism doesn't see diversity itself as a goal, but rather argues that diversity must be affirmed within a politics of cultural criticism and a commitment to social justice. It must be attentive to the notion of "difference." Difference is always a product of history, culture, power, and ideology. Differences occur *between* and *among* groups and must be understood in terms of the specificity of their production. Critical multiculturalism interrogates the construction of difference and identity in relation to a radical politics. It is positioned against the neo-imperial romance with monoglot ethnicity grounded in a shared or "common" experience of "America" that is associated with conservative and liberal strands of multiculturalism.

Viewed from the perspective of a critical multiculturalism, conservative attacks on multiculturalism as separatist and ethnocentric carry with them the erroneous assumption by white Anglo constituencies that North American society fundamentally constitutes social relations of uninterrupted accord. The liberal view is seen to underscore the idea that North American society is largely a forum of consensus with different minority viewpoints simply accretively added on. We are faced here with a politics of pluralism which largely ignores the workings of power and privilege. More specifically, the liberal perspective "involves a very insidious exclusion as far as any structural politics of change is concerned: it excludes and occludes global or structural relations of power as 'ideological' and 'totalizing'."[25] In addition, it presupposes harmony and agreement — an undisturbed space in which differences can coexist. Within such a space, individuals are invited to shed their positive characteristics in order to become disembodied and transparent American citizens, a cultural practice that creates what David Lloyd calls a "subject without properties."[26] In this instance, citizens are able to occupy a place of "pure exchangeability." This accords the universalized white subject a privileged status. Yet such a proposition is dangerously problematic. Chandra Mohanty notes that difference cannot be formulated as negotiation among culturally diverse groups against a backdrop of benign variation or presumed cultural homogeneity. Difference is the recognition that knowledges are forged in histories that are riven with differentially constituted relations of power; that is, knowledges, subjectivities, and social practices are forged within "asymmetrical and incommensurate cultural spheres."[27]

Homi K. Bhabha makes the lucid observation that in attributing the racism and sexism of the common culture solely to the "underlying logic of late capitalism and its patriarchal overlay," leftists are actually providing an alibi for the common culture argument. The common culture is transformed in this instance into a form of ethical critique of the political system that supposedly fosters unity within a system of differences. The concept of cultural otherness is taken up superficially to celebrate a "range of 'nation-centered' cultural discourses (on a wide axis from right to left)."[28] It is worth quoting at length Bhabha's notion of common culture as the regulation and normalization of difference:

> Like all myths of the nation's "unity," the common culture is a profoundly conflicted ideological strategy. It is a declaration of democratic faith in a plural, diverse society and, at the same time, a defense against the real, subversive demands that the articulation of cultural difference — the empowering of minorities — makes upon democratic pluralism. Simply saying that the "nation's cement" is inherently sexist or racist — because of the underlying logic of late capitalism and its patriarchal overlay — ironically provides the "common culture" argument with the alibi it needs. The vision of a common culture is perceived to be an ethical mission whose value lies in revealing, prophylactically, the imperfections and exclusion of the political system as it exists. The healing grace of a culture of commonality is supposedly the coevality it establishes between social differences — ethnicities, ideologies, sexualities — "an intimation of simultaneity across homogeneous empty time" that welds these different voices into a "unisonance" that is expressive of the "contemporaneous community of the national culture."[29]

Too often liberal and conservative positions on diversity constitute an attempt to view culture as a soothing balm — the aftermath of historical disagreement — some mythical present where the irrationalities of historical conflict have been smoothed out.[30] This is not only a disingenuous view of culture, it is profoundly dishonest. It overlooks the importance of engaging in some instances in dissensus in order to contest hegemonic forms of domination, and to affirm differences. The liberal and conservative positions on culture also assume that justice already exists and needs only to be evenly apportioned. However, both teachers and students need to realize that justice does not already exist simply because laws exist. Justice needs to be continually created, and constantly struggled for.[31] The question I want to pose to teachers is this: Do teachers and cultural workers have access to a language that allows them sufficiently to critique and transform existing social and cultural practices that are defended by liberals and conservatives as unifyingly democratic?

Critical Multiculturalism and the Politics of Signification

Since all experience is the experience of meaning, we need to recognize the role that language plays in the production of experience.[32] You don't have an experience and then search for a word to describe that experience. Rather, language helps to constitute experience by providing a structure of intelligibility or mediating device through which experiences can be understood. Rather than talking about experience, it is more accurate to talk about "experience effects."[33]

Western language and thought are constructed as a system of differences organized *de facto* and *de jure* as binary oppositions — white/black, good/bad, normal/deviant, etc. — with the primary term being privileged and designated as the defining term or the norm of cultural meaning, creating a dependent hierarchy. Yet the secondary term does not really exist outside the first, but, in effect, exists inside it, even though the phallogocentric logic of white supremacist ideology makes you think it exists outside and in opposition to the first term. The critical multiculturalist critique argues that the relationship between signifier and signified is *insecure* and *unstable*. Signs are part of an ideological struggle that attempts to create a particular regime of representation that serves to legitimate a certain cultural reality. For instance, we've witnessed a struggle in our society over the meaning of terms such as "negro," "black," and "African-American."

According to Teresa Ebert, our current ways of seeing and acting are being disciplined for us through forms of signification, that is, through modes of intelligibility and ideological frames of sense-making. Rejecting the Saussurian semiotics of signifying practices (and its continuing use in contemporary poststructuralism) as "historical operations of language and tropes," Ebert characterizes signifying practices as "an ensemble of material operations involved in economic and political relations."[34] She maintains, rightly in my view, that socioeconomic relations of power require distinctions to be made among groups through forms of signification in order to organize subjects according to the unequal distribution of privilege and power.

To illustrate the politics of signification at work in the construction and formation of racist subjects, Ebert offers the example of the way in which the terms "negro" and "black" have been employed within the racial politics of the United States. Just as the term "negro" became an immutable mark of difference and naturalized the political arrangements of racism in the 1960s, so too is the term "black" being refigured in the white dominant culture to mean criminality, violence, and social degeneracy. This was made clear in the Willie Horton campaign ads of George Bush and in the Bush and David Duke positions on hiring quotas. In my view, this was also evident in the verdict of the first Rodney King trial in Los Angeles.

Carlos Munoz Jr has revealed how the term "Hispanic" in the mid-1970s became a "politics of white ethnic identity" that de-emphasized and in some cases rejected the Mexican cultural base of Mexican-Americans. Munoz writes that the term "Hispanic" is derived from "Hispania" which was the name the Romans gave to the Iberian peninsula, most of which became Spain, and "implicitly emphasizes the white European culture of Spain at the expense of the nonwhite cultures that have profoundly shaped the experiences of all Latin-Americans." Not only is this term blind to the multiracial reality of Mexican-Americans through its refusal to acknowledge "the nonwhite indigenous cultures of the Americas, Africa, and Asia, which historically have produced multicultural and multiracial peoples in Latin America and the United States," it is a term that ignores the complexities within these various cultural groups.[35] Here is another example of the melting pot theory of assimilation fostered through a politics of signification. So, we might ask ourselves, what signifieds (meanings) will be attached to certain terms such as "welfare mothers"? Most of us know what government officials mean when they refer derisively to "welfare mothers." They mean black and Latino mothers.

Kobena Mercer recently described what he calls "black struggles over the sign." Mercer, following Volosinov, argues that every sign has a "social multiaccentuality" and it is this polyvocal character that can rearticulate the sign through the inscription of different connotations surrounding it. The dominant ideology always tries to stabilize certain meanings of the term. Mercer writes that for over four centuries of Western civilization, the sign "black" was "structured by the closure of an absolute symbolic division of what was white and what was nonwhite" through the "morphological equation" of racial superiority.[36] This equation accorded whiteness with civility and rationality and blackness with savagery and irrationality. Subaltern subjects themselves brought about a reappropriation and rearticulation of the "proper name" — Negro, colored, black, Afro-American — in which a collective subjectivity was renamed. Mercer notes that in the sixties and seventies, the term "ethnic minorities" connoted the black subject "as a minor, an abject childlike figure necessary for the legitimation of paternalistic idcologies of assimilation and integration that underpinned the strategy of multiculturalism."[37] The term "black community" arose out of a reappropriation of the term "community relations." The state had tried to colonize a definition of social democratic consensus designed to manage race relations through the use of "community relations."

The examples discussed above underscore the central theoretical position of critical multiculturalism: that differences are produced according to the ideological production and reception of cultural signs. As Mas'ud Zavarzadeh and Donald Morton point out, "Signs are neither eternally predetermined nor panhistorically undecidable: they arc rather 'decided' or rendered as 'undecidable' in the moment of social conflicts."[38] Difference is not "cultural obviousness" such as black versus white or Latino versus European or Anglo-American; rather, differences are historical and cultural constructions.[39]

Just as we can see the politics of signification at work in instances of police brutality, or in the way blacks and Latinos are portrayed as drug pushers, gang members, or the minority sidekick to the white cop in movies and television, we can see it at work in special education placement where a greater proportion of black and Latino students are considered for "behavioral" placements whereas white, middle-class students are provided for the most part with the more comforting and comfortable label of "learning disabled."[40] Here, a critical multiculturalist curriculum can help teachers explore the ways in which students are differentially subjected to ideological inscriptions and multiply-organized discourses of desire through a politics of signification.

A critical multiculturalism suggests that teachers and cultural workers need to take up the issue of "difference" in ways that don't replay the monocultural essentialism of the "centrisms" — Anglocentrism, Eurocentrism, phallocentrism, androcentrism, and the like. They need to build a politics of alliance-building, of dreaming together, of solidarity that moves beyond the condescension of, say, "race awareness week," which actually serves to keep forms of institutionalized racism intact. A solidarity has to be struggled for that is not centered around market imperatives, but develops out of the imperatives of freedom, liberation, democracy, and critical citizenship.

The notion of the citizen has been pluralized and hybridized, as Kobena Mercer notes, by the presence of a diversity of social subjects. Mercer is instructive in pointing out that "solidarity does not mean that everyone thinks the same way, it begins when people have the confidence to disagree over issues because they 'care' about constructing a common ground."[41] Solidarity is not impermeably solid but depends to a certain degree on antagonism and uncertainty. Timothy Maliqualim Simone calls this type of multiracial solidarity "geared to maximizing points of interaction rather than harmonizing, balancing, or equilibrating the distribution of bodies, resources, and territories."[42]

Whereas left-liberal multiculturalism equates resistance with destabilizing dominant systems of representation, critical multiculturalism goes one step further by asserting that all representations are the result of social struggles over signifiers and their signifieds. This suggests that resistance must take into account an intervention into social struggle in order "to provide equal access to social resources and to transform the dominant power relations which limit this access according to class privilege, race, and gender."[43] Differences *within* culture must be defined as political difference and not just formal, textual, or linguistic difference. Global or structural relations of power must not be ignored. The concept of totality must not be abandoned but rather seen as an *overdetermined structure of difference.* Differences are always *differences in relation,* they are never simply free-floating. Differences are not seen as absolute, irreducible, or intractable, but rather as undecidable and socially and culturally relational.[44]

Resistance or critical multiculturalism does not agree with those left-liberal multiculturalists who argue that difference needs only to be interrogated as a form of rhetoric, thereby reducing politics to signifying structures and history to textuality.[45] We need to go beyond destabilizing meaning, by transforming the social and historical conditions in which meaning-making occurs. Rather than remaining satisfied with erasing the privilege of oppressive ideologies that have been naturalized within the dominant culture, or with restating dangerous memories that have been repressed within the political unconscious of the state, critical multiculturalist praxis attempts to revise existing hegemonic arrangements. A critical multiculturalist praxis does not simply reject the bourgeois decorum that has consigned the imperialized other to the realm of the grotesque, but effectively attempts to remap desire by fighting for a linguistically multivalenced culture and new structures of experience in which individuals refuse the role of the omniscient narrator but rather conceive of identity as a polyvalent assemblage of (contradictory and overdetermined) subject positions. Existing systems of difference which organize social life into patterns of domination and subordination must be reconstructed.

We need to do more than unflaggingly problematize difference as a condition of rhetoric, or unceasingly interrogate the status of all knowledge as discursive inscription, because, as Ebert notes, this annuls the grounds of both reactionary and revolutionary politics. Rather, we need a rewriting of difference as *difference-in-relation* followed by attempts dramatically to change the material conditions that allow relations of domination to prevail over relations of equality and social justice. This is a different cultural politics than one of simply reestablishing an inverse hierarchical order of blacks *over* whites or Latinos *over* whites. Rather, it is an attempt to transform the very value of hierarchy itself, followed by a challenge to the material structures that are responsible for the overdetermination of structures of difference in the direction of oppression, injustice, and human suffering. However, this is not to claim that individuals are oppressed in the same ways since groups are oppressed nonsynchronously in conjunction with systems such as class, race, gender, age, ethnicity, sexuality, etc.[46] People can be situated very differently in the *same totalizing structures of oppression.* We need to analyze and challenge the specific enunciations of microdifferences within difference and the macrostructure of difference-in-relation.[47] We need to refocus on "structural" oppression in the forms of patriarchy, capitalism, and white supremacy — structures that tend to get ignored by liberal multiculturalists and their veneration of difference as identity. As educators and cultural workers, we must critically intervene in these power relations that organize difference.

Whiteness: The Invisible Culture of Terror

Educators need to examine critically the development of pedagogical discourses and practices that demonize Others who are different (through transforming them into absence or deviance). Critical multiculturalism calls serious attention to the dominant meaning systems readily available to students and teachers, most of which are ideologically stitched into the fabric of Western imperialism and patriarchy. It challenges meaning systems that impose attributes on the Other under the direction of sovereign signifiers and tropes. And this means not directing all our efforts at understanding ethnicity as "other than white," but interrogating the culture of whiteness itself. This is crucial because unless we do this — unless we give white students a sense of their own identity as an emergent ethnicity — we naturalize whiteness as a cultural marker against which Otherness is defined. Coco Fusco warns that "To ignore white ethnicity is to redouble its hegemony by naturalizing it. Without specifically addressing white ethnicity there can be no critical evaluation of the construction of the other."[48] White groups need to examine their own ethnic histories so that they are less likely to judge their own cultural norms as neutral and universal. The supposed neutrality of white culture enables it to commodify blackness to its own advantage and ends. It allows it to manipulate the "other" but not see this "otherness" as a white tool of exploitation. "Whiteness" does not exist outside of culture but constitutes the prevailing social texts in which social norms are made and remade. As part of a politics of signification that passes unobserved into the rhythms of daily life, and a "politically constructed category parasitic on 'blackness',"[49] "whiteness" has become the invisible norm for how the dominant culture measures its own worth and civility.

Using an ethnosemiotic approach as a means of interrogating the culture of whiteness and to understand ethnicity as a rhetorical form, Dean MacCannell, in his new book, *Empty Meeting Grounds,* raises the question: "In their interactions with others, how can groups in power manage to convey the impression that they are less ethnic than those over whom they exercise their power; in other words, how can they foster the impression that their own traits and qualities are correct, while the corresponding qualities of others are 'ethnic'?"[50] Furthermore, asks MacCannell, how does the consensus that is achieved in this matter structure our institutions? His answer leads us to explore the secret of power in discourse — that simply because language is essentially rhetorical (that is, free of all bias because it is pure bias) we cannot escape the fact that rhetoric and grammar always intersect in particular ideological formations which makes language unavoidably a *social relation.* And every social relation is a structurally located one that can never be situated outside of relations of power. MacCannell locates this power in the ability of the speaking subject to move into the position of "he" without seeming to leave the position of "I" or "you" (which are empty or "floating" signifiers that have no referent outside the immediate situation). The personal pronoun "he" refers to an objective situation outside of the immediate subjectively apprehended situation. MacCannell asserts that whites have mastered interactional forms that permit them to operate as *interactants* while seeming to be detached from the situation, to be both an "I" or a "you" and a "he" at the same time — both to operate within the situation and to judge it. Dominant groups will always want to occupy the grammatical power position; that is, assume the external objective and judgmental role of the "he" by suggesting that their use of language is free of bias. White culture, according to MacCannell, is an enormous totalization that arrogates to itself the right to represent all other ethnic groups. For instance, binary oppositions such as "white as opposed to nonwhite" always occupy the grammatical position of "him," never "I" or "you," and we know that in white culture, "whiteness" will prevail and continue to be parasitic on the meaning of "blackness."

Cornel West remarks that "'Whiteness' is a politically constructed category parasitic on 'blackness'."[51] He further asserts that "One cannot deconstruct the binary oppositional logic of images of blackness without extending it to the contrary condition of blackness/whiteness itself." According to Jonathan Rutherford

> Binarism operates in the same way as splitting and projection: the center expels its anxieties, contradictions and irrationalities onto the subordinate term, filling it with the antithesis of its own identity; the Other, in its very alienness, simply mirrors and represents what is deeply familiar to the center, but projected outside of itself. It is in these very processes and representations of marginality that the violence, antagonisms and aversions which are at the core of the dominant discourses and identities become manifest — racism, homophobia, misogyny and class contempt are the products of this frontier.[52]

Of course, when binarisms become racially and culturally marked, *white* occupies the grammatical position of *him,* never I or you and, notes MacCannell, "always operates *as if* not dependent on rhetoric to maintain its position."[53] Rhetoric is aligned with *nontruth* and whiteness is perceived as neutral and devoid of interest. Of course, "whiteness" projects onto the term "blackness" an array of specific qualities and characteristics such as wild, exotic, uncontrolled, deviant and savage. Whiteness is founded on the principle of depersonalization of all human relationships and the idealization of objective judgment and duty. MacCannell is worth quoting at length on this issue:

> To say that white culture is impersonal is not the same thing as saying that it does not function like a subject or subjectivity. But it is the kind that is cold, the kind that laughs at feelings while demanding that all surplus libido, energy and capital be handed over to it... White culture begins with the pretense that it, above all, does not express itself rhetorically. Rather, the form of its expression is always represented as only incidental to the truth. And its totalizing power radiates from this pretense which is maintained by interpreting all ethnic expression as "representative," and therefore *merely* rhetorical.[54]

When people of color attack white ground rules for handling disputes, or bureaucratic procedures, or specific policies of institutionalized racism, these are necessary oppositional acts, but insufficient for bringing about structural change because, as MacCannell notes, this work is "framed by the assumption of the dominance of white culture."[55] This is because white culture is predicated upon the universalization of the concept of "exchange values" — systems of equivalences, the transcribability of all languages, the translatability of any language into any other language, and the division of the earth into real estate holdings in which it is possible to calculate and calibrate precisely the worth of every person. MacCannell is quite clear on this. Within such a totalization brought about by white culture, indigenous groups can only belong as an "ethnicity." As long as white culture, as the defining cultural frame for white ethnic transactions, sets the limits on all thought about human relations, there can be no prospect for human equality.

Richard Dyer has made some useful observations about the culture of whiteness, claiming that its property of being "everything and nothing" is the source of its representational power in the sense that white culture possesses the power to colonize the definition of the normal with respect to class, gender, heterosexuality, and nationality.[56] Perhaps white culture's most formidable attribute is its ability to mask itself as a category. Whites will often think of their Scottishness, Irishness, or Jewishness, and so on, before they think of their whiteness. Michael Goldfield argues that white supremacy has been responsible for holding back working-class struggle in the United States, as labor groups tragically failed to grasp the strategic importance for labor in fighting the system of white supremacy, missing an opportunity — especially during the Reconstruction — for changing the face of United States politics.[57]

In her recent book, *Black Looks*, bell hooks notes that white people are often shocked when black people "critically assess white people from a standpoint where 'whiteness' is the privileged signifier." She remarks that

> Their [white people's] amazement that black people match white people with a critical "ethnographic" gaze is itself an expression of racism. Often their rage erupts

because they believe that all ways of looking that highlight difference subvert the liberal belief in a universal subjectivity (we are all just people) that they think will make racism disappear. They have a deep emotional investment in the myth of "sameness," even as their actions reflect the primacy of whiteness as a sign informing who they are and how they think. Many of them are shocked that black people think critically about whiteness because racist thinking perpetuates the fantasy that the Other who is subjugated, who is subhuman, lacks the ability to comprehend, to understand, to see the working of the powerful. Even though the majority of those students politically consider themselves liberals and antiracist, they too unwittingly invest in the sense of whiteness as mystery.[58]

hooks discusses the representation of whiteness as a form of terror within black communities and is careful not simply to invert the stereotypical racist association of whiteness as goodness and blackness as evil. The depiction of whiteness as "terrorizing" emerges in hooks' discussion, not as a reaction to stereotypes but, as she puts it, "as a response to the traumatic pain and anguish that remains a consequence of white racist domination, a psychic state that informs and shapes the way black folks see 'whiteness'."[59]

The Politics of Multicultural Resistance

Critical pedagogy needs to hold a nonreductionist view of the social order; that is, society needs to be seen as an irreducible indeterminacy. The social field is always open and we must explore its fissures, fault-lines, gaps, and silences. Power relations may not always have a conscious design, but they have unintended consequences which define deep structural aspects of oppression even though every ideological totalization of the social is designed to fail. This is not to affirm Schopenhauer's unwilled patterns of history but rather to assert that while domination has a logic without design in its sign systems and social practices, it does operate through overdetermined structures of race, class, and gender difference. Resistance to such domination means deconstructing the social by means of a reflexive intersubjective consciousness — what Freire terms "conscientization." With this comes a recognition that ideology is more than an epistemological concern about the status of certain facts, but the way in which discourse and discursive systems generate particular social relations as well as reflect them. A reflexive intersubjective consciousness is the beginning — but only the beginning — of revolutionary praxis.

We also need to create new narratives — new "border narratives" — in order to reauthor the discourses of oppression in politically subversive ways as well as create sites of possibility and enablement. For instance, we need to ask: How are our identities bound up with historical forms of discursive practices? It is one thing to argue against attacks on polyvocal and inassimilable difference and on narrative closure or to stress the heterogeneity of contemporary culture. But in so doing we must remember that dominant discourses are sites of struggle and their meanings are linked to social struggles and labor/economic relations and then naturalized in particular textual/linguistic referents. Consequently, self-reflection alone — even if it is inimically opposed to all forms of domination and oppression — is only a necessary but not nearly sufficient condition for emancipation. This must go hand in hand with changes in material and social conditions through counterhegemonic action.[60] The sociohistorical dynamics of race, class, and gender domination must never be left out of the education for social struggle or take a back seat to the sociology seminar room. We need a language of criticism as an antidote to the atheoretical use of "personal experience" in advancing claims for emancipatory action. Common sense consciousness is not enough. However, this needs to be followed by the development of truly counterhegemonic public spheres. We need more than rhetorical displacements of oppression but strategic and coordinated resistance to racist patriarchal capitalism and gender-divided labor relations. According to Teresa Ebert, what is needed is an intervention into the system of patriarchal oppression at both the macropolitical level of the structural organization of domination (a transformative politics of labor relations) and the micropolitical level of different and contradictory manifestations of oppression (cultural politics).[61]

Those of us working in the area of curriculum reform need to move beyond the tabloid reportage surrounding the political correctness debate and take the issue of difference seriously and challenge the dismissive undercutting of difference by the conservative multiculturalists. First, we need to move beyond admitting one or two Latin-American or African-American books into the canon of great works. Rather, *we need to legitimize multiple traditions of knowledge.* By focusing merely on diversity we are actually reinforcing the power of the discourses from the Western traditions that occupy the contexts of social privilege. Second, curriculum reform requires teachers to interrogate the discursive presuppositions that inform their curriculum practices with respect to race, class, gender, and sexual orientation. In addition, they need to unsettle their complacency with respect to Eurocentrism. Third, what is perceived as the inherent superiority of whiteness and Western rationality needs to be displaced. The very notion of the "West" is something that critical educators find highly problematic. Why is Toni Morrison, for instance, denounced as non-Western simply because she is African-American? (This is complicated by the fact that conservative multiculturalists often retort with the insinuation that any attack on Western culture is an attack against being American.) Fourth, curriculum reform means recognizing that groups are differentially situated in the production of Western high-status knowledge. How are certain groups represented in the official knowledge that makes up the curriculum? Are they stigmatized because they are associated with the Third World? Are we, as teachers, complicitous with the oppression of these people when we refuse to interrogate popular films and TV shows that reinforce their subaltern status? Educators would do well to follow hooks in dehegemonizing racist discourses such that "progressive white people who are antiracist might be able to understand the way in which their cultural practice reinscribes white supremacy without promoting paralyzing guilt or denial."[62] In addition, curriculum reform means affirming the voices of the oppressed; teachers need to give the marginalized and the powerless a preferential option. Similarly, students must be encouraged to produce their own oppositional readings of curriculum content. And lastly, curriculum reform must recognize the importance of encouraging spaces for the multiplicity of voices in our classrooms and creating a dialogical pedagogy in which subjects see others as subjects and not as objects. When this happens, students are more likely to participate in history rather than become its victims.

In taking seriously the irreducible social materiality of discourse and the fact that the very semantics of discourse is always organized and interested, critical pedagogy has revealed how student identities are differentially constructed through social relations of schooling that promote and sustain asymmetrical relations of power and privilege between the oppressors and the oppressed. And it has shown that this construction follows a normative profile of citizenship and an epistemology that attempts to reconcile the discourse of ideals with the discourse of needs. Discourses have been revealed to possess the power to nominate others as deviant or normal. Dominant discourses of schooling are not laws. Rather, they are strategies — disciplined mobilizations for normative performances of citizenship. Ian Hunter has shown that citizenry taught in schools has less to do with ethical ideals than disciplinary practices and techniques of reading and writing and the way students are distributed into political and aesthetic spaces.[63] We are being aesthetically and morally reconciled with the governing norms of a civic unconscious. The "unconscious" is not a semiotic puzzle to be opened through the discovery of some universal grammar but is rather an ethical technology designed to "complete" students as citizens. Pedagogically, this process is deceptive because it used liberal humanism and progressive education to complete the circuit of hegemony. The liberal position on pedagogy is to use it to open social texts to a plurality of readings. Because we live in an age of cynical reason, this pedagogy provides a "knowing wink" to students which effectively says "We know there are multiple ways to make sense of the world and we know that you know, too. So let's knowingly enter this world of multiple interpretations together and take pleasure in rejecting the dominant codes." Consequently, teachers and students engage in a tropological displacement and unsettling of normative discourses and revel in the semantic excess that prevents any meaning from becoming transcendentally fixed. The result of this practice of turning knowledge into floating signifiers circulating in an avant-garde text (whose discursive trajectory is everywhere and nowhere and whose meaning is ultimately undecidable) is simply a recontainment of the political. By positing undecidability in advance, identity is reduced to a form of self-indexing or academic "vogue-ing." Liberation becomes transformed into a form of discursive "cleverness," of postmodern transgressive-chic grounded in playfully high vogue decodings of always already constructed texts.

I would also like to argue, in conclusion, that students need to be provided with opportunities to construct border identities. Border identities are intersubjective spaces of cultural translation — linguistically multivalanced spaces of intercultural dialogue. It is a space where one can find an overlay of codes, a multiplicity of culturally inscribed subject positions, a displacement of normative reference codes, and a polyvalent assemblage of new cultural meanings.[64]

Border identities are produced in sites of "occult instability" and result in "un laberinto de significados." Here, knowledge is produced by a transrepresentational access to the real — through reflexive, relational understanding amidst the connotative matrixes of numerous cultural codes. It is a world where identity and critical subjectivity depend upon the process of translating a profusion of intersecting cultural meanings.[65] We need to remember that we live in a repressive regime in which identities are teleologically inscribed towards a standard end — the informed, employed citizen. A tension exists among students to "reterritorialize" this narrative in which schools have attempted to install in them through normative pedagogical practices and the nonlinear narratives that they "play out" in the world outside of the school. But students and even their often well-intentioned teachers are frequently incapable of intervening.

Especially in inner-city schools, students can be seen as inhabiting what I call "border cultures." These are cultures which, while there is a repetition of certain normative structures and codes, often "collide" with other codes and structures whose referential status is often unknown or only partially known. In Los Angeles, for instance, it is possible that an inner-city neighborhood will contain Latino cultures, Asian cultures, and Anglo cultures and students live interculturally as they cross the borderlines of linguistic, cultural, and conceptual realities. Students, in other words, have the opportunity to live multidimensionally. Living in border cultures is an anticentering experience as school time and space are constantly displaced and often a carnivalesque liminal space emerges as bourgeois linear time is displaced. Because the dominant model of multiculturalism in mainstream pedagogy is of the corporate or conservative variety, the notion of sameness is enforced and cultural differences that challenge white Anglo cultures are considered deviant and in need of enforced homogenization into the dominant referential codes and structures of Euro-American discourse.

I am in agreement with critics who assert that border identity cannot be subsumed under either dialectical or analytic logic.[66] It is, rather, to experience a deterritorialization of signification[67] in a postnationalist cultural space — that is, in a postcolonial, postnational space. It is an identity structure that occurs in a postimperial space of cultural possibility. The postcolonial subject that arises out of the construction of border identity is nonidentical with itself. It acquires a new form of agency outside of Euro-American Cartesian discourses. It is not simply an inverted Eurocentrism, but one that salvages the modernist referent of a liberation from oppression for all suffering peoples. I am here stressing the universality of human rights but at the same time criticizing essentialist universality as a site of transcendental meaning. In other words, I am emphasizing the universality of rights as historically produced. Social justice is a goal that needs to be situated historically, contextually, and contingently as the product of material struggles over modes of intelligibility as well as institutional and social practices. I need to be clear about what I mean by a referent for social justice and human freedom. I mean that the project underlying multicultural education needs to be situated from the standpoint not only of the *concrete other* but also the *generalized other*. All universal rights in this view must recognize the specific needs and desires of the concrete other without sacrificing the standpoint of a generalized other without which it is impossible to speak of a radical ethics at all. Seyla Benhabib distinguishes between this perspective — what she refers to as an "interactive universalism" — and a "substitutionalist universalism": "Substitutionalist universalism dismisses the concrete other behind the facade of a definitional identity of all as rational beings, while interactive universalism acknowledges that every generalized other is also a concrete other."[68] This position speaks neither exclusively to a liberal humanist ethics of empathy and benevolence nor a ludic postmodernist ethics of local narratives or "les petits recits," but one based on engagement, confrontation and dialogue, and collective moral argumentation between and across borders. It takes into account both macro and micro theory and some degree of normative justification and adjudication of choices. As Best and Kellner note, "one needs new critical theories to conceptualize, describe, and interpret macro social processes, just as one needs political theories able to articulate common or general interests that cut across divisions of sex, race, and class."[69] In this sense I take issue with "ludic" voices of postmodernism that proclaim an end to both self-reflective agenthood and the importance of engaging historical narratives and which proclaim the impossibility of legitimizing institutions outside of "practices and traditions other than through the immanent appeal to the self-legitimation of 'small narratives'."[70] Rather, a critical multiculturalism must take into account the "methodological assumptions guiding one's choice of narratives, and a clarification of those principles in the name of which one speaks."[71]

A border identity is not simply an identity that is anticapitalist and counterhegemonic but is also critically utopian. It is an identity that transforms the burden of knowledge into a scandal of hope. The destructive extremes of Eurocentrism and national-cultural identities (as in the current crisis in what was formerly Yugoslavia) must be avoided. We need to occupy locations between our political unconscious and everyday praxis and struggle but at the same time guided by a universalist emancipatory world view in the form of a provisional utopia or contingent foundationalism.[72] A provisional utopia is not a categorical blueprint for social change (as in fascism) but a contingent utopia where we anticipate the future through practices of solidarity and community. Such a utopian vision demands that we gain control of the production of meaning but in a postnationalist sense. We can achieve this by negotiating with the borders of our identity — those unstable constellations of discursive structures — in our search for a radical otherness that can empower us to reach beyond them.

Border identities constitute a bold infringement on normalcy, a violation of the canons of bourgeois decorum, a space where we can cannibalize the traces of our narrative repression or engage them critically through the practice of cultural translation — a translation of one level of reality into another creating a multidimensional reality that I call the *cultural imaginary*, a space of cultural articulation that results from the collision of multiple strands of referential codes and sign systems. Such collisions can create hybrid significations through a hemorrhage of signifiers whose meanings endlessly bleed into each other or else take on the force of historical agency as a new *mestizaje* consciousness. *Mestizaje* consciousness[73] is not simply a doctrine of identity based on cultural bricolage or a form of bric-a-brac subjectivity but a critical practice of cultural negotiation and translation that attempts to transcend the contradictions of Western dualistic thinking. As Chandra Talpade Mohanty remarks

> A *mestiza* consciousness is a consciousness of the borderlands, a consciousness born of the historical collusion of Anglo and Mexican cultures and frames of reference. It is a plural consciousness in that it requires understanding multiple, often opposing ideas and knowledges and negotiating these knowledges, not just taking a simple counterstance.[74]

Anzaldúa speaks of a notion of agency that moves beyond the postmodernist concept of "split subject" by situating agency in its historical and geopolitical specificity.[75] Borders cannot simply be evoked in an abstract transcendental sense but need to be identified specifically. Borders can be linguistic, spacial, ideological and geographical. They not only demarcate otherness but stipulate the manner in which otherness is maintained and reproduced. A *mestizaje* consciousness is linked, therefore, to the specificity of historical struggles.[76]

A critical multiculturalism needs to testify not only to the pain, suffering, and "walking nihilism" of oppressed peoples, but also to the intermittent, epiphanic ruptures and moments of *jouissance* that occur when solidarity is established around struggles for liberation. As I have tried to argue, with others, elsewhere,[77] we need to abandon our pedagogies of protest (which, as Houston Baker reminds us, simply reinforce the dualism of "self" and "other" and reinstate the basis of dominant racist evaluations and preserve the "always already" arrangements of white male hegemony) in favor of a politics of transformation. Those of us who are white need also to avoid the "white male confessional" that Baker describes as the "confessional *manqué* of the colonial subject."[78]

White male confessionals simply "induce shame" rather than convince people to change their axiology, yet still employ the language and shrewd methods of the "overseers." It is the type of confessional that proclaims that oppressed people of color are "as good as" white people. It simply asserts that subaltern voices measure up to dominant voices and that African-Americans are merely "different" and not deviant. In contrast, Baker calls for a form of *"supraliteracy"* or "guerrilla action" carried out *within* linguistic territories. This constitutes an invasion of the dominant linguistic terrain of the traditional academic disciplines — an invasion that he describes as a "deformation of mastery." From this perspective, critical pedagogy needs to be more attentive to the dimension of the vernacular — "to sound racial poetry in the courts of the civilized."[79] Teachers need to include nonliterary cultural forms into our classrooms — such as video, film, popular fiction, and radio — and a critical means of understanding their role in the production of subjectivity and agency.

Concentrating on the reflexive modalities of the intellect or returning to some pretheoretical empirical experience are both bad strategies for challenging the politics of the white confessional. The former is advocated mostly by academics while the latter is exercised by educational activists suspicious of the new languages of deconstruction and the fashionable apostasy of the poststructuralists whose intellectual home is in the margins. Academic theorists tend to textualize and displace experience to the abstract equivalence of the signified while activists view "commonsense" experience as essentially devoid of ideology or interest. We need to avoid approaches that disconnect us from the lives of real people who suffer and from issues of power and justice that directly affect the oppressed.

Critical social theory as a form of multicultural resistance must be wary of locating liberatory praxis in the realm of diachrony as something to be resolved dialectically in some higher unity outside of the historical struggle and pain and suffering to which we must serve as pedagogical witnesses and agents of radical hope. Yet at the same time, critical pedagogy needs to be wary of forms of populist elitism that privilege only the reform efforts of those who have direct experience with the oppressed. After all, no single unsurpassable and "authentic" reality can be reached through "experience" since no experience is preontologically available outside of a politics of representation.

As multicultural educators informed by critical and feminist pedagogies, we need to keep students connected to the power of the unacceptable and comfortable with the unthinkable by producing critical forms of policy analysis and pedagogy. In tandem with this, we must actively help students to challenge sites of discursive hierarchy rather than delocalizing and dehistoricizing them, and to contest the ways their desires and pleasures are being policed in relationship to them. It is important as critical educators, that we do not manipulate students simply to accept our intellectual positions nor presume at the same time to speak for them. Nor should our critical theorizing be simply a service to the culture of domination by extending student insights into the present system without at the same time challenging the very assumptions of the system. We cannot afford just temporarily to disengage students from the *doxa* — the language of common sense. If we want to recruit students to a transformative praxis, students must not only be encouraged to choose a language of analysis that is undergirded by a project of liberation but must affectively invest in it.

If we are to be redeemed from our finitude as passive supplicants of history, we must, as students and teachers, adopt more directly oppositional and politically combative social and cultural practices. The destructive fanaticism of present day xenophobia is only exacerbated by the current ethical motionlessness among many left constituencies. Insurgent intellectuals and theorists are called to steer a course between the monumentalization of judgment and taste and riding the postmodern currents of despair in a free-fall exhilaration of political impotence. And here I would agree with Cornel West and Henry Louis Gates that "a left politics that can imagine only an agonistic relation to real-world liberalism is a bankrupt politics" and, conversely, "[a] rights-based liberalism unresponsive to radical (and conservative) critiques is an impoverished one indeed."[80]

The present historical moment is populated by memories that are surfacing at the margins of our culture, along the faultlines of our logocentric consciousness. Decolonized spaces are forming in the borderlands — linguistic, epistemological, intersubjective — and these will affect the classrooms of the future. Here saints and Iwa walk together and the Orishas speak to us through the rhythms of the earth and the pulse of the body. The sounds produced in the borderlands are quite different from the convulsive monotones that echo from the schizophrenic boundaries of Weber's iron cage. Here it is in the hybrid polyrhythms of the drum that the new pulse of freedom can be felt. Within such borderlands our pedagogies of liberation can be invested once again with the passion of mystery and the reason of commitment. This is neither a Dionysian rejection of rationality nor a blind, prerational plunge into myth but rather an attempt to embrace and reclaim the memories of those pulsating, sinewed bodies that have been forgotten in our modernist assault on difference and uncertainty.

Notes

1 Slightly altered versions of this paper will appear in Christine Sleeter and Peter McLaren, eds, *Critical Pedagogy and Multiculturalism*, (Albany, NY: State University of New York Press); and Peter McLaren, Rhonda Hammer, Susan Reilly and David Sholle, *A Pedagogy of Representation* (New York: Peter Lang Publishers). Some sections of this paper have appeared in Peter McLaren, "Multiculturalism and the Postmodern Critique: Towards a Pedagogy of Resistance and Transformation." *Cultural Studies*, 7, (1993), pp. 118–46; and Peter McLaren, "Critical Pedagogy, Multiculturalism, and the Politics of Risk and Resistance: A Response to Kelly and Portelli," *Journal of Education*, 173, 3 (1991), pp. 29–59.

2 Cindi Katz and Neil Smith, "LA Intifada: Interview with Mike Davis," *Social Text*, 33 (1992), pp. 19–33.

3 Cited in Anders Stephanson, "Interview with Cornel West," in *Universal Abandon? The Politics of Postmodernism*, ed. Andrew Ross (Minneapolis: University of Minnesota Press, 1988), p. 276.

4 B. M. Cooper, "Cruel and the Gang: Exposing the Schomburg Posse," *The Village Voice*, 34 (1989), pp. 27–36.

5 Michele Wallace, "Multiculturalism and Oppositionality," *Afterimage* (October 1991), pp. 6–9.

6 Africa is still demonized as a land uncivilized, corrupt, and savage. It has been broken up into countries that are viewed as not evolved enough to govern themselves without Western guidance and stewardship. We shamefully ignore Africa's victims of war and famine in comparison, for instance, to the "white" victims of Bosnia. When the United States' media does decide to report on Africa, many of the images it reinforces are a land of jungle, wildlife, famine, poachers, and fierce fighting among rival tribal factions. The white supremacist and colonialist discourses surrounding the recent intervention in Somalia by heroic United States troops and relief workers (referred to by Colin Powell as sending the "cavalry") is captured in comments made by Alan Pfizzy of CBS when he described the intervention in "humanitarian" terms as "just a few good men trying to help another nation in need, another treacherous country where all the members of all the murderous factions look alike." Described as a land populated by helpless and history-less victims and drug-crazed thugs high on khat (a mild stimulant) who ride around in vehicles out of a Mad Max movie, an implicit parallel is made between Somalian youth and the cocaine-dealing gangs of toughs who participated in the LA rioting. Jim Naureckas, *Extra* (March 1993). This "othering" of Africa encouraged a preferred reading of Somalia's problems as indigenous and camouflaged the broader context surrounding the famine in Somalia and its subsequent "rescue" by United States marines. Occluded was the fact that the United States had previously obstructed United Nations peacekeeping efforts in Somalia, Angola, Namibia, and Mozambique because they were too costly — a factor absent in nearly all the media coverage (Naureckas, ibid.). From a United States foreign policy perspective, Somalia still plays an important role geopolitically, not simply because of its potential interest to Israel and Arab nations, but because of its rich mineral deposits and potential oil reserves. As Naureckas notes, Amoco, Chevron and Sunoco are engaged in oil exploration there (ibid.).

The media have rarely reported on other factors surrounding the famine in Somalia. For instance, they have virtually ignored the United States' support (to the sum of $200 million in military aid and half a billion dollars in economic aid) to the Siad Barre regime (1969–1991). The United States ignored its corruption and human rights abuses because the dictatorship kept

Soviet-allied Ethiopia embroiled in a war. Naureckas also points out that until the 1970s, Somalia was self-sufficient in grain and its agricultural land productive enough to withstand famine. However, United States and international agencies like the IMF pressured Somalia to shift agriculture from local subsistence to export crops (cited in Naureckas, ibid., p. 12).

7 Phillips Verner Bradford and Harvey Blume, *Ota Benga: The Pygmy in the Zoo* (New York: St Martin's Press, 1992).

8 *Observer*, 5, 2 (March 1992), p. 20.

9 Jan Nederveen Pieterse, *White on Black: Images of Africa and Blacks in Western Popular Culture* (New Haven: Yale University Press,1992).

10 Ibid., p. 220.

11 Donaldo Macedo, "Literacy for Stupidification: The Pedagogy of Big Lies," *Harvard Educational Review*. In press.

12 Michael Gardiner, *The Dialogics of Critique: M. M. Bakhtin and the Theory of Ideology* (London: Routledge, 1992), p. 186.

13 Stanley Fish, "Bad Company," *Transition*, 56 (1992), pp. 60–7.

14 Pieterse, *White on Black: Images of Africa and Blacks in Western Popular Culture*.

15 Michael E. Dyson *Reflecting Black: African-American Cultural Criticism* (Minneapolis: University of Minnesota Press, 1993), p. 158.

16 See Fish, "Bad Company."

17 Christopher Norris, *What's Wrong With Postmodernism?* (Baltimore, MD: The Johns Hopkins University Press, 1990).

18 Ibid.

19 Linda Hutcheon, *The Politics of Postmodernism* (London: Routledge, 1989), p. 145.

20 Stuart Hall, "Ethnicity: Identity and Difference," *Radical America*, 23, 4 (1991), pp. 9–20.

21 Henry A. Giroux, *Border Crossings* (London: Routledge, 1992); Joan Scott, "Experience," in *Feminists Theorize the Political*, eds Judith Butler and Joan W. Scott (New York: Routledge, 1992), pp. 22–40.

22 [This is] an issue that I have explored elsewhere. Peter McLaren, "Schooling the Postmodern Body," in *Postmodernism, Feminism, and Cultural Politics,* ed. Henry A. Giroux (Albany, NY: SUNY Press, 1990), pp. 144–73.

23 Scott, "Experience," p. 34.

24 Henry A. Giroux and Peter McLaren, "Media Hegemony," Introduction to *Media Knowledge* by James Schwoch, Mimi White, and Susan Reilly (Albany, NY: SUNY Press, 1991), pp. xv–xxxiv; Henry A. Giroux and Peter McLaren, "Leon Golub's Radical Pessimism: Toward a Pedagogy of Representation," *Exposure*, 28, 12 (1991), pp. 18–33.

25 Teresa Ebert, "Ludic Feminism, the Body, Performance and Labor: Bringing Materialism Back into Feminist Cultural Studies," *Cultural Critique*. In press.

26 David Lloyd, "Race Under Representation," *Oxford Literary Review*, 13, 1–2, (1991), p. 70; Joan Copjec, "The *Unvermogender* Other: Hysteria and Democracy in America," *New Formations* 14 (Summer 1991), pp. 27–41; Renato Rosaldo, *Culture and Truth: The Remaking of Social Analysis* (Boston: Beacon, 1989).

27 Chandra Talpade Mohanty, "On Race and Voice: Challenges for Liberal Education in the 1990s," *Cultural Critique* (Winter 1990), p. 181.

28 Homi K. Bhabha, "A Good Judge of Character: Men, Metaphors, and the Common Culture," in *Race-ing Justice, En-gendering Power*, ed. Toni Morrison (New York: Pantheon Books, 1992), p. 235.

29 Ibid., pp. 234–5.

30 Peter McLaren, "Border Disputes: Multicultural Narrative, Critical Pedagogy and Identity Formation in Postmodern America," in *Naming Silenced Lives*, eds J. McLaughlin and William G. Tierney (New York: Routledge, in press).

31 Antonia Darder, *Culture and Power in the Classroom* (South Hadley, MA: Bergin and Garvey, 1992); Peter McLaren and Rhonda Hammer, "Critical Pedagogy and the Postmodern Challenge: Towards a Critical Postmodernist Pedagogy of Liberation," *Educational Foundations*, 3, 3 (1989), pp. 29–62.

32 Peter McLaren, "Collisions with Otherness: Multi-Culturalism, the Politics of Difference, and the Ethnographer as Nomad," *American Journal of Semiotics* (in press); Henry A. Giroux and Peter McLaren, "Paulo Freire, Postmodernism, and the Utopian Imagination: A Blochian Reading," in *Bloch In Our Time*, eds Jamie Owen Daniel and Tom Moylan (London: Verso, in press).

33 Mas'ud Zavarzadeh and Donald Morton, "Signs of Knowledge in the Contemporary Academy," *American Journal of Semiotics*, 7, 4 (1990), pp. 149–60.

34 Teresa Ebert, "Political Semiosis in/of American Cultural Studies," *The American Journal of Semiotics*, 8, 1/2 (1991), p. 117.

35 Carlos Munoz, *Youth, Identity, Power* (London: Verso, 1989), p. 11.

36 Kobena Mercer, "1968: Periodizing Politics and Identity," in *Cultural Studies*, eds Lawrence Grossberg, Cary Nelson, and Paula Treichler (London: Routledge, 1992), p. 428.

37 Ibid., p. 429.

38 Zavarzadeh and Morton, "Signs of Knowledge in the Contemporary Academy," p. 156.

39 Teresa Ebert, "Writing in the Political: Resistance (Post)Modernism," *Legal Studies Forum*, xv, 4 (1991), pp. 291–303.

40 Peter McLaren, *Life in Schools* (White Plains, NY: Longman, 1989).

41 Kobena Mercer, "Welcome to the Jungle: Identity and Diversity in Postmodern Politics," in *Identity: Community, Culture, Difference*, ed. Jonathan Rutherford (London: Lawrence and Wishart, 1990), p. 68.

42 Timothy Maliqualim Simone, *About Face: Race in Postmodern America.* (Brooklyn, NY: Autonomedia, 1989), p. 191.
43 Ebert, "Writing in the Political: Resistance (Post)Modernism," p. 294.
44 Ibid.
45 Ibid.
46 Cameron McCarthy, "Rethinking Liberal and Radical Perspectives on Racial Inequality in Schooling: Making the Case for Nonsynchrony," *Harvard Educational Review*, 58, 3 (1988), pp. 265–79.
47 Ebert, "Political Semiosis in/of American Cultural Studies."
48 Cited in Wallace, "Multiculturalism and Oppositionality," p. 7.
49 Cornel West, "The New Cultural Politics of Difference," in *Out There: Marginalization and Contemporary Cultures,* eds Russell Ferguson, Martha Gever, Trinh T. Minh-ha and Cornel West (Cambridge: The MIT Press and The New Museum of Contemporary Art, New York, 1990), p. 29.
50 Dean MacCannell, *Empty Meeting Grounds: The Tourist Papers* (London: Routledge, 1992), pp. 121–2.
51 West, "The New Cultural Politics of Difference."
52 Ibid., p. 22.
53 MacCannell, *Empty Meeting Grounds: The Tourist Papers,* p. 131.
54 Ibid., p. 130.
55 Ibid., p. 131.
56 Richard Dyer, "White," *Screen*, 29, 4 (1988), pp. 44–64.
57 Michael Goldfield, "The Color of Politics in the United States: White Supremacy as the Main Explanation for the Peculiarities of American Politics from Colonial Times to the Present," in *The Bounds of Race,* ed. Dominick LaCapra (Ithaca, NY: Cornell University Press, 1992), pp. 104–33.
58 bell hooks, *Black Looks* (Boston, MA: South End Press, 1992), pp. 167–8.
59 Ibid., p. 169.
60 Rhonda Hammer and Peter McLaren, "Spectacularizing Subjectivity: Media Knowledges and the New World Order," *Polygraph,*5 (1992), pp. 46–66; Rhonda Hammer and Peter McLaren, "Rethinking the Dialectic," *Educational Theory,* 41, 1 (1991), pp. 23–46.
61 Ebert, "Ludic Feminism, the Body, Performance and Labor: Bringing Materialism Back into Feminist Cultural Studies."
62 hooks, *Black Looks,* p. 17.
63 Ian Hunter, *Culture and Government: The Emergence of Literary Education* (Houndmills, Basingstoke, Hampshire, and London: Macmillan,1988).
64 See Giroux, *Border Crossings;* McLaren, "Border Disputes: Multicultural Narrative, Critical Pedagogy and Identity Formation in Postmodern America,"; and McLaren, "Collisions with Otherness: Multi-Culturalism, the Politics of Difference, and the Ethnographer as Nomad."
65 D. Emily Hicks, *Border Writing* (Minneapolis: University of Minnesota Press, 1992).

66 Ibid.

67 Neil Larsen, "Foreword" to *Border Writing* by Emily Hicks (Minneapolis: University of Minnesota Press, 1991), pp. xi–xxi.

68 Seyla Benhabib, *Situating the Self: Gender, Community and Postmodernism in Contemporary Ethics* (London: Routledge, 1992), p. 165.

69 Steven Best and Douglas Keller, *Postmodern Theory: Critical Interrogations* (New York: The Guilford Press, 1991), p. 301.

70 Benhabib, *Situating the Self: Gender, Community and Postmodernism in Contemporary Ethics,* p. 220.

71 Ibid, p. 226.

72 See Judith Butler, "Contingent Foundations: Feminism and the Question of 'Postmodernism'." *Praxis International,* 11, 2 (1991), pp. 150–65.

73 Gloria Anzaldúa, *Borderlands/La Frontera* (San Francisco: Spinsters/Aunt Lute, 1987).

74 Chandra Talpade Mohanty, "Introduction. Cartographies of Struggle: Third World Women and the Politics of Feminism," in *Third World Women and the Politics of Feminism,* eds Chandra Talpade Mohanty, Ann Russo, and Lourdes Torres (Bloomington: Indiana University Press, 1991), pp. 34–5.

75 Ibid., p. 37.

76 Ibid., p. 38.

77 Peter McLaren and Rhonda Hammer "Media Knowledges, Warrior Citizenry, and Postmodern Literacies," *Journal of Urban and Cultural Studies,* 2, 2 (1992), pp. 41–77; Kelly Estrada and Peter McLaren, "A Dialogue on Multiculturalism and Democracy," *Educational Researcher* (April 1993), pp. 27–33.

78 Houston A. Baker, "Caliban's Triple Play," in *"Race," Writing and Difference,* ed. Henry Louis Gates Jr (Chicago: The University of Chicago Press, 1985) p. 388.

79 Ibid., p. 395.

80 Henry Louis Gates Jr, *Loose Canons: Notes on the Culture Wars* (Oxford: Oxford University Press, 1992), p. 192; West, "The New Cultural Politics of Difference."

2

The Politics of Recognition

Charles Taylor[1]

I

A number of strands in contemporary politics turn on the need, sometimes the demand, for *recognition*. The need, it can be argued, is one of the driving forces behind nationalist movements in politics. And the demand comes to the fore in a number of ways in today's politics, on behalf of minority or "subaltern" groups, in some forms of feminism, and in what is today called the politics of "multiculturalism."

The demand for recognition in these latter cases is given urgency by the supposed links between recognition and identity, where this latter term designates something like a person's understanding of who they are, of their fundamental defining characteristics as a human being. The thesis is that our identity is partly shaped by recognition or its absence, often by the *mis*recognition of others, and so a person or group of people can suffer real damage, real distortion, if the people or society around them mirror back to them a confining or demeaning or contemptible picture of themselves. Nonrecognition or misrecognition can inflict harm, can be a form of oppression, imprisoning someone in a false, distorted, and reduced mode of being.

Thus some feminists have argued that women in patriarchal societies have been induced to adopt a depreciatory image of themselves. They have internalized a picture of their own inferiority, so that even when some of the objective obstacles to their advancement fall away, they may be incapable of taking advantage of the new opportunities. And beyond this, they are condemned to suffer the pain of low self-esteem. An analogous point has been made in relation to blacks: that white society has for generations projected a demeaning image of them, which some of them have been unable to resist adopting. Their own self-depreciation, in this view, becomes one of the most potent instruments of their own oppression. Their first task ought to be to purge themselves of this imposed and destructive identity. Recently, a similar point has been made in relation to indigenous and colonized people in general. It is held that since 1492, Europeans have projected an image of such people as somehow inferior, "uncivilized," and through the force of conquest have often been able to impose this image on the conquered. The figure of Caliban has been held to epitomize this crushing portrait of contempt of New World aboriginals.

Within these perspectives, misrecognition shows not just a lack of due respect. It can inflict a grievous wound, saddling its victims with a crippling self-hatred. Due recognition is not just a courtesy we owe people. It is a vital human need.

In order to examine some of the issues that have arisen here, I'd like to take a step back, achieve a little distance, and look first at how this discourse of recognition and identity came to seem familiar, or at least readily understandable, to us. For it was not always so, and our ancestors of more than a couple of centuries ago would have stared at us uncomprehendingly if we had used these terms in their current sense. How did we get started on this?

Hegel comes to mind right off, with his famous dialectic of the master and the slave. This is an important stage, but we need to go a little farther back to see how this passage came to have the sense it did. What changed to make this kind of talk have sense for us?

We can distinguish two changes that together have made the modern preoccupation with identity and recognition inevitable. The first is the collapse of social hierarchies, which used to be the basis for honor. I am using *honor* in the ancien regime sense in which it is intrinsically linked to inequalities. For some to have honor in this sense, it is essential that not everyone have it. This is the sense in which Montesquieu uses it in his description of monarchy. Honor is intrinsically a matter of "préférences."[2] It is also the sense in which we use the term when we speak of honoring someone by giving her some public award, for example, the Order of Canada. Clearly, this award would be without worth if tomorrow we decided to give it to every adult Canadian.

As against this notion of honor, we have the modern notion of dignity, now used in a universalist and egalitarian sense, where we talk of the inherent "dignity of human beings," or of citizen dignity. The underlying premise here is that everyone shares in it.[3] It is obvious that this concept of dignity is the only one compatible with a democratic society, and that it was inevitable that the old concept of honor was superseded. But this has also meant that the forms of equal recognition have been essential to democratic culture. For instance, that everyone be called "Mr.," "Mrs.," or "Miss," rather than some people being called "Lord" or "Lady" and others simply by their surnames — or, even more demeaning, by their first name — has been thought essential in some democratic societies, such as the United States. More recently, for similar reasons, "Mrs." and "Miss" have been collapsed into "Ms." Democracy has ushered in a politics of equal recognition, which has taken various forms over the years, and has now returned in the form of demands for the equal status of cultures and of genders.

But the importance of recognition has been modified and intensified by the new understanding of individual identity that emerges at the end of the eighteenth century. We might speak of an *individualized* identity, one that is particular to me, and that I discover in myself. This notion arises along with an ideal, that of being true to myself and my own particular way of being. Following Lionel Trilling's usage in his brilliant study, I will speak of this as the ideal of "authenticity."[4] It will help to describe in what it consists and how it came about.

One way of describing its development is to see its starting point in the eighteenth-century notion that human beings are endowed with a moral sense, an intuitive feeling for what is right and wrong. The original point of this doctrine was to combat a rival view, that knowing right and wrong was a matter of calculating consequences, in particular, those concerned with divine reward and punishment. The idea was that understanding right and wrong was not a matter of dry calculation, but was anchored in our feelings.[5] Morality has, in a sense, a voice within.

The notion of authenticity develops out of a displacement of the moral accent in this idea. In the original view, the inner voice was important because it tells us what the right thing to do is. Being in touch with our moral feelings matters here, as a means to the end of acting rightly. What I'm calling the displacement of the moral accent comes about when being in touch with our feelings takes on independent and crucial moral significance. It comes to be something we have to attain if we are to be true and full human beings.

To see what is new here, we have to see the analogy to earlier moral views, where being in touch with some source — for example, God, or the Idea of the Good — was considered essential to full being. But now the source we have to connect with is deep within us. This fact is part of the massive subjective turn of modern culture, a new form of inwardness, in which we come to think of ourselves as beings with inner depths. At first, this idea that the source is within doesn't exclude our being related to God or the Ideas; it can be considered our proper way of relating to them. In a sense, it can be seen as just a continuation and intensification of the development inaugurated by Saint Augustine, who saw the road to God as passing through our own self-awareness. The first variants of this new view were theistic, or at least pantheistic.

The most important philosophical writer who helped to bring about this change was Jean-Jacques Rousseau. I think Rousseau is important not because he inaugurated the change; rather, I would argue that his great popularity comes in part from his articulating something that was in a sense already occurring in the culture. Rousseau frequently presents the issue of morality as that of our following a voice of nature within us. This voice is often drowned out by the passions that are induced by our dependence on others, the main one being *amour propre*, or pride. Our moral salvation comes from recovering authentic moral contact with ourselves. Rousseau even gives a name to the intimate contact with oneself, more fundamental than any moral view, that is a source of such joy and contentment: "le sentiment de l'existence."[6]

The ideal of authenticity becomes crucial owing to a development that occurs after Rousseau, which I associate with the name of Herder — once again, as its major early articulator, rather than its originator. Herder put forward the idea that each of us has an original way of being human: each person has his or her own "measure."[7] This idea has burrowed very deep into modern consciousness. It is a new idea. Before the late eighteenth century, no one thought that the differences between human beings had this kind of moral significance. There is a certain way of being human that is *my* way. I am called upon to live my life in this way, and not in imitation of anyone else's life. But this notion gives a new importance to being true to myself. If I am not, I miss the point of my life; I miss what being human is for *me*.

This is the powerful moral ideal that has come down to us. It accords moral importance to a kind of contact with myself, with my own inner nature, which it sees as in danger of being lost, partly through the pressures toward outward conformity, but also because in taking an instrumental stance toward myself, I may have lost the capacity to listen to this inner voice. It greatly increases the importance of this self-contact by introducing the principle of originality: each of our voices has something unique to say. Not only should I not mold my life to the demands of external conformity; I can't even find the model by which to live outside myself. I can only find it within.[8]

Being true to myself means being true to my own originality, which is something only I can articulate and discover. In articulating it, I am also defining myself. I am realizing a potentiality that is properly my own. This is the background understanding to the modern ideal of authenticity, and to the goals of self-fulfillment and self-realization in which the ideal is usually couched. I should note here that Herder applied his conception of originality at two levels, not only to the individual person among other persons, but also to the culture-bearing people among other peoples. Just like individuals, a *Volk* should be true to itself, that is, its own culture. Germans shouldn't try to be derivative and (inevitably) second-rate Frenchmen, as Frederick the Great's patronage seemed to be encouraging them to do. The Slavic peoples had to find their own path. And European colonialism ought to be rolled back to give the peoples of what we now call the Third World their chance to be themselves unimpeded. We can recognize here the seminal idea of modern nationalism, in both benign and malignant forms.

This new ideal of authenticity was, like the idea of dignity, also in part an offshoot of the decline of hierarchical society. In those earlier societies, what we would now call identity was largely fixed by one's social position. That is, the background that explained what people recognized as important to themselves was to a great extent determined by their place in society, and whatever roles or activities attached to this position. The birth of a democratic society doesn't by itself do away with this phenomenon, because people can still define themselves by their social roles. What does decisively undermine this socially derived identification, however, is the ideal of authenticity itself. As this emerges, for instance, with Herder, it calls on me to discover my own original way of being. By definition, this way of being cannot be socially derived, but must be inwardly generated.

But in the nature of the case, there is no such thing as inward generation, monologically understood. In order to understand the close connection between identity and recognition, we have to take into account a crucial feature of the human condition that has been rendered almost invisible by the overwhelmingly monological bent of mainstream modern philosophy.

This crucial feature of human life is its fundamentally *dialogical* character. We become full human agents, capable of understanding ourselves, and hence of defining our identity, through our acquisition of rich human languages of expression. For my purposes here, I want to take *language* in a broad sense, covering not only the words we speak, but also other modes of expression whereby we define ourselves, including the "languages" of art, of gesture, of love, and the like. But we learn these modes of expression through exchanges with others. People do not acquire the languages needed for self-definition on their own. Rather, we are introduced to them through interaction with others who matter to us — what George Herbert Mead called "significant others."[9] The genesis of the human mind is in this sense not monological, not something each person accomplishes on his or her own, but dialogical.

Moreover, this is not just a fact about *genesis,* which can be ignored later on. We don't just learn the languages in dialogue and then go on to use them for our own purposes. We are of course expected to develop our own opinions, outlook, stances toward things, and to a considerable degree through solitary reflection. But this is not how things work with important issues, like the definition of our identity. We define our identity always in dialogue with, sometimes in struggle against, the things our significant others want to see in us. Even after we outgrow some of these others — our parents, for instance — and they disappear from our lives, the conversation with them continues within us as long as we live.[10]

Thus, the contribution of significant others, even when it is provided at the beginning of our lives, continues indefinitely. Some people may still want to hold on to some form of the monological ideal. It is true that we can never liberate ourselves completely from those whose love and care shaped us early in life, but we should strive to define ourselves on our own to the fullest extent possible, coming as best we can to understand and thus get some control over the influence of our parents, and avoiding falling into any more such dependent relationships. We need relationships to fulfill, but not to define, ourselves.

The monological ideal seriously underestimates the place of the dialogical in human life. It wants to confine it as much as possible to the genesis. It forgets how our understanding of the good things in life can be transformed by our enjoying them in common with people we love; how some goods become accessible to us only through such common enjoyment. Because of this, it would take a great deal of effort, and probably many wrenching breakups, to *prevent* our identities being formed by the people we love. Consider what we mean by *identity*. It is who we are, "where we're coming from." As such it is the background against which our tastes and desires and opinions and aspirations make sense. If some of the things I value most are accessible to me only in relation to the person I love, then she becomes part of my identity.

To some people this might seem a limitation, from which one might aspire to free oneself. This is one way of understanding the impulse behind the life of the hermit or, to take a case more familiar to our culture, the solitary artist. But from another perspective, we might see even these lives as aspiring to a certain kind of dialogicality. In the case of the hermit, the interlocutor is God. In the case of the solitary artist, the work itself is addressed to a future audience, perhaps still to be created by the work. The very form of a work of art shows its character as *addressed*.[11] But however one feels about it, the making and sustaining of our identity, in the absence of a heroic effort to break out of ordinary existence, remains dialogical throughout our lives.

Thus my discovering my own identity doesn't mean that I work it out in isolation, but that I negotiate it through dialogue, partly overt, partly internal, with others. That is why the development of an ideal of inwardly generated identity gives a new importance to recognition. My own identity crucially depends on my dialogical relations with others.

Of course, the point is not that this dependence on others arose with the age of authenticity. A form of dependence was always there. The socially derived identity was by its very nature dependent on society. But in the earlier age recognition never arose as a problem. General recognition was built into the socially derived identity by virtue of the very fact that it was based on social categories that everyone took for granted. Yet inwardly derived, personal, original identity doesn't enjoy this recognition *a priori*. It has to win it through exchange, and the attempt can fail. What has come about with the modern age is not the need for recognition but the conditions in which the attempt to be recognized can fail. That is why the need is now acknowledged for the first time. In premodern times, people didn't speak of "identity" and "recognition" — not because people didn't have (what we call) identities, or because these didn't depend on recognition, but rather because these were then too unproblematic to be thematized as such.

It's not surprising that we can find some of the seminal ideas about citizen dignity and universal recognition, even if not in these specific terms, in Rousseau, whom I have wanted to identify as one of the points of origin of the modern discourse of authenticity. Rousseau is a sharp critic of hierarchical honor, of "préférences." In a significant passage of the *Discourse on Inequality*, he pinpoints a fateful moment when society takes a turn toward corruption and injustice, when people begin to desire preferential esteem.[12] By contrast, in republican society, where all can share equally in the light of public attention, he sees the source of health.[13] But the topic of recognition is given its most influential early treatment in Hegel.[14]

The importance of recognition is now universally acknowledged in one form or another; on an intimate plane, we are all aware of how identity can be formed or malformed through the course of our contact with significant others. On the social plane, we have a continuing politics of equal recognition. Both planes have been shaped by the growing ideal of authenticity, and recognition plays an essential role in the culture that has arisen around this ideal.

On the intimate level, we can see how much an original identity needs and is vulnerable to the recognition given or withheld by significant others. It is not surprising that in the culture of authenticity, relationships are seen as the key loci of self-discovery and self-affirmation. Love relationships are not just important because of the general emphasis in modern culture on the fulfillments of ordinary needs. They are also crucial because they are the crucibles of inwardly generated identity.

On the social plane, the understanding that identities are formed in open dialogue, unshaped by a predefined social script, has made the politics of equal recognition more central and stressful. It has, in fact, considerably raised the stakes. Equal recognition is not just the appropriate mode for a healthy democratic society. Its refusal can inflict damage on those who are denied it, according to a widespread modern view, as I indicated at the outset. The projection of an inferior or demeaning image on another can actually distort and oppress, to the extent that the image is internalized. Not only contemporary feminism but also race relations and discussions of multiculturalism are undergirded by the premise that the withholding of recognition can be a form of oppression. We may debate whether this factor has been exaggerated, but it is clear that the understanding of identity and authenticity has introduced a new dimension into the politics of equal recognition, which now operates with something like its own notion of authenticity, at least so far as the denunciation of other-induced distortions is concerned.

II

And so the discourse of recognition has become familiar to us, on two levels: First, in the intimate sphere, where we understand the formation of identity and the self as taking place in a continuing dialogue and struggle with significant others. And then in the public sphere, where a politics of equal recognition has come to play a bigger and bigger role. Certain feminist theories have tried to show the links between the two spheres.[15]

I want to concentrate here on the public sphere, and try to work out what a politics of equal recognition has meant and could mean.

In fact, it has come to mean two rather different things, connected, respectively, with the two major changes I have been describing. With the move from honor to dignity has come a politics of universalism, emphasizing the equal dignity of all citizens, and the content of this politics has been the equalization of rights and entitlements. What is to be avoided at all costs is the existence of "first-class" and "second-class" citizens. Naturally, the actual detailed measures justified by this principle have varied greatly, and have often been controversial. For some, equalization has affected only civil rights and voting rights; for others, it has extended into the socioeconomic sphere. People who are systematically handicapped by poverty from making the most of their citizenship rights are deemed in this view to have been relegated to second-class status, necessitating remedial action through equalization. But through all the differences of interpretation, the principle of equal citizenship has come to be universally accepted. Every position, no matter how reactionary, is now defended under the colors of this principle. Its greatest, most recent victory was won by the civil rights movement of the 1960s in the United States. It is worth noting that even the adversaries of extending voting rights to blacks in the southern states found some pretext consistent with universalism, such as "tests" to be administered to would-be voters at the time of registration.

By contrast, the second change, the development of the modern notion of identity, has given rise to a politics of difference. There is, of course, a universalist basis to this as well, making for the overlap and confusion between the two. *Everyone* should be recognized for his or her unique identity. But recognition here means something else. With the politics of equal dignity, what is established is meant to be universally the same, an identical basket of rights and immunities; with the politics of difference, what we are asked to recognize is the unique identity of this individual or group, their distinctness from everyone else. The idea is that it is precisely this distinctness that has been ignored, glossed over, assimilated to a dominant or majority identity. And this assimilation is the cardinal sin against the ideal of authenticity.[16]

Now underlying the demand is a principle of universal equality. The politics of difference is full of denunciations of discrimination and refusals of second-class citizenship. This gives the principle of universal equality a point of entry within the politics of dignity. But once inside, as it were, its demands are hard to assimilate to that politics. For it asks that we give acknowledgment and status to something that is not universally shared. Or, otherwise put, we give due acknowledgment only to what is universally present — everyone has an identity — through recognizing what is peculiar to each. The universal demand powers an acknowledgment of specificity.

The politics of difference grows organically out of the politics of universal dignity through one of those shifts with which we are long familiar, where a new understanding of the human social condition imparts a radically new meaning to an old principle. Just as a view of human beings as conditioned by their socioeconomic plight changed the understanding of second-class citizenship, so that this category came to include, for example, people in inherited poverty traps, so here the understanding of identity as formed in interchange, and as possibly so malformed, introduces a new form of second-class status into our purview. As in the present case, the socioeconomic redefinition justified social programs that were highly controversial. For those who had not gone along with this changed definition of equal status, the various redistributive programs and special opportunities offered to certain populations seemed a form of undue favoritism.

Similar conflicts arise today around the politics of difference. Where the politics of universal dignity fought for forms of nondiscrimination that were quite "blind" to the ways in which citizens differ, the politics of difference often redefines nondiscrimination as requiring that we make these distinctions the basis of differential treatment. So members of aboriginal bands will get certain rights and powers not enjoyed by other Canadians, if the demands for native self-government are finally agreed on, and certain minorities will get the right to exclude others in order to preserve their cultural integrity, and so on.

To proponents of the original politics of dignity, this can seem like a reversal, a betrayal, a simple negation of their cherished principle. Attempts are therefore made to mediate, to show how some of these measures meant to accommodate minorities can after all be justified on the original basis of dignity. These arguments can be successful up to a point. For instance, some of the (apparently) most flagrant departures from "difference-blindness" are reverse discrimination measures, affording people from previously unfavored groups a competitive advantage for jobs or places in universities. This practice has been justified on the grounds that historical discrimination has created a pattern within which the unfavored struggle at a disadvantage. Reverse discrimination is defended as a temporary measure that will eventually level the playing field and allow the old "blind" rules to come back into force in a way that doesn't disadvantage anyone. This argument seems cogent enough — wherever its factual basis is sound. But it won't justify some of the measures now urged on the grounds of difference, the goal of which is not to bring us back to an eventual "difference-blind" social space but, on the contrary, to maintain and cherish distinctness, not just now but forever. After all, if we're concerned with identity, then what is more legitimate than one's aspiration that it never be lost?[17]

So even though one politics springs from the other, by one of those shifts in the definition of key terms with which we're familiar, the two diverge quite seriously from each other. One basis for the divergence comes out even more clearly when we go beyond what each requires that we acknowledge — certain universal rights in one case, a particular identity on the other — and look at the underlying intuitions of value.

The politics of equal dignity is based on the idea that all humans are equally worthy of respect. It is underprinted by a notion of what in human beings commands respect, however we may try to shy away from this "metaphysical" background. For Kant, whose use of the term *dignity* was one of the earliest influential evocations of this idea, what commanded respect in us was our status as rational agents, capable of directing our lives through principles.[18] Something like this has been the basis for our intuitions of equal dignity ever since, though the detailed definition of it may have changed.

Thus, what is picked out as of worth here is a *universal human potential*, a capacity that all humans share. This potential, rather than anything a person may have made of it, is what ensures that each person deserves respect. Indeed, our sense of the importance of potentiality reaches so far that we extend this protection even to people who through some circumstance that has befallen them are incapable of realizing their potential in the normal way — handicapped people, or those in a coma, for instance.

In the case of the politics of difference, we might also say that a universal potential is at its basis, namely, the potential for forming and defining one's own identity, as an individual, and also as a culture. This potentiality must be respected equally in everyone. But at least in the intercultural context, a stronger demand has recently arisen: that one accord equal respect to actually evolved cultures. Critiques of European or white domination, to the effect that they have not only suppressed but failed to appreciate other cultures, consider these depreciatory judgments not only factually mistaken but somehow morally wrong. When Saul Bellow is famously quoted as saying something like, "When the Zulus produce a Tolstoy we will read him,"[19] this is taken as a quintessential statement of European arrogance, not just because Bellow is allegedly being *de facto* insensitive to the value of Zulu culture, but frequently also because it is seen to reflect a denial in principle of human equality. The possibility that the Zulus, while having the same potential for culture formation as anyone else, might nevertheless have come up with a culture that is less valuable than others is ruled out from the start. Even to entertain this possibility is to deny human equality. Bellow's error here, then, would not be a (possibly insensitive) particular mistake in evaluation, but a denial of a fundamental principle.

To the extent that this stronger reproach is in play, the demand for equal recognition extends beyond an acknowledgment of the equal value of all humans potentially, and comes to include the equal value of what they have made of this potential in fact. This creates a serious problem, as we shall see below.

These two modes of politics, then, both based on the notion of equal respect, come into conflict. For one, the principle of equal respect requires that we treat people in a difference-blind fashion. The fundamental intuition that humans command this respect focuses on what is the same in all. For the other, we have to recognize and even foster particularity. The reproach the first makes to the second is just that it violates the principle of nondiscrimination. The reproach the second makes to the first is that it negates identity by forcing people into a homogeneous mold that is untrue to them. This would be bad enough if the mold were itself neutral — nobody's mold in particular. But the complaint generally goes further. The claim is that the supposedly neutral set of difference-blind principles of the politics of equal dignity is in fact a reflection of one hegemonic culture. As it turns out, then, only the minority or suppressed cultures are being forced to take alien form. Consequently, the supposedly fair and difference-blind society is not only inhuman (because suppressing identities) but also, in a subtle and unconscious way, itself highly discriminatory.[20]

This last attack is the cruelest and most upsetting of all. The liberalism of equal dignity seems to have to assume that there are some universal, difference-blind principles. Even though we may not have defined them yet, the project of defining them remains alive and essential. Different theories may be put forward and contested — and a number have been proposed in our day[21] — but the shared assumption of the different theories is that one such theory is right.

The charge leveled by the most radical forms of the politics of difference is that "blind" liberalisms are themselves the reflection of particular cultures. And the worrying thought is that this bias might not just be a contingent weakness of all hitherto proposed theories, that the very idea of such a liberalism may be a kind of pragmatic contradiction, a particularism masquerading as the universal.

I want now to try to move, gently and gingerly, into this nest of issues, glancing at some of the important stages in the emergence of these two kinds of politics in Western societies. I will first look at the politics of equal dignity.

III

The politics of equal dignity has emerged in Western civilization in two ways, which we could associate with the names of two standard-bearers, Rousseau and Kant. This doesn't mean that all instances of each have been influenced by these masters (though that is arguably true for the Rousseauean branch), just that Rousseau and Kant are prominent early exponents of the two models. Looking at the two models should enable us to gauge to what extent they are guilty of the charge of imposing a false homogeneity.

I stated earlier, at the end of the first section, that I thought that Rousseau could be seen as one of the originators of the discourse of recognition. I say this not because he uses the term, but because he begins to think out the importance of equal respect, and, indeed, deems it indispensable for freedom. Rousseau, as is well known, tends to oppose a condition of freedom-in-equality to one characterized by hierarchy and other-dependence. In this state, one is dependent on others not just because they wield political power, or because one needs them for survival or success in one's cherished projects, but above all because one craves their esteem. The other-dependent person is a slave to "opinion."

This idea is one of the keys to the connection that Rousseau assumes between other-dependence and hierarchy. Logically, these two things would seem separable. Why can't there be other-dependence in conditions of equality? It seems that for Rousseau this cannot be, because he associates other-dependence with the need for others' good opinion, which in turn is understood in the framework of the traditional conception of honor, that is, as intrinsically bound up with "préférences." The esteem we seek in this condition is intrinsically differential. It is a positional good.

It is because of this crucial place of honor within it that the depraved condition of mankind has a paradoxical combination of properties such that we are unequal in power, and yet *all* dependent on others — not just the slave on the master, but also the master on the slave. This point is frequently made. The second sentence of *The Social Contract*, after the famous first line about men being born free and yet being everywhere in chains, runs: "Tel se croit le maitre des autres, qui ne laisse pas d'être plus esclave qu'eux [One thinks himself the master of others, and still remains a greater slave than they]."[22] And in *Emile* Rousseau tells us that in this condition of dependence, "maître et esclave se dépravent mutuellement [master and slave corrupt each other]."[23]

Rousseau often sounds like the Stoics, who undoubtedly influenced him. He identifies pride (*amour propre*) as one of the great sources of evil. But he doesn't end up where the Stoics do. There is a long-standing discourse on pride, both Stoic and Christian, that recommends that we completely overcome our concern for the good opinion of others. We are asked to step outside this dimension of human life, in which reputations are sought, gained, and unmade. How you appear in public space should be of no concern to you. Rousseau sometimes sounds as if he is endorsing this line. In particular, it is part of his own self-dramatization that he could maintain his integrity in the face of undeserved hostility and calumny from the world. But when we look at his accounts of a potentially good society, we can see that esteem does still play a role in them, that people live very much in the public gaze. In a functioning republic, the citizens do care very much what others think. In a passage of the *Considerations on the Government of Poland*, Rousseau describes how ancient legislators took care to attach citizens to their fatherland. One of the means used to achieve this connection was public games. Rousseau speaks of the prizes with which,

> aux acclamation de toute la Grèce, on couronnoit les vainqueurs dans leurs jeux qui, les embrasant continuellement d'émulation et de gloire, portèrent peur courage et leurs vertus à ce degré d'énergie dont rien aujourd'hui ne nous donne l'idée, et qu'il n'appartient pas même aux modernes de croire.

> [Successful contestants in Greek games were crowned amidst applause from all their fellow citizens — these are the things that, by constantly rekindling the spirit of emulation and the love of glory, raised Greek courage and Greek virtues to a level of strenuousness of which nothing existing today can give us even a remote idea — which, indeed, strikes modern men as beyond belief.][24]

Glory, public recognition, mattered very much here. Moreover, the effect of their mattering was highly beneficent. Why is this so, if modern honor is such a negative force?

The answer seems to be equality, or, more exactly, the balanced reciprocity that underpins equality. One might say (though Rousseau didn't) that in these ideal republican contexts, everyone did depend on everyone else, but all did so equally. Rousseau is arguing that the key feature of these events, games, festivals, and recitations, which made them sources of patriotism and virtue, was the total lack of differentiation or distinction between different classes of citizen. They took place in the open air, and they involved everyone. People were both spectator and show. The contrast drawn in this passage is with modern religious services in enclosed churches, and above all with modern theater, which operates in closed halls, which you have to pay to get into, and consists of a special class of professionals making presentations to others.

This theme is central to the *Letter to D'Alembert*, where again Rousseau contrasts modern theater and the public festivals of a true republic. The latter take place in the open air. Here he makes it clear that the identity of spectator and performer is the key to these virtuous assemblies.

> Mais quels seront les objets de ces spectacles? Qu'y montrerat-on? Rien, si l'on veut. Avec la liberté, partout où régne l'affluence, le bien-être y régne aussi. Plantez au milieu d'une place un piquet couronné de fleurs, rassemblez-y le peuple, et vous aurez une féte. Faîtes mieux encore: donnez les spectateurs en spectacle; rendez-les acteurs eux-mêmes; faîtes que chacun se voie et s'aime dans les autres, afin que tous en soient mieux unis.

> [But what then will be the objects of these entertainments? What will be shown in them? Nothing, if you please. With liberty, wherever abundance reigns, well-being also reigns. Plant a stake crowned with flowers in the middle of a square; gather the people together there, and you will have a festival. Do better yet; let the spectators become an entertainment to themselves; make them actors themselves; do it so that each sees and loves himself in the others so that all will be better united.][25]

Rousseau's underlying, unstated argument would seem to be this: A perfectly balanced reciprocity takes the sting out of our dependence on opinion, and makes it compatible with liberty. Complete reciprocity, along with the unity of purpose that it makes possible, ensures that in following opinion I am not in any way pulled outside myself. I am still "obeying myself" as a member of this common project or "general will." Caring about esteem in this context is compatible with freedom and social unity, because the society is one in which all the virtuous will be esteemed equally and for the same (right) reasons. In contrast, in a system of hierarchical honor, we are in competition; one person's glory must be another's shame, or at least obscurity. Our unity of purpose is shattered, and in this context attempting to win the favor of another, who by hypothesis has goals distinct from mine, must be alienating. Paradoxically, the bad other-dependence goes along with separation and isolation;[26] the good kind, which Rousseau doesn't call other-dependence at all, involves the unity of a common project, even a "common self."[27]

Thus Rousseau is at the origin of a new discourse about honor and dignity. To the two traditional ways of thinking about honor and pride he adds a third, which is quite different. There was a discourse denouncing pride, as I mentioned above, which called on us to remove ourselves from this whole dimension of human life and to be utterly unconcerned with esteem. And then there was an ethic of honor, frankly nonuniversalist and inegalitarian, which saw the concern with honor as the first mark of the honorable man. Someone unconcerned with reputation, unwilling to defend it, had to be a coward, and therefore contemptible.

Rousseau borrows the denunciatory language of the first discourse, but he doesn't end up calling for a renunciation of all concern with esteem. On the contrary, in his portrait of the republican model, caring about esteem is central. What is wrong with pride or honor is its striving after preferences, hence division, hence real other-dependence, and therefore loss of the voice of nature, and consequently corruption, the forgetting of boundaries, and effeminacy. The remedy is not rejecting the importance of esteem, but entering into a quite different system, characterized by equality, reciprocity, and unity of purpose. This unity makes possible the equality of esteem, but the fact that esteem is in principle equal in this system is essential to this unity of purpose itself. Under the aegis of the general will, all virtuous citizens are to be equally honored. The age of dignity is born.

This new critique of pride, leading not to solitary mortification but to a politics of equal dignity, is what Hegel took up and made famous in his dialectic of the master and the slave. Against the old discourse on the evil of pride, he takes it as fundamental that we can nourish only to the extent that we are recognized. Each consciousness seeks recognition in another, and this is not a sign of a lack of virtue. But the ordinary conception of honor as hierarchical is crucially flawed. It is flawed because it cannot answer the need that sends people after recognition in the first place. Those who fail to win out in the honor stakes remain unrecognized. But even those who do win are more subtly frustrated, because they win recognition from the losers, whose acknowledgment is, by hypothesis, not really valuable, since they are no longer free, self-supporting subjects on the same level with the winners. The struggle for recognition can find only one satisfactory solution, and that is a regime of reciprocal recognition among equals. Hegel follows Rousseau in finding this regime in a society with a common purpose, one in which there is a "'we' that is an 'I', and an 'I' that is a 'we'."[28]

But if we think of Rousseau as inaugurating the new politics of equal dignity, we can argue that his solution is crucially flawed. In terms of the question posed at the beginning of this section, equality of esteem requires a tight unity of purpose that seems to be incompatible with any differentiation. The key to a free polity for

Rousseau seems to be a rigorous exclusion of any differentiation of roles. Rousseau's principle seems to be that for any two-place relation R involving power, the condition of a free society is that the two terms joined by the relation be identical. x R y is compatible with a free society only when $x = y$. This is true when the relation involves the x's presenting themselves in public space to the y's, and it is of course famously true when the relation is "exercises sovereignty over." In the social contract state, the people must be both sovereign and subject.

In Rousseau, three things seem to be inseparable: freedom (nondomination), the absence of differentiated roles, and a very tight common purpose. We must all be dependent on the general will, lest there arise bilateral forms of dependence.[29] This has been the formula for the most terrible forms of homogenizing tyranny, starting with the Jacobins and extending to the totalitarian regimes of our century. But even where the third element of the trinity is set aside, the aligning of equal freedom with the absence of differentiation has remained a tempting mode of thought. Wherever it reigns, be it in modes of feminist thought or of liberal politics, the margin to recognize difference is very small.

IV

We might well agree with the above analysis, and want to get some distance from the Rousseauean model of citizen dignity. Yet still we might want to know whether any politics of equal dignity, based on the recognition of universal capacities, is bound to be equally homogenizing. Is this true of those models — which I inscribed above, perhaps rather arbitrarily, under the banner of Kant — that separate equal freedom from both other elements of the Rousseauean trinity? These models not only have nothing to do with a general will, but abstract from any issue of the differentiation of roles. They simply look to an equality of rights accorded to citizens. Yet this form of liberalism has come under attack by radical proponents of the politics of difference as in some way unable to give due acknowledgment to distinctness. Are the critics correct?

The fact is that there are forms of this liberalism of equal rights that in the minds of their own proponents can give only a very restricted acknowledgment of distinct cultural identities. The notion that any of the standard schedules of rights might apply differently in one cultural context than they do in another, that their application might have to take account of different collective goals, is considered quite unacceptable. The issue, then, is whether this restrictive view of equal rights is the only possible interpretation. If it is, then it would seem that the accusation of homogenization is well founded. But perhaps it is not. I think it is not, and perhaps the best way to lay out the issue is to see it in the context of the Canadian case, where this question has played a role in the impending breakup of the country. In fact, two conceptions of rights-liberalism have confronted each other, albeit in confused fashion, throughout the long and inconclusive constitutional debates of recent years.

The issue came to the fore because of the adoption in 1982 of the Canadian Charter of Rights, which aligned our political system in this regard with the American one in having a schedule of rights offering a basis for judicial review of legislation at all levels of government. The question had to arise how to relate this schedule to the claims for distinctness put forward by French Canadians, and particularly Quebeckers, on the one hand, and aboriginal peoples on the other. Here what was at stake was the desire of these peoples for survival, and their consequent demand for certain forms of autonomy in their self-government, as well as the ability to adopt certain kinds of legislation deemed necessary for survival.

For instance, Quebec has passed a number of laws in the field of language. One regulates who can send their children to English-language schools (not francophones or immigrants); another requires that businesses with more than fifty employees be run in French; a third outlaws commercial signage in any language other than French. In other words, restrictions have been placed on Quebeckers by their government, in the name of their collective goal of survival, which in other Canadian communities might easily be disallowed by virtue of the Charter.[30] The fundamental question was: Is this variation acceptable or not?

The issue was finally raised by a proposed constitutional amendment, named after the site of the conference where it was first drafted, Meech Lake. The Meech amendment proposed to recognize Quebec as a "distinct society," and wanted to make this recognition one of the bases for judicial interpretation of the rest of the constitution, including the Charter. This seemed to open up the possibility for variation in its interpretation in different parts of the country. For many, such variation was fundamentally unacceptable. Examining why brings us to the heart of the question of how rights-liberalism is related to diversity.

The Canadian Charter follows the trend of the last half of the twentieth century, and gives a basis for judicial review on two basic scores. First, it defines a set of individual rights that are very similar to those protected in other charters and bills of rights in Western democracies, for example, in the United States and Europe. Second, it guarantees equal treatment of citizens in a variety of respects, or, alternatively put, it protects against discriminatory treatment on a number of irrelevant grounds, such as race or sex. There is a lot more in our Charter, including provisions for linguistic rights and aboriginal rights, that could be understood as according powers to collectivities, but the two themes I singled out dominate in the public consciousness.

This is no accident. These two kinds of provisions are now quite common in entrenched schedules of rights that provide the basis for judicial review. In this sense, the Western world, perhaps the world as a whole, is following American precedent. The Americans were the first to write out and entrench a bill of rights, which they did during the ratification of their Constitution and as a condition of its successful outcome. One might argue that they weren't entirely clear on judicial review as a method of securing those rights, but this rapidly became the practice. The first amendments protected individuals, and sometimes state governments,[31] against encroachment by the new federal government. It was after the Civil War, in the period of triumphant Reconstruction, and particularly with the Fourteenth Amendment, which called for "equal protection" for all citizens under the laws, that the theme of nondiscrimination became central to judicial review. But this theme is now on a par with the older norm of the defense of individual rights, and in public consciousness perhaps even ahead.

For a number of people in "English Canada," a political society's espousing certain collective goals threatens to run against both of these basic provisions of our Charter, or indeed any acceptable bill of rights. First, the collective goals may require restrictions on the behavior of individuals that may violate their rights. For many nonfrancophone Canadians, both inside and outside Quebec, this feared outcome had already materialized with Quebec's language legislation. For instance, Quebec legislation prescribes, as already mentioned, the type of school to which parents can send their children; and in the most famous instance, it forbids certain kinds of commercial signage. This latter provision was actually struck down by the Supreme Court as contrary to the Quebec Bill of Rights, as well as the Charter, and only reenacted through the invocation of a clause in the Charter that permits legislatures in certain cases to override decisions of the courts relative to the Charter for a limited period of time (the so-called notwithstanding clause).

But second, even if overriding individual rights were not possible, espousing collective goals on behalf of a national group can be thought to be inherently discriminatory. In the modern world it will always be the case that not all those living as citizens under a certain jurisdiction will belong to the national group thus favored. This in itself could be thought to provoke discrimination. But beyond this, the pursuit of the collective end will probably involve treating insiders and outsiders differently. Thus the schooling provisions of Law 101 forbid (roughly speaking) francophones and immigrants to send their children to English-language schools, but allow Canadian anglophones to do so.

This sense that the Charter clashes with basic Quebec policy was one of the grounds of opposition in the rest of Canada to the Meech Lake accord. The cause for concern was the distinct society clause, and the common demand for amendment was that the Charter be "protected" against this clause, or take precedence over it. There was undoubtedly in this opposition a certain amount of old-style anti-Quebec prejudice, but there was also a serious philosophical point, which we need to articulate here.

Those who take the view that individual rights must always come first, and, along with nondiscrimination provisions, must take precedence over collective goals, are often speaking from a liberal perspective that has become more and more widespread in the Anglo-American world. Its source is, of course, the United States, and it has recently been elaborated and defended by some of the best philosophical and legal minds in that society, including John Rawls, Ronald Dworkin, Bruce Ackerman, and others.[32] There are various formulations of the main idea, but perhaps the one that encapsulates most clearly the point that is relevant to us is the one expressed by Dworkin in his short paper entitled "Liberalism."[33]

Dworkin makes a distinction between two kinds of moral commitment. We all have views about the ends of life, about what constitutes a good life, which we and others ought to strive for. But we also acknowledge a commitment to deal fairly and equally with each other, regardless of how we conceive our ends. We might call this latter commitment "procedural," while commitments concerning the ends of life are "substantive." Dworkin claims that a liberal society is one that as a society adopts no particular substantive view about the ends of life. The society, rather, is united around a strong procedural commitment to treat people with equal respect. The reason that the polity as such can espouse no substantive view, cannot, for instance, allow that one of the goals of legislation should be to make people virtuous in one or another meaning of that term, is that this would involve a violation of its procedural norm. For, given the diversity of modern societies, it would unfailingly be the case that some people and not others would be committed to the favored conception of virtue. They might be in a majority; indeed, it is very likely that they would be, for otherwise a democratic society probably would not espouse their view. Nevertheless, this view would not be everyone's view, and in espousing this substantive outlook the society would not be treating the dissident minority with equal respect. It would be saying to them, in effect, "your view is not as valuable, in the eyes of this polity, as that of your more numerous compatriots."

There are very profound philosophical assumptions underlying this view of liberalism, which is rooted in the thought of Immanuel Kant. Among other features, this view understands human dignity to consist largely in autonomy, that is, in the ability of each person to determine for himself or herself a view of the good life. Dignity is associated less with any particular understanding of the good life, such that someone's departure from this would detract from his or her own dignity, than with the power to consider and espouse for oneself some view or other. We are not respecting this power equally in all subjects, it is claimed, if we raise the outcome of some people's deliberations officially over that of others. A liberal society must remain neutral on the good life, and restrict itself to ensuring that however they see things, citizens deal fairly with each other and the state deals equally with all.

The popularity of this view of the human agent as primarily a subject of self-determining or self-expressive choice helps to explain why this model of liberalism is so strong. But we must also consider that it has been urged with great force and intelligence by liberal thinkers in the United States, and precisely in the context of constitutional doctrines of judicial review.[34] Thus it is not surprising that the idea has become widespread, well beyond those who might subscribe to a specific Kantian philosophy, that a liberal society cannot accommodate publicly espoused notions of the good. This is the conception, as Michael Sandel has noted, of the "procedural republic," which has a very strong hold on the political agenda in the United States, and which has helped to place increasing emphasis on judicial review on the basis of constitutional texts at the expense of the ordinary political process of building majorities with a view to legislative action.[35]

But a society with collective goals like Quebec's violates this model. It is axiomatic for Quebec governments that the survival and flourishing of French culture in Quebec is a good. Political society is not neutral between those who value remaining true to the culture of our ancestors and those who might want to cut loose in the name of some individual goal of self-development. It might be argued that one could after all capture a goal like *survivance* for a proceduralist liberal society. One could consider the French language, for instance, as a collective resource that individuals might want to make use of, and act for its preservation, just as one does for clean air or green spaces. But this can't capture the full thrust of policies designed for cultural survival. It is not just a matter of having the French language available for those who might choose it. This might be seen to be the goal of some of the measures of federal bilingualism over the last twenty years. But it also involves making sure that there is a community of people here in the future that will want to avail itself of the opportunity to use the French language. Policies aimed at survival actively seek to *create* members of the community, for instance, in their assuring that future generations continue to identify as French-speakers. There is no way that these policies could be seen as just providing a facility to already existing people.

Quebeckers, therefore, and those who give similar importance to this kind of collective goal, tend to opt for a rather different model of a liberal society. In their view, a society can be organized around a definition of the good life, without this being seen as a depreciation of those who do not personally share this definition. Where the nature of the good requires that it be sought in common, this is the reason for its being a matter of public policy. According to this conception, a liberal society singles itself out as such by the way in which it treats minorities, including those who do not share public definitions of the good, and above all by the rights it accords to all of its members. But now the rights in question are conceived to be the fundamental and crucial ones that have been recognized as such from the very beginning of the liberal tradition: rights to life, liberty, due process, free speech, free practice of religion, and so on. In this model, there is a dangerous overlooking of an essential boundary in speaking of fundamental rights to things like commercial signage in the language of one's choice. One has to distinguish the fundamental liberties, those that should never be infringed and therefore ought to be unassailably entrenched, on one hand, from privileges and immunities that are important, but that can be revoked or restricted for reasons of public policy — although one would need a strong reason to do this — on the other.

A society with strong collective goals can be liberal, in this view, provided it also is capable of respecting diversity, especially when dealing with those who do not share its common goals; and provided it can offer adequate safeguards for fundamental rights. There will undoubtedly be tensions and difficulties in pursuing these objectives together, but such a pursuit is not impossible, and the problems are not in principle greater than those encountered by any liberal society that has to combine, for example, liberty and equality, or prosperity and justice.

Here are two incompatible views of liberal society. One of the great sources of our present disharmony is that the two views have squared off against each other in the last decade. The resistance to the "distinct society" that called for precedence to be given to the Charter came in part from a spreading procedural outlook in English Canada. From this point of view, attributing the goal of promoting Quebec's distinct society to a government is to acknowledge a collective goal, and this move had to be neutralized by being subordinated to the existing Charter. From the standpoint of Quebec, this attempt to impose a procedural model of liberalism not only would deprive the distinct society clause of some of its force as a rule of interpretation, but bespoke a rejection of the model of liberalism on which this society was founded. Each society misperceived the other throughout the Meech Lake debate. But here both perceived each other accurately — and didn't like what they saw. The rest of Canada saw that the distinct society clause legitimated collective goals. And Quebec saw that the move to give the Charter precedence imposed a form of liberal society that was alien to it, and to which Quebec could never accommodate itself without surrendering its identity.[36]

I have delved deeply into this case because it seems to me to illustrate the fundamental questions. There is a form of the politics of equal respect, as enshrined in a liberalism of rights, that is inhospitable to difference, because (a) it insists on uniform application of the rules defining these rights, without exception, and (b) it is suspicious of collective goals. Of course, this doesn't mean that this model seeks to abolish cultural differences. This would be an absurd accusation. But I call it inhospitable to difference because it can't accommodate what the members of distinct societies really aspire to, which is survival. This is (b) a collective goal, which (a) almost inevitably will call for some variations in the kinds of law we deem permissible from one cultural context to another, as the Quebec case clearly shows.

I think this form of liberalism is guilty as charged by the proponents of a politics of difference. Fortunately, however, there are other models of liberal society that take a different line on (a) and (b). These forms do call for the invariant defense of *certain* rights, of course. There would be no question of cultural differences determining the application of *habeas corpus,* for example. But they distinguish these fundamental rights from the broad range of immunities and presumptions of uniform treatment that have sprung up in modern cultures of judicial review. They are willing to weigh the importance of certain forms of uniform treatment against the importance of cultural survival, and opt sometimes in favor of the latter.

They are thus in the end not procedural models of liberalism, but are grounded very much on judgments about what makes a good life — judgments in which the integrity of cultures has an important place.

Although I cannot argue it here, obviously I would endorse this kind of model. Indisputably, though, more and more societies today are turning out to be multicultural, in the sense of including more than one cultural community that wants to survive. The rigidities of procedural liberalism may rapidly become impractical in tomorrow's world.

V

The politics of equal respect, then, at least in this more hospitable variant, can be cleared of the charge of homogenizing difference. But there is another way of formulating the charge that is harder to rebut. In this form, however, it perhaps ought not to be rebutted, or so I want to argue.

The charge I'm thinking of here is provoked by the claim sometimes made on behalf of "difference-blind" liberalism that it can offer a neutral ground on which people of all cultures can meet and coexist. In this view, it is necessary to make a certain number of distinctions — between what is public and what is private, for instance, or between politics and religion — and only then can one relegate the contentious differences to a sphere that does not impinge on the political.

But a controversy like that over Salman Rushdie's *Satanic Verses* shows how wrong this view is. For mainstream Islam, there is no question of separating politics and religion the way we have come to expect in Western liberal society. Liberalism is not a possible meeting ground for all cultures, but is the political expression of one range of cultures, and quite incompatible with other ranges. Moreover, as many Muslims are well aware, Western liberalism is not so much an expression of the secular, postreligious outlook that happens to be popular among liberal *intellectuals* as a more organic outgrowth of Christianity — at least as seen from the alternative vantage point of Islam. The division of church and state goes back to the earliest days of Christian civilization. The early forms of the separation were very different from ours, but the basis was laid for modern developments. The very term *secular* was originally part of the Christian vocabulary.[37]

All this is to say that liberalism can't and shouldn't claim complete cultural neutrality. Liberalism is also a fighting creed. The hospitable variant I espouse, as well as the most rigid forms, has to draw the line. There will be variations when it comes to applying the schedule of rights, but not where incitement to assassination is concerned. But this should not be seen as a contradiction. Substantive distinctions of this kind are inescapable in politics, and at least the nonprocedural liberalism I was describing is fully ready to accept this.

But the controversy is nevertheless disturbing. It is so for the reason I mentioned above: that all societies are becoming increasingly multicultural, while at the same time becoming more porous. Indeed, these two developments go together. Their porousness means that they are more open to multinational migration; more of their members live the life of diaspora, whose center is elsewhere. In these circumstances, there is something awkward about replying simply, "This is how we do things here." This reply must be made in cases like the Rushdie controversy, where "how we do things" covers issues such as the right to life and to freedom of speech. The awkwardness arises from the fact that there are substantial numbers of people who are citizens and also belong to the culture that calls into question our philosophical boundaries. The challenge is to deal with their sense of marginalization without compromising our basic political principles.

This brings us to the issue of multiculturalism as it is often debated today, which has a lot to do with the imposition of some cultures on others, and with the assumed superiority that powers this imposition. Western liberal societies are thought to be supremely guilty in this regard, partly because of their colonial past, and partly because of their marginalization of segments of their populations that stem from other cultures. It is in this context that the reply "this is how we do things here" can seem crude and insensitive. Even if, in the nature of things, compromise is close to impossible here — one either forbids murder or allows it — the attitude presumed by the reply is seen as one of contempt. Often, in fact, this presumption is correct. Thus we arrive again at the issue of recognition.

Recognition of equal value was not what was at stake — at least in a strong sense — in the preceding section. There it was a question of whether cultural survival will be acknowledged as a legitimate goal, whether collective ends will be allowed as legitimate considerations in judicial review, or for other purposes of major social policy. The demand there was that we let cultures defend themselves, within reasonable bounds. But the further demand we are looking at here is that we all *recognize* the equal value of different cultures; that we not only let them survive, but acknowledge their *worth*.

What sense can be made of this demand? In a way, it has been operative in an unformulated state for some time. The politics of nationalism has been powered for well over a century in part by the sense that people have had of being despised or respected by others around them. Multinational societies can break up, in large part because of a lack of (perceived) recognition of the equal worth of one group by another. This is at present, I believe, the case in Canada — though my diagnosis will certainly be challenged by some. On the international scene, the tremendous sensitivity of certain supposedly closed societies to world opinion — as shown in their reactions to findings of, say, Amnesty International, or in their attempts through UNESCO to build a new world information order — attests to the importance of external recognition.

But all this is still *an sich*, not *für sich*, to use Hegelian jargon. The actors themselves are often the first to deny that they are moved by such considerations, and plead other factors, like inequality, exploitation, and injustice, as their motives. Very few Quebec independentists, for instance, can accept that what is mainly winning them their fight is a lack of recognition on the part of English Canada.

What is new, therefore, is that the demand for recognition is now explicit. And it has been made explicit, in the way I indicated above, by the spread of the idea that we are formed by recognition. We could say that, thanks to this idea, misrecognition has now graduated to the rank of a harm that can be hardheadedly enumerated along with the ones mentioned in the previous paragraph.

One of the key authors in this transition is undoubtedly the late Frantz Fanon, whose influential *Les Damnés de la Terre (The Wretched of the Earth)*[38] argued that the major weapon of the colonizers was the imposition of their image of the colonized on the subjugated people. These latter, in order to be free, must first of all purge themselves of these depreciating self-images. Fanon recommended violence as the way to this freedom, matching the original violence of the alien imposition. Not all those who have drawn from Fanon have followed him in this, but the notion that there is a struggle for a changed self-image, which takes place both within the subjugated and against the dominator, has been very widely applied. The idea has become crucial to certain strands of feminism, and is also a very important element in the contemporary debate about multiculturalism.

The main locus of this debate is the world of education in a broad sense. One important focus is university humanities departments, where demands are made to alter, enlarge, or scrap the "canon" of accredited authors on the grounds that the one presently favored consists almost entirely of "dead white males." A greater place ought to be made for women, and for people of non-European races and cultures. A second focus is the secondary schools, where an attempt is being made, for instance, to develop Afrocentric curricula for pupils in mainly black schools.

The reason for these proposed changes is not, or not mainly, that all students may be missing something important through the exclusion of a certain gender or certain races or cultures, but rather that women and students from the excluded groups are given, either directly or by omission, a demeaning picture of themselves, as though all creativity and worth inhered in males of European provenance. Enlarging and changing the curriculum therefore is essential not so much in the name of a broader culture for everyone as in order to give due recognition to the hitherto excluded. The background premise of these demands is that recognition forges identity, particularly in its Fanonist application: dominant groups tend to entrench their hegemony by inculcating an image of inferiority in the subjugated. The struggle for freedom and equality must therefore pass through a revision of these images. Multicultural curricula are meant to help in this process of revision.

Although it often is not stated clearly, the logic behind some of these demands seems to depend upon a premise that we owe equal respect to all cultures. This emerges from the nature of the reproach made to the designers of traditional curricula. The claim is that the judgments of worth on which these latter were supposedly based were in fact corrupt, were marred by narrowness or insensitivity or, even worse, a desire to downgrade the excluded. The implication seems to be that absent these distorting factors, true judgments of value of different works would place all cultures more or less on the same footing. Of course, the attack could come from a more radical, neo-Nietzschean standpoint, which questions the very status of judgments of worth as such, but short of this extreme step (whose coherence I doubt), the presumption seems to be of equal worth.

I would like to maintain that there is something valid in this presumption, but that the presumption is by no means unproblematic, and involves something like an act of faith. As a presumption, the claim is that all human cultures that have animated whole societies over some considerable stretch of time have something important to say to all human beings. I have worded it in this way to exclude partial cultural milieux within a society, as well as short phases of a major culture. There is no reason to believe that, for instance, the different art forms of a given culture should all be of equal, or even of considerable, value; and every culture can go through phases of decadence.

But when I call this claim a "presumption," I mean that it is a starting hypothesis with which we ought to approach the study of any other culture. The validity of the claim has to be demonstrated concretely in the actual study of the culture. Indeed, for a culture sufficiently different from our own, we may have only the foggiest idea *ex ante* of in what its valuable contribution might consist. Because, for a sufficiently different culture, the very understanding of what it is to be of worth will be strange and unfamiliar to us. To approach, say, a raga with the presumptions of value implicit in the well-tempered clavier would be forever to miss the point. What has to happen is what Gadamer has called a "fusion of horizons."[39] We learn to move in a broader horizon, within which what we have formerly taken for granted as the background to valuation can be situated as one possibility alongside the different background of the formerly unfamiliar culture. The "fusion of horizons" operates through our developing new vocabularies of comparison, by means of which we can articulate these contrasts.[40] So that if and when we ultimately find substantive support for our initial presumption, it is on the basis of an understanding of what constitutes worth that we couldn't possibly have had at the beginning. We have reached the judgment partly through transforming our standards.

We might want to argue that we owe all cultures a presumption of this kind. I will explain later on what I think this claim might be based. From this point of view, withholding the presumption might be seen as the fruit merely of prejudice or of ill will. It might even be tantamount to a denial of equal status. Something like this might lie behind the accusation leveled by supporters of multiculturalism against defenders of the traditional canon. Supposing that their reluctance to enlarge the canon comes from a mixture of prejudice and ill will, the multiculturalists charge them with the arrogance of assuming their own superiority over formerly subject peoples.

This presumption would help explain why the demands of multiculturalism build on the already established principles of the politics of equal respect. If withholding the presumption is tantamount to a denial of equality, and if important consequences flow for people's identity from the absence of recognition, then a case can be made for insisting on the universalization of the presumption as a logical extension of the politics of dignity. Just as all must have equal civil rights, and equal voting rights, regardless of race or culture, so all should enjoy the presumption that their traditional culture has value. This extension, however logically it may seem to flow from the accepted norms of equal dignity, fits uneasily within them, as described in Section II, because it challenges the "difference-blindness" that was central to them. Yet it does indeed seem to flow from them, albeit uneasily.

I am not sure about the validity of demanding this presumption as a right. But we can leave this issue aside, because the demand made seems to be much stronger. The claim seems to be that a proper respect for equality requires more than a presumption that further study will make us see things this way, but actual judgments of equal worth applied to the customs and creations of these different cultures. Such judgments seem to be implicit in the demand that certain works be included in the canon, and in the implication that these works have not been included earlier only because of prejudice or ill will or the desire to dominate. (Of course, the demand for inclusion is *logically* separable from a claim of equal worth. The demand could be: Include these because they're ours, even though they may well be inferior. But this is not how the people making the demand talk.)

But there is something very wrong with the demand in this form. It makes sense to demand as a matter of right that we approach the study of certain cultures with a presumption of their value, as described above. But it can't make sense to demand as a matter of right that we come up with a final concluding judgment that their value is great, or equal to others'. That is, if the judgment of value is to register something independent of our own wills and desires, it cannot be dictated by a principle of ethics. On examination, either we will find something of great value in culture C, or we will not. But it makes no more sense to demand that we do so than it does to demand that we find the earth round or flat, the temperature of the air hot or cold.

I have stated this rather flatly, when as everyone knows there is a vigorous controversy over the "objectivity" of judgments in this field, and whether there is a "truth of the matter" here, as there seems to be in natural science, or indeed, whether even in natural science "objectivity" is a mirage. I do not have space to address this here. I have discussed it somewhat elsewhere.[41] I don't have much sympathy for these forms of subjectivism, which I think are shot through with confusion. But there seems to be some special confusion in invoking them in this context. The moral and political thrust of the complaint concerns unjustified judgments of inferior status allegedly made of nonhegemonic cultures. But if those judgments are ultimately a question of the human will, then the issue of justification falls away. Properly speaking, one doesn't make judgments that can be right or wrong; one expresses liking or dislike, one endorses or rejects another culture. But then the complaint must shift to address the refusal to endorse, and the validity or invalidity of judgments here has nothing to do with it.

Then, however, the act of declaring another culture's creations to be of worth and the act of declaring oneself on their side, even if their creations aren't all that impressive, become indistinguishable. The difference is only in the packaging. Yet the first is normally understood as a genuine expression of respect, the second often as insufferable patronizing. The supposed beneficiaries of the politics of recognition, the people who might actually benefit from acknowledgment, make a crucial distinction between the two acts. They know that they want respect, not condescension. Any theory that wipes out the distinction seems at least *prima facie* to be distorting crucial facets of the reality it purports to deal with.

In fact, subjectivist, half-baked neo-Nietzschean theories are quite often invoked in this debate. Deriving frequently from Foucault or Derrida, they claim that all judgments of worth are based on standards that are ultimately imposed by and further entrench structures of power. It should be clear why these theories proliferate here. A favorable judgment on demand is nonsense, unless some such theories are valid. Moreover, the giving of such a judgment on demand is an act of breathtaking condescension. No one can really mean it as a genuine act of respect. It is more in the nature of a pretend act of respect given on the insistence of its supposed beneficiary. Objectively, such an act involves contempt for the latter's intelligence. To be an object of such an act of respect demeans. The proponents of neo-Nietzschean theories hope to escape this whole nexus of hypocrisy by turning the entire issue into one of power and counterpower. Then the question is no more one of respect, but of taking sides, of solidarity. But this is hardly a satisfactory solution, because in taking sides they miss the driving force of this kind of politics, which is precisely the search for recognition and respect.

Moreover, even if one could demand it of them, the last thing one wants at this stage from Eurocentered intellectuals is positive judgments of the worth of cultures that they have not intensively studied. For real judgments of worth suppose a fused horizon of standards, as we have seen; they suppose that we have been transformed by the study of the other, so that we are not simply judging by our original familiar standards. A favorable judgment made prematurely would be not only condescending but ethnocentric. It would praise the other for being like us.

Here is another severe problem with much of the politics of multiculturalism. The peremptory demand for favorable judgments of worth is paradoxically — perhaps one should say tragically — homogenizing. For it implies that we already have the standards to make such judgments. The standards we have, however, are those of North Atlantic civilization. And so the judgments implicitly and unconsciously will cram the others into our categories. For instance, we will think of their "artists" as creating "works," which we then can include in our canon. By implicitly invoking our standards to judge all civilizations and cultures, the politics of difference can end up making everyone the same.[42]

In this form, the demand for equal recognition is unacceptable. But the story doesn't simply end there. The enemies of multiculturalism in the American academy have perceived this weakness, and have used this as an excuse to turn their backs on the problem. But this won't do. A response like that attributed to Bellow which I quoted above, to the effect that we will be glad to read the Zulu Tolstoy when he comes along, shows the depths of ethnocentricity. First, there is the implicit assumption that excellence has to take forms familiar to us: the Zulus should produce a *Tolstoy*. Second, we are assuming that their contribution is yet to be made *(when* the Zulus produce a Tolstoy ...). These two assumptions obviously go hand in hand. If they have to produce our kind of excellence, then obviously their only hope lies in the future. Roger Kimball puts it more crudely: "The multiculturalists notwithstanding, the choice facing us today is not between a 'repressive' Western culture and a multicultural paradise, but between culture and barbarism. Civilization is not a gift, it is an achievement — a fragile achievement that needs constantly to be shored up and defended from besiegers inside and out."[43]

There must be something midway between the unauthentic and homogenizing demand for recognition of equal worth, on the one hand, and the self-immurement within ethnocentric standards, on the other. There are other cultures, and we have to live together more and more, both on a world scale and commingled in each individual society.

What there is is the presumption of equal worth I described above: a stance we take in embarking on the study of the other. Perhaps we don't need to ask whether it's something that others can demand from us as a right. We might simply ask whether this is the way we ought to approach others.

Well, is it? How can this presumption be grounded? One ground that has been proposed is a religious one. Herder, for instance, had a view of divine providence, according to which all this variety of culture was not a mere accident but was meant to bring about a greater harmony. I can't rule out such a view. But merely on the human level, one could argue that it is reasonable to suppose that cultures that have provided the horizon of meaning for large numbers of human beings, of diverse characters and temperaments, over a long period of time — that have, in other words, articulated their sense of the good, the holy, the admirable — are almost certain to have something that deserves our admiration and respect, even if it is accompanied by much that we have to abhor and reject. Perhaps one could put it another way: it would take a supreme arrogance to discount this possibility *a priori*.

There is perhaps after all a moral issue here. We only need a sense of our own limited part in the whole human story to accept the presumption. It is only arrogance, or some analogous moral failing, that can deprive us of this. But what the presumption requires of us is not peremptory and unauthentic judgments of equal value, but a willingness to be open to comparative cultural study of the kind that must displace our horizons in the resulting fusions. What it requires above all is an admission that we are very far away from that ultimate horizon from which the relative worth of different cultures might be evident. This would mean breaking with an illusion that still holds many "multiculturalists" — as well as their most bitter opponents — in its grip.[44]

Notes

1 Reprinted by permission of Princeton University Press and the author from *Multiculturalism and "The Politics of Recognition"* (Princeton: Princeton University Press, 1992).

2 "La nature de l'honneur est demander des préférences et des distinctions...." Montesquieu, *De l'esprit des lois,* Bk. 3, chap. 7.

3 The significance of this move from "honor" to "dignity" is interestingly discussed by Peter Berger in his "On the Obsolescence of the Concept of Honour," in *Revisions: Changing Perspectives in Moral Philosophy,* ed. Stanley Hauerwas and Alasdair MacIntyre (Notre Dame, IN: University of Notre Dame Press, 1983), pp. 172–81.

4 Lionel Trilling, *Sincerity and Authenticity* (New York: Norton, 1969).

5 I have discussed the development of this doctrine at greater length, at first in the work of Francis Hutcheson, drawing on the writings of the Earl of Shaftesbury, and its adversarial relation to Locke's theory in *Sources of the Self* (Cambridge: Harvard University Press, 1989), chap. 15.

6 "Le sentiment de existence dépouillé de toute autre affection est par lui-même un sentiment précieux de contentement et de paiz qui suffiroit seul pour rendre cette existence chère et douce à qui sauroit écarter de soi toutes les impressions sensuelles et terrestres qui viennent sans cesse nous en distraire et en troubler ici bas la douceur. Mais la pluspart des hommes agités de passions continuelles connoissent peu cet état et ne l'ayant gouté qu'imparfaitement durant peu d'instans n'en conservent qu'une idée obscure et confuse qui ne leur en fait pas sentir le charme." Jean-Jacques Rousseau, *Les Rêvereies du promeneur solitaire,* "Cinquième Promenade," in *Oeuvres complètes* (Paris: Gallimard, 1959), Vol. 1, p. 1047.

7 "Jeder Mensch hat ein eigenes Maass, gleichsam eine eigne Stimmung aller seiner sinnlichen Gefühle zu einander." Johann Gottlob Herder, *Ideen,* chap. 7, sec. 1, in *Herders Sämtliche Werke,* ed. Bernard Suphan (Berlin: Weidmann, 1877–1913), Vol. 13, p. 291.

8 John Stuart Mill was influenced by this Romantic current of thought when he made something like the ideal of authenticity the basis for one of his most powerful arguments in *On Liberty* (London, 1859). See especially chapter 3, where he argues that we need something more than a capacity for "apelike imitation": "A person whose desires and impulses are his own — are the expression of his own nature, as it has been developed and modified by his own culture — is said to have a character." "If a person possesses any tolerable amount of common sense and experience, his

own mode of laying out his existence is the best, not because it is the best in itself, but because it is his own mode." John Stuart Mill, *Three Essays* (Oxford: Oxford University Press, 1975), pp. 73–4, 83.

9 George Herbert Mead, *Mind, Self, and Society* (Chicago: University of Chicago Press, 1934).

10 This inner dialogicality has been explored by M. M. Bakhtin and those who have drawn on his work. See, of Bakhtin, especially *Problems of Dostoyevsky's Poetics*, tr. Caryl Emerson (Minneapolis: University of Minnesota Press, 1984). See also Michael Holquist and Katerina Clark, *Mikhail Bakhtin* (Cambridge: Harvard University Press, 1984); and James Wertsch, *Voices of the Mind* (Cambridge: Harvard University Press, 1991).

11 See Bakhtin, "The Problem of the Text in Linguistics, Philology and the Human Sciences," in *Speech Genres and Other Late Essays*, ed. Caryl Emerson and Michael Holquist (Austin: University of Texas Press, 1986), p. 126, for this notion of a "super-addressee," beyond our existing interlocutors.

12 Rousseau is describing the first assemblies: "Chacun commença à regarder les autres et à vouloir être regardé soi-même, et l'estime publique eut un prix. Celui qui chantait ou dansait le mieux; le plus beau, le plus fort, le plus adroit ou le plus éloquent devint le plus considéré, et ce fut là le premier pas vers l'inégalité, et vers le vice en même temps." *Discours sur l'origine et les fondements de l'inégalité parmi les hommes* (Paris: Granier-Flammarion, 1971), p. 210.

13 See, for example, the passage in the *Considerations sur le gouvernement de Pologne* where he describes the ancient public festival, in which all the people took part, in *Du contrat social* (Paris: Garnier, 1962), p. 345; and also the parallel passage in *Lettre à D'Alembert sur les spectacles*, in *Du contrat social*, pp. 224–5. The crucial principle was that there should be no division between performers and spectators, but that all should be seen by all. "Mais quels seront enfin les objets de ces spectacles? Qu'y montrera-t-on? Rien, si l'on veut. ... Donnez les spectateurs en spectacles; rendez-les acteurs eux-mêmes; faites que chacun se voie et s'aime dans les autres, que tous en soient mieux unis."

14 See Hegel, *The Phenomenology of Spirit*, tr. A. V. Miller (Oxford: Oxford University Press, 1977), chap. 4.

15 There are a number of strands that have linked these two levels, but perhaps special prominence in recent years has been given to a psychoanalytically oriented feminism, which roots social inequalities in the early upbringing of men and women. See, for instance, Nancy Chodorow, *Feminism and Psychoanalytic Theory* (New Haven: Yale University Press, 1989); and Jessica Benjamin, *Bonds of Love: Psychoanalysis, Feminism and the Problem of Domination* (New York: Pantheon, 1988).

16 A prime example of this charge from a feminist perspective is Carol Gilligan's critique of Lawrence Kohlberg's theory of moral development, for presenting a view of human development that privileges only one facet of moral reasoning, precisely the one that tends to predominate in boys rather than girls. See Gilligan, *In a Different Voice* (Cambridge: Harvard University Press, 1982).

17 Will Kymlicka, in his very interesting and tightly argued book *Liberalism, Community and Culture* (Oxford: Clarendon Press, 1989), tries to argue for a kind of politics of difference, notably in relation to aboriginal rights in Canada, but from a basis that is firmly within a theory of liberal neutrality. He wants to argue on the

basis of certain cultural needs — minimally, the need for an integral and undamaged cultural language with which one can define and pursue his or her own conception of the good life. In certain circumstances, with disadvantaged populations, the integrity of the culture may require that we accord them more resources or rights than others. The argument is quite parallel to that made in relation to socioeconomic inequalities that I mentioned above.

But where Kymlicka's interesting argument fails to recapture the actual demands made by the groups concerned — say Indian bands in Canada, or French-speaking Canadians — is with respect to their goal of survival. Kymlicka's reasoning is valid (perhaps) for *existing* people who find themselves trapped within a culture under pressure, and can flourish within it or not at all. But it doesn't justify measures designed to ensure survival through indefinite future generations. For the populations concerned, however, that is what is at stake. We need only think of the historical resonance of "la survivance" among French Canadians.

18 See Kant, *Grundlegung der Metaphysik der Sitten* (Berlin: Gruyter, 1968; reprint of the Berlin Academy edition), p. 434.

19 I have no idea whether this statement was actually made in this form by Saul Bellow, or by anyone else. I report it only because it captures a widespread attitude, which is, of course, why the story had currency in the first place.

20 One hears both kinds of reproach today. In the context of some modes of feminism and multiculturalism, the claim is the strong one, that the hegemonic culture discriminates. In the Soviet Union, however, alongside a similar reproach leveled at the hegemonic Great Russian culture, one also hears the complaint that Marxist-Leninist communism has been an alien imposition on all equally, even on Russia itself. The communist mold, in this view, has been truly nobody's. Solzhenitsyn has made this claim, but it is voiced by Russians of a great many different persuasions today, and has something to do with the extraordinary phenomenon of an empire that has broken apart through the quasi-secession of its metropolitan society.

21 See John Rawls, *A Theory of Justice* (Cambridge: Harvard University Press, 1971); Ronald Dworkin, *Taking Rights Seriously* (London: Duckworth, 1977) and *A Matter of Principle* (Cambridge: Harvard University Press, 1985); and Jürgen Habermas, *Theorie des kommunikativen Handelns* (Frankfurt: Suhrkamp, 1981).

22 *The Social Contract and Discourses*, tr. G. D. H. Cole (New York: E. P. Dutton, 1950), pp. 3–4.

23 Jean-Jacques Rousseau, *Emile* (Paris: Garnier, 1964), Bk. 2, p. 70.

24 *Considerations sur le gouvernement de Pologne*, p. 345; *Considerations on the Government of Poland*, tr. Wilmoore Kendall (Indianapolis: Bobbs-Merrill, 1972), p. 8.

25 *Lettre à D'Alembert*, p. 225; *Letter to M. D'Alembert on the Theatre*, in Jean-Jacques Rousseau, *Politics and the Arts*, tr. Allan Bloom (Ithaca, NY:Cornell University Press, 1968), p. 126.

26 A little later in the passage I quoted above from the *Considerations on the Government of Poland*, Rousseau describes gatherings in our depraved modern society as "des cohues licencieuses," where people go "pour s'y faire des liaisons

secrètes, pour y chercher les plaisirs qui séparent, isolent le plus les hommes, et qui relâchent le plus les coeurs." *Considerations sur le gouvernement de Pologne*, p. 346.

27 *Du contrat social*, p. 244. I have benefited, in this area, from discussions with Natalie Oman. See here "Forms of Common Space in the Work of Jean-Jacques Rousseau" (Master's research paper, McGill University, July 1991).

28 Hegel, *Phenomenology of Spirit*, p. 110.

29 In justifying his famous (or infamous) slogan about the person coerced to obey the law being "forced to be free," Rousseau goes on: "car telle est la condition qui donnant chaque citoyen à la Patrie le garantit de toute dépendance personnelle...." *Du contrat social*, p. 246.

30 The Supreme Court of Canada did strike down one of these provisions, the one forbidding commercial signage in languages other than French. But in their judgment the justices agreed that it would have been quite reasonable to demand that all signs be in French, even though accompanied by another language. In other words, it was permissible in their view for Quebec to outlaw unilingual English signs. The need to protect and promote the French language in the Quebec context would have justified it. Presumably this would mean that legislative restrictions on the language of signs in another province might well be struck down for some quite other reason

Incidentally, the signage provisions are still in force in Quebec, because of a provision of the Charter that in certain cases allows legislatures to override judgments of the courts for a restricted period.

31 For instance, the First Amendment, which forbade Congress to establish any religion, was not originally meant to separate church and state as such. It was enacted at a time when many states had established churches, and it was plainly meant to prevent the new federal government from interfering with or overruling these local arrangements. It was only later, after the Fourteenth Amendment, following the so-called Incorporation doctrine, that these restrictions on the federal government were held to have been extended to all governments, at any level.

32 Rawls, *A Theory of Justice* and "Justice as Fairness: Political Not Metaphysical," *Philosophy & Public Affairs* 14 (1985), pp. 223–51; Dworkin, *Taking Rights Seriously* and "Liberalism," in *Public and Private Morality*, ed. Stuart Hampshire (Cambridge: Cambridge University Press, 1978); Bruce Ackerman, *Social Justice in the Liberal State* (New Haven: Yale University Press, 1980).

33 Dworkin, "Liberalism."

34 See, for instance, the arguments deployed by Lawrence Tribe in his *Abortion: The Clash of Absolutes* (New York: Norton, 1990).

35 Michael Sandel, "The Procedural Republic and the Unencumbered Self," *Political Theory* 12 (1984), pp. 81–96.

36 See Guy Laforest, "L'esprit de 1982," in *Le Québec et la restructuration du Canada, 1980–1992*, ed. Louis Balthasar, Guy Laforest, and Vincent Lemieuz (Quebec: Septentrion, 1991).

37 The point is well argued in Larry Siedentop, "Liberalism: The Christian Connection," *Times Literary Supplement*, 24–30 (March 1989), p. 308. I have also discussed these issues in "The Rushdie Controversy, " in *Public Culture* 2, 1 (Fall 1989), pp. 118–22.

38 Frantz Fanon, *Les Damnés de la Terre (The Wretched of the Earth)* (Paris: Maspero, 1961).

39 *Wahrheit und Methode* (Tubingen: Mohr, 1975), pp. 289–90.

40 I have discussed what is involved here at greater length in "Comparison, History, Truth," in *Myth and Philosophy*, ed. Frank Reynolds and David Tracy (Albany: State University of New York Press, 1990); and in "Understanding Ethnocentricity," in *Philosophy and the Human Sciences* (Cambridge: Cambridge University Press, 1985).

41 See part 1 of Francis Hutcheson, *Sources of the Self* (Cambridge: Harvard University Press, 1989).

42 The same homogenizing assumptions underlie the negative reaction that many people have to claims to superiority in some definite respect on behalf of Western civilization, say in regard to natural science. But it is absurd to cavil at such claims in principle. If all cultures have made a contribution of worth, it cannot be that these are identical, or even embody the same kind of worth. To expect this would be to vastly underestimate the differences. In the end, the presumption of worth imagines a universe in which different cultures complement each other with quite different kinds of contribution. This picture not only is compatible with, but demands judgments of, superiority in a certain respect.

43 "Tenured Radicals," *New Criterion* (January 1991), p. 13.

44 There is a very interesting critique of both extreme camps, from which I have borrowed in this discussion, in Benjamin Lee, "Towards a Critical Internationalism" (forthcoming).

3

Introduction to "Critical Multiculturalism"

LAUREN BERLANT AND MICHAEL WARNER

"Critical Multiculturalism" was written in late 1990 and early 1991, a time when multiculturalism and cultural studies seemed to promise a great deal. So when our group came together to discuss these new developments, it surprised us that our discussions turned skeptical. We were puncturing our own new balloon. Not because of a distaste for utopian sentiment; we wanted to begin thinking about how to preserve the practical possibilities that interested us without becoming spokesintellectuals for what has turned out to be, as we already anticipated, liberal multiculturalism. As the coda to "Critical Multiculturalism" notes, this was before the American scene was dominated by the rhetoric of political correctness. (D'Souza's *Illiberal Education* appeared in 1991.) Soon the issues became — even more than we expected — the stuff of a national media drama. Many of our colleagues — and we ourselves in other contexts — lined up to defend cultural studies and multiculturalism against a right-wing attack that had the full support of the national and local media.[1]

Now, in 1994, as two of us reread the essay, we find that our concerns about multiculturalism and cultural studies have deepened, as have our ambitions for the possibilities they offered. Multiculturalism promised to make political culture open and responsible, not only to diverse viewpoints, but also to the conflicts that liberal procedures normally screen out; now, it easily appears to turn into a Clintonian fantasy of "looking like America." In this defanged version, "multicultural" identities are being conceived as genetic and iconizing sources of ethnicity, of political validity, and of authenticity. Multiculturalism could be taken to mean quite the opposite: a scene of complex and always changing histories that cannot be reduced rhymingly to a face, a postmodern place, or the heritage of an abandoned space.

Cultural studies promised (and still promises) to become an arena of intellectual activity in which these more unfamiliar stories could be told. As an academic program it sought to shake up the disciplinary and expert sureties of academic knowledge. It developed ways of reading "culture" as many competing scenes of knowledge-production and consumption, requiring inventive ways of explaining meaning and power. But in this still early moment, the impulse to justify academic work by claims about "culture" rather than about a "canon" has been merely thematized in ever so many mass-cultural readings, and in facile equations of consumption with agency. Mistaking the context of its own performance, confident in the power of readings as "interventions," much of cultural studies has led to intellectual pseudo-activity.

Even in their best versions, neither multiculturalism nor cultural studies has developed an international project that would be *critical* in the strong sense of our title (discussed on pp. 120–1). Both tend to assume Euro-American value terms and working conditions. Our criticisms of these tendencies have been amplified by others in the meantime, notably by John Guillory's *Cultural Capital* and Aijaz Ahmad's *In Theory*.[2]

We also see more clearly now that the problem set out in "Critical Multiculturalism," sometimes only partly articulated by the essay, was a larger issue of which multiculturalism and cultural studies were only the nearest examples to hand. And that is how to imagine any transnational context for a generally "left" criticism. In 1990, we were writing in the wake of one set of epochal changes in the world (in 1989) and just in advance of another (in 1991). Can criticism think its local conflicts as part of a project or stance that might make sense in more than one locale or in more than one conflict? In 1990 we asked this question to see if multiculturalism could generate a strong, transnational, comparative critique. Now, in the world still reeling and recombining its maps of culture and power in the post-cold war era, this question even more clearly describes the dilemma of anything that might be called left criticism.

We wrote "Critical Multiculturalism" at a time when Tiananmen and the disintegration of the Eastern Bloc suggested the vital energies of progressive criticism did not lie with marxism, at least by that name; for many, the whole project of organizing a critical culture primarily against capitalism, class exploitation, and consumer passivity seemed to have been either discredited or emptied of its practical and utopian force. In part, the sense of a break with the axioms of the traditional left spurred new kinds of leftism, especially around identity politics. The past five years have been boom times for queer theory, for example, in a way that was never possible under the domain of the academic leftism that was.

But the post-Cold War world has not turned out to be one in which a culturalist left could happily form its coherence around a concept like multiculturalism. Nor have the international frontiers of capitalism ceased to be an organizing problem. In "Critical Multiculturalism," we associate the new dominance of "market democracy" rhetoric and the international policing problems of the New World Order with George Bush. Since then, Clinton has embraced the same programs and, in the case of "market democracy," the same rhetoric. As a result it becomes more and more important to describe the systemic inequities of marketized society, distortions of possibilities for happiness in consumer culture, and restrictions of political activity in a world regulated by transnational wealth, technocracy, and national or international bureaucracies. "Market democracy," which falsely substitutes free consumption for free activity and legitimate citizenship, requires a kind of criticism not grounded in identitarianism which itself can too easily fall back into the consumption of identity and other new pseudofreedoms.

Any number of political events around the world could be cited as a way of showing what a transitional moment we live in, and how deeply these world transitions have shifted the grounds for intellectual self-understanding. Without falling back on the narrative form of the headline, with its blithely frenzied consumption of crisis, consider the following:

1. The end of cold war alignment has not only made it more difficult to support socialism, which looks tainted, but also to identify oneself with US-style liberal democracy, now trying to wipe its hands from the sordid police business of globalism.

    The end of that alignment also marked the end of "realignment" or "nonalignment." Rubble from the cold war sits around everywhere. Some of it is big and visible, like NATO. Some of it is radioactive, not only in a literal residue of armaments but in forms of toxicity we are just beginning to imagine, let alone measure. Some is conceptual, like the idea of the "Third World." Even George Bush's solutions to the problem of narrating a New World alignment of Order turn out to have been fitful and desperate gambits.

2. Now that the counterspecter of the socialist state no longer organizes the narrative of world conflicts, it becomes easier to see the fundamentally ambivalent nature of the systems that have given Europe, America, and Japan their cold war identities: the welfare state project, liberalism (broadly understood), and capitalism. All of these are continuing projects, expanding to new frontiers. All have antidemocratic tendencies, but are no longer opposed by systems of a similar scale that have any corresponding claims to advance equality and well-being. At least two of these — the welfare state and liberalism — are in deep internal conflict at the moment of their preeminence in the world. And in the vast parts of the world that are now being organized by capitalism, there are new ambivalent tendencies. On one hand, maneuvers like GATT and NAFTA are succeeding in transferring power from national publics to

international bureaucracies, even as work forces become more commonly diasporic. On the other hand, there are new reminders in China, Russia, Mexico, and elsewhere that the project of modernization remains unfinished. This "economic" lesson has generated particularly horrific spectacles of the state and of mass suffering in places such as Haiti, Brazil, and the Philippines.

3. Similar ambivalences surround the relation of media publics and identities. No one was prepared for the rush of populisms and nationalisms in the supposedly postnational era. While some of these have consolidated new nation-states with their own version of "public" media, information culture has displayed sporadic autonomy from national and international control, transforming both identities and the polities to which they supposedly belong (Hong Kong/Taiwan/China). In some places, such as South Africa, the centrality of mass media to the democratic transformation of national and local or specific identities has been enormous, though the postapartheid moment reveals, as always, intricate double binds in the relations between national racism and marketized identities. Many examples serve to remind us that the uneven deployment of identity politics — in its postmodern, liberal, or fundamentalist forms — can be dangerous as much for democratic culture as for the liberal nation-state that claims to be its armature.

4. Other world crises are disclosing the distortions and limits at once of national states, international bureaucracy, and local or transnational publics. Among these are public health issues — such as AIDS, postindustrial environmental sickness, and the priorities of health care distribution — as well as conflicts pitting capitalist development and the environment. These problems affect more than national peoples, and have no appropriate political frame. They prove unsettling to transnational management culture, to relations between rich and poor nations, and to liberal interest-group proceduralism within nations.

5. United States political culture is also undergoing some realignment. If it has become harder to say what the alignments are in the international world, it has also become harder to define the terms of progressive and conservative politics in the wake of Clinton's cannonball plunge into the liberal Democratic program. Whatever symbolic relief Clinton's doctrine of multiethnicity might have provided, the clarity of the "face of America" has been a substitute for social justice policy. The problem of orienting alliances is shared by liberals (and leftists, no longer even marginally acknowledged) and by conservatives who cannot agree on how to describe their opposition to Clinton's procapital, promilitary

program. The two-party system has long been a powersharing system, but it has usually functioned, in part, by allowing a much wider range of voices and positions than of actual policies. Since the end of the cold war, the range of legitimate conflicting positions has narrowed. Both parties now bound themselves within the "mainstream" of corporate populism.

Of course, at any moment in history it would have been possible to generate a list of problems around the world. We cite this list of epochal unsettlements, not to claim that history has entered unprecedented crisis, but to show that the current form of historical crisis is particularly unsettling for the self-positioning of cultural theory. In this context, theory cannot fall back on its own resources to generate new theoretical solutions, nor can it abandon, as merely archaic, the tasks of making criticism thorough and coordinating emergent wishes for a more equal world — the tasks that used to be called leftism.

The right has also been unsettled. It can no longer pose marxism as the enemy. But in the United States, the extravagant popularity of rhetoric about "political correctness" has succeeded in consolidating a new right wing, especially in sustaining a ghost image of liberalism. The new right can define itself against "special rights," "the gay agenda," or "feminazis" — the latter an especially brilliant coinage because it deflects attention away from the new right's own protofascist elements. But neither political correctness nor multiculturalism has succeeded to the same degree in defining a new left that can coherently stand against that insurgent right, attacking from the moral high ground. Political correctness is thought to describe a rampant, even dominant, left. The right opposes it in the name of free inquiry, open intellectual discussion, and respect for individuals over the prejudicial categories of identity. No leftist wants to repudiate these ideals — which are, after all, the very ones "political correctness" describes. But the right's success at distorting the antiviolence social ethics of the left has been paralyzing; there is no rhetoric available in the national media to throw the right into a similarly defensive ambivalence.

Meanwhile, in the anxiety to describe a postnational world, many intellectuals have taken up categories like the global, hybridity, alliance politics, the postmodern, and decentralized subjectivity. These analytic concepts were of special interest to us in "Critical Multiculturalism" because they represent efforts to identify some set of interests or forces in the world comparable in scale to the systemic patterns of inequality we want to challenge around the world. They are theoretical conceptions designed to give left theory and politics a purchase on radically different contexts. "Critical Multiculturalism" argues that there are deep flaws in each of these attempts to link up contexts of criticism and give them a politics. Concepts of the global and the postmodern, which tend to bypass the labor of writing new histories and redescribing local conflicts, too often occupy the monumentalized conceptual place of the nation-states whose memorials they (prematurely) declaim. The global and the postmodern are interpreted, fetishistically, as institutions and cultures with their own inner logic — as though they were facts to be analyzed rather than themselves analytic narratives. Likewise, a rhetoric of alliances and hybridity can work to proliferate and coordinate different forms of identity politics, but a formalism of hybridity does not necessarily break with a consumerist relation to identity. It just shops more freely. Like global postmodernism, it derives its linking power from the special vantage of theory. As we noted apropos of the related concept of the subaltern, when generalized from one context to another, hybridity loses its political significance.

Intellectual self-narration constantly requires us to make alignments and take positions on what are fundamentally ambivalent transformations. When we endorse what we take to be countercultures, insurgencies, and movements unpredicted by hegemonic systems, we make inevitably imperfect bargains. Not only can we force ourselves into historically false oppositions (for example, to liberalism), we also make peace with remainders of violence and unknowledge that are the price of our preferred narratives. Consoling ourselves with the illusion of activity in the drama of self-situation, we also situate ourselves into new complacencies. It is important to remind ourselves that any new narrative of these transitions — be it one of multiculturalism, of global flows, or of market democracy — must be alert to its uninevitability, and of the multiple conflicts surrounding its own terms.

There is a kind of hubris even in listing all the world-transformations of the contemporary moment as conditions for intellectual work. It implies that everything we happen to think now is an index of world history. We have offered our assessment of the complexities of transition, not because we think we understand their coherence or because we have a theory of them, but because these are the kinds of unsettled problems to which we want thinking to be responsible. In the coda to "Critical Multiculturalism," we wrote that the essay would not be true forever. We would not be simply committing the paradox of the Cretan liar to say: we were right.

Notes

1 We did more than burst balloons in "Critical Multiculturalism"; we suggested a number of lines of productive inquiry and useful change. Some of these we have pursued. The section on criticism and its publics, for example, helped direct many of us to experiment with our work — even though, like the rest of the essay, that section remains mired in the polemic mode of address of academic writing. Some members of the group became involved with the journal *Public Culture*; others started a book series called *Public Worlds*; others launched a nonacademic series for short paperbacks called *Public Planet Books*. The Center for Psychosocial Studies, which originally convened the group, has since changed its name to the Center for Transcultural Studies, and coordinates these publishing projects. The Center

continues to bring intellectuals from different parts of the world together, continuing the discussions begun in "Critical Multiculturalism." The "Chicago Cultural Studies Group," on the other hand, no longer exists. Writing the essay was its only act.

2 John Guillory, *Cultural Capital* (Chicago: University of Chicago Press, 1993); and Aijaz Ahmad, *In Theory* (London: Verso, 1992). Guillory's first chapter is a thorough critique of multiculturalism in school curricula. On Ahmad, see the special issue of *Public Culture*, 6, 1 (Fall 1993).

4

Critical Multiculturalism

CHICAGO CULTURAL STUDIES GROUP[1]

Perhaps because it is so empty as a description, the phrase "cultural studies" has proven to be a capacious vehicle for utopian thinking. It is invested with desires that range from the relatively petty — solving the crisis of English departments, for example — to the relatively great, such as linking the cultural criticism of subaltern movements in the West with that of postcolonial and postauthoritarian movements around the world.[2] Given the different registers of these desires, it is easy to see why they are often in conflict or, at best, remain unclarified and unreconciled. It is equally easy to see that these desires to bring critical knowledge to bear in, on, and beyond the academy are jeopardized by the pressure to fix cultural criticism, to make it a "studies," a method, a content, a reproducible knowledge, a canon, a discipline, a politics, or a curriculum. Cultural studies will only lose its utopian import — will become merely utopian, in other words — if its imagination of value is controlled either by the disciplines of knowledge in the Western academy or by the rhetoric of generalism against which academic disciplines are usually contrasted.

"Multiculturalism" has produced if anything an even greater rush for utopian thinking than "cultural studies." For its adherents, multiculturalism increasingly stands for a desire to rethink canons in the humanities — to rethink their boundaries and their function. It also stands for a desire to find the cultural and political norms appropriate to more heterogeneous societies within and across nations, including norms for the production and transmission of knowledges. Under the banner of multiculturalism fall phenomena as disparate as the permeability of any locale in the age of a global economy, imperial networks of knowledge, environmental crisis, the end of the cold war, European integration, and the growth of the Pacific rim. Multiculturalism and cultural studies have been, in part, a response to these New World conditions and to the Bush-era rhetoric of the "New World Order" which is designed to stabilize them.

Under the weight of such a seemingly endless diversity of empirical concerns, multiculturalism as a social movement gets its critical purchase because it seeks to challenge established norms, and to link together identity struggles with a common rhetoric of difference and resistance. In distinction, cultural studies as an academic movement proposes to reorder the world of expert knowledge, recasting method and pedagogy as elements of public culture. When newspapers and magazines amalgamate multiculturalism and cultural studies as a two-pronged drive to install political correctness, these utopian projects are the sprawling troublemakers the media describe.

But nonacademic corporate and administrative agencies have been working equally hard to adapt a "multicultural" logic to their own purposes, and the concept has begun to appear frequently in mass culture. It is far from clear whether a multicultural emphasis in education will result in a more democratically critical society or rather in one with more subtle international administrative abilities. Multiculturalism may therefore prove a poor slogan. Those who use it as a slogan seem to think that it intrinsically challenges established cultural norms. But multiculturalism is proving to be fluid enough to describe very different styles of cultural relations, and corporate multiculturalism is proving that the concept need not have any critical content. We could call this the Benetton effect.

Multicultural studies is vulnerable at this juncture, not only because of the reactionary attack on it in the popular press, but because of weaknesses in its own rhetoric: an overreliance on the efficacy of theory; a false voluntarism about political engagement; an unrecognized assumption of civil-society conditions; a tendency to limit grounds of critique to a standard brace of minoritized identities (for example, race, class, and gender); and a forgetfulness about how its terms circulate in Third World contexts which are often expected to provide raw material for integration in Western visions of multicultural pluralism. The temptation in the face of such problems is to resort to heroic fantasies about intellectual work. And certainly the multiculturalist conception of cultural studies implies an important (even world-historical) task for intellectuals. But in a culture where the derision of academics is a small industry, there are reasons to be skeptical about the imagined substitution of *engagé* intellectual for *dégagé* academic. It also is too easy to suppose that mere academics can rise to become activist intellectuals simply by force of moral will, or fail to do so by failure of will — rather than through the mediation of publics, media, institutions, roles, discourses, and other conditions. If cultural studies is, among other things, the expression of a desire for a broader intellectual role, what conditions will be needed to bring it about?

When our group began its discussions, we thought those conditions already existed. We thought that by bringing together different disciplines and different marginal voices — of nationality, gender, sexuality, and race — an alliance would emerge. But that alliance does not come about through common histories of marginalization, or intellectual good faith, or theory. The discursive space of multicultural critique cannot be presupposed. Different kinds of criticism occur in different contexts, different spaces of criticism. As our group's experience of our own national, disciplinary, and institutional diversity showed us, nothing guarantees that the different impulses toward or interpretations of multiculturalism will always be consonant with each other.

We would like to open some questions here about the institutional and cultural conditions of anything that might be called cultural studies or multiculturalism. By introducing cultural studies and multiculturalism many intellectuals aim at a more democratic culture. We share this aim. In this essay, however, we would like to argue that the projects of cultural studies and multiculturalism require: (a) a more international model of cultural studies than the dominant Anglo-American versions; (b) renewed attention to the institutional environments of cultural studies; and (c) a questioning of the relation between multiculturalism and identity politics. We seek less to "fix" these problems than to provide a critical analysis of the languages, the methods of criticism, and the assumptions about identity, culture, and politics that present the problems to us. Because the thickets entangling what our group calls cultural studies are so deeply rooted in Western academia, which to a large degree constitutes our own group, the counterexample of cultural criticism in other contexts can be more than usually instructive. We begin by considering the position of cultural studies in China, since our group includes a number of Chinese intellectuals, on whose experience the following section is largely based.

1. "Cultural Craze" or "Cultural Studies" in China

In China, during the protest movement of 1989, academic and nonacademic intellectuals, particularly those in the tradition of the May Fourth movement, proved spectacularly capable of critical intervention — no one needs to be reminded. It might therefore be expected that cultural studies would find an enthusiastic if hazardous reception among Chinese academics. But cultural studies of the Western type has a slight presence in the academy; where it exists at all, it tends to be read mostly by younger scholars and dismissed even by them when "real" questions of power arise. Whereas cultural studies often is perceived by Western academics as a style of engagement, it could hardly have that appeal in China where the boundary between "academic" and socially engaged intellectuals has little or no force. From the perspective of most Chinese intellectuals, attempts by even activist Western scholars such as Raymond Williams to "mediate" the academic theory/social praxis divide are still far too theoretical. Insofar as cultural studies is becoming institutionalized in Chinese academia, therefore, it seems to be a catchall for miscellaneous objects of inquiry, easily marginalized in the face of "real" questions about state power and who will exercise it.

Chinese intellectuals outside the academy do have, however, a different kind of cultural studies — one with a different object and function from those of its

Western counterpart — roughly translatable as "cultural craze" or "cultural frenzy" [*wenhua re*]. Cultural craze has been a movement predominantly among Chinese writers outside academia where analysis of culture has been the domain of traditional Marxist "ideology studies." These mostly younger writers have treated "culture" in conscious opposition to "politics" and "ideology." They have tried to provide an interpretation of the essence of Chinese culture, sometimes in order to emulate what is seen as the developmental progress of a monolithic Western society, sometimes to challenge the totalitarian state as a betrayal of Chinese tradition. One extreme of cultural craze was the television miniseries "River Elegy" shown to large audiences in 1988; it created for the first time at the national level a relatively open discussion of culture and politics, but its chauvinistic fervor also helped to reinvigorate the rhetoric of Mao-style Party discourse.

The suppression of cultural craze following 1989 can be seen as a sign of its threat to state discourse. In retrospect, it can be seen as having evoked the "antipolitical politics" articulated by Vaclav Havel; that is, it sought to delineate a realm of civil society that would be "depoliticized" in the sense of being removed from the power/knowledge monopoly of the Chinese state.[3] On its face, of course, this is an agenda exactly opposed to that of cultural studies in the United States which seeks to politicize the realm of civil society designated as "nonpolitical" by traditional liberalism.

The contrast with China shows how much the rhetoric of cultural studies has relied on the context of a civil-society tradition in which, among other things, "political" would mean "contested." The assumptions of that tradition include the autonomy of criticism as a field and its separation from sponsorship and control by the state. Together with other realms of discourse that belong to civil society in this sense, criticism helps to establish the self-definition of the liberal public sphere as an unconstrained space. The various discourses of Chinese cultural criticism, therefore, would seem anomalous if one is looking for Western-style civil society. But China, Eastern Europe, and other postcolonial or unstably authoritarian states are different contexts for deciding what will count as criticism. If a critical politics is to be elaborated (or even coordinated) across such different contexts, we will have to attend carefully to the context-specific inflections of categories like "politics" and "autonomy." A major limitation on the relevance of Western left-cultural theory to non-Western countries is the presupposition of a liberal-public discursive space in (and for) which domestic cultural theory has been formulated.

When Western academic intellectuals announce a plan to intervene politically, that desire is enabled by a civil-society matrix which is not often reflected in the plan. In this matrix, the autonomy of the academy is guaranteed by its separation from the state and public discourse, but many Western intellectuals risk doing without that separation, in effect asking that we not be too subtle to point out that we want to change the world again, that we not be afraid to speak in broad terms about basic things that we will have to do in order to mediate different civil-society and state contexts. But should "to intervene" mean to politicize directly the public sphere and the arena of critical discourse? One might suspect that if every academic were really a politician in the United States and were really subject to the political interactions of the nation-state, academics would be more vulnerable to state control and ideological orthodoxy. If politicization erases the boundary between the academy and public discourse, the result will not be a gain in relevance but the loss of the very ideal sought by politicization, the ideal of multiple cultural spaces all protected from invasion by each other or by the state.

The context of civil society is so thoroughly assumed in the structure of academic discourse that it tends to go unacknowledged and unthematized. The results are, on one hand, an enormous difficulty in recontextualizing Western theory in places like China where those assumptions interfere, and, on the other hand, a weakness within the cultural politics of Western nations where academics are put at a disadvantage by their reliance on unstated conditions and norms. In the United States, Britain, and some other nations, recent crises of censorship and right-wing (largely homophobic) campaigns against funding for the arts have driven home the realization that "politicization" is not a panacea; the boundary drawn in the civil-society tradition between the state and the realm of the arts is one that must be preserved in some form, and one that is under aggressive assault from the right. The "politicizing" called for in cultural studies, then, should not be allowed to obscure the basic autonomy of cultural production from regulation by the state. Because critics often have not taken these conditions into account, the resulting confusion of cultural politics and state politics has been the source of disarray and vulnerability for the left.

The Chinese (and perhaps more generally non-Western) intellectual's very different relationship to cultural and national politics has other consequences for cultural studies as well: whereas American cultural theorists rather easily have tended to assume an alliance between domestic subaltern identity movements and the cultural politics of non-Western nations (generally conceiving of the latter in terms of the former), many non-Western-trained intellectuals implicitly or explicitly reject such an alliance — seeing little in common between their own political agendas and, for example, those of the American feminist and gay movements. The prospect of alliance and the very category of identity politics, therefore, demand ample and continuous specification.

Recently some types of new social movements have begun appearing all over Southeast Asia — quite often coming out of the middle class, and often with nationalist tones. But intellectuals and the academy in Southeast Asia and East Asia do not have the same conditions for articulating a larger public consciousness in which these issues could be placed. In the United States and Western Europe, intellectual critique, in order to assert public relevance, has to be multileveled and multifaceted because it must coordinate contexts that otherwise are separated and sufficiently self-reproducing as to be relatively autonomous. For example, academic feminism has tried to be a coordinating ground for clarifying the position of women in contexts that otherwise would seldom if ever intersect, one of which is the context of academic feminism itself. This is what allows universities and theory to be a special site for political engagement. In China, the university does not respond to civil-society/state diremptions in the same way; it responds to state saturation of society. Academics, therefore, must engage the issues of cultural movements in a different way since the coordinating role is claimed by the state.

We have suggested that, because the posture and effect of criticism varies so widely from one cultural context to another, we should be wary of thinking there is a politics of intellectual work in general. Stanley Fish has argued against this political fantasy as it appears in New Historicism in literary studies; whatever its claims to "politicize" literature, Fish argues, New Historicism should not hope to effect real political change beyond the institution of literary studies itself. In saying this, he has been one of the few people in literary studies to call attention to the institutional conditions of discourse that govern what will count as political. He reminds us of the boundary between civil society — including academia — and the state, a boundary that has been one of the defining conditions of literary criticism in Western culture. Fish concludes it would be futile to challenge that boundary from within the language of literary criticism.[4]

Yet even if his conclusion were adequate for the context of the United States, it would have to be altered substantially in a different academic-institutional context, such as English studies in China, where a New Critical ideology of literary "autonomy" carefully has been preserved as an enclave against the Maoist state. In state-saturated societies, depoliticizing can be an important political strategy. If Fish seems to take for granted the position of intellectual work in the current conditions of civil society, treating that position as a more or less just limitation on change, a corresponding criticism might be made against American critics at the opposite pole — those who argue in favor of a broad "politicization" without considering the extent to which the civil-society tradition, thereby, would be abandoned.

There is also a tendency for some postmodern thinkers to think they have created a new basis for politics and alliance — through such notions as difference, popular culture, and fragmented subjectivity — that could be spread to other areas and applied across different dimensions.[5] Critical intellectual work, however, cannot simply be exported from one context to another; the contribution of Euro-American critical theory to contemporary Chinese cultural criticism, for example, has been neither predictable nor foundationally transformative. Because of the power of institutional settings and international relations, the uneven circulation of critical theories and cultures is as much a global phenomenon as is so-called global culture. Western theorists might think Chinese critics would be emancipated by Western critical theory, but the usefulness of any critical theory depends on the national and institutional sites that constitute the horizons of practice. Even within Western academic discourse, any multicultural linkage of criticism requires comparative contextualization. Comparative contextualization, in this sense, cannot be generated by mere comparison of objects; it requires sources in multiple cultural contexts so that the critical tools used as a wedge into understanding the production of norms themselves would become objects of scrutiny.

The concept of "difference," for example, is a master-trope across many contexts of cultural criticism. Its function has been to convert a liberal politics of tolerance which advocates empathy for minorities on the basis of a common humanity into a potential network of local alliances no longer predicated on such universals. But this insurgent way of valuing difference still presupposes the coordination of difference and, in this respect, is insufficiently distinguished from a pluralist tolerance with its minoritizing effects. It, therefore, might invite (re)assimilation to a reactionary cultural politics. Witness the statement by the National Association of Scholars, a reactionary organization, which recently placed advertisements in a number of intellectual journals to argue against multiculturalism. NAS argues that cultural difference makes no valuable sense without the liberal norm of tolerance, itself of Western origins. In one respect, NAS has a point. The mistake of NAS is to think that tolerance is the only solution.

If nothing, therefore, guarantees the progressive force of multiculturalism — neither theory, good will, nor "inclusiveness" — can there be any sense at all in speaking of a critical multiculturalism? What distinguishes it from a generally rigorous "critical inquiry"? Neither content nor method nor intention can suffice to give force to the word *critical* here. Nor can they be relied on to make multicultural theory exportable or even coherent. The self-articulation of "difference," for example, has become a norm for subaltern critical politics; yet while this gesture might be appropriate in some contexts, such as India, in others (for example, China) it might be ineffective or reactionary. But whatever their differences might be, postcolonial situations and identity movements in the United States and various other cultural movements have one thing in common: they are critical of a dominant Western-liberal discourse and are understood within that dominant discourse as threatening. The NAS statement neatly illustrates that sense of threat to Western-liberal discourse arising from many sources — Indian subaltern theory to British feminism to African-American studies. In all these different contexts, a challenge has arisen to that now-global discourse (and a discourse now globally congratulating itself on its global triumph). At the same time, because one of the key rallying cries across these different settings has been to insist on recognizing cultural differences and to invest them with critical force, it would be fitting to think about the differences involved in this alignment of contexts of criticism. A kind of common enemy, a common point of departure, and a norm of critical difference — these conditions give multiculturalism its intelligibility.

Given that Western and non-Western intellectuals are meeting more often in contexts staged by Western academia, what are the prerequisites for a noncolonial encounter in these new spaces? We need to remember that different cultures might have quite different uses for the same theory — or the same history. The problem has been that theory believes quite often that it creates its own linkages. The goal is not transposition of theory, but rather juxtapositions or alliances of differently contextualized critique. The creation of a space where a relatively noncolonial comparative contextualization could take place is the first necessity. The spaces that are ready to hand for Western intellectuals are the academic disciplines. Can they be used as the basis for a different contextualization?

2. Disciplines, Knowledges, and Forms of Critique

Given the context-dependence of what will count as cultural criticism, what would have to change so that a cultural studies, based on the academic disciplines of the West, could clarify or even comprehend cultural criticism in other contexts? How many of our most elementary concepts — not just widely challenged ones like "presence" and "authority," but potently talismanic ones like "politics" and "difference" — stand in a too-indicative relation to the civil-society foundation of Western academic knowledges? Disciplinary contexts as well as national-cultural ones constrain criticism, and the terms that are axiomatic to a discipline cannot be generalized predictably. Indeed, might not *culture* itself be such a term? Much of the appeal of "difference" comes from anthropology's tradition of demonstrating the irreducible differences of human cultures; yet that ability has been predicated historically on assumptions that many in cultural studies are now hasty to disavow.

Traditional cultural models of modernist anthropology stressed the organic unity, boundedness, and self-sufficiency of the object culture; in contrast, newer styles of postmodern anthropology emphasize (and indeed celebrate) the openness or permeability of cultural boundaries, the impurity of cultural poetics always already infected by other cultures, and the multiply-constituted nature of subjectivity. This new postmodern celebration of cultural impurity and interpermeability, however, runs the risk of effacing real difference and losing the subject into a global matrix of symbolic exchange. Traditionally, difference has acquired a certain solidity by its linking with culture, but the idea of culture can also dilute the critical force of the notion of difference when culture is understood as a site of shared or common significance. The critical potential of postmodern anthropology still lies in the fact that anthropological categories of cultural difference, though articulated from within a Western tradition, nevertheless make available perspectives of otherness. These categories, therefore, could function as tools for a radical critique of our own cultural formations and situations. But pointing out incommensurability and difference need not involve insisting on the boundedness either of Western culture or of the things that are incommensurate with the West.

As anthropologists have become more attentive to the political relations between cultural groups, they have become less willing to think of themselves as disinterested analysts of a unified object. But it is not yet clear what disciplinary matrix will emerge, nor is it clear how cultural studies would differ from anthropology in this respect.

It is certainly not to be expected that styles of cultural studies derived from literary or film criticism will solve these dilemmas. Literary studies, in general, assume a notion of "the text" as a given or fixed entity which can then have multiple or contested interpretations, even when the text is nominally a mass-cultural phenomenon or "practice." Yet this is a highly problematic assumption for anthropology and subaltern studies where the fixity of the object text is often precisely what is at stake. In the Indian context, for example, "subaltern consciousness" may look radically different, depending on which discourses are taken as the text, while much recent work in anthropology has been to fix various cultural practices as texts to be interpreted. Academic disciplines define themselves, in large part, by styles of constructing objects for knowledge, and cultural studies cannot escape the fact that there are different, sometimes incompatible ways of doing this.

Many anthropologists seeking a "native" perspective for the purposes of critiquing Western capitalist individualism tend to employ a notion of "fusion," of "face-to-face"; that is, some notion of a local community based on face-to-face interaction becomes the epistemological starting point for all critique. But one of the problems is the mediation and alienation that constitute the very nature of the community, of the "local" that these people continuously invoke. Does the authenticity of the local become a trope to escape the problem of mediation and alienation? Both "culture" and "the local" have been useful concepts in recent critical thinking. But the drift of these considerations is that the acts by which they are constituted as objects of knowledge also block from view some of the political conditions (mediations) of their existence — and especially the Western or postcolonial critic's relation to them. The whole idea of a presentness, of a collapse between the object level and the metalevel (the native's point of view and the interpreter's) seems to indicate an effort to avoid the issue of mediation.

The same problems have been encountered in the disciplines of literary studies. Cultural studies there has generally involved a challenge to the autonomy of literary texts from politics, a challenge now bitterly repudiated by cultural conservatives. But several problems follow from the strategy of asserting that the aesthetic is thoroughly political. Because this strategy often seems to entail the radical relativizing of all aesthetic norms and standards, it gives rise to a disciplinary gap, within cultural studies, between critics who follow the politicizing strategy and intellectuals based in the social sciences where politics and relativism have a different relation. There is some tension, for example, between the critic's assertion that there can be no aesthetic standards independent of cultural-historical context and, on the other hand, a linguistic anthropologist's task of observing regularities across cultural contexts. There is a tendency in cultural studies to assume that cross-cultural comparisons are universalizing and imperialist in their covert cultural and institutional horizons. And, therefore, cultural studies has sometimes thought to be the domain of the humanities as opposed to the social sciences. But those who assume this not only ignore the critical work being done in the social sciences, but also abandon the cross-contextualizing moment of comparison often heading, instead, for the metanarrative of the "global" and avoiding the specific intercultural patterns already in place. Cultural studies cannot presuppose that such differences in a disciplinary matrix will prove irrelevant.

In part, the disciplinary difference is one between the search for observable regularities and the search for normative regularities. Structural analysis might elucidate the former among different cultures, but these regularities may never be sufficient to generate norms for aesthetic or cultural judgment. A strong sense of local relativism, therefore, may be compatible with a certain form of universalism, though not a universalism that would lead to normative judgments. In anthropology, one must start from local critiques and then derive a larger picture of what critique would mean when articulated from different positions. But this is a very different standpoint from the universalism in the version of the Enlightenment defended by Jürgen Habermas who derives the effectiveness of critique from a transcendental standpoint and then tries to apply it.[6] One could say that universals only emerge out of comparisons and cannot be grounded except through radical comparisons and, while this comparison may resemble the effort to coordinate local perspectives from a transcendent standpoint, the difference is that radical comparison cannot presuppose that it will finally produce any universals. It may just produce a set of linkages.

There also is no reason to suppose that a translation from one local culture to another is symmetric and transitive. The common assumption is that one can translate from A to B to C to D, and A is translatable into D. Comparative work can be guided by a postulate of universality only if this set of translations is possible. But they might not be, and radical comparison cannot assume they will be. If it is to critique international liberal discourse, comparative work must resist the normative "universals" and the flattening effect typical of corporate multiculturalism; but it also may have to reject the faith in the unlimited critical power of relativism.

3. "Identity" in Intellectual Work

Much of the utopian project of multiculturalism lies in the notion that it will allow intellectual work to be the expression and medium of identity. To some extent, this is true whether the "identity" in question is that of postcolonial subjects or of national minorities. In either case, multiculturalism seems to offer the prospect of using intellectual discourse no longer as a means of dominant acculturation or international administration, but rather as the articulation of alternative points of view represented in the persons of the intellectuals themselves. It can do this only if it is a field for alliances, for different identity struggles to come into a comparative relation under the heading of multiculturalism. This is a powerful utopian project indeed, but it has some problems.

First, there is a tendency to obscure the enormous gulf between different styles of identity politics where, in most cases, only a few intellectuals are willing to see any potential alliance at all (for example, between the Chinese student movement and the American gay movement). Even within Western identity politics where so much of cultural studies has been based, there is a tension between separatist and alliance logics, and this tension makes even more problematic the notion of multicultural translation from one context to another.

Much commentary in subaltern studies has been devoted to these problems. The description of identity has been contested signally in the public discursive arena created by political insurgents collaborating with revisionist academics doing radical historiographies of India. The effects of this contest will be felt in universities and in national life, but the effects in these two realms will be different and the tasks of representing and transforming identities in a political context will be played against one another. Gayatri Spivak's work on subaltern studies argues that intellectuals can never make themselves adequate to the standard of representing the subaltern point of view, of simply giving it speech. Nor can they entirely do without that standard. The anthropologist or subaltern analyst (or more generally "the intellectual") finds him- or herself in a necessarily tragic position: inserted into a social field of heterogeneous, often contradictory voices and at the same time, representing (or at least addressing) a different field of voices, this individual may be in a position of inescapably bad faith — yet one that is nevertheless indispensable.[7]

Vinay Dharwadker, however, has suggested that a serious shortcoming of the Subaltern Studies group is its failure to include within its corpus any work by the "subalterns" in question — an omission that implicated the group's own project in a kind of academic neocolonialism.[8] Of fifty essays produced to date by the group, only a handful focus primarily on documents in languages other than English — even though English is an unlikely language in which the "subaltern consciousness" might express itself. An example would be the six million Dalit speakers of Marathi, one of the most thoroughly marginalized social groups in the Indian caste system who, nevertheless, have produced an independent body of self-analytic discourse in their native language. None of it finds any place in the writing of the Subaltern Studies group. The Subaltern Studies group has found itself drawn much more into Western European and American academic discourse, into a Western-language game.

Intellectual work on subalterns necessarily opens itself to this charge. The example of Chinese cultural politics again shows that the question of the native voice has to be contextualized. In China, there are intellectuals who, as in the Dalit example, are not interested in being heard by the West. But they tend to be aligned with a conservative, xenophobic ideology that supports the current regime. The Chinese government itself has employed a nativist and separationist rhetoric in defending the June crackdown, and the Bush administration very obligingly has picked this up.

The critical potential of a subaltern consciousness itself might be dependent on context, in its "coarticulation" with other elements. And the character or value of intellectual intervention, for example, in "speaking for" a subaltern group, might vary from case to case. In India, where cultural politics largely have divided along linguistically defined lines, acts of translation and deference of public podia can have a different meaning than they have elsewhere. In China, intellectuals themselves are products of the authoritarian political structure, and they in no way are innocent of this political reality. They might be enthusiastically groping for ways to break away from it, but there is always a dead end in the point of view that derives by negation from this authoritarian system. Many assume a "repressive hypothesis": "I am always the spokesman for Truth — so long as I utter something, it's always on the side of Justice and Truth"; or, "I am categorically divided from the government; everything I say is against the government." China is, in Vaclav Havel's term, a "post-authoritarian" society in which the dichotomy between oppressor and oppressed is not categorical.[9]

Cultural criticism runs two opposing dangers with respect to identity politics; on one hand, an overconfidence in the ability of theory to master and translate different points of view, resulting in criticism that confirms the elasticity of dominant discourse rather than providing a point of access for marginal groups; on the other hand, a romance of authenticity in which the intellectuals begin to consider any intervention or mediation — including that of the intellectuals themselves — a betrayal of the subaltern consciousness or voice. Where a subaltern group is defined by race or language, the boundedness of the group makes it easier to think of those subjects as preconstituted and defined and, therefore, to imagine they need only be represented transparently. In other cases, such a notion of authenticity is more difficult to sustain because the subaltern group is more dispersed and differently colonized; in feminist scholarship, in gay and African-American studies, among other places, the inside/outside boundary cannot be drawn in the same way, and the problem of intellectuals and their mediating roles becomes necessarily more prominent. The "authentic native voice" can only be a highly problematic category in any case, insofar as any instance of the subaltern voice speaking to or in the West would entail some kind of intermediary role such as that played by intellectuals or the news media.

Part of the problem lies in assuming that the category of subaltern is or should be transposable. Is it so easy to identify "the Indian subaltern" or "the Chinese subaltern"? The notion of the subaltern was generated to describe a specific colonial relation of power. The concept, however, like that of culture, has been appealing for its critical purchase in the way it makes a social difference available as a basis for criticism. Spivak argues that the project of "recovering" a subaltern consciousness is impossible as a project of authenticity; it necessarily encounters that consciousness as a reified object, thus effacing its dynamism and political agency. The kind of "subjectivity" constituted in any comparative analysis — in anthropology or comparative subaltern studies or elsewhere — can never simply be equivalent to native subjectivity. Spivak rightly points out that the process of intellectual knowledge production introduces a significant departure, not always reflected on in intellectual work, from the contexts it describes.[10] But no amount of reflection can close the gap between the context of subaltern consciousness and the context of intellectual comparison, as many postmodern critics seem to wish. What do subalterns have in common except that somehow they are dominated? — a statement so general as to be nearly useless.

Academic multiculturalism transposes one subaltern formation into another, in part, because of the way academic disciplines construct an object of knowledge as the source of their legitimacy. For cultural studies, the notion of the subaltern tends to play this role, serving as the object of which cultural studies tries to have adequate, even superior knowledge. But that way of legitimating the knowledge of cultural studies threatens to falsify its subject. Something that is not a socially objective fact — subalternity — has been taken up as though it has to be described systematically from the outside. We find ourselves struggling to transpose a subaltern position into generalizable descriptive terms, thus eliding precisely the moment of antagonism that makes it possible to describe them as subalterns in the first place. One impulse is to efface the need for the intellectual's intervention in the name of authentic and immediate speech; another and opposite impulse, equally bound to fail, would be a call for a general description of a social position in the mode of theory.

Invocations of Gramscian Marxism or Derridean deconstruction (or nativist authenticity) could be appropriate and effective in certain contexts, but they have to be seen as strategic invocations, rhetorical gestures, and not absolute or universalizing claims (so that several such invocations could coexist without necessarily contradicting each other). Any discourse about a subaltern group is already part of their transformation and, one hopes, will become part of their self-clarification — but, of course, "self" is the very thing that's at stake here. The consciousness and interests of subaltern subjects, far from being predefined by an objective structure or simply immanent to their own consciousness, are created through rhetoric and struggle, in which intellectual's work is one intervention among others.

Dharwadker's critique is a reminder that the separatist and alliance logics of identity politics remain in tension, whether in Indian subaltern movements or in Western identity movements. One need in such movements is to have a language in which to develop a self-understanding and an autonomous point of view; another need is to have a language that links such groups comparatively. These needs often conflict. Since neither can be pursued independently and since neither can easily be separated from the dominant discourse, we might expect conflicts over such strategies to be renewed continually. Multiculturalism is not a postconflictual state.

4. Criticism and Its Publics

Partly because multiculturalism aspires to develop and sustain political and cultural criticism outside the academy, in the United States the trend toward cultural studies has opened academics to a sharp reaction in the realms of politics and journalism. Not just the self-identified conservative press, but also a wide range of publications have led a reaction against cultural studies: the *Atlantic Monthly*, *The New York Times*, *The New Republic*, *The New York Review of Books*, *Time*, *Newsweek*, and many newspapers' op-ed pages have all followed the lead of *The New Criterion* and *The American Scholar*. In one attack after another on "political correctness," an alliance of conservative academics and liberal journalists have worked to reinforce an ideal of boundaries between academic and political spheres. In this climate of reaction, state restriction, and journalistic ridicule, it has become more important than ever to think through the strategies by which academic intellectuals have tried to link their work to nonacademic publics.

Left-cultural critics work from a significant disadvantage in this struggle. Their counterparts on the right are ideologically committed to a vision of a homogeneous and universally normative culture; conservative academics such as Allan Bloom, therefore, are comfortable with the idea of addressing a popular imaginary, of making their criticism continuous with the language and conceptual frameworks of journalism. Left-cultural critics, generally more committed to a society in principle diversified into different publics and languages, consider conservatives such as Bloom to be writing unrigorously or hysterically while conservatives see their counterparts on the left as speaking a jargon to be condemned in principle because it is not the language of a common public. Since multiculturalism also aspires to a broad public, this conflict over style and its social implications remains a difficult but productive problem.

Cultural studies based in the academic disciplines of the humanities seems therefore to have little purchase on middle-brow and mass publics. The problems are somewhat different among the social sciences. Social-scientific discourse, when it appears in a larger public context, remains a phenomenon of "expert" culture. Its knowledge can be invoked as expertise, but not as a style of criticism to be adopted by a public. Expertise in humanistic discourse has retained closer links to public discourse, especially when its task has been to disseminate a potentially universalizable "sensibility."

The problems also are different in other countries. In South Africa, the closure of certain disciplines around texts and around an idea of professionalism has been disturbed by the emergence of different cultural organizations and trade unions. People are saying, "We want academics to be cultural workers," meaning workers on the trade-union model — a confusion of terms and theories, to say the least. This demand for "cultural work" has infused South African cultural studies with a populist energy absent in the United States; yet at the same time the notion has played havoc with the traditional regimes of academic cultural knowledge.

In the United States and Britain, mass-cultural studies is attractive because it seems to offer a link between academic and public discourses. This is an aspiration of cultural studies in general, but at the moment mass culture seems specially capable of opening professional discourse because it has never been considered an archive or object of the kind that allows disciplinary closure. Current academic celebrations of "popular culture" — especially where a distinction between "mass" and "popular" has eroded — remain problematic: nostalgic, self-deluded, and possibly reactionary. Yet even at their worst they raise the possibility of a decredentialized knowledge, a possibility on which the academy looks with both longing and horror.

One also might say that cultural studies in general is a response to the way mass culture tries to empty out any space in which one might perform as a political agent. That is, mass culture tries to treat all conflicts as happening only in the very delocalized space of mass media. One of the continually renewed but continually frustrated impulses in cultural studies has been to enact or clarify conflicts and regenerate local contexts or publics that are responding to the evacuation of a mass public.

In the Western nations, that most often means identity politics. The attempt to focus criticism on race, gender, and sexuality, in part, has been a way of resisting the kind of nonlocation created by the mass media. In national contexts without liberal public spheres, delineating the specific features of a multiple identity might be problematic, as might the word *identity* itself. The idea of identity formation as a pedagogical project, for instance, virtually would be impossible in China given the political and ideological constraints and the absence of a concept of "the private" on which so much feminist discourse relies (if only by opposition). To the extent that cultural studies has taken shape as a critical response to the mass public, appealing to the locatedness of identity politics in an attempt to reshape public discourse, to that extent it will encounter static in contexts where the mass-cultural public is not the primary political object of critical response, and where the matrix of identity politics is not an available or appropriate alternative.

Within the Western academic context, identity politics opens intellectual work to the demands of nonacademic publics. There is immense pressure on academic feminists, for example, to speak with a kind of pragmatic impulse that would connect any feminist theory in the academy with feminist practice in other contexts. Many women, including nontheoretical feminists in the academy, perceive academic feminism's theoretical language as a barrier, and characterize their sense of exile as a kind of violence to them. In the late sixties and seventies, some feminists found little of use in poststructuralist models of fragmented subjectivity or utopian accounts of a radically other "feminine identity." Eventually, however, movements within academic feminist theory began to take the different self-understanding of women as its descriptive challenge and its political responsibility. In the early seventies certain Hispanic, African-American, and lesbian feminists — for example, Barbara Smith, Cherríe Moràga, and Gloria Anzaldúa — were already locating their particular embodiments between categories of identity. Concepts of the body as a concrete site of oppression and resistance, derived, in part, from subaltern and gay studies, also have helped to recast productively the stress among feminist discourses. So feminists' uses of "the body" have served a double function: as a standpoint for critique of theoretical discourses and as a point that allows identity politics, centered around categories of the body to engage instances of identification and its failure or crisis. To coordinate these movements within specific academic environments remains a problem.

Feminism, in short, already has an elaborate discourse about the problem of publics and discursive politics; cultural studies doesn't yet. Following the lead of racial and sexual minority movements, academic feminism has come around to an analysis of "women" and "woman" that is increasingly more complex and subtle in its enunciation of who constitutes the audience for the broadest range of feminist concerns. The multiple publics of feminism continue to pressure academic feminists not to become too invested in professional rhetorics of expertise, too limited by the norms of academic rational discourse, too constrained by values about what constitutes arguments and evidence, too focused on the pseudomeritocracy of ideas that academia promises.

Cultural studies has the same impulse toward multiple engagements, but because most of its practitioners teach, public discussion has focused on the classroom. Advocates of cultural studies see the classroom as a place for developing socially critical thought and for articulating identity politics. The right protests both of these as ways of soliciting students to a partisan cause. The danger is seen by the right as especially acute in English and history departments which have come to be defined as sites of identity-formation where citizens and well-rounded persons are born. This characterization of the classroom as a civic space traditionally has been bolstered by an ideology of humanistic universality. Critics of cultural studies worry that the "values" that mesh societies are being replaced with an analytics of power that split them apart at their many seams.

Clearly this violence is not an aim of multicultural studies whose practitioners try to make the classroom a safe space for experimental thinking, involving encounters with the Other, with "difference," and with theory. There is nonetheless a danger in seeing a new set of contents as itself liberating and affirmative. There is also a danger in assuming that the "new" knowledges have no authoritarian potential, in practice or in theory, just because professors are explicitly committed to producing the experience and the imagination of more fully democratic cultures. Thus cultural studies has tended to conjoin transformations in the norms of cultural literacy with more explicit attention to the conditions of knowledge, competence, and critique. But there are limits to what a classroom can do. To begin with, the conventional logic of the classroom is such that the introduction of multiculturalism can be seen as an opportunity to recultivate pluralist consensus while concern for critical thinking can be reduced to a fitness program in competence for future citizens. The classroom, moreover, is neither a typical public nor a place ideally capable of furnishing a heightened self-reflection that other public arenas lack. The criticisms of the right and the aspirations of the left overestimate the transposability of criticism from the classroom to other contexts. And both underestimate the intelligence and independence of the students whose identities are at stake. Nonetheless, the current media controversy is an opportunity for teachers not just to transmit knowledge but to transform what counts as knowledge in the culture at large. In this way cultural studies as an academic movement expresses a strong aim of multiculturalism.

5. Affiliated Knowledge

One of the primary ways of bracketing off politics is to deny that knowledge has any worldly affiliation. This becomes especially dangerous as corporate America designs itself for the next ten years around global markets, trying to retrain workers and corporate executives through programs of "multicultural studies." Cultural studies needs a notion of affiliation such that it would be extremely difficult for students and academics in a classroom context to think of themselves as engaged in a humanistic discourse unconnected to their organizations. Otherwise a cultural studies pedagogy might simply revert to an abstract exercise in the "critical faculties" that would be indistinguishable from classical humanism.

Affiliation describes the possibility of thematizing one's position and turning it into a site of conflict. It does not imply the voluntarism and the wish for pure autonomy that characterize modernist notions of politics. You are born partly into a set of affiliations you didn't choose; so the affiliation of your knowledge is less the product of a free choice than something to negotiate. Affiliations are relations you are already in, although they include affiliations you make, and part of the question is how you deploy the ones you're in. That is how identity politics may be fruitfully understood now: as sites of struggle, rather than as sites of "identity."

One reason why a certain postmodern, self-reflexive anthropology has gained popularity in the humanities is that it seems to aspire toward such a self-affiliation.[11] But neither in identity politics nor in an academic discourse such as anthropology can the affiliations of knowledge be reduced to the self-reflexive affiliations of its individual producers. "Postmodern" ethnographics often imply that the grounding point of their knowledge is a simple embodiment, a relationship of a writer to a text. But to locate a text self-reflexively, it is not enough to romanticize the field encounter, as many anthropologists are doing. The whole process of engagement in the fieldwork and the academic formations that make it possible would pinpoint the affiliation more clearly. Even a much more "complete" self-location would not be necessarily politically adequate. Gestures of self-location, however nuanced or elaborate, can be totally undone by the larger rhetoric of one's writing, or by the political inflection of one's approach to the object culture; and the self-congratulatory tone of much postmodern ethnography only makes these errors more likely.

The subjectivity of knowledge is not located simply in an author. Location must be a matter not only of the "dialogic encounters," but also of the history, media, and institutional destinations of knowledge produced by any confrontation. Postmodern ethnographers typically represent the dialogic encounter of the ethnographer as if it were the real locus of interaction, as if forms of cultural engagement could be reduced to a depoliticized "dialogue." Postmodern ethnographers' interest in the ethnographic dialogue, after all, itself reflects the construction of the "authentic," the cultural, the native, through a figure of "face-to-face" relations.

If the affiliations laid out in an autobiographical gesture could therefore only be inadequate, a more productive though more challenging form would be to indicate the goal of one's knowledge production. To do so seriously would partly disrupt one's claim to academic authority and authorial self-mastery. It is no surprise, after all, that knowledge originates from individuals who "really" have (private) interests of their own; the challenge is to think of knowledge as being openly produced not so much for a private interest as for the transformation of a problem such that one's interest in the outcome could only partly be described. Affiliation in this sense requires thinking about the metaproblem of the history of normativity in any particular field of knowledge. It also would include foregrounding one's own pedagogical authority as the present arbiter of normativity.

No amount of self-dramatization otherwise could challenge the "view from nowhere" that governs the American social sciences as well as much of the humanities. A substantial challenge to that theomorphic view has been mounted within several disciplines of the humanities, but the result tends to be an essentializing of pluralism (for example, Bakhtinian "dialogism" and "polyphony") which offers no better standpoint for substantive critique. Such pluralism, in fact, is quite compatible with — and even a product of — the "view from nowhere" itself.

Authoritative voices in the academy will appeal to the "view from nowhere" to justify their own nonlocation; one of the things we need to understand better is how this is accomplished. One way, for example, is by invoking a natural science methodology or, in the humanities, by relying on "the canon." But both of these moves have the same effect: by appearing to neutralize particular locations or affiliations, they perform expertise that turns out to orient all other distinctions. What these "voices from nowhere" always seem to do is to create a margin for what are understood to be nonneutral parties, special interests, or constraining conditions; and one of the interesting things about the margins that have been created is that now they are being resistant. In the classroom and elsewhere, that marginalization is being contested. But what hasn't really been worked out is how to develop a critique from the margins without reconfirming as reality the very rhetoric of center and margin. What seems to happen is that the centralized voices borrow from their experience with many different marginal positions. Their effective rhetoric against a single marginal position comes from their neutralization and creation of many marginal positions, each in evident relation only to the center rather than to the other margins. So it becomes very difficult for a single marginal position to gain a leverage of critique.

The operation by which expertise is constructed raises empirical questions; it needs to be addressed as a matter of research as well as pedagogy. One thing that differentiates anthropology from humanistic studies is the idea of writing an accurate account of something that is going on, an empirical project to be engaged in. Cultural studies is going to need that kind of empirical support because "views from nowhere" often use a certain set of empirical arguments against situated humanistic positions.

An effective critique of positivism would not situate positivistic knowledge within a more totalizing account, as Habermas does, but would instead challenge the disembodied "view from nowhere" mode of knowledge-production itself. That mode of producing knowledge at this point has been embedded in the internal history of every discipline so that it is difficult for anybody to get a purchase on and difficult to combat systematically.

An equally formidable problem is the global transmission of knowledge. The Western classroom is not the sole space for the production and dissemination of knowledges; in many ways the final destination of these knowledges is frequently the "Third World," as research programs and curricula there are often modeled after those of prestigious and dominant Western institutions. The history of normativity in knowledge also is a history of the dissemination of evidence, with its own specific institutional and geographical terrain. For the social sciences especially, normativity is built into notions of evidence, and it is the ideological norms of positivism that make social-scientific knowledges so readily exportable.

6. Corporate Multiculturalism

The problem of the transportation of knowledge is one of the most serious problems facing a critical multiculturalism in an age of corporate multiculturalism, and a great danger lies in thinking that multiculturalism could be exported multiculturally. In anthropology, where a politics of identity formation is less effective institutionally than it is in the humanities, a more crucial axis of critique might involve confrontation with international relations programs insofar as the latter impinge directly on academic restructuring outside of the United States. In all disciplines, as we have suggested earlier, we still lack the conditions that would allow multiculturalism to make good on its claims: forums, media, publics, and linkages with scholars' other cultural affiliations.

On an even more cautionary note, we should remember that the "view from nowhere" problematic extends much further than a particular academic/institutional mode of knowledge production. The disembodied character of the centralized knowledges is what allows them to embody a certain stance which is the stance of the modern nation-state in the last couple hundred years. Many who might oppose the "views from nowhere" would nevertheless find it hard to give up the stance of inclusive notions of equality and citizenship. Those nation-state ideologies are the hidden buttress behind the "views from nowhere" and are implicitly being appealed to without explicitly being brought into focus.

When a "view from nowhere" becomes the dominant view, "cultures" become pluralizing views that differentiate out from the central nowhere set up by modern science. Cultures become the self-same, the local, the particular, where the national/international frame of their relation does not. That frame is the *system* in Habermas's terms,[12] that is, the central organizing principle for what modern nation-states are all about, indeed for what the whole world order is about. It is not "culture," in this ideology's terms, but economics, politics, law, international relations.

It might seem that anthropologists would resist such an ideology because the strength of the discipline seems to lie in showing that all is cultural. But anthropologists formed their discipline by studying little societies that have a certain kind of culture, where a model of sameness tended to dominate, where a single, homogeneous, transmitted knowledge and way of life organized the community. When anthropologists went to places like the United States, they found little communities and neighborhoods that could be analyzed in the same way because that was what they were looking for. So the anthropological concept of culture got put into the position of being not the central organizing principle for something like modern nation-states, but for differentiation against the backdrop of the modern nation-state (and its anthropological knowledge) which itself was held together by different principles.[13]

This anthropological practice precipitates an ideology of what sociability is all about in the nation-state. It has been a very powerful ideology, building on a history that dates from Locke and Rousseau and is embedded in notions of human rights and equality under the law. The basic problem with the ideology is that it produces interchangeability — of cultures as well as persons. It is the Habermasian "system world" as opposed to these "life worlds" which are culture. The project that anthropology might have now would be analogous to the Boasian project; that is, to theorize the problem of culture not as a single-level, small-scale society based on homogeneity, but as involving imbricated levels of similarity and difference; and to see how one could attack an ideology of interchangeability by considering its own cultural and deculturing moments. It may be, of course, that the discipline of anthropology is itself too thoroughly implicated in the American nation-state ideology (by way of positivism and the "view from nowhere") to develop such a critique.

By this account, any argument for "cultural relativism" runs the risk of simply feeding into nation-state ideology. An overly simple relativism — that flattened, homogenized model of culture in anthropology, but also the essentialized notion of "difference" common to many deconstructive critiques — loses its critical purchase. "Difference" in contemporary nation-state formations is complexly mediated, multiple and overlapping, and mediated partly by a national perspective designed to recognize difference precisely so as to construct the locales it superinvests or coordinates. Without this insight such critiques cannot effectively counter the dominant, positivist ideology of knowledge production which actively seeks to subsume real difference through an abstract-statistical homogenization.

Coda

This essay will not be true forever. Not because it will be false, but because it describes what we see as a still-developing crisis in the relation between academic knowledge and cultural politics. The terms of this crisis — *culture, politics, identity* — are contested and ambiguous. The conditions we describe here also are changing rapidly enough to outstrip our own attempt to encapsulate them. When we began our discussions, for example, it seemed that the public campaign against cultural studies in the United States was designed mainly to conserve a liberal tradition: the principle that expertise should be autonomous from politics, credentialized as knowledge by its distance from influence or interests. This linked up with conservatives' critique of the multiculturalists as those soiling learned culture with mere "politics," undermining objectivity, reason, neutral pluralism, or human values. But these are no longer the main lines of battle. Now the vanguard of reaction in the popular press, notably Dinesh D'Souza and Roger

Kimball, have begun to call more or less overtly for the politicization of academic knowledge by the right in the name of "the mainstream" or of "Western civilization." This often self-acknowledged strategy lies behind the attack on "political correctness," the "defunding" initiatives of the National Endowments for the Arts and Humanities, and post-Gulf consensualism in general. Suddenly it is the Anglo-American multiculturalists who have to scramble to defend the autonomy of scholars and artists from state regulation and majority coercion. The liberal separation of state and civil society seems newly threatened, and more valuable than ever. At the same time, it is more imperative than ever to resist the inclination of all parties to claim their own ethnically pure marginality in the face of some insidious authoritarian Other.

We have tried to clarify this crisis, for example, by elaborating a variety of meanings for the idea of multiculture: the corporate multiculturalism of global capital; the interdisciplinary cultural criticism that conjoins different publics around discourse, identities, and difference; the international comparativism that crosses boundaries to produce new knowledge and new challenges to the means of knowledge; as well as countless local impulses that appear to derive from pluralism, nationalism, or insurgent subcultural formations and alliances. In America, we have suggested reemphasizing a distinction between the "politics" of contested aspects of culture and the "politics" of the state apparatus so that we can engage the one while rejecting the other as it currently exists. We have tried to exemplify and to advocate a cultural criticism that minds its proximity to the historical present and its different obligations to the variety of publics in which it circulates. Thus we have found ourselves struggling to keep up with the temporality of politics and journalism from within academic institutions and media oriented to a very different temporality.

The resulting lag is not the only constraint we have encountered in our effort to address the public crisis of cultural criticism. The attempt to bring academic discourse into interaction with politics and journalism has posed a threat to conventions of voicing, originality, authority, evidence, and expertise. We have authorized ourselves as this speaking "we," even where the group had significant disagreements, and even in a document expressly critical of disembodied knowledge; we have incorporated into this document the speeches of people who were summarizing work that in very important ways was "theirs," whether as professional positiontaking or as personal expression; we have addressed problems so close at hand that our estimate of them cannot be fully authorized by scholarship or research; and we have freely exerted ourselves in fields of knowledge unanticipated in our credentials. That we have severally felt uneasy about these things may be taken as an index of the crisis facing us — "us" as critical theorists, as national subjects, as political agents, and as specific persons who have come together to discuss a problem in common. One of our central contentions has been that a genuinely critical multiculturalism cannot be brought about by good will or by theory, but requires institutions, genres, and media that do not yet exist. Another is that, as critical multiculturalism redescribes the various public orders that are now undergoing change, it can help to realign what is now understood as simply insurgent or simply reactionary, simply dominant or simply marginal. The reaction it elicits from the guardians of dominant policies, canons, lexicons, and media suggests that the "rational" discourse of critical multiculturalism indeed might inhabit new worlds of *dis*order advancing changes dangerous and important.[14]

Notes

1 Reprinted by permission of The University of Chicago Press and the authors from *Critical Inquiry* 18 (Spring 1992), pp. 530–55. The Chicago Cultural Studies Group began meeting in June 1990. It includes Lauren Berlant, David Bunn, Vinay Dharwadker, Norma Field, Dilip Gaonkar, Marilyn Ivy, Benjamin Lee, Leo Ou-fan Lee, Xinmin Liu, Mathew Roberts, Sharon Stephens, Katie Trumpener, Greg Urban, Michael Warner, Jianyang Zha, and Jueliang Zhou. Our own way of posing questions about this topic has to do with our improbable convergence as a group. Aided by the Center for Psychosocial Studies and the Rockefeller Foundation, we came together in Chicago from schools across the United States; from departments not only in the humanities but also in area studies and the social sciences; from cultural backgrounds in India, China, and Africa, as well as North America; from kinds of praxis that range from "field work" to "identity politics." "Cultural studies" has served as a more comfortable tag for some of us than for others. The intensity and extent of our distance form its major version (see the work of Stuart Hall and the "Birmingham School"; of James Clifford and other postmodern anthropologists) also varies greatly among us. The same might be said for our diverse views about the emancipatory possibilities of identity and insurgent national politics. We share a stake in the potential changes that cultural studies heralds in academic work, but as a group we are inclined to look beyond any single theoretical argument, discipline, or contested category to define those changes and our stake in them. The dialogue and disagreement that took place around these matters has been rendered as critical dialectic in this essay, which has been compiled and edited from the minutes of our meetings by Mathew Roberts, Michael Warner, and Lauren Berlant.

2 The meetings on cultural studies and multiculturalism leading to this document resulted from several years of collective discussion of readings in literary and cultural theory, not all of which are listed here in notes. See note 14, "Works Consulted," which indicates the most immediate stimuli to our exchanges.

3 Vaclav Havel, "Politics and Conscience," *Open Letters* (New York: Random, 1981), p. 269.

4 See Stanley Fish, "Commentary: The Young and the Restless," in *The New Historicism*, ed. H. Aram Veeser (New York: Routledge, 1989), pp. 303–16.

5 See, for example, Aijaz Ahmad's critique of Fredric Jameson, "Jameson's Rhetoric of Otherness and the 'National Allegory'," *Social Text* 17 (Fall 1987): 3–25.

6 See Jürgen Habermas, *Theory of Communicative Action*, tr. Thomas McCarthy, 2 vols. (Boston: Beacon Press, 1984, 1987).

7 See Gayatri Chakravorty Spivak, "Subaltern Studies: Deconstructing Historiography," in *Selected Subaltern Studies*, eds Ranajit Guha and Gayatri Chakravorty Spivak (New York: Oxford University Press, 1988), pp. 3–32.

8 See Vinay Dharwadker, "The Future of the Past: Modernity, Modern Poetry, and the Transformation of Two Indian Traditions," 2 vols. (Ph. D. diss., University of Chicago, 1989), 2, pp. 278–97.

9 Vaclav Havel, "Politics and Conscience," p. 269.

10 See Spivak, "Subaltern Studies."

11 See *Writing Culture: The Poetics and Politics of Ethnography*, eds James Clifford and George E. Marcus (Berkeley: University of California Press, 1986).

12 See Habermas, *Theory of Communicative Action*.

13 This argument has been developed by Greg Urban, "Two Faces of Culture," University of Texas, Austin, typescript.

14 Works Consulted: Vito Acconci, "Public Space in a Private Time," *Critical Inquiry* 16 (Summer 1990), pp. 900–18; Judith Butler, *Gender Trouble: Feminism and the Subversion of Identity* (New York: Routledge, 1990); Partha Chatterjee, "More on Modes of Power and the Peasantry," in *Selected Subaltern Studies*, pp. 351–90; "Mayor Chen Xiton's Report on Putting Down Anti-Government Riot," *China Daily*; Cultural Studies Group, "Critical Multiculturalism Report," 1990; Embassy of the People's Republic of China Press Release 19, 29 June 1989; Johannes Fabian, "Presence and Representation: The Other and Anthropological Writing," *Critical Inquiry* 16 (Summer 1990), pp. 753–72; Jane Feuer, "The Concept of Live Television: Ontology as Ideology," in *Regarding Television: Critical Approaches—An Anthology*, ed. E. Ann Kaplan (Los Angeles: Greenwood Press, 1983), pp. 13–22; John Fiske and John Hartley, "Bardic Television," *Reading Television*, John Fiske and John Hartley (London: Methuen, 1978), pp. 85–108; Diana Fuss, "Reading Like a Feminist," *differences* 1 (Summer 1989), pp. 77–92; Nelson Goodman, "On Rightness of Rendering," in *Ways of Worldmaking*, Nelson Goodman (Indianapolis: Hackett, 1978), pp. 109–39; Jürgen Habermas, "Modernity — An Incomplete Project," in *The Anti-Aesthetic: Essays on Postmodern Culture*, ed. Hal Foster, tr. Seyla Ben Habib (Seattle: Bay Press, 1983), pp. 13–15; Stuart Hall, "Gramsci's Relevance for the Study of Race and Ethnicity," *Journal of Communication Inquiry* 10 (Summer 1986), pp. 5–27; Stuart Hall, "Encoding/Decoding," in *Culture, Media, Language: Working Papers in Cultural Studies*, eds Stuart Hall et al. (London: Routledge, 1980), pp. 128–38; Stuart Hall, "Cultural Studies: Two Paradigms," *Media, Culture and Society*, ed. Richard Collins (London: Sage, 1980), pp. 57–72; Stuart Hall, "Signification, Representation, Ideology: Althusser and the Post-Structuralist Debates," *Critical Studies in Mass Communication* 2 (June 1985), pp. 91–114; Stuart Hall, "The Emergence of Cultural Studies and the Crisis of the Humanities," *October*, 53 (Summer 1990), pp. 11–23; Daniel C. Hallin, "We Keep America on Top of the World,"in *Watching Television: A Pantheon Guide to Popular Culture*, ed. Todd Gitlin (New York: Pantheon, 1986), pp. 85–108; Donna J. Haraway, *Simians, Cyborgs, and Women: The Reinvention of Nature* (New York: Routledge, 1991); Nancy Hartsock, "Foucault on Power: A Theory for Women?" in *Feminism/Postmodernism*, ed. Linda J. Nicholson (New York: Routledge, 1990), pp. 157–75; Eugene W. Holland and Vassilis Lambropoulos, "The Humanities as Social Technology — An Introduction," *October*, 53 (Summer

1990), pp. 3–10; bell hooks, *Feminist Theory from Margin to Center* (Boston: South End Press, 1984); Fredric Jameson, "Postmodernism and Consumer Society," in *The Anti-Aesthetic: Essays on Postmodern Culture*, ed. Hal Foster, tr. Seyla Ben Habib (Seattle: Bay Press, 1983), pp. 111–25; Richard Johnson, "What Is Cultural Studies Anyway?" *Social Text* 6 (Winter 1986/87), pp. 38–80; Benjamin Lee, "Culture and Communication: An Initiative from the Center of Psychosocial Studies," typescript; Benjamin Lee and Leo Ou-fan Lee, "Rethinking Chinese Democracy," Center for Psychosocial Studies, Chicago, typescript; Leo Ou-fan Lee, "The Crisis of Culture," in *China Briefing 1990*, ed. Anthony J. Kane (Boulder, CO: Westview, 1990), pp. 83–105; Armand Mattelart, Xavier Delcourt, and Michele Mattelart, "International Image Markets," in *Global Television*, eds Cynthia Schneider and Brian Wallis (New York: Wedge Press, 1988), pp. 13–33; W. J. T. Mitchell, "The Violence of Public Art: Do the Right Thing," *Critical Inquiry* 16 (Summer 1990), pp. 880–99; Chandra Talpade Mohanty, "Under Western Eyes: Feminist Scholarship and Colonial Discourses," in *Third World Women and the Politics of Feminism*, eds Chandra Talpade Mohanty, Ann Russo, and Lourdes Torres (Bloomington: Indiana University Press, 1992); Louis Montrose, "Professing the Renaissance: The Poetics and Politics of Culture," in *The New Historicism*, ed. H. Aram Veeser (New York: Routledge, 1989), pp. 15–36; *This Bridge Called My Back: Writings by Radical Women of Color*, eds Cherríe Moràga and Gloria Anzaldúa (Watertown, MA: Kitchen Table Books, 1981); David Morley, *The "Nationwide" Audience: Structure and Decoding* (London: British Film Institute, 1980); Meaghan Morris, "Banality in Cultural Studies," typescript; Chantal Mouffe, "Radical Democracy; Modern or Postmodern?" tr. Paul Holdengraber, in *Universal Abandon? The Politics of Postmodernism*, ed. Andrew Ross (Minneapolis: University of Minnesota Press, 1988), pp. 31–45; Ashis Nandy, "Evaluating Utopias: Considerations for a Dialogue of Cultures and Faiths, and Towards a Third World Utopia," *Traditions, Tyranny, and Utopias: Essays in the Politics of Awareness* (Delhi: Oxford University Press, 1987), pp. 1–55; Cindy Patton, *Inventing AIDS* (New York: Routledge, 1990); Vijay Prashad, "Rethinking Peasant History: Who Is the Subaltern? A Genealogy of Becoming a Thing," University of Chicago, typescript; Elspeth Probyn, "Travels in the Postmodern: Making Sense of the Local," in *Feminism/Postmodernism*, ed. Linda J. Nicholson (New York: Routledge, 1990), pp. 176–89; Ellen Rooney, "Discipline and Vanish: Feminism, the Resistance to Theory, and the Politics of Cultural Studies," *differences* 2 (Fall 1990), pp. 14–28; John Searle, "The Storm over the University," *New York Review of Books*, 6 (December 1990), p. 19; Sharon Stephens, "Postmodern Anthropology: A Question of Difference," University of Chicago, typescript; Susan Stewart, "Ceci Tuera Cela; Graffiti as Crime and Art," *Life after Postmodernism: Essays on Value and Culture*, ed. John Fekete (New York: St Martin, 1987), pp. 161–80; "Televising the Discovery of India," eds Greg Urban and Benjamin Lee, *Center for Psychosocial Studies Working Paper*, 38 (1990); Cornel West, "The New Cultural Politics of Difference," in *Out There: Marginalization and Contemporary Cultures*, eds Russell Ferguson et al. (Cambridge: MIT Press, 1990), pp. 19–36; Iris Marion Young, "Polity and Group Difference: A Critique of the Ideal of Universal Citizenship," in *Feminism and Political Theory*, ed. Cass R. Sunstein (Chicago: University of Chicago Press, 1990), pp. 117–41; Iris Marion Young, *Justice and the Politics of Difference* (Princeton,

NJ: Princeton University Press, 1990); Iris Marion Young, "The Ideal of Community and the Politics of Difference," in *Feminism/Postmodernism*, ed. Linda J. Nicholson (New York: Routledge, 1990), pp. 300–323; and Jianying Zha, "Notes of Emergence of a Counter-Public in China," Center for Psychosocial Studies, Chicago, typescript.

5

Diversity's Diversity

JUDITH STIEHM

Introduction

Symbols, whether verbal or nonverbal, are wonderful things. They can be shared widely, passionately supported, and also encompass contradiction, fact and fancy, the possible and the impossible. They serve as a means of avoiding the complicated and the delicate and of evading the tests of logic and of data. For example, the yellow ribbons of the Gulf War made it possible for Americans to avoid any debate related to that war by making support for the troops — for the ordinary Americans who had volunteered to serve — the only salient issue.

Sometimes symbols emerge with apparent spontaneity; sometimes they are created with calculation. Often their use is intended to capitalize on emotion and to forestall reflection. Today, what may once have been a concept, "diversity," is rapidly becoming a symbol — a stimulus producing (at least for now) a positive response. I suspect that it has been carefully adopted as a replacement for the concept, "affirmative action," because the negative valence the latter acquired has made it no longer useful.

I suspect, also, that "diversity's" positive valence derives from the analogy which can be made to the biologists' argument that it is important to society to maintain the largest possible gene pool. Note that the gene pool argument is (1) future-oriented and (2) argues a social benefit. It is quite unlike the (1) immediate and (2) individual rights argument historically used to support demands for political and social inclusiveness. Note also that "diversity" principally refers to outcome while affirmative action refers to selection processes.

"Diversity" celebrates variety and implies inclusiveness. It skips over the fact (1) that selection may nevertheless occur and (2) that selection can involve the exclusion of individuals with superlative attributes — individuals whose only deficiency may be their inability to contribute to a desired, diverse outcome. Advocates of diversity need to acknowledge, then, that righting "under-representation" sometimes leads to the denial of opportunity to individuals who are considered members of "overrepresented" groups. It also puts one in the awkward position of using criteria positively to overcome patterns created by their use negatively when they would not be used at all ideally.

I expect that "diversity" will soon acquire a negative connotation. This is because it is being used as a symbol with the purpose of avoiding the complex and sensitive. Rushing in where others fear to tread, I am willing to assert first, that one should be committed to achieving diversity as a social policy; second, that if one is, one's commitment must go beyond using diversity as a means of gaining access for oneself and those like oneself; and third, that academics have an obligation to apply their skills and expertise to the task of thinking (and speaking and writing) carefully about the costs and benefits, rights and wrongs of diversity. It is not enough to rely on the biological analogy and symbolic communication.[1]

In teaching, I find it hard to get students to understand the difference between a generalization (what thinking is all about — the asking "of what is this an instance?") and a stereotype (the attributing of a general finding to particular individuals). Many students have learned so well the injunctions against prejudice, discrimination, and bigotry that they are reluctant to make any but particular judgments; that is, they are reluctant to think. Thus appropriate sensitivity has led to an inappropriate rejection of a crucial tool — reason. I am fully confident that I will embarrass myself in what follows. However, having urged an obligation to address the difficulties of diversity and having tweaked the silent, I am bound to offer some general propositions for others to critique and improve.

There are three specific contributions I would like to make to the discussion about diversity in higher education. The first is to note that students, faculty, and policymakers tend to be of quite different generations, to have had quite different experiences with and to face quite different challenges from diversity. The second is that different educational institutions operate in quite different environments. In particular, "elite" schools and "naturally" diverse schools do not fit the model usually assumed in discussions about diversity. The third is that symbolic thinking has led to the use of impoverished and inadequate concepts. "Diversity" requires new language and fresh conceptualization.

My concluding suggestions will be modest. They will involve tactics and experiments rather than strategies and solutions. My assumption is that the goal of harmonious diversity in which there is a general sense that "justice" is at least being pursued, requires an appreciation and willingness to tackle diversity's difficulties. Yellow ribbons can buy only a limited amount of time.

The Generations

Diversity issues affect students, faculty, and policymakers differently. A diagram using generational analysis can be helpful in understanding this.

University Generations

Position	Age	Imprinting	Challenge
Policymakers	50+	Cold War TV Emmett Till Lynching *Brown v. Board of Education*	Achieving diversity throughout institution but exempt from having the experience themselves
Faculty	35+	Civil Rights Act Vietnam War Women's Movement	Diversity in faculty and curriculum
Students	20	Reagan Era's Individualism, Materialism	Living with diversity, competing with everyone in conditions of scarcity

Let us assume policymakers — regents, chancellors, legislators — are 50 plus. Born by 1940 they were imprinted by the 1950s. In the 1950s, even at a "liberal" school like the University of Wisconsin, ethnic jokes were common, although they tended to be about Swedes or Jews (who were referred to as "New York Indians.") Women were the most underrepresented group of "qualified" students, discussions about "mixed marriages" meant Catholics and Protestants, and quotas were alive and well — as a way of limiting enrollments of Jewish students generally, and of women in professional and graduate schools. At that time, though, it was customary to take measures to achieve geographical diversity, prime targets being the likes of Montana and New Hampshire. In the policymakers' generation, men of Irish, Italian, and East European ancestry were often the first in their family to attend college. Many felt marginal there. Today, having succeeded with difficulty, they sometimes are annoyed, sometimes amused to find themselves classified as privileged and "Anglo." Today's policymakers, simply put, have had little firsthand or peer experience with the range of what we call diversity today.

The Emmett Till lynching was wrong and *Brown v. Board of Education* was right. In the 1950s, it seemed simple. Make everyone legally equal and enforce the law. Moreover, the handful of women and of minority men from that era who now have found their way into top policy positions adapted to the culture of the policymakers. To some, their value is that while they look different, they think alike. When this is the case, though, their contribution to diversity is merely visual.

I do know of one six-person university executive committee (the president and vice presidents) which was truly diverse. It included two African-Americans, one woman, an Hispanic, and two upwardly mobile white ethnic (Irish and Italian) men. Their interaction would be well worth detailing but, for now, it is enough to say that the mix did not work at all. The dominant white-male culture was missing entirely and each of the individuals had achieved success by adopting (and continuing to follow) quite different strategies. This led to much misunderstanding, the early departure of three of the vice presidents, and several reorganizations. In most circumstances, though, policymakers assume, think, and act similarly. Their mutual trust is rooted in their similarity; their teamwork is not threatened by different perceptions of the informal rules or by apparent unpredictability. Policymakers, though, are the ones who receive and must give direction related to diversity (and affirmative action) within their institutions. They are the ones who are responsible to outside constituencies and to political and legal requirements. They are expected to cause diversity, but they have been and continue to be exempt from attempting to live it.

Let us assume that faculty are in their late 30s. They were born in the 1950s, imprinted by the late 1960s, but did not finish their doctoral work until the 1970s — a time when academic jobs were very scarce. This is a generation which is likely to have a strong commitment to diversity as a concept — but it also is a generation which has a profound sense of the extended and arduous preparation required for a faculty position and of the rigorous competition for a limited number of positions. It is here that one hears, again and again, the refrain "I'd love to ... but I can't find any that are qualified."

Faculty hiring is decentralized. Periodically, a department has the opportunity to hire one individual — usually in a narrowly defined specialty; for example, surface tension physics. This can mean that, year after year, faculty can search in good conscience, can make the best and fairest individual hiring decisions they know how to make, and one plus one plus one will again and again add up to zero minority faculty.

In admitting a freshman class, admissions officers "build" or "sculpt" a class. Senior administrators now have learned that they also need to sculpt their faculties. This is why many administrators now offer departments a chance to hire "targets of opportunity" — individuals who may represent a fine and needed addition to the faculty, but who might not be the single best scholar in a narrow subspecialty at a particular moment in time.

In faculty hiring, scarcity (a word Americans deplore and repress) is hard at work in two ways.[2] First, there is a scarcity of "minority" (especially African-American and Latino) applicants for positions; second, there is often a scarcity of positions. The scarce set of applicants sometimes is attributed to the universities' failure to educate — but if educational failure is acknowledged at all, it is usually assigned to the precollegiate experience.[3] Further, when there are scarce positions and abundant applicants, those doing the hiring often focus on extremely narrow criteria for field and for merit simply reduce the applicant pool to a manageable size.[4] This narrowing results in conventional decisions which give great weight to invidious academic niceties, but little weight to the needs of the community, the students, or the institution as a whole.

Institutional needs which are rarely considered in department hiring include provision of role models, willingness to advise, knowledge about different cultures, and different perspectives on and different strategies for achieving success. Again, discussions about faculty hiring must not overlook the difference in assumptions between administrators and faculty as to just what is the appropriate level or appropriate unit for analysis. To administrators, it is the resulting whole faculty; to faculty, it is the process of filling each individual slot. The decentralized nature of hiring makes faculty relatively immune to external pressures, therefore, and liable to self-replication.

Universities pay scarce faculty more. This means they often pay faculty from "underrepresented" groups more because they are in short supply. The problem is that envy, which can be suppressed when a new accounting faculty member is paid double the salary of a new Spanish professor, is harder to swallow when the salary differential (even a small one) is experienced within a department rather than between schools.

Switching back and forth between holding that individuals are the proper unit of analysis and holding that some larger unit such as the family, the state, the nation, are of more import is frequent in political discourse. Our culture strongly emphasizes the individual; it is important to remember, though, that we have never accepted radical and unadulterated individualism as our national ethic. Again, honest debate requires that we substitute consistent and acknowledged assumptions about the unit of analysis for the usual shifting and unnoted assumptions.[5]

Today's students were born in 1970 and imprinted by the Reagan years' materialism, individualism and, I would say, fear of decline. Reagan's personal boosterism, optimism, and endorsement of competition had as a downside the creation of anxiety among the young who were experiencing a world in which (at least in theory) everyone was, for the first time, in competition with everyone else — including competition with those from other countries — who were "known" to be extraordinary drudges and who would do the work "no one else" would do, whether that was cleaning kitchens or doing meticulous laboratory science.

When women began to compete for advanced degrees and top positions, men found the competition doubled almost overnight. This led them to feel relatively deprived (as compared to their fathers, uncles, and older brothers) and it has made some of them insecure and angry. Meanwhile, neither women nor minority men believe that fairness has been finally achieved. Further, women and minority men continue to have to accept white men as the makers of most policy and decisions.

In short, they continue to have to trust that today's white male policymakers will behave differently from previous white male officials or differently than they themselves have behaved in the past. Again, in theory, substance is all that should matter. In practice, women and minority men continue to have to turn to white men for protection, direction, and approval; in virtually no institution have adult white men found themselves dependent on women or minority men. Pictorial representation may not "matter," but only white men have consistently enjoyed it. Few of them have experimented even voluntarily with being a minority; for example, by attending or teaching at a predominantly African-American college for a year.

The increased diversity of student bodies means that today's students are experiencing more scarcity and more competition than their elders. Most also see what they consider "preference" being given to others. Even white men are experiencing a demand that they acknowledge their ethnic and sex identity and allegiance. Many of them find this distasteful. They are not used to being marked as "other" and, if they should acknowledge their group identification with pride or actively seek to pursue their group interest (for example, in a "National Association for the Advancement of White Men"), they are attacked, isolated, and repudiated. Thus, one burden of being perceived as powerful is that one cannot openly promote oneself; one must advance one's interests as though they were generic. One must do so even as others are vigorously pointing out that they are *not,* in fact, generic.[6]

For students, then, scarcity and competition loom large. And so does sex. College years, after all, are also courting years. Sex is always tricky, but it becomes even trickier cross-culturally, because the rules of courtship are not the same in various cultures. Also, cross-cultural dating itself encounters hazards and reproofs from third parties. Again, students are likely to practice diversity (even with discomfort) far more than their elders, and it is important that we elders understand what it means to share intimacies cross-culturally, to actually listen to each other's music, to guard or choose not to guard one's tongue in a dormitory room, locker room, or other setting where one might feel it fair to be considered as "off duty." Meanwhile, many minority students are now asserting a new claim. They are not just asking for either tolerance or assimilation. They are asking to be accepted and respected as they are. They do not want always to be "on guard." Further, other students, those who have always been comfortable being themselves, are now being confronted and experiencing criticism for being themselves. These students are finding that behavior which was once approved as "self confident" is now being labeled "presumptuous" or even "oppressive." Again, when some groups reject the social controls which once kept them in "their place," other groups will inevitably experience new restraints — and will not like them.

Should everyone expect to encounter, to have to accept if not to relish some misunderstanding or discomfort? Should the goal be to distribute better, rather than to eliminate adversity? And is there a "dose" of discomfort or adversity which is actually therapeutic? Some might say that Jews, in the 1950s, had an achievement-producing dose of adversity. Do Asians receive a similar dose today? Do African-Americans receive too large and Anglos too small a dose?

In sum, the experiences, the responsibilities, and the challenges of diversity for the different generations within a single institution are different. Even if general diversity goals are agreed upon, the generations' motivation, costs, benefits, and views about the best way of reaching those goals may well be at odds.

Institutional Context

There is some sense that under ideal conditions, an institution's students, faculty, and administration should reflect the gender and ethnicity of the overall population. Few universities do. Few student bodies even reflect the pool of high school graduates. As a result, usual institutional behavior is to assert a commitment to diversity, to advertise its efforts to achieve it, to fall short, but to escape too much criticism. There are some interesting special cases. They are (1) schools with highly selective admission policies and (2) minority-majority schools. Both kinds can be either private or public.

While one might expect public schools to be committed to diversity, private schools — including many with exclusive admissions policies — are also committed to it. They face several problems. The first is that they are very expensive. The price of one year at a private school can be two-thirds of the median annual family income. To achieve diversity, therefore, many elite private schools have adopted a "need blind" policy for admitting students. This means admission decisions are made without regard to an applicant's ability to pay. A financial aid package which will make attendance possible is guaranteed with admission. This may encourage applications from students from low income families, but it has other consequences as well.

First, costs to those who can afford to pay go up; that is, tuition. Second, students are encouraged to take large loans and can graduate thousands of dollars in debt. Third, the very meaning of "private" is changed. Once a "private" school was contrasted to a "public" school as a way of purchasing a different or special education. Thus a specialty market existed for those able to pay. A "need blind" admissions policy means, though, that certain elite schools are trying to remove themselves from the marketplace. They are, essentially, advertising their product as a "free good." Instead of offering a special education and competing for paying students, these schools are seeking the very best students with the assurance that money doesn't matter.[7] The students then become, in effect, trophies — possessions to brag about. The focus, then, has shifted from the students' choosing of a product, an education, to the schools' capturing of the "best" customers (particular students). It is like the merchant who advertises "furrier to the Queen."

The customer (who may not pay at all) becomes the proof of the product rather than the product itself.

A second problem for (some) private (and some public) schools relates to their academic exclusiveness. First, there is some inherent dishonesty involved in institutional claims to have "the best" freshman class since adequate measures for establishing such a claim simply do not exist. Further, with only a limited number of freshmen slots at exclusive schools and thousands and thousands of annual high school graduates, large numbers of superbly qualified students are regularly rejected by elite schools. Many of the rejected are surprised and grieved. They seek an explanation. When they do, they find that the schools which rejected them have admitted ethnic minority students whose SATs and GPAs are lower than theirs. This is the source of many of the charges of "preference" given to minorities.

The feelings of the rejected are understandable. What is not understandable is the schools' reveling in their academic exclusiveness while failing to explain that their admissions policies are not now and never have been tied exclusively to conventional measures of academic merit. Also, these schools often fail to explain how very well qualified the admitted "minority" students are. They also fail to explain that the *majority* of the students who are below the average for the school's admissions standards are "Anglo," although only a few of those students are "known" (unless they have exceptionally high visibility, as did John F. Kennedy Jr and Dan Quayle). Again, the kid from Idaho, the trustee's and alumni's children, the pole vaulter, the soprano, the quarterback, the donor's twins are probably not visually identifiable. Many of them, though, have SATs and GPAs lower than the average of those admitted and also lower than many rejected applicants.[8] Because they are not visually identifiable, they suffer neither stigma nor stigmata. They are not blamed for having "taken" a rejectee's place. They are not resented. No campaigns are launched to change the criteria or process under which they gained admission.[9] Sadly then, it must be concluded that to attack "preference" only as it applies to the visually identifiable is racist.

Latinos and African-Americans bear the brunt of resentment and envy. Native Americans are so few in number that they are not usually perceived as displacing others. Also, in schools which largely fail to meet proportional goals, efforts to achieve diversity are not seen as occurring at others' expense. The problem, again, is rooted in the combination of the visibility of some but not all "diverse" students *and* of the scarcity of slots. If elite schools could admit *all* who met a particular standard, the "diversity" backlash would not be such a problem. Then, diversity efforts would be experienced as increasing inclusiveness rather than as increasing exclusiveness.

When schools set diversity goals to reflect the nation's population in their student bodies, they must confront the fact that when conventional measures are used, African-American and Hispanic scores are different and lower than those of Anglos (and Asians).

Therefore, if each school were to follow a policy of recruiting its "share" of minority students, and if the "best" schools could, in fact, buy or attract the "best" minorities, the overall effect would be similar to the now outlawed civil service policy of race-norming. That is, the effect would be to create everywhere a miniaturized version of the population as a whole in which the SATs of every school's minority students would lag behind those of Anglos. This would create everywhere an impression of generally lower competence and would likely lead to stress and discomfort for minority students. One response by many well-qualified minorities has been to choose not to be trophies and, instead, to attend historically minority colleges. Thus private (like Spelman) and public (like Florida A&M) African-American institutions continue to thrive.

Another strategy minorities could follow would be to seek out integrated schools where they could expect to be stars; for example, instead of choosing the most academically exclusive school that admitted him/her, an African-American might choose an excellent school where his/her scores predict high performance relative to other students. If minorities did select schools where their quantified accomplishments were relatively high, a message of their competence and of the homogeneity and remoteness of "elite" schools might replace the current perception of minority lag and special treatment.[10]

There are a set of schools which "naturally" have a diverse student body. Many of them are urban or western and public. As noted, some have historically been "majority-minority" schools and present a competing, public alternative for minority students. Some other public schools, though, like the University of California at Berkeley, have simultaneously and rapidly become diverse and exclusive (because they have capped enrollments).[11] Even though new institutions (for example, the University of California, Riverside) could provide access, they have not succeeded in making themselves as attractive as the older schools. The result is that for some, the ensuring of diversity creates a situation like that in the private schools — a situation in which the previously "overrepresented" now feel underrepresented, and rejected applicants perceive their "places" as "taken" by "less-qualified" minorities.

State schools are committed to educating states' citizens. When they cannot admit all who meet the (often) legislatively established minimum criteria, one response might be to say "first come, first served"; another solution could be to use a lottery and/or to abolish *all* (including athletic) special admissions. However, many public schools have chosen to behave like private schools by "building" their freshman classes and applying selective academic standards for admissions. By de-emphasizing the number of low-scoring students admitted and by ignoring altogether the effect of junior college transfers and admissions in the Summer and Spring, these schools end up experiencing the same contradictions as elite private schools.[12] However, as public schools, they are subject to a broader critique, and have a broader responsibility. Thus exclusivity is a double-edged sword. It may foster civic pride, but it also fosters decreased civic ownership. After all, the great state universities founded in the nineteenth century did not become great by imposing exclusive admissions requirements. Public schools make a mistake when they emulate private schools in this regard, and policymakers err when they encourage or permit invidious competition with private schools. It is educational opportunity, not hierarchy, which makes a nation, a state, a school great.

Schools with diverse student bodies are likely to produce strong student support for diversifying the faculty, the administration, and the curriculum as well.[13] Responsiveness to such demands varies, but students have limited time and resources, and do not usually grasp how university decisions are made. Students have had some effect on curriculum change and perhaps some on new hiring, but they rarely can influence a faculty tenure decision. More responsiveness to diversity with regard to hiring and tenuring occurs when the mandate comes from a budgeting or governing body.

To summarize: an institution's context poses different problems and provides different resources for working toward diversity. Where and when there is great underrepresentation, population proportionality may be a good measure because it is clear, simple, and sets a high goal.[14] However, as diversity succeeds, such goals can become dysfunctional. This is because even if all students met the same academic standards, the previously overrepresented population will experience relative deprivation. This problem is aggravated when opportunities are scarce relative to qualified applicants, and it becomes a severe problem for a few highly selective schools which must select beyond any rational capacity to do so. Thus a liberal, inclusive stance works when there are enough places to go around. When there are not enough, "diversity" can easily splinter into competition between groups seeking their own advantage. Further, when the rejected feel displaced, their discontent inevitably focuses on the visible "displacers."

Impoverished and Inadequate Concepts

The language, the concepts, and the programs for achieving diversity have been shaped by the black civil rights movement. This means that emphasis has been placed on individual entitlement — now! In the beginning, this interpretation was aided by a widely shared perception of severe legal and *de facto* discrimination against African-Americans. Indeed, in the 1960s, many groups seeking sympathy wrote an "X as Nigger" statement. Every group sought to capitalize on the analogue to blacks.[15] In particular, women were major "free riders" on the Civil Rights Bill of 1964. Some would even argue that the current generation of African-Americans are free riders on the last generation's experience. "Inferiority anxiety," "integration shock," and "meanness" are real. Shelby Steele argues, though, that while real, they are adversities that are manageable; that is, they challenge but are not so severe as to defeat.

This may be so. Still, I think it important to note that the existential situation for African-Americans in the United States is different from that of other groups which are underrepresented in policy-making positions. Studies about seeking employment, and a recent article in the *Journal of the American Medical Association* related to medical care demonstrate that this is so.[16] So do two other social indicators. One is residential segregation; that data consistently show that while other minority groups have areas of residential concentration, they also are distributed throughout urban and suburban areas. Blacks, though, almost always reside in distinctly bounded areas even when they move to the suburbs. The other measure is intermarriage. State laws against miscegenation were only struck down by the Supreme Court in 1967. At present, there are some 1,000,000 interracial marriages representing about two per cent of all United States marriages. Such marriages are common for Japanese, Chinese, and Native Americans. Black/white marriages number over 200,000 (up from 65,000 in 1970). Still, less than four per cent of black men and less than one per cent of black women marry whites. (The percentage of whites marrying blacks is infinitesimal.) The rate is significantly higher in the west and among higher income groups than it is elsewhere or in the middle- or lower-economic classes.

This social isolation suggests that the circumstances for African-Americans are sufficiently different that removing barriers to individual effort may not be easy or, even if removed, sufficient. It also forces one to confront the question of how to respond when racism is itself a significant part of a culture when there is a fundamental commitment to respect and encourage diverse cultures.[17]

Our concepts, then, are impoverished because they are drawn almost exclusively from the United States' white/African-American experience. Often, we have extended remedies designed to be responsive to that experience, to women (who are not a minority), and to other minorities who experience much less social distance from the dominant culture.

Further, many situations involve not two, but a number of ethnicities. The dynamics of multiethnic groups are little understood or even examined. Is there always a dominant group and an "out" group or do the groups establish an understood hierarchy? Are alliances stable or do they shift? Does multiplicity reduce or enhance ethnic self-consciousness? And is the traditional liberal remedy of providing for the socialization and inclusion of those whose "only difference is color" at odds with the fact that diversity does mean *difference*? The most acknowledged campus difficulties related to diversity occur between students and during "off-duty" time, a time when different groups may show little enthusiasm for each others' popular music, dress, style, and humor. However, different tastes and views of what is central and what is marginal should/could be a part of universities' on-duty time, too. Indeed, some would argue that an institution has not achieved diversity if those who look unlike do not think unlike as well.

Today social scientists can tell us a good deal about what whites think about blacks, and something about what they think about Asians and Hispanics.

However, they can tell us very little about what those groups think — either about whites or about each other. For example, whites stereotype other groups; is it right to assume that those groups also stereotype whites? Also, are the stereotypes of whites held by Chicanos, held by blacks, and by Asians congruent? If so, can one assume the "stereotypes" may have validity as generalizations? If not, what do we learn about the perceiving cultures from the different views they have of the same culture? Pretend that one group sees Anglos as high-achieving, model citizens, another as ethnically exclusive and above the law, and the third as materialistic and disdainful of productive work. Can such diverse views be taken into account intellectually? Is such a variety of views compatible with any set of shared values and/or allegiance to any common cause or course?

A favorite recurring example of the social value of diversity is the use of the Navajo language by military radio operators in the Pacific theater during World War II — their "code" was never cracked. Top managers are now urged to seek "complementarity" in their staff. Again, Mill and Milton argued that dissent/diversity should be tolerated, not because individuals have a "right," but because variation is, in itself, a benefit to society. Diversity, then, is real, it is multiple, and what we should be beginning to understand is that even if we are committed to its value, it is not easy and we lack even the concepts needed for thinking about the issues.

Multicultural research lacks the support of a tradition, of mentors, of trained scholars, and of institutional structures. Most intellectual work benefits from (in motion) inertia and from institutionalization. At present, diversity theory and practice lack institutionalization. They are treated generally as either marginal or "too hot" to handle. Nevertheless, the most serious problem may be our impoverished thinking. Consciousness of difference can invoke stormy emotion. Categories are often unclear; some (like gender and race) are perceived as enduring, but others (for example, "Irishness") may be in the process of being created (or of dissolving). Some, like Catholicism, may stem from shared cultural values, while others (for example, "people of color") may share little more than the experience of exclusion. Other distinct categories include language groups, social class, age, disability; others which may be relevant to educational institutions may include part-time students and nondegree candidates.

Finally, there is the question of diversity and proportionality. Is it enough to have some specimens of the national (or global) human variety to illustrate what is taught about, to expose them to the dominant culture, to teach mutual tolerance, and to teach future leaders to work with others? Or should diversity seek to be in proportion with diversity's reality? If so, why? As a measure that everyone's fullest potential is being tapped? Or to maintain (or to upset) the existing power equilibrium? And what is the relevant unit to determine proportion? Is it local, regional, the state, the nation, the world? In the 1950s, elite schools sought geographic representation. They gave priority to the academically able, but also to the able to pay and to alumni children. They restricted access for some academically able and able to pay (for example, Jews and women). Should universities ruthlessly exclude the academically untalented even if very rich or even if their parents are very powerful? Would they, even if they acknowledge they should? Do such schools have the courage to enforce familial downward mobility? Do they grasp the pain accompanying upward mobility?

Suggestions

Universities have as their unique charge education. One might expect that their central school, their keystone, the domain of their most honored scholars would be a School of Education. One might also expect universities to study themselves, to collect data to help them enhance their teaching and scholarship. The truth is that Schools of Education are low in most institutional hierarchies and the Offices of Institutional Research tend to address managerial issues rather than educational concerns. My first suggestion, therefore, is that universities direct increased attention and resources to education as a subject and to formulating the issues related to higher education which require public debate. Then they should assume responsibility for educating policymakers so that they (the policymakers) can make judicious policy.

Second, because any disciplined discussion requires consistent use of the unit of analysis, that unit should be made an explicit and conscious part of any diversity discussion. Related to this is the concept of "availability" and of "the pool" from which individuals should be drawn to work toward institutional diversity. "The pool" will differ for students, employees, faculty, administrators, and policymakers. It is important to ask constantly what a pool's requirements really are, and whether or not pools are too narrowly defined.

Third, one must ask whether and how one has a responsibility for helping to create the pool. For example, do universities have a responsibility to recruit minorities vigorously to attend their institutions? Does that include precollege programs? If so, for whom? Entering students? High school Juniors? Junior high school students? Elementary school students? Looking across the country, one sees many different efforts, some of which *do* extend all the way down to elementary school, but one has the profound sense that these programs exist so that schools which, in fact, are *not* diverse can say they are doing *something*. Sometimes these programs are more self-justifying than efficacious. It may be that more would be done for students if the same monies were put into providing full-time, on-campus, high-school counselors. At present, secondary schools struggle with as few as one counselor for 400 students — they do well to keep programs in place and files accurate. One might, then, question whether particular programs are actually designed to protect the higher institution, or whether they focus on programs which are most likely to accomplish the job. Having high-prestige institutions substitute or insert themselves into the work of the high schools because they have more funds may actually waste funds as well as demean those who know their jobs but who are frustrated by a lack of support.

Fourth, because universities' purpose is education and not mixing, or melting, or diversifying per se, and because ethnic and gender consciousness and declarations have become, in some places, so central to the college experience as to be distracting, perhaps all ethnic programs for recruiting, tutoring, or otherwise assisting minority students be redirected to any and all students who do not have a parent who completed a four-year degree. This would (1) crosscut ethnicities, (2) concentrate on a shared (or unshared) experience, and (3) provide support for the main thing — academic achievement. (All students requiring financial aid also might be given extra academic support.) Regardless of ethnicity, students whose parents did not get degrees and low-income students are the students most likely to lack skills, attitudes, habits, reinforcement, support, and information to sustain their efforts. As an example, some may hear fellow undergraduates brag that they "didn't study at all" and got an "A" and believe them — not realizing that the speaker may well have spent all night studying but, in the student culture, it just isn't couth to say so.

Fifth, faculties — aggregated at the departmental or, perhaps, the school level — should be assessed as to their record in being able to teach their discipline to the range of students. If it is shown, for instance, that one school has failed to train a substantial number of women, it would be evaluated for that failure.

Sixth, measures need to be developed for self-testing to guard against two things: (1) holding women and minority men to a higher standard because scrupulous efforts to be fair end by holding them to the ideal not the real; and (2) "positive discrimination," the favoring of an individual like oneself, one whose personal history is known, or who enjoys the halo of having come from a "good" school. In accordance with this, one needs to ensure that selectors are educated about how to interpret a vita. Thus, if one won a Rhodes when none were available to women or blacks, one did so with less than half of today's competition. Or if one entered into a commuting marriage to pursue one's career, that might mean *more* commitment rather than less to the job. Conversely, a refusal to commute may mean commitment to substantive achievement rather than prestige or income-maximizing. The point is: the same facts can have different meanings for different individuals. Their meaning for white males may not be identical to their meaning for women and minority men. Indeed, the "meaning" of particular facts can be quite varied.

Seventh, more attention should be given to informal procedures, sanctions, and self-defense as ways of restraining the intolerant. Legal proceedings, even student judicial proceedings, are rarely as effective as peer disapproval. A "climate for learning" is essential, but appeals to higher authority or to those "in loco parentis" are not sufficient. Individuals need to know how to act effectively themselves.

Conclusion

There are always several ways to accomplish a particular purpose and each, in turn, will generate new difficulties. Diversity almost guarantees complexity which, in turn, almost ensures misunderstanding and error. But diversity also stimulates, challenges, and increases the range of possibilities and responses. Its value, then, is not just political (accommodating an intense minority's ability to veto) or economic (ensuring the next generation can be economically productive enough to support us in our old age); it is not just moral (seeking justice); it also enhances the intellectual enterprise.

There is a danger in trying to smooth over difficulty and hurt by using "diversity" merely as a symbolic yellow ribbon. Acknowledging the pain and the adversity, which are a part of unshared assumptions and experiences, are important to managing and to benefiting from diversity. If intellectuals and educators shrink from addressing these issues, they marginalize themselves and their institutions. Equally important, if we expect flawless performance, we encourage such shirking.

John Stuart Mill is said to have brought utilitarianism to a premature death — that is, before its work of deconstructing feudalism had been completed. He did so by fully and convincingly analyzing utilitarianism's faults. Diversity may rapidly diminish in importance. If it does, I hope it will be because it has become natural and not because it has succumbed to backlash and its critiques.

One day in a Los Angeles neighborhood which had signs in every other shop in Russian (with Cyrillic alphabet), I stopped at a taco stand where a number of Asian-American students were also eating. The African-American waiter wore dreadlocks. No one seemed to notice.

Notes

1 The resounding silence with which many academics respond to discussions about affirmative action stems, in part, from not wanting to offend, *or* to be attacked, embarrassed, or misunderstood. This partly explains the offensive against "political correctness" taken by some individuals who were once able to speak freely without fear of contradiction or confrontation. Now, in some circumstances, those who were previously exempt are challenged, and so sometimes hold their tongues just as others have done for centuries (and continue to do daily). The previously unchallenged do not like being criticized and complain about being punished for their beliefs. "Well," many would respond, "welcome to the club." Being free to speak has never implied that one would be listened to, that one would be agreed with, or that one would not be criticized, or even sanctioned.

2 Another deplored concept is downward mobility; in our culture, mobility is nearly always discussed as "upward."

3 Typically, the response by universities to criticism of the composition of their student bodies has been to recruit earlier and earlier instead of considering how to make the early experience better. For instance, universities work with junior high school students themselves instead of giving priority to the training of and support for secondary school teachers.

4 Thus, a department might say, "We only hire from the top six departments nationally," and refuse even to consider other applicants.

5 Women are especially frustrated by discussions which consider men as individuals but women as family members, yet this frequently occurs in academic research because of the measures used for social class.

6 At another time it might be worth exploring a "lost ethnicity," German, which first raised the bilingual question in United States public education and which accounts for the wonderful orchestras of the Middle West, but which was consciously repressed during the two World Wars so that "German-Americans" have *de facto* become "Anglo."

7 The federal government recently charged that some private schools tried to remove themselves from the market in a second way — by agreeing among themselves about what aid package would go to particular students. This meant that sought-after students could not shop around for the best package, that is, one with more grant money and less loan burden.

8 A study of Harvard admissions for 1988 showed one of six freshmen was a "legacy," a child of an alum. Also, 40 per cent of alumni children are admitted against 14 per cent of nonalumni children. *The New York Times* (December 8, 1990).

9 There is sometimes discussion about admission standards for athletes. In 1989, twenty-seven per cent of football and basketball players at NCAA Division I-A schools were "special authority admissions." Only four per cent of the freshmen at those schools were "specials." *The Chronicle of Higher Education* (May 1, 1991).

10 Admission to UCLA Law School is now highly competitive. Much is made of the lower admission standards currently met by African-Americans and Hispanics, but it should be noted that those standards are higher than those met by Anglo students only a short time ago. The problem is not that the minorities admitted will not make fine lawyers, but that by routinely admitting women, competition doubled and the scarcity thus created has led to absurdly high admission standards for a public law school.

11 Only twenty years ago Berkeley could accept all qualified applicants (residents who graduated in the top one-eighth of the state's graduating seniors.) By five years ago, however, applications had increased by a multiple of almost five, while admissions had only doubled. Moreover, only five per cent of black and Hispanic high school graduates met UC eligibility requirements while 16 per cent of whites and 33 per cent of Asians did so. Achieving diversity and equity in the face of scarcity became a challenge. See the Berkeley Academic Senate's report, "Freshman Admissions at Berkeley," prepared by Jerome Karabel, May 14, 1989.

12 In making institutional comparisons, the admission scores used are for freshmen, full-time, and fall admits. Schools have already learned to require weaker students to begin in the Summer or to defer until Spring. The records of the many transfer

students are not considered at all. Thus, "entering freshmen SAT scores" mean different things at different schools. For example, almost all Oberlin students enter together as freshmen in September. The scores represent the student body. In the state university system of Florida, though, 70 per cent of juniors and seniors are community college transfers.

13 The great curriculum debate has been structured as though the struggle were over the substitution of "lesser" and "diverse" authors such as Zora Neale Hurston for Homer in a shared and required "core" curriculum. In fact, most students do not take a core curriculum. They may be required to show both "breadth and depth" in their course selection, but a majority of bachelors degrees go to students in education, engineering, and business. Their curricula are often very professionally focused. They may receive very little liberal arts education, whether nouveau/diverse or traditional.

14 Note that even women rarely argue that they should be proportionately represented as faculty and administrators even though they are a majority of college students. Real "minorities" can be proportionately incorporated without seriously changing an institution, but women's numbers mean men's opportunities and control would be dramatically altered if proportional representation occurred.

15 Norman Mailer even wrote an essay in *Dissent* titled "The White Negro," to call attention to the oppression of white males! They didn't get to have fun.

16 *The Los Angeles Times* (May 14, 15, 1991).

17 For example, how should policymakers relate to foreign (and domestic) groups which do not encourage or even accept a public role for half the population, women?

6

Ethnic Studies: Its Evolution in American Colleges and Universities

RAMON A. GUTIERREZ

Ethnic studies has recently emerged as a discrete discipline at institutions of higher education in the United States, Canada, and Europe. This development has been largely a response to heightened levels of political awareness regarding ethnic, racial, and religious conflict worldwide and as a program for the recognition of multiculturalism. In the most optimistic scenarios, ethnic studies offers a path for the peaceful management of differences over time; at worst, it is seen as exacerbating the importance of identity politics over time. This essay traces some of the important historical lineages that led to the creation of ethnic studies in the United States, outlines how the discipline is currently defined, charts the direction of contemporary scholarship, and lists the sites at which this scholarship is being generated.

Some thirty years ago in the mid-1960s, in the midst of the escalation of the war in Vietnam and the movement for civil rights in the United States, many colleges and universities created programs, centers, and departments devoted to the study of particular racial and ethnic groups. This development was motivated primarily by a crashing of the universities' gates by a popular challenge from below to what were imagined then as bastions of white Euro-American male ideals and privilege. As part of the democratizing project of the civil rights movement, young women and men of African, Mexican, Native American, and Asian ancestry started to arrive in unprecedented numbers on American campuses. As they did, they taxed the former habits and attitudes of institutions of higher education. Minority students demanded that the curriculum reflect their presence and that safe havens exist for them in what they rightly perceived as alien and hostile environs. They demanded that scholars from minority communities be hired to teach the culture and history of minorities in the United States. And they demanded that the study of race and ethnicity be removed from the disciplinary homes they had long occupied in departments of sociology and anthropology, where race and ethnicity were pathologized, problematized, or exoticized.

This demand for a separate space on college campuses devoted to the recognition of racial and ethnic differences in the United States mirrored larger political debates in the public realm. During the 1940s and 1950s civil rights movement, activists had sought slow, peaceful, change through assimilation, through petitions for governmental beneficence, and through appeals to white liberal guilt; trends that were reflected in scholarship as well. Talcott Parsons, for example, whose theories influenced not only the sociology of deviance, but also cultural anthropology, saw ethnicity as a social problem to be explained through careful study of the barriers preventing full assimilation into the mainstream of society.[1] Thus consensus historians such as Oscar Handlin[2] and Stanley Elkins[3] looked respectively at how immigrants had assimilated over time and how the institutional legacies of slavery slowly were being eroded. Scholars from marginalized communities responded to such perspectives in the 1950s by lauding the resourcefulness and ingenuity of racial and ethnic groups, noting their accomplishments and contribution to society, even in the face of overwhelming discrimination. John Hope Franklin's *From Slavery to Freedom: A History of Negro Americans*, Americo Paredes' *With His Pistol in His Hand: A Border Ballad and its Hero*, and Kenneth M. Stampp's *The Peculiar Institution*, were illustrative of this perspective.

The political turn in the mid-1960s from a movement for civil rights to nationalism was accompanied by a rejection of assimilation and a demand for cultural autonomy and national self-determination. In the public realm, black nationalists declared the creation of the Nation of Islam. Others called for the Black Belt Nation's independence. Chicanos declared that they wanted nation-state status for their ancestral land, Aztlan. And Native Americans militated for greater sovereignty rights over their own affairs. On college campuses, students translated self-determination as meaning the need for separate centers, programs, and departments devoted to the study of African, Asian, American Indian, and Mexican culture and history; a development that was quickly expressed in the production of a scholarship that chronicled the protest and resistance of the powerless to their domination and exploitation in the United States. Examples of this perspective abound: Vine Deloria's *Custer Died for Your Sins*, Rudolfo Acuna's *Occupied America: The Chicano's Struggle Toward Liberation*, Vincent Harding's *This Is a River: The Black Struggle for Freedom in America*, and Herbert Gutman's *The Black Family in Slavery and Freedom*. This scholarship concluded by elaborating distinctive values, institutions, and semiautonomous cultural realms generated internally by ethnic and racial communities, but constrained and shaped by external social forces.

The demography and cultural geography of constituencies generally dictated the ways faculty and college administrators responded to the programmatic and curricular demands raised by minority students. In areas of large African-American population density and at schools that had recruited large numbers of African-American students, the pressure for black studies and its more global analogue, Africana studies, dominated. In the southwestern and midwestern parts of the United States, in states where there was a large number of Mexican immigrants, the call for Mexican-American and Chicano studies was raised and addressed. Similar demographic pressures explain much of the spatial distribution of Asian-American and Native American studies programs throughout the United States.

If one surveys the degree of institutionalization that these ethnic and racial studies programs were able to attain in the 1960s and early 1970s, without a doubt, the movement for black studies, broadly defined, was by far the most successful. While a few academic departments of Chicano studies were created at the community college level, numerous black studies, Afro-American, and Africana studies programs blossomed as independent, autonomous, degree-granting departments. *The Directory of Afrikanamerican Research Centers* by 1980 listed 103 major departments with associated research institutes. The *Hispanic Resource Directory*, published in 1988, counted well over 100 programs in Chicano studies, Latino studies, Boricua studies, and Puerto Rican studies, but few academic departments.[4] The emergence of professional associations such as the National Council on Black Studies, the National Association of Interdisciplinary Ethnic Studies, the National Association of Chicano Studies, and the Association for Asian-American Studies further attested to the increasing permanence and professionalization of the study of race and ethnicity in the United States by the late 1970s.

The reason black studies programs were able to establish themselves on many campuses as independent departments undoubtedly was due to the strong moral and political arguments that the larger public was then willing to endorse regarding the history of slavery and the legacy of racial discrimination in the United States. Chicano studies and Asian-American studies activists tried to advance moral arguments for their curricular cause by imagining themselves as internal colonies dominated by white America. But in the end, the arguments that were most persuasive on their behalf were political. Educational institutions, particularly public ones, had to address the educational needs of the entire citizenry.

As was to be expected, programs in black studies and Chicano studies that began as formally recognized departments were the most successful and long-lasting. This was so because of the structural and organizational location that departments occupy in the business of colleges and universities. Resources are doled out by department, courses are listed by department, faculty are recruited and promoted by departmental criteria, and the degrees departments grant are largely governed by departmentally defined requirements.

By contrast, the multidepartmental program was the model most black, Chicano, Native American, and Asian-American studies programs created in the early 1970s took. These programs relied almost exclusively on the resources of established departments for their courses and personnel. Programs were pieced together by offering a hodgepodge curriculum: a course here and there on history, a sociology of race relations course, a course on deviance in minority communities, and perhaps a smattering of literature courses drawn from English and foreign-language departments. In the heat of the moment, the educational objectives of very few programs were carefully articulated and, instead, what they reflected was the curricular colonialism that had previously characterized the academic study of minorities. Many in the academy believed that professional upward mobility and national prominence was achieved by studying major problems as opposed to the minor problems of minorities. In the minds of skeptics and agnostics these programs had been created to deal with the "minority problem"; that is, with campus unrest and remedial education for the ill-prepared immigrants in the university.[5]

For the faculty who gave their skills and services to such minority studies programs, the work proved difficult, primarily because of the structural problem most programs face on university campuses — programs are usually dependent on the generosity of established departments. If departments did not deem the faculty who staffed the various ethnic studies programs' course offerings as essential to their particular departmental curriculum, or judged the whole area of scholarship as deficient, job vacancies went unfilled for years. Departments expected faculty working with the black studies, Chicano studies, or Asian-American studies programs to fulfill all of their departmental responsibilities. Programs expected just as much, thus requiring two full-time jobs instead of just one. Given that programs devoted to American racial and ethnic minorities included a large component of student remedial education, faculty in these programs also were asked to do the support services that few faculty in mainstream disciplines did. All of this further guaranteed that tenure would be even more difficult for faculty persons in these programs to attain. The end result of faculty vacancies that were not immediately filled by departments were course listings that were not taught, demoralized and overtaxed faculty, and programmatic curricula that were uneven and fragmented.

The creation of programs and departments of black, Chicano, Asian-American, and Native American studies naturally had mixed results. On the positive side, if any conclusion can be drawn from the educational research on the social and psychological effects of such educational programs on student learning and retention, it is that they significantly improved minority student self-image and identity, enhanced academic skills, and by making universities less alienating environments, led to greater retention and higher graduation rates.[6]

On the negative side, programs devoted to the study of race and ethnicity were particularly fragile and unpredictable. To begin with, the faculty members who were recruited initially into these programs in the early 1970s were young assistant professors working in heterodox and experimental topics that did not fit clearly into established disciplinary boundaries. Many of these scholars left university settings. They did so for a variety of reasons: for some, potently perceived social and political commitments kept them from producing the scholarship necessary to obtain tenure; for others, private industry and government employment offered better pay and demanded less; and others, particularly the better researchers, were lured away to more prestigious institutions where they entered into Afro-American, black, and Chicano studies departments. They chose moves into such departments because they had felt isolated in traditional departments as the sole minority member doing research colleagues often deemed "minor." In departments focused on the study of race and ethnicity, they found a critical mass of kindred intellects, and a more nurturing environment in which no one would question the validity or importance of their work.

If the 1960s and 1970s were the heydays for the genesis and maturation of programs and departments devoted to the study of American racial and ethnic groups, the 1980s proved to be the decade of retrenchment. In these years, under the presidencies of Ronald Reagan and George Bush, the ideal of fair access to housing, education, and employment was actively attacked by conservative Republicans and political forces on the Right. Affirmative action programs were caricatured as reverse discrimination, as reparations for slavery, and as racial quotas. Whereas in the previous decade affirmative action had been used to recruit faculty of color, now the program was used cynically to subvert governmental intent. Upper class Argentines and Peruvians, for example, were recruited to satisfy "Hispanic" hiring goals, as were West Indians in lieu of African-Americans. These were all recruitment and hiring practices that created a backlash against affirmative action policies. Discussions of Eurocentrism in the curriculum and the need to expand the range of voices represented in university courses fell largely on deaf, if not hostile, ears. Economically, these were years of dwindling resources for programs that studied race and ethnicity, matched attitudinally by apathy, and reflected in lower course enrollments and a decreasing number of majors in such programs.

The end of the 1980s saw attempts to rehabilitate, reorganize, and reinvigorate what had become moribund programs in black, Chicano, Native American, and Asian-American studies. This movement was a result of numerous developments at the international, national, and local levels. At the international level, the decolonialization of most areas of the world, save South Africa, led to an examination of the legacy that colonialism had wrecked on the nation state. What invariably was found was that when independence came to former colonies in the Third World and power was transferred to national elites, the old ethnic tensions and rivalries that had long been held in abeyance by the force of the imperial state,

suddenly exploded in open conflicts. Such latent tensions also increasingly came
to light as cracks started to appear in the Berlin Wall and as the Soviet empire
fragmented into warring nations.

The move to reimagine the structure and function of academic programs
devoted to the study of race and ethnic relations in the United States created in
the 1960s, was rooted in these larger global concerns and accelerated by a renewed
educational concern to articulate the theoretical intersections among the
epistemologies of black studies, Chicano studies, Asian-American studies, and
Native American studies. What united the study of these groups? How were the
experiences of these groups different? Was there a sufficiently distinct and well
articulated knowledge base to define these programs as a discipline?

Several institutions of higher education in the United States entered the
conversation. The University of California, Berkeley, initiated what is now
regarded as the first conceptualization of ethnic studies as a distinct
discipline-based department. Founded in 1969 at the end of several months of
student protest, the autonomous department of ethnic studies at UC–Berkeley
encompassed under its umbrella four independent and vertically separate
programs devoted to Afro-American studies, Asian-American studies, Chicano
studies, and Native American studies. According to Ling-chi Wang, one of the
early chairs of the UC–Berkeley department of ethnic studies, "the early advocates
of ethnic studies deliberately rejected the notion of curricular 'mainstreaming' or
'integration', favoring instead, autonomous academic programs built on the
principles of solidarity among racial minorities, interdisciplinary approach,
'self-determination', and 'educational relevance', unencumbered by failed
paradigms and biased scholarship of the past."[7]

The vertical structure that the UC–Berkeley department of ethnic studies chose
was particularly problem-prone, primarily because of the competition for
resources that each of the vertical components (that is, Chicano studies, Native
American studies, etc.) had to engage in. Resources won by one program in the
department were resented by the others, thus eventually leading to the secession
of Afro-American studies which eventually became an independent department.
In 1994, Native American studies similarly declared its independence and
currently is seeking departmental status. However, it was not until 1980 that the
ethnic studies department at Berkeley developed a more comprehensive vision of
what it could be when it established a Ph.D. granting program explicitly devoted
to comparative ethnic studies. Here the emphasis was to tie the department's
concerns about domestic minorities with Third World peoples, thus giving an
international component to the curriculum.

The desire to merge the various and distinct ethnic programs into one larger
unit was already well in the air of higher-education circles. By the mid-1970s,
scholars such as James A. Banks and Jack Bass had proposed the consolidation
of single-group ethnic programs into larger aggregations that could explore
commonalities and divergences in the experiences of racial and ethnic groups

domestically and worldwide.[8] Bowling Green State University took up this challenge in 1979, creating an ethnic studies department that was a hybrid between the older organizational model and the newer one imagined, thus integrating general ethnic studies with black studies and Latino studies.[9]

Despite these initial curricular transformations of older models for the study of race and ethnicity, little thought was given to an articulation of a more complicated model for ethnic studies, one that attempted to define the parameters of the discipline and its main propositions. In 1988, several faculty members in the Chicano studies, Asian American studies, and black performing arts programs at the University of California, San Diego, were brought together by this author to propose the formation of an ethnic studies department that incorporated the best of the ethnic studies movement, but avoided the problems that had plagued the UC–Berkeley ethnic studies department. We did this with a clear realization that the nature of knowledge and its use as a tool to understand the physical world and the human condition was then in radical flux. As new social and scientific discoveries were made every day, so too new fields and disciplines were being born. Clifford Geertz, the eminent cultural anthropologist, referred to this refiguration of knowledge as the "blurring of genres ... a phenomenon general enough and distinctive enough to suggest that what we are seeing is not just another drawing of the cultural map — the moving of a few disputed borders, the making of some more picturesque mountain lakes — but an alteration of the principles of mapping."[10] As a result of these changes, hybrid disciplines in the natural sciences codified as disciplines and departments of geophysics and biochemistry had emerged. In the sciences, the growth of transdisciplinary or supradisciplinary fields had led to the creation at the University of Chicago in 1984 of new departments of microbiology, biochemistry, and biophysics and theoretical biology which replaced the old departments of biochemistry and molecular biology and the department of molecular genetics and cell biology. The chair of the University of Chicago's committee charged with this reorganization stated that the change would "more accurately reflect ... the current principal areas of biological research."[11] There were many other relevant examples of the refigurations of social and scientific knowledge that were then taking place, but the rationale for the creation of departments of cognitive science worldwide sufficiently and spectacularly illustrated this trend.

It was in the light of these larger developments that the faculty at the University of California, San Diego, began to imagine ethnic studies as a distinct discipline. By our assessment, ethnic studies as a discipline had been born in the 1960s out of the cultural conflicts that occurred when blacks, Chicanos, American Indians, and Asian-Americans protested that their contributions to American society had been sorely ignored in the texts that Eurocentric middle-class white males historically had articulated. Ethnic studies scholars objected that the claims these men had advanced regarding the universalism of their perspectives and their freedom from particularistic commitments, claims that gave them a detached objectivity and a monopoly on truth, were actually strong reflections of the value the dominant culture gave to a rigid distinction between the mind and body, and the presumed advantages of detachment and distance from the object of study. Claims to objectivity had to be founded not on transcendent universalisms or sharp dichotomies between subjectivity and objectivity, but in the recognition of the importance of perspective; perspectives that were always partial and situated in relationship to power.

The perspectives that ethnic studies scholars brought to the debate on the meaning of America's past, and which uniquely defined the method and discipline of ethnic studies, looked at social relations from the bottom up, from the vantage point of those who were powerless or marginalized, and were rooted in the lived historical memories of slavery, racism, victimization, and physical and psychological damage.

Though ethnic studies scholarship had begun as "contributionism" aimed at overcoming historical neglect, it quickly had moved on to chronicle protest and resistance, finally elaborating distinctive values, institutions, and semiautonomous cultural realms generated internally by ethnic and racial communities, but constrained and shaped by external forces. Ethnic studies scholarship revealed the ways in which people gave meaning to their lives under even the most brutal conditions, thus in being, or becoming more than mere victims. Since so much of ethnic studies scholarship required the mining of unused empirical sources that had been ignored for generations, the discipline by necessity became cross-disciplinary, taking methods of intensive investigation from the social sciences, and enriching them with vantage points from the humanities, particularly with a concern for change over time.

The enduring methodological principles that had emerged from the study of racial and ethnic groups in the United States were: (1) all knowledge claims had to be viewed as situated and recognized as partial; (2) culture was not a unified system of shared meanings, but a system of multivocal symbols, the meanings of which were frequently contested, becoming a complex product of competition and negotiation between various social groups, such as between males and females, between masters and slaves, between blacks and whites, and between rich and poor; and (3) the study of race and ethnicity was best understood by using comparative interdisciplinary methods.

The 1989 proposal for the creation of an ethnic studies department at the University of California, San Diego (UCSD), approved in 1990, began by rejecting the vertical model of single ethnic-based programs and, instead, proposed a horizontal model that focused on common trends and experiences among social groups. Ethnic studies was thus the study of the social, cultural, and historical forces that have shaped the development of America's diverse ethnic peoples. Focusing on immigration, slavery, and genocide, the three social processes that combined to create in the United States a nation of nations, the ethnic studies department at UCSD was organized to examine intensively the histories, languages, and cultures of America's racial and ethnic groups in and of themselves, in their relationships to each other, and particularly, in structural contexts of power.

The goal of the ethnic studies department at the University of California, San Diego was to promote research, teaching, and community service in ethnic studies that: (1) focused intensively on the histories of different ethnic and racial groups, particularly on intragroup stratification, (2) drew larger theoretical lessons from comparisons among these groups, (3) sought to articulate general principles that shaped racial and ethnic relations presently and historically, and (4) explored how ethnic identity was constructed and reconstructed over time, internally and externally.

In the past, most ethnic studies scholarship focused on African-Americans, Asian-Americans, Chicanos/Latinos, and Native Americans. The numerous ethnic groups encompassed in these broad categories were studied as largely autonomous, as if their particular experiences were isolated and unique in American history. The ethnic studies department at UCSD expanded the scope of the study of race and ethnicity in the United States in two ways. First, comparative analysis was made a fundamental component of ethnic studies research and teaching. Second, to understand fully the power dynamics that had shaped relationships between dominant groups and minorities in the United States, the European-American immigrant experience would also be explored, thus making the department's focus comparative and relational.

Since the creation of the ethnic studies department at UC–San Diego, other colleges and universities have attempted to consolidate and reimagine their single-group ethnic programs into units that study the dynamics of race and ethnicity in global and comparative context. In 1991, for example, the University of Washington's department of American ethnic studies which grew out of their Afro-American studies program, began offering a degree in American ethnic studies.[12] Brown University's Center for the Study of Race and Ethnicity in America, a research center closely affiliated with the American studies program, has recently proposed a similar focus, moving from the study of American exceptionalism to the comparative study of the dynamics of race and ethnicity in the United States.[13] At a moment when nationalism is reemerging powerfully among students in the United States as well as many other nations and states around the globe, it seems imperative that we see that glorification of local systems of knowledge which are rooted in racial, religious, and ethnic distinctions, as fundamentally tied to the globalization, commodification, and massification of social life.

Notes

1 The influence of Talcott Parsons can be found in Robert E. Park, *Race and Culture* (Glencoe, IL: The Free Press, 1950); Louis Wirth, "The Problem of Minority Groups," in Ralph Linton, ed., *The Science of Man in the World Crisis* (New York: Columbia University Press, 1945); Milton Gordon, *Assimilation in American Life* (New York: Oxford University Press, 1964).

2 Oscar Handlin, *Boston's Immigrants* (Cambridge: Harvard University Press, 1941).

3 Stanley M. Elkins, *Slavery: A Problem in American Institutional and Intellectual Life* (Chicago: University of Chicago Press, 1959).

4 Bill Foster, *The Directory of Afrikanamerican Research Centers* (New York: Institute of AfriKan Research, 1980); Alan Edward Schorr, *Hispanic Resource Directory* (Juneau, AK: Denali Press, 1988), pp. 327–30.

5 The field of women's studies underwent rather similar developments on many American college campuses. On the similarities between ethnic studies and women's studies programs, see Johnella E. Butler and Betty Schmitz, "Ethnic Studies, Women's Studies, and Multiculturalism," in *Change* (January/February 1992), pp. 36–41; and Johnella E. Butler and John C. Walter, *Transforming the Curriculum: Ethnic Studies and Women's Studies* (Albany, NY: SUNY Press, 1991).

6 Henry L. Gates Jr, "Academe Must Give Black Studies Programs their Due," *The Chronicle of Higher Education*, 36, 3 (September 20, 1989), p. 56; Wilson Reed, "Some Implications of the Black Studies Movement for Higher Education in the 1970s," *Journal of Higher Education*, 44 (1973), pp. 191–216; Henry Sioux Johnson and William J. Hernandez-Martines, *Educating the Mexican American* (Valley Forge, PA: Judson Press, 1970), p. 2; Roberto Jesus Garza, "Chicano Studies: A New Curricular Dimension for Higher Education in the Southwest" (Ed.D. diss., Oklahoma State University, 1975), esp. pp. 75–6; Charles V. Willie and Arline Sakuma McCord, *Black Students at White Colleges* (New York: Praeger, 1972), p. 109; Winnie Bengelsdorf, *Ethnic Studies in Higher Education* (Washington, DC: American Association of State Colleges and Universities, 1972); Larry A. Braskamp and Robert D. Brown, "Evaluation of Programs on Blacks," *Educational Record*, 53 (1972), pp. 51–8; Allen H. Frerichs, "Relationship of Self-Esteem of the Disadvantaged to School Success," *Journal of Negro Education*, 40 (1971), pp. 117–20; Edmund W. Gordon and Doxey A. Wilkerson, *Compensatory Education for the Disadvantaged* (New York: College Entrance Examination Board, 1966); Harriet P. Lefley, "Effects of a Cultural Heritage Program on the Self-Concept of Miccrosulcee Indian Children," *The Journal of Educational Research*, 67 (1974), pp. 462–6; Margo K. McCormick and Juanita H. Williams, "Effects of a Compensatory Program on Self-Report, Achievement and Aspiration Level of 'Disadvantaged' High School Students," *Journal of Negro Education*, 43 (1974), pp. 47–52; Roger W. Buffalohead, "Native American Studies Programs: Review and Evaluation," in Convocation of American Indian Scholars, *Indian Voices* (San Francisco: Indian Historian Press, 1970), pp. 161–90; Vine Deloria Jr, "Indian Studies: The Orphan of Academia," *Wicazo Sa Review*, 2 (1986), pp. 1–7; Annette

M. Jaimes, "American Indian Studies: Toward an Indigenous Model," *American Indian Culture and Research Journal,* 11 (1987), pp. 1–16.

7 Ling-chi Wang, "Ethnic Studies and Curriculum Transformation at UC Berkeley: Our Past, Present, and Future" (unpublished paper), p. 2.

8 James A. Banks, *Teaching Strategies for Ethnic Studies* (Boston: Allyn and Bacon, 1975); Jack Bass, *Widening the Mainstream of American Culture: A Ford Foundation Report on Ethnic Studies* (New York: Ford Foundation, 1978).

9 Robert L. Perry and Susan May Pauly, "Crossroads to the 21st Century: The Evolution of Ethnic Studies at Bowling Green State University," *Explorations in Ethnic Studies,* 11, 1 (January 1988), pp. 13–22.

10 Clifford Geertz, "Blurred Genres: The Refiguration of Social Thought," in his *Local Knowledge: Further Essays in Interpretive Anthropology* (New York: BasicBooks, 1983), p. 34.

11 "Biological Sciences Reorganization Reflects Current Areas of Study," *University of Chicago Magazine,* 76 (Summer 1984), pp. 3–4.

12 Johnella E. Butler, "Ethnic Studies: A Matrix Model for the Major," *Liberal Education,* 77 (1991), pp. 26–32.

13 Rhett S. Jones, "Ethnic Studies: Beyond Myths and Into Some Realities (A Working Paper)" (unpublished paper, March 12, 1993).

7

Diminishing Returns: Can Black Feminism(s) Survive the Academy?

Barbara Christian[1]

When I was asked to speak at this conference on "Feminisms in the Twenty-first Century," at first I chose a topic that asked the question whether feminism in America is still largely conceived of as a white movement by most American institutions. Despite the impact the Anita Hill/Clarence Thomas hearings had on feminism in this country, I was amazed that when the media focused its attention on the women's movement as it did in 1992, it still featured primarily white women as its major spokespersons. For example, *Time Magazine* in 1992 featured on its oh-too-predictable March cover, Gloria Steinem and Susan Faludi, representing two generations of the second wave of feminism.[2] Even *The Atlantic*, by featuring Wendy Kaminer's "Feminism's Identity Crisis," got into the fray, perhaps because of first lady (a title I hate) Hillary Clinton's media profile. But while Wendy Kaminer's clearly conservative (backlash) piece did mention the white feminist theorist Carol Gilligan's work, it did not indicate that African-American women scholars had contributed anything of worth to American feminism(s).[3] Apparently Wendy Kaminer still thinks that feminism is a strictly-white upper-class phenomena emanating from prestigious universities such as Harvard.

So much for media writers. As I thought about the concerns of this conference, however, who my likely audience would be — that of the smarter and purer folk in the academy where I am situated — I decided it would be more appropriate, more honest for me to assess my own site, hence the title of this exploration, "Diminishing Returns: Can Black Feminism(s) Survive the Academy?"

I hope it is clear to everyone here that black feminisms have existed for a long time — that since the nineteenth century, black women such as activist Sojourner Truth, poet Frances Harper, and educator Anna Julia Cooper had articulated a position that stressed the interrelatedness of racism, sexism, and classism as central to this society's structure. I name these women's primary commitments because I want us all to be clear that African-American feminists have operated in many arenas, a fact that gets left out in cultural histories, even on the left.[4] Radical black women such as turn-of-the-century feminist Ida B. Wells' hard-hitting journalistic pieces about lynchings demonstrate how racism and sexism are not separate entities, but are interdependent modes of domination which affect us all, for contrary to much contemporary white feminist theorizing, racism often expresses itself in sexist terms and sexism in racist terms. Works on African-American women are not just examples of some cultural nationalist problem, but rather a mirror image of this country's inability to deal with its hierarchical inequities. Too often race issues are seen as the "problems" of blacks and people of color, gender issues as the "problems" of women.

Contemporary black feminists have continued and developed their foremothers' tradition — especially in the literature they have produced — in which they have claimed themselves as subjects. Scholar Deborah King put it this way in her essay, "Multiple Jeopardies, Multiple Consciousness": "A black feminist ideology fundamentally challenges the interstructure of the oppressions of racism, sexism, and classism both in the dominant society and within movements for liberation."[5]

I hope it is clear also that the second wave of black feminist thought and practice did not originate or does not now reside primarily in the academy despite all the hoopla about political correctness. Rather, its roots were in popular movements, in the civil rights, black power, and women's movements of the 1960s and early 1970s as exemplified by the many voices of black women collected in Toni Cade's edition of *The Black Woman* (1970). Black feminist thought and practice is very much alive outside the academy, whether its proponents use that label or not, although I could not prove that since most studies conducted by American white women demonstrate the incidence of feminism among American women without taking into account in any real way the ways in which African-American women might frame that concept quite differently. Some African-American women call themselves womanists, the word coined by writer Alice Walker to distinguish themselves and their specific perspective from white feminists. Other African-American women, like many of their women of color and white counterparts, may not call themselves feminists or even womanists, yet practice the tenets that that point of view signifies.[6]

As was true of the black women's rights movement of the nineteenth century, contemporary black feminisms have been articulated in many arenas, an important one being the literature of African-American women such as Alice Walker, Audre Lorde, Toni Morrison, and June Jordan. As I have already noted in my essay, "But

What Do We Think We're Doing Anyway? The State of Black Feminist Criticism(s) or My Version of a Little Bit of History,"[7] in the seventies, the academy scarcely acknowledged the existence of black women in major knowledge areas such as literature or history, nor had a black feminist inquiry been initially central to the establishment of African-American and women's studies in the academy. For much of that decade, the subject of race was usually associated with men and the subject of gender with white women for even the most astute intellectuals. The few black women scholars who existed in the university often fell between the cracks or just managed to straddle the apparently divided terrains of race and gender.

By the early eighties, however, scholars had established a small but influential place in the academy for black women's studies, mostly as a result of the intensity and quality of African-American women's literature and scholarship. A few of us were able to excavate the neglected histories and literatures of African-American women, to articulate the interrelatedness of race, class, and gender as the core of a black feminist inquiry, and to critique the male bias of race analysis and the white bias of gender studies. The number and quality of these studies are too vast for me to cite in this essay. Suffice it to say that black feminist inquiry in all of the major disciplines of the university as well as in interdisciplinary areas, such as women's studies, African-American studies, and diaspora studies, has been substantive. As well, in collaboration with other women of color, in anthologies such as *This Bridge Called My Back* and *Making Face, Making Soul*, African-American women writers and scholars have challenged the concept of a universalized woman. As a result, the editors of the book *Feminist Theory in Practice and Process,* a collection of essays published in the women's studies journal *Signs* during the decade of the 1980s, could note "the shift away from an undifferentiated concept of woman," in recent feminist theorizing:

> Just as one of the first acts in the development of a feminist theory was to reject the standpoint and experiences of white men as normative, so too, one of the first acts in developing black feminist theory has been to reject the perspectives of white women as normative, focusing instead on the concrete everyday experiences of black women as the basis for theory making.[8]

Black feminist inquiry also has had a major effect on the study of race, so that male African-American studies specialists increasingly include African-American women in their studies — to the extent that some of the major scholars in the area of African-American women's literature are African-American men. Some African-American women critics have noticed that contemporary societal institutions still tend to choose African-American men over African-American women to be the "real" experts and spokesmen when it comes to critiquing the relationship between race and gender, again reflecting the hierarchical structure of our society in which men are always better than women.[9]

Fortunately, some male scholars are beginning to explore the other side of African-American women's studies, that constructions of masculinity in relation to race are often camouflaged in our society. Major contemporary African-American male writers such as John Wideman and Clarence Major credit African-American women's intellectual questionings in the 1970s with opening spaces for them to investigate themselves as men in relationships with family and female and male lovers, as opposed to the white/black border wars, relegated to black male writers of the past. Such an anthology is Joseph Beane's *Brother to Brother*. Some of my graduate students are engaged in this endeavor. An important anthology called *The African-American Black Male, His Person, Status and Family*, edited by Richard Myers and Jacob Gorden, which places the intersection of race and gender in relation to men, is about to be published. As well, major intellectuals such as Cornel West and Manning Marable have used black feminist ideological positions in their analyses of black community contexts, and possibilities for liberation.[10]

African diasporic and postcolonial feminist studies also have developed in the last decade. Because of its marginality in US studies and its long tradition of subjugation to colonial/racial points of view that extend even beyond the celebration of left male critics' idealization of male Caribbean writer Frantz Fanon's writings, this field has understood the importance of one of the first tenets of black feminist scholarship — that of intervention and change. Postcolonial scholar Chandra Mohanty has pointed out that feminist scholarship:

> is not the mere production of knowledge about a certain subject. It is a political praxis which counters and resists the totalizing imperative of age-old "legitimate" and "scientific" bodies of knowledge.[11]

Critiques originating in black feminist thought, then, have had a sure effect on the restructuring of traditional disciplines. Positioned at the vortex of so many discourses that seem to be vying with one another for centrality, black feminist critics have had to rethink traditional constructs in the academy and the world. Many of my sister/colleagues, as well as graduate students with whom I work, have often asked ourselves the question, "To whom do I belong? Black studies? Women's studies? A specific discipline such as English or sociology? Black feminist scholar Patricia Hill Collins recalls that she:

> found [her] training as a social scientist inadequate to the task of studying the subjugated knowledge of a black woman's standpoint. This is because subordinate groups have long had to use alternate ways to create independent self-definitions and self-valuations and to rearticulate them through our own specialists.[12]

In creating alternate systems, black feminist critics have helped to validate the necessity for interdisciplinary approaches, such as those of cultural studies as well as the possibility of redefining the very concept of what it means to be an intellectual, since so many of our thinkers have resided outside the academy or even outside traditional black institutions.

But not only has black feminist inquiry critiqued the race bias of white feminisms, the gender bias of race matters, the usually neglected subject of class, the too-rigid boundaries of academic systems, it exists also for itself. In other words, black feminist thought is not only a critique of other systems that is at the service of "the real" points of view, it is also a distinctive, one is tempted to say, a coherent perspective which places black women, including those from the rest of this hemisphere and Africa, at the center of its inquiry. That distinctiveness is obvious especially in the literature that African-American women have produced during the last two decades in which I would insist they have been major theorizers about gender, race, class, and sexual preference. Toni Morrison's receipt of the 1993 Nobel Prize for Literature — the first time a black woman, and an African-American — has been so honored is a sign that African-American women finally are being perceived as intellectuals within their own right, nationally and internationally. Increasingly, black feminist thought is also being articulated in critical works such as bell hooks' *Talking Back: Thinking Feminist, Thinking Black;* Patricia Hill Collins' *Black Feminist Thought;* and anthologies such as *Home Girls,* edited by Barbara Smith; *Wild Women in the Whirlwind,* edited by Braxton and McLaughlin; and *Changing Our Own Words,* edited by Cheryl Wall.

Without question, as the applications to the Ph.D. Program in ethnic studies at my university indicate, more and more students are studying African-American women's thought, especially in the area of literature. I, for example, now find myself, as I am sure most of my sister/colleagues do, "an academic mother to more children than I could have possibly imagined, and to types of children beyond my conjuring ... at a time when my white counterparts are already academic grandmothers."[13]

Clearly black feminisms no longer are completely absent in the academy and have had some effect on the ways in which we think about the intersections of race, gender, and class, as well as the accomplishments and thought of black women. And yet — I have entitled this essay "Diminishing Returns: Can Black Feminisms Survive the Academy?" for, though there have been some advances, they have been achieved at much cost and have not really changed the landscape or the population of the academy. What central problems do black women and, therefore, black feminisms face in the academy in the last decade of this century?

One especially important dilemma we face is who black feminist academics of the future will be. My experience during the last few years is that although African-American women's thought and literature, and intersections of race, class, gender, and even sexual preference are being focused on by some graduate students, few of them are black women or men. Of course, not all black women in the academy do feminist scholarship, nor is all black feminist scholarship done by black women. Yet, although black women are not all the same, they do bring a certain urgency to this area of study precisely because it affects them directly and emanates from their personal and historical contexts since black feminist thought, for them, is not only and primarily an artifact to be studied. It would be a tremendous loss, a distinct irony, if some version of black feminist inquiry exists in the academy to which black women are not major contributors.

My experience that there are few African-Americans entering graduate school, is verified by statistics. In 1991, according to *The Journal of Blacks in Higher Education*, only 2.3 per cent of the Ph.D.s in all academic disciplines awarded in this country went to blacks, a percentage far below that of Ph.D.s awarded in the 1970s to blacks, such as myself. There was a slight gain in overall black graduate enrollments in the late 1980s, but progress occurred mostly at professional schools such as business, law, and medicine. The *Journal* also included a survey of the status of African-Americans on the faculties of American colleges and universities. Although there were gains in the 1970s, there was a slowdown, then an abrupt drop during the Reagan/Bush years of the percentage of blacks at predominantly white institutions. The *Journal* points out that roughly half of the 19,000 black professors in the United States teach at the predominantly black colleges and universities — that is, one hundred colleges as opposed to the 3,000 "historically white" colleges and universities.[14] Even then, only 2.5 per cent of all professors in the country, 4.2 per cent of associate professors, 6.0 per cent of assistant professors, and 6.7 per cent of instructors were black.[15] How are African-American women faring? In 1987, African-American women received 54 per cent of the doctoral degrees awarded blacks, that is two per cent of the doctorates awarded that year. In 1985, 0.6 per cent of all full professors were black women, 1.4 per cent were associate professors, 2.5 per cent were assistant professors, and 3.2 per cent were instructors.[16]

Even I, suspicious of numbers and statistical studies, could see that the situation for African-American women graduate students and faculty is dismal. While I could have some measure of pride in the fact that such a small percentage of black feminist academics had had such a significant impact on intellectual inquiry in the 1970s and 1980s, any optimism I have about our situation was greatly outweighed by the reality of the minuscule number of black women entering the academy. Why are African-Americans, and especially women, not going into academic areas at a time when issues of race and gender have become increasingly acknowledged as central to intellectual inquiry?

I recall the many students I've worked with, very bright, intellectually oriented, and interested in graduate study, who decided to go into business, law, or medicine. I think about the many African-American students who didn't have the opportunity to make such a choice since they had not finished high school or did not have *access* even to the knowledge about these choices. For them, making it big in music or sports continues to be their only options out of poverty or the violence of an early death.

Some of us African-American academics have focused much of our attention on those students who manage to graduate from high school. I've learned in my

20 years at University of California, Berkeley, that students of color who supposedly could not succeed in college often did very well when they learned about, were inspired by, the possibilities that other students had taken for granted from the time they were born. Still, many of those students, though interested in pursuing graduate study, moved into more "practical" areas such as the professional schools, community activism, and journalism. They felt, for some reason, that life in the academy would be unrewarding. While life in the professions might be difficult, at least they could make some money and pay back the debts their education incurred, even as they might be able possibly to effect our contemporary society.

As I was working on this essay, a new volume was published, exploring specifically the issue of black women faculties' survival in white universities. Called *Spirit, Space and Survival: African-American Women in (White) Academe*, this anthology, a collection of black women's voices from inside the academy, voices concerns that we black women faculty talk about when we see each other at conferences, usually the only time we do see each other since so many of us are the only black woman, or one of a few at our respective universities. In fact this volume grew out of such a meeting at a conference. The editors, Joy James and Ruth Farmer, say that the objective of the volume is to examine the voices of African-American women "struggling with Eurocentric disciplines, students, faculty and administrators in predominantly white institutions." Most African-American women faculty, they inform us, are at the bottom of the academic hierarchy and, even in comparison to the fewer black male academics, are paid less, have higher workloads, and get fewer returns. For most African-American academics, research and writing does not come easy, beleaguered as they are by demands within their institutions as well as in their families and communities, demands that they feel they must meet if they are to fulfill their many roles in their diverse communities.

I am aware of how better off African-American women are in the academy than they are in many sectors of our community. After all, we have the possibility of doing work we like to do, an opportunity that probably only two per cent of the planet has got. Still it is important that we raise our voices about the inequities we face in our terrain and how it affects our daily lives, for our "complaints" nuance a site of possible resistance.

In their introduction to their courageous volume, Joy James and Ruth Farmer remind us that African-American women academics work in environments which often are not only nonsupportive but, at times, outright hostile. They (we) are expected to perform mightily — with little reward — and to be grateful that we are allowed in the halls of learning. Overworked and underrecognized, we are forced to cope with office and university politics as well as the racism, sexism, and homophobia inherent in these environments and the larger society.[17]

Perhaps my students are smarter than I think. Salaries paid to business, law, and medical graduates are considerably more than those paid to nontenured, even tenured professors. For African-Americans, most of whom come from families who are struggling to survive, the issue of monetary returns is not a mercenary concern but a communal one. In addition, as Martin Anderson, a senior fellow at the Hoover Institution at Stanford University, has pointed out,

> the time necessary to earn a Ph.D. has gradually lengthened in recent years ... that after receiving a bachelor's degree, the median time it takes to earn a Ph.D. is now 10.5 years. For women the median time to earn a Ph.D. has reached 12.5 years ... the time it takes for black Americans to earn the Ph.D. stretches out to 14.9 years.[18]

Pursuing one's intellectual interests might seem frivolous to many African-American students, especially women, who are generally perceived as necessary contributors to their family and community's financial well-being.

In the essay "Balancing the Personal and the Profession," Adrienne Andrews extends the knowledge we have about African-American women academics by interviewing a number of black women faculty at different universities around the country about their lives. Inevitably she found they faced issues of concern to Euro-American women, but also issues specifically related to being black and female in the academic environment:

> [t]he issues they felt were the most pressing ones facing them as black women, were not only the impact of gender and salary discrimination based on male dominance in the profession, and struggling to get tenure, but racial discrimination and a type of role conflict and professional burnout that was compounded by the fact of race, as well.[19]

One respondent noted:

> Most women have family responsibilities, and when black women have family responsibilities, they're even more difficult for us than for the white woman because for us many of us are the first, second generation at best. In university life....[20]

Other respondents described how the black woman professor is often called upon to serve as mentor, mother, and counselor in addition to educator to African-American students who experience the academy as a hostile and alien place and that she often is expected to serve on committees to make certain the minority and woman perspective are represented. Some of my sister/colleagues refuse to be what they call "academic mules"; yet they are also aware that it is usually our communities who lose if we do not attempt to fulfill the demands of our respective institutions.

Many of the women in this study also are struggling with the issue of finding a suitable mate who could contend with a woman who has a doctorate, and whose professional life would involve much of her time. The question as to whether the feminist movement has negatively affected women's marital status or whether that idea is a media hype is one that Susan Faludi explores in her book *Backlash*. The situation in African-American communities perhaps might be different, an example of how an important mainstream "theory" might take on different ramifications if it is viewed from the point of view of African-Americans, and possibly other people of color. African-American men have been under severe attack from the judicial system, levels of poverty that affect their ability to be breadwinners. I note that in the last month, my local paper *The Oakland Tribune* ran a Sunday feature article about the fact that one-third of African-American women in the ages from 18 to 50 who express heterosexual desires are not able to find a mate. Whether that fact is true or not (I always doubt newspaper articles), the experiences of many of my colleagues, as well as my own personal experience, indicate that African-American women academics very often are single, or single mothers, with little prospect of intragroup heterosexual relationships, if that is what they desire. As well, African-American women academics, whether they are heterosexual or homosexual, often are living in areas where there is no vibrant African-American presence so that they suffer from cultural isolation.

But the problems of monetary returns, time concerns, probable work overload, and distorted personal relationships are not the only issues confronting an African-American woman who might want to go into the academy. When *The Journal of Blacks in Higher Education* asked black feminist scholar Professor Johnnetta Cole why there is a shortage of black professors, she not only cited these restraints but also that:

> Many African-Americans entering the academy today do so because they have been lured by the promise of alternative models of research and action-oriented scholarship ... [But] anything not fitting the traditional model is considered less than scholarly.[21]

While some African-American women are willing to endure financial and personal lifestyle sacrifices because they love intellectual inquiry and understand its importance, some are deterred by the realization that they will likely have to do the *kind* of work they want to do in a hostile environment, or they might have to change their sense of themselves and the position from which they explore ideas if they are to succeed in the academy.

In her essay "Teaching Theory, Talking Community," Joy James, who teaches courses on African-American women in political movements in Women's Studies, University of Massachusetts–Amherst, passionately delineates this theoretical dilemma:

> If it is assumed that we only speak as "black" women — not as *women* — or "black" people — not as *human beings* — our stories and theorizing are considered irrelevant or not applicable to women or people in general; they are reduced to descriptions of a part rather than analyses of a whole (humanity).[22]

The way in which the writings of bell hooks is viewed by some white scholars, female and male, is one example of this reduction. While my graduate students use her work extensively and cite her quite extensively in their dissertations, while her books are widely used in sociology and literature classes as well as in women's studies and African-American studies class, I have heard many a white scholar, female and male, insist that hooks does not articulate theories. Rather she reacts to others' theories, uses inappropriate language, and has no scholarly methodology. I believe, although it is never really said, that her work is suspect because it is so popular. While I certainly do not agree with everything hooks has ever written, I consider her work to be an example of theorizing, of making connections between many different forms of intellectual disciplines, as well as between the so-called popular cultural terrain and intellectual marketplaces. She has emphasized how she has consciously chosen to locate her work "in the margin." Not one "imposed by oppressive structures" but one she has chosen as a "site of resistance — as location of radical openness and possibility."[23]

Perhaps some academics' assessment of bell hooks and other black intellectuals has to do with another bias. Professor Andrew Hacker, the author of the much celebrated study *Two Nations: Separate, Hostile and Unequal*, believes that many black intellectuals "rely on more discursive modes of analysis as opposed to the more schematic linear method embodied in the multiple-choice matrix and — later on — the formats expected for academic research." Thus, "they are seen as failing to internalize and adapt to white mental ways," that is, of not assimilating intellectually.[24] Whether all African-American intellectuals can be so characterized is a question for debate. The point, however, that Hacker is making has more to do with the monolithic standard as to what "real" scholarship is and how it should be expressed.

Can one be a *successful* academic, artist, or writer and still be seen as an African-American woman? I recall the many times television and radio commentators stated, on the occasion of Toni Morrison's recent receipt of the Nobel Prize for Literature, that she was not *just* an African-American woman writer, she was a universal writer. I wrote a piece on Morrison's receipt of the Nobel Prize which emphasized that she wrote as an African-American woman writer. I got letters in response from white women readers who were upset that I had "limited" her by locating her in that tradition. In other words, if you're really good, you somehow are no longer an African-American woman. African-American writers have had to contend with such responses, ones that have "limited" their access to the literary establishments of the West and, thus, to other "Third World" countries whose educational systems take their cue from the West. Clearly, the literary tradition is surviving that assault, and I suspect that black feminism(s) in the academy will, too.

Besides, the point is, and it is an important point, that there is joy in struggle, a fact that a few genuinely wonderful students of mine, female and male, African-American, colored, and white, have understood and have demonstrated

178   *Diminishing Returns: Can Black Feminism(s) Survive*

in their teaching, writing, and campus and community activism, thus regenerating these old bones of mine. We will survive in the academy.

Still, it is important that those of us who understand the importance of black feminist thought's role in the academy be clear about the dire situation that African-American women academics face; in other words, praxis is central to our survival. We need not only fancy treatises on *Beloved* or smart feminist theses that include black feminisms. We need nuts and bolts action. We need to ask questions that at first glance may seem to have nothing to do with scholarship but are central to our survival. For example, how many African-American women and men graduate students are there at my institution? Can we conceive of that idea that oftentimes their projects and the ways in which they pursue them might be incomprehensible to our sense of what scholarly enterprises should be about? Can we think about how narrowly defined our own definition of scholarship might be? Do we really subscribe to the idea the feminist scholarship should be interventionist, should change our view of society, and therefore of our site, the university?

I fear that if we do not engage these issues, potential black feminist scholars, faced with diminishing returns, may have to reconsider whether the academy is a suitable site for them or whether more gains in scholarship and intellectual inquiry may lie elsewhere. If that occurs, the academy will be the loser.

Notes

1 This paper was originally written for a conference entitled "Figuring Feminism at the Fin-de-Siecle," sponsored by Scripps College Humanities Institute and the Claremont Graduate Humanities Center, to be published by Stanford University Press, edited by Kari Weil.

2 See "The Backlash Debate," *Time*, 139, 10 (March 9, 1992), pp. 50–7. Also see "'I'm Not a Feminist, But …'," *San Francisco Chronicle, This World* section (February 23, 1992), pp. 7, 9–11.

3 Wendy Kaminer "Feminism's Identity Crisis," *The Atlantic*, 272, 4 (October 1993), pp. 51–68. Even Susan Faludi's more respectable study, *Backlash* (New York: Crown, 1991) does not pay much attention to African-American women's contributions to the development of feminist concepts.

4 See Paula Giddings' *When and Where I Enter* (New York: W. Morrow, 1984), a marvelous historical study of African-American women except that it gives short shrift to the women involved in cultural transformation, such as Frances Harper.

5 Deborah King, "Multiple Jeopardy, Multiple Consciousness: The Context of a Black Feminist Ideology," in *Feminist Theory in Practice and Process*, eds Micheline R. Malson, Jean F. O'Barr, Sarah Westphal-Wihl, and Mary Wyer, (Chicago: The University of Chicago Press, 1989), p. 105.

6 For a popular view of the way in which most white women in this country do not call themselves feminist, while a good proportion of them believe in and/or practice

its basic tenets, take a look at Wendy Kaminer's quite conservative article in *The Atlantic*, October 1993. See also Susan Faludi's *Backlash*.

7 Barbara T. Christian, "What Do We Think We're Doing," in Changing Our Own Words: Essays on Criticism, Theory and Writing by Black Women, ed. Cheryl Wall (New Brunswick, NJ: Rutgers University Press, 1991), pp. 58–74.

8 "Introduction," to *Feminist Theory in Practice and Process*, eds Macheline R. Malson, Jean F. O'Barr, Sarah Westphal-Wihl and Mary Wyer (Chicago: University of Chicago Press, 1989).

9 See Barbara T. Christian et al. "Conference Call," *differences*, 2 (Fall, 1990), pp. 52–108. For a comprehensive and brilliant analysis on this issue published after I completed this essay, see Ann duCille, "The Occult of True Black Womanhood: Critical Demeanor and Black Feminist Studies," *Signs: Journal of Women in Culture and Society*, 19, 3 (Spring 1994), pp. 591–629.

10 See Patricia Hill Collins, *Black Feminist Thought: Knowledge, Consciousness and the Politics of Empowerment* (Boston: Unwin Hyman Publishers, 1990).

11 Chandra Talpade Mohanty, "Under Western Eyes: Feminist Scholarship and Colonial Discourses," *Boundary 2*, 12, 3 (1984), pp. 333–58.

12 Patricia Hill Collins, *Black Feminist Thought*, p. 202.

13 Barbara T. Christian, "Polylogue on Feminism and the Institution," *Differences: A Journal of Feminist Cultural Studies*, 2 (Fall 1990), p. 57.

14 Andrew Hacker, "Why the Shortage of Black Professors?" *The Journal of Blacks in Higher Education*, 1, 1 (Autumn 1993), p. 32.

15 *The Journal of Blacks in Higher Education*, 1, 1 (Autumn 1993), pp. 23–5.

16 "Introduction," *Spirit, Space and Survival: African-American Women in (White) Academe*, eds Joy James and Ruth Farmer (New York: Routledge, 1993), p. 2.

17 Ibid., p. 3.

18 Martin Anderson in "Why the Shortage of Black Professors," *The Journal of Blacks in Higher Education*, 1 (Autumn 1992), p. 34.

19 Adrienne Andrews, "Balancing the Personal and the Professional," *Spirit, Space and Survival*, p. 183. See also: Yolanda Moses' study, *Black Women in Academia: Issues and Stratus* (Baltimore: Project on the Status of Education of Women, August 1989).

20 Ibid., p. 190.

21 Johnnetta B. Cole, "Why the Shortage of Black Professors?" *The Journal of Blacks in Higher Education*, 1, 1 (Autumn 1993), p. 30.

22 Joy James, "Teaching Theory, Talking Community," *Spirit, Space and Survival*, p. 121.

23 bell hooks, *Yearning: Race, Gender and Cultural Politics* (Boston: South End Press, 1990), p. 153.

24 Andrew Hacker, "Why the Shortage of Black Professors," p. 33.

8

On Being a Role Model

Anita L. Allen[1]

I. The Journalist's Question

In the spring of 1990, Harvard Law School students demanding faculty diversity[2] took over the Dean's office.[3] Derrick Bell, Harvard's first and most senior black law professor, announced that he would sacrifice his $120,000 annual salary until the Law School tenured a black woman.[4] Bell's action soon became a mass media event, and my telephone began to ring.

Most callers were friends who knew that a month before the students' protests and Bell's announcement, I had accepted Dean Robert Clark's offer to teach at Harvard as a Visiting Professor of Law. Clark's offer had been flexible; I would be welcome any time within the next few years. A variety of personal and professional considerations had seemed to point toward visiting sooner rather than later. Therefore, in consultation with the husband I would have to leave behind and my Georgetown dean, I had made arrangements to teach at Harvard during the 1990–91 academic year. Now friends wondered whether I regretted my plans. They inquired whether, as a black woman, I viewed the unresolved, nationally publicized diversity drama as a reason to renege on my agreement to begin at Harvard in September 1990.

One memorable caller was not a friend, but a savvy newspaper reporter. She phoned to ask what I thought of the "role model argument" Professor Bell purportedly used in urging his school to hire black women. The journalist explained that, according to the role model argument, the primary justification for adding black females to a law faculty that may already include black males and white females is that black female law students need black female role models.[5] The reporter's pointed question caught me off guard. I resorted to equivocation, mouthing something mildly approving of the role model argument, followed by something mildly critical of it.

After the call, I began to think seriously about the case for black female role models in American law schools. I pondered a stance which at first seemed ambivalent, then inconsistent, and finally correct. Black women law teachers have unique contributions to make as role models for black female law students. Yet, incautious, isolated appeals to role modeling capacities are potentially risky. They can obscure the wider range of good reasons institutions have for recruiting black women to their faculties. They also can obscure the fact that some very accomplished black women may fit no one's ideal description of the "positive" minority role model.

I believe there are good reasons for hiring black women that have little or nothing to do with role modeling. It abundantly is evident that black women can teach, write, and do committee work as well as anyone else. Individual black women, in fact, often excel at one or more of these tasks. To be sure, individual black women also often excel as role models. It is nonetheless misleading to single out role modeling and purport to rank it as the "primary" or "only" reason schools have for appointing black women to their faculties.

The significance to black women of black women teachers must be more widely understood if there is to be serious public discussion of the role model argument for faculty diversity. In the first three sections of this essay, I share what my personal experiences suggest to me about the value of black women teachers and role models to black women students. In the remaining three sections, I elaborate my sense of the adverse implications of premising the recruitment of black women law teachers solely or primarily on their role modeling potential. The fate of women of color in higher education depends upon recognizing the power and the limitations of the role model argument.

II. Meritocracy and Suspicion

Black women teachers have never been found in great numbers in higher education outside of historically black colleges and universities.[6] Not everyone looks to the ugly legacy of American race relations to explain our conspicuous absence. Some, instead, attribute our absence to the failure of civil rights legislation or affirmative action policies to produce an adequate pool of qualified applicants. Some believe that taking advantage of whatever black women have to offer is not worth the affront to the principle of meritocracy that our inclusion would supposedly entail.

The idea that higher education should reflect the nation's cultural diversity is sometimes referred to as "multiculturalism." As interpreted by its most heartfelt supporters, multiculturalism requires much more than that colleges and universities lower formally-unjust barriers to admission. It requires affirmative efforts on the part of faculty and administrators to insure that the cultural perspectives, histories, and contributions of minority groups receive appropriate emphasis. It also requires efforts that aid the struggles of minority students to achieve up to their individual capacities. So conceived, the multicultural ideal may seem to justify the policy of providing same-kind minority role models — such as black female teachers for black female students — who can contribute curricular diversity while attending the special needs of minority students. However, many of the egalitarian impulses that underlie multiculturalism are compromised by popular uses of the role model argument for faculty diversity.

As developed below, the role model argument is deeply problematic. It mischaracterizes black women's actual and potential contributions. The argument encourages the inference that black women are inferior intellectuals and that white teachers have no role to play in addressing the special needs of black students. The quest for "positive" minority role models demanded by the role model argument risks stereotyping minorities on the basis of race and gender, imposing upon black women teachers the felt obligation to be perfectly "black" and perfectly "female."

History teaches that the seemingly sacred principle of meritocracy has often been applied selectively as a rule of convenience. At one time, the putative principle was ignored to the detriment of the Jewish-Americans who sought admission to elite schools. Earlier in the century, former President Abbott L. Lowell of Harvard defended quotas designed to exclude Jews on the ground that whatever superior intellectual accomplishment they had to offer over less intelligent white Christian students was not worth the affront to the ideal of the well-rounded character demanded by American business and government.[7]

In the past, traditionalists criticized schools like Harvard for opening their doors to Jews. These schools paid a price in lost alumni donations. Institutions that hire white women and minorities still pay a price. A law student I know recently participated in a telephone fundraising campaign on behalf of Harvard Law School. She reports contacting a number of older alumni who flatly refused to contribute on the ground that the law school faculty now includes women and blacks.

As an activist for faculty diversity, Derrick Bell pays a price, too. Professor Bell's controversial decision to give up his salary until Harvard tenures a black woman law teacher was viewed widely as not only coercive, but ridiculous. How could anyone seriously expect Harvard Law School to award tenure on demand? And to a black woman! The ridicule Bell drew for his "woman of color" emphasis underscored the fact that including black women in higher education arouses inherent suspicion.

The concept of black women teaching in white schools is suspect in part because the experience of having black women as teachers is unfamiliar to many faculty and students. Lack of familiarity is how I explain an undergraduate's hostile challenge on the first day of the first class I ever taught. The year was 1976. I was a doctoral student in philosophy and a teaching fellow at the University of

Michigan. "What gives you the right to teach this class?" the young white man asked, when I introduced myself as his instructor.

Ironically, distrust of black women infects minority students as well as whites. This accounts for why an ambitious black law student in Washington, DC told me he would not dream of taking a class from a black professor of either gender. He said he wanted to learn "the same thing the white boys are learning."

The academics and media pundits who have been most strident in their opposition to the role model argument have probably rarely, if ever, been taught by a black woman. The same is probably also true of many supporters of the role model argument, and many of the young black women, born in the 1960s, on whose behalf the role model argument is currently advanced. Both sides lack personal experience with what black women have to offer in the classroom. I am scarcely better off. If I can boast first-hand experience with black women teachers, it is only because certain childhood memories have stubbornly resisted oblivion.

III. My Teachers

A. Black Educators

My first school teacher was a black woman. Reaching her was not easy. Each weekday morning, a military bus, the brown-green color of my father's fatigues, arrived on our block. We climbed aboard, black and white playmates together, headed with all deliberate speed to our separate but equal schools in the next town. The long trip from Fort McClellan to Anniston, Alabama, was saddening, especially when I travelled alone. Most of the time I was the only child making the special journey required of five-year-old children of Negro servicemen needing kindergarten.

The Jim Crow journey began when the federal government's school bus dropped me off on a street corner near my teacher's house.[8] She met me promptly and took me to her bungalow. Inside, we waited. She filled those hours nursing her elderly mother and tidying her clutter. I sat still or moved cautiously among ceramic figurines and delicate needlework. When it was time, this teacher, whose name is long forgotten, drove the two of us to school — the windowless basement of a red-brick Presbyterian church.

Private Negro education in the year 1958 cost my parents five dollars per month. Their money got me an ample desk squeezed between church things: boxes of abandoned hymnals and dusty stacks of folding chairs. My teacher assigned painful, real work. Pupils of promise, with parents able to buy books, read and wrote, added and subtracted, seriously. At recess a swarm of children, friends from the neighborhood, laughed and played out of doors under relaxed supervision. But I stood in the shade of an enormous oak tree, a xenophobic stranger, overwhelmed and overdisciplined, combatting tears.

At the end of the school day, the journey was reversed. I travelled from church to teacher's house; house to bus stop; bus to base; then, home, to family and friends. Safe again, I soared beside my baby sister Pumpkin in a backyard swing, belting out radio songs about purple people-eaters and that clown Charlie Brown.

My second school teacher was also a black woman. Everything she was supposed to teach me, I had already learned in the church basement. So, her bright classroom at E. C. Clements public elementary school in Atlanta was a picnic. From my great-grandmother's house I eagerly walked the half mile to school with Red Cynt, Garney Perkins, and cousins who straightened their hair with Vaseline. In class, I broke sugar cookies into tiny enough pieces to sweeten the days of anyone stuck with mayonnaise sandwiches for lunch and whispered the answers to test questions, all in the innocent spirit of sharing. When my mother gave birth to her first son and we were finally able to fly to Hawaii to join my father, I was not anxious to go.

My third school teacher was also a black woman. Miss Bradley was to be my last black teacher until I enrolled at Harvard Law School twenty years later. At Harvard I would be assigned to Clyde Ferguson's course on Civil Procedure, and I would sign up for Christopher Edley's courses on tax and administrative law. But when I was new to Oahu, the elementary school at Wheeler Air Force Base, and Miss Bradley's rainbow of Caucasian, Hispanic, Asian, Pacific Island, and African ancestry first-graders, I preferred standing close by the teacher to joining in unfamiliar games. But Miss Bradley pushed me away, exhorting me to "go and play with the other children." Wounded, I took her sage advice. Years later, standing too close, too long by Professor Ferguson at law school orientation, he would seem to send essentially the same message. I tried to take his advice, too.

The black women teachers of my childhood were wholly credible. They taught demeanor and responsibility. They defied the odds, worked extra hard, and cared. Both because of who they were and who I am, it is impossible for me to share, or even to comprehend, others' automatic suspicions that women of color in higher education are inferior.

B. White Educators

While males are the dominant group in American higher education, they are the most numerous academic role models for black women. For most women of my generation who pursued higher education, white males were just about the only academic role models we had. In addition to the seven years I spent in college and law school, I spent four years in graduate school earning a Ph.D. In those eleven years, I had no black female professors. I had only three white female professors, two black male professors, and one Korean male professor. The rest, dozens, were white males.

My white male college teachers at New College in Sarasota, Florida, were, by and large, good academic role models. One of the best admitted that, when he saw me walk into an advanced philosophy class freshman year, he did not think I belonged there. He was right. At 17, I was overconfident. He concealed his skepticism until I returned two decades later to deliver the commencement address. To help me along he tutored me outside of class, invited me into his family home, sponsored my senior thesis, and helped me choose a graduate school.

One of the worst white male academic role models I encountered at New College was a professor who suggested, before getting to know me or my work, that I should become an airline stewardess rather than try to complete college. This same professor privately accused me of plagiarizing an independent study project. He could not believe I was the author of what he regarded as a very good paper.

For the longest time, there were so few professional women in my life to serve as role models that I did not have a clue as to how an aspiring female scholar should behave. Once, when I was a first-year graduate student, I crocheted a lace doily during a guest lecture by a famous philosopher. A friendly professor advised me against further public needlework until I had "established [myself] in the field."

I never crocheted again, and increasingly looked to my professors and classmates — virtually all white men — to figure out how to comport myself. I ate what they ate; spoke as they spoke; wrote as they wrote. When I went into philosophy teaching at Carnegie–Mellon University in the late 1970s, it took me a year to figure out that my students would be more cooperative if I simply took off the blue jeans and button-down collar shirts I had learned to wear, imitating white males, and put on a dress.

Today, as in the 1970s and 1980s when I was a student, white male college, university, and professional school teachers are often poor role models for black female students. Whites fail as positive role models when they communicate a lack of confidence in black students or simply ignore them. A white male law teacher at Harvard once told me point blank that he aimed his classes at the conservative white males whom he wished to rattle with progressive sensibilities before they took off for Wall Street. He had defined a pedagogical agenda that expressly excluded blacks.

Several of my white male professors were poor role models because they allowed their alcoholism, their drug dependencies, and their psychological problems to interfere with their teaching and scholarship or because they were curiously indifferent to students with such problems. Needless to say, white males are also poor role models for black women when they engage in sexual harassment. White women are not the sole victims of sexual harassment in the university. Two of my graduate school teachers at the University of Michigan flunked the positive role model test on this score, including the man I dropped as an advisor after he kissed me on the mouth the first time we got together to discuss my work.

The ethos of significant segments of mainstream intellectual culture includes distrust of ethnicity-specific and feminist studies. Professors who never mention relevant work of people of color, our history, our problems, our contributions, and our perspectives cannot be nurturing, positive role models. Professors, of whatever gender or hue, who sneer, roll their eyes, or become impatient when a student wants to know the value of a line of inquiry for people like her, are not positive academic role models. Professors who dismiss black females' perspectives and are hostile to efforts to bring scholarly tools to the interpretation of our experiences are not positive role models. Regrettably, a black woman looking for mentors runs a gauntlet of teachers who subtly communicate that it is inappropriate for a serious academic or lawyer to care about black women, and even worse to be one.

IV. The Case for Black Women Role Models

It will sound self-serving to insist upon this point, but black women teachers have something special to offer students. Some of what black women law teachers do, say, and write is indistinguishable from the contributions of their black, white, brown, red, or yellow male colleagues. It does not follow, however, that black women law teachers are superfluous.

Black female students deserve teachers who will assume their competence. They deserve teachers who will motivate them to do their best work, listen with understanding, and validate their life experiences. Black female students deserve teachers who will sponsor special events and provide insight into how to deal professionally and sanely with the problems women of color inevitably face in legal practice and the academy. Many black women teachers are interested in helping black female students in just these ways.

I believe that certain experiences black women law professors have had, precisely as black women, have led to the development of personal skills, social perspectives, and concerns to which law students are beneficially exposed. As a student, lawyer, and teacher, I have had more than one experience that has challenged my professionalism and taught me lessons I am now prepared to share with students. Consider the time a white male professor told me that as a black woman I would "have to pee on the floor" at job interviews not to get hired. Consider my first day as a summer associate at a Wall Street law firm: a partner asked me to write a memorandum explaining why private clubs have a constitutional right to exclude women and minorities from membership. When I expressed my disapproval of race and gender discrimination, he cheerily replied that he was not interested in the "sociological considerations."

Consider, too, the time a white female student in a class I taught told me that she did not get along with black people. Or the time another of my students announced to a racially diverse group discussing affirmative action that "there are no intelligent black people in Oklahoma." Her evidence? She explained that the public school system in her home town, previously headed by a black woman, had gone bankrupt.

And then there was the time my husband and I attended a Georgetown basketball game at the invitation of faculty colleagues. An irate white fan seated behind me screamed, "Nigger, nigger," as a black official escorted unruly white youths out of the auditorium. My mild-mannered spouse leapt to his feet and grabbed the fan by the collar, daring him to repeat further epithets. The fan muttered something about keeping our noses out of his business, but quickly backed down. Situations like these simultaneously place dignity, safety, and careers on the line.

Racial insensitivity, prejudice, and racism are facts of life. For women of color, sexism and sexual harassment magnify race-related burdens. Black female students have much to learn from black female teachers. We know what it is to experience insecurity about the stereotypes of black women as fit only for sex and servitude, or as having faces that belong on cookie jars or syrup bottles rather than on the pages of bar journals.

Last spring, a middle-aged white college professor who attended a presentation I made to the American Association of University Professors on the problem of discriminatory harassment on campuses, told me that I should not mind being called a "jungle bunny." "After all," he said, "you are pretty cute and so are bunnies." Once, an eminent white scholar with whom I was dining suddenly took my chin into his hand to inspect my face. He told me, approvingly, that I resembled his family's former maid.

In a different vein, on a hot day on which I had my kinky hair tied back in a bandanna, a white colleague innocently remarked that I looked liked comedian Eddie Murphy's parody of "Buckwheat." My valued friend was unaware of the negative connotations the unkempt, wild-haired, inarticulate "Our Gang" character has for me as a southern black. However, I felt slighted by the comparison, as did my incredulous black female secretary, who sputtered, "But, but Buckwheat is ugly!"

Black women may be better able to take themselves seriously as intellectuals knowing that others like them are concerned professors, deans, provosts, and university presidents. Black female law students benefit from opportunities in law school to relate precisely as black women to some of their teachers. Recent encounters at Georgetown Law Center, where I am a professor, have persuaded me of the value of dealing closely with women students. These encounters have breathed new life into the adage that educated blacks must be role models for the next generation.

Last year I attended a meeting called by students to discuss why many women feel alienated in law school and silenced in the classroom. The significance of gender was on everyone's mind. But it was plain that the group of mainly white women was barely aware of the significance of class and racial divisions among women. For example, a white student stated that she had heard enough of a Hispanic classmate's criticism of our school's meager loan repayment assistance program and wished to return to the subject of alienation in the classroom. She added that should the Latina have financial problems after law school stemming from a decision to pursue public interest law, she could always contact her, "a person of privilege and increasing privilege," for help.

After this meeting I was anxious to focus attention on diversity among women. I invited a multiracial group of about twenty female Georgetown law students to my home to view a Hollywood film about black, white, and mulatto women struggling in New York City in the 1950s. The crowded, informal meeting in my living room was the most ethnically diverse group one of the white women who came said she had ever experienced. Another white student said that, prior to our evening together, she had never before been part of the racial minority in any social setting. The next week this same student wrote me a thank-you note. The moving note enclosed a photocopy of a page from her diary recounting a remarkable dream she had had months before while she was a student in my torts class. The dream was about "a tall, beautiful black woman with dreadlocks" trying to give her some important information "disruptive to the status quo," when a threatening, obese white man in his fifties "pulls out a revolver and shoots her in the stomach."[9] It seems that our students think about race and gender whether we discuss it with them or not.

Several of the black women who came to my home said that interacting that evening with white classmates was new to them. One black woman revealed that she did not initiate conversations with whites at law school except to conduct business. A black professor on the faculty of an elite New England college told me a few days later that she, too, rarely strikes up conversations with whites. Black students in my classes who had never spoken to me or participated in class poured forth their perspectives as law students, but also as wives, mothers, and workers. Thereafter, one of them began stopping by my office and became more animated in class. She did very well on my anonymously-graded jurisprudence examination.

V. Against the Role Model Argument

A. Attenuated Support for Affirmative Action

Against the background of the compelling case for black women role models, the role model argument for hiring black women teachers has a certain appeal. In the age of racially integrated higher education, the role model argument acknowledges that black women are indispensable. The argument provides a pragmatic link for affirmative action proponents between the case for affirmative action in student admissions, on the one hand, and the case for affirmative action in faculty hiring, on the other. According to the role model argument heard today, white institutions that now admit significant numbers of black females need energetic black women to teach, counsel, mentor, and inspire.

Affirmative action policies that increase black admissions proportionately increase the need for black female role models. Affirmative action policies that increase admissions opportunities for blacks also potentially increase the overall number of black role models available to future generations.[10] But the relationship between the case for affirmative action and the case for black role models is not as close as one might suppose. Logically speaking, the soundness of the role model argument does not entail or presuppose the soundness of the argument for affirmative action. A stern opponent of affirmative action could favor hiring black female role models to improve the educational experiences of students "wrongly" admitted on an affirmative action basis.

Black teachers, like black students, may be fitting beneficiaries of affirmative action. But the role model argument defends employing black women on utilitarian grounds referring to student and institutional need, rather than on grounds referring to compensatory justice or to our own remedial desert.[11] It is worth noting also that, because the role model argument does not entail the justice or prudence of affirmative action, it follows that the role model argument is neutral as among each of the proposed rationales for affirmative action — racism, inequality, and past injustice.[12]

Affirmative action arguments are sometimes premised on the perceived importance of empowering blacks economically, politically and socially. Advocates also discuss black empowerment as an important objective quite apart from the fate of affirmative action programs. As individuals and as communities, blacks undeniably need more and better political representation, and more and better economic resources. Blacks need healthier and more harmonious social lives. Without these forms of empowerment, pluralist ideals of democratic self-government lack real meaning.

Empowerment presupposes education. Black female role models are potential power enhancers. Black female educators can help black citizens manage autonomous communities, share power with other groups, and give voice to blacks' concerns. Black women's presence in higher education promises to help lift the political and economic status of blacks. The presence of black women professors is also evidence of our actual power as minority group members situated to help set educational and scholarly priorities.

However, the romantic image of black women as inherent power-enhancers is misleading. If, as sometimes happens, black women professors are either disaffected or marginalized by colleagues and scholarly associates, then our presence does not truly indicate that blacks are sharing or will someday significantly share power with other groups. Keeping black women out of academia surely thwarts black empowerment. But, regrettably, letting us in does not guarantee it.

B. Ambiguity: Templates, Symbols and Nurturers

The role model argument loses some of its initial luster when one begins to appreciate the attenuated character of its logical ties to arguments for affirmative action and black community empowerment. Even a racist can embrace the role model argument, and adding black women teachers to university faculties does not guarantee significant empowerment. The role model argument loses additional appeal upon appreciation of the ambiguity it tolerates. In some senses of the popular term, being a black woman is neither a necessary nor a sufficient condition for being a role model for black women students.

All teachers are role models. But not every teacher is a role model in every sense. All teachers are role models in one familiar sense. They "model" their roles as teachers. They are what I will call "ethical templates," men and women whose conduct sets standards for the exercise of responsibilities. Only some teachers are role models in the stronger, equally familiar senses I will label "symbols" of special achievement and "nurturers" of students' special needs.

Like other teachers, law school teachers are role models in the "ethical template" sense. The manner in which faculty members exercise their responsibilities as teachers sets standards for how responsibilities ought to be exercised. As ethical templates, teachers can set high standards or low ones. What law school teachers say and do suggests something to their students about what law school teachers ought to say and do. The conduct of law professors also carries general messages about the exercise of responsibility in adult roles other than teaching, especially the roles of attorney and judge.

Educators are not the only role models in the "ethical templates" sense. However, notorious acts of professional misconduct have led to fears that youth have few credible, laudable ethical templates for adult roles in any field. The virtual national crisis over the decline in ethical standards led a reporter for the *New York Times* recently to make a grim survey: "[W]ho are the role models? Mayor Marion Barry of Washington? Michael Milken of Wall Street? Ben Johnson, the disqualified Olympic sprint champion? Defrauders of savings and loans institutions?"[13]

A laudable template need not be viewed as laudable. Derrick Bell's poor reception as a visiting professor at Stanford Law School several years ago can perhaps be explained as students' devaluation of his modeling of the constitutional law professor role.[14] Disgruntled students rounded up a white male professor to teach them supplementary classes from which Bell was excluded. As a black visiting professor, Bell represented a new kind of template. Students assigned to his class wanted to be taught constitutional law from a "traditional" professor's perspective.

Law students may resist teachers for reasons unrelated to race and tradition. They sometimes reject academic lawyers as poor ethical templates for the roles of practicing attorney and judge. Harvard law student Brian Melendez was recently quoted in the American Bar Association Journal doing just that. He said he "wouldn't really call [professors who expound theory and develop new approaches to the law] role models because most of them have never practiced."[15] In hiring judges and practicing attorneys onto their faculties, law schools provide experts students can readily embrace as role models in the term's "ethical template" sense. The ability of students to embrace their teachers as credible templates may be critical for successful clinical legal education.[16]

Law teachers are ethical templates, but they can be role models in another sense. They can be symbols of special achievement. Indeed, in the only sense acknowledged by philosophers Judith Thomson and George Sher, role models are individuals who inspire others to believe that they, too, may be capable of high accomplishment.[17] Kent Greenawalt had this understanding in mind when he described the utilitarian, "role models for those in the minority community" argument for racial preferences.[18] Minority group members and white women are not the only ones who can be symbols of special achievement, of course. A white man from a poor, troubled home who succeeds through hard work in a chosen profession can serve as a role model for others of his same background.[19]

Law teachers who directly engage students through mentoring, tutoring, counselling, and sponsoring special cultural or scholarly events are role models in a third sense. They are nurturers. Educators sometimes assume nurturing roles as supererogatory commitments to students they believe would not be adequately served by mere templates and symbols.

Blacks hired as symbols may turn out to be nurturers. Robert K. Fullinwider suggested that implicit in the rationale for placing blacks in "visible and desirable positions" is the possibility that we will provide "better services to the black community."[20] This is not to overlook the existence of intensive programs that take the provision of nurturing role models, as opposed to mere symbols, as among their central purposes.[21]

The roles of template, symbol, and nurturer are often conflated in using role model arguments for including black women in higher education. As a practical matter, it is not always important to distinguish between the template, the symbol, and the nurturer. As templates, our mere presences can reshape conceptions of who can teach law, and of what law teachers appropriately do and say. Moreover, many black women teachers serve willingly and well, both as symbols and as nurturers.

However, some black women "symbols" do not give a "nurturer's" priority to the advancement of the interests of black students and wider black communities. And a few nonsymbol white males do. In arguments for academic role models for black women, the tasks one expects the role model to perform must be clearly specified. Not every black woman will be willing or able to perform every task.

C. Whispers of Inferiority

Whether premised on the template, the symbol or the nurturer conception, the role model argument for recruiting black women faculty has serious limitations. One problem with the role model argument is that while it trumpets our necessity, it whispers our inferiority. Black women, like black men, often are presumed to be at the bottom of the intellectual heap. Employing us is perceived as stepping over the deserving in favor of the least able. Unlike arguments that aggressively contest mainstream notions of merit, qualification, and competence, the role model argument gives white males a reason for hiring minority women that is perfectly consistent with traditional assumptions of white male intellectual superiority.

Unassisted by other arguments, the role model argument leaves intact the presumption that black women have third-rate intellects. The argument makes it possible to assume that black women can be more competent than whites only insofar as they are better role models. The inability of many academics to communicate with blacks and women is indeed an incompetence, but not one of which the society teaches anyone who is not black or female to be especially ashamed. If schools are encouraged to premise hiring black women primarily or solely on the ground that we are better than others at guiding our kind, faculties may avoid confronting the truth that black women think, research, and write as well as whites.

Institutions that employ role model arguments cannot avoid issues of merit entirely. Not every black woman has the same educational credentials. Some black women will be better symbols or nurturers than others. Schools may believe they are looking for flawless symbols, or symbols who are also tireless nurturers. This, I take it, is what is meant when the quest for role models to hire, promote, and tenure is described as a quest for positive role models.

Sadly, being a positive black role model often seems to require acting as much like an educated upper-middle-class white person as possible, consistent with an ability to participate meaningfully in elite African-American community life. Looking and speaking like whites has always helped would-be positive role models. In the 1970s to be viewed as a positive academic role model at some institutions required eschewing scholarly interest in black studies. By contrast, some faculty members seem willing to defend overt ethnic identification as a precondition for serving as positive role models for black students.

In the 1980s, blacks and whites were heard to advance the claim that there is no point to employing as a law professor a black without a culturally different "voice." Being a diversity symbol, it was argued, is not enough for minority educators. The ideal positive black role model would have ties to the black community, manifest in scholarship and in a willingness to work closely with black students. She would project an image or approach teaching in a way that would aggressively forge new ethical templates for the teaching role. Faculties may feel pressure to hire a certain kind of black by students who complain, as one did a few years ago in my presence, about faculty who are not "black enough." Incredibly, a white professor in New York wrote a letter to his school's affirmative action office in October 1990 complaining that the role model argument did not justify the appointment of a certain fair-skinned black professor, because he was too fair.[22]

In addition to ethnic self-identification and commitments, wearing her feminism on her sleeve and showing a willingness to work with female students sometimes have seemed to be further requirements of the positive black female role model. Thus, when combined with the inevitable quest for positive role models — unfailing symbols and nurturers — the role model argument risks imposing stereotypes of race and gender in the name of accommodating diversity.

D. Fraudulent Undervaluation

Understandably, some black female academics resent the role model argument. We resent it in the way that we resent all faint praise. It undervalues. Black women may want badly to help educate and inspire black students. But we know we are smarter and more valuable even than our status as role models implies. Black women are valuable to students of all races and to our institutions generally. We teach classes, write, and serve on committees just like our colleagues. At some institutions we publish more and get better teaching evaluations than do our average white colleagues, many of whom were hired when standards were lower than they are now.

I have heard black women teachers swear that they spend more time talking to white students than their white colleagues do, and that they talk about a greater variety of personal and professional problems. My black students at Georgetown have rarely claimed as much of my time as have my white students. Black students stay away, explaining that they do not want to presume special privileges with black faculty. They worry about how it would look if they regularly spoke to black faculty after class or appeared to monopolize office hours. Some black students use the same rationale for not actively participating in class discussion.

Abstracted from the full spectrum of our capacities and contributions, the role model argument is thus a damning understatement. Our utility includes our contribution to black students, but is greater still. Moreover, the role model argument is a kind of "bait and switch." We are hired ostensibly to be templates, symbols and nurturers. Then we are expected to do scholarship and much more for which we are seldom separately recognized or separately compensated.

E. Psychological Burdens

In candid conversation with black women teachers, one learns that the "role model" label, even willingly embraced, can be a special psychological burden. It makes those of us who take it seriously worry that we have to be perfect — perfectly black, not just black; perfectly female, not just female. Since we are told that our reason-for-being is that we are role models, we attach undue weight to everything we do.

Not only how and what we choose to teach — corporations versus race relations versus family law — but even how we wear our hair takes on special importance. If we straighten our hair, we fear black female students will infer that it is necessary for black female lawyers to have straight hair. If we braid our hair, we fear black female students will infer that they should take their braids to the Justice Department.

At the University of Pittsburgh, the Black Law Students Association sponsored a party to welcome me as the school's first black female law professor. When male members of the student group boycotted the party, I discovered that an aspiring role model's choice of spouse can interfere with her function. A white male colleague in whom the black males confided explained that the students' discovery that my husband is white had played a role in creating the misimpression that I did not "speak" to blacks. I was annoyed; but I was genuinely concerned that my personal life had permanently undercut my ability to nurture some black students.

In sum, the role model argument seems to imply that black women are intellectual inferiors, unqualified for anything but serving as role models for blacks. Serving as role models for blacks is splendid, urgent service. But the role model argument downplays the other important teaching, scholarly, or institutional contributions black women make. It ignores that our employers pile on duties besides role modeling. Demanding that we be precisely as black as others want us to be, the role model argument imposes taxing ideals of perfection based, in part, on stereotypes of our cultures and identities.

F. White Men Off the Hook

In media coverage of the diversity debates spawned by events at Harvard Law School in 1990, the role model argument sometimes stood alone as a provocative "sound bite." The argument is not at its best as a stand-alone. It casts too tall a shadow, obscuring the full range of good reasons schools have for hiring black women and we black women have for valuing ourselves.

A final problem with the role model argument is that it signals to faculty members who are not black females that they may abandon efforts to serve as positive role models for black women. The logic of the role model argument is such that it lets most faculty off the hook when it comes to educating black women.

The argument implies that some blacks are simply unreachable — unteachable — by nonblacks. While it may be viewed as responsibly recognizing the reality of racial and gender differences, the role model argument must also be seen as providing teachers who are not black women with a convenient excuse to remain inept at dealing with black women in their classrooms. The role model argument justifies hiring black female teachers, but it also condones a degree of indifference toward black female students. Black women have much to learn from white faculty who care to extend themselves. Thus, trying to hire black females solely as role models looks disturbingly close to something privileged Americans have always done: hire black women to perform the tiresome, unappealing tasks.

G. Honest Rhetoric

In the final analysis, it is plain that we should applaud black female role models, but reject the journalist's version of the role model argument — that the principal reason for adding black women to a faculty that may already include white women and black men is that they are role models. We should not pretend that we can rank-order the many good reasons for hiring black women any more than we should pretend that we can rank-order the many good reasons for hiring other categories of teachers. We should also reject any version of the role model argument that portrays role modeling capacities as the only reason to hire black women. It is futile scholasticism to speculate about whether role modeling capacities could be a sufficient reason for hiring a black woman since they, in fact, never would be.

Rejecting exclusive use of role model arguments to persuade schools to hire black women is consistent with the reality that all teachers, black women included, are role models in the "ethical template" sense. It also is consistent with the moral expectation that blacks will take responsibility, as symbols and nurturers, for educating blacks. Concern for black students is paramount among reasons for rejecting exclusive reliance on role model arguments. Black students must understand the full range of demands that black teachers face and that they, too, will someday face should they assume comparable roles.

The point of raising and clarifying concerns about the role model argument is neither to cripple activism on behalf of diversity nor to silence progressive voices fighting for the inclusion of black women. What I am after is something I believe students and faculty concerned about diversity are also after, namely, supporting minority communities through fairness and honesty in the reasons institutions give for hiring black women. If progressives' arsenal of political rhetoric is to include role model arguments, the limitations of those arguments must be well understood.

VI. Uncommon Faces

Even successful black women students have felt out of place within higher education. And in the post-civil rights era, black women educators have been made to feel unwelcome. Long before the media caught wind of the controversy over hiring women of color, black women knew that many on campus privately raised the question I was once asked publicly: "What gives you the right to teach this class?" Learned communities will continue to ask it until the fruits of our determination and diversity have ripened and our faces are so common among them that the question becomes as unthinkable as it is generally, but not always, unspeakable.

Notes

1 In addition to participants in the June and October 1990 meetings of the Northeast Corridor Black Women Law Teachers' Collective, I would like to thank the many friends and colleagues who read drafts of this essay and encouraged me to publish it. For their generous written comments I would like to thank Professors Giradeaux Spann, Martha Minow, David Strauss, and Robert Nozick; and Georgetown law students Ms. Lee Llambelis and Ms. Michele Beasley. I owe special gratitude to Professor Charles Ogletree and the Harvard Law School students who, along with Professors Randall Kennedy and Derrick Bell, attended the Saturday School program on September 22, 1990, at which I was allowed to present this essay. I am also grateful to the University of South Florida for permitting me to deliver this essay on February 11, 1991, as part of its university lecture series. This essay is dedicated to the memory of my great grandmother, Clemmie Glass Cloud (1889–1981). An earlier version of this article appeared in *Berkeley Women's Law Journal,* 6 (1990–1).

2 Harvard Law School students moved their diversity protests from the campus to the court in the fall of 1990. A group of students filed a lawsuit in Massachusetts state court alleging that Harvard's failure to hire additional women, racial minorities, and openly gay and lesbian faculty violated state human resource laws. The complaint specifically alleged that the law school's hiring practices constituted a continuing pattern and practice of discrimination, disproportionately excluding women, racial minorities, openly gay or lesbian people and people with disabilities from tenured and tenure-track faculty positions, in violation of Massachusetts law prohibiting employment discrimination and discrimination in the enjoyment of basic rights. *Harvard Law School Coalition for Civil Rights v President and Fellows of Harvard College,* Complaint No. 90-7904 (Massachusetts Superior Court, Middlesex County, Cambridge Division, November 20, 1990). The lawsuit was dismissed for lack of standing on February 25, 1991. See Robert Arnold, "Discrimination Suit Dismissed," 92 *Harvard Law Record* I (March 1, 1991).

3 See Fox Butterfield, "Harvard Law Professor Quits Until Black Woman Is Named," *New York Times* (April 24, 1990), p. 1, col. 1. The students' rallies and "sit-ins" pressed law school administrators for a commitment to a "diverse" faculty broadly conceived. However, media reports often focused on the question of a permanent, tenured appointment for a particular black woman, Professor Regina Austin, a visiting professor at Harvard during the 1989–90 academic year. See *id.* (quoting discordant students perspectives on Austin's teaching).

Critical of the tenor of the *New York Times* coverage, a group of prominent black women law teachers wrote a letter to the editor stressing that by appointing Austin, Harvard "would [not] depart from its usual standards of quality." See Paulette M. Caldwell, et al., "Law School Standards: The Old and the New: 'A Superb Scholar'," *New York Times* (May 11, 1990), p. 34, col. 5. Professor Austin returned home to the University of Pennsylvania Law School without an offer to join the Harvard faculty.

4 Butterfield, "Harvard Law Professor Quits Until Black Woman Is Named," p. 1.

5 As of this writing, there has never been a tenured or tenure-track black woman on the Harvard Law School faculty. At the time of the student protests and lawsuit in 1990, see notes 1 and 2, Professor Derrick Bell was one of three tenured black men on the faculty. (The other two were Christopher Edley Jr and Randall Kennedy.) The faculty also included five tenured white women, and two untenured black men. (David Wilkins and Charles Ogletree were the black men; Martha Field, Elizabeth Bartholet, Mary Ann Glendon, Martha Minow, and Kathleen Sullivan, the white women.) Another black man, Scott Brewer, had accepted a tenure-track faculty position that he is expected to assume after a judicial clerkship. The tenured and tenure-track faculty included a Brazilian citizen, Roberto Unger, but no Hispanic-Americans, Asian-Americans, or open gays or lesbians.

6 For data on blacks in law teaching see generally Richard H. Chused, "The Hiring and Retention of Minorities and Women on American Law School Faculties," 137 *University of Pennsylvania Law Review* 537 (1988). See also Edward J. Littlejohn, "Black Law Professors: A Past ... A Future?" *Michigan Bar Journal* 539, (June 1985).

7 See Ronald Dworkin, *Taking Rights Seriously* (Cambridge: Harvard University Press, 1977), p. 230.

8 Since at least the 1950s, large military installations that house the families of active duty service personnel also provide free, racially integrated schools. I attended such a school at Wheeler Air Force Base in Hawaii. Fort McClellan had no schools of its own, but provided transportation on government buses to nearby civilian schools. These schools were racially segregated.

9 Gillian Caldwell, unpublished journal (entry on file with author).

10 Bernard Boxill suggested that even if affirmative action (in his words, "reverse discrimination") "sins against a present equality of opportunity, [it may be acceptable because it] promotes a future equality of opportunity by providing blacks with their own successful 'role models'." Bernard Boxill, *Blacks and Social Justice* (Totowa, NJ: Rowman and Allanheld, 1984), p. 171.

11 This is not to say that there are only utilitarian arguments for hiring role models or for affirmative action. See, by analogy, Dworkin, *Taking Rights Seriously,* p. 232 (discussing *Sweatt v Painter*, 339 US 629 (1945) and *DeFunis v Odegaard*, 416 US 312 (1974)) (in some cases discriminatory policy which puts some individuals at

disadvantage may be justified because average welfare of community improved or because community rendered more just or ideal).

12 See generally Robert K. Fullinwider, *The Reverse Discrimination Controversy: A Moral and Legal Analysis* (Totowa, NJ: Rowman and Littlefield, 1980); *Equality and Preferential Treatment*, eds Marshall Cohen, Thomas Nagel, and Thomas Scanlon (Princeton: Princeton University Press, 1977); Kent Greenawalt, *Discrimination and Reverse Discrimination* (New York: Alfred A. Knopf, 1983); Boxill, *Blacks and Social Justice*, pp. 147–72.

13 Fred Hechinger, Education, *New York Times* (September 26, 1990), p. B8, col. 1.

14 Derrick Bell, "The Price and Pain of Racial Perspectives," *Stanford Law School Journal*, 5 (May 9, 1986); Derrick Bell, "Strangers in Academic Paradise: Law Teachers of Color in Still White Schools," 20 *USF Law Review* 385 (1986). See also Derrick Bell, "Memorandum to Harvard Law School Record" (November 22, 1987) (on file at *Cornell Law Review*) (recounting incidents at Stanford Law School).

15 Maria Morocco, "Law Students on Law School: The Job Chase," *ABA Journal*, 66 (September 1990).

16 See Minna J. Kotkin, "Reconsidering Role Assumption in Clinical Education," 19 *New Mexico Law Review*, 185 (1989), pp. 199–202 (proposing role model-based learning as alternative to role assumption-based learning in clinical legal education).

17 The role model-as-symbol argument acknowledged by Judith J. Thomson in her essay, "Preferential Hiring," in *Equality and Preferential Treatment*, eds Marshall Cohen, Thomas Nagel, and Thomas Scanlon, pp. 19, 22 was the argument that:

> [W]hat is wanted is role models. The proportion of black and women faculty members in the larger universities (particularly as one moves up the ladder of rank) is very much smaller than the proportion of them amongst recipients of Ph.D. degrees from those very same universities. Blacks and women students suffer a constricting of ambition because of this. They need to see a member of their own race or sex who are [sic] accepted, successful, professional. They need concrete evidence that those of their race or sex can become accepted, successful, professionals. (Emphasis in the original.)

In the same book, George Sher acknowledged and severely criticized the "symbolic" role model argument that:

> [P]ast discrimination in hiring has led to a scarcity of female "role models" of suitably high achievement. This lack, together with a culture that inculcates the idea that women should not or cannot do the jobs that ... men do, has in turn made women psychologically less able to do these jobs. ... [T]here is surely the same dearth of role models ... for blacks as for women.

George Sher, "Justifying Reverse Discrimination in Employment," in *Equality and Preferential Treatment*, eds Marshall Cohen, Thomas Nagel, and Thomas Scanlon, pp. 49, 58.

18 If blacks and other members of minority groups are to strive to become doctors and lawyers, it is important that they see members of their own groups in those roles. Otherwise they are likely to accept their consignment to less prestigious, less

demanding roles in society. Thus an important aspect of improving the motivations and education of black youths is to help put blacks into positions where blacks are not often now found so that they can serve as effective role models. Greenawalt, *Discrimination and Reverse Discrimination,* p. 64.

19 Still, public attention has generally focused on the especially difficult problems of role models for white women and racial minorities. Efforts abound to present young people with white female and minority role models who are "symbols" of special achievement. See, for example, Kathleen Teltsch, "Schools to Share Grant on Teaching," *NewYork Times* (September 23, 1990), p. 31, col. 1 ("The [General Electric] Foundation has tried to underscore its message about the rewards of research and the gratifications of teaching in a 17-minute videotape presenting six people who chose university careers as possible role models — two white women, two black women, a black man and a Hispanic man.").

20 Fullinwider, *The Reverse Discrimination Controversy: A Moral and Legal Analysis,* p. 18.

21 Larry Hawkins, President of the Institute for Athletics and Education, appears to be a "nurturer" who aspires to provide youth with many other nurturing role models. His sports programs "provide youngsters with a sense of belonging, after-school activities, discipline, group skills, motivation to attend school and do well academically, adult role models and ultimately ... self-esteem." Karen M. Thomas, "Coach-principal Seen as Vital Inner-City Education Motivator," *Chicago Tribune* (September 23, 1990), Chicagoland section, p. 3.

22 Letter of anonymous professor to Affirmative Action Office of John Jay College, New York, New York, October 8, 1990, on file with author. Observing that "color has been — and is still — used as a basis for discrimination," the professor protested that:

> ... I very much doubt whether Dr. _____ adequately instantiates the requirement of the role model argument. ... [U]ntil I made some inquiries about him subsequent to his appointment [I] did not know that he belonged to a "protected class." ... Dr. _____ fails to display to any but the most "discerning" the characteristics that formally commend him to those who appointed him.

Names have been omitted for reasons of privacy.

PART II:
BREAKING THE BOUNDS
OF DISCIPLINES

9

Good-Bye, Columbus?
Notes on the Culture
of Criticism[1]

HENRY LOUIS GATES JR

"We must remember that until very recently Nigeria was British," said Miss
Spurgeon. "It was pink on the map. In some old atlases it still is." Letty felt
that with the way things were going, nothing was pink on the map any more.

Barbara Pym, *Quartet In Autumn*

1

I recently asked the dean of a prestigious liberal arts college if he thought that his
school would ever have, as Berkeley has, a majority nonwhite enrollment.
"Never," he replied candidly. "That would completely alter our identity as a center
of the liberal arts."

The assumption that there is a deep connection between the shape of a college
curriculum and the ethnic composition of its students reflects a disquieting trend
in American education. Political representation has been confused with the
"representation" of various ethnic identities in the curriculum, while debates about
the nature of the humanities and core curricula have become marionette theaters
for larger political concerns.

The cultural right, threatened by these demographic shifts and by the demand
for curricular change, has retreated to a stance of intellectual protectionism,
arguing for a great and inviolable "Western tradition" which contains the seeds,

fruit, and flowers of the very best that has been thought or uttered in human history. The cultural left demands changes to accord with population shifts in gender and ethnicity (along the way often providing searching indictments of the sexism and racism that have plagued Western culture and to which the cultural right sometimes turns a blind eye). Both, it seems to me, are wrongheaded.

As a humanist, I am just as concerned that so many of my colleagues, on the one hand, feel that the prime motivation for a diverse curriculum is these population shifts as I am that those opposing diversity see it as foreclosing the possibility of a shared "American" identity. Both sides quickly resort to a grandly communitarian rhetoric. Both think they're struggling for the very soul of America. But if academic politics quickly becomes a *bellum omnium contra omnes,* perhaps it's time to wish a *pax* on both their houses.

What *is* multiculturalism, and why are they saying such terrible things about it? We've been told it threatens to fragment American culture into a warren of ethnic enclaves, each separate and inviolate. We've been told that it menaces the Western tradition of literature and the arts. We've been told it aims to politicize the school curriculum, replacing honest historical scholarship with a "feel good" syllabus designed solely to bolster the self-esteem of minorities. As I say, the alarm has been sounded, and many scholars and educators — liberals as well as conservatives — have responded to it. After all, if multiculturalism is just a pretty name for ethnic chauvinism, who needs it?

Well, there is, of course, a liberal rejoinder to these concerns, which says that this isn't what multiculturalism is — or at least, not what it ought to be. The liberal pluralist insists that the debate has been miscast from the beginning and that it's worth setting the main issues straight.

There's no denying that the multicultural initiative arose, in part, because of the fragmentation of American society by ethnicity, class, and gender. To make it the culprit for this fragmentation is to mistake effect for cause. Mayor Dinkins' metaphor about New York as a "gorgeous mosaic" is catchy but unhelpful, if it means that each culture is fixed in place and separated by grout. Perhaps we should try to think of American culture as a conversation among different voices — even if it's a conversation that some of us weren't able to join until recently. Perhaps we should think about education, as the conservative philosopher Michael Oakeshott proposed, as "an invitation into the art of this conversation in which we learn to recognize the voices," each conditioned, as he says, by a different perception of the world.[2] Common sense says that you don't bracket 90 per cent of the world's cultural heritage if you really want to learn about the world.

To insist that we "master our own culture" before learning others only defers the vexed question: what gets to count as "our" culture? What makes knowledge worth knowing? There's a wonderful bit of nineteenth-century student doggerel about the great Victorian classicist Benjamin Jowett which nicely sums up the monoculturalist's claims on this point.

Here I stand, my name is Jowett
If there's knowledge, then I know it.
I am the master of this college:
What I know not, is not knowledge.

Unfortunately, as history has taught us, an Anglo-American regional culture too often has masked itself as universal, passing itself off as our "common culture" and depicting different cultural traditions as "tribal" or "parochial." So it's only when we're free to explore the complexities of our hyphenated-American culture that we can discover what a genuinely common American culture might actually look like. Is multiculturalism un-American? Herman Melville — canonical author and great white male — didn't think so. As he wrote in *Redburn*, "We are not a narrow tribe, no.... We are not a nation, so much as a world."[3] Common sense (Gramscian or otherwise) reminds us that we're *all* ethnics and the challenge of transcending ethnic chauvinism is one we all face.

Granted, multiculturalism is no magic panacea for our social ills. We're worried when Johnny can't read. We're worried when Johnny can't add. But shouldn't we be worried, too, when Johnny tramples gravestones in a Jewish cemetery or scrawls racial epithets on a dormitory wall? It's a fact about this country that we've entrusted our schools with the fashioning and refashioning of a democratic polity: that's why the schooling of America has always been a matter of political judgment. But in America, a nation that has theorized itself as plural from its inception, our schools have an especially difficult task.

The society we have made simply won't survive without the values of tolerance, and cultural tolerance comes to nothing without cultural understanding. In short, the challenge facing America in the next century will be the shaping, at long last, of a truly common public culture, one responsive to the long-silenced cultures of color. If we relinquish the ideal of America as a plural nation, we abandon the very experiment that America represents.

2

Or so argues the liberal pluralist. But it's a position that infuriates the hard left as much as the conservative rhetoric of exclusion distresses the liberal pluralist. The conservative (these are caricatures, and I apologize), extolling the achievement of something narrativized under the rubric "Western civilization," says: "Nobody does it better." We liberal reformists say: "Do unto others as you would have them do unto you ... and hope for the best." The hard left says: "Let's do unto you what you *did* unto Others and then see how you like that."

For the hard left, what's distasteful about the ideology of pluralism is that it disguises real power relations while leaving the concept of hegemony unnamed

— that it presents an idyllic picture of coexistence that masks the harsh realities. Pluralism, for them, fails to be adequately emancipatory; it leaves oppressive structures intact.

There are at least two things to notice here. First, if the hard left is correct, then the hard right has nothing to worry about from the multicultural initiative. Second, the hard left distinguishes itself from the liberal pluralist position in its frank partisanship; it subsists on a sharp division between hegemons and hegemonized, center and margin, oppressor and oppressed, and makes no bones about which side it's on.

Finally, there is something more puzzling than it first appears about the more general objective: the redistribution of cultural capital, to use the term made familiar by Pierre Bourdieu.[4] I think it's clarifying to cast the debate in his terms, and faithful to what's at the core of these recent arguments; I also think there's a reason that participants in the debate have been reluctant to do so. Again, let me enumerate.

First, the concept of "cultural capital" makes an otherwise high-minded and high-toned debate sound a little ... sordid. The very model of cultural capital — by which the possession of cultural knowledge is systematically related to social stratification — is usually "unmasked" as an insidious mechanism; it's held to be the bad faith that hovers over the "liberal arts." You don't want to dive into this cesspool and say, "I want a place in it, too."

Second, a redistributionist agenda may not even be intelligible with respect to cultural capital. Cultural capital refers us to a system of differentiation; in this model, once cultural knowledge is redistributed so that it fails to mark a distinction, it loses its value. To borrow someone else's revision of Benjamin, this may be the work of reproduction in an age of mechanical art.[5] We've heard, in this context, the phrase "cultural equity," a concept that may well have strategic value, but that is hard to make sense of otherwise, save as an illicit personification (the transferral of equal standing from people to their products). What could confer "equity" on "culture"? The phrase assumes that works of culture can be measured on some scalar metric — and decreed, from some Archimedean vantage point, to be equal. The question is why anybody should care about "culture" of this sort, let alone fight for a claim upon its title.

Third, the question of value divides the left in two. On the one hand, the usual unself-conscious position is to speak in terms of immanently valuable texts that have been "undervalued" for extrinsic reasons. On the other hand, the more "theorized" position views the concept of "value" as essentially mystified. That position has shrewdly demonstrated that our usual *theories* of value are incoherent, unintelligible, or otherwise ill-founded; the only error it made was to assume that our *practices* of evaluation should, or could, fall by the wayside as well, which is surely a non sequitur. Indeed, the minute the word "judgmental" became pejorative, we should have known we had made a misstep. This is not for a moment to concede that anybody actually stopped judging. Literary evaluation merely ceased to be a professionally accredited act.

In the end, neither left nor right escapes the dean's dilemma. In short, we remain mired in the representation quandary.

3

The interplay between the two senses of the word "representation," indeed, has been foundational to the now rather depleted argument over the "canon." On the one hand, it has dawned on most of us that the grand canon — this fixed repository of valuable texts — never existed, which is why it was such a pushover. On the other hand, more scholars have come to see that the conflation of textual with political representation fueled a windily apocalyptic rhetoric that had nowhere to go when its putative demands were granted. (It tended to sponsor a naively reductionist mode of reading as well: Alice Walker as the black Eternal Feminine on two legs.) As John Guillory, perhaps our most sophisticated scholar of canon formation, has remarked,

> this sense of representation, the representation of groups by texts, lies at a curious tangent to the concept of political representation, with which it seems perhaps to have been confused, a confusion which is the occasion of both the impasse of cooptation and the very cachet of the noncanonical, contingent as it is upon the delegitimation of the canon.... The work of recovery has for the most part been undertaken as though the field of writing were a *plenum*, a textual repetition of social diversity. In fact, as is quite well known, strategies of exclusion are employed historically most effectively at the level of access to literacy.[6]

But the tension between the two senses of "representation" isn't restricted to arguments about the canon; in the minority context, the same issues resurface as an issue about the "burdens of representation" of the black artist. If black authors are primarily entrusted with producing the proverbial "text of blackness," they become vulnerable to the charge of betrayal if they shirk their duty. (The reason that nobody reads Zora Neale Hurston's *Seraph on the Suwannee* isn't unrelated to the reason that everybody reads *Their Eyes Were Watching God.*) Isaac Julien and Kobena Mercer, the black British filmmaker and media theorist, have focused on the tension "between representation as a practice of depicting and representation as a practice of delegation. Representational democracy, like the classic realist text, is premised on an implicitly mimetic theory of representation as correspondence with the 'real'."[7] (As one of a small number of black filmmakers, Julien has felt the pressure, in some sense, to be "representative" so that his theoretical objections have an additional polemical edge.)

And while most of us will accept the point, I think many of us haven't appreciated the significance of this breach when it comes to the highly mediated relation between critical debates and their supposed referents.

Indeed, with the celebrated turn to politics in literary studies in the past decade, there's been a significant change in the register of reproach. Pick up any issue of *Modern Philology* in the 1950s, and turn to the review section. You'll find that in those days, one would typically chastise a study for unpardonable lapses in its citations or for failing to take full account of the insight yielded by other scholarship, and judge the author to be a slipshod ignoramus. Today, for equivalently venial offenses, the errant scholar can be reproached as a collaborationist — accused of unwitting complicity with the ideologies and structures of oppression, of silencing the voice of the Other, of colluding with perpetrators of injustice: "Thus Heywood's study only reinstates and revalorizes the very specular ideologies it appears to resist...." The culprit, some fresh-faced young academic from the Midwest, stands exposed for what she is, a collaborator and purveyor of repression, a woman who silences entire populations with a single paragraph, who, in view of fatal analytic conflations, has denied agency to all the wretched of the earth.

Politics never felt so good.

It's heady stuff. Critics can feel like the sorcerer's apprentice, unleashing elemental forces beyond their control. But we know, on some level, that it's mostly make-believe — that the brilliant Althusserian unmasking of the ideological apparatus of film editing you published in *October* won't even change the way Mike Ovitz treats his secretary, let alone bring down the house of patriarchy.

I suppose that's why these levels of criticism often get mixed up. I've seen readers' reports on journal manuscripts that say things like: "Not only does so-and-so's paper perpetuate a logic internal to the existing racist, patriarchal order, but footnote 17 gives page numbers to a different edition than is listed in the bibliography." Well, we can't have that, now can we?

The dilemmas of oppositional criticism haunt the fractured American academic community. The 1980s witnessed not only a resurgence of what I'll call the New Moralism, but the beginnings of its subsidence. And this, too, is bound up very much with the problematic of representation, such that the relation between the politics of theory and the politics of politics became a question to be indefinitely deferred or finessed.

Seventies-style hermeneutics killed the author; eighties-style politics brought the author back. The seventies sponsored a hedonic vocabulary of "free-play," *jouissance,* the joys of indeterminacy. The eighties brought back a grim-faced insistence on the hidden moral stakes: New Historicist essays on the English Renaissance, for instance, regularly turned out to be about Indians and empire.

Oppositional criticism in the early seventies offered us a sort of "wacky packs" version of literary history as a procession no longer of laureled heads, but of clay feet. Later critiques of the canon went on to dispute its patterns of inclusion and exclusion. And, as Guillory also has pointed out, the reason the debate over the canon entailed the resurrection of the author was simply that it required representatives of a social constituency: The debate over canon formation was concerned, in the first instance, with *authors,* not texts.[8]

And we "minority" critics came to play a similar role in the marionette theater of the political that I referred to earlier. We shouldn't wonder at the accompanying acrimony. Edward Said has indicted what he describes as the "badgering, hectoring, authoritative tone" that persists in contemporary cultural studies, adding, "The great horror I think we should all feel is toward systematic or dogmatic orthodoxies of one sort or another that are paraded as the last word of high Theory still hot from the press."[9] It is merely the uncanny workings of the old "imitative fallacy" that account for the authoritarian tonalities of scholarship and professional intercourse where issues of domination are foregrounded?

Again, I want to stress the way in which minority criticism can become a site for larger contestations. Robert Young, an editor of the *Oxford Literary Review*, ventured an intriguing proposition in a recent paper entitled "The Politics of 'The Politics of Literary Theory'." He notes that literary Marxism in contemporary America (as opposed to that in Britain) has "few links with the social sciences or with a political base in the public sphere. You can make almost any political claim you like: you know that there is no danger that it will ever have any political effect." "At the same time," he continues, "the pressure of feminism, and more recently Black Studies, has meant that today the political cannot be ignored by anyone, and may be responsible for the white male retreat into Marxism. Marxism can compete with feminism and Black Studies insofar as it offers to return literary criticism to its traditional moral function, but can, more covertly, also act as a defence against them...."[10] The elided social referent of struggle returns, but now it is merely a struggle for the moral high ground. And I think you could argue that this return to a gestural sort of politics reflects a moralizing strain in contemporary criticism that has lost faith in its epistemological claims. If we can't tell you what's true and what's false — the thought goes — we'll at least tell you what's right and what's wrong. What's wrong? Racism, colonialism, oppression, cultural imperialism, patriarchy, epistemic violence.... So we lost facts, and we got back ethics — a trade-in, but not necessarily an upgrade.

4

One problem is, as I've suggested, that the immediate concern of the "politics of interpretation" is generally the politics of interpreters. Another is that we tend to equivocate between, on the one hand, what a text *could* mean — the possibilities of its signification, the "modalities of the production of meaning," as Paul de Man has it — and on the other hand, what a text *does* mean — the issue of its actual political effectivity. Political criticism usually works by demonstrating the former and insinuating the latter. Now, the pleasurable political frisson comes from the latter, the question of reception and effects (as an old newsroom slogan has it, if it bleeds, it leads). But critics are reluctant to engage in actual sociology: it isn't what they were trained to do; it's not what they were raised to value. Still, as political critics, we usually *trade* on the ambiguity.

Let me give you an example of a now familiar version of such political reading. In the course of elaborating a theory of the "corporate populist," a recent critical essay accused filmmaker Spike Lee of being responsible, though perhaps indirectly, for the death of black youths.[11] The chain of causality begins with Spike Lee, who makes television commercials promoting Air Jordans; it ends with the inner city — devastated by crack and consumerism — and a black youth with a bullet through the brain, murdered for his sneakers. All because Spike said that he's gotta have it. You think Mars Blackmon is funny? Those commercials have a body count.

I want to insist that this was not an aberration, but a state-of-the-art critical essay, one that represents the impasse we've reached in the American academy. This is how we've been taught to do cultural politics: you find the body; then you find the culprit. It's also where the critique of the commodity will lead you. This is an old phenomenon on the right and the left — and certain kinds of Marxism can be very theological on this point: commodification is a kind of original sin, and any cultural form it touches is tainted. These critiques, to be sure, are usually anchored to semiorganicist notions of authenticity.

The old leftist critique of the commodity has a usefully confining tendency: it sets up a cunning trap that practically guarantees that the marginalized cultures it glorifies will remain marginalized. They knew just how to keep us in our place. And the logic was breathtakingly simple: if you win, you lose.

And that's because it's just a fact about what we quaintly label the "current conjuncture" that if a cultural form reaches a substantial audience, it has entered the circuits of commodification. What Paul Gilroy calls "populist modernism" stays in good ideological standing so long as it doesn't get too popular. And one of the most important contributions of a younger breed of cultural theorists has been a critique of the old critique of the commodity form. Mercer, for example, explores ways in which commodity forms have been expressively manipulated by the marginalized to explore and explode the artificiality of the identities to which they've been confined.

I want to propose that it's worth distinguishing between morality and moralism, but I do so with trepidation. As Logan Pearsall Smith has observed: "That we should practise what we preach is generally admitted; but anyone who preaches what he and his hearers practise must incur the gravest moral disapprobation."[12] At the same time, I worry that the critical hair shirt has become more of a fashion statement than a political one.

A friend of mine suggested that we institutionalize something we already do implicitly at conferences on "minority discourse": award a prize at the end for the panelist, respondent, or contestant most oppressed; at the end of the year, we could have the "Oppression Emmy" Awards.[13] For what became clear by the end of the past decade was that this establishment of what J. G. Melquior calls an "official marginality" meant that minority critics are accepted by the academy but, in return, they must accept a role already scripted for them: once scorned, now exalted. You think of Sally Field's address to the Motion Picture Academy when she received her Oscar, "You like me! You really, really like me!" We authorized Others shriek into the microphone, exultation momentarily breaking our dour countenances. (We can, of course, be a little more self-conscious about it and acknowledge our problematic positionality: "You like me, you really, really like me — you racist patriarchal Eurotrash elitists!") But let's face it. It takes all the fun out of being oppositional when someone hands you a script and says, "Be oppositional, please — you look so cute when you're angry."

What feel-good moralism had to confront was the nature of commodified postmodern ethnicity — which we could describe as the Benetton's model: "All the colors of the world"; none of the oppression. It was a seductive vision: cashmere instead of power relations.

And it *was* a change. Usually, the Third World presented itself to us as the page people turn when the *Time* magazine ad says, "You can help little Maria or you can turn the page." It was a tropological locale of suffering and destitution. Now little Maria's wearing a purple Angora scarf and a black V-neck sweater, and the message is: "You can have style like Maria and shop at Benetton's — or don't you even care about ethnic harmony?"

To be sure, the Benettonization of culture was not without its ironies: in New York, as Patricia J. Williams has pointed out, the shops may not buzz you in if you actually look like one of those "ethnic" models. But as the eighties came to a close, a nagging doubt began to surface: was academic politics finally a highbrow version of what *Women's Wear Daily* would call the "style wars"? I think that too easily lets us off the hook of history; I want to talk about the ways we've been betrayed by our two-decade-long love affair with theory. Oscar Wilde once quipped that when good Americans die, they go to Paris. I think in Paris, when good theories die, they go to America.

In retrospect, it was easy to point to blunders, some of which I've mentioned. Righteous indignation became routinized, professionalized, and, in so doing, underwent an odd transformation. Back in the 1930s, a magazine editor wondered aloud if there was a typewriter at the *Partisan Review* with the word "alienation" on a single key. At the moment, I'm on the lookout for a typewriter that has "counterhegemonic cultural production" on a single key.

5

And one of the most interesting developments in the past decade took place when theoretically sophisticated minority scholarship parted company with its left-theoretic mentors. I want to take my example here not from literature, but law, and the field of critical legal studies in particular. The participants include the legal scholars Maria Matsudo, Richard Delgado, and Patricia J. Williams, and the philosopher Cornel West.[14] What was revealed was a principled distrust of a "radically utopian strain" in Critical Legal Studies (CLS). West took to task American leftism for its undialectical, purely antagonistic relation to liberalism: if you don't build on liberalism, he argues, you build on air. In this vein the minority legal scholars pointed out that those rudiments of legal liberalism — the doctrine of rights, for example, formality of rules and procedures, zones of privacy — that CLS purists wanted to demolish as so much legalistic subterfuge was pretty much all they had going for them. So the irony was, when all the dust had cleared (I'm oversimplifying of course, but not hugely), that the left-minority scholars had retrieved and reconstituted liberalism. Some may well dismiss this as just another example of "uneven theoretical development," the minoritarian resistance to universalizing theory. It is, in fact, one of the most telling intellectual twists of recent memory.

And one that also points to the way in which critical theory has failed to keep pace with the larger world. The very notion of an ethical universal — for years dismissed as hopelessly naive — is beginning to make a comeback in the works of a number of feminist theorists. We had so much fun deconstructing the liberal ideology of "rights," for example, that we lost sight of how strategically — humanly — valuable the notion proved in, for example, much Third World politics (as Francis Mading Deng, Abdullahi Ahmed An-Na'im, and others have shown).

Turning a baleful eye to its fellow disciplines, literary criticism has spent the last two decades singing "Anything You Can Do, I Can Do Better," rather like a scratched Ethel Merman recording, which makes the difficulty literary critics have had in grasping some elementary ideas rather poignant. What was once a resistance to theory has turned into a resistance to anything not packaged as theory.

The oppositional style of criticism has failed us, failed us in our attempt to come to grips with an America that can no longer be construed as an integral whole. What Richard Hofstadter famously called the "paranoid style" of American politics has become the paranoid style of American studies.

None of this is of recent vintage, of course. In 1930, Lionel Trilling could write, "There is only one way to accept America, and that is in hate; one must be close to one's land, passionately close in some way or other, and the only way to be close to America is to hate it…. There is no person in the United States, save he be a member of the plutocratic class … who is not tainted, a little or much, with the madness of the bottom dog, not one who is not in sympathy of disgust and hate with his fellows." For these are "the universally relevant emotions of America."[15]

Today, success has spoiled us, the right has robbed us of our dyspepsia, and the routinized production of righteous indignation is allowed to substitute for critical rigor.

And nothing more clearly marks our failure to address the complexities of the larger world than the continuing ascendancy, in contemporary criticism, of what could be called the colonial paradigm. Colonialism, more as metaphor than as a particularized historical phenomenon, has proven astonishingly capacious; Fanon is blithely invoked to describe the allegedly "colonizing" relation between English departments and history departments. The irony is that, in the meantime, the tendency in subaltern studies has been to pluralize the notion of "colonization," to insist on the particularity of its instances and question the explanatory value of the general rubric. So too with the concept of "neocolonialism" which is increasingly regarded as exculpatory of despotic Third-World regimes and, 30 years after independence, too vague to be helpful in characterizing the peculiarities of these states in the world economy.[16]

But the sovereign-colony relation is simply another instance of the spatial topography of center and margin on which oppositional criticism subsists. And it is just this model that, I want to suggest, has started to exhaust its usefulness in describing our own modernity.

6

Let me say at once that I do not have in mind what some people have trumpeted as the new Pax Americana. In his recent "reflections of American equality and foreign liberations," David Brion Davis remarks, apropos of the recent decline of Eastern bloc communism, that "[n]othing could be more fatuous than to interpret these developments ... as a prelude to the Americanization of the world." He reminds us of Marx's view that capitalism itself is "permanently revolutionary, tearing down all obstacles that impede the development of productive forces, the expansion of needs, the diversity of production and the exploitation and exchange of natural and intellectual forces."[17] But to view recent events as a triumph of American corporate capitalism, which has failed to abate the immiseration of the so-called underclass in its own backyard, is simply to misread history. (The Chinese students at Tianenman Square quoted Locke and Jefferson, not Ayn Rand or Lee Iaccocca.) At the same time, I think Davis establishes that the historiographical tradition that depicts America univocally as a force of reaction in a world of daisy-fresh revolutionary ferment reduces a history of complex ambivalence to a crude morality tale.

A great deal of weight has been assigned to the term "cultural imperialism"; I do not know that much time has been spent thinking about what the phrase should mean. Should the global circulation of American culture always be identified as imperialism, even if imperialism by other means? In an era of transnational capital, transnational labor, and transnational culture, how well is the center-periphery model holding up?

The distinguished anthropologist Arjun Appadurai has drawn our attention to that "uncanny Philippine affinity for American popular music": "An entire nation," he writes, "seems to have learned to mimic Kenny Rogers and the Lennon sisters, like a vast Asian Motown chorus."[18]

All this, in a former US colony racked by enormous contrasts of wealth and poverty, amounting to what he felicitously describes as "nostalgia without memory." And yet the usual remarks about "cultural imperialism" fail to acknowledge the specificity of cultural interactions. An American-centered view of the world blinds us to the fact that America isn't always on center stage, whether as hero or as villain. As Appadurai writes,

> [I]t is worth noticing that for the people of Irian Jaya, Indonesianization may be more worrisome than Americanization, as Japanization may be for Koreans, Indianization for Sri Lankans, Vietnamization for the Cambodians, Russianization for the people of Soviet Armenia and the Baltic Republics. Such a list of alternative fears to Americanization could be greatly expanded, but it is not a shapeless inventory: for polities of smaller scale, there is always a fear of cultural absorption by polities of larger scale, especially those that are nearby. One man's imagined community is another man's political prison.[19]

What we are beginning to see, in work that proceeds under the rubric of "public culture," is that, as Appadurai concludes, "the new global cultural economy has to be seen as a complex, overlapping, disjunctive order, which cannot any longer be understood in terms of existing center-periphery models (even those which might account for multiple centers and peripheries)."[20] Again, I want to suggest that the spatial dichotomies through which our oppositional criticism has defined itself prove increasingly inadequate to a cultural complex of traveling culture. Once more, the world itself has outpaced our academic discourse.

Melville's America retained a strong sense of its marginality vis-à-vis its former sovereign and colonizer, and yet his assertion that we are "not a nation, so much as a world" has *become* true, as a geopolitical fact. As a result, the disciplinary enclave of American studies is surely the proper site to begin a study of the globalization of America and the Americanization of the globe; but, equally, the resistance bred by both of these trends. I think this is a project worth pursuing even if it does not come without a price. Surely it is clear to us all that the ritualized invocation of Otherness is losing its capacity to engender new forms of knowledge, that the "margin" may have exhausted its strategic value as a position from which to theorize the very antinomies that produced it as an object of study.

Or as Audre Lorde writes in her poem "Good Mirrors are Not Cheap,"

It is a waste of time hating a mirror
or its reflection
instead of stopping the hand
that makes glass with distortions[21]

But I've been misunderstood in the past, so I want to be very clear on one point. While I may be taken to have argued for the retrieval of liberalism, however refashioned, as a viable, reformable agenda, I distrust those — on the left, right, or center — who would erect an opposition between leftism and liberalism. West has rightly argued that a left politics that can imagine only an agonistic relation to real-world liberalism is a bankrupt politics,[22] but the converse is true as well; a rights-based liberalism unresponsive to radical (and conservative) critiques is an impoverished one indeed. So let me make it clear that my remarks are primarily aimed at those massively totalizing theories that marginalize practical political action as a jejune indulgence. It's a critique I made a few years back about Luce Irigaray — that her conception of the amazing fixity of patriarchy, the complete unavailability of any external purchase, is more likely to send us to the margins of Plato, Freud, and Lacan than to encourage anything so vulgar as overt political action. The embrace of systematicity — and this is something common to a certain structural/functional tradition of social thought, a tradition whose grand paranoias have made it particularly seductive to literary criticism — rules out humble amelioration.[23] And while some of the masters of grand totalizing theory will concede the need to struggle for such unglamorous things as "equal wages and social rights," the fact that they feel obliged to make the (rather left-handed) concession indicates the difficulty; their Olympian, all-or-nothing perspective cannot but enervate and diminish the arena of real politics. In short, my brief — and that of many minority intellectuals today — is against the temptations of what I call Messianic pessimism.

Nor, however, can we be content with the multiplication of authorized subjectivities, symbolically rewarded in virtue of being materially deprived. Perhaps we can begin to forgo the pleasures of ethnicist affirmation and routinized resentment in favor of rethinking the larger structures that constrain and enable our agency. In an increasingly polycentric world, our task may be to prepare for a world in which nothing is pink on the map.

Notes

1 Reprinted from *American Literary History* (1991) by permission of the author.
2 Michael Oakeshott, *The Voice of Liberal Learning: Michael Oakeshott on Education*, ed. Timothy Fuller (New Haven: Yale University Press, 1989).

3 Herman Melville, *Redburn, His First Voyage,* ed. Harold Beaver (Harmondsworth, NY: Penguin, 1976).

4 Pierre Bourdieu and Jean-Claude Passeron, *Reproduction in Education, Society and Culture,* tr. Richard Nice (London: Sage, 1977).

5 Arjun Appadurai, "Disjuncture and Difference in the Global Cultural Economy," *Public Culture,* 2, 2 (1990), p. 17.

6 John Guillory, "Canonical and Non-canonical: A Critique of the Current Debate." *ELH,* 54 (1987), pp. 484–5.

7 Isaac Julien and Kobena Mercer, "Introduction — De Margin and De Centre," *Screen,* 29, 4 (1988), p. 4.

8 John Guillory, "Canon, Syllabus, List: A Note on the Pedagogic Imaginary," *Transition,* 52 (1991), p. 40.

9 Edward Said and Raymond Williams, "Media, Margins, and Modernity," *The Politics of Modernism: Against the New Conformists,* ed. Tony Pinkney (London: Verso, 1989), p. 182.

10 Robert Young, "The Politics of 'The Politics of Literary Theory'," *Oxford Literary Review,* 10, 1–2 (1988), p. 137.

11 "For Lee to deny the potential connection between the indiscriminate hawking of shoes and a climate of indiscriminate crime is incredibly to render his advertising as the commercial version of the Air Force's vaunted surgical strike," Jerome Christensen maintains. Jerome Christensen, "Spike Lee, Corporate Populist," *Critical Inquiry,* 16, 2 (1990), p. 593.

12 Logan Pearsall Smith, *All Trivia* (New York: Ticknor & Fields, 1984).

13 I don't think this is much of an extrapolation. In an issue of *Screen,* for instance, Yvonne Rainer, a distinguished avant-garde filmmaker, helpfully listed her conferential Others: "Starting with the most victimised (alas, even the most noble fantasy of solidarity has its pecking order), they were: blacks, Lesbians, Latina women, Asians, and gay men." (She apologized that Latino men "got lost in the shuffle." Bérénice Reynaud and Yvonne Rainer, "Responses to Coco Fusco's 'Fantasies of Oppositionality'," *Screen,* 30, 3 (1989), pp. 91–2.

14 "There simply is no intellectually acceptable, morally preferable, and practically realizable left social vision and program that does not take liberalism as a starting point," West argues. "I find it ironic that as a black American, a descendant of those who were victimized by American liberalism, I must call attention to liberalism's accomplishments. Yet I must do so.... Liberalism is not the possession of white male elites in high places, but rather a dynamic and malleable tradition.... In this regard, liberalism signifies neither a status quo to defend ... nor an ideology to thrash ... but rather a diverse and complex tradition that can be mined in order to enlarge the scope of human freedom." Cornel West, "Colloquy: CLS and a Liberal Critic," *Yale Law Journal,* 97 (1988), p. 757; see also Patricia J. Williams, *The Alchemy of Race and Rights* (Cambridge: Harvard University Press, 1991), pp. 146–65; Richard Delgado, "The Ethereal Scholar: Does Critical Legal Studies Have What Minorities Want?" *Harvard Civil Rights-Civil Liberties Law Review,* 22 (1987), p. 301; and the selection presented in Minority Critiques of the Critical Legal Studies Movement. Special issue of *Harvard Civil Rights-Civil Liberties Law Review,* 22 (1987), pp. 297–447. Cf. my "Contract Killer," *Nation,* 10 (June 1991), pp. 766–70.

15 Lionel Trilling "The Promise of Realism," *Speaking of Literature and Society,* ed. Diana Trilling (New York: Harcourt, 1980), pp. 29, 32; see also Mark Krupnick, *Lionel Trilling and the Fate of Cultural Criticism* (Evanston: Northwestern University Press, 1986), pp. 40–6.

16 For a more extended discussion of the colonial paradigm, see my "Critical Fanonism," *Critical Inquiry,* 17 (1991), pp. 457–70.

17 David Brion Davis, *Revolutions: Reflections on American Equality and Foreign Liberations* (Cambridge: Harvard University Press, 1990), p. 6.

18 Appadurai, "Disjuncture and Difference in the Global Cultural Economy," p. 3

19 Ibid., pp. 5–6. Further, as Appadurai argues, "the simplification of these many forces (and fears) of homogenization can also be exploited by nation-states in relation to their own minorities, by posing global commoditization (or capitalism, or some other such external enemy) as more real than the threat of its own hegemonic strategies." Ibid., p. 6.

20 Ibid., p. 6.

21 Audre Lorde, "Good Mirrors Are Not Cheap," *From a Land Where Other People Live* (Detroit: Broadside, 1973), p. 15.

22 Cornel West, "Between Dewey and Gramsci: Unger's Emancipatory Experimentalism," *Northwestern University Law Review,* 81 (1987), pp. 941–51.

23 See my "Significant Others," *Contemporary Literature,* 29 (1988), pp. 606–24.

10

Essentialism and the Complexities of Racial Identity[1]

MICHAEL ERIC DYSON

Contemporary African-American culture is radically complex and diverse, marked by an intriguing variety of intellectual reflections, artistic creations, and social practices. Its vibrant diversity cautions against portraying the constitutive experiences of African-American culture in monolithic terms. And yet, there exists an unfailing precedent to cast black culture in a distorted light and to view it through the prisms of racist stereotype or racial essentialism. The former is the attempt to apply inferior science to undisciplined social observation, fueled by the effort to foist overdrawn generalizations about individual character onto entire racial groups. The latter often occurs as black intellectuals oppose the strangling of black culture by caricature offering, instead, cultural standards to help define racial authenticity.

Ironically the crude half-light that escapes through stereotype and the well-meaning but illusory absolutes generated by essentialism share similar traits: both ignore black culture's relentless evolutions and metamorphoses. Any substantial investigation of the protean meanings of African-American culture must take these factors into account.

Of course, any serious contribution to African-American cultural criticism must reckon decisively with the vulgar effects associated with a certain species of criticism long dishonored in black communities. Although critical consciousness has traced the resilient circumference of black culture, deep suspicions about criticism's worth and function roil incessantly beneath the cultural surface. This is a direct consequence of the thinly veiled malevolence that characterized much of what passed for criticism of black culture from outside its precincts early on in our national history.

Most early criticism of black culture was vicious and unjust, reflecting the self-validating sciolism of cultural imperials whose prejudice clouded their reason. Most white public figures and men of letters habitually castigated black culture, viewing blacks as ugly and savage. And when conveniently vexed by pangs of charitable guilt, white intellectuals believed blacks to be captives of racial infantilism. In many early forms, then, criticism of black culture was indistinguishable from racist assumptions about black intelligence, beauty, and humanity which are deeply premised in American life. In this light, black skepticism about criticism, itself involving an implicit critical judgment, is understandable and even healthy.

A damaging consequence of racist judgments about black culture being passed off as "objective" cultural criticism is their success in portraying black culture as inferior to white society. In the wake of such claims, black cultural creativity often acquired a protective ideological function, shielding African-American culture from the lambasting of its detractors. Phyllis Wheatley's poetry, Alexander Crummell's lectures, Frederick Douglass' orations, and Ida B. Wells' journalism were never *merely* artistic creations of sharp and resourceful intelligences. Rather, they provided models of cultural excellence in an ethos of white disbelief in black humanity and, in other instances, they served to thaw the frozen regions of white indifference to black life.

African-American cultural expression often served propagandistic and practical intellectual ends as well, demonstrating the political dimensions of cultural expression. Black cultural expression continually reinforced the idea that culture must be understood within the environment of its material production and in relation to forces like political change, economic evolution, and religious transformation. African-American culture has taken shape in the defining interplay of historical contingency and the pursuit of a humane racial identity that have been the heart of black culture's growth.

Unfortunately, the ideological function that attached to black cultural expression fed off of the energies of an evolutionary cultural trait that long ago exhausted its founding logic and many of its redemptive uses: the demand of racial unity. Conceived in the mid-nineteenth century, as manumitted and fugitive slaves acquired literacy and public voice, racial unity was a socially useful way of speaking about the need of consolidated cultural resources to offset slavery's divisive effects on black culture. To this day, the narrative of racial unity has survived mainly as a rhetorical strategy of black intellectuals, artists, and leaders to impose provisional order on the perplexing and chaotic politics of racial identity.

Strands of that narrative have usefully recounted how tactics of white racial tyranny, employed by slave masters and political demagogues alike, undermined black racial solidarity and molded the unavoidable dependence of blacks on the diffuse forms of white culture. Still other fragments of the racial unity narrative recount how unity was complicated by diversities in tongue among slaves in the earliest stages of slavery, and made still more difficult by the differences in culture, region, and nation, these linguistic dissimilarities embodied. Eventually, however, the commonalities of black racial experience, which were fashioned under the rigorous and, in some instances, almost immediate decline of African identity in slavery, precipitated the emergence of a distinct racial identity in American culture. The dynamics of this burgeoning racial identity prompted many blacks to lament a lack of intraracial regard, intimacy, and cooperation, qualities that are prized and encouraged within the symbolic universe of racial unity.

The quest for racial unity has represented largely the desperate effort to replace a cultural uprooting that should never have occurred with a racial unanimity that actually never existed. While clan, community, and nation were central to African societies, only a cultural catastrophe the magnitude of chattel slavery could impose upon blacks an artificial and single racial identity. Blacks responded by asserting their racial identity in defense of their humanity and against the claims of worthlessness advanced by racist intellectuals. Once on American soil, the intricate interactions and forced symbiosis of African and American cultures produced a hybrid worldview whose cultural and social dimensions continue to be vividly explored.

Under the rhetoric of racial unity, the undeniable commonalities of racial experience have been recast in mythic and homogeneous terms, a project fueled by the utopic and romanticizing visions of race most notably espoused by black nationalists. But the difficulties of racial unity — the weight of its exponents' narrow understanding of racial cooperation and their ignoble infelicities in defining "in" and "out," "friend" and "enemy," and "us" and "them" — were overlooked in the desperate search for an enabling explanation of the evils of racial extirpation and debasement. It was not long, though, before the lacerating contradictions of racial history and memory undercut the overarching impulses of racial unity making it increasingly apparent that homogeneous racial images are an untenable source of African-American identity.

The peculiar complexions of racial identity — which inherit their distinctive hues from the specific and cumulative conditions of black life from plantation to suburb — mean that black folk do have a history and memory in common. The incalculable grief and titanic inhumanities of chattel slavery; the unsayable trauma brought on by the erosion of embryonic liberties after Reconstruction; the sometimes acoustic, sometimes muted pain borne in response to the chafing indignities imposed by Jim Crow law; the stunning affirmation of race and culture that accompanied the transformation of social relations in the civil rights movement; and the inviolable courage and unshakable hope that ripple from religious faith all form, in part, the content of common racial history and memory from which black culture is fashioned.

But black culture is not static or one-dimensional. Neither is it drawn forward by a single historical end. While historical memory permits the identification of characteristics of black culture that make it singular and unto itself, historical experience — which is generated and shaped by cultural renewal and decay, and the ongoing encounter by black culture with new social and cultural forces that impact its future — provides a basis to resist essentialist modes of expression. An essence is an immutable, history-transcending characteristic of, for instance, art objects, religions, and cultures. It does not reflect the historical, social, and cultural forces that produce black culture and that continue to inflect the tenor of contemporary black cultural practices from painting to basketball. While one may cherish black cultural norms, values, and ideals — or even wish to protect them from rejection, irrelevance, or extinction — such desires must not be realized through appeals to an unvarying racial or cultural essence that remains unaffected by vicissitude or chance.[2]

Hence, the desire to promote love, friendship, and mutual cooperation among black folk is a laudable cultural goal, especially in light of the vicious and paralyzing forms of self-hatred and mutual contempt that have riddled black culture from its fragile origins in slavery through present postindustrial urban conditions. One might even describe such an aspiration as the quest for an enabling solidarity. And how is an enabling solidarity to be distinguished from most varieties of black unity? It will only appeal to the richly varied meanings of cultural practices, the diversity of authentic roles one may express within the repertoire of black cultural identities, and the ever-expanding context of historical experience in supporting its vision of racial cooperation.

An enabling solidarity should not appeal to truncated understandings of authentic racial identity or place an ideological noose of loyalty around the necks of critical dissenters from received ideas about racial unity. The proponents of racial unity have often operated on the assumption that black people have one overriding vision, purpose, and destiny. While it is true that our common history of slavery and racial oppression signifies a common goal of freedom from oppression for black people, broadened horizons of racial experience and more sophisticated conceptions of racial identity make the articulation of a single, unitary, racial goal highly problematic.

Black culture is not simply formed in the response to forces of oppression. Its purposes do not easily reduce to resisting racism. Although black cultural creativity and agency are profoundly influenced by racist oppression, their rich range of expressions are not exhausted by preoccupation with such oppression. And even when due consideration is paid to the oppressive forces that constrain black life, we must transcend the gaze of race and look to a more ecumenical constellation of forces — age, gender, and class among them — that crisscross the landscape of cultural identity and that affect the shape of life and racial destinies of black Americans. Most versions of racial unity have failed to engage these issues in liberating or illuminating fashion.

Complicating matters more, the rhetorics of race loyalty and racial authenticity are almost naturally clustered around the rhetoric of racial unity. Taken together, these rhetorics compose the moral center of a politics of racial propriety, used by some black intellectuals to determine what is legitimate and acceptable for a widening body of black cultural expression. Loyalty to race has been historically construed as primary and unquestioning allegiance to the racial quest for freedom and the refusal to betray that quest to personal benefit or the diverting pursuit of lesser goals. Those who detour from the prescribed path are labeled "sellouts," "traitors," or "Uncle Toms."

At various times in African-American history, race loyalty has meant refusing to reveal slave plans to revolt or escape; empathy for emigrationist movements back to Africa in the Conventionist Era; support for various strategies of mass civil disobedience and other tactics of racial rebellion and protest developed during the Civil Rights and Black Power movements; holding radical class-based interrogations of racial politics at arm's length; repudiating neoconservative criticism of black culture, especially attacks on black liberal or nationalist race ideology; refraining from public criticism of black leaders, especially elected officials; and chastising black women writers for "betraying" black men with "negative" literary portraits.

The rhetoric of racial authenticity has been employed to reveal the ostensibly authentic bases of black intellectual and artistic expression. Those who deviate from familiar forms of racial identity and cultural expression are termed "oreos," or "incognegroes." Debates about racial authenticity have questioned whether black cultural icons like Michael Jackson and Whitney Houston have rejected enabling expressions of blackness in their art; whether black politicians like Douglas Wilder, David Dinkins, and Wilson Goode have abandoned the goals of historic black politics in their bid for the political mainstream; whether a black literary critical theory should enlarge upon a black aesthetic that is grounded in a black or Afrocentric worldview, or traffic in avant-garde theories rife with French prefixes, German suffixes, and British cognates.

It is in the crossfire between unprincipled assaults upon black culture's *raison d'etre* from outside its ranks, the debilitating decline in intellectual acuity in American culture at large, and the romantic and myth-producing impulses of African-American culture, that black critical consciousness has been fatefully wedged. Because black critical consciousness has been unable to find its best voice at the center of black culture, it has found fruitful exile on black culture's creative margins, inspiring varying degrees of support within academic and literary circles, ecclesiastical organizations, and vernacular cultural traditions.

But the peripheral position of criticism means that it is often expressed in disenabling forms as well. The deflection of the critical impulse into destructive expressions is poignantly symbolized in the legendary crab barrel metaphor of intraracial strife. This familiar black cultural metaphor compares the plight of African-Americans to crabs in a barrel that, instead of pooling their resources to help free each other, prevent the successful escape of any member through the self-defeating activity of mutual clawing. More specifically, the comparison captures the untamed envy on the part of some blacks for another black's social mobility, economic well-being, or educational accomplishment, assuming the form of hostile hints of personal defect or outright character assassination. A deflected critical reaction is transparent as well in the elliptic criticism that is expressed in signifying speech and in the often humorous, but sometimes lethal, linguistic put-down of the "dozens."

Aside from criticism's disenabling expressions, veiled criticism is also employed by persons who suffer exclusion from official authority, or by those who fear that explicit criticism is likely to incur penalty or scorn. Such concealed criticism is manifest, for example, in church gossip that slows or interrupts the harmful effects that antidemocratic leadership may have on ecclesiastical life. This variety of criticism is especially directed at pastors who view even gentle criticism as disloyalty, or boards of deacons or trustees who view the legitimation of any voice other than their own as institutional treason.

The cultural realities I have discussed reinforce the need of a mature and oppositional criticism of black culture. Such criticism revels in black culture's virtues, takes pleasure in its achievements, laments its failed opportunities, and interrogates its weaknesses. An oppositional African-American cultural criticism is engaged in resisting the labored seductions of all narrow views of black life, whether they be racist, essentialist, or otherwise uncritically disposed toward African-American culture.

Moreover, an oppositional African-American cultural criticism is open in its search for truth about black culture wherever it may be found. It views black folk not merely as victims of history but, in limited manner, as agents of their own jubilation and pain and creators of worlds of meaning through art, thought, and sport that fend off the prospects of personal and social absurdity. An oppositional African-American cultural criticism roots critical reflection in a racial maturity that acknowledges the differentiation of black life. The expansion of criticism upon the basis of such racial maturity appeals to criticism's best history and works toward the most progressive possibilities for its richest future. Three principles guide my understanding of an oppositional African-American cultural criticism.

Such a criticism must be antiessentialist about black racial and cultural identity. Racial essences have been promoted through literary critical theories that attempt to mine the conceptual riches of blackness as sign and symbol; through philosophical arguments intent on rebutting the denial of humanity to Africans and African-Americans by tracing racial identity to a unitary cultural source in Africa; through everyday criticism of crossover music; and through black films that aspire to an archetypal representation of black life.

An oppositional African-American cultural criticism holds that identity is socially and culturally constructed from the raw materials of the individual and social, the private and public, and the domestic and civic. Racial identity is not exhausted by genetic inheritance. The processes by which the meanings of race are shattered and reconstituted over time and place in American culture convincingly make the case against a narrow understanding of racial identity.

Although it is undeniably rooted in pigment and physiology, racial identity transcends their boundaries. It is created and remade in a network of conflicting and converging social relations, political options, civil limits, gender politics, economic crises, religious narratives, and moral choices. Given the variety of elements and the complexity of means by which racial identity is constructed, there can be no essential black identity because racial identity is relentlessly reshaped. Also, the intellectual, empirical and material strata of black culture — from which racial identity can be usefully excavated — challenge the politics of essentialism. The differences that geography, sexual preference, gender, and class position generate within black culture cannot be captured by essentialist thought.

Of course, I don't mean that there are not distinct black cultural characteristics that persist over space and time, but these features of black life are the products of the historical and social construction of racial identity. For instance, we may point to patterns of verbal and artistic invention identified as call and response that are threaded through various dimensions of black culture. Evidences of call and response can be glimpsed in the rhetorical improvisations of ministers in the black pulpit. Black preachers refine their craft in sacred settings where their verbal performances are shaped by a responsive audience that employs either ecstatic vocal support or silent rejection of the preacher's declared truth. Call and response also may be viewed in concerts where vocal artists' performances evoke affirmative applause or signs of disruptive disapproval, responsive elements that are often creatively woven into the fabric of the live and electric performed moment.

But call and response and countless other characteristics of black life, as well, are socially created, culturally improvised, and historically transmitted. These distinct features of black life nuance and shape black cultural expression from the preaching of Martin Luther King to the singing of Gladys Knight. They, however, do not form the basis of a black racial or cultural essence. Nor do they indicate that *the* meaning of blackness will be expressed in a quality or characteristic without which a person, act, or practice no longer qualifies as black. Rigid racial essentialism must be opposed.

Oppositional African-American cultural criticism must also acknowledge the broad range of American experiences that influence its makeup, shape its expression, and challenge its existence. Although it must always keep track of the effects of racism, an oppositional criticism also describes how class and gender affect African-American culture while creating strategies to reveal their importance as categories of social theory, criticism, and struggle. For instance, as intellectuals have charted the gargantuan forces that circumscribe African-American life, class politics have been largely ignored. Of course, exceptions prevail. W. E. B. Du Bois, Paul Robeson, and Oliver Cromwell Cox, among others, argued for the prominence of class politics in an earlier day, while Barbara Fields, Manning Marable, Cornel West, and William Julius Wilson have made more contemporary claims. Class politics and conflicts constitute a crucial ideological juncture in African-American intellectual history, proving that a methodological loyalty to race *only* analysis — versus a race *specific* analysis — fails fully to illumine our current cultural crises.

Given the renaissance of black nationalist discourse, and a concomitant revival of explicit race hatred on college campuses and in ethnic communities across America, the difficulty of pushing past narrow understandings of our condition become more difficult but no less urgent. Class differentiation complicates simple and reductive cultural versions of unified racial action. Many significant differences between blacks follow the axis of class and are shaped by its unyielding persistence. Although, for example, Bill Cosby's and a black shoeshiner's lives are intertwined by race, their perceptions of the world also are bounded by differences of class location and economic stability.

Gender similarly has been neglected as a useful category for organizing social resistance or for comprehending vital aspects of black culture. The presumed primacy of eliminating racism as a black cultural goal — a crucial ideological pillar in integrationist and nationalist racial politics — has obscured the distinctive voices of black women who suffer the cruel jeopardies of multiple oppression and who skillfully have had to criticize the constitutive elements of black feminist identities. Sojourner Truth, Ida Wells Barnett, Harriet Tubman, Harriet Jacobs, Anna Julia Cooper, Alice Walker, Michele Wallace, Audre Lorde, and bell hooks have mapped the enormously difficult route to full voice for black women. Gender figures prominently in a healthy African-American cultural criticism that, in the past, has mostly failed to oppose an ironic black patriarchy; on the one hand, a faded reflection of white patriarchy in regard to black men wielding institutional power and, on the other hand, is a faithful imitation of white patriarchy's worst effects, felt most severely in domestic violence by black men aimed at women and children.

An oppositional African-American cultural criticism also is public and receptive to the best critical insights available from all responsible and reasonable quarters. It does not observe a tedious etiquette of racial manners that maintains that negative, controversial, or critical news about black folk — especially if its source is other blacks — must be handled in secrecy away from the omniscient gaze of white society. We may term this protective response to the harmful white surveillance of black culture as the "dirty laundry theory" of racial politics.

Of course, it made sense for slaves to handle their business in their own domain, not exposing their differences to the threat of exploitation by white masters. But even in slavery, the conditions for successful privacy — an intimate geographical environment where information flow could be controlled, with all relevant parties having access to conversation in a relatively democratic space — were barely available. Moreover, slaves held conflicting views on how best to cope with their condition: some wanted to revolt (Turner, Vesey); some advocated escape (Tubman); some preferred subtler forms of subversion (hymns, spirituals); some believed remaining under white rule was a greener pasture than the wilderness of black escape (so-called "Toms"); and many advocated enduring slavery while rebelling in small but significant symbolic rituals of resistance (for example, mixing in unsavory elements during food preparation).

Under contemporary conditions of African-American diaspora, exile, and differentiation, attempting to emulate such racial privacy and secrecy is clearly detrimental. When it is secret and closed, cultural criticism threatens to become elitist and antidemocratic. Making criticism public encourages the widest possible participation of a diverse audience of potential interlocutors. The dirty laundry theory of racial politics has recently surfaced at three cultural sites: the controversy surrounding Spike Lee's production of his third film *School Daze*, the political controversy occasioned by former Washington Mayor Marion Barry's drug case, and the tragic racial fiasco involving New York's Tawana Brawley.

Spike Lee's third film *School Daze*, a morality play about black intraracial conflict, was roundly criticized in many quarters as a harsh and punitive peek into ugly black racial identity politics, such gestures that, many believed, were better left to the black pulpit, beauty salon, or classroom. Lee's film, a minor *succes de scandale*, was staged during a Homecoming Weekend celebration at a historically black college and revealed the lethal confrontations black folk have over hair texture, skin complexion, class status, and educational attainment. During the course of filming, Lee was forced off the campus of his alma mater, Morehouse College. The move was allegedly due to crossed signals regarding the availability of dorm space for filming, but a more likely explanation may be retaliation by Morehouse's administration against Lee's critical look at the rituals of black self-hate dramatized in full color and sketched on a film canvas that the entire public was invited to view. Such narrowness of racial vision embodied in Morehouse's response and the racial insecurity that feeds it must be addressed and opposed.

The alleged rape of Tawana Brawley by a gang of white men illustrated the pernicious consequences of the dirty laundry theory of racial politics. After it became likely that Ms. Brawley was ominously entangled in a web of deceit, most segments of the black (leadership) community were unable to offer public criticism of Brawley or her handlers, Alton Maddox, C. Vernon Mason, and Al Sharpton. Most tragically, the likely reason for Brawley's desperate public disregard for truth — the fear of domestic violence by her mother's male companion as reprisal for Tawana's disobedience — was obscured in the scattered and weak black public criticism of the Brawley case. The confused black response contributed once again to the silencing of the black female voice about a significant source of its repression and helped divert attention from the sometimes brutal consequences of the sexism and patriarchy that are deeply entrenched in black culture.

The case of Barry is more complex but, nonetheless, exemplary. Barry was videotaped smoking crack cocaine, and answered for his behavior in a highly publicized criminal trial. Remarkably, with few exceptions, there was little black public criticism of Barry's behavior or of his flagrant abuse of his black supporters' stringent and sometimes colorful loyalty. Of course, this silence was achieved in part because of the wide black cultural perception of the general attack on prominent black political leadership by federal, state, and local government officials.

Unfailingly, many black leaders are denigrated for alleged political, moral, or legal indiscretions, a pattern of attack that began in recent times with the varied personal and political troubles of Adam Clayton Powell. Thus, Barry became the highly charged symbol of black political power under assault, which exacerbated the public resentment of black citizens across America. Interestingly, there was not a commensurate public criticism of Barry motivated by the evidence of his political decline prior to his public downfall. Undoubtedly, many believed that silence about Barry's foibles was the most eloquent emblem of racial solidarity. But given the corruption of contemporary American politics and the political hustling from which black political leadership is not exempt, such forces must be energetically opposed.

By contrast, the riveting and repulsive drama of O. J. Simpson's freakish unraveling before our very eyes contained many ironies. An athlete whose brilliant moves on the football field were marked by beauty and grace, O. J. now left an international audience aghast at his ungainly flight from the law. A champion who played Prometheus to a nation of Walter Mittys now shrank in stature to a shriveled, self-defeating parody of his former strength. An icon with an ingenious talent for turning gridiron glory into Hollywood fame and fortune was now bedeviled by the media that helped make him a national figure.

And a man whose face and initials were broadly familiar became, in an instant, a stranger with a secret history of spousal abuse that may prove to have been an unseemly rehearsal for murder. But one of the most remarkable ironies of the commentary around Simpson's sad situation is the way in which race, in its deliberate denial, has been made even more present. Like Poe's purloined letter, race lies hidden in plain sight.

On the face of things, such a denial signals a praiseworthy attempt by the media to balance its racially skewed reporting of news events. That's not easy when politicians and pundits are obsessed with negatively linking race to everything from welfare reform to crime. But in denying the role of race in the Simpson ordeal, media critics reveal the faulty assumptions behind efforts to get beyond race by pretending it's not there.

The goal should not be to transcend race, but to transcend the biased meanings associated with race. Ironically, the very attempt to transcend race by denying its presence reinforces its power to influence perceptions because it gains strength in secrecy. Like a poisonous mushroom, the tangled assumptions of race grow best in darkness. For race to have a less detrimental effect, it must be brought into the light and openly engaged as a feature of the events and discussions it influences, even if in subtle ways.

In the case of O. J. Simpson, the fingerprints of race are everywhere. First, his spectacular rise to fame was aided not only by his extraordinary gifts but, because he fit the mold of a talented but tamed black man who was known in his youth as a "respectable Negro." O. J. received brownie points throughout his playing career as much for who he wasn't as for how he performed. He wasn't considered, like football star-turned-actor Jim Brown, a black "buck," an "uppity nigger," an arrogant, in-your-face threat because of his volatile presence and unpredictable behavior. From the beginning, O. J. Simpson was marketed to white society as a raceless figure whose charisma drew from his sophisticated, articulate public persona. In this light, horrified, disbelieving gasps of "not him" unleashed at O. J.'s public disintegration take on new weight.

That Simpson's second wife Nicole Brown Simpson — whom O. J. has been accused of brutally murdering — was a beautiful blonde white woman has gone virtually unremarked upon, though her now ubiquitous picture has made it hard not to notice. By marrying Nicole, O. J. transgressed one of the remaining taboos of race and sex in our nation.

When a black man marries a white woman, it irks KKK types ("he's spoiled one of *our* women"); grieves many black mothers ("when a black son brings home a white woman, it's an insult to his mama"); angers many white men ("she's throwing her life away"); disappoints many black women ("with all these single black women, why would he choose a white woman?"); unnerves some white women ("I could never see myself with a black man"); and raises some black men's ire ("why do all these brothers, when they become successful, have to marry a white woman?"). This small sample of anecdotal responses to interracial relationships provides a glimpse of the furious passions and unresolved conflicts that continue to haunt love in black and white. Were O. J. and Nicole completely immune to such concerns? Probably not. Does the fact that O. J. is charged with killing his *white* wife make a difference in our world? Probably so. Can we seriously doubt that if O. J. had been accused of murdering his *black* wife and not the ultimate symbol of ideal white beauty we wouldn't be learning of it with a similar degree of intensity, its details adorned in such gaudy omnipresence?

The attempt to negotiate the politics of race by negating its presence causes us to overlook the irony of how O. J.'s abrupt decline embodies the plight of more black men now than he did at his heroic height. (After all, there are thousands more black men in prison than in the Hall of Fame.) Less than a week before his fall, O. J. appeared to be a lifetime away from the heartless siege of troubles that vex millions of black men.

But his current condition has added O. J.'s name to a growing list of (in)famous black men whose personal problems have made them poster boys for the perversions of (white) patriarchal culture. Mike Tyson and date rape. Clarence

Thomas and sexual harassment. Michael Jackson and child molestation. And now, O. J. Simpson and spousal abuse. Each of these problems merits serious action, and these men, if guilty, should be held responsible and punished accordingly. But serious, probing questions — questions that can only be raised when race is above board — must be asked in explaining how such a circumstance could occur in a nation where millions of white men, well-known and anonymous alike, commit the same offenses, though often without stigma or punishment. Even the moral and legal consequences of crime appear to be determined by race.

Many argue that Simpson's troubles have nothing to do with race, that his fall instead is an *American* tragedy. Of course it is, because all black citizens are Americans, and all of our problems, therefore, are American problems. But we don't have to embrace our American identity at the expense of our race. The two are not mutually exclusive. We simply have to overcome the limitations imposed upon race to make sure that privilege is not viciously, arbitrarily assigned to racial difference. To erase race is to erase ourselves and to obscure how race continues to shape American perceptions and lives. As the commentary on O. J. Simpson proves, that which is denied may not become popular, but it certainly becomes powerful.

In broad compass, an oppositional African-American cultural criticism is concerned to examine the redemptive and unattractive features of African-American culture, to pass fair but critical judgment on a variety of cultural expressions and historic figures, from popular music to preaching, from black nationalist politics to the political economy of crack, from Jesse Jackson to Michael Jordan. It promotes the preservation of black culture's best features, the amelioration of its weakest parts, and the eradication of its worst traits.

Notes

1 This essay is adapted from the introduction to Michael Eric Dyson's *Reflecting Black: African-American Cultural Criticism* (The University of Minnesota Press, 1993).

2 For more discussion of my views on the relation between essentialism and identity politics, see my "Contesting Racial Amnesia: From Identity Politics Toward Post-Multiculturalism," in *Higher Education Under Fire*, eds Michael Berube and Cary Nelson (New York: Routledge, 1994).

11

Black Vernacular Representation and Cultural Malpractice

TOMMY L. LOTT

The unfortunate thing about American thought is the habit of classifying first and investigating after. As a result this misrepresentation of the temper and spirit of Negro folk lore has become traditional, and for all we know, permanent.

Arthur Huff Fauset

If we are a race we must have a race tradition, and if we are to have a race tradition we must keep and cherish it as a priceless — yes, as a holy thing — and above all not be ashamed to wear the badge of our tribe.

Alain L. Locke

Witnessing black comedians perform acts of self-denigration sometimes can be a painful experience for black spectators. Many prominent black leaders expressed outrage at Ted Danson's use of blackface comedy in his roast of Whoopi Goldberg. Several black celebrities in attendance claimed to have been deeply offended by Danson's minstrel show humor, which they thought viciously objectified and ridiculed black people whether it was intended to do so or not. Being told that Whoopi Goldberg collaborated with Danson to write the skit did not affect this judgment. Some maintained that such humor perpetuates racism whether presented by a white or a black comedian.[1] This public outcry by black leaders marks a recent break with a familiar pattern of officially protesting apparently racist humor by white performers while refraining from officially protesting a very similar humor by black performers. A major difficulty faced by those who believe an official protest ought to be possible in either case is the lack of agreement, especially in the latter instances, about what constitutes racism and self-denigration. By focusing on some of the perennial criticisms of black vernacular representation, I aim to highlight a much neglected discussion of this problem in the discourse on black culture. I want to draw attention to the inadequacy of the criteria used to identify self-denigrating aspects of black vernacular culture. Political ideology is a major factor influencing judgments of this sort. I argue that to identify a particular instance of black vernacular representation as self-denigrating is tantamount to rendering a judgment regarding the ideological orientation of the artist.

The term "black vernacular" refers primarily to the oral and paralinguistic activity of the speakers of a black dialect. Here, I use it to include the idioms employed in various media to represent these speakers. Black artists have been charged with cultural malpractice whenever they have been taken to employ these idioms in a fashion that misrepresents black people. This misrepresentation occurs at several levels. The material image might include phenomena such as misspelled or mispronounced words, Sambo and mammy caricatures, simianized portrayals or even gorillas themselves, as a sign of the inferiority of black people. The material image, however, does not always reveal its underlying ideology; that is, whether beneath this surface there are elements of accommodationism, resistance, or perhaps even both. On the view I shall advance in support of the black cultural norm against malpractice, the accusation that black vernacular culture has been misrepresented at a deeper ideological level is most often a perceptual claim standing in need of a justification. Historically, the charge of cultural malpractice has been leveled by an illustrious group of intellectuals. To what criteria did they appeal to justify their various *perceptions* that a misrepresentation of black vernacular culture had occurred?

The Cultural Malpractice Charge

One type of vernacular misrepresentation at the material level of transcription involves the spelling of the words used to represent a black dialect. Sojourner Truth's famous quote, for instance, is sometimes rendered as *Ain't I A Woman* or *Ar'n't I A Woman,* depending on the author.[2] If Truth spoke with a Dutch accent, however, it is a misrepresentation to attribute a black southern speech pattern to her. Moreover, if it is racist for a white transcriber to impute a black literary dialect to her, it seems equally racist for a black transcriber to do this. Sojourner Truth's speech will be misrepresented if rendered in standard English, in a conventional literary black dialect, or in any other dialect we invent for her.[3] This is due to the fact that an accurate transcription of her lost dialect is needed to gain access to the idiom captured by her manner of speech. But is this generally so?

Sterling Brown, an accomplished dialectal poet, wrote a cautionary note to the WPA regarding the collecting of slave narratives in dialect.[4] He made two recommendations. He insisted that standard English be used, arguing that because most Americans speak with a dialect there is no need to adopt a special spelling of words for African-American speech patterns. He even provided a list of words that were not to be used. Unlike the Sojourner Truth case of a lost dialect, Brown's recommendation seems to presuppose a common familiarity among the readers of the WPA narratives with the pronunciation used by speakers of a black dialect.

Brown also insisted that the editorializing should be minimal, with the words "darky" and "nigger" omitted. He stipulated that these words are permitted only where the ex-slave herself used them. Apparently, Brown was addressing not only an issue of transcription, or the spelling of words, but also a political concern with racism. Notwithstanding a common awareness that in the context of a legally segregated South the connotation of terms such as "nigger" or "darky" were quite different when stated by a white person, it is remarkable that Brown remained more concerned with the representation of black dialect than with the racial identity of the transcriber. He maintained that "Truth to idiom is more important ... than truth to pronunciation" and cited Erskine Caldwell, Ruth Suckow, and Zora Neale Hurston as authors who could "get a truth to the manner of speaking without excessive misspellings."[5]

In his book *The Cool World,* Warren Miller recorded the speech patterns of the black urban males he observed on the streets of Harlem.[6] Critics have suspiciously viewed Miller's book not only with regard to his literary representation of black dialect but with equal regard to his reproduction of popular mainstream conceptions.[7] Since, for most, the dialect he employed requires translation, his story undoubtedly would have been more accessible had he followed Brown's advice regarding the spelling of words in standard English. Although, just as in the above cases, Miller's use of black dialect can be criticized by specifically citing the linguistic criterion of spelling, he might have replied that he used a particular spelling in order to capture the black urban idiom more accurately. This shows that disagreement about whether the spelling Miller adopted constitutes a misrepresentation is not precluded, and perhaps what is really at issue is a question of ideology. Given the social norm that dictates a white-authored version of a black dialect is always to be suspected of latent racism, such disagreements cannot be resolved on wholly scientific grounds.[8]

There have been occasions, however, on which scientific evidence has been persuasively employed to resolve such disagreements when suspicions about a black person's use of dialect were raised. In her typical eloquence, Anna Julia Cooper accused Paul Robeson of misrepresenting black dialect. According to Cooper,

The story has gone the rounds of the press that Paul Robeson, who himself tells us that he has toiled and spent to attain the accent not offensive to Mayfair, sometimes slips into the "soft slur of the Southern Negro" and even at the tragic moment of Othello's sublime fury demands: "Where am dat handkerchief, Desdemona?"

Reporters and critics must sell their stuff and one should not grudge them their little joke. Nothing helps like a bit of local color to heighten tone effects. This story listens well for heart interest on this side of the Atlantic, where a black man is not true black unless he says "am dat." Mr. Robeson in his impersonation of the noble blackamoor may on his own part deliberately allow himself the racial touch, not at all inconsistent to my mind with a highly artistic effect. If he did so, be sure it was not a slip; he had been instructed and believed that such a departure would give just the original flavor he was expected to create. But speaking *ex cathedra* I claim, as one who ought to know, that no artist who has intelligently analyzed the Negro folk-speech, whether he be poet, novelist, or impersonator, can ever accept "am dat" as a possibility in Negro or Southern vocalization.[9]

Cooper goes on to provide a detailed physiological explanation of the impossibility of this verbal construction in Southern black speech. She supported her cultural malpractice charge against Robeson's use of dialect by relying on sociolinguistic evidence and facts about the physiological production of speech. Her insight was derived from her long experience as a Southern black teacher as well as from her formal study of languages at the Sorbonne.[10]

Notice that Cooper accused Robeson of using an invented dialect to emphasize his black identity. This is similar to the cultural malpractice charge against Sojourner Truth's transcribers. In both cases the pronunciation is deliberately changed to accord with a more stereotypical representation. Further, the misrepresentation originates with a white author but it is perpetuated by a black author or performer. The black cultural norm against accepting white-authored black dialect by writers such as Warren Miller must be viewed in the light of a history of deliberate misrepresentations by white transcribers. Cooper's cultural malpractice charge against Robeson makes clear that such misrepresentations involve more than a matter of misspelled words, but also involve a political problem of idioms being manufactured to fit a certain stereotype of black people.

Alain Locke's Remarks on the Representation of Black Folk Culture

In his analysis of the literary uses of black dialect, Dillard noted that among all of the black writers he had surveyed, Hurston and Richard Wright were the best at reproducing authentic black dialect.[11] But how do we square this praise from a sociolinguist with the well-known criticisms of Hurston's use of dialect by some of her literary cohorts?[12] Given Hurston's training as an anthropologist, it is difficult to imagine how she could have produced either an inaccurate transcription of black dialect or misrepresented the Southern black idioms of her hometown. Yet her mentor, Alain Locke, had the following to say in his review of her book *Their Eyes Were Watching God:*

> Her gift for poetic phrase, for rare dialect, and folk humor keep her flashing on the surface of her community and her characters and from diving down deep either to the inner psychology of characterization or to sharp analysis of the social background. It is folklore fiction at its best, ... But when will the Negro novelist of maturity, who knows how to tell a story convincingly — which is Miss Hurston's cradle gift, come to grips with native fiction and social document fiction? Progressive southern fiction has already banished the legend of these entertaining pseudo-primitives whom the reading public still loves to laugh with, weep over and envy. Having gotten rid of condescension, let us now get over oversimplification![13]

Locke's criticism has an aesthetic and a political dimension. From his aesthetic standpoint, he praised Hurston's ability to accurately represent the dialect and idioms of her folk characters. What he questioned was her lack of social consciousness in presenting these characters. He was concerned that she merely perpetuated the sentimentalist dialectal tradition of caricature rather than what he considered to be "genuine folk portraiture."[14] Locke's distinction between caricature and portraiture, however, is far from clear.

Scholars have sometimes conceived certain folkloric aspects of black vernacular culture as retentions traceable to West Africa.[15] In his book *The Signifying Monkey,* Gates juxtaposes black vernacular oral literature and a "formal black Literature."[16] This dichotomy of folk culture and high culture sometimes conveys a transhistorical notion of dialectal speakers as bearers of an authentic black culture.[17] This idea was quite prominent in Alain Locke's social theory and a cornerstone of his account of the evolutionary development of African-American art. With regard to African-American drama he claimed that "the timeless beauty of Negro folk life and tradition, including that taproot of it which leads back to the vast traditions of Africa, must someday yield its dramatic treasures."[18] Locke was keenly aware of the social transformation of African retentions under the brutal influence of slavery and their continual transformation as the ex-slaves developed an African-American folk culture from their peasant lifestyles. He recognized that, due to the large migrations of blacks from the rural South to urban centers in the North at the turn of the century, most of their preindustrial folk beliefs and folkways would be lost.[19] His theory of folk art aimed to provide an account of the metamorphosis of surviving Africanisms from their earliest forms as folklore to their more mature forms as high tragedy or comedy. According to Locke, "One can scarcely think of a complete development of Negro dramatic art without some significant artistic reexpression of African life, and the tradition associated with it."[20]

Locke's concern with African retentions in African-American folklore is most vividly presented in a series of manuscript notes he sent to Hurston regarding her field studies of Southern black folklore.[21] In some cases, he rejected her stories as being of a non-African origin or he requested a more accurate or more complete explanation of an alleged retention, whereas, in other cases, he endorsed their African elements or origin. Taken as a whole, Locke's remarks suggest that he thought the authenticity of African-American folk culture is ultimately established by reference to verifiable African retentions.[22]

In his Fisk University lecture on Paul Laurence Dunbar, Locke explained the importance of field studies, such as Hurston's, for the advanced development of a black literary tradition.

> [T]he Negro must reveal himself if the true instincts and characteristics of the race are ever to find their place in literature. In Ireland now some of the greatest literary men of our time are hard at work, visiting the lumber cabins of the Irish peasants collecting their folk tales, their stories, and writing them into literature.[23]

Locke often drew this parallel between African-American folk culture and other folk cultures throughout the world. He held that to carry out the social function of revitalizing the cultural life of the race, African-American art must develop an organic tradition by drawing on the "ancestral sources of African life and material."[24]

Although Locke believed there were African retentions, he rejected the notion of an atavistic "race-soul" that contributed to the primitivism formula so prevalent in American fiction and drama about black people.[25] He maintained that "the Negro's primitivism is nine-tenths that of the peasant the world over and has only a remote tropical flavor."[26] He held a strictly sociohistorical notion of race that emphasized cultural rather than biological traits. Hence, he used the notions of "race" and "folk" interchangeably, identifying African-Americans as a race with the spoken tradition that developed from their isolation in the rural South and the rigors of agricultural life.[27] According to Locke, "We are a race because we have a common race tradition, and each one of us becomes such just in proportion as he recognizes, knows and reverences that tradition."[28] He considered Dunbar to be an exponent of this race tradition because of Dunbar's interest in preserving the plantation folk beliefs and folkways that were gradually vanishing. Locke believed that maintaining this tradition was the only means of transmitting the valuable lessons of the forebears to a younger generation.

Locke's criticism of Hurston does not seem to square with his praise of Dunbar's contribution to the African-American literary tradition. He attributed to Dunbar a sense of social responsibility concerning the race tradition. Given that Hurston could easily be viewed as having Dunbar's sense of social responsibility, Locke's point had more to do with the relation between her work and its social context than with the work itself.[29] During the period of Dunbar's writing career, his poetry served the useful purpose of adding an absent black voice to the sentimentalist plantation literature, whereas, several decades later at the time Hurston wrote, the dialectal tradition had degenerated into minstrelsy.

In his critique of minstrelsy, Locke recognized that the sentimentalist tradition fostered by white authors such as Joel Chandler Harris, as well as Dunbar, included portrayals of the Southern black peasant that were really "vital."[30] He also recognized that the influence of the public demand for more and more stereotypes had led to disproportionate caricature. His criticism of Hurston meant to draw in question her intention in presenting characters who simply perpetuated this caricature. Perhaps the force of this objection to Hurston can be appreciated by comparing it with his equally nuanced criticism of white authors who wrote in dialect. For example, he criticized DuBose Heywood for using the primitivism formula of an atavistic race-soul while in the same breath he claimed that "*Porgy* was the first Negro play that moved with real primitive force instead of the fake primitivism imposed on the Negro cast by directors trying to force them into preconceived moulds."[31] But with regard to Gershwin's opera version of *Porgy*, Locke protested that the director "was guilty of overworking his own discovery with set mannerisms."[32] The dissatisfaction Locke expressed here with the representation of black folk culture by white authors seems to parallel his criticism of Hurston.

Locke was critical of white dramatists for relying on stock formulas that produced "an overstudied situation lacking spontaneity and exuberant vitality."[33] Many of his reservations about the black folk drama of white playwrights stemmed from his belief that only the black playwright can reveal the inner stresses and dilemmas of black folk characters. For Locke, this was "not a question of race, but of intimacy of understanding."[34] Although white dramatists such as Paul Green had "unimpeachable artistic motives" and came close to a genuine representation of black folk idioms, Locke believed that only a black dramatist could provide the requisite touch.[35] In his review of Hurston's play *Moses: Man of the Mountain*, however, he again gave a scathing critique of her treatment of black folk characters. "What if the stereotyping is benign instead of sinister, warmly intimate instead of cynical or condescending, it is still caricature for all that instead of portraiture."[36] Locke generally expected something more from black playwrights than what he expected from white playwrights. His criticisms of Hurston, nevertheless, seem somewhat unfair by comparison with his more favorable comments on Heywood's *Porgy*.

Given his dismissal of Hurston, what more did Locke expect from black dramatists? He claimed that Hurston's treatment of black folk characters was caricature rather than portraiture. This criticism was tantamount to his political objection to minstrelsy. Keep in mind here that Locke does not object to Hurston's characters as such; rather, he thought Hurston's shortcoming was that she failed to provide "a sharp analysis of the social background."[37] This objection, however, is out of line with Locke's more notorious criticism of black writers whose work he considered to be political propaganda.[38] Locke seems to have commented more favorably on white dramatists because he considered the black dramatist's advantage of psychological intimacy to be more than offset by the disadvantage of insufficient aesthetic distance which inclined so many to seek racial vindication in their work.

To clarify Locke's political concern with minstrelsy, some explanation is needed of the discontinuity between his commentary on Hurston's black folk characterizations and his commentary on similar folk characterizations by white authors. He seems to have criticized Hurston inconsistently for not providing a social analysis he labeled as propaganda in the work of other black writers leaving us to wonder about some of the political implications of his aesthetic notion of genuine folk portraiture for his general view of high folk art. When he spoke in praise of the "dramatic treasures" that would come from "the timeless beauty of Negro folk life and tradition" and more harshly of the "un-actable propaganda plays" of black dramatists, he set up a time-honored dichotomy between aesthetics and propaganda. He believed, however, there was a social and political justification for "the more purely aesthetic attitudes."[39] His periodic evaluations of the growth and development of Negro artistic expression rested on his sociological view of group progress. Because he believed that life was becoming less of a problem and more a "vital process" for the younger black person, Locke thought that the purely artistic point of view and vision was also becoming more of a possibility.[40] In this regard, Locke's criticisms of Hurston seem to reflect his dissatisfaction with her lack of artistic maturity. In his earlier review of her first novel *Jonah's Gourd Vine,* he stated, "For years we have been saying we wanted to achieve 'objectivity' — here it is."[41]

There was a political dimension to the aesthetic principle underlying Locke's critique of minstrelsy. He saw his view of folk drama as being compatible with Marxism.[42] In response to the criticism that his view was a reversion to aestheticism and art-for-art's-sake, he pointed out that "a reawakening of an oppressed people is spiritually impossible without restored pride and cultural self-respect."[43] He compared his proposal that folk culture provide a source of materials for high art with the policy of the Soviet national theaters. According to Locke, "The social yield of such ethnic art is as great or greater than its artistic yield."[44] But what exactly was the social yield Locke had in mind?

As the drama of "free expression and imaginative release," according to Locke, folk drama, "has no objective but to express beautifully and colorfully the folk life of the race ... to cover life with the illusion of happiness and spiritual freedom."[45] While it is far from clear how this would break down false stereotypes and stimulate black cultural life, Locke's remarks regarding the objectives of folk drama, nonetheless, help shed light on his notion of genuine folk portraiture. He tells us that,

But when our serious drama shall become as naive and spontaneous as our drama of fun and laughter, and that in turn genuinely representative of the folk spirit which it is now forced to travesty, a point of classic development will have been reached."[46]

Here again we are left to wonder what, if anything, could have possibly satisfied Locke's criteria for a genuine representation of the folk spirit.

Surprisingly, his clearest statement of this achievement is reserved for the Hollywood film *Hearts in Dixie*.[47] After noting certain lapses in the film, Locke cited several outstanding features of its representation of black folk culture. He claimed that "[t]he absence of the clownish leer and the minstrel's self-pity are real steps toward the genuineness of Negro emotion."[48] He also claimed that in a film such as this, which managed to "cut away from all dependence on stock pantomime, the Negro voice achieves an artistic triumph, and for the reason that it is purely Negro than ever, a fine peasant thing in a genuine setting."[49] Locke's praise of this film is quite remarkable when compared with the views of film critics who straightforwardly dismissed it as minstrelsy. Consider, for example, Locke's claim that "Stepin Fetchit in this picture is as true as instinct itself, a true mirror of the folk manner."[50] Film critic Gary Null saw something different. According to Null, "Stepin Fetchit led the songs and played the very incarnation of the irresponsible nigger who knew his place, loved his master, and just grinned for joy every time his laziness was rewarded by a kick in the pants."[51] The fact that Locke's judgment of the representation of black folk culture in this film is contested in almost the same terms as his own criticism of Hurston shows, I think, that his attempt to ground his critique of minstrelsy on aesthetic principles was inadequate. The disagreement between Locke and Null indicates that what Locke considered genuine portraiture is sometimes viewed by others as caricature. Locke's aesthetic criteria for identifying genuine portraiture failed to render it distinguishable from caricature. In what follows, I will argue that this failure is due to the highly politicized nature of black vernacular representation.

The Paradox of Minstrelsy

Despite Locke's desire to use wholly aesthetic criteria to distinguish between racist and nonracist white authors who wrote in the folk-dialectal tradition, he invariably made reference to their *intentions*. Saunders Redding followed Locke's rationale regarding this distinction, showing even more concern with the political motivation of white authors who used black dialect. In a manner that echoed Locke's commitment to genuine folk representation, Redding championed a view of integrity and honest exploration of the black experience. Much more than Locke, however, he viewed the folk-dialectal tradition as a manifestation of Booker T. Washington's accommodationist ideology which perpetuated the image of the contented ex-slave and supported the views of white apologists for segregation.[52] For this decidedly political reason, Redding's view quickly shifted from a criticism of individual practitioners of the folk-dialectal tradition to a rejection of the dialectal genre entirely, whereas Locke saw in the genre the aesthetic possibility of a transformation of folk expression into high art. Hence, Redding dismissed Dunbar's dialectal poetry while Locke saw worthier elements in it.

Does the intentionality criterion invoked by Locke and Redding against white authors who wrote in black dialect apply to black authors as well, and to what extent? Interestingly, Redding was critical of Dunbar's dialectal poetry, but not of Dunbar. He acknowledged that Dunbar was urged by his sponsor William Dean Howell to write in dialect against his wishes.[53] Dunbar was against writing in dialect because he understood that his dialectal poetry functioned socially to reinforce the stereotype of illiterate blacks who lack the intellectual capacity to use language properly. Redding tells us,

> Thus a Negro character, like Black Samson of Brandywine, could be ever so heroic and noble so long as he "talked nigger" and was ignorant of what nobility meant. Thus, too, the loftiest precepts could fall from the lips of a black woman, so long as she was in the white folk's kitchen and spoke her maxims in dialect. This was incongruous, like a monkey with table manners, and just as amusing, and therefore, so far as whites were concerned, permissible.[54]

To the extent that Dunbar produced dialectal poetry under social pressure his cultural malpractice can be excused on the intentionalist ground that he wrote in dialect against his will.

There is no reason to suppose, however, that an appeal to Redding's intentionalist criterion can always succeed in distinguishing between representations of folk dialect by black and white authors. Redding supported his malpractice charge against Dunbar by comparing Dunbar's representation of black dialect with that of his African-American predecessor James Edwin Campbell. He concluded that

> Paul Dunbar's dialect is a bastard form, modeled closer upon James Whitcomb Riley's colloquial language than upon the speech it was supposed to represent. Campbell's ear alone dictated his language. Dunbar's five senses (as they should) controlled his.[55]

Even in the absence of overt social pressure, as in the case of Robeson's invented dialect, a black authored representation of folk dialect can sometimes voluntarily display the oppressive aspects of a racist white author.

Although minstrelsy always carries the burden of proof, from the standpoint of black audiences there is sometimes disagreement about whether to count it as a misrepresentation of vernacular culture. In some instances where audience reactions are divided along class lines, the charge of cultural malpractice is grounded on a judgment about the representation's underlying political ideology. Cinematic representations provided by minstrel characters from television programs such as *Amos 'n Andy* or *In Living Color* can project ambiguous images that suggest at once accommodation and resistance. By signifying on themselves, these characters will sometimes elicit a favorable response from an appreciative segment of the black audience.[56] The audience split arises from the perception by a dissenting segment that a social critique employing certain images can function sometimes as another form of minstrelsy, despite any element of resistance it ambiguously may express.

To speak of a given minstrel performance, or work, as constituting or expressing resistance is to make an implicit appeal to some intentionalist criterion. For how do we know whether a particular instance of minstrelsy should count as resistance unless we also know the intention of the author or performer? The use of dialect itself does not signal this given that some representations of black vernacular culture aim to empower oppressed black people while others aim to perpetuate their oppression. The paradoxical nature of minstrelsy derives from its dual social function as well as from the fact that minstrel behavior alone is an inadequate sign of the agent's intention. Subversive elements often entered the performances of black minstrels.[57] On what basis, however, can we attribute an act of resistance to a minstrel's performance given that, to succeed, the behavior has to be sufficiently ambiguous for the subversive intent to go unnoticed?

A similar consideration applies to the question of whether Dunbar's dialect poetry was minstrelsy. The underlying presupposition of this question is that minstrelsy is, by its very nature, accommodationist, therefore, it always stands in juxtaposition with more oppositional acts of resistance.[58] This presupposition can be challenged, however, when we take into account the manner in which minstrelsy can be employed to resist racial oppression. Some interpreters of Dunbar, for instance, take his use of dialect to implicate him as a plantation apologist; others maintain that his use of dialect was a subversive means of raising black consciousness.[59] What must be acknowledged by proponents of the view that Dunbar's dialect was, as it were, a mask; once this guise was adopted, it may have functioned as accommodationism, despite Dunbar's intent to use it for subversive purposes.

There is not much disagreement about whether the use of blackface, whether for derogatory purposes or not, is inherently offensive to a majority of black people. In the minds of most black spectators, however, dialect can range from closely representative to crudely manufactured. Even among scholars, there does not seem to be a settled view of whether the various forms of dialect used in minstrelsy were historically accurate representations of black speech patterns. Dillard, for instance, claims "Everyone knows that the minstrel shows used phony dialect, although some of the earlier ones might have been more nearly accurate."[60] Mahar is less reserved in his claim that "The discovery of common characteristics in blackface song and black English shows that there was much truth to the contention that the early minstrels borrowed from black culture."[61] What exactly did the early minstrels "borrow" from black culture? To understand this disagreement as only a debate about whether certain speech patterns have been accurately represented, I think, is to overlook the politico-economic role of white intervention.

Consider, for instance, ex-Los Angeles Police Chief Daryl Gates' response to a statement that his new video game *Police Quest: Open Season,* might be viewed as racist, given the *Amos 'n Andy*-style dialect of the game's black suspects. Gates pointed out that he was against using some of the dialogue written by Tammy Dargan, a former segment producer for *America's Most Wanted.* According to Gates, "I told [Dargan] that these people use the same language that you and I use. A lot of that was changed. It's not intended to offend anyone."[62] Apparently, Dargan won out and much of the potentially offensive dialect remained. Dargan justified keeping it in by claiming that it was "inspired" by Fab 5 Freddy's record *Fresh Fly Flavor.* What if, however, we were to view the dialect used by Fab 5 Freddy as only an adopted dialect, a mask used for signifying, or even for theatrical purposes? This has been an option for many rap artists seeking to profit from the large white audience demand for the latest, most controversial, rap records. Gates' video game responds to a strong market incentive to exploit mass media constructions of hip-hop culture as a criminal underclass.[63] Dargan's decision to use a black dialect to represent black people appears somewhat pernicious in the context of Gates having insisted that blacks and whites use the same language.

Dargan's appropriation of Fab 5 Freddy's dialect for minstrel purposes shows the difficulty that underlies the question of whether Dunbar's dialectal poetry was minstrelsy. To provide an answer, we must first determine for whom the dialect was written. Because so much of Dunbar's dialectal poetry was heavily influenced by the plantation tradition, even when he employed it as a subversive mode of resistance, it ran the risk of being interpreted as accommodationist.[64] We know from his public testimony that Dunbar preferred not to write in dialect.[65] Moreover, his protest literature makes clear that he was not entirely an accommodationist.[66] But to resolve the ambiguity of Dunbar's dialectal poetry on the side of resistance by appealing to various documentations of his nonaccommodationist political ideology is to choose to treat his protest literature as a better indication of his real aims.[67] The debate about whether Dunbar's dialectal poetry was a form of minstrelsy indicates quite clearly that each poem has to be judged separately. Given that Dunbar's dialectal poetry exemplifies the ambiguity of the minstrel, Locke's endorsement of it as a form of race conscious literature was tantamount to an endorsement of minstrelsy.

The Aesthetic of Cultural Resistance

What about Dunbar's lyric poetry written in conventional English? Since Dunbar preferred to write in standard English, it seems odd to consider his nondialectal verse to be a less "authentic" form of African-American cultural expression than his dialectal poetry. "Authentic" cultural expression means here a genuine dialect spoken by black people on the plantations. Dunbar's dialect was not genuine in this sense. But given the political thrust of Dunbar's appropriation of white-authored literary black dialect, perhaps his political orientation was on a par with the dialectal form of expression for which he was known. Insofar as Dunbar's poetry written in conventional English aimed to express the true sentiments and aspirations of African-Americans, whether or not he employed dialect as a sign of blackness seems irrelevant.[68]

Consider, for instance, slave narratives written by African-Americans in standard English. By comparison with those written in dialect, they offer another paradigm of African-American cultural resistance. House slaves were enabled by their class position within the social system of slavery to acquire the skills by which to document their aspirations. In the narratives of Harriet Jacobs and Frederick Douglass, many of the ideas expressed as well as their general style of expression were thoroughly Eurocentric. Douglass' discussion of his consciousness as a slave, his references to the natural rights of slaves, as well as the structure of the narrative itself is closer to an Anglo-American tradition in literature, distinguished only by the fact that the author is a black person.[69] In a very similar fashion, Jacobs patterned her narrative after the sentimental Victorian novel. Both works, nonetheless, constitute a form of cultural resistance to slavery by African-Americans.

There seems to be something both correct and misleading about the reference to these narratives as a form of "African-American" cultural resistance. Given their Eurocentric mode of expression, they do not represent what is commonly understood to be a distinctive idiom of African-American culture. If, however, African-American-authored slave narratives played an important consciousness raising role in the abolitionist movement, the political agenda of the authors seems sufficient to alleviate the concern about the status of their narratives as a form of cultural resistance. This worry seems to derive from the misguided idea that cultural assimilation and cultural resistance are contrary notions. Jacobs and Douglass each represent highly assimilated African-Americans who employed their acculturated status to engage in resistance to slavery. Although their narratives constituted a form of cultural resistance by African-Americans, they do not count as an African-American form of cultural expression where this implies some unique form of expression.

Spirituals and coded sermons presented in the social context of the slave's religious practices are often touted as unique forms of African-American cultural resistance.[70] The Harlem-based negritude movement, spearheaded by Locke, also is taken sometimes to be a form of African-American cultural resistance because of its appropriation of the black southern folk traditions, some of which already had been transplanted to the North.[71] The use of dialect by Zora Neale Hurston and Langston Hughes aimed to capture in literary fashion a distinctive feature of the African-American oral tradition. Dialect earmarks a distinctive aspect of African-American culture by representing an African linguistic component that has been syncretized, along with other mainstream elements, into African-American cultural practices.[72] Spirituals, sermons, and literature written in dialect are held to be forms of cultural expression that are distinctly African-American because they contain elements of African-American culture (viz., transformed retentions) that are distinguishable from the Eurocentric mainstream.

This notion of a unique form of African-American cultural expression fits the prevailing characterization of rap music as a distinctly African-American cultural practice whose roots can be traced to the oral and musicmaking traditions of West Africa.[73] By contrast with slave narratives written in standard English, rap music provides a paradigm of African-American cultural resistance involving transformed African retentions. For obvious political reasons, cultural resistance cannot always be overtly oppositional. In the nineteenth century, the sentimentalist dialectal tradition was overtly racist, hence, many black writers were politically motivated to eschew it as a form of cultural expression. To the extent that the aim of Dunbar's appropriation of black dialect was to foster group consciousness among black people and institute a race tradition in literature, we can allow a subversive reading of his works. A similar line of argument can be applied to various forms of twentieth-century minstrelsy. The era of legal segregation provided the social context for the legal battle waged by the NAACP to ban the television version of *Amos 'n Andy.*[74] Ironically, in the racial climate of postdesegregation, black urban youth have appropriated a black dialect as an overtly oppositional form of cultural expression. The sign of blackness used in an earlier era by mass media to rationalize the oppression of African-Americans, when appropriated and incorporated into hip-hop culture, implies a form of collective resistance to the cultural hegemony sustained by mass media.

Unlike slave narratives that were authored by a single person, rap music involves the joint activity of a group of artists. The fact that rap musicmaking is a shared cooperative activity, however, does not mean that it can be taken as a whole to be a form of cultural resistance. To do so would be to treat a cultural practice that ranges over twenty years as though it were a single collective act. The creation of conventions regarding the use of various idioms, including dress, dance, and posturing, involves activity that rap artists as a group have engaged in over a certain period of time. Although the making of records by various rap artists throughout the history of rap music involves a series of specific collective acts, such acts are a part of the shared cooperative activity constituting a musical tradition. The cultural practice established by many groups of rap artists over a long period constitutes a hip-hop tradition which can be distinguished from a collective act of a particular group at any given time during this period. This distinction is important if we are to remain clear about which specific performances or recordings should count as resistance and which should not.

A similar distinction within hip-hop culture itself has been made between so-called "hardcore" rap and "commercial" rap. Hardcore rap is sometimes viewed as more "authentic" in the sense that it emanates directly from the streets and does not disguise or "sell out" its messages in order to increase record sales. Commercial rap is supposed to be less "authentic" in the sense that it eschews the politics of opposition expressed so frequently in hardcore rap and, instead, attempts to be more appealing to a mainstream audience. This distinction has proven to be somewhat untenable given that hardcore artists such as Snoop Dog, Ice Cube, Ezy-E, Niggaz With Attitude, and Naughty by Nature have had phenomenal record sales. Politics accounts for the distinction between the lyrical content of hardcore and commercial rap. Hence, hardcore rap tunes deliver messages of a gritty reality, sometimes even revolution, and thereby embody acts of resistance when performed or played. Commercial rap tunes emphasize style over substance to avoid such messages in an effort to gain a wider appeal with mainstream audiences. A rap tune's status as resistance turns on whether the intention of the artist is to communicate a political ideology that addresses issues of concern to black urban youth.[75]

What about some of the messages in hardcore rap that seem to denounce politics? Ezy-E, a member of the gangsta rap group, Niggaz With Attitude, has been quoted as having made the statement "Fuck that black power shit: we don't give a fuck. Free South Africa: we don't give a fuck," with reference to tunes by politically motivated artists from the Afrocentric school.[76] The group's producer Dr. Dre elaborated by pointing out that he valued being crazy more than he valued being political. Bev Francis, the host of *Our Voice*, a talk show on Black Entertainment Television, expressed a black middle-class concern with some of the lyrics in hardcore rap. She asked two women guests from the rap group Bytches With Problems about the potentially destructive influence of their music on black youth. Francis was concerned with the rap group's embracing of and communicating nihilistic values that, when internalized by black youth, might exacerbate the violence that plagues black communities. What this concern indicates, whether we share it or not, is the idea that hardcore rap music as a form of cultural resistance stands in need of further examination.

Whether groups such as BWP and NWA are engaged in an oppositional form of cultural resistance can be ascertained by considering more generally the target of resistance in hardcore gangsta rap. There seems to be several: the black nationalist focus on Africa by politically minded rappers (rather than a greater focus on the local situation of African-Americans), the government's role in the international drug trade, the racist hypocrisy of capitalism, the success of the black middle class, and the problem of police brutality. The recent controversy resulting from black women and black political and religious organizations publicly protesting the mass marketing of the violence and pornography in hardcore gangsta rap has shifted the media's overriding focus to gender issues.[77] Since a critique of global capitalism sometimes may be given by the same artist who also performs tunes that are extremely misogynistic, each tune must stand on its own, rendering it extremely difficult to ascertain the political significance of a gangsta rap artist.

Matters are made even more difficult by the fact that the aesthetic qualities of a rap tune can sometimes overshadow the politics it displays. When asked what he thought of the latest album by NWA (*Niggaz 4 Life*), former group member Ice Cube responded by pointing out that it was not well-conceived from the standpoint of its political message. He added, however, that he thought "[t]heir production is dope."[78] This expression metaphorically captures the problem of musical technique dominating political content and reveals the difficulty the aesthetic aspects of rap music poses for ascertaining elements of resistance. Many progressive people enjoy dancing to rap music. Are young women "hypocritics," for instance, when they denounce the misogyny in the lyrical content of a hardcore rap tune while deriving pleasure from its other musical qualities? How are we to understand this phenomenon of progressive people enjoying music they would otherwise find objectionable for political reasons? The key to resolving this puzzle is to understand an important implication of the claim that the production is dope, namely, that the music has the aesthetic power to cause pleasure, perhaps even against the wishes of the listener.

This suggestion about rap music's aesthetic appeal also accounts for the related phenomenon that the premier political rap group Public Enemy has the status of being the favorite rap group in racist white communities such as South Boston and Bensonhurst. The truth contained in Ice Cube's remark is that rap messages need not be the only reason certain audiences listen to rap music. The aesthetic qualities of the music can be an overriding factor. He points out that "[t]o white kids rap ain't nothing but a form of entertainment, for blacks it's a strategy on how to maneuver through life."[79] How then do we assess rap music as a form of cultural resistance when the mediating role of its aesthetic characteristics can sometimes guide us away from political messages we might want to endorse or condemn?

The Political Ambiguity of Bad Nigga Narratives

Some commentators have argued that we should view the practice of making rap music in relation to the record industry.[80] By sampling, scratching, and remixing recorded music, rap artists are engaged in a political struggle with the commercial culture industries that control the production of African-American music. The difficulty with this line of thought is that the recording industry seems to have accommodated the production of rap music with very little difficulty. Even the so-called underground channels for rap music have been incorporated into a distribution network that permits the calibration of record sales.[81] With the commercializing of gangsta rap we no longer can speak in a totalizing manner of rap music as a form of cultural resistance. Instead, this designation must be reserved for specific rap tunes.

The denial of values that pervades the worldview presented by gangsta rappers has sometimes perplexed commentators who view rap as a form of cultural resistance.[82] At other times, this amoral lapse in gangsta rap is taken to be only a certain phase in hip-hop culture's evolution towards becoming a genuine social movement.[83] The Afrocentric values in New York-centered hardcore rap represent elements of cultural resistance that promotes a political agenda consistent with a legacy of black political struggle dating from early nineteenth-century slave revolts and abolitionism to the more recent civil rights movement and urban riots. The emergence of a nihilistic school of Los Angeles-centered gangsta rappers represents a break with this tradition, an unparalleled rupture that is to be understood in terms of the social conditions that fostered it.

The nihilism expressed in gangsta rap music is deceptive. A much celebrated element of resistance in gangsta rap, for instance, is the appropriation of the term "nigga." Gangsta rappers effectively have recoded the social meaning of this term. In public discourse, its use is a social taboo although what the term connotes is reiterated on daily newscasts of crime and violence. On the news program, *Nightline,* Ice T, a popular gangsta rapper, engaged in a long drawn-out debate with Harvard professor Alvin Poussaint about whether the use of the term "nigger" by any group of black people, even among ourselves, is always self-denigrating.[84] Finally, Ice T drove home the point of his disagreement by capping on Poussaint's view with the signifying expression, "Nigga, please!" Poussaint's self-hatred account of the black vernacular use of the term "nigger" was challenged by Ice T's *demonstration* of its appropriateness as a term of defiance. When used in black vernacular culture, such a reversal of meaning allows this term to function as a source of pride rather than denigration.[85]

Poussaint, of course, was also concerned that, although the appropriation of the term "nigger" by gangsta rappers aims to recode its racist meaning, there remains a question of whether such an appropriation can change the racist connotation, or whether it serves only to reinforce a negative image of African-Americans. This concern, however, tends to ignore the social significance of the term's newly acquired meaning. The appropriated use by gangsta rappers adds an ambiguity that shifts, depending on whether the term is used in a white racist discourse or whether it is constructed as an idiom of a resistive mode of African-American cultural expression. To capture the class consciousness of a distinctly black male lumpenproletariat, gangsta rappers revised the spelling of the racist version of the term "nigger" to the vernacular version, "nigga." The vernacular version permits a distinction to be made between black urban youth who constitute a so-called "black underclass" and other black middle-class professionals. Poussaint's analysis failed to acknowledge that gangsta rappers such as Ice T have been extremely outspoken about their belief that some African-Americans in positions of institutional authority are responsible for perpetuating the plight of the black urban poor. The appropriation and respelling of the term "nigga" by gangsta rappers displays resistance by embracing *and* rejecting the social meaning of this term. NWA's top selling *Niggaz4Life* was spelled backwards on the record cover to avoid censorship. This maneuver succeeded in subverting, by means of a socially transgressive black idiom, the taboo Poussaint defends.

A political distinction remains between hardcore and nonhardcore rap music, despite the commercial success of gangsta rap. The fury over Ice T's "Cop Killer" tune reflected the cultural politics governing the relationship between rap-music production and the record industry. Although Ice T "voluntarily" withdrew his album *Body Count* from distribution, the incident called to attention the constitutional grounds of free speech. The subsequent suppression of rap music by corporate decision makers has been justified by their judgment of whether the lyrical content is socially harmful. The economic factor also seems to have been of some importance to Ice T and Times-Warner, a sure indication that profit was the bottom line for their "agreement" to renege on the First Amendment. Ice T's capitulation to the record industry's economic pressure contrasts sharply with the "no sellout" aspect of his bad nigga persona.[86]

The fact that Ice T aimed for a white youth audience with a heavy metal album that contained socially transgressive lyrics regarding interracial sex and retaliatory violence against racial bigots was, no doubt, a factor contributing to the corporate pressure to suppress "Cop Killer." But once we acknowledge that some of the controversies surrounding hip-hop personalities frequently serve to increase the market value of their records, it is difficult to ignore the question of whether the bad nigga persona adopted by gangsta rappers is mostly an exaggerated defiance feigned for commercial purposes. When gangsta rap is viewed in its politico-economic context, it displays an ambiguous mock nihilism that parallels the ambiguous accommodationism displayed in subversive forms of minstrelsy.[87]

One important consequence of the transnational commodification of hip-hop culture is that it made possible the introduction of an ambiguous meaning of the term "nigga" into a global context. Alain Locke's claim that "the Negro's primitivism is nine-tenths that of the peasant the world over" is borne out by the international appeal of rap music. There is reason to believe that its widespread appeal is due to more than just the music. Even cross-culturally, the political ideology expressed in some of the bad nigga narratives that dominate gangsta rap's lyrical content are often perceived to contribute to an emancipatory political agenda.[88] Within the local context of black urban youth, however, the gangsta rapper's appropriation of the term "nigga" as a source of pride rather than degradation resonates with a tradition of black urban folklore in which the counterpart to the gangsta rapper's "real nigga" is the "bad nigger" who personifies defiance, brutality, and ruthlessness.[89] The corporate suppression of Ice T's "Cop Killer" was an acknowledgment that, by exceeding the social limits of gangsta rap's bad nigga, this tune had disrupted the music industry's transnational system of commodification.[90]

There is an aesthetic dimension to this disruption that is of equal political significance. Locke's praise for Richard Wright's "Zolaesque" style of social realism in *Native Son* shows Locke's willingness, by the early 1940s, to allow a notion of the urban proletariat in place of the rural peasant as the subject of black literature and art. It also indicates the extent to which he continued to place a greater value on aesthetics. In his review of *Native Son,* Locke quotes a crucial passage from Wright's essay "How Bigger Was Born," but failed to appreciate the fact that Bigger Thomas was conceived by Wright as a "bad nigger," a character Wright intended to be aesthetically displeasing.[91] In the passage Locke quotes, Wright claims that Bigger Thomas was capable of becoming either communist or fascist, but was neither. According to Wright,

> But, granting the emotional state, the tensity, the fear, the hate, the impatience, the sense of exclusion, the ache for violent action, the emotional and cultural hunger, Bigger Thomas, conditioned as his organism is, will not become an ardent, or even a lukewarm, supporter of the status quo.[92]

Locke completely disregarded Wright's stated aim to write a book that no banker's daughter could weep over. His criticism of *Native Son* urged a more romantic tragedy in the face of Wright's explicit rejection of that. With regard to Locke's proposal to elevate black folk expression to high art, it was held in abeyance by Wright's construction of Bigger Thomas as a "bad nigger" who unromantically profanes mainstream values.

Locke's frequent references to Emile Zola indicate his strong commitment to a nineteenth-century European standard for judging the aesthetic merit of black social realist literature.[93] He believed that portrayals of black urban existence by social realists, such as Wright, were aesthetically limited due to their preoccupation with sociology and psychoanalysis. When Locke's concern with aesthetic pleasure is applied to gangsta rap it has an interesting political twist because Wright's appropriation of the "bad nigger" figure from black urban folklore was in keeping with Locke's urging of black writers to return to folk culture as a source for artistic self-expression. In a manner similar to Wright's Marxist framing of the nihilism represented by Bigger Thomas, the gangsta rapper's image of the "bad nigger" is often employed for political purposes. The point of Locke's critique of minstrelsy was that it was not a form of genuine folk expression representative of the true sentiments of the Southern black peasant. This critique was consistent with his objection to Wright because he considered both to be distortions of authentic folk expression. It seems that, as in the case of Hurston, Locke is committed to endorsing the use of bad nigga narratives by authors or artists who aim solely to produce aesthetic pleasure.

The political ambiguity of bad nigga narratives in gangsta rap arises from the fact that the nihilism represented is only a mask employed by various rappers for political and commercial purposes.[94] For this reason we must be wary of equating all of the gangsta rap music offered under the rubric of cultural resistance simply because of the nihilism expressed. As an oppositional form of cultural expression, gangsta rap music is constituted by inherently resistive elements. But how does this aspect of the aesthetic of gangsta rap fit with the fact that not every tune aims to engage in resistance? The political use of a form of cultural expression does not rule out other uses. The mock nihilism in gangsta rap music is an inherently resistive element that also has been a key element in its commercial exploitation. The choice of title for MC Ren's album *Kiss My Black AZZ* (Ruthless/Priority, 1992) shows the extent to which, as a resistive element, the representation of nihilism in gangsta rap has been commodified.[95] The aim of MC Ren's version of the bad nigga seems to have been to provide aesthetic pleasure for a thrill-seeking audience. Commodification of gangsta rap's bad nigga idiom leaves unclear how the concept of resistance can provide a basis for a distinction between tunes that are political and those that are commercial.

Jon Michael Spencer appeals to a well-known distinction between various genres of black folklore to provide a ground on which to condemn the nihilism in gangsta rap. Spencer claims "the black community knows how to tell the difference between the 'bad nigger' and the heroic badman."[96] Following John Roberts, he maintains that, unlike the badman, the "bad nigger" is motivated by a narcissistic hedonism that is genocidal and threatens the safety and moral stability of the black community. For this reason, the "bad nigger" is never viewed as a hero by the black community. This claim does not appear to be well grounded given that some gangsta rappers who have adopted this guise are quite popular with black audiences.[97] Roberts and Spencer have failed to realize that, under the influence of mass media, their highly questionable distinction between the badman and the "bad nigger" lapses into a troublesome conflation given that both are sometimes represented indiscriminately as violent criminals. We can notice this conflation, for example, in the film *Trespass*. The heroic badman is Ice T portraying a gang leader who considers himself a responsible businessman; the sociopathic "bad nigger" is Ice Cube portraying an impetuous gangbanger who values nothing but ruthless violence. In accordance with the film's existentialist theme, both die violently as black criminals in the end.

The conflation of the figures of the moralistic badman and the amoral "bad nigger" into a composite image of the violent black criminal occurs in the context of mass media's politicizing the image of the "bad nigger." By appropriating the term "nigga" and recoding its social meaning, gangsta rappers have imbued mass media's criminal image of black urban youth with a political ambiguity akin to all the subversive nuances of the minstrel's Sambo image. What clearly distinguishes Ice Cube's use of bad nigga narratives from their use by other gangsta rappers, such as Ezy-E, is his well-known intention to promote a political agenda. The gangsta idiom nonetheless remains the same in both cases. In the case of Ezy-E, this idiom facilitates an accommodationist ideology that appears as a form of cultural resistance. Because the bad nigga idiom encompasses Ezy-E's amoral "I don't give a fuck!" attitude as well as Ice Cube's strongly felt nationalist desire, resolving the political ambiguity of bad nigga narratives in gangsta rap music trades on a judgment regarding the intention of the artist.

The black cultural norm that justifies a suspicion of the intention of a white author or artist when a racist material image, such as the black criminal stereotype, is employed rests on the underlying assumption that, in a racist social context, this image will serve to perpetuate racism. But what distinguishes a black author's or artist's employment of a similar image? The cultural malpractice charge justifies a similar suspicion regarding the intention of a black author or artist. In unclear cases involving subversive strategies, the audience orientation of the author or artist is paramount. With regard to concerns about the social harmfulness of gangsta rap, there is no need to deny that the black criminal image may very well reproduce, accommodate, or perpetuate a racist ideology among some white audiences. This concern does not outweigh the consideration that, at the same time, its recoded ideology can be emancipatory for some black audiences. Ice Cube's album *The Predator* (Priority, 1992) provides a politically conscious gangsta rapper's interpretation of the 1992 uprising in Los Angeles.[98] Similarly, Da Lench Mob's album *Guerrillas in the Mist* (Street Knowledge/East West, 1992) appropriated the racist police image of black people as gorillas to provide a view of the Los Angeles rebellion as guerilla warfare. It seems undeniable that, by articulating an ideological frame for urban rebellion, gangsta rap music such as this has moved the hip-hop generation toward social action.

Notes

1 "Blacks Fail to See Humor in Ted Danson's Blackface Tribute to Whoopi Goldberg," *Jet,* 84, 1 (November 1, 1993), pp. 56–9.
2 See Deborah Gray White, *Ar'n't I A Woman* (New York: W. W. Norton, 1985); and bell hooks, *Ain't I A Woman: Black Women and Feminism* (Boston: South End Press, 1982); but also see the rendering of some of Sojourner Truth's speeches in standard English in *Black Women in White America: A Documentary History,* ed. Gerda Lerner (New York: Vintage, 1972), pp. 566–72; and in conventional southern black dialect in Olive Gilbert, comp., *Narrative of Sojourner Truth, A Bondwoman of Olden Time* (New York: Arno, 1968). For a critical discussion of the ideological orientation of Sojourner Truth's transcribers, see Nell Irvin Painter, "Sojourner Truth in Feminist Abolitionism: Difference, Slavery, and Memory," in *An Untrodden Path:*

Antislavery and Women's Political Culture, eds Jean Fagan Yellin and John C. Van Horne (Ithaca: Cornell University Press, 1993).

3 Arthur Fauset criticized the earlier authors for inaccurately transcribing Truth's speech. "[W]hen in the following pages quotations are made from these later sources, it may seem that her English was normal at the beginning of her life and degenerated as she grew older. This, of course, is not the case. In her childhood, she spoke a Dutch jargon which, even if we knew the language, we probably could not transcribe." Arthur Huff Fauset, *Sojourner Truth: God's Faithful Pilgrim* (Durham:University of North Carolina Press, 1938), p. vii.

4 Sterling A. Brown, "On Dialect Usage," in *The Slave's Narrative,* eds Charles T. Davis and Henry Louis Gates Jr (New York: Oxford University Press, 1985), pp. 37–9.

5 Ibid., p. 35.

6 Warren Miller, *The Cool World* (New York: Fawcett World Library, 1969).

7 A similar suspicion was raised by June Jordan with regard to Miller's book and Shirley Clarke's film version of the story. June Jordan, *Civil Wars* (Boston: Beacon Press, 1981), pp. 3–15.

8 According to Dillard, "Virtually every articulate Black critic has argued that the white writer ignores the meaning of the Negro's language, as well as of his experience in general." J. L. Dillard, *Lexicon of Black English: The Words the Slaves Made* (New York: Seabury Press, 1977). Conversely, the charge of racism against Mark Twain has to be rethought in the light of new evidence that the voice of Huck Finn (and, hence, his use of the term "nigger") may have been influenced by a ten-year-old black servant. Anthony DePalma, "Huck Finn's Voice Is Heard as Twain Meets Black Youth," *New York Times* (July 7, 1992), pp. A1, A9.

9 Anna Julia Cooper, "The Negro's Dialect" in Anna Julia Cooper Papers, Folder #35 (Washington, DC: Moorland-Springarn Research Center, Howard University), pp. 23–4.

10 In addition to receiving her doctorate from the Sorbonne, Cooper published in Latin and French. For a biographical account, see Louis Daniel Hutchinson, *Anna Julia Cooper: A Voice from the South* (Washington, DC: Smithsonian Institution Press, 1982).

11 According to Dillard, "Zora Neale Hurston's writings come close to being the ultimate source for a rural Black lexicon." J. L. Dillard, "Can We Trust Literary Sources," in his *Lexicon of Black English,* p. 153.

12 Gale Jones remarked, "the problem with Hurston is how does one write of ordinary people without making the story seem trivial, without making the writer's concerns seem likewise?" "Breaking out of the Caricatures of Dialect," in *Zora Neale Hurston,* eds Henry L. Gates Jr and Kwame A. Appiah (New York: Amistad, 1993), p. 147. Richard Wright claimed, "Miss Hurston seems to have no desire whatever to move in the direction of serious fiction.... Her dialogue manages to catch the psychological movements of the Negro folk-mind in their pure simplicity, but that's as far as it goes. Miss Hurston voluntarily continues in her novel the tradition which was forced upon the Negro in the theater, that is the minstrel technique that makes the 'white folks' laugh." "Review of *Their Eyes Were Watching God,*" in *Zora Neale Hurston,* p. 17.

13 Alain L. Locke, "Jingo, Counter-Jingo and Us" in *The Critical Temper of Alain Locke,* ed. Jeffrey C. Stewart (New York: Garland, 1983), p. 260.

14 Alain L. Locke, "Dry Fields and Green Pastures" in *The Critical Temper of Alain Locke,* ed. Jeffrey C. Stewart (New York: Garland, 1983), p. 288.

15 See, for instance, Roger Abrahams, *Deep Down in the Jungle* (Chicago: Aldine Publishing Co., 1970), p. 3; John W. Roberts, *From Trickster to Badman* (Philadelphia: University of Pennsylvania Press, 1989), p. 35. For an interesting debate about the African origins of African-American folklore, see Daniel J. Crowley ed., *African Folklore in the New World* (Austin: University of Texas, 1977).

16 Henry L. Gates Jr, *The Signifying Monkey* (New York: Oxford University Press, 1988), p. xxii.

17 See R. D. G. Kelley, "Notes on Deconstructing 'The Folk'," *American Historical Review* (December 1992), p. 1400.

18 Alain L. Locke, "The Drama of Negro Life," Locke Papers, Box 107, p. 14, Moorland-Springarn Research Center, Howard University. Locke wrote several somewhat different versions of this paper under the same title, some of which were never published or were slightly altered for publication. In subsequent notes, reference will be made to: Locke Papers, "The Drama of Negro Life," followed by a designation of his five-page version, his sixteen-page typescript version, or his published version appearing in Stewart's *The Critical Temper of Alain Locke,* pp. 87–91. See also Locke's essay, "The Negro and the American Theatre," in *Theatre: Essays on the Arts of the Theatre,* ed. Edith J. R. Isaacs (Freeport, NY: Books for Libraries Press, 1927), pp. 249–56.

19 Locke queried, "Is the dance hall in the city as innocent an amusement as the plantation dance in the corn crib?" Dunbar Lecture delivered at Fisk University, date unknown, Locke Papers, Box 125, File #46, p. 15.

20 Alain Locke, "The Negro and the American Stage," *The Critical Temper of Alain Locke,* p. 85; Alain Locke, "The Negro and the American Theatre," *Theatre: Essays on the Arts of the Theatre,* p. 301. Locke coauthored a scenario for a Negro folk play in which the opening scene is set in the African jungle and the closing scene is set in a New York concert hall. Nokomis Cobb and Alain L. Locke, *Scenario Outline of a Negro Folk Play for Dramatic and Motion Picture Presentation,* 1933, in Locke Papers, miscellaneous file.

21 Locke–Hurston Correspondence, June 13–16, 1929, Locke Papers, Folder 163, File #28. Later Locke criticized Hurston's published field work *Tell My Horse* as "anthropological gossip." Locke, "The Negro: 'New' or Newer. A Retrospective Review of the Literature of the Negro for 1938," *The Critical Temper of Alain Locke,* p. 279.

22 See, for instance, Locke's review of N. N. Puckett, *Folk Beliefs of the Southern Negro,* date unknown, Locke Papers, Box 164-133, Folder 33, in which he criticized Puckett's inability to ascertain "genuine survivals." Similarly, he criticized the conclusions of a report by the Virginia WPA. "In their present shape they suggest a little too strongly the thesis of straight African survivals, and need to be gone over carefully from the acculturation angle as composite folkways and folklore which, in the main, they seem to represent." Alain Locke, "Of Native Sons: Real and Otherwise," *The Critical Temper of Alain Locke,* p. 306.

23 Locke Papers, Dunbar Lecture, p. 6.

24 Locke Papers, "The Drama of Negro Life," five-page version, p. 4.

25 Locke Papers, "The Drama of Negro Life," sixteen-page version, p. 5.

26 Ibid., p. 6.
27 See Locke Papers, Dunbar Lecture, pp. 12–13. Locke presents a fuller account of his sociohistorical view of race in Alain LeRoy Locke, *Race Contacts and Interracial Relations*, ed. J. Stewart (Washington, DC: Howard University Press, 1992) and in the editorial sections of *When Peoples Meet*, eds Alain Locke and Bernard J. Stern (New York: Progressive Education Association, 1942).
28 Locke Papers, Dunbar Lecture, p. 13.
29 It is worth noting that Locke's authorized interpreter Margaret Just Butcher presented a more evenhanded assessment of Hurston. According to Butcher, "The work of such present-day writers as Guy Johnson, Julia Peterkin, and Zora Neale Hurston (to name but three out of many) has done a great deal to establish the folk tale in legitimate perspective." Margaret Just Butcher, *The Negro in American Culture* (New York: New American Library, 1956), p. 45.
30 Locke Papers, "Folk Tale Lecture," Box 164-133, pp. 2–3.
31 Locke Papers, "The Drama of Negro Life," sixteen-page version, p. 7.
32 Ibid.
33 Ibid., p. 16.
34 Locke Papers, "The Drama of Negro Life," five-page version, p. 4.
35 Ibid., p. 5.
36 Alain Locke, "Dry Fields and Green Pastures," p. 288.
37 Alain Locke, "Jingo, Counter-Jingo and Us," p. 260.
38 See, for instance, Alain Locke, "The Negro and the American Theatre," *The Critical Temper of Alain Locke*, pp. 297 and 58; Alain Locke, "The Eleventh Hour of Nordicism: Retrospective Review of the Literature of the Negro for 1935," p. 229; Alain Locke, "The Negro: 'New' or Newer," *The Critical Temper of Alain Locke*, p. 274, and Alain Locke, "From *Native Son* to *Invisible Man*: A Review of the Literature of the Negro for 1952," *The Critical Temper of Alain Locke*, p. 385. For Locke's main argument against propaganda, see Alain Locke, "Art or Propaganda?" in *The Critical Temper of Alain Locke*, pp. 27–8 and Alain Locke, "Propaganda — or Poetry?" in *The Critical Temper of Alain Locke*, pp. 55–61.
39 Locke Papers, "The Drama of Negro Life," five-page version, p. 4.
40 According to Locke, "And a test of the achievement of such a point of view will not only be the changed position of the Negro in the picture but the altered values — as the painters say, with which he will have to be painted." Locke Papers, "The Drama of Negro Life," five-page version, p. 4.
41 Alain Locke, "The Eleventh Hour of Nordicism," p. 230.
42 Locke complained of "an unfortunate insistence of proletarian poetry on being drab, prosy and inartistic, as though the regard for style were a bourgeois taint and an act of social treason." Alain Locke, "Propaganda — or Poetry?" p. 57. He included some of the poetry of Langston Hughes and Richard Wright among this propagandistic proletarian school. While speaking favorably about the successful run of the play *Stevedore*, he remarked that "Only a driving, pertinent theme could carry such amateurish dialogue and technique...." Alain Locke, "The Eleventh Hour of Nordicism," pp. 231–2. And, after giving Wright's *Native Son* a favorable review, Locke cited his communist ideology as a major flaw. Alain Locke, "From *Native Son* to *Invisible Man*: A Review of the Literature of the Negro for 1952," p. 385.
43 Locke Papers, "The Drama of Negro Life," sixteen-page version, p. 7.

44 Ibid.

45 Alain Locke, "The Negro and the American Theatre," p. 300.

46 Ibid., p. 302. Elsewhere Locke states this point in relation to his general theory of folk art. According to Locke, "it (Negro drama) learns how to beautify the native psychological idioms of our folk life and recovers the ancestral folk tradition, it will express itself in a poetic and symbolic style of drama that will remind us of Synge and the Irish Folk Theatre or Ansky and the Yiddish Theatre. There are many analogies, both of temperament, social condition and cultural reactions, which suggest this." Alain Locke, "The Drama of Negro Life," reprinted in Stewart's *The Critical Temper of Alain Locke,* p. 90.

47 Alain Locke and Sterling A. Brown, "Folk Values in a New Medium" in *Black Films and Filmmakers,* ed. Lindsay Patterson (New York: Dodd, Mead & Co., 1975), pp. 26–7. There is a typescript of Locke's contribution to this joint article in the Locke Papers at the Moorland-Springarn Center. Apparently he wrote the section on *Hearts in Dixie* and Sterling Brown wrote the section on *Hallelujah.* Locke Papers, Box 65. In his review of the play *Cabin in the Sky,* Locke wrote in a similar praiseworthy fashion. He claimed that it "does convey an authentic and characteristic Negro feeling" and that "Its comedy is inoffensive ... and its tempo and emotional tone are set true to real folk values." Alain Locke, "Of Native Sons: Real and Otherwise," p. 305. He also spoke highly of the play *The Rider of Dreams* as "showing for the first time a way of poetizing humble folk characters and extracting comedy without farce." Locke Papers, "The Drama of Negro Life," sixteen-page version, p. 4. It is worth noting that Locke wrote a letter agreeing to be a consultant on *Song of the South* with Disney Studios. See Locke's letter to Walter Wanger, September 4, 1944, Locke Papers. Box 164-133.

48 Alain Locke and Sterling A. Brown, "Folk Values in a New Medium," p. 26.

49 Ibid.

50 Ibid.

51 Gary Null, *Black Hollywood* (Secaucus, NJ: Citadel Press, 1975), p. 27.

52 Saunders Redding, "The Negro Writer and American Literature," in *Anger, and Beyond,* ed. Herbert Hill (New York: Harper and Row, 1968), p. 7.

53 Ibid., p. 4.

54 Saunders Redding, "The Problems of the Negro Writer," in *Black & White in American Culture,* eds Jules Chametzky and Sidney Kaplan (Amherst: University of Massachusetts Press, 1969), p. 363. For a discussion of the link between apes and the Sambo image, see Joseph Boskin, *Sambo* (New York: Oxford University Press, 1986), p. 123.

55 Saunders Redding, *To Make a Poet Black* (College Park, MD: McGrath Publishing Company, 1968), p. 52.

56 The term "signifying" derives its meaning from African-American folklore, specifically the trickster tale "The Signifying Monkey and the Lion." According to Roger Abrahams, "The name 'signifying' shows the monkey to be a trickster, signifying being the language of trickery, that set of words or gestures achieving Hamlet's 'direction through indirection' and used often, especially among the young, to humiliate an adversary." Roger Abrahams, *Deep Down in The Jungle* (Chicago: Aldine Publishing Company, 1963/70), pp. 66–7. In his well-received attempt "to lift the discourse of Signifyin(g) from the vernacular to the discourse of literary

criticism," Henry Louis Gates offers the following revision of the term: "When one
text Signifies upon another text, by tropological revision or repetition and difference,
the double-voiced utterance allows us to chart discrete formal relationships in
Afro-American literary history. Signifyin(g), then, is a metaphor for textual
revision." Henry Louis Gates Jr, *The Signifying Monkey* (New York: Oxford
University Press, 1988), pp. xi, 88.

57 Cf. Robert C. Toll, *Blacking Up: The Minstrel Show in Nineteenth-Century America*
(Oxford: Oxford University Press, 1974), pp. 246–8; and Joseph Boskin, "The Life
and Death of Sambo: Overview of an Historical Hang-Up," in *Remus, Rastas,
Revolution,* ed. Marshall Fishwick (Bowling Green, OH: Bowling Green Popular
Press, n.d.), p. 147.

58 See, for instance, Howard McGary, "Resistance and Slavery," in Howard McGary
and Bill E. Lawson, *Between Slavery and Freedom* (Bloomington: Indiana
University Press, 1992), pp. 38–9. Piersen has cautioned against using this
conceptual dichotomy. According to Piersen, "A more African perspective, on the
other hand, would permit us to understand that the black bondsmen intended their
musical satire as a basic and primary weapon in their arsenal of resistance against
oppression." William D. Piersen, *Black Legacy America's Hidden Heritage*
(Amherst: University of Massachusetts Press, 1993), p. 54.

59 This interpretation of Dunbar's work was originally maintained by George W. Ellis
in his early essay, "The Mission of Dunbar," *The Boston Citizen,* 2 (1915); but has
been supported recently by John Brown Childs, *Leadership, Conflict, and
Cooperation in Afro-American Social Thought* (Philadelphia: Temple University
Press, 1981), p. 92; Marcellus Blount, "The Preacherly Text: African-American
Poetry and Vernacular Performance," *Proceedings Modern Language Association,*
107, 3 (May 1992), p. 586; and Gossie Harold Hudson, "Paul Laurence Dunbar:
Dialect Et La Negritude," *Phylon,* IV, 3 (September 1973), p. 242.

60 J. L. Dillard, *Lexicon of Black English,* p. 148.

61 William J. Mahar, "Black English in Early Blackface Minstrelsy: A New
Interpretation of the Sources of Minstrel Show Dialect," *American Quarterly* (1984)
p. 284.

62 Joseph V. Tirella, "Video Vigilante," *Vibe,* 2, 3 (April 1994), p. 23.

63 John Michael Spencer refers to the white audience for rap as "resentment listeners."
See "The Emergency of Black and the Emergence of Rap," *Black Sacred Music,* 5,
1 (Spring 1991), p. 5. David Samuels proclaimed gangsta rappers to be nothing more
than cartoonish minstrels entertaining white kids. See "The Rap on Rap," *The New
Republic* (November 11, 1991), pp. 24–6. See also J. D. Considine, "Fear of a Rap
Planet," *Musician* (February 1992), p. 57.

64 Sterling Brown justified his interpretation of Dunbar as an accommodationist by
reference to "his omission of the hardships that the Negro folk met with." *Negro
Poetry and Drama* (New York: Atheneum, 1978), p. 36. See also Saunders Redding,
"Negro Writer," p. 6.

65 Sterling Brown cites the testimony of Dunbar's friends to show that it is not clear
what Dunbar thought of his dialectal poetry. Brown also cites Dunbar's well-known
autobiographical line from "The Poet" in which he expressed regret that his
nondialectal verse had been ignored. *Negro Poetry and Drama,* p. 47.

66 Although Dunbar was sometimes criticized for not speaking out against racial injustice, he wrote a letter on race riots and lynchings that was widely published. "Negro Author Voices Protest," *Chicago Tribune* (July 10, 1903), p. 3. Revell points out that Dunbar risked the goodwill of his editor to get his poem on lynching, "The Haunted Oak," printed in the *Century*. See Peter Revell, *Paul Laurence Dunbar* (Boston: Twayne Publishers, 1979), p. 172.

67 See, for instance, Peter Revell, *Paul Laurence Dunbar*, p. 168.

68 Sterling Brown noted that "When Dunbar dealt with the harsher aspects of Negro life, he discarded not only dialect, but also directness and simplicity." *Negro Poetry and Drama*, p. 48. Locke argued that Dunbar's race consciousness extended to his poetry written in standard English as well. Locke Papers, Dunbar Lecture, pp. 9–11.

69 Frederick Douglass is reported to have been pressured by white abolitionists to speak in a dialect to prove that he had really been on a plantation. See Leon F. Litwack, *North of Slavery: The Negro in the Free States, 1790–1860* (Chicago: University of Chicago Press, 1961).

70 Vincent Harding, "Religion and Resistance among Antebellum Negroes, 1800–1860," in *The Making of Black America*, Vol. 1, eds August Meier and Elliot Rudwick (New York: Atheneum, 1969), pp. 179–97; Raymond Bauer and Alice Bauer, "Day to Day Resistance to Slavery," in *Old Memories, New Moods*, ed. Peter I. Rose (New York: Atherton, 1970), pp. 5–29.

71 John Brown Childs is quite critical of this feature of the New Negro movements. John Brown Childs, *Leadership, Conflict, and Cooperation in Afro-American Social Thought*, pp. 69–80. Gates' claim "that dialect ceased to be a major form in the Harlem Renaissance" should not be taken to imply that Locke's advocacy of folk art went unheralded. See Henry Louis Gates Jr, *Figures in Black* (New York: Oxford University Press, 1987), p. 180.

72 Gates seems to want to deny this. He states, "Afro-American dialects exist between two poles, one English and one lost in some mythical linguistic kingdom now irrecoverable." Ibid., p. 172.

73 David Toop, *Rap Attack 2 African Rap to Global Hip Hop* (London: Serpent's Tail, 1991). See also Cornel West, "On Afro-American Popular Music: From Bebop to Rap," *Black Sacred Music*, 6, 1 (Spring 1992), p. 292.

74 See Melvin Patrick Ely, *The Adventures of Amos 'n Andy* (New York: The Free Press, 1991), pp. 194–244; and Thomas Cripps, "*Amos 'n Andy* and the Debate over American Racial Integration," in *American History/American Television*, ed. John E. O'Connor (New York: Frederick Ungar Publishing Co., 1983), pp. 33–54.

75 Ice Cube gave the following response to an interviewer's question of whether he aimed to educate whites as well: "Yeah, if they're educated too, then that's fine; if they're not, that's fine too…. As long as I get to *my* brothers and sisters who are spilling blood on the streets." Lisa Anthony, "Lyrics of Fury," *Hip-Hop Connection*, 36 (January 1992), p. 15.

76 Frank Owen, "Hanging Tough," *Spin*, 6, 1 (April 1990), p. 34.

77 Kierna Mayo Dawsey, "Caught Up in the (Gangsta) Rapture," *The Source*, 57 (June 1994), pp. 58–62. See also Clarence Lusane, "Rap, Race and Politics," *Race and Class*, 35, 1 (July–September, 1993), pp. 52–5.

78 Ras Baraka, "Mo' Dialogue," *The Source*, 24 (September 1991), p. 32.

79 Lisa Anthony, "Lyrics of Fury," p. 15.

80 Paul Gilroy, *There Ain't No Black in the Union Jack* (London: Hutchinson, 1987), pp. 209–17; and Tricia Rose, *Black Noise: Rap Music and Black Culture in Contemporary American Popular Culture* (Hanover, NH: Wesleyan University Press, 1994).

81 See Lusane, "Rap, Race and Politics," p. 44.

82 Ibid., pp. 49–55; and Robin D. G. Kelly, "Kickin' Reality, Kickin' Ballistics: The Cultural Politics of Gangsta Rap in Postindustrial Los Angeles," in *Dropin' Science: Critical Essays on Rap Music and Hip Hop Culture,* ed. Eric Perkins (Philadelphia: Temple University Press, 1994).

83 See, for instance, Cornel West, "On Afro-American Popular Music: From Bebop to Rap," p. 294; Michael E. Dyson, *Reflecting Black* (Minneapolis: University of Minnesota Press, 1993), p. 15; James Barnard, "The Rise of Rap: Reflections on the Growth of the Hip Hop Nation," *African Commentary* (June 1990), p. 50, cited in Spencer, "The Emergency of Black and the Emergence of Rap," p. 7..

84 For a defense of the claim that motives are irrelevant, see Michael Philips, "Racist Acts and Racist Humor," *Canadian Journal of Philosophy,* XVI, 1 (March 1984), p. 82.

85 With regard to the social meaning of "bitch" and "whore" a similar line of thought has been argued by members of the female gangsta rap group, Hoez With Attitude. See Rob Marriott, "Studio Hoez," *The Source,* 56 (May 1994), p. 46.

86 Ice Cube illuminates what it means to be a "sellout" in the following remarks: "I think you compromise your integrity to sell records to a pop crowd, that's when you've gone pop.... I'm on the pop charts, but I ain't poppin' shit!" Cleo H. Choker, "Down for Whatever," *The Source,* 53 (February 1994), p. 62.

87 Clarence Lusane makes this point in his statement that "[t]he commodification of black resistance is not the same as resistance to a society built upon commodificaton." Lusane, "Rap, Race and Politics," p. 45.

88 Ibid., p. 42.

89 For a selection of these narratives see Daryl Cumber Dance, *Shuckin' and Jivin'* (Bloomington: Indiana University Press, 1978), pp. 224–46. See also H. Nigel Thomas, *From Folklore to Fiction: A Study of Folk Heroes and Rituals in the Black American Novel* (New York: Greenwood Press, 1988), pp. 71–9.

90 I owe this point to Ronald Judy.

91 See H. Nigel Thomas, *From Folklore to Fiction: A Study of Folk Heroes and Rituals in the Black American Novel,* pp. 71–2.

92 Quoted in Stewart, *Critical Temper,* p. 300.

93 For Locke's references to Zola, see Stewart, ibid., pp. 299–300, 323, 329–30, and 332.

94 According to Ezy-E, "The way I see it, as long as you're being talked about, people still remember you. All publicity is good publicity whether it's bad or good." Carter Harris, "Easy Street," *The Source,* 58 (July 1994), p. 89. Ezy-E is the owner of Ruthless Records, a company that has sold over twenty million records since 1986. A recent dispute with Dr. Dre led Ezy-E to make the following remarks: "Dr. Dre's claimin' he's from a place he ain't really from.... He ain't never gangbanged or sold dope. Never, never in his life. All of a sudden he know gankin' and robbin' and all this chronic and low ridin'. He ain't never done that shit in his life." Carter Harris, "Easy Street," *The Source,* 58 (July 1994), p. 76.

95 MC Ren is reported to have converted to Islam.
96 Spencer, "The Emergency of Black and the Emergence of Rap," p. 7.
97 Snoop Dogg and Dr. Dre, for instance.
98 See James Bernard, "The LA Rebellion: Message Behind the Madness," *The Source*, 35 (August 1992), pp. 38–48.

12

The Search for the "Good Enough" Mammy: Multiculturalism, Popular Culture, and Psychoanalysis

Michele Wallace

By now I suppose everybody knows on the right, left, and in the middle that multiculturalism is not the promised land.

As employed by universities, museums, and advertising companies, the utopian idealism of a multicultural philosophy becomes a pragmatic institutional technique for neutralizing the myriad economic, political, and social demands of diversity. As we can readily see in such institutional practices from the Whitney Biennial to a Benetton ad campaign, multiculturalism doesn't necessarily redistribute power or resources. Although a few individual people of color may achieve employment, or rise higher in the ranks than they might have otherwise, collectively, people of color aren't necessarily empowered by multiculturalism. Rather, an ambiance of cultural diversity (a subaltern mise-en-scène, if you will) can serve to obscure the fact that nothing at all has changed for the diverse populations in question. More importantly, there may be little alteration in how the dominant group — or the oppressed groups, for that matter — conceptualize diversity.

And yet while we're slapping the wrists of the Whitney Museums or the Benettons (mostly for being pretentious and holier than thou), let us not forget that the Whitney is doing better than the Museum of Modern Art and that Benetton's ads led the way for the recent increase in the use of models of color in ads for Oil of Olay, Ralph Lauren, the Gap, and other companies;[1] which is to say that, even at its most cynical and pragmatic, there is something about multiculturalism which continues to be worth pursuing. For all sorts of reasons — in order to save the planet and live at peace — we do need to find many ways of publicly manifesting the significance of cultural diversity, of integrating the contributions of people of color into the fabric of our society.

But the problem with multiculturalism, in general, is that it tends to lump people of color together. People of color don't think of themselves as people of color, for the most part. Perhaps we should (for global reasons) but most of us don't. Most of our problems seem, at least to us, very specific and very local. So perhaps the real problem is that unified, monological identities such as people of color or whiteness are always unrepresentative fictions, just as globalizing, totalizing theories never work. Since we conceptualize our problems in terms of unworkable fictions (that is, whiteness, people of color), is it inevitable that our solutions will also be ultimately unworkable (from multiculturalisms to Rainbow Coalitions)? I'm not sure.

A year or so ago when I put together the Black Popular Culture Conference at the Dia Center for the Arts, I thought that a focus on popular culture in cultural analysis would help cultural critics to deal with the material, historical, and emotional specificity of populations of color. I also thought that using popular culture as primary cultural texts would help to draw African-American cultural analysis, in general, to a higher level of engagement with contemporary social, political, and economic issues. I suspect that's been true, perhaps because African-American cultural analysis is always inclined in this direction in any case, but there were some unanticipated limitations to this approach as well.

First, popular culture is not some obscure subsidiary of contemporary cultural production. Given the global revolution that's taking place in telecommunications and computer technology, popular culture is *the* main event on the world stage. As such, it is not a cohesive or singular entity nor can it be effectively described at this point since it is still, I suspect, in a relatively early stage of development. The point about popular culture, or mass culture, or the overlap of the two, is that it is overwhelming, drowning out, and subsuming other forms of cultural production. In particular, so called fine art — from opera to painting and sculpture — is being irreversibly affected by contact with popular culture.

But what I've come to realize is that the way in which one regards (or disregards) such issues is symptomatic of one's approach to cultural analysis in general. Without taking the global cultural and economic revolution of telecommunications and computer technology into account, we can simply read black popular culture, or indeed any popular culture, precisely the same way we've always read Shakespeare or Milton — not in their social or cultural context. Popular culture isn't inherently a subversive text. We needn't necessarily read it as a living, unfolding drama. It is just as subject to slaughter through analysis as Shakespeare, or, indeed, precisely because we imagine that it encompasses only the desires of the "low," we can allow ourselves to take shortcuts and liberties in analysis that we could scarcely imagine in dealing with so-called high culture.

I've gotten really interested in the possibility of a creative use of psychoanalysis in combination with multiculturalism and popular culture to think about issues of race conjoining gender and sexuality in the relationship of culture to society. This area of potential study seems to me particularly suggestive because feelings about race, and the relationship of race to gender and/or sexuality, tend to work so unconsciously in cultural representation and social relations in the West.

I am well aware that a lot of people feel as though psychoanalysis of any kind is utterly useless in social analysis because of its developmental ahistoricism but what continues to draw me back to it, after all, is the idea of the "unconscious" as a generalizable repository of all those social and psychological impulses which don't fall comfortably under the heading of the intentional. When I suggest the "unconscious" should be generalizable, it is not because I think there is only one kind of unconscious and that it can only function in a single way. In fact, I think it more than likely that if there is an unconscious, it is plural, variegated, and probably somewhat alterable by historical time and geographical space, although not at the rate of history or culture themselves.

For example, when we suggest that an Oedipal Complex might have made more sense for the nineteenth-century Viennese bourgeoisie, Freud described, than for twentieth-century Vietnamese youth, we are taking into account that the psychological operations described by the Oedipal Complex, indeed, are altered by context, environment, culture, and history. This doesn't mean, however, that the identity formation accounted for by an Oedipal Complex shifts with each permutation of context, environment, culture, and history. In other words, psychological functions may alter in time although not necessarily in precise synchronization with history, culture, and environment. Crosscutting the other systems, the unconscious, nevertheless, is less sensitive to change.

Because the idea of an unconscious is still fairly controversial in most circles, there hasn't been a lot of work done on diversifying notions of the unconscious. But so many processes in culture and society operate at the unconscious level — the economy, social change, individual and collective psychology, gender, race, sexuality, hegemony, our knowledge of grammar — that the reality of some kind of unconscious realm seems to me fairly certain.

Of course, the problems in psychoanalysis arise in terms of the specific descriptions of how the unconscious is constructed and how it functions, particularly in terms of gender, sexuality, and race formation. Although there is a great deal of debate in regard to most of the major tenets of psychoanalytic thought, all of the approaches still flaunt their color blindness. I think that the general failure to take into account the impact of "race" or cultural diversity is not necessarily owing to anything intrinsic to psychoanalysis but, rather, it has to do with who uses psychoanalysis and what it is generally used for. It is very rare for anybody of color to write about psychoanalysis. The most prominent exception has been Frantz Fanon. (Because of his sexism, misogyny, and his misguided ideas about revolution, Fanon's work was extremely limited.) Also, since white psychoanalysis hasn't been interested in people of color, in general, or thought that "race" played an important role in identity formation, certain kinds of questions having to do with race never get posed.

Let's face it. "Race" isn't taken seriously as a category by most academic or intellectual discourse in the West, so why should psychoanalysis be any different? Furthermore, since people of color, when perceived as mentally ill, are generally thought to fall into the category of those who are too sick to be reached by psychoanalysis, what would be the point of trying to think through ways of describing "race" in psychoanalytic terms? In order to communicate with whom?

But there are already lots of different kinds of psychoanalysis and there could be a lot more. There is the feminist psychology of Phyllis Chesler and Dorothy Dinnerstein and the feminist psychoanalysis of Nancy Chodorow and Carol Gilligan and, embedded in such practices, a reconsideration of issues having to do with the failure of Freudian psychoanalysis to deal with the reality of his patients' stories of incest and sexual abuse. There's the object relations theories of Melanie Klein and W. D. Winnicott and others, and the very important question of whether or not the mother-child dyad, as formulated by Adrienne Rich and other feminists, is actually the cite of primary identity formation in men and women instead of the Oedipal Complex. Further, did Freud really scrap the Seduction Theory because he couldn't deal with history, social reality, and the reality of trauma?

Moreover, in current practices of psychoanalysis and in radical theories of psychoanalysis, the question often asked is how accurate are victims in reporting their experience of trauma? At what age do we become accurate witnesses? What is the role of fantasy and the unconscious in the experience, recollection, or memory of trauma? Moreover, what kind of psychological damage does trauma cause and can such victims be reached by psychoanalysis? If one thinks about Toni Morrison's novels *The Bluest Eye* or *Beloved* or Alice Walker's *Meridian* or Toni Cade Bambara's *The Salteaters*, such questions take on an even greater resonance.

Who can be reached by psychoanalysis? Perhaps even more to the point, what causes mental illness? Can talk therapy reach people who are mentally ill? Can psychoanalysis be used as a means of social revolution, as some radicals have suggested? Are the mentally ill being unfairly oppressed by our categorization of them as mentally ill?

Is psychoanalysis accurately understood, itself, as a form of repression? Or is it just that we've been paralyzed much too long by the mistaken assumption that psychoanalysis designates a limited and narrow bourgeois Eurocentric problematic? Is it possible that, instead, psychoanalysis simply stands in for an entire, unconscious level of experience most of us have barely begun to explore?

Moreover, there is the way in which cultural analysis has appropriated various forms of psychoanalysis. In particular, I have been interested in feminist literary and film criticism and the use of feminist readings of Lacan's readings of Freud to reconsider the role of fantasy and the unconscious in cultural texts. Also, more to the point, Michel Foucault's description of psychoanalysis as the definitive context for the development of the human sciences in the late nineteenth century in *The Order of Things*[2] is highly compelling.

Such questions and observations to me seem to be highly suggestive for thinking about problems of African-American cultural and social analysis. Large numbers of African-Americans (as well as other peoples of color) continue to be traumatized by the American experience. Moreover, a great deal of discussion about the African-American aptitude for progress continues to circulate around speculation regarding the structure of our families, the frequency of female-headed households, teenage pregnancy, and drug-addicted babies in our communities.

In *Disfigured Images: The Historical Assault On Afro-American Women,* historian Patricia Morton traces this preoccupation with African-American family structure back to the myth of the black female slave as invented by American historians. The deviance of the black woman in the slave quarters (her physical strength, her sexual promiscuity, her propensity for dominance in the household, and her emotional callousness toward her children and her mate)[3] became the linchpin of theories of black inferiority first, in the historical accounts of white and black historians, and then in sociological accounts.

Not only did sociological accounts become social policy in the form of the Moynihan Report, when we turn to the "Mammy" specifically, the most prominent and long lasting of "disfigured images" of the black female, we begin to see how social policy and analysis converge with popular culture production. From *Birth of a Nation* in 1915 to *Gone With The Wind* in 1939 to *Raisin in the Sun*, the most important myth of the black woman — the "Mammy" — configures, and thus delimits black female cultural participation.

On the other hand, as Morton suggests, "Mammy" is not just a myth. Or rather the power of her mythology is that she is both real and unreal. There is no question that there has always been and there continues to be a strong black woman who provided profoundly crucial services to the black community and the black family. There can be little question that she also provided myriad essential services to the white community. Useful people tend to be useful to all those with whom they come in contact.

The point for me, however, is that there is a great deal of self-destructive, masochistic hostility for the myth of "Mammy" in the black community as a stereotype, hostility which quite commonly overflows to embrace most contemporary black women, and black mothers, perhaps teenage mothers in particular. In reading Morton's account of the stereotype and how it rests upon presumptions of black male inferiority and the dysfunction of the black family, one can understand the hostility. Nevertheless, aiming the hostility at contemporary black women constitutes an attack upon the "body" of the self or the race.

Feminist psychoanalytic conceptions of the "mother" could prove useful in exploring this phenomenon since general cultural trends of simultaneously loathing and worshiping the "mother" are not only at play in African-American self-perception but also in the way in which African-American culture is regarded by the dominant culture. First, one might want to think about what psychological role the mother actually plays in the black family. Does race make a difference in the identity formation of the child and to whether or not a mother is "good enough?" What difference does "race" make? What, for instance, is the psychological future of the children who are raising themselves in the Sudan and in Ethiopia? What are the long-range costs of such crisis management? What are the long-range costs of what is happening to many black children today in poor black communities?

The way feminist cultural analysis uses psychoanalysis could provide ways of reading cultural stereotypes of black women more fully, or against the grain. I'll admit it is still hard for me to imagine how current feminist uses of Lacan might come into play but there is no question that textual representations of black women, particularly of "Mammy," could benefit from deconstruction and analysis. Current feminist uses of Lacan seem to me too fashion-bound, too divorced from problems of social policy, and too accepting of the structures of white domination and male supremacy.

Since I, myself, am neither a psychologist or a psychoanalyst, I am not prepared to work through all the implications of psychoanalysis taking "race" seriously, although I hope somebody will someday. I would like to propose that psychoanalysis might prove quite useful to a multicultural black popular-culture analysis. The goal for me in such cultural analysis is to combine, or at least to establish a connection between, social analysis and cultural interpretation simply because this is what oppressed minorities need cultural analysis to do. I can provide three examples of how this can be done.

My first example is taken from history: the construction of race and gender in Hollywood films in the 1940s and 1950s such as *Gone with the Wind*, *Pinky*, and *Imitation of Life*. Such matters are inherently difficult for analysis because black producers (such as Oscar Micheaux) were generally so powerless and peripheral to the mainstream that black performers were made to play such marginal roles. Current practices of social segregation, economic disenfranchisement, and conventions of stereotypical images all serve to further trivialize our attempt to focus on race. And yet it is crucial to analyse the relationship of race to gender in this period in the film precisely because it sets the standard for everything that was to follow. Ideals of imagery and narrative were established then.

The question a psychoanalytic approach allows one to ask is how was the virtual "invisibility" of blacks then central to the function of American hegemony expressed through the classic Hollywood cinema of this period? If you look at *Gone with the Wind*, for example, obviously, in a very real sense, this film is not about blacks at all but about a fantasy notion white Americans had of the antebellum South. It was about the screen chemistry of Vivian Leigh and Clark Cable, the film's innovative set design and lighting techniques, and David Merrick's megalomania. On the other hand a psychoanalytic approach allows us to suggest, as well, that this film is also about slavery, about a certain kind of historical narrative, and the social and economic status of blacks in the antebellum South. Most importantly, the film reflects directly upon the status of blacks at that moment in 1939 in the United States and projections for their future. Also, a psychoanalytic approach might lead us to reflect upon the subliminal effects of constructions of race on black and white spectators, as well as spectators of color.

Now these may seem like obvious observations for many of you but you would be hard pressed to find much film analysis to corroborate it. As a child I remember viewing *Gone with the Wind* and being really taken aback by the realization that it had something to do with race at the same time that none of the discussions of the film, in books or in the press, seemed to take its racial content seriously. The most that might ever be said, reluctantly, if you brought it up was that the racial stereotypes were rather unfortunate. It reminds me of how American democracy was explained in my introduction to US Politics course — it was an otherwise perfect system except for the negligible flaw of slavery. Thanks to Freud, Derrida, and Foucault, we know now that systems don't really work that way. As likely as not, the negligible flaw provides the crucial clue to what's up.

In particular, extending upon Morton's work, one might look at the successful attempt to trivialize "Mammy's" role in comic terms in *Gone with the Wind*. Where were blacks then? Where were they going? How does this aspect of the film, the "Mammy" stereotype, reject our focus, and subvert our thinking about "race" or about any of the historical realities of the period?

My second example proposes a possible reading of the contemporary black film scene. There are many novel and new ways in which a psychoanalytic reading of the unconscious might be employed here, in terms of texts, audiences, authors, or institutional practices. It's all still pretty much virgin territory. For instance, if one looks at the representation of black female protagonists in such films as *Just Another Girl on the IRT, Poetic Justice,* and *What's Love Got to Do with It*, one might dismiss such representations as insignificant, either on the grounds that these weren't such great films or on the grounds that black women were relatively powerless to determine their content. Although *Just Another Girl on the IRT* was written, directed, and produced by Leslie Harris, a black woman, it would also appear that her struggle to get the film produced forced her to make commercial compromises which rendered the film not a reliable indication of what she might have done if she'd had more control. But a psychoanalytic approach to such matters might take all of this and more into account. How was her compromise staged?

In *Just Another Girl on the IRT*, the protagonist is a foul-mouthed teenager from black Brooklyn who wants to finish high school in three years and become a doctor but she accidentally gets pregnant. Unable to make up her mind about whether or not to have an abortion, she uses the $500 her boyfriend offers her to pay for it to go on a shopping spree with her girlfriend. Yet when she goes into labor early and the baby is accidentally born in the boyfriend's house, she commands him to dispose of the baby in the trash. Fortunately, he fails to do so and the picture ends with boyfriend, protagonist, and baby happily reunited.

There are many confusing aspects to the portrayal of this young woman, but the key one for me is why she refuses to consider getting rid of the baby (legally in the form of an abortion before it is born), and yet so readily disposes of it (illegally in the form of murder) once it is born. On the other hand, this representation fits well with Morton's stereotype of the black "Mammy" or mother. And the formal criteria of the maternal melodrama, in regard to the protagonist's antagonistic relationship with her mother, comes into play as well.

I saw this film on a Sunday afternoon in a ghetto movie theater in Louisville, Kentucky. The sparse audience consisted of mostly black teenage girls (a number of whom were accompanied by their own infant children) who laughed uncontrollably during the protagonist's painful and bloody labor scene, yet grew silent when she commanded her boyfriend to throw the baby away. I suspect these inconsistencies in plot and in audience response reflect profound ambivalences in the views of the director and the Louisville, Kentucky black female teenager audience about abortion and motherhood, ambivalences which it might be fascinating to pursue and connect.

On the other hand, neither *Poetic Justice* nor *What's Love Got to Do with It* were written or directed by black women and yet texts by black women (poetry by Maya Angelou and an autobiography by Tina Turner) were, to some degree, influential. How are *Poetic Justice* and *What's Love Got to Do with It* not black women's films? How do these films reflect upon the status of black women in our society?

The protagonist in *Poetic Justice*, Justice as played by Janet Jackson, is supposed to be a hairdresser poet yet we never see her write or recite poetry. As a character she is sketchy and ill-formed and seems to have no ideas whatsoever. Moreover, why did John Singleton choose the mostly lyrical, upbeat poetry of Maya Angelou over the work of one of the more profound black feminist poets such as June Jordon, Lucille Clifton, Audre Lorde, or Alice Walker? In the end, this film is quite disturbing because of what Singleton is trying to say about violence and dissension in the black community and in the black family. How can he raise such issues without taking black women more seriously? Moreover, what does his treatment of this matter in *Poetic Justice* (as well as the commercial success of the film) tell us about the ongoing success of black boyz/gangster films?

Of course, *What's Love Got to Do with It* is a much more satisfying film for women primarily because of the compelling performances of Larry Fishburne as

Ike and Angela Bassett as Tina, and because of the endlessly fascinating voice of Tina Turner, herself, on the soundtrack. Although the story of Turner's physical abuse would seem to provide an opportunity to publicly deal for the first time in film with the identity formation of a black woman, in fact, we have, instead, a narrative which frolics carelessly from bravura performance to musical number to bravura performance. The narrative dimension of this film never really takes off and, as in most musicals (although the film is not a musical), there is no sustained drama. Of course, part of the problem is that Tina Turner is still alive and seems not in favor of any kind of intensive public thoughtfulness about her experiences.

My final example of using psychoanalysis in cultural analysis would be to use it to consider contemporary events such as the dissemination of the videotape of the beating of Rodney King, the court trial in Simi Valley of the police who beat him in Simi Valley, the subsequent response to the verdict in the form of a riot and/or rebellion in the streets of Los Angeles, etc. First, I'd like to point out the way in which the revolution in telecommunications irreversibly impacts on all the events connected with the LA rebellion and all the texts resulting from it. It seems to me impossible and useless to consider King's beating independent of issues of representation.

The major point to be made about the whole Rodney King matter is that the videotape changed everything about how we discuss police brutality. The fascinating thing, however, was the resistance of the courts and the jury to the videotape as reliable documentary evidence, and the manner in which mostly conservative forces in the society began to behave as though they had always taken for granted that video imagery could be subject to an endless series of interpretations. Of course, in fact, this hasn't been the case at all in the past. The lesson for me here is that interpretation, itself, is always ideologically motivated.

There's no end to how psychoanalytic approaches might be used to examine the impact of "race" and gender on contemporary events for unconscious motivations, ambivalent impulses, repression, and possibly contradictory truth content. For example, consider King's question "Why can't we all get along?" Why was this innocuous question immediately taken up by everybody far and wide, as though it had never before occurred to anyone, or as though it were precisely the question that had been on everybody's mind all along? Why was a society which ordinarily would have had no interest in anything a Rodney King had to say suddenly convulsed by his rather simple question? What does this all mean? What can it tell us about "race," about popular culture, about the possibilities for multiculturalism, and about ourselves?

A probing psychoanalysis, which took its natural link between the humanities and the social sciences more seriously in general, might allow African-American cultural analysis to become more sophisticated, to respond more directly to social policy. Cultural shame over black women as mothers is a cultural construction older than we realize. And the problem can be addressed at myriad levels through an adaptive psychoanalytic approach: through individual and group therapy and counselling addressing personal and psychological issues; through financial and/or educational relief;[4] through deconstruction of stereotypes at the cultural level by means of direct cultural production, as well as through cultural analysis, criticism, and pedagogy.

Notes

1 In a recent (September 1993) article called "The Ugly Side of the Modeling Business" in *Essence Magazine,* Deborah Gregory and Patricia Jacobs write about the first press conference of The Black Girls Coalition, a protest group consisting of some of the top black models who complain that they are grossly underrepresented in fashion advertising, designer shows, and the editorial pages of consumer magazines. "A paltry 3.4 per cent of all consumer-magazine advertisements depicted African-Americans," Gregory and Jacobs write, "despite the fact that we comprise approximately 11.3 per cent of the readership of all consumer magazines and 12.5 per cent of the US population." Jacobs and Gregory take their statistics from a City of New York Department of Consumer Affairs report on the use of people of color in magazine and catalog advertising called "Invisible People" and issued in 1991. Of course, there are those who think that having blacks in ads is worse than not having them, that their presence serves to obscure the pernicious character of economic power. To this I would counter: while we're waiting for the ultimate socialist revolution, what's wrong with spreading the wealth around? Is it better that only whites work in advertising? If so, why is it okay for blacks to teach in universities or work in government and not okay for blacks to work in advertising? Universities, governments, and advertising are linked by the same money, the same power, and the same system of domination. It seems foolish, impractical, and naive to me to participate in one and not the other.
2 Michel Foucault, *The Order of Things* (New York: Random House, 1970).
3 Patricia Morton, *Disfigured Images: The Historical Assault on Afro-American Women,* (Westport, CT: Greenwood Press, 1991).
4 The idea that the goal of life for all black teenagers, and all black people, should be lifelong work seems to me not to take into account the limited capacities of the planet. I'll agree that a work-based identity can be socially useful and psychologically fulfilling but there may not be enough useful work for all of us. As such, we may need to consider other constructive avenues for our energies and current workfare policies are misguided, at best. On the other hand, financial relief and educational support seems essential.

13

"Chicana! Rican? No, Chicana-Riqueña!" Refashioning the Transnational Connection[1]

ANGIE CHABRAM DERNERSESIAN

Yo soy tu hij[a]/I am your daughter
de una migración ... /from a migration ...
ahora regreso, Puerto Rico ... /Now I return, Puerto Rico ...
por uno de tus/through one of your
muchos callejones./many passageways.[2]

Following in the tradition of alternative ethnographies which self-consciously reference situated knowledges, global travels, and the reflexive commentary of a socially constructed author-coproducer, I begin by explaining why I chose to speak about transnational identities within Chicana/o discourse in the manner described in the title. In reality, I must admit that the explanation became the paper, that this paper displaced another one referencing a transnational connection with México. While it could be stated that I willfully entered into a forbidden space by seriously interrogating *why* I was expending my intellectual and physical labor in a particular manner when academia leaves one so little room for doing so, I had no way of knowing that once I elaborated the rationale, I would enter another forbidden space: an unsanctioned transnational migration within Chicana/o discourse.

I am referring to a transnational migration: Chicana-Riqueña!, which intersects with México, which crisscrosses Chicanas/os in the contemporary world order, and which I believe should be engaged, at least considered, if the Eurocentric bent of multicultural paradigms is to be newly challenged. From within the field of Chicana/o studies this type of interrogation is timely because Chicanas/os are assuming their founding discourses in a critical fashion, as discourses which have "not only liberated us, but also gagged and disempowered many of us," to extend the language of Anzaldúa.[3] This endeavor is also relevant for a feminist theory which is deconstructive in character and as Barrett and Phillips point out, "seeks to destabilize, — challenge, subvert, reverse, overturn — some of the hierarchical binary oppositions ... of western culture"[4] along the lines of the "local, the specific, the particular."

It is important to note that these thoughts on transnational identities[5] coalesced as I prepared to visit Los Angeles, an urban space known for its "Third World" extensions, glimpse of the future, and irreverent cultural and ethnic border crossings.[6] For me, the trip to "Our Lady of" Los Angeles offers more than a delicious and much awaited escape from the heart of agribusiness and the grip of the ivory tower *"al norte"* (to the North) — it is also a connection with my past, my family, and with a strategic body/*cuerpo* foregrounded in the area: Chicana/o studies. Not surprisingly, what is examined in this entrance into the field is a particular claim to representation, for it is within this slippery territory that I labor along with many others refashioning fractured identities and community linkages, retracing critical histories, and reconfiguring social and political geographies. Given this context, it should not come as a surprise that the autobiographical should be foregrounded within this consciously assumed inquiry-turned-paper, because, to a large extent, that's what Chicana/o studies claims to be, a self-representation, a conscious and strategic doubling of oneself and each other, a way of affecting not only the content but also the relations and politics of representation.[7]

In this paper I choose to register my own autobiographical impulses, the ones that complicate earlier schemes of Chicana/o identity, the ones that prefigure the kinds of transnational multicultural linkages anticipated in Chicana/o Latina/o, a problematic, yet forward looking attempt to forge semantic linkages between peoples and cultures of the Americas, here and there. Examining these kinds of transnational linkages interrupts traditional multicultural constructions, which revisit melting-pot theories of assimilation in an effort to ward off a presumed "tribalism"[8] and/or apprehend ethnic difference through simplified relations between dominant and subordinate groups without accounting for the differences between them, for the complex ways in which they negotiate these differences in daily life.[9]

❋ ❋ ❋ ❋

The seed that generated the thoughts for this paper were planted while I was on a postdoctoral fellowship at the Chicana/o Research Center at UCLA. Shortly after having made the acquaintance of a colleague and delivering to him the familiar Chicana/o salutation: a mode of opening up discourse around a narrative of one's origins, he responded to me: "Chicana! Riqueña? You aren't a Puerto Rican, you're a Chicana!" To be sure, this bothered me for I had voiced my plurality as a way of formulating a connection, not a disruption. Implicit in his statement is the idea that I had to be one or another, a Chicana or a Puerto Rican, but not both, certainly not a hybrid, hybrids aren't authentic, they have no claim to a fixed set of ethnic categories. Implicit in the statement is the idea that I might pass for a Puerto Rican in appearance, but no one could seriously mistake me for a Puerto Rican. At least no one who knew Puerto Ricans, no one who could really distinguish between Latinas/os, no one who could identify specific Latina/o roots.

I didn't talk like a Puerto Rican, I had never lived in New York or on the Island, *everything* about me spoke Chicana! That is a particular rendering, a refashioning of Chicanas/os along singular Mexican/American lines. The fact that I was raised single-handedly by a Chicana from El Paso, Texas, grew up in La Puente, California, lived in Occupied México and not Occupied Boriquen.... The fact that I had reconstituted myself through strategic Chicana revisions of the nineties.... The fact that I taught Chicana/o studies at Davis.... All of this only served to reframe my identity within this unitary mode of Chicana/o.

Since by this I was made akin to a card-carrying Chicana, there was no question about my Chicana*ness*, no dispute about this being a problem, about being on the *inside* of that representation, hence the exclamation point. The problem was with the selected ethnic equation, the particular framing of Chicana, the Rican who intersected it, the Rican who spoke to a continuity and a difference simultaneously, the Rican who interrupted the socially acceptable polarity, the mode of writing Chicana/o history, the mode of experiencing Chicana subjectivity, the mode of drawing "American" relations. In retrospect, I know I was being challenged like other Chicanas/os know they are being challenged when we are called *pochas* (half-breeds) and not *Méxicanas, marxistas y feministas* and not Chicanas, and inhabitants of the *United States* of America instead of inhabitants of the other America. The one José Martí termed, *"NuestraAmérica"*/"Our America" to retain the plural character of this geopolitical space.

Yes, I had been administered the acid test which would confirm a particular claim to authenticity, and in all honesty, this type of ethnic containment was commonplace. However, I wasn't about to masquerade as a Puerto Rican national or a Nuyorican, to engage in the business of inventing ready made identities the way Chicano nationalists did when they celebrated a glorious Aztec past with questionable relations to the present, but neglected to map vital relations with contemporary *indígenas* and other local underrepresented groups. I was, after all, a Chicana-Riqueña, a particular type of Chicana-Riqueña, a West Coast one with a Chicana-Méxicana foundation. I had no patent on the identity or the multiple ways of assuming this identity delivered by histories, social experiences, and human subjects. And to be fair, I wasn't being singled out, it was not as if I hadn't heard similar things about being Mexican — that I wasn't really a Mexican either because I was a second-generation Chicana, because my mother had grown up in El Paso and lived through the aftermath of her parent's migration into the United States as a result of the violence associated with the Mexican Revolution.

For years I had witnessed Central Americans, Latinas/os, even Spaniards/*Españoles* joining the ranks of the Chicana/o movement, consciously assuming a Chicano political identity and strategically glossing over their ethnic and cultural distinctions, and being expected to do so for a chance to join in to forge an alliance, *una relación con la causa chicana/o* relationship with the Chicana/o cause. But they were not alone in this endeavor, there was already a blueprint for containing ethnic differences engraved in important documents such as in the epic poem/book *I am Joaquín/yo soy joaquín*,[10] where the speaking subject infers that *la raza*: Méxicanos, Españoles, Latinos, Hispanos, and Chicanos; Yaquis, Tarahumaras, Chamulas, Zapotecs, Mestizos, and indios, are all the same because of *his* authenticating universal discourse of the Chicano.[11] This masculine construction in and around whose body and social location and ideological purview these particular multiethnic constructions converge and are diluted, can be read as a "Chicano" rendition of pluralism although it is framed within a nationalist perspective that opposes assimilation and white "melting-potism." Artistic representations of *mestizaje*, in which the Chicano/male/*mestizo* is framed on the one side by the conquistador and on the other by the *indígena*, making *mestizaje* the preferred ethnic construction, have furnished a way also of containing ethnic pluralities within brown masculinities.

Even today this model of *mestizaje* presupposes a confluence, based on equal mixtures, with the Chicano as the confluence and the other two, the indians and the *españoles,* as the tributaries. This type of *mestizaje* is the age-old political embodiment of the Mexican national who has traditionally occupied this central space and is the subject of contention by many *indígenas* for whom *mestizaje* means inequality, a concerted dilution of indianness, and partnership with the Mexican State. Yet, this "native" multiculturalism has gained much currency among Chicana/o and Méxicana/o writers because, as Rosaura Sánchez points out, "writers such as Octavio Paz and Carlos Fuentes have made a fetish of *mestizaje*, attributing to this notion essentialist monocausality to explain Mexican identity and history." She explains that:

> [F]rom this we are to understand that the struggle between warring Spanish conquistadores and hermetic, stoic Indians is ongoing in the blood of all Mexicans,

a mixture that explains not only the contradictory national character but even problems in socioeconomic development. *Mestizaje* then serves all too conveniently to explain away a multitude of economic, political, and social sins. The manipulation of essentialist discourses like *mestizaje* is thus another hegemonic strategy which we need to disarticulate and reject, just as in the United States, notions such as the "melting pot" of American culture need to be debunked.[12]

Yet as Sánchez points out, far from rejecting these ideas around *mestizaje*, Chicana/o writers have privileged them within essentialist discourses, "unwittingly perhaps repeating Mexican hegemonic discourses which have become, to a degree at least, part of the dominant political rhetoric there and served to distort and obfuscate the oppression and exploitation of thousands of Mexican Indians."[13]

For those seeking to reference the contemporary social realities and new ethnicities that mark a fully transculturated context, this type of native multiculturalism has little to offer. Given the prevailing ethnic absolutism which marked so much of the thinking around issues of identity and subjectivity within Chicana/o discourse, it is not then surprising that aside from the unsatisfactory discourse of *la raza*, there are so few possibilities for referencing the kind of "local" transnational plurality with which I was contending at UCLA within an already constituted body of Chicana/o discourse.[14] In its authoritative renditions, this discourse is largely fashioned around a Mexican-American binary, only disrupting this model occasionally with cultural productions registering Latino metanarratives: border crossings in other geographical directions that often maintain the interpellated ethnicities at a comfortable distance from one another.[15] Within dominant productions, the situation is worse since these groups are either artificially polarized or else blended into an unrecognizable mass.

It is ironic that while we live in a period which prizes the multiplicity of identities and charts border crossings with borderless critics, there should be such a marked silence around the kinds of divergent ethnic pluralities that cross gender and classed subjects within the semantic orbit of Chicana/o. So powerful is the hegemonic reach of dominant culture that fixed categories of race and ethnicity continue to be the foundation, the structuring axis around which Chicana/o identities are found. Few are those who have cut through the nationalist or pluralist registers which promote an "all-or-nothing approach" to writing the intersections between underrepresented transnational ethnic groups and their heterogeneous social movements towards one another.

I am the first to admit that to modify this scenario in ways that do not signal complicity with the nullifying gestures of the dominant culture is to enter a territory where strategic maneuvers are required at every turn, especially given the different kinds of multicultural scenarios that are present within the national context and implicate Chicanas/os in competing ways. Yet the cost of not confronting the new ethnicities that frame Chicana/o in 1994 is very high, for it is to accept what is seemingly unacceptable from a Chicana/o studies viewpoint: that we are not only unable, but also *unwilling* to engage the social panorama, the community, the *reason* for Chicana/o representation. For even though an academic Chicana/o discourse may lag far behind the continual refurbishing of global transnational identities in fashioning particular ethnic subjects, social reality has not; it is speeding ahead as the geopolitical boundaries of this territory extend north and south in an unrelentless march towards the twenty first century. And Los Angeles has lead the way in this regard. There, if anywhere, the binary structure which manages distinct cultural and ethnic groups is destabilized within the social formation by a series of mixed racial and ethnic identities that speak to the wide range of possibilities that frame Chicana/o:

> Chicana/o African-American; Chicana/o Asian-American, Chicana/o Native American; Chicana/o Central-American; Chicana/o Latin-American; Chicana/o white, Chicana/o Middle Eastern, and the list goes on, breaking down the familiar blocks that follow the term, Chicana/o here, expanding beyond them with such configurations as Chicana/o Ukrainian, Chicana/o Armenian, Chicana/o Indian.[16]

I am referring to the new ethnicities of this generation,
to our relatives,
to our forebears,
to ourselves, *a nos otros*
to the *human panorama* across which we experience and socially construct our identities,
to the *unacknowledged* generations silenced by ethnic absolutism of the Mexican-American binary.

Can we afford to keep us/them within an ethnic closet? How will we/they write our/their herstories and histories and draw a connection to the past? To an alternative tradition of resistance and contestation? It seems to me that we/they have no choice: we/they must break out of the prisonhouse of nationalism if we/they are to engage our/their socially intersected ethnicities "on the inside." And this is, of course, only a narrow reference to "ethnicities," a category which itself is problematic if not recoded in a critical fashion because, historically, this term does not address any number of other pluralities at work in the formation of socially constructed identities. Instead it tends to subsume them into an essentialist frame that promotes a notion of Americanness that survives by an imaginary notion of the nation as a unified cultural community, "by marginalizing, dispossessing, displacing and forgetting other ethnicities."[17]

I do not recall this context as a way of reinscribing racialized ethnic categories as primary, nor as a way of reinventing the primacy of race through an acknowledgment of another hybridity: Chicana-Riqueña. Neither do I seek to expand the circumference of an oppressive nationalistic mode of writing Chicana/o identity, by unproblematically adding Caribbean or Central American or Latin American linkages to it, by making the fatal move into an unmarked collectivity. This Chicana-Riqueña frame is a social identity constructed through any number of experiences and discursive practices that extend beyond what is illustrated here by way of an introduction; it intersects with Chicana/o in any number of ways implicating not only race and ethnicity but also gender and class. Thus it is susceptible to competing modes of interpretation, themselves changing and intersected. Rather than inscribing monocausality, a one-dimensional view of oppression, it forecasts an articulation of other intersected and overlapping categories.

I appeal to this framing of social identity as a way of opening up a discussion around "the diversity of identities within ourselves and our communities,"[18] and as a way of acknowledging the transnational perspectives which must be figured into a more "diverse concept of ethnicity" which "is theorized through differences: the relations among and between different social groups" and which *does* recognize the role that an alternative reframing of the discourses of national origin can play in contesting the dominant notion of ethnicity which has coupled itself "with nationalism, imperialism, racism, and the state."[19] Instead of seeking recognition of Chicana-Riqueña identity through a logic of exceptionalism, one appeals to unique circumstances: the important struggles for self- determination within the "belly of the monster" which bring Chicanas/os and Puerto Ricans into an important political convergence, I appeal to the Chicana- Riqueña modality because of its significance for an alternative mode of writing social identities and agencies within the larger context in which we live as we approach the year 2000 in the purview of the so-called "New World Order."

Within this fully transculturated reality, where newspapers forecast an unprecedented browning of California (according to the US Census Bureau, 36 per cent of the ten million immigrants estimated in California in the next quarter century will be Latino[20]) and where even the governor has launched his infamous anti-immigrant rights campaign, doubling his forces with liberal democrats and an angry constituency and creating hysteria over *their* borders and *our* numbers, there is little doubt that the subordinated ethnic pluralities to which we are being partnered are *here* in unprecedented numbers. There is little doubt that these socially constructed identities are being worked out in ways that beg for a rethinking of the politics of one's location and one's contestation/*una respuesta* as well as a refashioning, perhaps even the coding of a new critical language to reference alongside, between, and through Chicana/o.[21] Compared to the current scenario, the largely simplified Mexican-American dilemma that was the staple of a nationalist ideology which combatted Anglo-Saxon purism might seem manageable enough, easily referenced and consumed, and not at all like the complex relations inscribed through the hyphens above. However, that is until we begin to deconstruct a state generated *Mexican* identity, claim its absented presences: the underrepresented multiethnic communities *en México*, and voice the other intersected ethnic pluralities that link us to the *American of the Americas.*

And that is until we attempt to forge our complex historical relationships to both sides of the deconstructed binary.

In my own case, I was motivated along this line of thinking, not only by the heterogeneous social panorama and my unspoken circumstance, but also by the children, the ones who are well on their way to adulthood and to forging cultural and political identities. I am referring to those who live well out of the limits proscribed by Chicana/o discourse and its traditional notions of *"mestizaje."* In particular, I am motivated by my nieces and nephews, the sons and daughters of my brothers and sister,[22] who, like me, have counterparts with Mexican Puerto Rican linkages. I am referring to siblings who *did* grow up on the island, who *do* speak like Puerto Ricans, and who are rarely mistaken as Mexicans or Chicanas/os. This situation is not all that unique; it may well be the norm. While these types of social identities have not occupied a strategic place within Chicana/o discourse, there is no reason why they should not.

Given this context, there is no reason why the Puerto Rican, for instance, should be othered as *another* within this space, where historic social and ethnic intersections have been prominent at least at the symbolic level, where even the Spanish and Yankee colonizers have earned recognition amidst a critique of the violence that their conquests incurred. Within Chicana/o discourse, assuming a claim to representation means staking out a territory based on historical and political entitlements. This claim involves a strategy of reversal commonly activated by Chicanas who contest exclusion within mainstream and alternative sectors. From this vantage point, the counter position: Chicana-Riqueña is a response to those who would silence the pluralities marking alternative subject positions and histories. It is a counterposition to those who would suggest that the intersected Riqueña (and by extension, the African-American or the Native American or the Asian-American) was/were not there: *aquí* (here), and that therefore their/our intersected herstories and histories — local or global — should not be written within, throughout, or across Chicana/o.

This position involves a passionate form of "talking back," *"lanzando la palabra,"* throwing the word back like you would throw a rock. This speech intersects with a tradition of defiance that extends beyond the dualistic limits of resistance inscribed by the ballad of the border hero who negotiates a political boundary between México and the United States, and it entails an interrogation of socially-accepted subject positions that do not script the relations between underrepresented ethnic groups. To throw the word back in this particular case (Chicana-Riqueña) can be construed as a response to the original ethnic dislocation and absolutism contained in the violent phrase: "You're not a Puerto Rican!,"[23] a response with an alternative mapping of an ethnic ancestry, one that I refashion on the basis of a partial life story rendered in the tradition of the *testimonio*/testimony with the *contestación* (answer and contestation): Who?

Who has the right to deny me this ethnicity, a particular history, mediated by the contemporary experiences of rupture, conquest, migratory cycles, and divorce? Who dare tell me that my first and most formative experiences with collectivity didn't constitute a cultural identity worthy of a presence and a place within a Chicana/o genealogy of difference? Who could dispute the fact that my *abuelos*/grandfathers, the one who cut lawns in El Paso and the one who taught women on the island, weren't both my *abuelos*? Who could dispute the fact that María, who migrated from Arecibo to Monterey, California, and Chavela, who migrated from Chihuahua to El Paso, Texas, would not anticipate a kind of transnational migration that their granddaughters would consciously assume generations later as a way of tracing different subordinated ethnic ancestries and cultural identities denied to them through the state-sanctioned borders of t.v. and public education? Those identities that complicate the Chicana-Riqueña frame many times over with other hyphenated spaces filled with four or five transnational migrations through nation states and occupied territories that share an uneven distribution of the wealth of the globe.

Who would erase my *tía*, my wonderful Puerto Rican aunt turned Chicana-Riqueña in the seventies, she who modeled a Chicana/o studies identity for me and provided a much-needed path from literature to Chicana/o studies? Who would censure the life histories of all of those Central Americans, Puerto Ricans, and Latinas/os who are in Chicana/o studies classes, calling themselves Chicanas/os in the tradition of my *tía*?[24] Those students who live a strategic connection between different histories and peoples, a connection that is often relegated to the private realm or the back burner as exclusionary and ready made notions of Chicana/o are consumed within the academy.

Will these transnational migrations through Chicana/o be written? Or will they be perceived as ripping away at the core of Chicana/o studies, a domain being contested under the deconstructive insights of gender and cultural studies and where the glue that is generally accepted as "holding it all together in spite of it all" is often a specific notion of race or ethnicity? Will the tensions that mediate political alliances and/or ruptures between Chicanas/os, Méxicanos and other Central and Latin American groups be silenced within the age-old multicultural discourse of Chicanas/os? Will we disseminate the impression that the inherited notion of *"mestizaje"* is a "natural" phenomenon and not a discourse? That this framing of the mixture is at all desirable — that it should not give way to others — just because there exist shared histories among Chicanas/os, Latinas/os, and *indígenas* referencing colonialism and imperialism and which also inscribe important differences that are often repressed by native multiculturalisms.

Will we insist that this type of multiculturalism is enough to usher away the tensions between Chicanas/os and any other Latinos or Hispanos? Especially between Chicanas/os and their hyphenated Latina/o *indígena* coalitions, and those who dispense with this intersected group because of its problematic relationship to Spanish-speaking communities and linkage to colonized nations or tribes, because the Chicana/o denomination deliberately strays from the Hispanic ethnic flock by attaching specific political conditions and ideological sequences to the notion of ethnic identity. Or, finally, because Chicanas/os and Méxicanas/os and the rest are a majority of working poor to be contended with locally, to be assisted and joined in alliances and life-long commitments?

These kinds of problematic situations emerge when native multiculturalisms fail to account for how Chicanas/os are impugned because of their bilingual expressions, their filial relationship to a territory annexed by the United States, and are accused of being alingual or illiterate because their particular code of Spanish is not the official language in this region and is not reaccentuated by the dominant form of linguistic capital: Euro/Their-American. Reinscribing a brown smorgasbord is a risky business, not only when Central Americans, Latin Americans, or Cubanos are added to the equation; multiple tensions also emerge when Chicanas/os are unproblematically partnered with Méxicanos along an essentialist transnational route, without consideration for the disruptive influences of history, class, race, or gender. As Rosaura Sánchez points out, "representation on the basis of national origin alone continues nonetheless to be unidimensional and to bracket other forms of oppression and exploitation in society." She continues:

> There is an excellent antidote to this essentialist discourse, a practice that shatters all notions of collectivity or identity purely on the basis of national origin. And that practice is interactional, requiring only that one come in contact with upper-class Mexicans. It is then that the myth of a shared cultural identity goes up in smoke for Chicanos, who at that moment experience the same class-based rejection to which they are subject in the US.[25]

This is not to suggest that, for example, the children of those who most vehemently promote linguistic purism (in terms of Spanish or English) and other class-based attitudes from a position of social and economic privilege aren't also capable of partaking in the type of racial discrimination launched at Chicanas/os once they cross the border. It is this type of a convergence that has often led Chicanas/os into multicultural paradigms that only promise to exclude them down the road along with many others. As a way of censuring the native element over here, institutions of dominant culture frequently anchor transnational "hegemonic" multiculturalisms under the leadership of a foreign-born and socially-privileged Spanish-speaking elite.

By invoking these examples, I do not wish to undermine the histories of those working-class Central Americans, Puerto Ricans, and Latinas/os whose life histories and social conditions converge strategically with Chicanas/os and who bring important lessons of resistance that are often ignored by Chicana/o nationalists who walk a more separatist and exclusionary path even while appealing to global notions of *"la raza."* I offer these examples as a way of demonstrating the complex relations that are to be negotiated between those whom government documents loosely refer to as "Hispanic," "Spanish," or "Latino," as if they all shared the same social, cultural, and ethnic characteristics, and as if they all sought natural coalitions with one another. All too often predominant multicultural paradigms sin by virtue of casting these social constituencies as homogeneous elements which only encounter difference when relating to other subordinated ethnic groups (that are not Spanish-speaking) or when coming into contact with dominant ethnic groups in the United States. This kind of faulty thinking has important repercussions because, without accounting for their differences, it is impossible to comprehend, for instance, why some Chicana-Riqueña coalitions are desirable within an alternative subject position recording intersected political agencies while others are not. The same holds true for other Chicana/o Latina/o, Latina/o Chicana/o connections. Marking these types of positionalities within identities is not entirely new to Chicana/o discourse where, from the very beginning, lines were drawn between Chicanas/os and Mexican-Americans, those who claimed the subordinated ethnicity and the benefits to be reaped from Chicana/o struggles and Chicana/o sufferings but not the politics inscribed in these divergent identities or the controversial mode of self-naming that still raises eyebrows. The difference is that native multiculturalisms have rarely been scrutinized, thus these amorphous essentialist constructions of race and national identity prevail.

If it is true that the differences among and between Chicanas/os and Latinas/os are commonly factored out of predominant multicultural paradigms, it is also true that within these paradigms, the different subordinated social and ethnic groups are often cut off from the *trans*national context so that crucial relations between competing nation states are factored out of the social panorama. The result is that these groups are deprived of the vital connections that make diverse ethnic communities part of a local as well as globalized cultures in contact. Forging the connections outside of the proscribed limits of national culture (at home and abroad) offers the possibility of apprehending viable transnational and multicultural linkages that have generally gone unexplored. This approach also promises to shed light on the complexity of the unconventional narrative of ethnic ancestry contained in Paul Gilroy's eye catching title: "It Ain't Where You're From, It's Where You're At."[26] "Where You're At" involves a necessary and oftentimes continuous reconfiguration of "Where You're From" or, as I see it, "Where You've Been." In the case of Chicanas/os, Méxicanas/os, and Puerto Ricans, for instance, this is particularly relevant, especially since the notion of the nation — "Where You've Been" — is itself under dispute. Thus, it is not only a question of navigating across water and borders and joining multiethnic communities over there, it is not only a question of charting immigration or reverse migrations towards México or Puerto Rico or other parts of "Aztlán." This type of recovery also involves contending with the realities of conquest; with having state-sanctioned borders being crossed over you and your ancestors; and with being labelled a legal or an illegal alien; and retaining a viable memory of another type of political geography, one that is sustained through strategic multicultural and multiethnic linkages.

Forging viable transnational linkages that operate in a dynamic manner also involves acknowledging the various forms of multiculturalism that coexist within a global culture outside of the US national context and addressing a series of competing notions of what constitutes "multiculturalism." Most "multicultural" readers offer little insight into these "other worlds" and even within ethnic studies there is a tendency to focus on how multiethnic populations here experience their dislocations, their strategic relocations, instead of focusing on how these human movements are also inscribed at their points of origin, the local communities and nation states from which migration takes place. Within Chicana/o studies, a much needed project involves looking at how different Mexican and indigenous communities have incorporated Chicana/o political agencies and modes of writing culture, how multiculturalism takes place through a transnational Mexican register that also "talks back" to Chicanas/os through a Méxicana/o Chicana/o dialogue.

Recently, an important novel, *Paletitas de Guayaba* (*Guayaba Suckers*) by Erlinda Gonzalez Berry, staged some of these complexities around a female protagonist who repatriates herself to Mexico City through memory, journey, and sexual desire.[27] She travels as a way of reclaiming her connection to her past and making sense of her present. Rather than encountering the ready made, unproblematic, mimetic identities furnished by Movement narratives, her identity is contested at every turn. She struggles with the stigma of being called a *"pocha"* or a *"pochita"* (a female half-breed/outsider in its diminutive form, "little") by Mexican males who would deny her partnership with a national identity; she struggles with the stigma of being *"manita"* with Chicano nationalists who interrogate her Chicananess because of regionalism: her New Mexican affiliation; and she challenges received notions of New Mexican identity for being Spanish-centered and for ignoring the necessary Mexican-Chicana/o working-class connection.

In addition, she explores the sexual nuances that are attached to any number of these terms by competing masculinities (white, Méxicano, Chicano) who would rob her of her agency and reify her as a sex object. Assuming social relations within a world fractured by split identities means that she negotiates her relations with others through different subject positions, acquiring power over discourse through extensive monologues and definitions that must be rendered as a kind of pedagogy of resistance in light of the rampant ignorance about her mode of living out a Chicana/o Méxicana/o transnational experience. This also involves reformulating a number of heterosexual displacements moving from their space into her own space and connecting to other Méxicana subjects and icons.

While the novel does threaten to reinscribe a *mujer*/woman-centered essentialism and only tangentially deals with class, it reverses the strategy of multicultural paradigms that speak to a Mexican ancestry only as a way of figuring a distant past from the position of the United States. In fact, all too often the

Mexican disappears quickly once the Chicana/o emerges within the annals of Chicana/o history. This does not occur in *Paletitas,* for the scene of the multicultural encounter is *there,* in México, and the protagonist does not leave her baggage behind once she arrives — she does not instantaneously receive a new fictitious identity and it isn't presumed that she'll be nourished in spirit automatically. She negotiates from the *inside* of a Chicana representation and these negotiations are often painful, ironic, sarcastic, and humorous. She travels through layers of contestation: this means responding to national dynamics, to regional dynamics, to gender dynamics, to racial dynamics, to sexual dynamics, to the politics of the Movement, and it means confronting the discourse of the brown female other: *"pochita"* at the point of origin.

A point where one is susceptible to insult, a point where one is disrupting another hegemonic construction of national identity, from the inside, as someone who carries different traces of Mexicanness that are foreign to accepted notions of *mestizaje.* This is a radically different location than that offered Joaquín, in the movement poem "I Am Joaquín," for his immersion is an adaptation of a ready-made epic of México's official history — it does not offer the possibility of a Mexican rejection, of someone else (*otro Méxicano,* for instance) talking back to him as he claims a Mexican space through various levels of *mestizaje.* Nor does it offer the possibility of someone offering a rampant distortion of who he is. This poem lacks the kinds of tensions involved in making coalitions that we see in *Paletitas* because Joaquín's act of poetic self-constitution involves identifying with the conquerors *and* the conquered and he is spared the kind of gender objectification experienced by Chicanas/os and Méxicanas within the national space and its masculinist orientation. By relocating the Chicana/o subject positions into México, *Paletitas* offers a kind of forum, a limited possibility of a multicultural paradigm that seeks to be participatory at many levels, at least to talk back, and where speaking across difference does involve risks, contradictory processes of reterritorialization, and where dialogues and even coalitions are temporarily imagined.

Berry's novel offers a glimpse of the types of transnational complexities that mark a Chicana Méxicano border crossing, and yet this is only one location from which such a transnational connection can be made. Multiple border crossings are possible outside of the text in every day life, where local transnational migrations from Chicana/o to Méxicana/o and back again take place all over the Southwest, in Michigan, Chicago, and other places as well. In the greater Sacramento area, for example, it is common to see Mexican farmworkers from specific regions in México settled in Chicana/o communities, marking out separate as well as shared terrains of coexistence, of difference and similarity. The kinds of transnational linkages which they refashion in daily life in the factories, in the fields, on the street corners, and in the schools, are rich but they are a far cry from the epic narratives that are commonplace in Chicana/o discourse. Suffice it to say these local connections rarely make their way into multicultural paradigms even when

Mexican linkages are actively sought across transnational lines. It is even rarer to encounter alternative narratives of ethnic ancestry in Chicana/o discourse that chart transnational migrations towards two or more points of ethnic origin and geopolitical spaces.

The transnational migration through *Paletitas* offers an example of how one aspect of a transculturated connection can be written from Chicana/o to Méxicanas/os through an international register that reverses the terms of the old-style multiculturalism. An admittedly partial and highly interpretative glimpse of my own transnational connection to Puerto Rico offers a different example, a local example, of how another side of these connections can be traced through a narrative of ethnic ancestry which intentionally deviates from quantifiable bilingual constructs, pretending to measure how much one is one thing and not another and naively assuming that hybrid identities necessarily operate from stable or "equal mixtures" of two ethnic groups.

Drawing partially on Kobena Mercer's reinterpretation of Walter Benjamin's phrase, "I seek not so much as to rearticulate the past the way it really was," but "to seize hold of a memory as it flashes up at a moment of danger."[28] I do so at this moment where Chicanas/os are being interpellated by hegemonic discourses urging them to reject immigrants (their families), at a time when defensive nationalistic frameworks reemerge in the alternative sector, inscribing once again unsatisfactory multiculturalisms with which to counter the effects of capitalism and racism. However, in contrast to Mercer's articulation, this memory is woven through a representation of a family history, one of the many starting points for a critical elaboration of our imagined communities, and for rethinking the terms of the counter hegemonic struggles that have prevailed within Chicana/o.

I newly assume the term *retomo la palabra* in the manner familiarized in the Chicana/o oral tradition by stating that in my childhood I crossed the border many times, but not only the border to México. I never travelled to Puerto Rico, but it was there, *here*, it was all around me although he, the Puerto Rican national, my father, he was not there/here. I experienced Puerto Rico from a Chicana-centered household on Eldon Street, from a Chicana/o barrio of household and domestic workers and of commuters who worked in downtown Los Angeles and "made ends meet" to send their children to Catholic school.[29] At home, the connection was there in our *"platicas"* as we revisited the historical and economic junctures that brought our parents together that fateful day in the *parque* in El Paso, Texas, and later in Fort Bliss; the connection was there as we rotated *frijoles* with *habichuelas, arroz blanco con sopa de arroz, sofrito* with *salsa méxicana,* and the connection was there as we listened to Javier Solís sing *"En mi viejo San Juan,"* ("In my Old San Juan"), transporting us once again from Mexicanness to Puerto Ricanness with somber, passionate tunes, with the nostalgic desire of the immigrant who has left to "a strange nation" but dreams of the return, of the day he will search for his love, of the day he will dream once again there, in his "Old San Juan."[30]

Javier's refashioning of an island, vibrant in memory is nourished by a contradictory *despedida (me voy, adiós, adiós,)* and a return *(pero algún dia volveré,* but one day I'll return), one that I experienced, not as a Puerto Rican immigrant, but as a member of an extended family of Méxicana/o and Puerto Rican immigrants. For me the song was a return, a way of contending with historical, geographical, and emotional displacements, it was a way of making Puerto Rico present. And it *was* present beyond the nostalgia of the song, but it was present in an unusual form. It was there, coexisting, at times interrupting and intermingling, and it was spoken from the interstices of Chicana/o, irreverently recreating itself through a family narrative of Chicana/o discourse that would do for me what the Chicano movement discourse had not done and would not do. The Puerto Rican and the Chicana were partnered in the contrasting narratives of how my *papás* negotiated their ethnic and political differences, in how the linguistic imaginations of a first-generation bilingual Chicana and a Puerto Rican migrant, whose tongue was primarily Spanish, converged, many times only to diverge.[31] The Chicana and the Riqueña were partnered in the rest home where *mis abuelos*/grandparents worked in La Puente. There grandpa, Rafael Chabrán, gave *mi hermano*/my brother by the same name, his first lessons *en literatura* by recounting the necessary *declamaciones y repeticiones* and all the while smoking his *puro* (cigar) *cubano* and *saboreando* (tasting) the day he would return to Puerto Rico. Grandpa got his wish, he returned to Arecibo, but not before instilling in us grandchildren the desire to teach, something that we would instill in other *Chicana/o* subjects.

And, the Chicana-Riqueña narrative was reinscribed again, indelibly marked on my imagination through the narratives of divorce, the ones that are rarely talked about even as the gates of sexuality are opened wide and rupture is now preferred to continuity. I am referring to the narratives around *"la ruptura"*/the rupture *y "la sobrevivencia"*/survival, around how we would pull together and around how the *vecinos*/neighbors were an integral part of the process.[32] And, I am referring to all of the *mujer*-centered theories that were born at home about what this meant for a mother of four in the late 1950s and early 1960s. A mother who was indisputably on her own and the first in her family bravely to assume the Texas–California migration by then already in full swing, to make her own life work on her own terms before there was a socially acceptable feminism to legitimate her path. Through her cluster of narratives, she anticipated poststructuralist dynamics, carefully marking the absence/presence dynamic, a movement of continuity and discontinuity, which marked complex negotiations with this gendered Puerto Rican ethnicity. She did so through her narrative that framed *her* cry *"Si se puede"* within a Chicana–Tejana imaginary which insisted that it was *necessary* for women to work outside the home, that one need not be married to survive, that one (women) could do without men if that's what one wanted to do, and that the children of divorced parents need not be juvenile delinquents as was commonly assumed in those days.[33]

   The first lesson in Chicana resistance, the most important lesson in self-fashioning, was framed around a dialogue between a Chicana and a Puerto Rican body, a body that encapsulated an individual and a collective. There she framed the contested identity with her own self-styled positioning, offering a daring and forward-looking conscious assumption of masculine and feminine roles and rendering an account of those aspects of Puerto Rican culture which she would pass on to her children. There the working class origins, her unforgettable heroic struggle for survival and historic entrance into the labor force as a factory worker, were counterposed with another Puerto Rican's ascending middle-class lifestyle and privilege. Yes, class and gender are definitely a part of this ethnic equation, an inescapable part of this transnational ethnic connection, and this is, of course, not the only way of encountering them within a Chicana-Riqueña frame.

   It does not cease to amaze me that it was *she* who nurtured a sense of Puerto Ricanness in me — she who had all the right to be a nationalist following the purist dictates associated with this politics, for she was a Chicana, she was not mixed in my way with the Riqueña.[34] In retrospect, it occurs to me that what she presented me with throughout one of the trajectories of our lives as mother and daughter was a pedagogy of Chicanas/os, a mode of knowing Puerto Rico from the inside of Chicana/o, a way of speaking across fractured ethnicities, a way[35] of initiating a dialogue among and between different ethnic groups. As an astute community theorist, she furnished a way of giving Puerto Rico and México another decisive connection, another border crossing beyond those which are naturally assumed when ethnic and cultural identities are automatically derived from the contexts of rapidly diminishing two-parent households, where intersected and subordinated ethnicities are believed to be represented equally within the immediate geopolitical space, and outside of the socioeconomic constraints of gender. While this narrative of ethnic ancestry cannot begin to approach the kinds of political negotiations that are required when these intersections (the hyphens) are marked by political identities: collective histories, specific programs for social change, and diverse subject positions enlisted in such a struggle, it does open a window into the kinds of irreverent ways in which people disrupt prevailing ethnic absolutions, stray from the chauvinistic gateways of racial and ethnic dominance, the ones Chicana/o discourse is theoretically committed to eradicating for ourselves and for others.

   If it is true, as Stuart Hall has suggested, that we live in a period of a new cultural politics which engages rather than suppresses difference and which depends, in part, on the construction of new ethnic identities, then writing the repressed within Chicana/o discourse in terms that far exceed the bordered ethnicity described here by means of a personal illustration, is entirely appropriate at this period in time. A contemporary refashioning of subordinated and underrepresented transnational subjects from the inside of another politics of Chicana/o offers the opportunity to renegotiate the other pluralities silenced by the Mexican-American binary; to begin really to acknowledge the Indians who are contained by the PRI's[36] ideology of *mestizo* nationalism; to offer another ideological contestation to the state-generated metaphysics of Americanness; to activate dynamic ways of speaking across culturally and ethnically subordinated groups, particularly African-Americans, Asian-Americans, Native Americans, etc. — across those groups and their subgroups. The ones that cannot be so easily avoided now that they are on the inside of representation, *a diestra* and *siniestra*/on the right and on the left, and not divided by walls separating the major ethnic studies departments. These walls are there to remind us that if we really engage each other, we'll be fused together and all lose. Unfortunately, all too often the warning is heeded: It is not uncommon that individual ethnic studies programs have more to say to Spanish, English, history, or French departments than they do to each other.

Encountering the new ethnicities that frame Chicana/o can also be border crossings in the positive sense. Now that these ethnicities are intersecting Chicanas/os in a variety of ways, we have the opportunity to reconfigure *una relación* with our América, *desde a dentro*/from the inside, *desde afuera*/from the outside, *de otra manera*/in a different way, and to begin to problematize the pan-ethnic Latino essentialist identity which proposes an undifferentiated collectivity. This configuration stresses the Latin and not indigenous identities and nonchalantly fuses the political claim of Chicanas/os by constructing it along a singular ethnic axis. Without a linguistic path to guide the strategic relations within Latino, and to a much needed changing transnational project of Chicana/o, this configuration: Latino can offer little more than a dose of brown brotherhood, and this is a highly questionable effect.

However, by examining specific intersections, we can begin to answer crucial questions such as how Chicana/o Latino expresses itself in relation to particular social and historical movements. Engaging in this form of multiculturalism not only involves naming a collectivity, but marks its strategic relations and a connection with our América, *con nuestras historias chicanas*/with our Chicana/o herstories/histories, *con otras historias de Américas*/with other herstories and histories of the Américas, *que a veces se acompanan*/that at times accompany one another, *y otras veces se cruzan*/and at other times cross one another/*y se mezclan*/and mix with one another, *y a veces se separaran para el bien de todos*/and that at times separate from one another for everyone's good.

In encouraging the refashioning of unregistered transnational migrations through Chicana/o, I appeal to the idea of *un movimiento*/a movement, since the idea is central to Chicana/o discourse, which effects a number of strategic relocations through contested territories that are coded in the word *Chicana/o*. However, unlike many of my predecessors who are claimed as cultural gurus, I dispute the claim that says we can be anywhere or anyone we want be, that we can speak for anyone, acritically usurp anyone's position, because our ancestors traveled transnationally, because we cross the border with México both ways, because we cross the border internally in any number of different ways and with any variety of cultural and ethnic groups. To admit our *cuerpos*/bodies are actually crossed with multiple histories of domination that are not restricted to an original indigenous-Spanish/or a Mexican-Anglo *encontronazo*/crash[37] is positive, because, after all, there are many historical and political contexts which mark our borders and because there are international borders at every corner, and the corner has moved down to Central America.

The question is how do we encounter these borders within Chicana/o discourse? It is doubtful that we can encounter the new socially constructed ethnicities inscribed in Chicana/o from the founding narratives of Chicano or Latino which tend to be universal in scope and shadow a privileged selection. It is more likely that these identities will be encountered from particular social and historical locations, from situated knowledges, from ethnographic experiences of rupture and continuity, and from a complex web of political negotiations with which people inscribe their social and historical experiences and deliver their self-styled counter narratives. I do not think we need to celebrate the transnational movement for its own sake. Just having a transnational identity is not something to be romanticized or something only we have: *everyone* in the world has one, thanks to the global culture of communications and the far reaching grip of capitalist formations.

So the crucial question is: Whose transnational movements will we narrativize in Chicana/o discourse, and why? All the while remembering what happened with the North American Free Trade Agreement (NAFTA), remembering how the borders were crossed by two dominant cultures without regard for many on either side of the border. Maybe upon reflecting on the symbolic value of how NAFTA was countered by the *indígena* women who got their own informal economy going by using the Zapatista movement to sell their own wares (thus evading the US corporate move to usurp most of the benefits by displacing Japan), it will be possible to gain insight into the kinds of limits and possibilities that can be afforded by transnational movements and identities. We might begin to see that transnational movements function along contrary axes of resistance and subordination, and thus choose a path of transnational resistance that is destined to fortify us, not disempower us. For after all, like many other theorists who walk a public path among our borders, we are in the purview of forging a counter discourse.

I am referring to a counter discourse that is capable of contesting *many* dominant cultures, including the ones that are supported by upper-class Latinas/os, who resist being interpellated by Chicanas and the new ethnicities they partner, who contest being made to share in the linguistic, social, and economic conditions of *campesinos, indocumentados*, and factory workers and their children who abhor the presence of a newly hyphenated Chicana/o Latina/o and its forecasting of solidarity. Until Latina/o is intersected by a political mediation inscribing resistance, it will continue to promote confusion and unexpected border disputes and it will deprive Puerto Ricans, Central Americans, Latin Americans, and Chicanas/os of a much-needed social agency that interrogates relations of power within systems that breed oppression, at home and abroad, through a number of social intersections.

Insofar as Chicana/o studies is concerned, this is *not* to suggest that we displace the idea of having a Chicana/o discourse or area of study, even when it appears that the job is too big and too complex and even when it is now common knowledge that Chicana/o studies can never be a home to us in the same old unproblematic mimetic way many naively once thought it was when it was written, Chicano. However, Chicana/o studies must be interrogated, it cannot remain the same. Chicana/o studies has oftentimes unwittingly reinforced an insular attitude by constructing its object of analysis: Chicana/o identity, Chicanas/os, on the basis of differences between dominant and subordinated cultures with little in the way of mapping the vital relations to other subordinated ethnic communities. It goes without saying that this is an artificial rendition of Chicana/o subjects; in reality people don't live in these types of compartments.

To be sure, these trends in Chicana/o studies are part of an overall strategic reaction to the way in which dominant culture has diluted ethnic cultural and racial difference or else privileged particular socioethnic identities, overlooking others in the construction of national episodes and historical events which inscribe the national body or community. For a recent example of this we can turn to representations of the LA riots which continue to be constructed through a black/white overdetermination which suggests that this difference is the *diff*erence which counts, even when the visual images revealed something else.

The academic context has also had its impact on this particular construction of Chicana/o subjects. Historically, Chicana/o studies programs have been intentionally subverted by watered-down ethnic studies requirements, garden-variety multicultural programs, mainstream "Spanish for Native Speakers Programs" that edit the voices of the natives to suit the tastes of colonial masters, and even postmodern frameworks that divorce Chicana/o studies of its political content as well as its relationship to lived Chicana/o Latina/o communities. Or, in the worst of cases, this procedure has led to tokenism or to editing out the Chicano subject altogether in favor of a Hispanic construction with the assistance of Spanish-speaking groups vying for institutional power from the position of economic privilege and a brown rendition of whiteness.[38] Here, the promise of plurality has been revealed to be the reality not of difference, but of absence, invisibility, and repeated marginality. While the effort to reinscribe a racial, ethnic opposition to dominant culture along nationalist lines may be constructed as an act of resistance to hegemonic discourse, this is destined to fail since this approach doesn't apprehend the nature of the pluralities that frame Chicana/o. In fact, this approach assumes that you need to confront a plurality: them, the dominant culture, with a singularity: us.[39] If the Chicana/o Movement has taught anything, it is that this is just not the case.[40] We should also be "wary of any attempt to reduce us to one identity" because, as Sánchez points out, "no single subject position defines us."[41]

Within Chicana/o studies it is not uncommon to hear that one of the greatest threats to this area of studies and praxis comes from *their* brand of multiculturalism, the one that circulates within the institutions of dominant culture. If this is true, then there is no doubt that a political refashioning of our own viable pluralities on the inside and next door is one of the most valuable and most important endeavors that can be undertaken. For what we would be doing is none other than providing the basis for a counterhegemonic mode of plurality and difference, one that doesn't cancel us out, one that engages us from every corner, and one that can settle the score with those who would deprive us of a global representation.

One of the ideas or premises behind multiculturalism is the notion that this configuration involves a mixture on the outside of us, that it is something that is not inside. Therefore it is not uncommon to hear university administrators counterpose their culturally-dominant multiculturalism with particular ethnic studies programs and even to assume an attitude while doing so, an arrogant attitude, accompanied by a desire for an expanse of territory. The territory of these programs is claimed under the erroneous assumption that because they don't have the plural inside them, and because they won't relinquish their singular underrepresented ethnic identity, then they need someone else to come in and do it for them, to forge global relations that look like the world does: intersected and not polarized.[42]

This line of thinking is plagued with faulty assumptions, although the maneuvers are skillful and this US construction of multiculturalism does target weak spots. To begin with, Chicana/o does engage pluralities, it engages them at the very core within the social formation, even though this worldliness has never been able fully to achieve its potential as a counterhegemonic force within Chicana/o discourse and displace the real subtext of the hegemonic multicultural discourse. I am referring to the subtext that says that "we are all the same" so it doesn't matter if we are fused into "them." Inscribing an alternative type of transnational multiculturalism within the core of Chicana/o studies means fortifying these sites of study and practice in ways that are unusual, for it means further extending the scope of one's analysis, countering our presumed singularity with our historically verifiable pluralities, the ones that are intersected, and do engage positions from diverse fields of contestation. And, as I pointed out before, this counterhegemonic multiculturalism won't be encountered readily, nor in a vacuum, but from somewhere, from the social, political, and historical contexts in which we live, from the diverse subject positions and linguistic markers we have developed in our progressive movement toward self-representation and social reform.[43] This not only entails looking forward to an ethnically transformed California/America, but looking backward, too.

Seeing what happened to the subordinated ethnic pluralities within Chicana/o discourse, asking whether the Mexican-American binary really ever had the power to make our/their other social identities fully disappear. Armed with the idea that they hadn't, I returned to early Chicana/o texts and I found many references to other subordinated groups, even among the most nationalistic of documents.[44] But these texts also framed a discourse of Chicana/o difference which negatively marked relations to these groups, creating a distance from Chicana/o. Other social groups were there alright, but they had been cancelled out through a language of difference that stressed racial, cultural, and ethnic similarities between Chicanos and differences between this group and all others. There was no way to cross this "unbridgeable binary."[45] Within such a structure, how could we encounter the differences between Chicanas/os and the similarities they shared with other subordinate groups whose lives they would affect? It was impossible to do so.

This is why the project of critical cultural studies must be complemented with a timely and much-needed rearticulation of the varied social relations which mark the subordinated ethnic groups who are intersected through competing social registers and modes of political subjectivity that have only been tangentially explored here. This endeavor is not marginal to Chicana/o studies, it is fundamental to this area, for at this historic juncture, Chicana/o studies need not be "bound by fixed categories or histories, by the fictitious categories of oneself and others, by the limits of traditional disciplines, by unchanging intellectual requirements...."[46]

As many of us see it, "C.S. breaks with the equivalence between the discipline and the nation state, especially insofar *as it draws its object of analysis from diverse national settings....* C.S. views *shifting social and ethnic borders as being central to its mode of apprehending divergent communities that refurbish and frame Chicana/o populations."* Chicana/o studies can be a border crossing between Chicana/o and other underrepresented groups, a way of speaking about the internal and transnational connections between Chicanas/os and other peoples of the Americas.

Arriving at this type of an approach involves a significant complication of the current attempts "to recognize the plurality and diversity of actors and identities" at play in contemporary politics, in a period in which many of our cultural studies practitioners are also working against what Kobena Mercer calls "the race, class, and gender mantra."[47] According to Mercer, this mantra posits that "serial acknowledgment of various sources of identity is sufficient for an understanding of how different identities get articulated into a common project or don't."[48]

We also face the effective limitations of the current rhetorical strategies in which identities are articulated and "the challenge ... to go beyond the atomistic and essentialist logic of 'identity politics' in which differences are dealt with only one at a time and which therefore ignores the conflicts and contradictions that arise in the relations within and between the various movements, agents, and actors in the contemporary forms of democratic antagonism."[49] However partial our responses are to this incredible challenge at this point in time, we nevertheless count with a powerful legacy that inscribes a notion of dramatic change and intellectual growth; with community linkages that are fashioning our paths where academic and nationalistic roadblocks prevail; and with an area studies that has managed to retain the notion of intellectual growth premised on collaborative perspectives of thinkers, students, communities, and binational frameworks.

At this point in time, it is ludicrous to imagine that these challenges will be assumed only through Chicana/o studies, that our transnational identities also won't be refashioned through women's studies, Native American studies, Latin American studies, Latina/o studies, Puerto Rican studies, cultural studies, Asian-American studies, African-American studies, and gay and lesbian studies, and/or other geopolitical sites where alternative knowledges have emerged and promise to emerge. Considering the impact which the cultural and ethnic discourses of Chicana/o studies have had on the "politics of Chicana/o representation," considering the rhetorical and practical frames which have *re*limited many of the grass-roots struggles for Chicana/o studies departments and programs in California and the movements against the immigration backlash, this is a strategic location from which to refashion a transnational connection to ourselves and one another, and to contribute to a widening of imagined communities and spheres of contestation.

It is in this vein I posit that expanding the horizons of Chicana/o studies can subvert the question mark after the Rican and replace it with an exclamation point, a marker signalling "how it is possible to struggle" *beyond* the quandary of biculturalism, *beyond* the crossroads of two discordant cultures and arrive at "yet another border generation and a different pattern of migration and settlement,"[50] to the point of the repressed: the silenced and the discarded "we's" that we are.

Juan Flores suggests that Puerto Rican culture today is a culture of commuting, a back-and-forth transfer. Chicana-Riqueña is then a refashioning of a transnational connection. It takes us from the Mexican to the Chicana/o; from the Puerto Rican to the Nuyorican to the LA Rican and back again through other sites of "mutually intruding differences."[51] To those sites occupied by people whose lives hang on the hooks of the question marks *¿allá, acá?*/there? here?[52] This is but a rearticulation of the other territories that are there to reclaim, for these are spaces between us, from where we draw borders, from where we speak to one another and struggle, and from where we migrate, commuting across transnational and multiethnic communities and cultural frameworks *de éste y del otro lado*, from this side of the political spectrum, from where we refashion a connection to Our/*Nuestra* América.

Notes

1 *A mi mamá:* Angeliña "Lita" Gonzalez Chabram, *a quien se lo debo todo, incluso esta etnicidad; a mi abuelo,* Rafael C., *que en paz descanse, que se conserve su memoria; y a mi comadre y amiga,* Inés H. *y a los que viven las otras caras de México desde estos callejones.*

2 This is inspired by a poem entitled "Nuyorican" by José Luis Gonzáles, quoted by Juan Flores in "Cortijo's Revenge: New Mappings of Puerto Rican Culture," in *On Edge*, eds George Yúdice, Jean Franco, and Juan Flores (Minneapolis: University of Minnesota Press, 1992), pp. 198–9, as a way of appealing to a third space of political and ethnic identification which marks a *mujer*'s/woman's counter discourse.

3 See Gloria Anzaldúa, "Haciendo caras, una entrada," in *Making Face, Making Soul*, ed. Gloria Anzaldúa (San Francisco: Aunt Lute Books, 1990). For another example of these trends in Chicana/o studies, see "Chicana/o Cultural Representations: Reframing Alternative Critical Discourses," special issue of *Cultural Studies*, eds Rosa Linda Fregoso and Angie Chabram, 4, 3 (1990).

4 Michèle Barrett and Anne Phillips, "Preface," *Destabilizing Theory*, eds Michèle Barrett and Anne Phillips, (Cambridge: Polity Press, 1992), p. 1.

5 Cultural studies critics have called for "transnational perspectives" from different contexts and intellectual traditions. See Kobena Mercer, "1968: Periodizing Politics and Identity," in *Cultural Studies*, eds Lawrence Grossberg, Carey Nelson, and Paula Treichler (New York: Routledge, 1992), pp. 424–37 for an example of the usage of this concept in the black context; George Yúdice, Jean Franco, and Juan Flores, eds, *On Edge* (Minneapolis: University of Minnesota Press, 1992) for the Latin American context; and a forthcoming version of Rosaura Sánchez's pivotal essay, "The Politics of Representation in Chicana/o Literature," in *Chicana/o Cultural Studies: New Directions*, eds Mario Garcia and Ellen McCraken (forthcoming).

6 I would like to thank Raymond Rocco for offering me the opportunity to present these ideas at UCLA and to offer the Chicana/o Research Center a belated thank you for supporting the production of the above-mentioned special issue of *Cultural Studies* and other projects.

7 I am indebted to Stuart Hall for this type of framing. See "The New Ethnicities," in *'Race', Culture and Difference*, eds James Donald and Ali Rattansi (London: Sage Publications in association with the Open University, 1992), pp. 252–9.

8 For a discussion of the multicultural debate, see Wahnemma Lubiano, "Multiculturalism: Negotiating Politics and Knowledge," *Concerns* 2, 3 (1992), pp. 11–21.

9 Chandra Talpade Mohanty has argued for this type of cross-cultural work in her wonderful essay, "Feminist Encounters: Locating the Politics of Experience," in *Destabilizing Theory*, eds Michele Barrett and Anne Phillips, pp. 74–92.

10 Rodolfo Gonzalez, *I am Joaquín* (New York: Bantam, 1972), p. 39.

11 Ibid., p. 98.

12 Sánchez, "The Politics of Representation in Chicana/o Literature," p. 17.

13 Sánchez posits this in relation to the essentialist discourse that prevails around *mestizaje*, continuing later on: "It is the discourse of mestizaje that is fetishistic because it posits the existence of a particular identity, a particular human nature based as much on blood lines as on posited cultural practices of past modes of production. Blood is posited as a carrier of cultural material which allows one to view the world in a particular way...." But she also posits that: "[s]elf-representation on the basis of *mestizaje* and language, if viewed historically and dialectically rather than in an essentialist fashion, can undoubtedly play a counterhegemonic role in a country where the discourses of color and origin have been instrumental in our oppression and exploitation." Sánchez, ibid., pp. 17–18. Unfortunately, this dialectical view of

mestizaje is rare in Chicana/o discourse where revisionist notions of José Vasconcelos' *La Raza Cósmica* dominate.

14 It is important to note that other types of transnational perspectives, other than the ones examined here, inscribed resistance through a political contestation aimed at curbing the effects of capitalism and racism. I am referring to the grass-roots movements which incorporated political philosophies from Fidel, Ché, and Fanon, in an effort to formulate alliances with Third-World liberation movements. This political current in Chicana/o representation did break away from the ethnic absolutism of nationalism, but it did not emerge as the authoritative discourse and it rarely incorporated issues of gender or the reality of local ethnic intersections in its purview.

15 One of the few journals to initiate a move against this grain and to popularize the Chicano Riqueña connection was the journal *Revista Chicano Riqueña* which offered an important comparative approach, fashioning a transnational objective across "Latino" borders: "a cross section of opinion through poetry, prose, and graphics of Latinos throughout the country who proclaim their cultural heritage, examine their lives in the cities, and towns where they reside, and further enliven the telling of our historical presence." In an important issue, the editors clarify that the journal looks at the United States "from the perspective of the literature of the Latino minorities," taking positions "on our status in the USA." They explicitly mention the heterogeneous populations affected by this circumstance, groups such as Chicanos, Méxicanos, Puerto Ricans, Cubans, Dominicans, and other Latinos living in the United States. As a response to mainstream celebrations of the bicentennial, the editors elaborate that the Revista Chicano-Riqueña serve as a forum "for clarifying the historical past, for proclaiming our cultural heritage," in a context where "our ancestors experienced the loss of their lands and patrimony, the invasion of their islands, massive forced migrations and even the flagrant imposition of colonial rule...." See Nicolás Kanellos and Luis Dávila, "Preface," in *Revista Chicano Riqueña*, 4, 4 (1971), pp. 1–2. While *Revista Chicano Riqueña* anticipates an important coalition and did offer a forum from which a cross-cultural dialogue could be forged, this type of articulation does not inscribe the hybrid identities of today that are intersected not only by histories of colonialism but also by the dictates of gender and work in the so-called New World Order. However, analyzing the way the journal promotes multiculturalism is an important part of formulating an alternative vision of our cultural and ethnic relations.

16 It is not my intention to furnish a comprehensive list of the mixtures nor to suggest that all of these mixtures will be equally represented in a contested Chicana/o Latina/o *Indígena* identity that counters the hegemonic practices of dominant culture. Undoubtedly the diverse social, historical, and geographical contexts in which these identities are produced will determine how these new ethnicities are refashioned across different social registers. However, it is important to call attention to the problematic nature of these intersected identities as they are commonly scripted through the denominations: Chicana/o Asian-American; Chicana/o Latin American; Chicana/o African-American, according to the familiar groupings. As Hollinger has argued elsewhere, this move threatens to reinscribe an essentialist frame in that it refers to blocks of people and these blocks erase the diversity between the subgroups that comprise the block. By appealing to the Chicana Riqueña frame in this paper, I

am targeting an internal diversity, offering a breakdown of the block. Hollinger offers a conservative approach to the topic in "Postethnic America," *Contention*, 2, 1 (1992), pp. 79–96.

17 I have elaborated my critique on the basis of the insights delivered by Stuart Hall, Rosaura Sánchez, and Paul Gilroy. Hall explains: "I am familiar with all of the dangers of 'ethnicity' as a concept and have written myself about the fact that ethnicity, in the form of a culturally constructed sense of Englishness and a particularly closed, exclusive and regressive form of English national identity, is one of the core characteristics of British racism today." Hall, "The New Ethnicities," p. 256. Sánchez points out how "the discourse of ethnicity may in some cases be a way of sidestepping the more problematic discourses of race and class since the term is all-encompassing, used now as much to refer to European immigrant groups as to all underrepresented minorities." Sánchez, "The Politics of Representation in Chicana/o Literature," p. 16. Paul Gilroy adds another viewpoint by discussing how certain absolutist notions of ethnicity mask racism: "We increasingly face a racism which avoids being recognized as such because it is able to link 'race' with nationhood, patriotism and nationalism, a racism which has taken a necessary distance from crude ideas of biological inferiority and superiority and now seeks to present an imaginary definition of the nation as a unified cultural community." Paul Gilroy, "The End of Antiracism," in *Race, Culture and Difference*, eds James Donald and Ali Rattansi (London: Sage, 1992), p. 53.

Notwithstanding his critique, Hall calls for a new contestation over the term "ethnicity," a contestation that involves "a retheorizing of difference, a more diverse concept of ethnicity, an ethnicity of the margins, of the periphery, which is not doomed to survive by marginalizing." He advocates a splitting away from the dominant notion which connects it to nation and race. Hall, "The New Ethnicities," pp. 257–8. Sánchez responds to this second characterization thus: "Hall suggests contestation on the basis of ethnicity, devoid of its connections to race and nation and linked to the concept of marginality or peripheralization, a discourse that would build on diversity and difference…. Hall's proposal then for 'freeing' ethnicity of its racial and Third-World connotations fits in well with other models … which advocate positing constructs of difference, otherness, diversity and pluralism as the basis for the creation of counterhegemonic affinity groups. My problem with these proposals is that they displace exploitation and cleverly conceal class stratification. In fact these spatial models of periphery and marginality do not really constitute a threat to hegemonic discourses or to the dominant social and political structures of society…." Sánchez, "The Politics of Representation in Chicana/o Literature," pp. 20–1. Sánchez's discussion of Hall deserves further attention than I can render here and it is not limited to a critique of this notion of ethnicity.

18 I am recasting Sánchez here.

19 I have revised Stuart Hall here according to the conditions of the context in which I work.

20 Cited in "Increasing Diversity in California," *The Sacramento Bee* (April 20, 1994), p. B4.

21 Raymond Rocco's description of the communities surrounding the urban core of Los Angeles is, in this sense, instructive: "in the area immediately surrounding the urban core ... to the west, only a few blocks from the financial district, the Pico-Union area has been completely transformed into a Central American environment. Further to the south, around Figueroa and Martin Luther King Boulevards, neighborhoods have entire blocks populated by Mexican and Central American families. To the southeast are the cities of Huntington Park and South Gate, which went from being four per cent Latino in 1960 to 90 per cent in 1990. And, of course, to the east is the oldest and largest barrio of East Los Angeles, and to the northeast the Lincoln Heights and Highland Park areas which are over 70 per cent Latino. Colombian communities have been established in neighborhoods around the corners of Third Street and Vermont Avenue as well as in South Gate, Long Beach, Huntington Park, Glendale. Cubans, Puerto Ricans, and Colombians have established a sizeable presence in the Echo Park and Silverlake area as well as immediately adjacent to Pico-Union...." Fregoso and Chabram eds, *Cultural Studies,* p. 324.

22 You know who you are, Missy, Rhonda, Marissa, Rafael, Paco, and Gabriel.

23 I am very well aware that many Nuyoricans hear this upon returning to the island.

24 Or subverting the essentialist framing of Chicano with other hyphenated intersections.

25 Sánchez, "The Politics of Representation in Chicana/o Literature," p. 16.

26 Paul Gilroy, "It Ain't Where You're From ... It's Where You're At ...: The Dialectics of Diasporic Identification," *Third Text,* 13 (1991), pp. 3–16.

27 Erlinda Gonzales Berry, *Paletitas de Guayaba* (Albuquerque: El Norte Publications, 1991).

28 Mercer quotes Walter Benjamin's phrase [1940], in "1968: Periodizing Politics and Identity," p. 427.

29 This is my interpretation of the order of things and it is but one of my interpretations. My account does not necessarily apply to anyone else and I do not pretend to speak for any other family members in recognition of the fact that they have their own memories of our imagined communities and their own rich ways of giving these communities style within discourse.

30 Javier Solís, *"En mi viejo San Juan,"* *Sombras.* Audiotape. 1049, Caytonics, CBS International, n.d. The song was written by Noel Estrada.

31 Such as the times my *amá* would say "hi there" to her male friends and my *papa* would hear "hi dear."

32 I take this opportunity to thank these neighbors on Eldon Street for their support.

33 This page was discussed with her, but this is my construction and any economic gain that comes from this essay will go to her. There are many twists to this narrative that I will keep to ourselves in the tradition of Rigoberta.

34 It was as much a question of solidarity with her as it was the constraints of Chicana/o discourse that delayed my arrival into this type of a Chicana- Riqueña interrogation. But she taught me as she has always taught me that I could transgress that particular Puerto Rican border, that I could encounter a collective not bound by the same decisive ruptures, and that to do so was not a betrayal of my Mexicanness: my Chicananess, but rather an affirmation of its permeable borders. And, she paved the

way for me at age 65 plus, when she finally boarded a plane and reclaimed *her* Puerto Rican relatives, met the extended family, and gave her received memories of Puerto Rico definitive forms, visual images. She even began her own self-styled migration to Puerto Rico. Without my mother's historic revisions, my own subsequent trips to Puerto Rico would have been something quite different than what they turned out to be: part of a life-long and culturally-decisive experience.

35 Certainly this is not the only way to dialogue across ethnic borders and I do not mean to suggest that it is *the way* for all of us to do it.

36 The *Partido Revolucionario Institucional*, México's dominant political party.

37 *Encontronazo* is a term which contests the friendly multicultural encounter that is often used to describe Columbus and his conquest.

38 Kobena Mercer's proposal that "cultural difference was used as a means of fragmenting the emergence of a collective black identity" is valid for Chicanas/os even today, especially in Chicana/o studies, where it is not uncommon that university administrators deconstruct nationalist paradigms as a way of collapsing these programs and underfunding them. Kobena Mercer, "1968: Periodizing Politics and Identity," p. 39.

39 By using the plural "us" I wish to point out the contradiction in these terms.

40 It is common knowledge that it was the pluralities that gave the struggle its power, the strategically placed alliances with other political movements: Third-World liberation movements, the black civil rights movements, and the feminist movements, for example. However, the "pluralities" within Chicana/o bodies were often repressed as race took precedence over class and gender and Chicanas/os were constructed along the purviews of masculine collectives.

41 Sánchez, "The Politics of Representation in Chicana/o Literature," p. 29.

42 The *encargado*/one in charge to do this is generally someone who proposes to create an identity: a mode of multiculturalism, that no one can identify as being uniquely anyone's.

43 I have taken this idea of what I see as a critical genealogy from Mercer's retrospective discussion of 1968 ("1968: Periodizing Politics and Identity").

44 See, for example, Armando Rendon's, *The Chicano Manifesto* (New York: MacMillan, 1972). I discuss this topic in an essay entitled, "Out of the Labyrinth, into the Race," which will appear in a subsequent issue of *Cultural Studies* featuring Latinas/os in the United States.

45 For a discussion of how these binaries are constructed through the black context, see Mercer's essay, "1968: Periodizing Politics and Identity."

46 These quotes are extracted from our working document for departmental status of Chicana/o studies at UC Davis.

47 See Mercer, "1968: Periodizing Politics and Identity," pp. 425–6.

48 Ibid., p. 442.

49 Ibid., p. 425.

50 I am rephrasing a point made by Juan Flores, "Cortijo's Revenge: New Mappings of Puerto Rican Culture," p. 201, to accommodate this third space of ethnic identification.

51 Ibid., p. 201.

52 This is a point quoted by Flores from Luis Rafael Sánchez's "Air Bus," ibid., p. 201.

14

Contested Histories: Eurocentrism, Multiculturalism, and the Media

ROBERT STAM AND ELLA SHOHAT

An awareness of the intellectually debilitating effects of the Eurocentric legacy forms an indispensable backdrop for understanding the contemporary debates about multiculturalism.[1] Naturalized as "common sense," Eurocentrism is endemic in present-day thought and education. The "best that is thought and written" is assumed to have been thought and written by Europeans. (By Europeans, we mean also the "Neo-Europeans" of the Americas, Australia, and elsewhere.) History is assumed to be European history, everything else being reduced to what historian Hugh Trevor-Roper (in 1965!) patronizingly called the "unrewarding gyrations of barbarous tribes in picturesque but irrelevant corners of the globe."[2] The residual traces of centuries of axiomatic European domination inform the general culture, the everyday language, and the media, engendering a fictitious sense of the innate superiority of European-derived cultures and peoples.

Although neoconservatives caricature multiculturalism as calling for the violent jettisoning of European classics and of "western civilization as an area of study,"[3] multiculturalism is actually an assault not on Europe or Europeans but on Eurocentrism — on the procrustean forcing of cultural heterogeneity into a single paradigmatic perspective in which Europe is seen as the unique source of meaning, as the world's center of gravity, as ontological "reality" to the rest of the world's shadow. Eurocentrism, like Renaissance perspective in painting, envisions the world from a single privileged point, attributing to the "West" an almost Providential sense of historical destiny. It maps the world in a cartography that centralizes and augments Europe while literally "belittling" Africa.[4] Eurocentrism bifurcates the world into the "West and the Rest"[5] and organizes everyday language into binaristic hierarchies implicitly flattering to Europe: *our* "nations," *their* "tribes"; *our* "religions," *their* "superstitions"; *our* "culture," *their* "folklore"; *our* "defense," *their* "terrorism."

Eurocentrism is the discursive residue or precipitate of colonialism, the process by which the European powers reached positions of economic, military, political and cultural hegemony in much of Asia, Africa, and the Americas. Colonization per se preexisted European colonialism, having been practiced by Greece, Rome, the Aztecs, the Incas and many other groups. But while nations had often annexed adjacent territories, what is new in European colonialism is its planetary reach, its affiliation with institutional power, and its imperative mode, its attempted submission of the world to a single "universal" regime of truth and power. Eurocentrism is ethnocentrism gone global. As an ideological substratum common to colonialist, imperialist, and racist discourse, Eurocentrism is a form of vestigial thinking which permeates and structures *contemporary* practices and representations even after the formal end of colonialism. Although colonialist discourse and Eurocentric discourse are intimately intertwined, the terms have a distinct emphasis. While the former explicitly justifies colonialist practices, the latter embeds, takes for granted, and "normalizes" the hierarchical power relations generated by colonialism and imperialism without necessarily even thematizing those issues directly. Although generated by the colonizing process, Eurocentrism's links to that process are obscured in a kind of buried epistemology.

Eurocentric discourse is complex, contradictory, historically unstable. But in a kind of composite portrait or "ideal type," Eurocentrism, as a mode of thought, might be seen as engaging in a number of mutually-reinforcing intellectual tendencies or operations. (1) Eurocentric discourse projects a linear historical trajectory leading from the Middle East and Mesopotamia to classical Greece (constructed as "pure," "western," and "democratic")" to imperial Rome and then to the metropolitan capitals of Europe and the United States. It renders history as a sequence of empires: Pax Romana, Pax Hispanica, Pax Britannica, Pax Americana. In all cases, Europe, alone and unaided, is seen as the "motor" for progressive historical change: democracy, class society, feudalism, capitalism, the industrial revolution. (2) Eurocentrism attributes to the "West" an inherent progress toward democratic institutions (Torquemada, Mussolini, and Hitler must be seen as aberrations within this logic of historical amnesia and selective legitimation). (3) Eurocentrism elides non-European democratic traditions while obscuring the limitations of western formal democracy and masking the West's part in subverting democracies abroad. (4) Eurocentrism minimizes the West's oppressive practices by regarding them as contingent, accidental, exceptional. Western colonialism, slave trading, and imperialism are not seen as fundamental causes of the West's disproportionate power. (5) Eurocentrism appropriates the cultural and material production of non-Europeans while denying their achievements and its own appropriation, thus consolidating its sense of self and glorifying its own cultural anthropophagy. In sum, Eurocentrism sanitizes Western history while patronizing and even demonizing the non-West; it thinks of itself in terms of its noblest achievements — science, progress, humanism — but of the non-West in terms of its deficiencies, real or imagined.

Needless to say, our critique of Eurocentrism is addressed not to Europeans as individuals but rather to dominant Europe's historically oppressive relation to its internal and external "others." We are in no way suggesting, obviously, that non-European people are somehow "better" than Europeans, or that Third-World and minoritarian cultures are inherently superior. There is no inborn tendency among Europeans to commit genocide, as some "ice people" theorists would suggest, nor are indigenous or Third-World peoples innately noble and generous. Nor do we believe in the inverted European narcissism that posits Europe as the source of all social evils in the world. Such an approach remains Eurocentric ("Europe exhibiting its own unacceptability in front of an antiethnocentric mirror," in Derrida's words) while exempting Third-World patriarchal elites from all responsibility.[6] Such "victimology" reduces non-European life to a pathological response to western penetration; it merely turns colonialist claims upside down. Rather than saying that "we" (that is, the First World) have brought "them" civilization, it claims instead that everywhere "we" have brought Diabolical Evil, and everywhere "their" enfeebled societies have succumbed to "our" insidious influence. The vision remains Promethean, but here Prometheus has brought not fire but the Holocaust, reproducing what Barbara Christian calls the "West's outlandish claim to have invented everything, including Evil."[7] Our focus here, in any case, is less on intentions than on institutional discourses, less on "goodness" and "badness" than on historically configured relations of power. The question, as Talal Asad puts it, is not "how far Europeans have been guilty and Third-World inhabitants innocent but, rather, how far the criteria by which guilt and innocence are determined have been historically constituted."[8]

The word "Eurocentric" is sometimes taken as a synonym for "racist." But although Eurocentrism and racism are historically intertwined, they are in no way equatable, for the simple reason that Eurocentrism is the "normal" view of history that most First Worlders and Second Worlders, along with many Third Worlders and even Fourth Worlders learn at school and imbibe from the media. As a result of this normalizing operation, it is quite possible to be antiracist at a conscious and practical level, and still be Eurocentric. Rather than attack Europe per se, an anti-Eurocentric multiculturalism, in our view, relativizes Europe, seeing it as a geographical fiction that flattens the cultural diversity and hybridity even of Europe itself. Europe has always had its own peripheralized regions and stigmatized ethnicities, classes, and genders (Jews, Irish, Gypsies, Huguenots, peasants, women, minorities of color). And since Eurocentrism is a historically-situated discourse and not a genetic inheritance, Europeans can be anti-Eurocentric, just as non-Europeans can be Eurocentric. Europe has always spawned its own critics of empire. Some of the European cultural figures most revered by today's neoconservatives, ironically, themselves condemned European colonialism. Samuel Johnson, the very archetype of the neoclassical conservative, wrote in 1759 that "Europeans have scarcely visited any coast but to gratify avarice, and extend corruption; to arrogate dominion without right and practice cruelty without incentive."[9] Even Adam Smith, the patron saint of capitalism, wrote in his *Wealth of Nations* (1776) that for the natives of the East and West Indies, all the commercial benefits resulting from the discovery of America "have been sunk and lost in the dreadful misfortunes which they have occasioned."[10] Yet, when contemporary multiculturalists make the same points, they are accused of "Europe-bashing."[11] Or the critiques are acknowledged, but then turned into a compliment to Europe, in a kind of "fallback position" for Euronarcissism: "Yes, Europe did all those cruel things, but then, only Europe has the virtue of being self-critical."

While the fashionability of the word multiculturalism might soon pass, the issues to which it points will not soon fade for these contemporary quarrels are but the surface manifestations of a deeper "seismological shift" — the decolonization of global culture. The concept of "multiculturalism" is, admittedly, open to various interpretations and subject to diverse political force fields; it has become a slippery signifier onto which diverse groups project their hopes and fears. In its more coopted version, it easily degenerates into a state or corporate-managed United-Colors-of-Benetton pluralism whereby established power promotes ethnic "flavors of the month" for commercial or ideological purposes. For us, multiculturalism means seeing world history and contemporary social life from the perspective of the radical equality of peoples in status, intelligence, and rights. Multiculturalism decolonizes representation not only in terms of cultural artifacts — literary canons, museum exhibits, film series — but also in terms of power relations between communities. While aware of the ambiguities of the term, then, we would hope to prod "multiculturalism" in the direction of a radical critique of power relations, turning it into a rallying cry for a more substantive and reciprocal intercommunalism.

What is missing in much of the discussion of multiculturalism is a notion of ethnic relationality and community answerability. Neoconservatives accuse multiculturalists of Balkanizing the nation, of emphasizing what divides people rather than what brings them together. That the inequitable distribution of power *itself* generates violence and divisiveness goes unacknowledged; that multiculturalism offers a more egalitarian vision of social relations is ignored. A radical multiculturalism calls for a profound restructuring and reconceptualization of the power relations between cultural communities. Refusing a ghettoizing discourse, it links minoritarian communities, challenging the hierarchy that makes some communities "minor" and others "major" and "normative." Thus what neoconservatives, in fact, find threatening about the more radical forms of multiculturalism is the intellectual and political regrouping by which different "minorities" become a majority seeking to move beyond being "tolerated" to forming active intercommunal[12] coalitions.

We would distinguish, therefore, between a co-optive liberal pluralism, tainted at birth by its historical roots in the systematic inequities of conquest, slavery, and exploitation,[13] and what we see as a more relational and radical *polycentric multiculturalism*. The notion of polycentrism, in our view, globalizes multiculturalism. It envisions a restructuring of intercommunal relations within and beyond the nation state according to the internal and partially overlapping imperatives of diverse communities.[14] Within a polycentric vision, the world has many dynamic cultural locations, many possible vantage points. The emphasis in "polycentrism," for us, is not on spatial points of origin but on fields of power, energy, and struggle. The "poly," for us, does not refer to a finite list of centers of power but rather introduces a systematic principle of differentiation, relationality, and linkage. No single community or part of the world, whatever its economic or political power, is epistemologically privileged.

Polycentric multiculturalism differs from liberal pluralism in the following ways. First, unlike a liberal-pluralist discourse of ethical universals — freedom, tolerance, charity — polycentric multiculturalism sees all cultural history in relation to social power. Polycentric multiculturalism is not about "touchy-feely" sensitivity toward sentimentalized "others"; it is about dispersing power, about empowering the disempowered, about transforming institutions and discourses. Second, polycentric multiculturalism does not preach a pseudoequality of viewpoints; its affiliations are clearly with the underrepresented, the marginalized, and the oppressed. Third, whereas pluralism is premised on an established hierarchical order of cultures and is grudgingly accretive — it benevolently "allows" other voices to add themselves to the mainstream — polycentric multiculturalism thinks and imagines "from the margins," seeing minoritarian communities not as "interest groups" to be "added on" to a preexisting nucleus but rather as active, generative participants at the very core of a shared, conflictual history. Fourth, polycentric multiculturalism grants an "epistemological advantage" to those prodded by historical circumstance into what Dubois called "double consciousness," to those familiar with "margins" and "center" (or even with many margins and many centers), and thus ideally placed to "deconstruct" dominant or narrowly national discourses. Fifth, polycentric multiculturalism rejects a unified, fixed, and essentialist concept of identities (or communities) as consolidated sets of practices, meanings, and experiences. Rather, it sees identities as multiple, unstable, historically situated, the products of ongoing differentiation and polymorphous identifications and pluralizations.[15] Sixth, polycentric multiculturalism goes beyond narrow definitions of identity politics, opening the way for informed affiliation on the basis of shared social desires and identifications. But these affiliations are not natural or inevitable; they have to be forged. Seventh, polycentric multiculturalism is reciprocal, dialogical; it sees all acts of verbal or cultural exchange as taking place not between essential discrete bounded individuals or cultures but rather between mutually permeable, changing individuals and communities. (Henceforth, we will use the term "multiculturalism" in the more radical sense we have outlined here.)

Polycentric multiculturalism tries, above all, to make connections. It makes connections, first, in temporal terms. While the media treat multiculturalism as a recent bandwagon phenomenon unrelated to colonialism, it is important to ground the discussion in a longer history of multiply-located oppressions. And where many literary studies of culture and empire privilege the nineteenth and twentieth centuries, it is important to trace colonialist discourse back to 1492, and even beyond. It makes connections, second, in spatial/geographical terms, placing debates about representation in a broader context which embraces the Americas, Asia, and Africa. Third, it makes connections in disciplinary terms, forging links between usually compartmentalized fields (media studies, literary theory, reflexive ethnography, Third-World feminism, postcolonial studies, Afrodiasporic studies, the diverse "area studies"); and fourth, in intertextual terms, envisioning the media as part of a broader discursive network ranging from the erudite (poems, novels, history, performance art, cultural theory) to the popular (commercial television, pop music, journalism, theme parks, tourist ads). Although progressive literary intellectuals sometimes disdain the lower reaches of popular culture, it is precisely at the popular level that Eurocentrism generates its mass base in everyday feeling. Fifth, in conceptual terms, it links issues of colonialism, imperialism, and Third-World nationalism on the one hand, and of race, ethnicity, and multiculturalism on the other, attempting to place often ghettoized histories and discourses in productive relation (avoiding, for example, the conventional "delinking" of issues of racism from issues of anti-Semitism).

Since all political struggle in the postmodern era necessarily passes through the simulacral realm of mass culture, the media are absolutely central to any discussion of multiculturalism. The contemporary media shape identity; indeed, many argue that they now exist close to the very core of identity production. In a transnational world typified by the global circulation of images and sounds, goods and peoples, media spectatorship complexly impacts on national identity and communal belonging. By facilitating a mediated engagement with distant peoples, the media "deterritorialize" the process of imagining communities. And while the media can destroy community and fashion solitude by turning spectators into atomized consumers or self-entertaining monads, they also can fashion community and alternative affiliations. Just as the media can exoticize and "otherize" cultures, they can also promote multicultural coalitions. And if dominant cinema historically caricatured distant civilizations, the media today are more multicentered with the power not only to offer countervailing representations but also to open up parallel spaces for symbiotic multicultural transformation.

Our interest, then, is in a theorized and historicized discussion of Eurocentrism as perpetuated and challenged by the media. What narrative and cinematic strategies have privileged Eurocentric perspectives, and how have these perspectives been subverted or interrogated? Our goal is not only to look at dominant media through multicultural eyes but also to decenter the discussion by calling attention to other traditions, other cinemas, other audiovisual forms. Our approach entails a dialectical interplay of the critique of Eurocentrism and the promotion of multiculturalism. On the one hand, it aims to expose the unthinking, taken-for-granted quality of Eurocentrism as a kind of bad epistemic habit informing mass-mediated culture and intellectual reflection on that culture. On the other, it hopes to illuminate the many cognitive, political, and aesthetic alternatives to Eurocentrism in the media. In a double operation, it critiques the Eurocentric tendencies within dominant discourse while celebrating the transgressive utopianism of multicultural texts and practices. (We do not mean "utopia" in the sense of scientist "blueprint" utopias or totalizing metanarratives of progress, but rather in the sense of "critical utopias" which seek what Moylan calls "seditious expression of social change" carried on in a "permanently open process of envisioning what is not yet.")[16] Rather than construct a purist notion of correct texts or immaculate sites of resistance, we would propose a positively predatory attitude which seizes aesthetic and pedagogic potentialities in a wide variety of cultural practices, finding in them germs of subversion that can "sprout" in an altered context.

Imperial Media: From Tarzan to the Gulf War

Here we can only begin to explore this dialectic by exploring on the one hand the ways the dominant media have formed part of the culture of empire, and evoking on the other the ways that alternative practices have challenged Eurocentric discourses. It is most significant for our discussion, for example, that the beginnings of cinema coincided with the giddy heights of the imperial project, with a time when Europe held sway over vast tracts of alien territory and hosts of subjugated peoples. The first film screenings by Lumiere and Edison in the 1890s closely followed the "scramble for Africa" that erupted in the late 1870s, the Battle of "Rorke's Drift" (1879) which opposed the British to the Zulus (memorialized in the film *Zulu*, 1964), the British occupation of Egypt in 1882, the Berlin Conference of 1884 that carved up Africa into European "spheres of influence," the massacre of the Sioux at Wounded Knee in 1890, and countless other imperial misadventures. The most prolific film-producing countries of the silent period — England, France, the United States, Germany — also "happened" to be among the leading imperialist countries in whose clear interest it was to laud the colonial enterprise. The cinema emerged exactly at the point when enthusiasm for the imperial project was spreading beyond the elites into the popular strata, partially thanks to popular fictions and exhibitions. For the working classes of Europe and Euro-America, photogenic wars in remote parts of the empire became diverting entertainments, serving to "neutralize the class struggle and transform class solidarity into national and racial solidarity."[17] The cinema adopted the popular fictions of colonialist writers like Kipling for India, Rider Haggard, Edgar Wallace and Edgar Rice Burroughs for Africa, and absorbed popular genres like the "conquest fiction" of the American Southwest. The cinema entered a situation where European and American readers had already devoured Livingston's *Missionary Travels* (1857); Edgar Wallace's "Sanders of the River" stories; Rider Haggard's *King Solomon's Mines* (1885); and Henry Morton Stanley's *How I Found Livingston* (1872), *Through the Dark Continent* (1878), and *In Darkest Africa* (1890). English boys especially were initiated into imperial ideals through such books as Robert Baden-Powell's *Scouting for Boys* (1908). The practical survivalist education of Scouting combined with the initiatory mechanisms of the colonial adventure story were designed to turn boys, as Joseph Bristow puts it, into "aggrandized subjects," an imperial race who imagined the future of the world as resting on their shoulders.[18] While girls were domesticated as homemakers, boys could gambol, if only in their imaginations, in the open fields of empire. Adventure films, and the "adventure" of going to the cinema, provided a vicarious experience of passionate fraternity, a playground for the self-realization of the white European male. Just as colonized space was available to empire, so was this expansive space available as a kind of psychic *Lebensraum* for the play of the virile spectatorial imagination.

The dominant European/American form of cinema not only inherited and disseminated a hegemonic colonial discourse, but also created a powerful hegemony of its own through monopolistic control of film distribution and exhibition in much of Asia, Africa, and the Americas. Eurocolonial cinema thus mapped history not only for domestic audiences but for the world. For the European spectator, the cinematic experience mobilized a rewarding sense of national and imperial belonging. For the colonized, the cinema (in tandem with other colonial institutions such as schools) produced a deep sense of ambivalence, mingling the identification provoked by cinematic narrative along with intense resentment, for it was they who were being otherized. African spectators, for example, were prodded to identify with Cecil Rhodes and Stanley Livingstone against Africans themselves, thus engendering a battle of national imaginaries within the fissured colonial spectator.

A situation in which colonized Africans and Asians went to European-owned theaters to watch European and Hollywood films thus encouraged a kind of spectatorial schizophrenia in the colonized subject who might, on the one hand, internalize Europe as ideal ego and on the other resent (and often protest) offensive representations. Some of the major figures within anticolonial and postcolonial discourse, interestingly, return in their writing to colonial spectatorship as a kind of traumatic primal scene. The Martiniquian revolutionary theorist Frantz Fanon, the Ethiopian-American filmmaker Haile Gerima, and the Palestinian-American cultural critic Edward Said have registered the impact of Tarzan on their impressionable young selves. Gerima recalls the "crisis of identity" provoked in an Ethiopian child applauding Johnny Weissmuller as he cleansed the "dark continent" of its inhabitants: "Whenever Africans sneaked up behind Tarzan, we would scream our heads off, trying to warn him that 'they' were coming."[19] In *Black Skin, White Masks*, Fanon, too, brings up Tarzan to point to a certain instability within cinematic identification:

> Attend showings of a Tarzan film in the Antilles and in Europe. In the Antilles, the young negro identifies himself de facto with Tarzan against the Negroes. This is much more difficult for him in a European theater, for the rest of the audience, which is white, automatically identifies him with the savages on the screen.[20]

Fanon's example points to the ambivalent, situational nature of colonized spectatorship: the colonial context of reception, and the consciousness of the possible negative projections of other spectators triggers an anxious withdrawal from the film's programmed pleasures.

While novels could play with words and narrative to engender an "aggrandized subject," the cinema entailed a new and powerful apparatus of the gaze. By prosthetically extending human perception, the apparatus grants the spectator the illusory ubiquity of the "all-perceiving subject" enjoying an exhilarating sense of visual power. From the Diorama, the Panorama, and the Cosmorama up through NatureMax, the cinema has amplified and mobilized the "virtual gaze" of photography, bringing past into present, distant to near. It has offered the spectator a mediated relationship with imaged others from diverse cultures. And although imperialism was not inscribed either in the apparatus or in the celluloid, the context of imperial power did inevitably shape the uses to which apparatus and celluloid were put. In an imperial context, the apparatus tended to be deployed in ways flattering to the imperial subject as invulnerable observer, as what Mary Louise Pratt calls the "monarch-of-all-I-survey." The cinema's ability to "fly" spectators around the globe gave them a subject position as film's audiovisual masters. The "spatially-mobilized visuality"[21] of the I/Eye of Empire spiraled outward around the globe, creating a visceral, kinetic sense of imperial travel and conquest, transforming European spectators into armchair conquistadors, affirming their sense of power while making the inhabitants of the colonies objects of spectacle for the metropole's voyeuristic gaze.

The colonial/imperial paradigm inaugurated in the early decades of this century did not die with the end of the imperial era. In the Reagan–Bush era, dominant cinema rediscovered the charms of the imperial/frontier narrative. *Red Dawn* (1984) returns to the encirclement imagery of the western, but this time it is the Cubans, the Soviets, and the (presumably Sandinista) Nicaraguans who take over the functional slot of the Indians. *Mountains of the Moon* (1989), meanwhile, recapitulates the Victorian explorer Richard Burton's search for the sources of the Nile, with weirdly colorful savages, presumably incapable of "discovering" the sources of the Nile for themselves, as his witnesses. The 1980s and 1990s witness a wave of elegiac narratives about the closing of the imperial period. The Raj nostalgia genre, exemplified by the TV series *The Jewel in the Crown*, and by such films as *Staying On* (1980), *Passage to India* (1984), *Gandhi* (1982), *Heat and Dust* (1982), and *Kim* (1984) was denounced by Salman Rushdie as a transparent Thatcherite attempt to refurbish the image of Empire, forming the "artistic counterpart of the rise of conservative ideologies in modern Britain."[22]

More often, colonialist imagery has been remarketed under the guise of humor and genre parody. Thus in a moment of apparent imperial decline, Hollywood resuscitates the imperial romance where the presumably parodic filmmaker celebrates the extinguished glories of "imperial conquest and dominion, of virtually magical mobility and power, and of exotic life at the outposts of empire."[23] The "Indiana Jones" series recycled Rider Haggard and Kipling for the Reagan/Bush era, resurrecting the colonial adventure genre with insidious charm. Even the films' adolescent qualities recall the pubescent energies of imperial adventure tales for boys. Set in the 1930s, the very heyday of the imperial film, the series, like comic books, is premised on an imperialized globe in which archaeology professors can "rescue" artifacts from the colonized world for the greater benefit of science and civilization. "Indy" operates with ease only in colonized countries, portrayed as ontologically corrupt, awaiting western salvation. The series assumes an uncontested empire with no trace of any viable anticolonial opposition. In the world of Indiana Jones, Third-World cultures are synopsized as theme-park cliches drawn from the orientalist repertoire: India is all dreamy spirituality as in the Hegelian account; Shanghai is all gongs and rickshaws. Third-World landscapes becomes the stuff of dreamy adventure. In a classical splitting operation, the Third World is demonized and infantilized: Non-Western adult characters are evil (Mola Ram, Chattar Lal, Lao Che) while children (Short Round and Little Maharajah) are eager, innocent, and pro-Western. The blame-the-victim paradigm inherited from the western is globalized: the civilized West is threatened by the savage East.

This same paradigm was reactivated in the case of the Persian Gulf War. The ground for the "popularity" of that war was prepared for by a long intertextual chain: crusading anti-Islamic tales, captivity narratives, the imperial adventure novel, the "manifest destiny" western, and more recent militaristic films like *Star Wars* (1977), the *Rambo* series (1982, 1985, 1988), and *Top Gun* (1988). The Gulf War was presented as macroentertainment, one with a beginning (Desert Shield), a middle (Desert Sword), and an End (Desert Storm), all undergirded by a fictive telos: The "New World Order." The futuristic overtones of "New World Order" meshed anachronistically with the medievalist connotations of "shield" and "sword," evocative of a religious substratum of crusades against muslim infidels. Network logos — "Countdown to War," "Deadline in the Desert," "America at the Brink" — communicated a throbbing sense of inevitability, of an inexorable slouching toward war, provoking, even, a kind of spectatorial desire for war. With the Gulf War, an already powerful media apparatus became "wedded" to another apparatus of the gaze — that of military simulation and surveillance. As a consequence, telespectators were encouraged to "enjoy" a quantum leap in prosthetic audiovisual power. Television news offered its spectator what Donna Haraway, in another context, calls the "conquering gaze from nowhere," a gaze that claims "the power to see and not be seen, to represent while escaping representation."[24] During the Gulf War, the media coaxed spectators to spy, thanks to an almost pornographic kind of surveillance, on a whole geographical region, whose nooks and crannies lay open to the military's panoptic view.[25] Much as the encirclement imagery model in the western film engages a literal point of view — the looking through scopes of a rifle, or through the windows of the fort — Gulf War "spectators" were made to see through the point of view of American pilots, and even through that of "smart bombs." Media coverage endowed the spectatorial eye with what Paul Virilio calls the "symbolic function of a weapon."[26] The Gulf War telespectator, vicariously equipped with night-vision technology, infrared vision capable of zapping "enemy" tanks, planes, buildings, and heads of state, was prodded into feeling infinitely powerful. In a war where the same pilot's hand that released the missile simultaneously tripped the camera shutter, spectators were teleguided to see from the bomber's perspective, incorporated into the surveillance equipment, sutured into the sights of high-tech weaponry.

While the media on the one hand forced a "dirty handed" complicity with the war by positioning viewers among the soldiers — Ted Koppel placing us in the cockpit of a Saudi fighter, Diane Sawyer putting us inside a tank — they also symbolically cleansed those very same hands. The spectator was prompted to indulge infantile dreams of omnipotence, made to feel allied to immense destructive forces, but also to feel fundamentally pure and innocent. Any word or image implying that the American spectators or their tax dollars were somehow responsible for mass suffering would have destroyed the shaky edifice of nonculpability. The Gulf War was fought in the name of American victimization, in the tradition of the many wars in which reiterated claims of self-defense have masked overwhelming, disproportionate power. That President Bush had been figuratively in bed with the dictator Hussein merely betrays the binaristic splitting off of one's own impulses onto a phantasmatic other that is so typical of colonialist thinking. Our point is not that some national essence induces the American public into war — obviously antiwar protest and antimilitarism are equally part of the American tradition — nor to suggest that Hussein was anything less than a despicable tyrant. It is rather to map the ways point-of-view conventions and a powerful media apparatus can be mobilized to shape public opinion for militaristic purposes. But these televisual tactics would not have "worked" so effectively had spectators not already been "primed" by innumerable westerns, adventure films, and imperial epics.

Alternative Histories

At the same time, there are also myriad alternative texts and resources for combatting the imperial imaginary. In the face of Eurocentric historicizing, Third-World and minoritarian filmmakers have rewritten their own histories, taken control over their own images, spoken in their own voices. It is not that their films substitute a pristine "truth" for European "lies," but that they propose countertruths and counternarratives informed by an anticolonialist perspective, reclaiming and reaccentuating the events of the past in a vast project of remapping and renaming. This rewriting has operated within a double time frame: the reinscription of the past inevitably also rewrites the present.

We find a good example of this remapping in the recent spate of critical films bearing on the Columbus quincentennial. The Columbus debate is important because the so-called Voyages of Discovery inaugurated modernity, catalyzing a new epoch of European colonial expansion which culminated in its domination of the globe. For many revisionist historians, 1492 installed the mechanism of systematic advantage which favored Europe against its African and Asian rivals. Prior to 1492, according to J. M. Blaut, a movement toward modernization was taking place in various parts of Europe, Asia, and Africa. "Protocapitalist" centers, equal to Europe in demographic, technological, commercial, and intellectual terms, were developing and linked in a network of mercantile-maritime centers stretching from western Europe to eastern and southern Africa and Asia. After 1492, however, the massive injection of wealth from the New World, the use of forced indigenous-American and African labor, and the advantage of new markets in the Americas, gave Europe the "edge" that turned it into a capitalist and colonialist giant.[27]

The Columbus story is crucial to Eurocentrism not only because Columbus was a seminal figure within the history of colonialism, but also because idealized versions of his story have served to initiate generation after generation into the colonial paradigm. For many children in North America and elsewhere, the tale of Columbus is totemic; it introduces them not only to the concepts of "discovery" and the "New World," but also to the idea of history itself. The vast majority of school textbooks, including very recent ones, as Bill Bigelow points out, describe and picture Columbus as handsome, studious, pious, commanding, audacious. Young pupils are induced to empathize with what are imagined to be his childhood dreams and hopes, so that their identification with him is virtually assured even before they encounter the New-World others, who are described variously as friendly or as fierce, but whose perspective is rigorously elided.[28] Only some voices and perspectives, it is implied, resonate in the world.

The 1992 Columbus debate was played out not only in the pages of newspapers and academic journals, but also in the realms of the visual media and popular culture. The quincentennial period brought not only two adulatory Hollywood superproductions but also a number of critical, revisionist features and protest documentaries whose titles reveal their anti-Columbus thrust: *Surviving Columbus* (1990), *Columbus on Trial* (1992), *The Columbus Invasion* (1992), and *Columbus Didn't Discover Us* (1991). Cinematic re-creations of the past reshape the imagination of the present, legitimating or interrogating hegemonic memories and assumptions. The mainstream films devoted to Columbus prolong the pedagogic role of the pro-Columbus textbooks. Indeed, such films exercise more influence over the representation of Columbus, and thus over perceptions of colonial history than could any number of debates and protests. There is surprisingly little difference, in this respect, between the 1949 (British) David Macdonald film *Christopher Columbus* and the recent (1992) Salkind superproduction *Columbus: the Discovery*. Although almost a half century separates the two films, their idealizations of Columbus are virtually identical. Both films portray Columbus as an avatar of modernity and the Christian faith, a man of vision struggling against obstacles of superstition, ignorance, and envy. Both films relay the old chestnut that "they all laughed at Christopher Columbus, when he said the world was round," when in fact most educated Europeans (and Arabs) knew very well the world was round.[29] Both emphasize European antagonists, especially the aristocrat Bobadilla, and thus displace attention from the more fundamental antagonism of Europe and the indigenous peoples.

The very title of the 1992 Salkind film — *Columbus: The Discovery* — betrays its makers' contempt for all those who have objected to the term "discovery." According to its producer, the film is an "adventure picture" combining "aspects of *Lawrence of Arabia* and *Robin Hood*" and featuring "no politics."[30] The generic choice of adventure film, the intertextual reference to an orientalist classic, and the tendentious use of "no politics" to mean "no opposition politics" are in keeping with the general tone of the film. That the Salkinds were the producing team behind the first *Superman* films (1978, 1981), *The Three Musketeers* (1974), and *Santa Claus — the Movie* (1985), and that the chosen director (John Glen) was a veteran of several James Bond films might have forewarned us about the heroic paradigm into which Columbus was about to be placed. Since the film covers only Columbus' campaign to win Queen Isabella's support, his first voyage, and his return in glory to Spain, it can ignore the death by massacre or disease that befell thousands of Indians after Columbus' second voyage. From the beginning, Columbus is portrayed as the personification of individual initiative overcoming bureaucratic inertia. Despite the historical Columbus' arcane views about so many subjects (mermaids, cannibals, devils), he is portrayed as the voice of modern rationality. That the role is incarnated by a handsome actor (George Corraface) further enforces spectatorial identification. Symphonic European music constantly supports the swelling ambition of Columbus' enterprise, while virtually every scene adds a humanizing touch. At one point, Columbus gives a young

Jewish cabin boy a free ticket out of anti-Semitic Spain. The natives, meanwhile, are reduced to mute, admiring witnesses who regard white men as gods.

Ridley Scott's *1492: The Conquest of Paradise*, meanwhile, is erratically revisionist, yet fundamentally protective of Columbus' good name. Here the scintillating beauty of the cinematography enfolds the violence of conquest into the ideology of the aesthetic. The film makes token acknowledgements of the present-day controversies surrounding Columbus, but in highly ambiguous ways. Once again, Columbus (Gerard Depardieu) is the central figure, subjectivized through voice-over, sycophantic close-ups, and empathetic music, and once again he is the voice of faith, science, and modernity. *1492* covers a greater number of Columbus' voyages (although the four voyages are reduced to three) and portrays him as being occasionally brutal as well as magnanimous. With sets built in Seville and Grenada, the film shows the final siege of the Moors in Grenada, and on the basis of no known historical evidence, portrays Columbus as outraged by the Inquisition. Throughout we are sutured into his vantage point while the music encodes binarist perspectives; choral music with ecclesiastical overtones cues sympathy for Columbus while brooding dissonance subliminally instructs us to fear the natives despite an otherwise positive portrayal. Indeed, on some levels, the film does pay respect to indigenous culture. The Indians speak their own language and complain that Columbus has never learned it. A native shaman takes care of the European sick and, in general, the natives act with gentleness and dignity, although there is no hint that Columbus helped eradicate complex civilizations. What looks like forced labor is shown, but Columbus' crucial role in it is obscured; the film scapegoats an underling figure, a scheming Spanish nobleman who happens to look very much like an Indian, as the racist, and Columbus as his antagonist. With the upgrading of the native image goes a parallel upgrading of Columbus. An enlightened version of the traditional figure, he sympathizes with the Indians and treats them just as he treats Spanish noblemen. It is as if the film combined the personalities and ideologies of Columbus and Bartolome de las Casas, as if the "discoverer" had been retroactively endowed with the conscience of the radical priest.[31]

Some recent revisionist historical films, set in the initial period of conquest, relativize and even invert colonialist perspectives on the Conquest. The Mexican film *Cabeza de Vaca* (1989) tells the story of Alvar Nunez Cabeza de Vaca, the shipwrecked Spaniard who went by foot from Florida to Texas. The film's source text, Alvar Nunez' *Relacion de los Naufragios,* already relates the Conquest as a story of failure. Inverting the usual roles, Nunez portrays the Spaniards as vulnerable, as losing control, weeping, supplicating. And while a phantasmatic cannibalism usually serves to justify European exploitation, here it is the Spanish who cannibalize one another and the natives who watch in horror.[32] Although the film version fails to humanize the Indians, it does expose the underside of European religious proselytizing, and shows the Conquistadors, not the natives, as the real cannibals. The Venezuelan film *Jericho*, meanwhile, largely adopts the indigenous perspective while respecting the languages, histories, and cultural styles of the indigenous groups portrayed. *Jericho*'s story evokes what was actually a frequent occurrence during the first centuries of conquest — the case of the European who "goes native." (In Mexico, Gonzalo Guerrero, a Spaniard kidnapped by Indians in the Yucatan, ultimately became a Cacique with tattooed face and pierced ears[33] while in North America, as Hector de Crevecoeur noted, thousands of Europeans became "white Indians" — to the point that some colonies passed laws against "Indianizing" — while "we have no examples of even one of these Aborigines having become, from choice, Europeans.")[34]

Jericho concerns Franciscan priest Santiago, the lone survivor of a sixteenth-century expedition led by the cruel conquistador Gascuna, in search of the mythic Mar del Sur. Although Santiago hopes to spiritually conquer the Indians, he, in fact, is spiritually conquered by them. While their captive, he comes to question European attitudes toward religion, the body, the earth, and social life, and finally renounces his evangelical mission. Whereas most Hollywood films have the "indians" speak a laughable pidgin English, here the natives laugh at the priest's garbled attempt to speak *their* language. In the end, Santiago is retaken by the Spaniards who regard his "going native" as a form of madness and heresy. What makes this revisionist captivity narrative so subversive is that it transforms what official Europe regarded with fear and loathing — indigenous culture — into a seductive pole of attraction for Europeans. (The real purpose of the Inquisition, suggests Jorge Klor de Alva, was not to force the indigenes to become Europeans, but to keep Europeans from becoming *indigenes*).[35]

A number of revisionist films assert links between past and contemporary oppressions and resistances. The Cuban-Peruvian epic *Tupac Amaru* (1984) evokes indigenous resistance to Spanish-European domination in Peru, specifically the Inca rebellion led by Jose Gabriel Condorcanqui Tupac Amaru whose story is told in flashbacks from his trial by the Spanish.[36] A direct descendant of an Inca emperor whose name he borrowed, Tupac Amaru led a broad-based messianic rebellion against Spanish rule. (The first Tupac Amaru was beheaded by the Spanish in 1572.) In 1781, he entered the main plaza of Cuzco and announced that he was condemning the royal Corregidor Antonio Juan de Arriaga to the gallows. A few days later, he issued a decree liberating the slaves and abolishing all taxes (*encomienda*) and forced labor (the *mita*). After a number of victories, he was betrayed and given over to the royalists who had him drawn and quartered in the four directions of the Inca empire, symbolically dismembering the indigenous reign which he was trying to install. The film begins and ends in Cuzco's central square, for within Inca cosmology, Cuzco was the center or navel of a universe that stretched anthropomorphically across a vast territory. The Spanish conquest, by decapitating the Inca, introduced a period of confusion and darkness, transforming the anthropomorphic figure of the Inca empire, the *Inkarri* in Quechua, into a grimacing, contorted figure of pain, and delegitimizing Cuzco as a center of power.[37] The film shows the Spanish punishment of Tupac Amaru and his family, watched by a distressed, benumbed indigenous crowd. We hear a pronouncement in Spanish: "The proceedings of this trial shall be destroyed. Not a trace shall remain of these unfortunate events nor a vestige of this accursed race." The camera swirls vertiginously, as if translating the despair of the crowd, after which the film segues into a black-and-white flashforward to a similar crowd, this time a modern-day political rally in 1975 being held in the same square where Tupac Amaru was assassinated. The film thus contradicts the Spanish prophecy that "not a trace shall remain" and instead installs the terms of Inca prophecy just as a poem speaks of the head and body of the dismembered *Inkarri* coming back together in an apotheosis of liberation.

The Venezuelan film *Cubagua* (1987), an adaptation and update of the 1931 novel by Enrique Bernardo Nunez, meanwhile, uses tripled characters to move back and forth between the sixteenth century, the 1930s, and the present, to show the continuities of exploitation. Cubagua's male protagonist lives three different lives in three different periods: in 1520 as Lampugnano, an Italian helping the Spaniards extract pearls; in 1930 as an engineer helping North American oil companies; and in 1980 as an engineer working for a transnational company extracting minerals in the Amazon. His female counterpart Nila is a victim of the Spanish in the 1500s, a resistant chief's daughter in the 1930s, and an anti-imperialist journalist in the 1980s. Together, the characters help compose a portrait in transhistorical time of a country which has been colonized and neocolonized, but which has also displayed diverse forms of cultural and political resistance.[38] The Brazilian film *Ajuricaba* (1977), similarly tells the story of Ajuricaba, eighteenth-century chief of the Manau tribe who fought against his people's enslavement and finally leapt to his death rather than be captured. The film stresses historical continuities by shuttling between Indian resistance in the eighteenth century to resistance against multinational companies in the present.

Other films deploy avant-garde-inflected tactics to critique European conquest. Lourdes Portillo's *Columbus on Trial* (1992) has the Chicano group Culture Clash perform a contemporary indictment of a Don Corleone-like Columbus. Kidlat Tahimik's work-in-progress *Magellan's Slave*, whose alternate title is *Memories of Overdevelopment,* is premised on the speculation that the first man to actually circumnavigate the globe was a Filipino slave that Magellan picked up in Spain who completed Magellan's project after Magellan died. But the most outrageously avant-gardist of the antiquincentennial films is Craig Baldwin's *O No Coronado!* (1992). Framed as a historical flashback within Coronado's mind as he falls off his horse — an apt metaphor for the carnivalesque dethroning performed by the film. Baldwin focuses on one of the more inept and deluded of the conquistadors, the one whose desperate search for the chimerical Seven Cities of Cíbola led him into a fruitless, murderous, journey across what is now the Southwest of the United States. To relate this calamitous epic, Baldwin deploys not only costumed dramatizations but also the detritus of the filmic archive: swashbucklers, pedagogical films, industrial documentaries. Found footage from diverse costume epics takes us back to the Old World origins of New World Conquest in the Crusades and the *reconquista*. Educational footage of an atomic test site — located in the same region perambulated by Coronado — is accompanied by a female voice-over pronouncing the prophecies of Native American seers ("Earthquakes shook the world ... fear was everywhere"). Coronado is portrayed as a Eurotrash exemplar of colonialism whose avatars are evoked through the "prior textualizations" of tacky costume dramas and sci-fi films: Vincent Price (incarnating the Inquisition), the Lone Ranger, Charles Bronson. The film ends with images of nuclear explosions, evocative of the apotheosis of instrumental reason, and of a lone Indian using a reflecting mirror as a weapon, an evocation of the minimal resistant means available to the weak.

Native Americans have also begun to make historical films from an indigenous point of view. George Burdeau's *Surviving Columbus* (1990) narrates the initial encounter between the Conquistadors and the Zuni, giving pride of place to Zuni narratives and perspectives within a communal atmosphere of domesticated storytelling. The conquistadors, as seen from a Zuni perspective, become abstracted, depersonalized Goyaesque figures of menace. Bob Hick's *Return of the Country* (1984) provocatively overturns Eurocentric assumptions, reversing an oppressive situation long familiar to Native Americans — but this time it is Anglo language and culture that are outlawed, and the courts, congress, and the presidency are all in indigenous hands. A number of didactic documentaries finally tell the story of the Conquest from the perspective of the Conquered: Tainos, Mayas, Aztecs, Mohawks. *The Columbus Invasion: Colonialism and the Indian Resistance* combines sixteenth-century images with contemporary interviews of Native Americans to convey the indigenous perspective on the conquest, citing a Maya prophecy that indigenous peoples, after 500 years of suffering, will unite as the "eagle of the north meets the condor of the south." *Columbus Didn't Discover Us* cinematically "realizes" that prophecy by recording a panindigenous encounter held in the highlands of Ecuador in July 1990. The British documentary *Savagery and the American Indian* sees the puritans from an indigenous perspective, inverting the trope of savage "wildness" by positing the Europeans rather than the Native Americans as wild, and at the same time, satirizing the litany of ethnocentric prejudice by having it pronounced by the backlit, bearded mouths of the "hairy men."

Oppositional cinemas also have explored a wide spectrum of alternative aesthetics. This spectrum includes films (and videos) that bypass the formal conventions of dramatic realism in favor of such modes and strategies as the carnivalesque, the anthropophagic, the reflexive modernist, and the resistant postmodernist. These alternative aesthetics often are rooted in nonrealist, non-Western, or para-Western cultural traditions featuring other historical rhythms, other narrative structures, other views of the body, sexuality, spirituality, and the collective life. Haile Gerima's *Sankofa* (1993), for example, synthesizes the modern and the traditional through an Afromagical *egungun* aesthetic, that is, an aesthetic that invokes the spirits of the ancestors as embodiments of a deep sense of personal and collective history.[39] Named after an Akan word for "recuperating what's lost," the film begins with a drummed invocation exhorting the ancestral spirits to "rise up, step out, and tell your story." An urgent whispered voice-over says: "Spirit of the dead, rise up and possess your bird of passage, come out, you stolen Africans, spirits of the dead, you raped, castrated, lobotomized." This device of a collective call by a presiding spirit, turned into a structural refrain, authorizes a transgenerational approach that mingles the present (a bewigged black fashion model posing against the backdrop of the Mina slave fort) and the past (the fort's former historical atrocities). In a kind of psychic and historical time machine, the fashion model becomes possessed by Shola, a nineteenth-century house slave, and is made to experience the cruelties of slavery, the rapes and the brandings, and to acknowledge her own kinship with her own enslaved ancestors. Gerima repeatedly pans over friezes of black faces, evoking an ocular chorus, bypassing an individualizing point of view structure to evoke a community of the gaze. The narrative forms a multifocal, communitarian *bildungsroman*: the fashion model confronts the sources of her own alienation; the "headman" who beats slaves becomes a double agent working for liberation. Nor is this a monolithic community since it includes field slaves and house slaves, even foremen who whip other slaves. The cultural facets of African life (communal child care, herbal remedies, the primordial role of music and stories) are constantly stressed. Orality exists as a diegetic presence — characters literally tell stories/histories of Africa, of the middle passage — and as a metacinematic device structuring the entire film as a collective narration where disembodied voices exhort, prophesy, exorcise, criticize, all in a "polyrhythmic" style where avant-garde-inflected moments of aesthetic contemplation alternate with dramatic moments of decisive action.

A number of films focus on the pathologies generated by the hegemonic white-is-beautiful aesthetic inherited from colonialist discourse, an aesthetic which exiled people of color from their own bodies. Until the late 1960s, the overwhelming majority of Anglo-American fashion journals, films, TV shows, and commercials promoted a canonical notion of beauty within which white women (and secondarily white men) were the only legitimate objects of desire. In so doing, the media extended a longstanding philosophical valorization of whiteness. For Gobineau, the "white race originally possessed the monopoly of beauty, intelligence and strength."[40] For Buffon, "[Nature] in her most perfect exertions made men white."[41] Fredrich Bluembach called white Europeans "Caucasians" because he believed that the Caucasus mountains were the original home of the most beautiful human species.[42]

The hegemony of this Eurocentric gaze, spread not only by First-World media but even at times by Third-World media, explains why morena women in Puerto Rico, like Arab-Jewish (sephardi) women in Israel, paint their hair blond, why Brazilian TV commercials are more suggestive of Scandinavia than of a black-majority country, why "Miss Universe" contests can elect blond "queens" even in North African countries, and why Asian women perform cosmetic surgery to appear more western. The mythical norms of Eurocentric aesthetics come to inhabit the intimacy of self-consciousness. A patriarchal system contrived to generate neurotic self-dissatisfaction in all women (whence anorexia, bulimia, and other pathologies of appearance) becomes especially oppressive for women of color by excluding them from the realms of legitimate "starring" erotic images. (Recently one finds reverse currents linked to the central role of African-Americans in mass-mediated culture: whites who thicken their lips and sport dreadlocks, fades, or cornrows.) Multicultural feminists, meanwhile, have criticized the internalized exile of Euro-"wannabees" (who transform themselves through cosmetic surgery or by dying their hair) while at the same time seeking an open, nonessentialist approach to personal aesthetics.

Many Third-World and minoritarian feminist film and video projects suggest strategies for coping with the psychic violence inflicted by Eurocentric aesthetics, calling attention to the racialized body as the site of brutal oppression and creative resistance. Black creativity turned the body, as a singular form of "cultural capital," into what Stuart Hall calls a "canvas of representation."[43] A number of recent independent films and videos — notably Ayoka Chenzira's *Hairpiece: A Film for Nappy-Headed People* (1985), Ngozi A. Onwurah's *Coffee Coloured Children* (1988), Shu Lea Cheang's *Color Schemes,* Pam Tom's *Two Lies* (1989), Maureen Blackwood's *Perfect Image?* (1990), Camille Billop's *Older Women and Love* (1987), and Kathe Sandler's *A Question of Color* (1993) meditate on the racialized body to narrate issues of minoritarian identity. These semiautobiographical texts link fragmented diasporic identities to larger issues of representation, recuperating complex identities in the face of the hostile condescension of mass-mediated culture.

Given the construction of dark bodies as ugly and bestial, resistance takes the form of affirming black beauty. The Black Power movement of the 1960s, for example, transformed kinky hair into proud, Afro, hair. Sandler's *A Question of Color* traces tensions around color-consciousness and internalized racism in the African-American community, a process summed up in the popular dictum: "If you're white, you're all right/if you're yellow, you're mellow/if you're brown, stick around/ but if you're black, stay back." Hegemonic norms of skin color, hair texture, and facial features are expressed even within the community through such euphemisms as "good hair" (that is, straight hair), and "nice features" (that is, European-style features), and in inferentially prejudicial locutions like "dark *but* beautiful" or in admonitions not to "look like a Ubangi." The film registers the impact of the "Black is Beautiful" movement while regarding the present moment as the contradictory site of the resurgent Afrocentrism of some rap music along with lingering traces of old norms. One interview features a Nigerian cosmetic surgeon who de-Africanizes the appearance of black women while the film reflects on the valorization of light-skinned black women in rap video and MTV. Sandler also probes intimate relations in order to expose the social pathologies rooted in color hierarchies; the darker-skinned feel devalorized and desexualized, the lighter-skinned, to the extent that their own community assumes they feel superior to it, are obliged to "prove" their blackness. Filtering down from positions of dominance, chromatic hierarchies sow tensions among siblings and friends, all caught by Sandler's exceptionally sensitive direction.

In all these films, internalized models of white beauty become the object of a corrosive critique. Not coincidentally, many of the films pay extraordinary attention to hair as the scenes of humiliation ("bad hair") and of creative self-fashioning, a "popular art form" articulating "aesthetic solutions," in Kobena Mercer's words, to the "problems created by ideologies of race and racism."[44] Spike Lee, even before the "conking" scene in his 1992 *Malcolm X*, had addressed the subject of hair in *School Daze*. Rather than satirize the feminine beautifying process in general, Lee's musical focuses on "white" (European) versus black (African) models of beauty. One stylized production number, set in a beauty salon, foregrounds the politicized perception of hair within the Afro-American community. While the white-aspiring "wannabees" reject the African look — "Don't you wish you had hair like this/then the boys would give you a kiss ... caint cha, don't cha hair stand on high/caint cha comb it and don't you try" — the politically conscious "Jigaboos" mock them: "Don't you know my hair is so strong/it can break the teeth out the comb ... I don't mind being BLACK/go on with your mixed-up head/I ain't gonna never be 'fraid."[45] The dancers, respectively, hold Vivien Leigh and Hattie McDaniel-style fans, reflexively alluding to Hollywood representations of race relations and, implicitly, to their impact on the Afro-American self-image. The number lends an aesthetic corollary to Malcolm X's dictum that the white man's worst crime was to make the black man hate himself.

Ayoka Chenzira's ten-minute animated short *Hairpiece: A Film for Nappy-Headed People* similarly addresses hair and its vicissitudes to narrate African-Americans' history of exile from the body as well as the utopia of empowerment through Afro-consciousness. In a dominant society where beautiful hair is that which "blows in the wind," *Hairpiece* suggests an isomorphism between vital, rebellious hair that refuses to conform to Eurocentric norms and the vital, rebellious people who "wear" the hair. Music by Aretha Franklin, James Brown, and Michael Jackson accompanies a collage of black faces. Motown tunes underscore a quick-paced visual inventory of relaxers, gels and curlers, devices painfully familiar to black people, particularly to black women. The film's voice-over and "happy ending" might seem to imply an essentialist affirmation of "natural African beauty," but as Kobena Mercer points out in another context, "natural hair" is not itself African; it is a syncretic construct.[46] Afrodiasporic hair styles, from the "Afro" style of the 1960s–1970s to cornrows, dreadlocks, and fades, are not emulations of "real" African styles but rather neologistic projections of diasporic identity. The styles displayed at the film's finale, far from being examples of "politically correct" hair, assert a cornucopia of diasporic looks, an empowering expression of a variegated collective body. Satirizing the black internalization of white aesthetic models, the film provokes a comic catharsis for spectators who have experienced the terror and pity of self-colonization.[47]

Many of the films just mentioned perform a kind of "media jujitsu." They appropriate the force of the dominant discourse only to deploy that force against domination. Such an "excorporation" steals elements of the dominant culture and redeploys them in the interests of oppositional praxis. Indeed, the very names given to evoke alternative aesthetics — from the Brazilian Modernists' "anthrophogic aesthetic" to Rocha's "aesthetic of hunger" and the Tropicalists' "aesthetics of garbage," from Claire Johnston's feminist "Counter Cinema" to Henry Louis Gates' signifying-monkey aesthetic and Paul Leduc's "salamander" (as opposed to dinosaur) aesthetic, from Jean Rouch's cine-transe and Teshome Gabriel's "nomadic aesthetics" to Kobena Mercer's "diaspora aesthetics," from Deleuze/Guattari's "minor" aesthetic to Espinosa's *cine imperfecto* — have in common the twin anthropophagic notions of revalorizing what had been seen as negative and of turning strategic weakness into tactical strength. (Even "magic realism" inverts the traditional condemnation of magic as irrational superstition.)

A number of texts perform media jujitsu by coercing Hollywood films and commercial TV into indicting themselves, deploying the power of the dominant media against their own retrogade and Eurocentric premises. The ludicrous catalogue of media Arabs (assassins, terrorists, fanatics), drawn from cartoons, newscasts, fiction films, and even game shows, in Elia Suleiman's *Muqaddima Li Nihayat Jidal* (An Introduction to the End of an Argument, 1990) hilariously deconstructs mass-media orientalism. Set against more critical materials, the sheer repetition of the caricatural images makes the stereotypes fall of their own weight. The performances of Spiderwoman Theater, a group of three Native American (Cuna/Rappahanock) sisters, as documented in *Sun, Moon and Feather* (1989), carnivalize Hollywood stereotypes by having two of the sisters mimic and sing along with Nelson Eddy and Jeanette MacDonald performing "Indian Love Call" in such a way as to break open the Eurocentric frame and "re-Indianize" a Hollywood caricature. And Sherry Milner and Ernest Larsen's *The Desert Bush* (1991) combines pop culture images and artifacts — Lawrence of Arabia, war movies, toys, George Bush speeches, Thousand and One Nights intertitles — to critique the Persian Gulf War.[48] In *From Hollywood to Hanoi* (1993), Tiana Thi Thanh Nga performs jujitsu by absorbing clips of her own orientalized performances in commercial films (as B-movie karate queen, as oriental sexpot) into her own guerrilla filmmaking portrayal of her odyssey from reflex anticommunist — as a child she learned that Ho Chi Minh would devour her if she did not eat her vegetables — into diasporic struggler for reconciliation between Vietnam and the United States.

It might be objected that jujitsu tactics place one in a perpetually reactive or parasitic posture of merely deconstructing or reversing the dominant. We would argue, however, that these films are not merely defensive. Rather, they express an alternative sensibility and shape an innovative aesthetic. By defamiliarizing and reaccentuating preexisting materials, they rechannel energies in new directions, generating a third conceptual space of negotiation outside of the binaries of domination and subordination. We are not suggesting, in any case, that jujitsu should ever be the only alternative strategy. We would argue, rather, for multiple strategies, for infiltrating the dominant, transforming the dominant, kidnapping the dominant, creating alternatives to the dominant, even ignoring the dominant. In a context of marginalization, however, jujitsu becomes crucial. Since minoritarian and anti-Eurocentric discourse has historically been placed in a defensive position, it is virtually obliged to turn the dominant discourse against itself. All systems of domination, we assume, are "leaky"; our responsibility is to turn such leaks into a flood. Instead of waiting passively for the culture industry to deliver its blockbusters, therefore, instead of waiting for the next Madonna music video with its possibly recuperable subversions instead of letting the industry do our cultural politics for us, we might create and support popular culture along a wider spectrum which would include the kinds of films and videos we have discussed here: critical First-World mass-media texts, Third-World films and video, rap music video, the politicized avant-garde, didactic documentaries, the camcorder militancy of media activists, the self-mocking minimalism of public access cable such as "Paper Tiger" or "Deep Dish."

In their respect for difference and plurality, and in their self-consciousness about their own status as simulacra, and as texts that attempt to connect with a contemporary, mass-mediated sensibility without losing their sense of activism, the best of the jujitsu films constitute examples of what Hal Foster has called "resistance postmodernism." Jorge Furtado's *Isle of Flowers* (1990) brings Brazil's "garbage aesthetic" into the postmodern era. Described by its author as a "letter to a Martian who knows nothing of the earth and its social systems," Furtado's fifteen-minute short uses Monty Python-style animation, archival footage, and parodic/reflexive documentary techniques to indict the distribution of wealth and food around the world. The "isle of flowers" of the title is a Brazilian garbage dump where famished poor are allowed ten minutes to scrounge for food. But this denunciatory material is woven into an ironic treatise about pigs, tomatoes, racism, and the Holocaust (where Jews, garbage-like, are thrown into death-camp piles). Furtado invokes the old carnival motif of pigs and sausage, but with a political twist; here the pigs eat better than people. Here we are given a social examination of garbage; the truth of a society is in its detritus. Rather than having the margins invade the center as in carnival, here the center creates the margins, or better, there are no margins; the urban bourgeois family is linked to the rural poor via the sausage and the tomato within a web of global relationality.

But one need not look so far to find examples of resistant postmodernism. Popular music, now almost invariably accompanied by visuals, offers countless examples. Unlike classical music which requires a distanced and contemplative attitude, popular music encourages movement and tries to abolish the separation between performer and spectator, often in dissident ways, all within a kinetic, energizing, percussive style. In the 1980s, Robert Mugge's *Black Wax* featured Gil Scott Heron satirizing Ronald Reagan in such media-conscious songs as "B-Movie." The rap videos of Ziggy Marley, the Jungle Brothers, Public Enemy, Queen Latifah, KRS One, and Arrested Development, similarly, show awareness of the media-saturated nature of the contemporary imaginary, yet do not fall into cynical nihilism. Marley's "Bold Our Story" offers a crash course in Afroliteracy (complete with a reading list). Queen Latifah's "Ladies First" dishes out Afrofeminism, while Public Enemy's rap-video "Burn, Hollywood, Burn" satirizes the stereotypical images proffered by Hollywood. "Can't Truss It" invokes the historical continuities in a postmodern age supposedly indifferent to history between the racialized terror of slavery and contemporary police brutality. Such work, as Manthia Diawara points out, has helped create a vibrant black public sphere disdainful of integration yet attracting, paradoxically, a host of white admirers and imitators.[49] And in Brazil pop musician intellectuals like Chico Buarque de Holanda with his samba allegories, Gilberto Gil with his musical essays on the politics of syncretism (for example, "From Bob Dylan to Bob Marley"), and Caetano Veloso in songs like "Something is Out of Order in the New World Order," provide a model of pleasurable, danceable political/artistic praxis.[50] For decades at the cutting edge of political and aesthetic innovation (and of reflection on the cultural moment and their own practice), these artists are actively engaged in the political issues of their time. "Popular" in the box-office sense and in the Bakhtinian carnivalesque sense, they constitute a contemporary version of Gramsci's "organic intellectuals." Brazilian musical groups like Olodum and Ile Aiye, meanwhile, not only make their own music videos but also create community schools for practical and anti-Eurocentric education while constructing "carnival factories" to provide jobs.[51] Their audiovisual-musical texts demonstrate art's capacity to give pleasurable form to social desire, to open new grooves, to mobilize a sense of possibility, to shake the body-politic, to appeal to deeply rooted but socially frustrated aspirations for new forms of work and festivity and community, crystallizing desire in a popular and mass-mediated form.

Within postmodern culture, the media not only set agendas and frame debates but also inflect desire, memory, phantasy. By controlling popular memory, they can contain or stimulate popular dynamism. The challenge, then, is to develop a media practice and pedagogy by which subjectivities may be lived and analyzed as part of a transformative, emancipatory praxis.[52] The question of the correctness of texts, in this sense, is less important than the question of mobilizing desire in liberatory directions. The question then becomes: How can we transform existing media so as to mobilize adversary subjectivity? Given the libidinal economy of media reception, how do we crystallize individual and collective desire for emancipatory purposes? An anti-Eurocentric pedagogy, in this sense, must pay attention to what Guattari calls the "production machines" and "collective mutations" of subjectivity. As right-wing forces attempt to promote a superegoish "conservative reterritorialization" of subjectivity, those seeking change in an egalitarian direction must know how to crystallize individual and collective desire.

We would also argue for a kind of pedagogic jujitsu in the form of the classroom highjacking or "*detournement*" of media texts. With the help of a VCR, teachers and students can raid the mass-media archive. Canonical Eurocentric texts can be snapped out of their original context to be reread and even rewritten by teachers and students. Rather than remaining passive spectators, students can "decanonize" the classics, rescripting or reediting films according to alternative perspectives. Students might write a paper or produce a video imagining *Imitation of Life*, for example, from the perspective of the Louise Beavers or the Freddi Washington character rather than that of the white mistress played by Claudette Colbert. They might imagine a film from the perspective of an apparently minor subaltern character (the "squaw," for example, in *The Searchers*). Whole genres could be revised: the Western could be rewritten from a Hopi or Cheyenne perspective, the Hollywood musical from an African-American perspective, the "raj nostalgia" film from an anticolonialist Indian perspective. Video-editing techniques — split frame, voice-over against image, freeze-frame, new voice-overs, changed music — could stage, on an audiovisual level, the clash of perspectives.

Speaking more generally, we would recommend a relational pedagogical strategy that would shuttle constantly between dominant and resistant, and between Euro-American cinema and alternative cinemas, so as to enable a contrapuntal reading of a shared, conflictual history. A film teacher or programmer might show a paternalist film about Africa like *Out of Africa* (1987) or *Mister Johnson* (1990), but counterpoint it with an anticolonialist film by an African like *The Camp at Thioraye* (1987). Teach Vidor's orientalist *Bird of Paradise* with its exoticized and eroticized pseudo-South Seas woman next to *Nice Coloured Girls*. Teach an all-white 1940s musical like *Girl Crazy* (1943) alongside *Illusions* which pinpoints precisely the racial subtexts and elisions of such films. Teach *Fame* (1980) where the minority characters abandon their ethnicity in favor of art and social mobility, but juxtapose it with Leon Ichaso's *Crossover Dreams* (1985) where a myth of success is debunked and shown as hollow. Teach *Imitation of Life* alongside Muriel Jackson's *The Maids* (1985) as a reflection on domestic labor since slavery. Juxtapose the Hollywood film *Glory* (1989) and its white-oriented focalization with *The Massachusetts 54th Colored Infantry* (1991), Jacqueline Shearer's black-focalized documentary on the same topic. Show *Gone with the Wind* (1939) but compare it to Sergio Giral's *El Otro Francisco*, a deconstruction of another sentimental abolitionist novel. In this way, cinema studies or history teachers become activist programmers, orchestrating illuminating clashes of perspectives and aesthetics, intellectual montages not of shots but of films and discourses.

A media-based pedagogy, at the same time, could empower "minorities" and build on privileged students' minimal experience of otherization to help them imagine alternative subject positions and divergent social desires.[53] An experimental pedagogy could thus embody multicultural ideals in symbolic forms. Since cultural identity, as Stuart Hall has pointed out, is a matter of "becoming" as well as "being," belonging to the future as well as the past,[54] multicultural media studies could provide a nurturing space where the secret hopes of social life are played out, a laboratory for the safe articulation of identity oppressions and utopias, a space of community fantasies and imagined alliances. Media pedagogy of this kind joins and parallels the realm of "indigenous media" as a means for "reproducing and transforming cultural identity among people who have experienced massive political, geographic, and economic disruption."[55] Speaking of the camcorder activism of the Kayapo in Brazil, Terence Turner stresses how their video work concentrates not on the retrieval of an idealized precontact past but on the processes of identity construction in the present. The Kayapo use video to communicate between villages, to record and thus perpetuate their own ceremonies and rituals, to record the official promises of Euro-Brazilian politicians and thus hold them accountable, and to disseminate their cause around the world in what Turner calls a "synergy between video media, Kayapo self-representation, and Kayapo ethnic self-consciousness."[56] Just as people all over the world have turned to cultural identity as a means of mobilizing the defense of their social, political, and economic interests, multicultural media activism and pedagogy might serve to protect threatened identities or even create new identities, a participant not only in the public sphere assertion of particular cultures, but also in fostering the "collective human capacity for self-production."[57] We might see media in this sense as exercising a tribalizing power, as potentially increasing a community's ache (Yoruba for "power of realization") with art as the catalyst for an emergent community or coalition.

The example of indigenous media suggests that a radical, polycentric multiculturalism cannot simply be "nice" like a suburban barbecue to which a few token people of color are invited. Any substantive multiculturalism has to recognize the existential realities of pain, anger, and resentment, since the multiple cultures invoked by the term multiculturalism have not historically coexisted in relations of equality and mutual respect. It, therefore, is not merely a question of communicating across borders but of discerning the forces which generate the borders in the first place. Multiculturalism has to recognize not only difference but bitter, even irreconcilable difference. The Native American view of the land as a sacred and communal trust, as Vine Deloria points out, is simply not reconcilable with a view of land as alienable property.[58] The descendants of the slave ships and the descendants of the immigrant ships cannot look at the Washington Monument, or Ellis Island, through exactly the same viewfinder. But these gaps in perception do not preclude alliances, dialogical coalitions, intercommunal identifications and affinities. Multiculturalism and the critique of

Eurocentrism, we have tried to show, are inseparable concepts; each becomes impoverished without the other. Multiculturalism without the critique of Eurocentrism runs the risk of being merely accretive — a shopping mall boutique summa of the world's cultures while the critique of Eurocentrism without multiculturalism runs the risk of simply inverting existing hierarchies rather than profoundly rethinking and unsettling them.

Notes

1 This essay is based largely on selected passages from our forthcoming book, *Unthinking Eurocentrism: Multiculturalism and the Media* (New York: Routledge, 1994).

2 Hugh Trevor-Roper, *The Rise of Christian Europe* (New York: Harcourt Brace Javonivich, 1965), p. 9.

3 For Roger Kimball, multiculturalism implies "... an attack on the ... idea that, despite our many differences, we hold in common an intellectual, artistic, and moral legacy, descending largely from the Greeks and the Bible [which] preserves us from chaos and barbarism. And it is precisely this legacy that the multiculturalist wishes to dispense with." See Roger Kimball, *Tenured Radicals: How Politics Has Corrupted Higher Education* (New York: Harper Collins, 1990), postscript.

4 The world map designed by German historian Arno Peters corrects the distortions of traditional maps. The text on the map, distributed by the UN Development Programme, Friendship Press, NY, points out that traditional maps privilege the Northern hemisphere (which occupies two-thirds of the map), that they make Alaska look larger than Mexico (when, in fact, Mexico is larger), Greenland larger than China (although China is four times larger), Scandinavia larger than India (which is, in fact, three times larger than Scandinavia).

5 The phrase "the West and the Rest" to the best of our knowledge, goes back to Chinweizu's *The West and the Rest of Us: White Predators, Black Slaves and the African Elite* (New York: Random House, 1975). It is also used in *Formations of Modernity*, eds Stuart Hall and Bram Giebe, (Cambridge: Polity Press, 1992).

6 See Jacques Derrida, *De la Grammatologie* (Paris: Minuit, 1967), p. 168.

7 Barbara Christian, from a paper presented at the "Gender and Colonialism Conference" at University of California, Berkeley (October 1989).

8 Talal Asad, "A Comment on Aijaz Ahmad's *In Theory*," *Public Culture*, 6, 1 (Fall 1993).

9 Samuel Johnson, "The World Displayed," quoted in the Yale edition of *The Works of Samuel Johnson*, Vol. 10, *The Political Writings*, ed. Donald J. Greene (New Haven, CT: Yale University Press, 1977), p. 421.

10 Adam Smith, *The Wealth of Nations* (New York: Random House, 1937), p. 590.

11 Thomas Jefferson, similarly, called in his own time for the study of Native American culture and languages in schools, yet the multiculturalist's call for a "curriculum of inclusion" is caricatured as "therapy for minorities." On Jefferson's interest in Native Americans, see Donald A. Grinde Jr and Bruce E. Johansen, *Exemplar of Liberty:*

Native America and the Evolution of Democracy (Los Angeles: American Indian Studies Center, 1991).

12 The phrase "intercommunalism," to the best of our knowledge, was first used by the Black Panthers.

13 See Y. N. Bly's *The Anti-Social Contract* (Atlanta: Clarity Press, 1989).

14 Samir Amin speaks of economic polycentrism in similar terms in his book *Delinking: Towards a Polycentric World* (London: Zed, 1985).

15 For a similar view, see Joan Scott, "Multiculturalism and the Politics of Identity," *October,* 61 (Summer 1992), pp. 12–19; and Stuart Hall, "Minimal Selves," in *Identity: The Real Me,* ed. Lisa Appignanesi (London: ICA, 1987), pp. 44–6.

16 Tom Moylan, *Demand the Impossible: Science Fiction and the Utopian Imagination* (New York: Methuen, 1986), p. 213.

17 See Jan Pietersie's chapter on "Colonialism and Popular Culture" in his book *White on Black* (New Haven, CT: Yale, 1992), p. 77.

18 Joseph Bristow, *Empire Boys: Adventures in a Man's World* (London: Harper Collins, 1991) p.19.

19 Haile Gerima, interview with Paul Willemen, *Framework,* 7–8 (Spring 1978), p. 32.

20 Frantz Fanon, *Black Skin, White Masks* (New York: Grove Press, 1967), pp. 152–3.

21 For more on the "mobilized gaze" of the cinema, see Anne Friedberg's discussion in *Window Shopping: Cinema and the Postmodern* (Berkeley: University of California Press, 1993).

22 Salman Rushdie, "Outside the Whale," in his book *Imaginary Homelands* (London: Penguin, 1992).

23 The words are John McClure's, from *Late Imperial Romance* (London: Verso, 1994).

24 Donna Haraway, "Situated Knowledge: The Science Question in Feminism and the Privilege of Partial Perspective," included in her *Simians, Cyborgs and Women* (London: Free Association Books, 1990), p. 188.

25 We focus here on the mechanisms of promoting identification; we do not suggest that these mechanisms were experienced in identical ways by, for example, Baghdadis or New Yorkers, Kuwaitis or Israelis, Christians or Muslims, leftists or rightists. Although the experience of war is mediated, there are differences within spectatorship. These spectatorial differences will be the subject of the last chapter in our book, *Unthinking Eurocentrism.*

26 See Paul Virilio, *War and Cinema: The Logistics of Perception* (London: Verso, 1989).

27 J. M. Blaut, "The Theory of Cultural Racism," *Antipode,* 24, 4 (1992), pp. 153–213.

28 Bill Bigelow, "Discovering Columbus, Rereading the Past," in "Rethinking Columbus," a special quincentenary issue of *Rethinking Schools* (1991).

29 See Hans Konig, *Columbus, His Enterprise: Exploding the Myth* (New York: Monthly Review Press, 1976), pp. 29–30.

30 See Bernard Weinraub, "It's Columbus Against Columbus, with a Fortune in Profits at Stake," *New York Times* (May 21, 1992), p. C17.

31 For a similar critique of the Ridley Scott film, see Andrew Cornell's review in *Turtle Quarterly* (Winter 1993).

32 For a critical analysis of Alvar Nunez' and other Spanish accounts of the Conquest, see Beatriz Pastor, *Discurso Narrativo de la Conquista de America* (Havana: Casa de las Americas, 1983).

33 Quoted in Stephen Greenblatt, *Marvelous Possessions: The Wonder of the New World* (Chicago: The University of Chicago Press, 1991), p. 141.

34 From Hector St John de Crevecoeur, *Letters from an American Farmer*, quoted in James Axtell, *The European and the Indian: Essays in the Ethnohistory of Colonial North America* (New York: Oxford, 1981), p. 172.

35 Lecture, New York University, October 9, 1992.

36 In Quechua, *tupac* means the "real thing," while *amaru* refers to "serpent." "Tupac Amaru" is also the name of a rap group denounced by Dan Quayle.

37 We are indebted to Miriam Yataco and Euridice Arataia for their interpretations of the film in the light of Andean cosmology. For more on the *Inkarri*, see Gordon Brotherston, *Book of the Fourth World: Reading the Native Americans Through Their Literature* (Cambridge: Cambridge University Press, 1992).

38 We would like to thank Emperatriz Arreaza-Camero for providing us with a videotape of *Cubagua*. Her essay "*Cubagua*, or the Search for Venezuelan National Identity," provides a historically-informed, in-depth study of the film. See *Iowa Journal of Cultural Studies* (1993).

39 *Egungun*, as practiced in Brazil, calls up representations of male ancestors. It was founded, interestingly, as a response to the preponderant role of women in candomble. For a documentary presentation of Egungun, see the Carlos Brasbladt film entitled, simply, *Egungun*.

40 Quoted in Brian V. Street, *The Savage in Literature* (London: RKP, 1975), p. 99.

41 Georges-Louis Leclerc de Buffon, *The History of Man and Quadrupeds*, tr. William Smellie (London: T. Cadell and W. Davies, 1812), p. 422. Quoted in Todorov, *On Human Diversity* (Cambridge: Harvard University Press, 1992), p. 105.

42 George Mosse, *Toward the Final Solution: A History of European Racism* (London: Dent, 1978), p. 44.

43 Stuart Hall, "What is this 'Black' in Black Popular Culture?" in *Black Popular Culture,* ed. Gina Dent (Seattle: Bay Press, 1992), p. 27.

44 Kobena Mercer, "Black Hair/Style Politics," *New Formations,* 3 (Winter 1987), pp. 33–54.

45 The lyrics are cited in Spike Lee (with Lisa Jones), *Uplift the Race: The Construction of School Daze* (New York: Simon and Schuster, 1988).

46 Kobena Mercer, "Black Hair/Style Politics."

47 Not surprisingly, the film has been screened in museums and churches, and even for social workers and hair stylists, as a provocative contemplation of the intersection of fashion, politics, and identity.

48 We would like here to call attention to the Media Alternatives Project (MAP), established in 1990 to introduce multicultural perspectives into American history teaching through the use of independent film/video. See B. Abrash and C. Egan, eds, *Mediating History: The Map Guide to Independent Video* (New York: NYU Press, 1992).

49 Manthia Diawara, "Black Studies, Cultural Studies: Performative Acts," *Afterimage,* 20, 3 (October 1992).

50 For more on Brazilian popular music, see Charles Perrone, *Masters of Contemporary Brazilian Song: MPB 1965–1985* (Austin: University of Texas, 1989); and Robert Stam, *Subversive Pleasures: Bakhtin, Cultural Criticism, and Film* (Baltimore: John Hopkins University Press, 1988).

51 Jeff Decker develops the notion of rap artists as "organic intellectuals" in his "The State of Rap," *Social Text,* 34 (1993). The expression strikes me as equally if not more appropriate to the Brazilian artists mentioned here. The Brazilian artists have also avoided the homophobia and misogyny that often have marred rap music.

52 See Rhonda Hammer and Peter McLaren, "The Spectacularization of Subjectivity: Media Knowledges, Global Citizenry and the New World Order," *Polygraph,* 5 (1992), pp. 46–66.

53 Charles Ramirez Berg makes this suggestion in his extremely useful essay "Analyzing Latino Stereotypes," in *Multicultural Media in the Classroom,* eds Lester Friedman and Diane Carson (Urbana: University of Illinois Press, 1992).

54 Stuart Hall, "Cultural Identity and Cinematic Representation," *Framework,* 36 (1989), pp. 68–81.

55 Faye Ginsburg, "Indigenous Media: Faustian Contract or Global Village?" *Cultural Anthropology,* 6, 1 (February 1991), p. 94.

56 Terence Turner, "Defiant Images: the Kayapo Appropriation of Video," Forman Lecture, RAI Festival of Film and Video, Manchester 1992.

57 Terence Turner, "Anthropology and Multiculturalism: What is Anthropology that Multiculturalists Should Be Mindful of It?" [Ch. 19 in this volume — ed.]

58 Interview with Vine Deloria in the film *Savagery and the American Indian.*

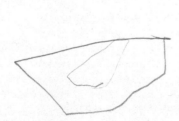

15

Insurgent Multiculturalism and the Promise of Pedagogy

HENRY A. GIROUX

Introduction

Multiculturalism has become a central discourse in the struggle over issues regarding national identity, the construction of historical memory, the purpose of schooling, and the meaning of democracy. While most of these battles have been waged in the university around curriculum changes and in polemic exchanges in the public media, today's crucial culture wars increasingly are being fought on two fronts. First, multiculturalism has become a "tug of war over who gets to create public culture."[1] Second, the contested terrain of multiculturalism is heating up between educational institutions that do not meet the needs of a massively shifting student population and students and their families for whom schools increasingly are perceived as merely one more instrument of repression.

In the first instance, the struggle over public culture is deeply tied to a historical legacy that affirms American character and national identity in terms that are deeply exclusionary, nativist, and racist. Echoes of this racism can be heard in the voices of public intellectuals such as George Will, Arthur Schlesinger Jr, and George Gilder. Institutional support for such racism can be found in neoconservative establishments such as the Olin Foundation and the National Association of Scholars.

In the second instance, academic culture has become a contested space primarily because groups that have been traditionally excluded from the public school curriculum and from the ranks of higher education are now becoming more politicized and are attending higher education institutions in increasing numbers. One consequence of this developing politics of difference has been a series of struggles by subordinate groups over access to educational resources, gender and cial equity, curriculum content, and the disciplinary-based organization of academic departments.

While it has become commonplace to acknowledge the conflicting meanings of multiculturalism, it is important to acknowledge that in its conservative and liberal forms multiculturalism has placed the related problems of white racism, social justice, and power off limits, especially as these might be addressed as part of a broader set of political and pedagogical concerns. In what follows, I want to reassert the importance of making the pedagogical more political. That is, I want to analyze how a broader definition of pedagogy can be used to address how the production of knowledge, social identities, and social relations might challenge the racist assumptions and practices that inform a variety of cultural sites, including but not limited to the public and private spheres of schooling. Central to this approach is an attempt to define the pedagogical meaning of what I will call an insurgent multiculturalism. This is not a multiculturalism that is limited to a fascination with the construction of identities, communicative competence, and the celebration of tolerance. Instead, I want to shift the discussion of multiculturalism to a pedagogical terrain in which relations of power and racialized identities become paramount as part of a language of critique and possibility.

In part, this suggests constructing "an educational politics that would reveal the structures of power relations at work in the racialization of our social order" while simultaneously encouraging students to "think about the invention of the category of whiteness as well as that of blackness and, consequently, to make visible what is rendered invisible when viewed as the normative state of existence: the (white) point in space from which we tend to identify difference."[2] As part of a language of critique, a central concern of an insurgent multiculturalism is to strip white supremacy of its legitimacy and authority. As part of a project of possibility, an insurgent multiculturalism is about developing a notion of radical democracy around differences that are not exclusionary and fixed, but that designate sites of struggle that are open, fluid, and that will provide the conditions for expanding the heterogeneity of public spaces and the possibility for "critical dialogues across different political communities and constituencies."[3]

Multiculturalism and White Racism

If ... one managed to change the curriculum in all the schools so that [Afro-Americans] learned more about themselves and their real contributions to this culture, you would be liberating not only [Afro-Americans], you'd be liberating white people who know nothing about their own history. And the reason is that if you are compelled to lie about one aspect of anybody's history, you must lie about it all. If you have to lie about my real role here, if you have to pretend that I hoed all that cotton just because I loved you, then you have done something to yourself. You are mad.[4]

What James Baldwin, the renowned Afro-American novelist, is suggesting in the most immediate sense is that issues concerning multiculturalism are fundamentally about questions of race and identity. A more penetrating analysis reveals that multiculturalism is not only about the discourse of racialized identities, but is also fundamentally about the issue of whiteness as a mark of racial and gender privilege. For example, Baldwin argues that multiculturalism cannot be reduced to an exclusive otherness that references Afro-Americans, Hispanics, Latinos, or other suppressed "minorities," as either a problem to be resolved through the call for benevolent assimilation or as a threat to be policed and eliminated. For Baldwin, multiculturalism is primarily about whiteness and its claims to a self-definition that excludes the messy relations of race, ethnicity, power, and identity. Baldwin highlights how differences in power and privilege authorize who speaks, how fully, under what conditions, against what issues, for whom, and with what degree of consistent, institutionalized support. In this sense, multiculturalism raises the question of whether people are speaking within or outside a privileged space, and whether such spaces provide the conditions for different groups to listen to each other differently to address how the racial economies of privilege and power work in American society.

I want to argue that educators need to rethink the politics of multiculturalism as part of a broader attempt to engage the world of public and global politics. This suggests challenging the narratives of national identity, culture, and ethnicity as part of a pedagogical effort to provide dominant groups with the knowledge and histories to examine, acknowledge, and unlearn their own privilege. But more is needed in this view of multiculturalism than deconstructing the centers of colonial power and undoing the master narratives of racism. A viable multicultural pedagogy and politics must also affirm cultural differences while simultaneously refusing to essentialize and grant immunity to those groups that speak from subordinate positions of power. As Graff and Robbins point out, the most progressive aspect of multiculturalism "has been not to exalt group 'particularism' but to challenge it, to challenge the belief that blackness, femaleness, or Africanness are essential, unchanging qualities."[5]

Within the current historical conjuncture, the struggles over national identity, race, and what it means to be an "American" have taken place largely within discussions that focus on questions of self- and social representation. While a politics of representation is indispensable in creating a multicultural and multiracial society, educators must also address the systemic, structural changes that are needed to produce such a social order. In part, this demands an approach to multiculturalism that addresses "the context of massive black unemployment, overcrowded schools, a lack of recreational facilities, dilapidated housing and racist policing."[6] Cornel West builds upon this position by arguing that white

America needs to address the nihilism that permeates black communities in the United States. He defines such nihilism as "the lived experience of coping with a life of horrifying meaninglessness, hopelessness, and (most important) lovelessness."[7] In this scenario, the black community is depicted as a culture that has lost the moral strength, hope, and resistance once provided by the institutions of black civil society: "black families, neighborhoods, schools, churches, mosques."[8]

I want to extend West's argument and suggest that if the depiction of black nihilism is not to reproduce the culture of poverty thesis made popular among conservatives, then educators must attempt to understand how white institutions, ethnicity, and public life is structured through a nihilism that represents another type of moral disorder, impoverishment of the spirit, and decline of public life. In this analysis, cultural criticism moves from a limited emphasis on the effects of racism and the workings of black nihilism to the origins of racism in the political, social, and cultural dynamics of white "supremacy." More specifically, a critical multiculturalism must shift attention away from an exclusive focus on subordinate groups, especially since such an approach tends to highlight their deficits, to one that examines how racism in its various forms is produced historically, semiotically, and institutionally at various levels of society. This is not meant to suggest that blacks and other subordinate groups do not face problems that need to be addressed in the discourse of multiculturalism. On the contrary, it means that a critical analysis of race must move beyond the discourse of blaming the victim in which whites view multiculturalism as a code word for black lawlessness and other "problems" blacks create for white America. Viewing black people in this manner reveals not only white supremacy as the discursive and institutional face of racism, but it also presents us with the challenge of addressing racial issues not as a dilemma of black people but as a problem endemic to the legacy colonialism rooted in "historical inequalities and longstanding cultural stereotypes."[9]

In opposition to a quaint liberalism, a critical multiculturalism means more than simply acknowledging differences and analyzing stereotypes; more fundamentally, it means understanding, engaging, and transforming the diverse histories, cultural narratives, representations, and institutions that produce racism and other forms of discrimination. As bell hooks points out, for too long white people have imagined that they are invisible to black people. Not only does whiteness in this formulation cease to mark the locations of its own privileges, it reinforces relations in which blacks become invisible in terms of how they name, see, experience, and bear the pain and terror of whiteness. hooks puts it succinctly:

> In white supremacist society, white people can "safely" imagine that they are invisible to black people since the power they have historically asserted, and even now collectively assert over black people, accorded them the right to control the black gaze....[And yet] to name that whiteness in the black imagination is often a representation of terror. One must face written histories that erase and deny, that

reinvent the past to make the present vision of racial harmony and pluralism more plausible. To bear the burden of memory one must willingly journey to places long uninhabited, searching the debris of history for traces of the unforgettable, all knowledge of which has been suppressed.[10]

It is worth noting that many educational commentators who address the issue of multiculturalism have ruled out any discussion of the relationship between race and class and how they are manifested within networks of hierarchy and subordination in and out of the schools. This particular silence, coupled with the popular perception bolstered by the media that recent racial disturbances and uprisings such as the rape of the female jogger in Central Park, the murder of Michael Jordan's father, and the LA uprising can be explained by pointing to those involved as simply thugs, looters, and criminals, makes it clear why the multicultural peril is often seen as a black threat; it suggests what such a belief shares with the dominant ideological view of the "other" as a disruptive outsider. In this scenario, multiculturalism is seen as an impediment rather than an essential condition for the survival of democratic public life.

To understand fully the conservative response to multiculturalism, it is crucial to situate the debates around the politics of cultural difference within the broader assault on democracy that has taken place in the last decade. But before I address this issue, I want to suggest that public schooling and higher education are crucial sites in which the relationship between multiculturalism and democracy should be acknowledged and incorporated into the curriculum. A democratic or insurgent multiculturalism is one that offers a new language for students and others to move between disciplinary borders and to travel within zones of cultural difference. This is a language that challenges the boundaries of cultural and racial difference as sites of exclusion and discrimination while simultaneously rewriting the script of cultural difference as part of a broader attempt to expand and deepen the imperatives of a multicultural and multiracial democracy.

An insurgent multiculturalism takes as its starting point the question of what it means for educators and cultural workers to treat schools and other public sites as border institutions in which teachers, students, and others engage in daily acts of cultural translation and negotiation. For it is within such institutions that students and teachers are offered the opportunity to become border crossers, to recognize that schooling is really an introduction to how culture is organized, a demonstration of who is authorized to speak about particular forms of culture, what culture is considered worthy of valorization, and what forms of culture are considered invalid and unworthy of public esteem. Drawing upon Homi Bhabha, I want to contend that schools, in part, need to be understood as sites engaged in the "strategic activity of 'authorizing' agency," of exercising authority "to articulate and regulate incommensurable meanings and identities."[11] Within this perspective, pedagogy is removed from its exclusive emphasis on management and is defined as a form of political leadership and ethical address. The pedagogical imperative here is to weigh cultural differences against the implications they have for practices that disclose rather than mystify, democratize culture rather than close it off, and provide the conditions for people to believe that they can take risks and change existing power relations. Translated into a critical pedagogical practice, multiculturalism pluralizes the spaces for exchange, understanding, and identity formation among a variety of dominant and subordinate groups. It is precisely because of the possibility of rewriting dominant cultural narratives and social relations that multiculturalism appears so threatening to conservatives and liberals. One of the most frank expressions of this position came from the 1975 Trilateral Commission report *The Crisis of Democracy* which boldly alleged that a substantive democracy represents an unwarranted challenge to government authority and existing configurations of power. Viewed in this context, the current assault on multiculturalism must be understood as a part of a broader assault on democracy itself.

Multiculturalism and the Perils of Democracy

Within the last decade, cultural authority and legislative policy have combined to extend massively the influence of domination to increasing numbers of subordinate groups in America. In the face of escalating poverty, increasing racism, growing unemployment among "minorities," and the failure of an expanding number of Americans to receive adequate health care and education, the Reagan/Bush administrations invoked a wooden morality coupled with a disdain for public life by blaming the nation's ills on the legislation of the Great Society, TV sitcom characters such as Murphy Brown, and the alleged breakdown of family values. Within this scenario, poverty is caused by the poverty of values, racism is seen as a "black" problem (lawlessness), and social decay is rectified by shoring up the nuclear family and social relations of the alleged free market.

Abandoning its responsibility for political and moral leadership, the federal government, during the last decade, reduced its intervention in public life to waging war against Iraq, using taxpayers' money to bail out corrupt bankers, and slashing legislation that would benefit the poor, the homeless, and the disadvantaged. There is a tragic irony at work when a government can raise 500 billion dollars to bail out corrupt bankers and 50 billion to fight a war in Iraq (put in perspective, the combined costs of these adventures exceeds the cost of World War II, including veterans benefits) while at the same time that same government cuts back food stamp and school lunch programs in a country in which nearly one out of every four children under six live in poverty. But there is more at stake here than simply the failure of moral and political leadership. The breadth and depth of democratic relations are being rolled back at all levels of national and daily life. For example, this is seen in the growing disparity between the rich and poor, the ongoing attacks by the government and courts on civil rights and the welfare system, and the proliferating incidents of racist harassment and violence on college and public school sites.

The retreat from democracy is evident also in the absence of serious talk about how as a nation, we might educate existing and future generations of students in the language and practice of moral compassion, critical agency, and public service. The discourse of leadership appears trapped in a terminology in which the estimate of a good society is expressed in indices that measure profit margins and the Dow Jones Average. Missing in this vocabulary is a way of nourishing and sustaining a popular perception of democracy as something that needs to be constantly struggled for in public arenas such as the schools, churches, and other sites which embody the promise of a multiracial and multicultural democracy.

This current assault on democratic public life has taken a new turn in the last few years. At one level, American conservatives have initiated a long-term project of discrediting and dismantling those institutions, ideologies, and practices that are judged incompatible with the basic ideology of the market place with its unswerving commitment to the principles of individualism, choice, and the competitive ethic. Accompanying this attempt has been a parallel effort to reprivatize and deregulate schools, health care, the welfare system, and other public services and institutions.

Part of the attempt to rewrite the terms of a discourse of democratic public life can be seen in the emergence of a new breed of intellectuals, largely backed by conservative think tanks such as the Madison Group, the Hoover Institute, Heritage Foundation, and a host of other conservative foundations. With access to enormous cultural resources infused by massive financial backing from the Olin, Scaife, and Smith Richardson foundations, right-wing think tanks have begun to mount mammoth public campaigns to promote their cultural revolution. Many of the major right-wing intellectuals who have helped to shape popular discourse about educational reform in the last decade have received extensive aid from the conservative foundations. These include intellectuals such as Diane Ravitch, Chester Finn Jr, Dinish D'Souza, and Thomas Sowell; all of whom have targeted public schools and higher education as two principal spheres of struggle over issues of curricula reform, privatization, choice, and difference. To understand the model of leadership these intellectuals provide, it is important to examine how some of their underlying ideological concerns relate to the broader issues of democracy, race, and public accountability.

For many conservatives, the utopian possibility of cultural democracy has become dangerous at the current historical conjuncture for a number of reasons. Most important, cultural democracy encourages a language of critique for understanding and transforming those relations that trap people in networks of hierarchy and exploitation. That is, it provides normative referents for recognizing and assessing competing political vocabularies, the visions of the future they presuppose, and the social identities and practices they produce and legitimate. Clearly, such a position poses a challenge to right-wing educators whose celebration of choice and the logic of the market place often abstracts freedom from equality and the imperatives of citizenship from its historical grounding in the public institutions of modern society.

In fact, many conservatives have been quite aggressive in rewriting the discourse of citizenship *not* as the practice of social responsibility but as a privatized act of altruism, self-help, or philanthropy. It is crucial to recognize that within this language of privatization, the disquieting, disrupting, interrupting difficulties of sexism, crime, youth unemployment, AIDS, and other social problems, and how they bear down on schools and subordinated groups, are either ignored or summarily dismissed as individual problems caused, in part, by the people who are victimized by them. This position accentuates individual character flaws and behavioral impediments to economic and social mobility to elide the political and economic conditions that produces the context of victimization and the systemic pressures and limits that must be addressed to overcome it. By focusing on the privatized language of individual character, conservatives erase the moral and political obligation of individuals, groups, and institutions to recognize their complicity in creating the racial problems that multicultural critics have addressed. In this scenario, we end up with a vision of leadership in which individuals act in comparative isolation and without any sense of public accountability. This is why many right-wing educators praise the virtues of the competition and choice but rarely talk about how money and power, when unevenly distributed, influence "whether people have the means or the capacity" to make or act on choices that inform their daily lives.[12]

Choice in this case serves to rewrite the discourse of freedom within a limited conception of individual needs and desires. What disappears from this view of leadership is the willingness to recognize that the fundamental issues of citizenship, democracy, and public life can neither be understood nor addressed solely within the restricted language of the marketplace or choice. Choice and the market are not the sole conditions of freedom, nor are they adequate to constituting political subjects within the broader discourses of justice, equality, and community. In fact, no understanding of community, citizenship, or public culture is possible without a shared conception of social justice, yet it is precisely the notion of social justice that is missing in mainstream discussions of multiculturalism and school reform.

Conservatives not only view multiculturalism as a threat to national identity, they have actively attempted to remove it from the language of community and social justice. Rather than asserting the primacy of the ethical in responding to the suffering of subordinated groups in America's schools and other social institutions, conservatives have developed educational and public policies that expand cost-benefit analyses and market relations at the expense of addressing major social problems such as racism, poverty, crime, and unemployment. For example, it is worth noting that 45 per cent of all "minority" children live in poverty while the dropout rate among "minority" students has attained truly alarming proportions, reaching as high as 70 per cent in some major urban areas. These problems are compounded by an unemployment rate among black youth that is currently 38.4 per cent. In the face of these problems, conservatives are aggressively attempting to enact choice legislation that would divert funds away from the public schools to private schools. Against these efforts, it is worth noting, as Peter Drier, points out that:

> since 1980 the federal government has slashed successful urban programs — public works, economic development, health and nutrition, schools, housing, and job training — by more than 70 per cent.... In 1980, federal dollars accounted for 14.3 per cent of city budgets; today, the federal share is less then five per cent.... To avert fiscal collapse, many cities have been closing schools, hospitals, police and fire stations; laying off of essential employees; reducing such basic services as maintenance of parks and roads; neglecting housing and health codes, and postponing or canceling capital improvements.[13]

The claim by conservatives that these problems can be solved by raising test scores, promoting choice, developing a national curriculum, and creating a uniform standard of national literacy is cruel and mean-spirited. But, of course, this is where the discourse of critical democracy becomes subversive; it makes visible the political and normative considerations that frame such reforms. It also offers a referent for analyzing how the language of excessive individualism and competitiveness serves to make social inequality invisible, promoting an indifference to human misery, exploitation, and suffering. Moreover, it suggests that the language of excellence and individualism when abstracted from considerations of equality and social justice serves to restrict rather than animate the possibilities of democratic public life. Increasingly, conservatives also have used the language of individual rights; that is, the right of individuals to think and act as they please, to attack any discourse or program that questions the existence of social inequalities. As Joan Scott points out, there is more at stake here than what the conservatives call the existence of dangerous orthodoxies in the university.

> We are experiencing another phase of the ongoing Reagan–Bush revolution which, having packed the courts and privatized the economy, now seeks to neutralize the space of ideological and cultural nonconformity by discrediting it. This is the context within which debates about political correctness and multiculturalism have taken shape.[14]

Rather than engage the growing insistence on the part of more and more groups in this country to define themselves around the specificity of class, gender, race, ethnicity, or sexual orientation, conservatives have committed themselves simply to resisting and subverting these developments. While conservatives rightly recognize that struggles over the public school curriculum and the canon in higher education are fueled, in part, over anxiety about the issue of national identity, they engage this issue from a largely defensive posture and in doing so appear to lack any understanding of how the curriculum itself is implicated in producing relations of inequality, domination, and oppression. For example, even moderate liberals who adopt a conservative stance on multicultural issues resort to rhetorical swipes that share ideological ground with nativist writing against Catholics and immigrants in the 1920s. For example, Schlesinger refers to the multiculturalists in the United States as part of an "ethnic upsurge" that threatens to become a full-fledged counterrevolution against the alleged common culture and the "American ideal of assimilation."[15] Schlesinger is quite clear, as are many of his conservative allies, that as soon as public schools refuse to serve as vehicles for cultural assimilation, they have betrayed their most important historically-sanctioned role. Unfortunately, Schlesinger does not see anything wrong with the schools producing social identities in which cultural differences are seen as a deficit rather than a strength. That the assimilation model of schooling maintains its hegemony through the racist, class-specific dynamics of tracking and cultural discrimination appears to Schlesinger to be unworthy of critical attention. When critical multiculturalists criticize how the curriculum through a process of exclusion and inclusion privileges some groups over others, such critics are summarily dismissed as being political, partisan, and radically anti-American by critics such as Schlesinger.

It is difficult to imagine what is either unpatriotic or threatening about subordinate groups attempting to raise questions such as: "Whose experiences, histories, knowledge, and arts are represented in our educational and cultural institutions? How fully, on whose terms, and with what degree of ongoing, institutionalized participation and power?"[16] Nor in a democratic society should subordinate groups attempting to fashion a pedagogy and politics of inclusion and cultural democracy be derisively labeled as particularistic because they have raised serious questions regarding how the canon and public school curriculum work to secure specific forms of cultural authority or how the dynamics of cultural power works to silence and marginalize specific groups of students. Responding to these concerns, academic conservatives such as William Kerrigan simply recycle their own beliefs about the superiority of the established canon without revealing the slightest element of self criticism. Kerrigan argues that "an undergraduate education that *saddles* (my emphasis) students with 'cultural diversity' requirements encourages them to flit incoherently from this concentration to that major."[17] That the knowledge that constitutes the academic disciplines is neither universal nor the highest expression of scholarship given its exclusion of women and "minorities" does not seem to bother Kerrigan. In this case, the claims that subordinate groups make upon the shaping of cultural memory and the promise of democratic pluralism are dismissed by Kerrigan through the arrogant, self-serving assertion that "educators have become pathologically sensitive to complaints of ethnocentrism. Rather than elevating the minds of students from historically oppressed groups, the whole educational system is sinking."[18] This emerging critique of schools and other cultural institutions is based on the elitist and racist assumptions that the enemy of democracy is not intolerance, structured inequality, and social injustice, but cultural differences.

In treating cultural narrative and national history in fixed and narrow terms, conservatives relinquish one of the most important defining principles of any democracy; that is, they ignore the necessity of a democratic society to rejuvenate itself by constantly reexamining the strengths and limits of its traditions. In the absence of a critical encounter with the past and a recognition of the importance of cultural diversity, multiculturalism becomes acceptable only if it is reduced to a pedagogy of reverence and transmission rather than a pedagogical practice that puts people in dialogue with each other as part of a broader attempt to fashion a renewed interest in cultural democracy and the creation of engaged and critical citizens. Bhikhu Parekh rightly argues that such an uncritical stance defines what he calls demagogic multiculturalism. For Parekh, the traditionalists' refusal of cultural hybridity and differences and the fixity of identity and culture promotes a dangerous type of fundamentalism. He writes:

> When a group feels besieged and afraid of losing its past in exchange for a nebulous future, it lacks the courage to critically reinterpret its fundamental principles, lest it opens the door to "excessive" reinterpretation. It then turns its fundamentals into fundamentalism, it declares them inviolate and reduces them to a neat and easily enforceable package of beliefs and rituals.[19]

Parekh's fear of demagogic multiculturalism represents a pedagogical problem as much as it does a political one. The political issue is exemplified in the conservative view that critical multiculturalism with its assertion of multiple identities and diverse cultural traditions represents a threat to democracy. As I have mentioned previously, the fatal political transgression committed here lies in the suggestion that social criticism itself is fundamentally at odds with democratic life. Indeed, this is more than mere rhetoric, it is a challenge to the very basic principles that inform a democratic society. Pedagogically, demagogic multiculturalism renders any debate about the relationship between democracy and cultural difference moot. By operating out of a suffocating binarism that pits "us" against "them" conservatives annul the possibility for dialogue, education, understanding, and negotiation. In other words, such a position offers no language for contending with cultures whose boundaries cross over into diverse spheres that are fluid and saturated with power. How this type of fundamentalism will specifically impact the schools can be seen in the increased calls for censorship as well as in the bleaching of the curriculum to exclude or underrepresent the voices and histories of various subordinate groups.

Instead of responding to the increasing diversity of histories, ethnicities, and cultures complexly layered over time, dominant institutions and discourses appear increasingly indifferent to the alarming poverty, shameful school dropout rate, escalating unemployment and a host of other problems that accentuate the alienation, inequality, and racial segregation that fuel the sense of desperation, hopelessness, and disempowerment felt by many "minorities" in the United States. It appears morally careless and politically irresponsible to define multiculturalism as exclusively disruptive and antithetical to the most fundamental aspects of American democracy. Such a position fails to explore the potential that multiculturalism has as a critical referent for linking diversity and cultural democracy while simultaneously serving to ignore the social, economic, and political conditions that have spurned the current insurgency among "minorities" and others around the issue of multiculturalism.

Toward an Insurgent Multiculturalism

To make a claim for multiculturalism is not … to suggest a juxtaposition of several cultures whose frontiers remain intact, nor is it to subscribe to a bland "melting-pot" type of attitude that would level all differences. It lies instead, in the intercultural acceptance of risks, unexpected detours, and complexities of relation between break and closure.[20]

Multiculturalism like another broadly signifying term is multiaccentual and must be adamantly challenged when defined as part of the discourse of domination or essentialism. The challenge the term presents is daunting given the way in which it has been appropriated by various mainstream and orthodox positions. For example, when defined in corporate terms it generally is reduced to a message without critical content. Liberals have used multiculturalism to denote a pluralism devoid of historical contextualization and the specificities of relations of power or they have depicted a view of cultural struggle in which the most fundamental contradictions "implicating race, class, and gender can be harmonized within the prevailing structure of power relation."[21] For many conservatives, multiculturalism has come to signify a disruptive, unsettling, and dangerous force in American society. For some critics, it has been taken up as a slogan for promoting an essentializing identity politics and various forms of nationalism. In short, multiculturalism can be defined through a variety of ideological constructs, and signifies a terrain of struggle around the reformation of historical memory, national identity, self- and social representation, and the politics of difference.

Multiculturalism is too important as a political discourse to be exclusively appropriated by liberals and conservatives. This suggests that if the concept of multiculturalism is to become useful as a pedagogical concept, educators need to appropriate it as more than a tool for critical understanding and the pluralizing of differences; it must also be used as an ethical and political referent which allows teachers and students to understand how power works in the interest of dominant social relations, and how such relations can be challenged and transformed. In other words, an insurgent multiculturalism should promote pedagogical practices that offer the possibility for schools to become places where students and teachers can become border crossers engaged in critical and ethical reflection about what it means to bring a wider variety of cultures into dialogue with each other, to theorize about cultures in the plural, within rather than outside "antagonistic relations of domination and subordination."[22]

In opposition to the liberal emphasis on individual diversity, an insurgent multiculturalism also must address issues regarding group differences and how power relations function to structure racial and ethnic identities. Furthermore, cultural differences cannot be merely affirmed to be assimilated into a common culture or policed through economic, political, and social spheres that restrict full citizenship to dominant groups. If multiculturalism is to be linked to renewed interests in expanding the principles of democracy to wider spheres of application, it must be defined in pedagogical and political terms that embrace it as a referent and practice for civic courage, critical citizenship, and democratic struggle. Bhikhu Parekh provides a definition that appears to avoid a superficial pluralism and a notion of multiculturalism that is structured in dominance. He writes:

> Multiculturalism doesn't simply mean numerical plurality of different cultures, but rather a community which is creating, guaranteeing, encouraging spaces within which different communities are able to grow at their own pace. At the same time it means creating a public space in which these communities are able to interact, enrich the existing culture and create a new consensual culture in which they recognize reflections of their own identity.[23]

In this view, multiculturalism becomes more than a critical referent for interrogating the racist representations and practices of the dominant culture, it also provides a space in which the criticism of cultural practices is inextricably linked to the production of cultural spaces marked by the formation of new identities and pedagogical practices that offers a powerful challenge to the racist, patriarchal, and sexist principles embedded in American society and schooling. Within this discourse, curriculum is viewed as a hierarchical and representational system that selectively produces knowledge, identities, desires, and values. The notion that curriculum represents knowledge that is objective, value free, and beneficial to all students is challenged forcefully as it becomes clear that those who benefit from public schooling and higher education are generally white, middle-class students whose histories, experiences, language, and knowledge largely conform to dominant cultural codes and practices. Moreover, an insurgent multiculturalism performs a theoretical service by addressing curriculum as a form of cultural politics which demands linking the production and legitimation of classroom knowledge, social identities, and values to the institutional environments in which they are produced.

As part of a project of possibility, I want to suggest some general elements that might inform an insurgent multicultural curriculum. First, a multicultural curriculum must be informed by a new language in which cultural differences are taken up not as something to be tolerated but as essential to expanding the discourse and practice of democratic life. It is important to note that multiculturalism is not merely an ideological construct, it also refers to the fact that by the year 2010, people of color will be the numerical majority in the United States. This suggests that educators need to develop a language, vision, and curriculum in which multiculturalism and democracy become mutually reinforcing categories. At issue here is the task of reworking democracy as a pedagogical and cultural practice that contributes to what John Dewey once called the creation of an articulate public. Manning Marable defines some of the essential parameters of this task.

> Multicultural political democracy means that this country was not built by and for only one group — Western Europeans; that our country does not have only one language — English; or only one religion — Christianity; or only one economic philosophy — corporate capitalism. Multicultural democracy means that the leadership within our society should reflect the richness, colors and diversity expressed in the lives of all of our people. Multicultural democracy demands new types of power sharing and the reallocation of resources necessary to great economic and social development for those who have been systematically excluded and denied.[24]

Imperative to such a task is a reworking of the relationship between culture and power to avoid what Homi Bhabha has called "the subsumption or sublation of social antagonism ... the repression of social divisions ... and a representation of the social that naturalizes cultural difference and turns it into a 'second'-nature argument."[25]

Second, as part of an attempt to develop a multicultural and multiracial society consistent with the principles of a democratic society, educators must account for the fact that men and women of color are disproportionately underrepresented in the cultural and public institutions of this country. Pedagogically this suggests that a multicultural curriculum must provide students with the skills to analyze how various audio, visual, and print texts fashion social identities over time, and how these representations serve to reinforce, challenge, or rewrite dominant moral and political vocabularies that promote stereotypes that degrade people by depriving them of their history, culture, and identity.

This should not suggest that such a pedagogy should solely concentrate on how meanings produce particular stereotypes and the uses to which they are put. Nor should a multicultural politics of representation focus exclusively on producing positive images of subordinated groups by recovering and reconstituting elements of their suppressed histories. While such approaches can be pedagogically useful, it is crucial for critical educators to reject any approach to multiculturalism that affirms cultural differences in the name of an essentialized and separatist identity politics. Rather than recovering differences that sustain their self-representation through exclusions, educators need to demonstrate how differences collide, cross over, mutate, and transgress in their negotiations and struggles. Differences in this sense must be understood not through the fixity of place or the romanticization of an essentialized notion of history and experience but through the tropes of indeterminacy, flows, and translations. In this instance, multiculturalism can begin to formulate a politics of representation in which questions of access and cultural production are linked to what people do with the signifying regimes they use within historically-specific public spaces.

While such approaches are essential to giving up the quest for a pure historical tradition, it is imperative that a multicultural curriculum also focus on dominant, white institutions and histories to interrogate them in terms of their injustices and their contributions for "humanity." This means, as Cornel West points out that

to engage in a serious discussion of race in America, we must begin not with the problems of black people but with the flaws of American society — flaws rooted in historical inequalities and longstanding cultural stereotypes.... How we set up the terms for discussing racial issues shapes our perception and response to these issues. As long as black people are viewed as "them," the burden falls on blacks to do all the "cultural" and "moral" work necessary for healthy race relations. The implication is that only certain Americans can define what it means to be American — and the rest must simply "fit in."[26]

In this sense, multiculturalism is about making whiteness visible as a racial category; that is, it points to the necessity of providing white students with the cultural memories that enable them to recognize the historically- and socially-constructed nature of their own identities. Multiculturalism as a radical, cultural politics should attempt to provide white students (and others) with the self-definitions upon which they can recognize their own complicity with or resistance to how power works within and across differences to legitimate some voices and dismantle others. Of course, more is at stake here than having whites reflect critically on the construction of their own racial formation and their complicity in promoting racism. Equally important is the issue of making all students responsible for their practices, particularly as these serve either to undermine or expand the possibility for democratic public life.

Third, a multicultural curriculum must address how to articulate a relationship between unity and difference that moves beyond simplistic binarisms. That is, rather than defining multiculturalism against unity or simply for difference, it is crucial for educators to develop a unity-in-difference position in which new, hybrid forms of democratic representation, participation, and citizenship provide a forum for creating unity without denying the particular, multiple, and the specific. In this instance, the interrelationship of different cultures and identities become borderlands, sites of crossing, negotiation, translation, and dialogue. At issue is the production of a border pedagogy in which the intersection of culture and identity produces self-definitions that enables teachers and students to authorize a sense of critical agency. Border pedagogy points to a self/other relationship in which identity is fixed as neither Other nor the same; instead, it is both and, hence, defined within multiple literacies that become a referent, critique, and practice of cultural translation, a recognition of no possibility of fixed, final, or monologically authoritative meaning that exists outside of history, power, and ideology.

Within such a pedagogical cartography, teachers must be given the opportunity to cross ideological and political borders as a way of clarifying their own moral vision, as a way of enabling counterdiscourses, and, as Roger Simon points out, as a way of getting students "beyond the world they already know in order to challenge and provoke their inquiry and challenge of their existing views of the way things are and should be."[27]

Underlying this notion of border pedagogy is neither the logic of assimilation (the melting pot) nor the imperative to create cultural hierarchies, but the attempt to expand the possibilities for different groups to enter into dialogue to understand further the richness of their differences and the value of what they share in common.

Fourth, an insurgent multiculturalism must challenge the task of merely re-presenting cultural differences in the curriculum; it must also educate students of the necessity for linking a justice of multiplicity to struggles over real material conditions that structure everyday life. In part, this means understanding how structural imbalances in power produce real limits on the capacity of subordinate groups to exercise a sense of agency and struggle. It also means analyzing specific class, race, gender, and other issues as social problems rooted in real material and institutional factors that produce specific forms of inequality and oppression. This would necessitate a multicultural curriculum that produces a language that deals with social problems in historical and relational terms, and uncovers how the dynamics of power work to promote domination within the school and the wider society. In part, this means multiculturalism as a curricula discourse and pedagogical practice must function in its dual capacity as collective memory and alternative reconstruction. History, in this sense, is not merely resurrected but interrogated and tempered by "a sense of its liability, its contingency, its constructedness."[28] Memory does not become the repository of registering suppressed histories, albeit critically, but of reconstructing the moral frameworks of historical discourse to interrogate the present as living history.

Finally, a multicultural curriculum must develop, in public schools and institutions of higher education, contexts that serve to refigure relations between the school, teachers, students, and the wider community. For instance, public schools must be willing to develop a critical dialogue between the school and those public cultures within the community dedicated to producing students who address the discourse and obligations of power as part of a larger attempt at civic renewal and the reconstruction of democratic life. At best, parents, social activists, and other socially-concerned community members should be allowed to play a formative role in crucial decisions about what is taught, who is hired, and how the school can become a laboratory for learning that nurtures critical citizenship and civic courage. Of course, the relationship between the school and the larger community should be made in the interest of expanding "the social and political task of transformation, resistance, and radical democratization.[29] In both spheres of education, the curriculum needs to be decentralized to allow students to have some input into what is taught and under what conditions. Moreover, teachers need to be educated to be border crossers, to explore zones of cultural difference by moving in and out of the resources, histories, and narratives that provide different students with a sense of identity, place, and possibility. This does not suggest that educators become tourists traveling to exotic lands; on the contrary, it points to the need for them to enter into negotiation and dialogue around issues of nationality, difference, and identity so as to be able to fashion a more ethical and democratic set of pedagogical relations between themselves and their students while simultaneously allowing students to speak, listen, and learn differently within pedagogical spaces that are safe, affirming, questioning, and enabling.

In this instance, a curriculum for a multicultural and multiracial society provides the conditions for students to imagine beyond the given and to embrace their identities critically as a source of agency and possibility. In addition, an insurgent multiculturalism should serve to redefine existing debates about national identity while simultaneously expanding its theoretical concerns to more global and international matters. Developing a respect for cultures in the plural demands a reformulation of what it means to be educated in the United States and what such an education implies for the creation of new cultural spaces that deepen and extend the possibility of democratic public life. Multiculturalism insists upon challenging old orthodoxies and reformulating new projects of possibility. It is a challenge that all critical educators need to address.

Notes

1 Alice Kessler-Harris, "Cultural Locations: Positioning American Studies in the Great Debate," *American Quarterly,* 44, 3 (1992), p. 310.
2 Hazel Carby, "The Multicultural Wars," in *Black Popular Culture,* ed. Gina Dent (Seattle: Bay Press, 1992), pp. 193–4.
3 Kobena Mercer, "Back to my Routes: A Postscript on the 80s," *Ten.8,* 2, 3 (1992), p. 33.
4 James Baldwin, "A Talk to Teachers," in *Multicultural Literacy: Opening the American Mind,* eds Rick Simonson and Scott Waler (Saint Paul, MN: Graywolf Press, 1988), p. 8.

5 Gerald Graff and Bruce Robbins, "Cultural Criticism," in *Redrawing the Boundaries,* eds Stephen Greenblat and Giles Gunn (New York: MLA, 1992), p. 435.

6 Alan O'Connor, "Just Plain Home Cookin'," *Borderlines,* 20/21 (Winter 1991), p. 58.

7 Cornel West, *Race Matters* (Boston: Beacon Press, 1993), p. 14.

8 Ibid. , p. 16.

9 Cornel West "Learning to Talk of Race, " *The New York Times Magazine,* 6 (August 2, 1992), p. 24.

10 bell hooks, *Black Looks: Race and Representation* (Boston: South End Press, 1992,) p. 168.

11 Homi K. Bhabha, "The Postcolonial Critic — Homi Bhabha interviewed by David Bennett and Terry Collits," *Arena,* 96 (1991), pp. 50–1.

12 Stuart Hall and David Held, "Citizens and Citizenship," in *New Times: The Changing Face of Politics in the 1990s,* eds Stuart Hall and Martin Jacques (London: Verso, 1989), p. 178.

13 Peter Drier, "Bush to the Cities: Drop Dead," *The Progressive* (July 1992), p. 22.

14 Joan Scott, "Multiculturalism and the Politics of Identity," *October,* 61 (Summer 1992), p. 13.

15 Arthur Schlesinger Jr, *The Disuniting of America* (Knoxville, TN: Whittle District Books, 1992), pp. 21, 78.

16 James Clifford, "Museums in the Borderlands," in *Different Voices,* ed. Association of Art Museum Directors (New York: Association of Art Museum Directors, 1992), p. 119.

17 William Kerrigan, "The Falls of Academe," in *Wild Orchids and Trotsky,* ed. Mark Edmundson (New York: Penguin Books, 1993), p. 166.

18 Ibid., p. 167

19 Homi K. Bhabha and Bhikhu Parekh, "Identities on Parade: A Conversation," *Marxism Today* (June 1989), p. 3

20 Trinh T. Minh-Ha, *Woman, Native, Other: Writing Postcoloniality and Feminism* (Bloomington: Indiana University Press, 1989), p. 232.

21 E. San Juan Jr, *Racial Formations/Critical Transformations: Articulations of Power in Ethnic and Racial Studies in the United States* (Atlantic Highlands, NJ: Humanities Press, 1992), p. 101.

22 Hazel Carby, "Multi-Culture," *Screen Education,* 34 (Spring 1980), p. 65.

23 Bhabha and Parekh, "Identities on Parade: A Conversation," p. 4.

24 Manning Marable, *Black America: Multicultural Democracy* (Westfield, NJ: Open Media, 1992), p. 13.

25 Homi K. Bhabha, "A Good Judge of Character: Men, Metaphors, and the Common Culture" in *Race-ing Justice, Engendering Power: Essays on Anita Hill, Clarence Thomas, and the Construction of Social Reality,* ed. Toni Morrison (New York: Pantheon, 1992), p. 242.

26 Cornel West, "Learning to Talk of Race," p. 24.

27 Roger I. Simon, *Teaching Against the Grain* (New York: Bergin and Garvey Press, 1992), p. 17.

28 Henry Louis Gates Jr, "The Black Man's Burden," *Black Popular Culture,* ed. Gina Dent (Seattle: Bay Press, 1992), p. 76.

29 Judith Butler, "Contingent Foundations: Feminism and the Question of 'Postmodernism'," in *Feminists Theorize the Political*, eds Judith Butler and Joan Scott (New York: Routledge, 1992), p. 13.

16

Is Science Multicultural?
Challenges, Resources,
Opportunities, Uncertainties[1]

SANDRA HARDING

I. Challenges and Resources

Are the natural sciences multicultural? Could they and should they be? Such questions initially may seem ignorant or, at least odd, since it is exactly the lack of cultural fingerprints that conventionally is held responsible for the great successes of the sciences. The sciences "work" — they are universally valid, it is said, because they transcend culture. They can tell us how nature really functions instead of only how the British, Native Americans, or Chinese fear or want it to work.

There are good reasons to wonder if one should regard this universal science claim as ending the matter, however. Multicultural perspectives are providing more comprehensive and less distorted understandings of history, literature, arts, and social sciences. They are beginning to reshape public consciousness as they are disseminated through television specials, new elementary and high school history and literature textbooks and, indeed, daily news reports of perspectives on the West (or should one say the "North"?) that conflict with the conventional beliefs that many Westerners now understand to be Eurocentric. Do the challenges raised by multicultural perspectives in other fields have no consequences for the natural sciences?

We can identify three central questions for anyone who wishes to explore this issue. First, to what extent does modern science have origins in non-European cultures? Second, have there been and could there be other sciences, culturally-distinctive ones, that also "work" and thus are universal in this sense? Third, in what ways is modern science culturally European or European-American? Fortunately, pursuit of these questions has been made easier by the appearance in English recently of a small but rich set of writings on such topics. These "postcolonial science studies," as I shall refer to them, are authored by scientists and engineers, a few anthropologists, and historians of science. These authors are of European and Third-World descent; the latter live in the Third and First Worlds.

The proceedings of two recent conferences give a sense of the increasing international interest in these topics. *Science and Empires: Historical Studies About Scientific Development and European Expansion* contains about one-third of the 120 papers presented at an UNESCO-sponsored conference in Paris in 1986. The conference was organized by the French government's National Center for Scientific Research and these proceedings are published by one of the most prestigious and largest science studies publishers in the world. *The Revenge of Athena: Science, Exploitation and the Third World* contains 20 of the 35 or so papers presented at a 1986 conference in Penang, Malaysia, where Asian scientists, engineers, and science policy analysts were joined by several historians of science of European descent. The final version of the conference's policy statement, the Third World Network's *Modern Science in Crisis: A Third World Response*, has been published separately.[2]

Now is none too soon to note that the terms of this discussion are and must be controversial, for who gets to name natural and social realities gets to control how they will be organized. Moreover, it is not just language at issue but also a "discourse" — a conceptual framework with its logic linking my words in ways already familiar to readers — that is adequate to the project of this essay.[3] For example, for conventional science theorists, it is controversial to use the term "science" to refer to sciences' social institutions, technologies and applications, metaphors, language, and social meanings. They insist on restricting the term's reference to sciences' abstract cognitive core — the laws of nature — and/or the legendary scientific method, thereby excluding the other parts of sciences' practices and culture which many contemporary science theorists insist also are fundamental constituents of sciences.[4]

Moreover, the terms of multicultural discourse are and must be controversial. Do my references to "Western" replicate dualistic, orientalist thinking that has been so widely criticized? Isn't it precisely from the borderlands between "Western" and "non-Western" that this paper and the thought of its cited authors arises?[5] How "Western" is Western science anyway (a topic to be pursued below)? Moreover, which of the diverse peoples currently living in Europe and North America get to count as Western? And is Japan "non-Western" and "Third World"? Additionally, Third-World cultures are immensely diverse, and they are internally heterogeneous by class, gender, ethnicity, religion, politics, and other features. Doesn't ignoring or marginalizing these differences disseminate characteristic

Eurocentric tendencies to homogenize and refuse to think carefully about peoples that Westerners have constructed as their Others? Furthermore, doesn't "neocolonial" designate better than "postcolonial" the present relations between the West and its former colonies? And are African-Americans and indigenous Americans appropriately thought of as "colonized"? What are the politics of continuing to refer to the First and Third Worlds when this contrast is the product of the Eurocentric Cold War? Finally, should the knowledge traditions of non-Western cultures be referred to as "sciences" rather than only as "ethnosciences" (a topic I take up below)?

We cannot settle such questions easily. In some cases, it is the familiar languages that are at issue in the questions raised in this essay. In other cases, less controversial terms have not yet been found or have not yet reached general circulation. Moreover, changing language sometimes advances the growth of knowledge but, in other cases, it simply substitutes an acceptable veneer under which ignorance and exploitative politics can continue to flourish. Discourses, conceptual schemes, paradigms, and epistemes are at issue, not just words. I hope readers can hear beyond these inadequate languages to the issues that can help us develop less problematic thinking, speech, and actions. I shall primarily use the terms the postcolonial authors use, though their own usages are diverse and sometimes conflicting.

One term worth clarifying, however, is "Eurocentrism." Here I refer to a cluster of assumptions, central among which are that peoples of European descent, their institutions, practices and conceptual schemes, express the unique heights of human development, and that Europeans and their civilization are fundamentally self-generated, owing little or nothing to the institutions, practices, conceptual schemes, or peoples of other parts of the world.[6] If Western sciences and science studies turn out to be Eurocentric, we are likely to discover possibilities of multiculturalism in the natural sciences that have been hidden from view.

One last issue: who is the "we" of this paper? In relation to its topics, I am positioned as a woman of European descent, and economically privileged. But the "we" I invoke is meant to include all people, regardless of their ethnicity, "race," nationality, class, gender, or other significant features of their location in local and global social relations, who are concerned to rethink critically those social relations past and present, the role of sciences in them, and who wish to bring about more effective links between scientific projects and those of advancing democratic social relations.

The universal science view — that modern sciences are uniquely successful exactly because they have eliminated cultural fingerprints from their results of research — contains some important insights, but it also incorporates some assumptions that are probably false but, at any rate, have not been supported by evidence. For example, it assumes that no other sciences could generate the laws of gravity or antibiotics; that modern science also does not "work" for producing human and natural disasters; that what has worked best to advance the West will and should work best to advance other societies; that modern sciences are the best ones to discover all of the laws of nature; and that the kinds of projects for which modern sciences have worked best in the past are the ones at which any possible sciences, past, present, and future, should want to succeed.[7] In spite of these problematic assumptions, the conventional view contains important insights. Such insights are more reasonably explained, however, in ways that give up these problematic assumptions and locate modern sciences on the more accurate historical and geographical maps produced by the postcolonial accounts.[8]

Let us turn to the three questions that will help to determine the degree to which science, or the sciences, may be multicultural.

II. Does Modern Science Have Non-Western Origins?

Least controversial is to acknowledge that modern sciences have borrowed from other cultures. Most people are aware of at least a couple of such examples. However, the borrowings have been far more extensive and important for the development of modern sciences than the conventional histories reveal. Modern sciences have been enriched by contributions not only from the so-called "complex" cultures of China, India, and others in east-Asian and Islamic societies, but also from the so-called "simpler" ones of Africa, pre-Columbian Americas, and others that interacted with the expansion of European cultures.

To list just a few examples, Egyptian mystical philosophies and premodern European alchemical traditions were far more useful to the development of sciences in Europe than is suggested by the conventional view that these are only irrational and marginally valuable elements of immature Western sciences.[9] The Greek legacy of scientific and mathematical thought was not only fortuitously preserved but also developed in Islamic culture, to be claimed by the sciences of the European Renaissance.[10] Furthermore, the identification of Greek culture as European is questionable on several counts. For one thing, the idea of Europe and the social relations such an idea made possible came into existence centuries later. Some would date the emergence of "Europe" to Charlemagne's achievements, others to fifteenth-century events. Another point here is that through the spread of Islam, diverse cultures of Africa and Asia can also claim Greek culture as their legacy.[11]

Some knowledge traditions that were appropriated and fully integrated into modern sciences are not acknowledged at all. Thus the principles of pre-Columbian agriculture, that provided potatoes for almost every European ecological niche and thereby had a powerful effect on the nutrition and subsequent history of Europe, was subsumed into European science.[12] Mathematical achievements from India and Arabic cultures provide other examples. The magnetic needle, rudder, gunpowder, and many other technologies useful to Europeans and the advancement of their sciences (were these not part of scientific instrumentation?) were borrowed from China. Knowledge of local geographies, geologies, animals, plants, classification schemes, medicines, pharmacologies, agriculture, navigational techniques, and local cultures that formed significant parts of European sciences' picture of nature were provided in part by the knowledge traditions of non-Europeans. ("We took on board a native of the region, and dropped him off six weeks further up the coast," report the voyagers' accounts.) Summarizing the consequences for modern sciences of British imperialism in India, one recent account points out that in effect "India was added as a laboratory to the edifice of modern science."[13] We could say the same for all of the lands to which the "voyages of discovery" and later colonization projects took the Europeans.[14]

Thus modern science already is multicultural, at least in the sense that elements of the knowledge traditions of many different non-European cultures have been incorporated into it. There is nothing unusual about such scientific borrowing. It is evident in the ordinary, everyday borrowing that occurs when scientists revive models, metaphors, procedures, technologies, or other ideas from older European scientific traditions, when they borrow such elements from the culture outside their laboratories and field stations, or from other contemporary sciences.[15] After all, a major point of professional conferences and international exchange programs, not to mention "keeping up with the literature," is to permit everyone to borrow everyone else's achievements. As we shall see shortly, without such possibilities, sciences wither and lose their creativity. What is at issue here is only the Eurocentric failure to acknowledge the origins and importance to "real science" of these borrowings from non-European cultures, and also, thereby, to trivialize the achievements of their scientific traditions.

To give up this piece of Eurocentrism does not challenge the obvious accomplishments of modern sciences. Every thinking person should be able to accept the claim that modern science is multicultural in this sense. Of course it is one thing to accept a claim that conflicts with one's own, and quite another to use it to transform one's own thinking. To do the latter would require that historians of science and the rest of us locate our accounts on a global civilizational map rather than only on the Eurocentric map of Europe that we all learned.

There are implications here also for philosophies and social studies of science. For example, the standard contrasts between the objectivity, rationality, and progressiveness of modern scientific thought versus the only locally valid, irrational, and backwards or primitive thought of other cultures begins to seem less explanatorily useful and, indeed, accurate after the postcolonial accounts. Whether overtly stated or only discretely assumed, these contrasts damage our ability not only to appreciate the strengths of other scientific traditions but also to grasp the real strengths and limitations of modern sciences.

These accounts of multicultural origins do not directly challenge conventional beliefs that modern sciences uniquely deserve to be designated sciences, however, or that they are universally valid because their cognitive/technical core transcends culture. Other arguments in the postcolonial accounts do.

III. Have There Been or Could There Be Other, Distinctive Sciences that "Work"?

Do any other knowledge traditions deserve to be called sciences? The conventional view is that only modern sciences are entitled to this designation. In such accounts, science is treated as a cultural emergent in early modern Europe. While a shift in social conditions may have made it possible in the first place, what emerged was a form of knowledge-seeking that is fundamentally self-generating; its "internal logic" is responsible for its great successes. This "logic of scientific research" has been characterized in various ways — as inductivism, crucial experiments, the hypothetico-deductive method, a cycle of normal science–revolution–normal science. Whatever the logic attributed to scientific research, it is conceptualized as "inside" science and not "outside" it "in society." Though Chinese or African astronomers may have made discoveries before Europeans, this is not sufficient to indicate that the former were really doing what is reasonably regarded as "science."[16] Thus while science is said to need a supportive social climate to flourish, the particular form of that climate is claimed to leave no distinctive cultural fingerprints on science's results of research.

Is this a reasonable position? Is the content of the successes of modern sciences due entirely to the sciences' "internal" features? For one, not all of the successes attributed to Western sciences are unique to it. In many cases,

> what has been ascribed to the European tradition has been shown on closer examination to have been done elsewhere by others earlier. (Thus Harvey was not the first to discover the circulation of blood, but an Arabic scientist was; Paracelsus did not introduce the fourth element "salt" and start the march towards modern chemistry, but a twelfth-century alchemist from Kerala did so teaching in Saudi Arabia.)[17]

Many other cultures made sophisticated astronomical observations which were repeated centuries later in Europe. For example, many of the observations that Galileo's telescope made possible were known to the Dogon peoples of West Africa more than 1,500 years earlier. Either they had invented some sort of telescope, or they had extraordinary eyesight.[18] Many mathematical achievements of Indians and other Asian peoples were adopted or invented in Europe much later. Indeed, it is as revealing to examine the ideas European sciences *did not* borrow from the knowledge traditions they encountered as it is to examine what they did borrow. Among the notions "unborrowed" are the ability to deal with very large numbers (such as 10^{-53}), the zero as a separate number with its own arithmetical logic, and irrational and negative numbers.[19] Needham points out that "between the first century BC and fifteenth century AD Chinese civilization was much more efficient than the occidental in applying human natural knowledge to practical human needs ... in many ways this was much more congruent with modern science than was the world outlook of Christendom."[20] Thus other knowledge traditions "worked" at projects Western sciences could not accomplish until much later. If the achievements of modern science should be attributed to its "internal logic," then evidently this logic is not unique to it.

This brings us to a second point. Nobody has discovered an eleventh commandment handed down from the heavens specifying what may and may not be counted as a science. Obviously the project of drawing a line between science and nonscience is undertaken because it emphasizes a contrast thought to be important. Belief in the reality of this demarcation, as in the reality of the science versus pseudoscience duality, is necessary to preserve the mystique of the uniqueness and purity of the West's knowledge-seeking. Thus the sciences, as well as the philosophies that are focused on describing and explaining that kind of rationality so highly valued in the modern West, have been partners with anthropology in maintaining a whole series of Eurocentric contrasts, whether or not individual scientists, philosophers, or anthropologists so intended. The self-image of the West depends on contrasts not only between the rational and irrational, but also between civilization and the savage or primitive, the advanced or progressive and the backwards, dynamic and static societies, developed and undeveloped, the historical and the natural, the rational and the irrational, and other contrasts through which the European Self has constructed its Other, and thereby justified its exploitative treatment of various peoples.[21] My point here is that even though there clearly are obvious and large differences between modern sciences and the traditions of seeking systematic knowledge of the natural world to be found in other cultures, it is useful to think of them all as sciences to gain a more objective understanding of the causes of Western successes, the achievements of other sciences, and possible directions for future local and global sciences.[22]

One cannot avoid noticing, moreover, that European scholars disagree on the exact distinctive features responsible for the success of European sciences. It is instructive to look at four accounts of Western scientific uniqueness made by distinguished and otherwise progressive Western analysts — ones whose work has in important ways challenged conventional Eurocentric assumptions. Anthropologist Robin Horton, who has shown how African traditional thought is surprisingly similar to Western scientific thought, attributes the residual crucial differences to the fact that modern scientific thought takes a critical stance toward tradition and is aided in this project by its rejection of magical relations between language and the world; it holds that we can manipulate language without changing the world.[23] However, as philosopher J. E. Wiredu points out, Horton undervalues the extent of noncritical and dogmatic assumptions in modern

Western scientific thought. After all, "classical" British empiricism is "traditional thought" for Western scientific communities and those who value scientific rationality, the once-radical claims of Locke and Hume have become uncontroversial assumptions for us. An anthropologist from another culture might refer to them as our "folk beliefs." So how accurate is it to claim that a critical approach to tradition is responsible for the successes of modern sciences? Moreover, if science is modern in its rejection of magical relations between language and the world, scientists surely aren't, Wiredu continues, since many also hold religious beliefs that invest in just such magical relations.[24] Many commentators have noted that sacred — dare one say "magical" — faith in the accuracy and progressiveness of modern science characteristic of many scientists and the "educated classes" more generally.

Historian Thomas Kuhn would agree with Wiredu's assessment that Western sciences are in significant respects uncritical of conventional assumptions; indeed, he argues that they are dogmatic in rejecting a thoroughgoing critical attitude. However, he has explained that this scientific dogmatism is not an obstacle to scientific progress but, instead, a crucial element in its success. A field becomes a science only when it no longer questions a founding set of assumptions within which it can then get on with the business of designing research projects to resolve the puzzles that such assumptions have brought into focus. He attributes the unique successes of modern sciences to the distinctive (progressive?) organization of Western scientific communities:

> ... only the civilizations that descended from Hellenic Greece have possessed more than the most rudimentary science. The bulk of scientific knowledge is a product of Europe in the last four centuries. No other place and time has supported the very special communities from which scientific productivity comes.[25]

Though one might think that a social community is not "internal" to the logic of science, Kuhn insists that in an important sense it is; the very special scientific communities are ones trained to follow modern science's success-producing internal logic of paradigm creation, puzzle-solving with anomaly tolerance, paradigm breakdown, and then, eventually, another paradigm shift. Kuhn directed attention to the importance of the distinctive social organization of modern scientific communities. However, one can also see that Kuhn's problematic here — his concern to identify a different, distinctive cause of modern science's successes — is inseparable in his thought from the widespread Eurocentric assumptions he articulates about the origins and virtues of European civilization.

Historian Joseph Needham refers to Chinese knowledge traditions as sciences when comparing them to those of the modern West. He would contest Kuhn's characterization of non-European sciences as primitive and the West's as uniquely descended from the Greek, and proposes yet another kind of cause of the success of modern European sciences.

> When we say that modern science developed only in Western Europe at the time of Galileo in the late Renaissance, we mean surely that there and then alone there developed the fundamental bases of the structure of the natural sciences as we have them today, namely the application of mathematical hypotheses to Nature, the full understanding and use of the experimental method, the distinction between primary and secondary qualities, the geometrization of space, and the acceptance of the mechanical model of reality. Hypotheses of primitive or medieval type distinguish themselves quite clearly from those of modern type.[26]

For Needham, it is not the attitudes on which Horton focuses, or the organization of scientific communities that appears so important to Kuhn, but a specific set of assumptions about the nature of reality and appropriate methods of research.

Finally, sociologist Edgar Zilsel, asking why modern science emerged only in Renaissance Europe rather than in China or some other "high culture," claims that the emergence of a new social class that, in contrast to the classes of aristocratic or slave societies, was permitted to combine a trained intellect with willingness to do manual labor, allowed the invention of experimental method. Only in early modern Europe where there was an absence of slavery and challenges to aristocracy was there a progressive culture, he implies, that gave individuals reasons to want to obtain intellectual and manual training.[27]

No doubt one could find additional features of the cultures and practices of modern sciences to which other historians would attribute their successes. These different purported causes are probably not entirely independent of each other, and some readers will find one more plausible than another of such proposals. However, my point is that there is no general agreement even among the most distinguished and progressive Western science theorists about the distinctive causes of modern science, and that the search for such an explanation and the kinds of accounts on which such scholars settle usually remain tied to Eurocentric dualisms.

A third source of skepticism about conventional claims for the unique efficacy of Western sciences arises from an oft-repeated argument in the postcolonial accounts. European sciences advanced because they focused on describing and explaining those aspects of nature's regularities that permitted the upper classes of Europeans to multiply and thrive, especially through the prospering of their military, imperial, and otherwise expansionist projects. Interestingly, evidence for this claim now can be gathered easily from many of the museum exhibits and scholarly publications associated with the 1992 quincentennial of the Columbian encounter. They drew attention, intentionally or not, to the numerous ways European expansion in the Americas advanced European sciences. A detailed account of how British colonialism in India advanced European sciences is provided by Kochhar. The British needed better navigation, so they built observatories, funded astronomers, and kept systematic records of their voyages. The first European sciences to be established in India were, not surprisingly, geography and botany.[28] Nor is the intimate relation between scientific advance in the West and expansionist efforts only a matter of the distant past (or only of expansion into foreign lands, as noted earlier). By the end of World War II, the development of US physics had been almost entirely handed over to the direction of US militarism and nationalism, as historian Paul Forman has shown in detail.[29]

Thus European expansionism has changed the "topography" of global scientific knowledge, causing the advance of European sciences and the decline or underdevelopment of scientific traditions of other cultures:

> The topography of the world of knowledge before the last few centuries could be delineated as several hills of knowledge roughly corresponding to the regional civilizations of, say, West Asia, South Asia, East Asia and Europe. The last few centuries have seen the levelling of the other hills and from their debris the erection of a single one with its base in Europe.[30]

These arguments begin to challenge the idea that the causes of modern sciences' achievements are to be located entirely in their purported inherently transcultural character. It turns out that what makes them "work," and to appear uniquely to do so, is at least partly a consequence of their focus on the kinds of projects that European expansion could advance and benefit from while simultaneously clearing the field of potentially rival scientific traditions. To make such claims is not to deny that Western sciences can claim many great and, so far, unique scientific achievements. Instead, it is to argue, contrary to conventional views, that scientific "truths," no less than false beliefs, are caused by social relations as well as by nature's regularities and the operations of reason.[31]

But could there be other, culturally-distinctive sciences that also "work"? The postcolonial accounts have shown the rich and sophisticated scientific traditions of Asia, Islam, and "simpler" societies of the past. But what about the future? We return to this issue shortly.

IV. Is Modern Science Culturally "Western"?[32]

The very accounts describing the histories of other scientific traditions also show the distinctive cultural features of modern sciences. These features are precisely, for better and worse, the features that are responsible for their successes, as the discussions above began to reveal. That is, the distinctive social/political history of the development of modern sciences is not external to their content; it appears in the image of nature's regularities and underlying causal tendencies they produce, including the "laws of nature" that form their cognitive/technical core. Here, I can identify only five of the distinctively "Western" features persistently noted in the postcolonial literature.

First, as indicated above, which aspects of nature modern sciences describe and explain, and how they are described and explained, have been selected, in part, by the conscious purposes and unconscious interests of European expansion. Of course, these are not the only purposes and interests shaping these sciences — androcentric, religious, local bourgeois, and others also have had powerful effects as many recent accounts have shown — but they are significant. The "problems" that count as scientific are those for which expansionist Europe needed solutions; conversely those aspects of nature about which the beneficiaries of expansionism have not needed or wanted to know have remained uncharted. Thus, the culturally-distinctive patterns of systematic knowledge and systematic ignorance in modern sciences' picture of nature's regularities and their underlying causal tendencies can be detected from the perspective of cultures with different preoccupations. For example, modern sciences answered questions about how to: improve European land and sea travel; mine ores; identify the economically useful minerals, plants, and animals of other parts of the world; manufacture and farm for the benefit of Europeans living in Europe, the Americas, Africa, and India; improve their health and occasionally that of the workers who produced profit for them; protect settlers in the colonies from settlers of other nationalities; gain access to the labor of the indigenous residents; and do all this to benefit only local European citizens — the Spanish versus the Portuguese, French, or British. These sciences have not been concerned to explain how the consequences of interventions in nature for the benefit of Europeans of the advantaged gender, classes, and ethnicities would change the natural resources available to the majority of the world's peoples, or what the economic, social, political, and ecological costs to less-advantaged groups in and outside Europe would be of the interventions in nature and social relations that sciences' experimental methods "foresaw" and to which it directed policymakers. Sciences with other purposes — explaining how to shift from unrenewable to renewable natural resources, to maintain a healthy but less environmentally destructive standard of living in the overdeveloped societies, to clean up toxic wastes, to benefit women in every culture, etc. — could generate other, perhaps sometimes conflicting, descriptions and explanations of nature's regularities and underlying causal tendencies.

Second, early modern sciences' conception of nature was distinctively Western or, at least, alien to many other cultures. For the resident of medieval Europe, nature was enchanted; the "disenchantment of nature" was a crucial element in the shift from the medieval to the modern mentality, from feudalism to capitalism, from Ptolemaic to Galilean astronomy, and from Aristotelian to Newtonian physics.[33] Modern science related to a worldly power in nature, not to power that lay outside the material universe. To gain power over nature for modern man would violate no moral or religious principles.

Moreover, the Western conception of laws of nature drew on Judeo–Christian religious beliefs and the increasing familiarity in early modern Europe with centralized royal authority, with royal absolutism. Needham points out that this

Western idea that the universe was a "great empire, ruled by a divine Logos"[34] was never comprehensible at any time in the long history of Chinese science since a common thread in the diverse Chinese traditions was that nature was self-governed, a web of relationships without a weaver, with which humans interfered at their own peril.

> Universal harmony comes about not by the celestial fiat of some King of Kings, but by the spontaneous cooperation of all beings in the universe brought about by their following the internal necessities of their own natures.... [A]ll entities at all levels behave in accordance with their position in the greater patterns (organisms) of which they are parts.[35]

Compared to Renaissance science, the Chinese conception of nature was problematic, blocking their interest in discovering "precisely formulated abstract laws ordained from the beginning by a celestial lawgiver for nonhuman nature."

> There was no confidence that the code of Nature's laws could be unveiled and read, because there was no assurance that a divine being, even more rational than ourselves, had ever formulated such a code capable of being read.[36]

Of course, such notions of "command and duty in the 'Laws' of Nature" have disappeared from modern science and have been replaced by the notion of statistical regularities that describe rather than prescribe nature's order — in a sense, a return, Needham comments, to the Taoist perspective. And yet other residues of the earlier conception remain. Evelyn Fox Keller has pointed to the positive political implications of conceptualizing nature simply as ordered rather than as law-governed.[37] My point here is that Western conceptions of nature have been intimately linked to historically-shifting Western religious and political ideals.

Third, the European-Christian conception of the laws of nature was just one kind of regional resource used to develop European sciences. Elements of medieval scientific and classical Greek thought, and other religious, national, class, and gender metaphors, models, and assumptions also were available for use in developing European sciences. The adoption of these cultural resources are familiar from the writings of conventional historians of Western sciences. In the context of the postcolonial literatures, these now appear as distinctively European cultural elements, ones that make modern sciences foreign to peoples in many other cultures.

Another kind of regional resource available only in Europe was created through the intermingling and integration of non-European elements with each other and with resources already available in Europe to make more useful elements for modern science. That is, those non-European elements indicated above were not only borrowed, but also were frequently transformed through processes possible only for a culture at the center of global exchanges. Thus the map and route of

European expansion could be traced in the expansion of the content of European sciences. Prior to European expansion African, Asian, and indigenous American cultures had long traded scientific and technological ideas among themselves as they exchanged other products, but this possibility was reduced or eliminated for them and transferred to Europe during the "voyages of discovery."[38]

Fourth, the way peoples of European descent distribute and account for the consequences of modern sciences appears distinctively Western. The benefits are distributed disproportionately to already overadvantaged groups in Europe and elsewhere, and the costs disproportionately to everyone else. Whether one looks at sciences intended to improve the military, agriculture, manufacturing, health, or even the environment, the expanded opportunities they make possible have been distributed predominantly to small minorities of already privileged people primarily but not entirely of European descent, and the costs to the already poorest, racial and ethnic minorities and women located at the periphery of local and global economic and political networks.[39]

The causes of this distribution are not mysterious or unforeseen. For one thing, it is not "man" whom sciences enable to make better use of nature's resources, but only those already positioned in social hierarchies. As Khor Kok Peng puts the point, the latter already own and control nature in the form of land with its forests, water, plants, animals, and minerals as well as having the tools to extract and process such resources. These people are in a position to decide "what to produce, how to produce it, what resources to use up to produce, and what technology to use."

> We thus have this spectacle, on the one hand, of the powerful development of technological capacity, so that the basic and human needs of every human being could be met if there were an appropriate arrangement of social and production systems; and, on the other hand, of more than half the world's population (and something like two-thirds of the Third-World's people) living in conditions where their basic and human needs are not met....[40]

Not only are the benefits and costs of modern sciences distributed in ways that disproportionately benefit elites in the West and elsewhere, but sciences' accounting practices are distorted to make this distribution invisible to those who gain the benefits. All consequences of sciences and technologies that are not planned or intended are externalized as "not science."[41] The critics argue that such an "internalization of profits and externalization of costs is the normal consequence when nature is treated as if its individual components were isolated and unrelated...."[42]

Finally, even if modern sciences bore none of the above cultural fingerprints, their value-neutrality would itself mark them as culturally distinctive. Of course, this is a contradiction ("If it's value-free, then it's not value-free.") or, at least highly paradoxical. The point is that maximizing cultural neutrality, not to mention claiming it, is itself a culturally specific value; the reality and the claim are at issue here. Most cultures do not value neutrality, so one that does is easily identifiable. Moreover, the claim to neutrality is itself characteristic of the administrators of modern Western cultures organized by principles of scientific rationality.[43] Surprisingly, it turns out that abstractness and formality express distinctive cultural features, not the absence of any culture at all. Thus when modern science is introduced into many other societies, it is experienced as a rude and brutal cultural intrusion precisely because of this feature. Modern sciences' "neutrality" devalues not only local scientific traditions, but also the culturally-defining values and interests that make a tradition Confucian rather than Protestant or Islamic. Claims for modern sciences' universality and objectivity are "a politics of disvaluing local concerns and knowledge and legitimating 'outside experts'."[44]

Interesting issues emerge from the discovery of the cultural specificity of modern sciences. For example, the conventional understanding of the universality of modern science is contested in two ways in these accounts. First, these accounts argue that universality is established as an empirical consequence of European expansion, not as an epistemological cause of valid claims, to be located "inside science" — for example, in its method. As pointed out by one author:

> The epistemological claim of the "universality of science" ... covers what is an empirical fact, the material and intellectual construction of this "universal science" and its "international character." The "universality of science" does not appear to be the cause but the effect of a process that we cannot explain or understand merely by concentrating our attention on epistemological claims.[45]

Second, a wedge has been driven between the universality of a science and its cultural neutrality. The laws of nature "discovered" by modern sciences that explain, for instance, how gravity and antibiotics work, will have their effects on us regardless of our cultural location, but they are not the only possible such universal laws of nature; there could be many universally valid but culturally-distinctive sciences.

> ... [I]f we were to picture physical reality as a large blackboard, and the branches and shoots of the knowledge tree as markings in white chalk on this blackboard, it becomes clear that the yet unmarked and unexplored parts occupy a considerably greater space than that covered by the chalk tracks. The socially structured knowledge tree has thus explored only certain partial aspects of physical reality, explorations that correspond to the particular historical unfoldings of the civilization within which the knowledge tree emerged.
>
> Thus entirely different knowledge systems corresponding to different historical unfoldings in different civilizational settings become possible. This raises the possibility that in different historical situations and contexts sciences very different

from the European tradition could emerge. Thus an entirely new set of "universal" but socially determined natural science laws are possible.[46]

These accounts thus provide additional evidence for the claim that fully modern sciences could be constructed within other cultures — the argument I left incomplete in the last section. Significant cultural features of modern sciences have not blocked their development as fully modern, according to the postcolonial accounts; indeed, they are responsible for these successes.[47] Moreover, one can now ask: which of the original cultural purposes of modern sciences that continue today to shape their conceptual framework are still desirable? Should we want to continue to develop sciences that, intentionally or not, succeed by extinguishing or obscuring all other scientific traditions, directing limitless consumption of scarce and unrenewable resources, distributing their benefits internally and their costs externally, and so forth? These questions show that if culture shapes sciences, then changes in local and global cultures can shape different sciences "here" as well as "there."

V. Future Sciences: Opportunities and Uncertainties

We live in one world, and the scientific choices made by each culture have effects on others. Class, gender, ethnicity, religion, and other social forces produce different and conflicting approaches to science and technology issues in the metropolitan centers as they do in the cultures at local and global peripheries. It would be a mistake to suggest that all of the difficulties Third-World cultures face at this moment in history are the doings of the West or its sciences; that is not the message of the postcolonial accounts or of this essay. These cultures, too, have historical and philosophic legacies of indigenous forms of inequality and exploitation, they have followed policies that turned out not to be wise, and they have suffered from natural and social processes they could not escape. The point, instead, is that the balance sheet for modern sciences and those of other knowledge traditions looks different from the perspective of the lives of the majority of the world's peoples than it does from the lives of advantaged groups in the West and elsewhere, and there are good reasons to think that, in some respects, the perspectives of the elites are not less objective.[48] We should also recollect that sciences of European or other civilizational histories have different effects on the lives of women and men and of peoples in different classes and ethnicities.[49] This important issue cannot be pursued further here but has to be kept in mind when thinking about the very general options that I turn to review.

Projects Starting in the Third World

One's location in local and global social relations makes pressing partially different projects and gives one access to different resources. In the balance of this essay, I wish to consider some of these different priorities and resources though, of course, those who value advancing democracy and, especially, bringing modern sciences under more democratic social controls, will share a great deal. One's social location enables and limits what one can see and do. Here I wish to focus on the resources of certain kinds of social locations. (As stressed earlier, the "Third World" and "the West" are socially diverse.) Of course, no one would deny there are aspects of modern sciences, their cultures and practices that can and should be used to benefit all peoples living in every society. What is at issue is not that claim, but a host of others having to do with who will decide which aspects these are, how they should be used in different cultures, and how the benefits and costs of their production and use are to be distributed.

To begin with, we must note that for the small middle classes in most Third-World societies, modern sciences represent desirable resources for the ways these groups participate in industry, agriculture, medicine, and state organization of social life, and for the higher status and increased power that is awarded there as well as here to most things of European origin. Moreover, it is modern scientific practices that are demanded as a condition of economic aid by such international organizations as the World Bank and International Monetary Fund. Thus, many people of Third-World descent whose voices reach Western ears are no more critical of modern sciences than are many Westerners. However, great social changes often have been stimulated by the farsighted projects of a few visionaries. (Think, for example, of the effects of the work of such people recently regarded as "kooks" such as Rachel Carson, critics of "passive smoking", and vitamin advocates.) Many features of postcolonial critical analyses express perspectives that appear in virtually every Third-World culture — and are rapidly gathering support in the West. What is needed is more extensive respectful public discussion of the issues raised in and by these writings.

What are the alternatives envisioned in Third-World postcolonial science analyses to continued suppression of indigenous scientific goals, practices, and cultures by Western ones? One proposal is to integrate endangered Third-World sciences into modern sciences. The continued expansion of European social relations and their modernization pressures are rapidly causing the extinction of many non-Western cultures, possibly losing for humanity the unique and valuable kinds of knowledge they have achieved.

> ... just as forest peoples possess much knowledge of plants and animals that is valid and useful, regional civilizations possess stores of elaborate knowledge on a wide variety of topics. These stores, the results of millennia of human enquiry, were lost

from view because of the consequences of the European "discovery." But now it appears they will be increasingly opened up, foraged for valid uses and what is worthy opportunistically used. The operative word should be "opportunistically," to guard against a mere romantic and reactionary return to assumed past golden ages of these civilizations.[50]

Just as modernization pressures are reducing the diversity of plant, animal, and even human genetic pools, so, too, they are reducing the diversity of cultures and the valuable human ideas developed in them. These scientific legacies are interesting and valuable to preserve for their own sake. But they also can make even greater contributions to modern sciences.

This proposal raises many questions. If this were the only strategy for using other scientific legacies, would it not be a self-fulfilling one, offering no resistance to the eventual extinction of all "free standing" non-Western scientific traditions? Is it presumed that only those non-Western elements that *could* be incorporated without dissonance into modern sciences would be, abandoning other kinds of valuable knowledge because it conflicted with modern scientific paradigms, and thus leaving one global science that is distinctively the product of the European civilizational tradition? Is it inevitable that modern science/culture end up the global one? How should Westerners feel about extracting for the benefit of their cultural legacy the resources that become available from cultures that are dying as a consequence of the policies of overadvantaged groups? (But how much should it matter what Westerners feel about such things?)

A second proposal is to integrate in the other direction. Thus indigenous scientific traditions around the world would be strengthened through adopting those parts of modern sciences that could be integrated into *them*. This kind of process has already occurred in many places. For example, one report describes how modern sciences were integrated into local knowledge systems in China.[51] Indian anthropologist Ashis Nandy argues for a comprehensive program of this sort. He points out that India

... is truly bicultural. It has had six hundred years of exposure to the west and at least two hundred years of experience in incorporating and internalizing not merely the west but specifically western systems of knowledge. It need not necessarily exercise the option that it has of defensively rejecting modern science *in toto* and falling back upon the purity of its traditional systems of knowledge. It can, instead, choose the option of creatively assessing the modern system of knowledge, and then integrating important segments of it within the frame of its traditional visions of knowledge. In other words, the Indic civilization today, because it straddles two cultures, has the capacity to reverse the usual one-way procedure of enriching modern science by integrating within it significant elements from all other sciences — premodern, nonmodern and postmodern — as a further proof of the universality and syncretism of modern science.[52]

In this scenario, there would be many culturally-distinctive scientific traditions that shared some common elements with modern Western sciences. Here there could again be "many hills" of scientific knowledge. Both forms of multiculturalism would be advanced: culturally-diverse sciences around the globe, and diverse cultural origins within each local science. Is this proposal possible? Few of the marginalized cultures are strong enough to resist the continued expansion of Western-originated modernization, but some may be able to do so. And Western societies are not static; they may find their own reasons to want a more democratic balance of their own and other cultures' projects.

A third proposal argues that Third-World scientific projects should be "delinked" from Western ones.[53] This is thought to be necessary if Third-World societies are to construct fully modern sciences within their indigenous scientific traditions. Otherwise capitalism inevitably succeeds in turning Third-World cultures into markets that can increase profits for elites in the West (just as it continually extends into more and more aspects of daily life in the West). The Third World Network puts the issue this way:

> Only when science and technology evolve from the ethos and cultural milieu of Third-World societies will it become meaningful for our needs and requirements, and express our true creativity and genius. Third-World science and technology can only evolve through a reliance on indigenous categories, idioms and traditions in all spheres of thought and action.[54]

This strategy makes sense when one recognizes there are many more "universal laws of nature" that such delinked sciences could discover if they were permitted to develop out of civilizational settings different from those that have been directed by European projects. Such a delinking program could make a world of different but interrelated culturally-diverse sciences.

How delinked can the cultures that make up our shrinking world become? Like earlier proposals, this one, too, raises knotty issues. However, even if a complete social, political, and economic delinking proves impossible, does not attempting to delink as much as possible — even just daring to think about it! — enable more creative strategizing? Let us begin to try to imagine what scientific culture and practices in the West would or should look like if the Third World no longer provided so much of the raw materials, "laboratories," or markets, voluntary or involuntary, for modern sciences and the kinds of "development" they have advanced.

A fourth proposal goes even further in revaluing non-Western scientific traditions. It argues that Third-World sciences and their cultures can provide useful models for global sciences of the future. Many elements of the distinctively-modern scientific ethic not only are unsuitable for disadvantaged peoples in the Third World and elsewhere, but also for any future human or nonhuman cultures at all. For example, modern sciences' commitments to a utilitarian approach to nature, to externalizing the costs and internalizing the benefits of scientific advances, and to an ethic of increasing consumption ("development") are not ones that can support future life on earth.

> [M]odern science has become the major source of active violence against human beings and all other living organisms in our times.... Third World and other citizens have come to know that there is a fundamental irreconcilability between modern science and the stability and maintenance of all living systems, between modern science and democracy.[55]

Thus non-Western scientific traditions that do not share such problematic commitments can provide models for the kinds of global sciences that our species must have for it and the rest of nature to survive. As two biologists put the point, Western sciences should realistically be assessed as a transitional stage in scientific development.[56] The point here is not that non-Western cultures and their scientific traditions are all good and Western ones all bad, but that all of us can learn and benefit from the achievements of non-European civilizations' traditions also.

For example, some Third-World societies have learned to negotiate with a powerful West. The forms of multiculturalism they have chosen or been forced to adopt give them valuable knowledge about how to live in a world where they, unlike Western elites, can't afford the illusion that they are dependent on no other culture, can take what they wish from nature and other peoples, are the one model of the uniquely and admirably human, and that their ideas are uniquely and universally valid. Third-World scientific traditions can offer valuable models for global sciences here, too.

In this scenario, presumably Western groups would integrate into their sciences and culture precisely those Third-World cultural elements that would transform modern sciences. In contrast to the first proposal, it would be precisely some of the elements of Third-World cultures most incompatible with modern sciences that are to be valued: the Third-World forms of democratic, pacific, life-maintaining, and communal tendencies so at odds with imperialistic, violent, consuming, and possessively individualistic ones that critics find in Western sciences and culture. Obviously the former are not always well-practiced in Third-World cultures prior to the expansion into them of European culture, nor are they absent from First-World cultures, as postcolonial critics are perfectly aware and always caution. There would be many culturally different sciences, each with culturally-diverse origins. But central among the elements most valued in each case would be those that advance cooperation, democracy, the richness of indigenous achievements, and sustainable development.

Is this a real possibility? Will people of European descent be able to accept the idea that their democratic traditions are not the only viable ones? It is time to turn to examine what those living in the West can contribute to the development of sciences that have greater validity and are less imperial.

Projects Starting in the West

There are important and unique contributions to viable future sciences that can be made by those of us who value important features of the European tradition, but are opposed to the history of modern science's service to antidemocratic social relations. Progressives in the West do not have to retreat to stoicism when the topic of science is raised or regard our appropriate responses to criticisms of Eurocentrism in the sciences and science studies as only defensive ones. Instead, we, too, can recognize the opportunity and challenge of critically and "opportunistically" (as the Third-World thinkers put the point) retrieving and developing the best in European cultural traditions for sciences suitable for the emerging postcolonial world. Obviously, adding to our local environments — our classrooms, faculties, conferences, syllabi, footnotes, policy circles, television interviewees, and the like — the voices and presence of peoples whose groups have less benefitted from modern sciences will immeasurably enable the rest of us. But there are important steps we can take beyond "add[ing] postcolonials and stir[ring]" (to borrow a phrase from feminist writings). I mention here just three contributions that appear fairly obvious (though not uncontroversial); we should make it a project to identify more of them.

First, we can relocate the projects of sciences and science studies that originate in the West on the more accurate historical map created by the new postcolonial studies, instead of on the familiar one charted by Eurocentric accounts of mainly European and US history. This will require rethinking what it is that sciences and science studies should be describing and explaining and how they do so — in "rational reconstructions" of scientific progress and historical, sociological, and ethnographic accounts of sciences (their cultures and practices), for example. In what ways have the existing projects in physics, chemistry, engineering, biology, geology, and the history, sociology, anthropology, and philosophies of the sciences been excessively contained by Eurocentric assumptions and goals? Moreover, we can disseminate these accounts outside of university circles — for example, in the new diversity-focused US and global history texts currently being produced for elementary and high school students in the United States; in media accounts reaching the general public; and in journals, conferences, and other forms of communication that reach scientists.

Second, to this kind of new "science education" about the history of scientific traditions we can add a new kind *in* the sciences for both schoolrooms and for public discussion in journals, newspapers, television, and other resources through which a citizenry educates itself. Obviously, one important assistance in this project will be to achieve more culturally-diverse science communities, especially including their directors and funders; in terms of what happens in the lab as well as later, "science communities" are far more extensive than only those who work in labs. However, other equally-important transformations are necessary here. "Science criticism" that draws on the postcolonial analyses needs to be introduced into all science education programs inside and outside classroom contexts, media accounts, and museum exhibits. Existing science programs are supposed to instill in students a commitment to the most rigorous criticism of traditional assumptions, but the postcolonial accounts show that Eurocentric assumptions have blocked a crucial range of such criticisms. Scientists and humanists usually have spoken as if intellectual life should be divided between their two kinds of projects, as if the sciences and humanities are parallel projects.[57] But they are not. The sciences are parallel to the arts, and the humanities to the social studies of science, which is not considered a part of science at all. Someone well-educated in the humanities is expected to have a good training in literary, art, drama, and other forms of humanist *criticism* — in the "history, theory, and sociology" *about* these arts, but we do not expect them to be accomplished poets, sculptors, or playwrights. And this humanist critical education is not considered to be a lesser field than the performance of the arts. It is not an introductory project of explaining "arts for nonmajors"; it is an equal and different project with its own principles and goals — one in which poets, sculptors or playwrights can gain greater resources through exposure to the achievements and limitations of past efforts in their fields. It is a kind of parallel program for the sciences that I suggest is needed.

There are lots of reasonable answers to the question why no such field of "science criticism" already exists within science departments: "the history of physics is not physics," "the methods of history and sociology are not really scientific," "not enough time in the curriculum," "where are the faculty to teach such courses?" etc. And, of course, some may reasonably object to my drawing this parallel between the arts and sciences at all since artists, in contrast to scientists, are not primarily trained in universities. My point here is that these answers are *not reasonable enough.* Failing to locate any significant critical studies of the sciences in universities and, especially in science departments, indicates to students that no one thinks critical studies of the sciences important for learning to do science or for making reasoned decisions about scientific issues in public life. This is unfortunate since, as the postcolonial accounts show, philosophical, sociological, and historical assumptions form part of scientific understanding *about nature*. Scientists unknowingly use distorting cultural assumptions as part of the *evidence* for their results of research if they are taught that social studies of science are irrelevant to doing science, and that they should assiduously "avoid politics" rather than learn how to identify cultural features in their scientific assumptions, and how to sort the distorting and knowledge-limiting from the knowledge-enlarging cultural values and interests. Of course, the kinds of philosophy and social studies of science needed for this project are not widely practiced. These fields have enthusiastically adopted the goal of serving as "handmaids to the sciences," as John Locke put the point, and lack the empirical and theoretical adequacy required to come to terms with postcolonial histories and critiques. But my point here is that, nevertheless, more accurate and critical studies of sciences in their historical context should form an important part of science education as well as of general education.

Imagine if every science department contained the proportion of "science critics" to scientists that there are of literary critics in English Departments to creative writers anywhere in the world. Imagine having scientists, science policymakers, and the rest of us educated in "The Role of Biology, Chemistry and Physics in the Modern European Empire — and Vice Versa"; "Chinese (Islamic, South Asian, African, indigenous American, etc.) Sciences: Past, Present and Future"; "The Sexual Meanings of the Scientific Revolution in the European Expansion"; "From Craft to Factory Production of Twentieth-Century Science: Benefits and Losses"; "Objectivity as Ideal and Ideology"; "The Science and Political Economy of the Human Genome Project"; "Science and Democracy: Enemies or Friends?" and, especially, a course on the meanings and effects that our scientific projects come to have that we never intended, entitled "After the 'Death' of the Scientist."[58] Here would be a start on educations that could vastly improve the empirical and theoretical adequacy of modern sciences, as well as their politics.

Third, we can think of these and other such distinctive tasks as a progressive project for constructing fully modern sciences that creatively develop key elements of the Western cultural legacy — that, one could say, modernize them (or should one say "postmodernize" them?). One striking feature noted earlier of some of the Third-World analyses is that they propose what we can think of as *principled* ethnosciences when they contemplate constructing fully-modern sciences that conscientiously and critically use their indigenous cultural legacies, rather than — as they point out — only European ones. Those of us who value features of the European tradition can similarly strengthen notions of objectivity, rationality, and scientific method — notions central not only to our scientific tradition but also to such other Western institutions as the law and public policy.[59] Paradoxically, these postcolonial analyses that can appear to come from outside modern science are also very much inside its historical processes, as I have been arguing throughout. They are exactly what is called for by modern science's conventional goal of increasing the growth of knowledge through critical examination of cultural superstitions and unwarranted assumptions.

To conclude, asking questions about the hidden but real multiculturalism of global sciences can lead to far more accurate and valuable understandings not only of other cultures' scientific legacies but also of rich possibilities in the legacy of European culture and practice.

Notes

1 To appear also in *Configurations: A Journal of Literature, Science, and Technology,* 2, 2 (1994). Support for writing this essay has been provided by a sabbatical leave from the University of Delaware, an appointment as Research Associate at the UCLA Center for the Study of Women, and an appointment as Visiting Professor of Gender Studies at the Swiss Federal Institute of Technology, Zurich. I thank especially Kate Norberg and Karen Sacks at UCLA and Marlis Buchmann at ETH. Many friends, lecture audiences, classes, and seminars over the last few years have improved my thinking on these issues, and I greatly appreciate their responses. For especially helpful comments, I thank Paola Bacchetta, Karen Barad, Nancy Brickhouse, David Goldberg, Laurel Graham, Frances Hanckel, Donna Haraway, and V. Y. Mudimbe. The errors and problematic claims that remain are my own.

2 Patrick Petitjean et al., *Science and Empires: Historical Studies about Scientific Development and European Expansion* (Dordrecht: Kluwer, 1992); Z. Sardar, ed., *The Revenge of Athena: Science, Exploitation and the Third World* (London: Mansell, 1988); Third World Network, *Modern Science in Crisis: A Third World Response* (Penang, Malaysia: Third World Network, 1988). Many of the works cited below are useful far beyond the particular claim I cite. Additional writings I also have found especially useful in thinking about the possible multiculturalism of science include Michael Adas, *Machines as the Measure of Man* (Ithaca: Cornell University Press, 1989); Donna Haraway, *Primate Visions: Gender, Race, and Nature in the World of Modern Science* (New York: Routledge, 1989); Charles Moraze, ed., *Science and the Factors of Inequality* (Paris: UNESCO, 1979); Vandana Shiva, *Staying Alive: Women, Ecology and Development* (London: Zed Press, 1989); Sharon Traweek, *Beamtimes and Life Times* (Cambridge: MIT Press, 1988). See also my *The Science Question in Feminism* (Ithaca: Cornell University Press, 1986) and "After Eurocentrism: Challenges for the Philosophy of Science," in *Philosophy of Science Association 1992 Proceedings,* eds David Hull, Micky Forbes, and Kathleen Okruhlik, Volume Two (East Lansing: Philosophy of Science Association, 1993) in addition to other works cited below.

3 Laurel Graham pointed this out.

4 For examples of the latter, see Andrew Pickering, ed., *Science as Practice and Culture* (Chicago: University of Chicago Press, 1992).

5 The term "borderlands" is from Gloria Anzaldúa's *Borderlands/La Frontera: The New Mestiza* (San Francisco: Spinsters/Aunt Lute Book Company: 1987). The notion appears in the writing of many other "borderlands" thinkers.

6 See, e.g., Samir Amin, *Eurocentrism* (New York: Monthly Review Press, 1989).

7 Scientists usually claim that all they mean by the statement that "science works" is that it makes accurate predictions. However, in the next breath they usually defend the extraordinarily high US investment in scientific establishments on what I take to be the only grounds anyone could find reasonable in a society professing a commitment to democratic social relations; namely, that the results of science improve social life. Thus "science works" in this enlarged sense which is conflated

with the more technical sense of the phrase. As we shall see below, the success of science's empirical predictions depends in part on social relations; there are good historical reasons for the conflation.

8 I am tempted to keep inserting "Western" into "modern science" — modern *Western* science — to avoid the standard Eurocentric assumption that non-Western traditions, including their scientific practices and cultures, are static; that only Western sciences are dynamic and thus have developed since the fifteenth century. However, that locution has other problems; it emphasizes the dualistic "West versus the rest" framework, and ignores the non-Western components of modern science.

9 Frances Yates, *Giordano Bruno and the Hermetic Tradition* (New York: Vintage, 1969).

10 Donald F. Lach, *Asia in the Making of Europe*, Vol. 2 (Chicago: University of Chicago Press, 1977); Seyyed Hossein Nasr, "Islamic Science, Western Science: Common Heritage, Diverse Destinies," in *The Revenge of Athena*, ed. Z. Sardar, pp. 239–48.

11 See Martin Bernal, *Black Athena: The Afroasiatic Roots of Classical Civilization*, Vol. I (New Brunswick: Rutgers University Press, 1987); Cheikh Anta Diop, *The African Origin of Civilization: Myth or Reality?* tr. M. Cook (Westport, CT: L. Hill, 1974); Lacinay Keita, "African Philosophical Systems: A Rational Reconstruction," *Philosophical Forum*, 9, 2–3 (1977–78), pp. 169–89; Lach, *Asia in the Making of Europe;* I. A. Sabra, "The Scientific Enterprise," in *The World of Islam*, ed. B. Lewis (London: Thames and Hudson, 1976); E. Frances White, "Civilization Denied: Questions on *Black Athena*," *Radical America*, 21, 5 (1987), pp. 38–40.

12 Jack Weatherford, *Indian Givers: What the Native Americans Gave to the World* (New York: Crown, 1988).

13 R. K. Kochhar, "Science in British India," Parts I and II, *Current Science* (India), 63, 11, p. 694. Cf. also 64, 1 (1992–93), pp. 55–62.

14 And, as V. Y. Mudimbe pointed out to me, of Europe itself, for European sciences also constituted European lands, cities, and peoples as their laboratories. Consider, for example, the way women, the poor, children, the sick, the mad, rural and urban populations, and workers have been continuously studied by natural and social sciences.

15 Susantha Goonatilake makes this point in "The Voyages of Discovery and the Loss and Re-Discovery of 'Other's' Knowledge," *Impact of Science on Society*, 167 (1993), pp. 241–64.

16 For one thing, Westerners note that Chinese or African astronomy is done within culturally-local projects of a sort devalued by scientific rationality, such as (in some cases) astrology, or culturally local meanings of the heavens or other natural phenomena. So, whatever their accuracy, such astronomical discoveries could not be admitted as "real science" without permitting the possibility of assigning such a status also to astrology or Confucian religious beliefs. Alternatively, one could say that any but only those discoveries of other cultures that are duplicated by Western sciences count as scientific; this has the paradoxical consequence that as Western sciences develop, other cultures also (retroactively!) get more scientific. Nancy Brickhouse's questions helped me to clarify this point.

17 Goonatilake, "A Project for Our Time," in *The Revenge of Athena*, ed. Z. Sardar, p. 226.

18 See the section on astronomy in Ivan Van Sertima, *Blacks in Science* (New Brunswick: Transaction Press, 1986).

19 Goonatilake, "The Voyages of Discovery," p. 256.

20 Joseph Needham, *The Grand Titration: Science and Society in East and West* (Toronto: University of Toronto Press, 1969), p. 55–6.

21 See, e.g., Susan Bordo, *The Flight to Objectivity* (Albany: State University of New York Press, 1987); Genevieve Lloyd, *The Man of Reason* (Minneapolis: University of Minnesota Press, 1984); Tzvetan Todorov, *The Conquest of America: The Question of the Other*, tr. Richard Howard (New York: Harper and Row, 1984).

22 See Needham's discussion of seven conceptual errors in standard Western thought about "universal science" that lead to erroneous devaluations of the scientific achievements of non-European sciences in *The Grand Titration*.

23 Robin Horton, "African Traditional Thought and Western Science," parts 1 and 2, *Africa*, 37 (1967), pp. 50–71, 155–87.

24 J. E. Wiredu, "How Not to Compare African Thought with Western Thought," in *African Philosophy*, ed. Richard Wright, 3rd ed. (Lanham, MD: University Press of America, 1984), pp. 149–62.

25 Thomas S. Kuhn, *The Structure of Scientific Revolutions*, 2nd ed. (Chicago: University of Chicago Press, 1970), p. 167.

26 Needham, *The Grand Titration*, p. 14–15.

27 Edgar Zilsel, "The Sociological Roots of Science," *American Journal of Sociology*, 47 (1942), pp. 544–62.

28 Kochhar, "Science in British India"; Alfred Crosby, *Ecological Imperialism: The Biological Expansion of Europe* (Cambridge: Cambridge University Press, 1987); V. V. Krishna, "The Colonial 'Model' and the Emergence of National Science in India: 1876–1920," in *Science and Empires*, Petitjean et al., pp. 57–72; Deepak Kumar, "Problems in Science Administration: A Study of the Scientific Surveys in British India 1757–1900," in *Science and Empires*, Petitjean et al., pp. 69–80.

29 Paul Forman, "Behind Quantum Electronics: National Security as Bases for Physical Research in the US, 1940–1960," *Historical Studies in Physical and Biological Sciences*, 18 (1987) pp. 149–229.

30 Susantha Goonatilake, "A Project for Our Times," p. 235–6. (Should not African and indigenous American civilizations also count as regional ones containing scientific traditions?)

31 The "Strong Programme" in the sociology of knowledge has developed this analysis. See, e.g., David Bloor, *Knowledge and Social Imagery* (London: Routledge and Kegan Paul, 1977).

32 This section reviews the arguments of my "Is Western Science an Ethnoscience?" (forthcoming).

33 See, e.g., Morris Berman, *The Reenchantment of the World* (Ithaca: Cornell University Press, 1981); Bordo, *The Flight to Objectivity*; Carolyn Merchant, *The Death of Nature: Women, Ecology and the Scientific Revolution* (New York: Harper and Row, 1980); Nasr, "Islamic Science, Western Science."

34 Needham, *The Grand Titration*, p. 302.

35 Ibid., p. 323.

36 Ibid., p. 327.

37 "[L]aws of nature, like laws of the state, are historically imposed from above and obeyed from below." In contrast, "the concept of order, wider than law and free from its coercive, hierarchical, and centralizing implications has the potential to expand our conception of science. Order is a category comprising patterns of organization that can be spontaneous, self-generated, or externally imposed." Evelyn Fox Keller, *Reflections on Gender and Science* (New Haven: Yale University Press, 1984), p. 131–2. See also the interesting discussion of Needham's argument in Jatinder K. Bajaj, "Francis Bacon, the First Philosopher of Modern Science: A Non-Western View," in *Science, Hegemony and Violence: A Requiem for Modernity*, ed. Ashis Nandy (Delhi: Oxford, 1990).

38 See Bruno Latour's discussion of the importance to science of "centres of calculation," in Chapter 6 of his *Science in Action* (Cambridge: Harvard University Press).

39 The complexity of these sentences arises from the fact that elites in Third-World cultures also enjoy luxurious access to the benefits of modern sciences, and the majority of citizens in most First-World cultures — that is, the poor and other disadvantaged groups — do not.

40 Khor, Kok Peng, "Science and Development: Underdeveloping the Third World," in *The Revenge of Athena*, ed. Z. Sardar, p. 207–8.

41 Claude Alvares, "Science, Colonialism and Violence: A Luddite View," in *Science, Hegemony and Violence: A Requiem for Modernity*, ed. Ashis Nandy, p. 108.

42 J. Bandyopadhyay and V. Shiva, "Science and Control: Natural Resources and their Exploitation," in *The Revenge of Athena*, ed. Z. Sardar, p. 63.

43 Dorothy Smith is especially eloquent on this point. See *The Conceptual Practices of Power* (Boston: Northeastern University Press, 1990) and *The Everyday World as Problematic: A Feminist Sociology* (Boston: Northeastern University Press, 1987). However, abstractness is not unique to such cultures. As Paola Bachetta pointed out (by letter), certain forms of ancient Hinduism are based on philosophical abstractions.

44 Bandyopadhyay and Shiva, "Science and Control," p. 60.

45 Xavier Polanco, "World-Science: How is the History of World-Science to Be Written?" in *Science and Empires*, Petitjean et al., p. 225.

46 Susantha Goonatilake, *Aborted Discovery: Science and Creativity in the Third World* (London: Zed Press, 1984), p. 229–30.

47 This kind of critique enables one to see that sleeping in the feminist science analyses lies a direct challenge to conventional assumptions about the necessity of value-neutrality to the universality of science. A form of this challenge has been to the necessity of value-neutrality to the maximal objectivity of science. Cf. my "After the Neutrality Ideal: Science, Politics and 'Strong Objectivity'," *Social Research*, 59, 3 (Fall 1992), pp. 568–87; reprinted in *The Politics of Western Science, 1640–1990*, ed. Margaret Jacob (Atlantic Highlands: Humanities Press, 1994).

48 Some readers may be troubled by my retention of notions that seem so central to modern science and its mentality, such as objectivity, less distorted, valid, and the like. I cannot take the space here to discuss the reasons why I, like many other science critics, find these important terms to appropriate, "reoccupy," and strengthen as we try to relink sciences to projects of advancing democratic social relations. Let me just say, first, that not all imagined ways of working toward greater democracy are

equally compatible with nature's constraints upon human activity (as the postcolonial critics themselves point out, after all). Second, as I discuss below, these notions (objectivity, etc.) are central in many other Western institutions besides the natural sciences, for example, the social sciences, the law, and public policy. We can't "just say no" to such notions without abandoning a central moral and social value of many Westerners — not just a scientific or epistemological one. See my discussion of "strong objectivity" in *Whose Science? Whose Knowledge? Thinking From Women's Lives* (Ithaca: Cornell University Press, 1991), and "After the Neutrality Ideal," pp. 568–87

49 One particularly good discussion of this is in Bina Agarwal, "The Gender and Environment Debate: Lessons from India," *Feminist Studies*, 18, 1 (1992), pp. 119–58.

50 Goonatilake, "Voyages of Discovery," pp. 259–60. This approach is by no means unique to Third-World theorists; it has been appearing even in Western popular accounts of "endangered societies." (Notice the extension to non-Western peoples of language initially used to describe animals.) For example, *Time* magazine ran a cover story in 1992 reporting on the "endangered knowledge" Western culture should gather from cultures disappearing under modernization and development pressures. ("Modernization" and "development" for whom?)

51 Elizabeth Hsu, "The Reception of Western Medicine in China: Examples from Yunnan," in *Science and Empires*, Petitjean et al., p. 89.

52 Ashis Nandy, "Introduction" to *Science, Hegemony and Violence*, ed. Nandy, p. 11.

53 This language has been developed by Samir Amin. See, e.g., *Eurocentrism*.

54 Third World Network, "Modern Science in Crisis," reprinted in *The "Racial" Economy of Science: Toward a Democratic Future*, ed. Sandra Harding (Bloomington: Indiana University Press, 1993), p. 324–5.

55 Ibid., p. 496.

56 Richard Levins and Richard Lewontin, "Applied Biology in the Third World," from *The Dialectical Biologist* (Cambridge: Harvard University Press, 1988); reprinted in Harding, *The "Racial" Economy of Science*, pp. 315–25.

57 See, e.g., C. P. Snow, *The Two Cultures, and a Second Look* (Cambridge: Cambridge University Press, 1964). The following argument draws from my "Women and Science in Historical Context," in *National Women's Studies Association Journal*, 5, 1 (1993), p. 49–55.

58 I refer here to the discussion of the meanings and other effects that authors never intended their works to have that is indicated by the phrase "the 'death' of the author."

59 The last two decades of feminist and antiracist critiques in philosophy, science studies, political theory, and the social sciences will provide especially useful resources here since they have focused on just such projects of transforming standards of objectivity, rationality, and method into ones more effective at distorting cultural assumptions and conceptual frameworks from shaping the results of research and public policy.

17

Identity: Cultural, Transcultural, and Multicultural

PETER CAWS

We thought we were dealing with sociologists; our mistake: they were entomologists.

Jean-Paul Sartre[1]

It has come to be a familiar claim of some advocates of multiculturalism that a culture of one's own (that is, one not imposed from without) is one of the conditions or the achievement of an authentic identity. In what follows I shall examine this claim and some of the arguments it has generated. Along the way, it will be necessary to clarify what might be meant by a culture in the first place, in what sense such a thing might be one's own, and how that might be connected to having an identity. It may be helpful to state at the beginning the guiding conviction that underlies this inquiry. I put the point categorically rather than hypothetically for the sake of definiteness, not because I think it beyond argument — though there may not be room for all the necessary arguments in the space of this paper.

My point of departure, then, is this: that every "first" or "native" culture in the singular (by analogy with the first or native language) *is* "imposed from without," willy-nilly: although it is "one's own" in a weak sense (one's background, upbringing, family, country), the possessive relation proves, when thought through, to go the other way — one belongs rather to it, it is not something one has freely chosen or worked to acquire, which would make it "one's own" in a strong sense. Consequently an identity that depends on it cannot be *one's own* identity in the strong sense either. The dialogical process of the development of an authentic identity (as Charles Taylor puts it[2]) will therefore require the transcendence of one's culture of origin. That one might settle back into an identity associated uniquely with that very culture is not ruled out *a priori*, but it is not to be expected — and certainly not to be insisted upon, especially not by others having an interest in the maintenance or strengthening of the culture in question. Nor is it to be expected that the identity eventually achieved will be associated with any recognizable single culture.

Given that the mature individual is likely to leave his or her culture of origin behind as limiting to the development of personal identity, what are the most fruitful sources for the construction of that identity, apart from purely interpersonal ones? First, I shall argue, the testing and strengthening of the self against constant features of the natural world — the body, the environment: I call these (and the culture-independent forms of knowledge that derive from them) *transcultural*; second, the enrichment of the self through acquaintance with and cultivation of what is found to be the most rewarding in all the human products and practices with which one comes in contact: I call this *multicultural*.

* * * * *

Some preliminary remarks on culture — necessarily sketchy, and touching on only a few of the multitude of issues the term evokes. Apart from its bacteriological sense which can safely be left aside, there are two or three main lines of development of the idea, implicitly in play in the multicultural debate, that are worth distinguishing. Culture has its roots in the practice of careful attention to the gods who were cultivated (as people are still said to cultivate the acquaintance of powerful or influential figures) to ward off their anger and invite their blessing. The cult of the gods of growth and fecundity, Persephone, Demeter, and the rest, involved invocations and ceremonies connected with the land; singing and sacrificing — but also ploughing and planting: whence agriculture, literally "the culture of fields." The transition from cultivation in this sense (which eventually became purely technical — horticulture, arboriculture, pisciculture, etc. — leaving its religious connotations behind) to the metaphorical cultivation of fields of idea, of the arts, of power, etc., is easy enough to understand.

From activities specific to particular domains, the concept comes to extend, by Kant's time, to rational action generally; he defines culture as "the bringing out of the aptitude of a rational being to reach any end it likes without restriction (consistently with its freedom)."[3] Since the nineteenth century at least, the term has had a normative sense at the individual level and a descriptive sense at the group level. The standard representative of the normative sense is Matthew Arnold who, in *Culture and Anarchy,* says that culture is "a pursuit of our total perfection by means of getting to know, on all the matters that most concern us, the best which has been thought and said in the world";[4] this, in his opinion, is all that will keep the barbarians at bay. The descriptive sense is to be found, for example, in von Virchow's characterization of the struggle between the Prussian State and the Catholic church as a clash of cultures in *Kulturkampf*[5] as well as, almost a century later, in C. P. Snow's evocation of "the two cultures," literary and scientific.[6] One thing that did *not* play a role in any of these senses of "culture" was what has come to be called ethnicity. The barbarians, in Matthew Arnold, are not tribesmen halfway around the world but British aristocrats close to home with their heavy hand on the institutions of art and education. It was the description by ethnographers of societies in which the connection between cult, ideology, power, and practice was still overt that led to the more recently dominant anthropological sense of culture as a body of beliefs, habits, products, and observances encountered in the daily and seasonal practice of some more or less localized group, usually geographically, linguistically, and technologically remote. This is the sense that was popularized in books like Ruth Benedict's *Patterns of Culture*,[7] and whose meaning was struggled over in the anthropological journals; Alfred Kroeber and Clyde Kluckhohn, in their almost exhaustive (and still pertinent) review of concepts of culture, reported having found 164 different definitions of the term.[8]

There were, it seems to me, two main factors that helped to bring this concept of culture to center stage in the West as modern began to yield to postmodern. First, some moderns in the arts turned to exotic cultures for inspiration, particularly in painting, music, and dance, thus drawing to them attention and increased respect. Second, some articulate minorities (whose aspirations might theretofore have been in the direction of assimilation) began to emphasize their own genetic links to such cultures, finding in them a source of identity with something other than the dominant culture by which they were surrounded.

* * * * *

The value of alternative cultures and their utility as vehicles for self-identification in the face of an oppressive dominant culture are two of the key elements of multiculturalism. About the first, there can be no doubt and I take it as given. The second engages the main topic of this paper but poses a subsidiary question as well, which I will deal with first. The question is whether it is properly speaking a *culture* which is dominant or, to put it in another way, whether the dominant culture has the unity and coherence that make it recognizably a single culture. For with respect to the problem of identity, if the dominant culture is not the culprit perhaps an alternative culture is not the cure.

Something dominates, to be sure: unassimilated minorities have been economically and socially disadvantaged, and the reasons for this (indeed for their nonassimilation in the first place), when not outright racist, often have seemed to be due to cultural differences — language, religious practice, manners, dress. But it is quite possible for an advantaged group to reject something as "the other" when there is no very clear view of "the same," and what looks like monolithic oppression from the outside may be riddled with variation and even contradiction on the inside. A good case might be made for the claim that while it was opening up to exotic cultures — though not for that reason — so-called Western culture was at the same time losing its own coherence so that only members of subcultures (religious, social, military, academic) could any longer find in it a basis for their own identity.

I do not wish to belabor the point, but on the very issue of the curriculum and without invoking C. P. Snow's somewhat simplistic view of the matter, the centrifugal and weakly-connected character of Western culture has been evident for a long time. The curriculum has been the main battleground of multiculturalism; as Arnold Krupat has written,

> multiculturalism refers to an order of instruction concerned to present that which a dominant culture has defined as "other"and "different" — usually, of course, minor and inferior as well — in such a way that it may interrogate and challenge that which the dominant culture has defined as familiar and its own — and so, to be sure, major and superior.[9]

But consider the real content of what is "familiar and its own" and how successfully this is communicated to those who, quite unproblematically, are supposed to belong to the dominant culture. Consider the frequent laments that students do not know the landmarks of their own history and literature; consider the virtual irrelevance of the curriculum to what is eventually remembered by those who pass through it. A few decades ago, a couple of irreverent Englishmen called Sellar and Yeatman published comic send-ups of the history — and then of all the other subjects — taught in British schools under the titles *1066 and All That* and *And Now All This*;[10] they defined the cultural residue of education as the "absolutely unforgettable," most of which in their version turned out, of course, to be hilariously wrong. Under the humor there was a serious point: people do *not* remember most of what they are exposed to for their own cultural good — and how much of the culture is that in any case?

A bit of anecdotal evidence comes from a conversation I once had with a student in which something about racism, or jealousy perhaps, prompted me to ask her if she had read *Othello*. "No," she said — "we read *Macbeth*." The point hardly needs elaboration: perhaps the *only* common element *all* college graduates can be expected to have had in their English literature classes is a play of Shakespeare — but not necessarily the same one. When one reflects that even that one play will have been read and remembered differently by people who were "taught" it in the same class, the *complete* idiosyncrasy of cultural formation no longer seems so implausible.

The irrelevance of the curriculum — to a debate in which it is considered central! — shows up even more clearly when I ask: if it was reasonable for me to expect that the student, as a cultured English-speaking person, *should* have read *Othello*, when should she have done it? The obvious answer is: on her own time, as soon as she became aware that that *was* a reasonable expectation. And how might she have acquired this awareness, given that the work had not been assigned as part of the curriculum? (The curriculum might have included a sensible curriculum would include — some second-order considerations about what it would take to be cultured, in various cultures: a debate about the canon, if you will, which would *not* take the form of a Hirsch-type list but would raise what are now recognized as the issues of multiculturalism itself.) Might she have acquired it as part of the development of her own identity? And yet she did not seem to be in much doubt about that — she was, as I remember, a perfectly self-possessed and articulate person.

I will not try to get further mileage out of this case; the lesson I draw from it is that the connection between cultural identity and the curriculum is far weaker than is generally supposed, hence that if a culture is dominant it is not necessarily the instructional establishment that makes it so. Instruction in the conventional sense must be supplemented by self-instruction — by persistent reading far beyond the boundaries of any received canon — if a genuine cultural identity is to be achieved, and the motivation for this does not come from the establishment whose system of rewards is inimical to it. This opens up another line of argument which cannot be followed here; the aim of this part of the paper has simply been to challenge the notion of a monolithic dominant culture as responsible for inequalities that follow racial, or linguistic or economic cleavages in the body politic.

There are other arguments that might be deployed along the same general line: to the effect, for example, that as far as the internalization of cultural content goes, differences between two individuals belonging to the same culture may often be as great as, or greater than, differences between two individuals belonging to different cultures; or to the effect that in any society only a very few individuals can ever seriously be said to be bearers or transmitters of the relevant culture in any but a superficial sense. Also there is a culture of attitude that transmits, on the one hand, piety towards the dominant canon and, on the other, a set of social prejudices that help to perpetuate oppression, and there is a mass culture, including sports, popular music, best sellers and the like, that is very generally diffused by the media but is on the whole nonoppressive (indeed, it was multicultural before the fact). But both of these tend to operate outside the curricular establishment and, hence, to be tangential to this part of the argument.

*   *   *   *   *

At this point perhaps it can safely be said that if there is oppression (and there is), the best target to attack in attempts to overcome it may not, after all, be "the dominant culture"; also that if there is a need for an identity of one's own (which is not quite as obvious, at least not just in those terms), the best place to look for it may not be a single culture of any kind, minority or otherwise. The suggestion, that the need for an identity of one's own is not so obvious, requires some explanation. I do not mean that identities, however defined, could be dispensed with or are unimportant — though I do think that the more secure one is in one's own identity the less one thinks about it as such, and perhaps, turning the argument around, that the more one worries about it the less secure it will prove to be. Rather, I question the emphasis on identity as something *needed*, hence, by implication, as something *lacking*. The allegation of needs in cases like this — usually, it is to be noted, the needs of others (it is hard to imagine the people who make this kind of argument admitting to deficiencies in their own identities) — seems to me to run a great risk of being patronizing.

Even if the case is put in the broadest cultural terms, I find something forced about it. Here is Steven C. Rockefeller in his comment on Charles Taylor's *Multiculturalism and "The Politics of Recognition"*:

> The call for recognition of the equal value of different cultures is the expression of a basic and profound universal need for unconditional acceptance. A feeling of such acceptance, including affirmation of one's ethnic particularity as well as one's universally shared potential, is an essential part of a strong sense of identity. As Taylor points out, the formation of a person's identity is closely connected to positive social recognition — acceptance and respect — from parents, friends, loved ones, and also from the larger society. A highly developed sense of identity involves still more. Human beings need not only a sense of belonging in relation to human society. Especially when confronted with death, we also need an enduring sense of belonging to — of being a valued part of — the larger whole which is the universe. The politics of recognition may, therefore, also be an expression of a complex human need for acceptance and belonging, which on the deepest level is a religious need.[11]

The claim that "an affirmation of one's ethnic particularity ... is an *essential* part of a strong sense of identity" (emphasis added) seems to me simply false, and the theme of cosmic union at the end to be an exercise in pious fantasy. But then I am always suspicious of the invocation of "we" in such contexts — it too often means the others, those with whom the speaker or writer is deigning, for the moment, to make common cause. (I remember an exchange after a lecture once with a questioner who said accusingly "We have lost our sense of values!" Really, I asked had he lost *his* sense of values? "No," he replied, "but I'm different.") For my own part, I would wish to argue that an affirmation of ethnic particularity tends to *weaken* one's sense of identity: the more the reliance on the group, the less the development of the individual.

Suppose it were admitted that everyone always already has as full an identity as anyone else, what would be the consequences for the multiculturalist argument? Perhaps it would be better to say that everyone should be *credited* with such an identity (it must always be possible for a free agent to express dissatisfaction with his or her own identity, though anyone who did this, in my view, would be giving evidence paradoxically enough, of a well-developed identity since it takes a fairly robust sense of self to admit to shortcomings in oneself). The multiculturalist argument would presumably take the line that this is precisely what the dominant culture denies, or refuses to credit. But not having one's identity *acknowledged* is not at all the same as not *having* it. As must be clear by now, I do not consider the dominant culture to be in a position to affirm or deny anything; what is done in its name by representatives of the forces of reaction (who thereby, often no doubt unconsciously, put themselves at the service of the forces of repression) is another matter, but not its fault (whatever that might mean).

But, the argument might proceed, it is just in our identity *as* members of the oppressed minority that the dominant culture rejects us. But is it really? Is a member of a minority required to adopt the corresponding identity? This is often expected, on pain of accusations of class disloyalty (the Uncle Tom, the Oreo cookie), but the question is worth examination: why should someone who is trying to escape personally from the domination of one culture be compelled to carry the banner of another? Also there is a risk in this context of confusing identity with other related concepts — identification, individuation, classification. That I should be *identified* by others as grey-haired, male, white, etc., need affect me in my *identity* not at all — though it may do so if I let it. (Anybody who exclaimed at this point "ah! a white male!" — with the implication that being an apparent member of the dominant culture in some way disqualifies me from dealing with this topic — would be guilty of an offense as racist and sexist as any on the multiculturalist index; mildly so, but purely so. I state it as a matter of fact, which anyone may dispute who is in a position to do so, that these attributions are not essential to my identity.)

Again, objective characteristics individuate and can be used as a basis for classification; one technique of individuation is precisely to keep classifying until just that intersection of classes is found to which only the individual in question belongs. But when I have been assigned to my unique and individual place in the scheme of classification, *nothing* has yet been established about my identity. Indeed, it is a general (though also a generally neglected) principle in the theory of social groups that, apart from the mere possession of the identifying properties that permit assignment to the group in the first place, *nothing follows about an individual from any fact, actual or alleged, about a group of which that individual is a member.* For example: it actually is the case that the median height of males is greater than the median height of females, but this gives me no information about the height of any particular male, nor does it tell me in advance that a given male will be taller or shorter than a given female. In a sufficiently large population it will be generally true that for any male there is a taller female, and the question of whether the tallest person is male or female can only be answered empirically. There are many imagined group differences that follow a logical pattern of this type, and if no conclusion follows about the individual from a real difference, this holds even more strongly for postulated differences based on prejudice or wish-fulfillment. *This* is the principle that needs to be deployed to combat racism, sexism, and the rest, and if followed out consistently it would do the job alone.

*   *   *   *   *

From the suggestion that "everyone always already has as full an identity as anyone else" it might seem to follow that I think identity is fixed and unchanging, and that there is, as it were, nothing to choose between one identity and another. Neither is the case. To take the latter point first: if identities change at all, they may change for the better; looking back, I can see that the person I was, before I met someone significant, or read some crucial text, or had some striking experience, was a shallower or less-complete person. Two caveats, however: on the one hand, it would seem inappropriate to take this as a matter of self-congratulation; on the other, I am not sure one is ever in a position to make this sort of judgment about another person. It is not my business to be judgmental about anyone else's identity — I do not know what he or she may have had to go through to attain it, even if it seems to be an identity I could not myself live with — and the strategy of crediting everyone with a full identity in every moment still seems the right one.

On the former point, I agree with Charles Taylor that identity is developed "in dialogue with, sometimes in struggle against, the things our significant others want to see in us,"[12] though I do not think that that is the whole story, nor do I find some of Taylor's characterizations of identity particularly helpful (for example: "Consider what we mean by *identity*. It's who we are, 'where we're coming from'. As such it is the background against which our tastes and desires and opinions and aspirations make sense"[13]). Identity, psychologically as well as logically, is a *reflexive* relation, a relation of myself to myself, but it can be a mediated relation: I relate to myself through my interaction with others *and with the world*. It is this last component that tends to be overlooked in the dialogical view of identity and whose importance, it seems to me, is seriously and even damagingly underrated when disadvantaged individuals are encouraged to find their identities in cultural identification alone. Nothing I say here is meant to belittle any particular culture, and if a member of a minority who has been subject to prejudice is able to replace a part of his or her identity that has been affected by negative stereotypes with a positive identification, say with the arts or other achievements of fellow inheritors of the culture, that is surely to the good — though in line with the principle enunciated above, it is not really up to me to make that judgment. What I do want to suggest is that a more direct and less derivative way to some aspects of a strong identity may lie in confrontation with and knowledge of the natural world.

There is a sense — the existentialists were good at dramatizing it, but I think they were also right — in which I am alone in the world and have to forge my identity in isolation. Granted that, human development being what it is, I cannot do this except on the basis of a security derived from primary human relations (it would be appropriate here to involve a sequence of Eriksonian stages) still, others cannot do everything for me and, in due course, I have to come to terms with my physical embodiment and situation as well as with the flood of ideas that come to me from my culture and from other cultures. What I urgently need as I confront this complexity is all the knowledge I can lay my hands on: on the one hand, about my own physiology, emotions, sexuality, prejudices, and so on — that is, a healthy self-knowledge — and, on the other, about general principles of psychology, language, symbolism, nutrition, climate, the properties and uses of materials, and so on and so on — in short, the usual contents of a scientific and humanistic education.

Now some of this no doubt will be culturally marked, but one of the claims I want to make is that much of it, by now, is a common heritage of all human cultures — is, if you will, culturally neutral or transcultural. I refer mainly, of course, to the gradual emergence and convergence of science since the Greeks and Arabs, with its spectacular acceleration in the last three or four hundred years. People from every cultural background have been persuaded by and have contributed to this, and learning it is the single most powerful agent of liberation and, hence, of the formation of identity free from any imposed cultural imprint to have been made available since the human enterprise began. That is why one of the main demands of those who see themselves as culturally oppressed ought, I believe, to be for the best possible training in the natural and human sciences. It is the analogue at a higher level of the literacy that Frederick Douglass so passionately understood to be the key to his own liberation.[14]

It is popular in some postmodernist circles to say that science does not converge, and that it is one cultural formation, among others, relativized to its own culture of origin which happens to be Western. At the level of the most abstract theorizing the convergence, it is true, remains to be consolidated and history may yet take a divergent turn; but at the level of the modeling of everyday phenomena for explanatory and predictive purposes, there is a ramified body of confirmed and teachable knowledge available to anyone irrespective of culture or origin, the mastery of which can, I am persuaded, do far more for the initiate's sense of identity, for his or her self-relation mediated by an enduring object domain, than can any rediscovered ancestral roots.[15]

Might this whole edifice prove flawed? — of course it might. But so might any specific cultural belief; indeed, the latter is far more likely. Can we be ultimately sure of the objectivity of the domain? — no, we cannot, but, again, its relative stability far exceeds that of any more-localized knowledge. Science, it is true, is a generalization from the local; how could it not be, since all knowledge is local in the first instance and comes back to being that on application. But if forms of knowledge from different localities generalize to the same conclusion in some respect, it looks as if we are in touch with something nonlocal, and that is what has happened historically. Meanwhile scientific results immediately are intelligible to people from diverse cultural backgrounds.

If I may be permitted an autobiographical note: I grew up in a primitive culture[16] with primitive beliefs, fundamentalist Judeo–Christian, antirationalist, absolutist, and was *saturated* with it during my formative years. But, when I was about eleven or twelve, the minute I came upon serious mathematics and physics, I saw that they had to be right in their way, independently of my own or any other cultural background. True, this was in school, and a Western school at that. But I do not accept the view that it, therefore, was culturally bound because there were many other things I was taught in school that I found quite unconvincing. People from cultures all over the world have had similar experiences. And except for moral or political *reasons* — which, as I have suggested repeatedly, must be addressed but which must not be confused with epistemological ones — they will not be found complaining that science is Western, or culture-specific at all.

Scientific literacy gives the subject a sense of his or her location in and adequacy to a world that transcends the individual; as such, it answers perhaps to the desideratum expressed in the passage from Steven Rockefeller cited earlier, with the crucial difference that the subject is not asking for acceptance but claiming understanding. That claim must of course be accompanied by appropriate disclaimers to the effect that the understanding is provisional, limited, and so on, but this is no reason not to make the claim in the first place or to mistrust the sense it warrants of being made to the measure of the universe.

Such transcultural elements of identity, since they derive from constant features of the world, bodily or environmentally, would tend to make individuals like one another — but even they will have a very modestly convergent effect as against the wide divergence that determines the radical idiosyncrasy of the human subject. It is difficult to convey graphically enough how deep this idiosyncrasy goes. Consider that every newborn human child (with the exception of monozygotic twins) begins life with a unique genetic endowment; consider that the characteristically human aspect of its existence will be mediated by a brain that is equipped with a hundred billion neurons, each multiply connected to thousands of the others; consider that chemical changes take place within and between adjacent neurons millions of times a second; consider that this goes on day and night beginning *in utero* and continuing without respite for the whole of the individual's life. Even monozygotic twins, though they begin with a high degree of similarity, may differ enough by the time epigenetic and experiential factors are taken into account to put them in very different corners of the multidimensional universe of human possibilities.

* * * * *

Each person's identity is built up on a wholly idiosyncratic basis; the number of dimensions of individual variability and of possibilities within each dimension, compared with the total number of actual human beings who have ever existed, are large enough to make it quite conceivable that nobody has any really near neighbors. We do not experience things this way because of the smoothing-over — and, I may add, the banality — that is effected by language and culture, though as we have seen the similarities produced by these, at best, are rough and approximate. Yet arguments about culture and about education seem to assume a uniformity and a pliability that would make everyone alike and similarly susceptible to influence and indoctrination, curricular or otherwise. That is the force of the epigraph from Sartre that I have put at the head of the paper: such assumptions would be justified if we were talking about the social insects, but they are wholly inappropriate as applied to free individuals, who are freely taking their places in human society. To confine the development of one's identity within the variables of any single culture seems to me to be a wanton neglect of the vast riches that are available in the world, a choice of the entomological rather than the genuinely sociological (though Sartre clearly thought that sociology was very far from having lived up to its potential as a theory of free agents in freely-chosen relations to one another).

If even the transcultural components of identity, worked out in relation to relatively constant features of an objective world, allow for such variation, consider how abundant the opportunities become when we turn to the genuinely multicultural. Is this the "multicultural" of "multiculturalism"? I have used these terms informally in the course of the paper but the answer to that question is not straightforward, partly because multiculturalism came along before the usage of its root adjective had had a chance to establish itself. I shall assume that a positive answer is defensible because it would be a shame if multiculturalism failed to take advantage of the multicultural in the sense in which I use the term — if it became an exercise in repressive correctness rather than in expansive celebration.

"Multicultural" is a good adjective: it has a generous feel to it, it is welcoming, inclusive, embracing; like "international" or "pluralist" or "ecumenical" it suggests a largeness of conception, a transcendence of sectional interest, an openness to the variety of human pursuits and achievements. This remark, of course, is not an argument for anything; it represents my own reaction to the idea, and is not necessarily shared by others. There are plenty of chauvinists, analytic philosophers, and fundamentalists who have felt equally strongly that internationalism and pluralism and ecumenism represent attacks on national interest or intellectual rigor or doctrinal purity, and who have been prepared to defend cultural hegemony on the basis of a conviction of the genuine superiority of their way of life or thought or worship. But these are the attitudes of single-culture people; even if a given culture were to prove superior to others in some respect (whatever "superior" might be taken to mean), it could hardly claim to be exhaustive in all respects so that there would be room for elements of other cultures in supplementary roles — and once allowed, the challenge of another culture might undermine the conviction of superiority. Nothing, it is true, prevents single-culture people from regarding their own culture as self-sufficient, which means turning a blind eye to those respects in which it is not exhaustive, with a consequent impoverishment of opportunities for experience. This attitude always has been known by the name of parochialism; it becomes harder to maintain the more permeable the boundaries of the parish.

The transcultural and the multicultural cannot always be sharply separated; even though the common content of scientific knowledge can expect to be mutually translatable between cultures, there may be something about one culture's formulation that throws light on that content in a distinct way. But multiculturalism comes into its own when it is matter not of translatable propositions about an objective world but of propositions, objects, and practices which, at best, may be structurally transformable from culture to culture but, in many cases, will be culture-specific, fully appreciable only by those who can assume the horizon of the culture in question. The enlargement of individual horizons is one of the characteristics of a multicultural identity. What is found beyond the old limited horizon may appear to be in conflict with what lies within it; cultures may be, as is sometimes said (borrowing an image, none too helpfully, from Greek mathematics) "incommensurable." But this need not be an occasion for despair since incommensurables can be comfortably accommodated in lifeworlds not dedicated to monocultural ideals of completeness and consistency. It is hard to resist quoting Whitman here, clichéd as the passage may have become: "I contradict myself: very well, I contradict myself. I am large, I contain multitudes."[17]

Completeness and consistency, like objectivity itself, might be entertained as ideals of the transcultural, though, even there, with the constitutive unattainability of the ideal. It at least can be said that the transcultural converges. The multicultural, on the other hand, diverges — without limit. No form of cultural novelty can be ruled out *a priori*; if I remain open to experience I shall certainly continue to be surprised by what I encounter and find I can appreciate. And because such new experiences, if I enter into them, mediate my relations to myself, they can add new facets to my identity. Some people have the experience of a radical transformation of identity under a new cultural influence, though this transformation can take pathological forms — in the "normal" case (with all due caution in the use of such a potentially repressive term) changes will be slight in relation to the stability of the self over time or, at the very least, there will be a traceable genidentity between earlier and later states.

It may have been remarked how closely my initial characterization of multicultural contributions to identity resembled Matthew Arnold's definition of the cultural; the crucial difference is that I leave it to the individual to decide what is most rewarding in his or her own case and context, whereas Arnold thought there was a kind of objectivity to the best. The individual, as Taylor's model for the development of identity suggests, almost inevitably will make that decision in dialogue with other individuals. What is best or most rewarding is certainly not beyond discussion, and I may be convinced by others to try something of which I was previously ignorant which moves forthwith to the top of my list. (This was in fact what happened to me, for example, when I was persuaded to read Alice Walker and found myself compelled without further prompting to make my way back through Toni Morrison to Zora Neale Hurston, thus opening up one of the richest unexplored cultural domains I had ever encountered.) But there is no single list — nothing canonical and nothing sacrosanct, as I try in a very different context to impress upon my students in philosophy.

Under the multicultural, single cultures may continue to exist in their pure forms. The few individuals to whom I referred earlier as the "bearers and transmitters" of a given culture may, if that is all they are (for pure cultures may well continue to be borne and transmitted in a multicultural context), represent a particularly disadvantaged class; in their commitment to the details of particular cultural practices, they may become stunted or atrophied along the multicultural dimension. It is not hard to think of examples, in life or literature, of priests, schoolteachers, rabbis, professors, indeed fanatics of any temple,[18] who fit this description.

One of the perversions of multiculturalism has been the attempt to legitimize, under its auspices, new fanaticisms of single (alternative) cultures. As I have been implicitly suggesting, to offer such a single culture as a main route to self-identification is really to practice a kind of deception on those to whom it is most likely to appeal since what they need is liberation from *any* single culture. *Caveat emptor:* individuals are free and nothing can or should prevent anyone, old conservative or new convert, from being fanatically monocultural if he or she wishes. But a more humane and generous approach would be to try to acquaint everyone, especially those whose identities are in the formative stage, with the common heritage of the transcultural and the rich variety of the multicultural. That is surely the real challenge to the curriculum.

The reaction of monocultural conservatives to this eclectic line, of course, will be one of alarm and horror. But I repeat: the pure forms of single cultures can survive in spite of general mixing. It is a bit like the Hardy–Weinberg law in genetics: no matter how thoroughly interbred a population may become, the pure original strains persist at the limits in predictable quantities. Furthermore, those enthusiastic about the pure form of a culture other than their culture of origin — having first encountered it, perhaps, in a multicultural context — may be able to do more to preserve it more intelligently and more effectively than its monocultural remnant. There are hundreds of languages, literatures, crafts, musical forms, artistic practices, and the like that would now be extinct if it had not been for the dedication of professionals (and of amateurs in the strong sense) who have devoted their time and resources to the preservation of what they found of value in cultures originally alien to them and have made elements of these cultures chosen aspects of their identities.

* * * * *

"Chosen aspects of their identities": in the end it is this matter of choice that I wish to emphasize. It is the mark of a free agent that he or she chooses, within the limits of possibility — which are flexible though not eliminable altogether — both identity and cultural affiliation. The choice can be made in bad faith;[19] as Sartre suggests in *Being and Nothingness*, if I make up an identity for myself on the basis of some external given — if I "take myself for someone else," to use another formulation of his[20] — and come to think of myself as *that*, then, as it were, I have broken faith with myself. This stricture would include the case in which I simply accept without critical reflection the identity with which I am provided by family and culture of origin — and also the case in which I adopt a full-blown identity from an alternative culture with no more critical reflection than is involved in a passionate rejection of the dominant one. In either case, I may come to see (or I may not — bad faith can be lived with all one's life) that I am deceiving myself. The crises of identity that plague adolescents who have never had a chance to experience themselves outside the suburban cocoon represent perhaps a first step towards that recognition.

I began by saying that any native culture will be an imposed one: we do not choose to be born when, where, and to whom we are born, and the fact that it has always been thought right for parents to determine the cultural formation of their children does not mean that it *is* right. On the contrary, I believe it to be an obligation upon parents to help free their children of their culture of origin if that is what the children decide they want — certainly to make them aware of alternatives, and to equip them with the critical resources (as free of cultural bias as may be) necessary to make judgments about their own eventual identities. The idea of a culture — Jewish culture comes to mind — once born into which a child, by the common consent of members *and nonmembers alike,* simply is not permitted to disavow his or her identification with, seems to me incompatible with human freedom. Granted that, as I have insisted, identification does not determine identity — but the forces at work in cases of this sort, from inside and from outside the cultural community (think of the race laws under Hitler), are of awesome power and, unless the apostate is prepared for total rejection, the part of significant others they may be impossible to resist. (That is a price some of us have had to pay for the cultural autonomy that should be everyone's right.)

Transcending one's culture of origin does not mean turning one's back on it. We live in a world that is irreversibly plural where culture is concerned, but a basis for the harmonious coexistence of cultures can be found in the mutual sharing of what is convergent in the sense specified above and in a mutual respect for what is divergent[21] — where this does not involve the oppression of individuals or groups. Such a mutuality is again an ideal — it is still all too frequently the case that the relations between two given cultures are asymmetrical, either because one side is unwilling to be as open as the other, or because the individuals who have managed to encourage their horizons to take in both cultures all come from only one of them. And this assumes at least a peaceful relationship; often enough the encounter has taken the form of a bloody opposition, something I have altogether left out of account in this essay. So a happy outcome in this respect is far from certain. As I put the finishing touches to these remarks, there comes to hand an unexpected text, one of the last Bertrand Russell ever wrote, which concludes:

> There could be a happy world, where cooperation was more in evidence than competition ... and where to promote joy is more respected than to produce mountains of corpses. Do not say this is impossible: it is not. It waits only for men to desire it more than the infliction of torture. There is an artist imprisoned in each one of us. Let him loose to spread joy everywhere.[22]

I end therefore on a note of hope — for the transcultural and for the multicultural; the former for its power of uniting, the latter for its power of enrichment. Such hope may seem Utopian, as indeed it is, construing Utopia as a good place rather than a nonplace which, if it is never to be fully realized, at least points the way along which our energies may be directed. I think individuals — all individuals — are capable of transcending not only their cultures of origin but also their cultures of identification under oppression; I think the robust knowledge that we do have of the natural world is capable of being shared by everyone; I think no avenue of cultural exploration can be assumed to be closed to anyone. I have not invoked the concept of rationality in this connection, but I find in some remarks of Renford Bambrough — from an article in which he expresses confidence that reason can afford a workable basis for a dialogue among civilizations — a reflection of this attitude to hope so admirably expressed that I had already decided to cite them in closing before coming upon the passage from Russell given above. The two texts reinforce one another; here then is Bambrough's:

> One who sets the bounds of reason as wide as I have drawn them must become inured to charges of excessive optimism. The complaint arises from confusion between actualities and possibilities. To say that there is a path is not to say that we shall have the skill to trace it and the stamina to follow it as far as it could lead us. To believe that there could be a chart of the unknown territory is not to believe that it will ever be charted. But there is all the same an important connection between

the actuality and our view of the possibilities. To deny that there is a path or that there could be a chart is to stifle the efforts and aspirations of oneself and others to undertake the necessary exploration.[23]

It is on grounds like these that I resist skepticism about the possibility of convergence in the sciences, the possibility of overcoming what I think must be a temporary resurgence of racial separatism, the possibility of realizing a worldwide moral community under a multiplicity of cultural values. The challenge to anyone who seeks to work in these direction is to be at once informed about the world, accepting of the stranger, and open to the new — to be, in short, an individual with an identity unconstrained by cultural particularity or prejudice. A multicultural identity, not a pancultural one: nobody is going to be at home everywhere. But it is one of the rewards of postmodernity to have many homes, not just one.

Notes

1 Jean-Paul Sartre, *The Communists and Peace,* tr. Martha H. Fletcher with the assistance of John R. Kleinschmidt (New York: George Braziller, 1968), p. 91.
2 Charles Taylor, "The Politics of Recognition," in *Multiculturalism and "The Politics of Recognition,"* eds Amy Gutmann, Steven C. Rockefeller, Michael Walzer, and Susan Wolf (Princeton: Princeton University Press, 1992), p. 32. [See chapter 2, p. 79, in this volume — ed.]
3 Immanuel Kant, *The Critique of Judgment,* tr. James Creed Meredith (Oxford: the Clarendon Press, 1952 [1928]), p. 94: "The production in a rational being of an aptitude for any ends whatever of his own choosing, consequently of the aptitude of a being in his freedom, is *culture.*" Because this version seems less than satisfactory I have retranslated the passage from *Kritik der Urtheilskraft,* in *Kants Werke: Akademie-Textausgabe* (Berlin: Walter de Gruyter, 1968 [1908]), Band V, p. 431 [original publication 1790].
4 Matthew Arnold, *Culture and Anarchy,* ed. and with an introduction by J. Dover Wilson (Cambridge: The University Press, 1937 [1932; original publication 1869]), p. 6.
5 My source for this usage is Ernst Wasserzieher, "Kultur," in *Woher? Ableitendes Worterbuch der deutschen Sprache* (Bonn: Ferd. Dummlers Verlag, 1959) p. 266.
6 C. P. Snow, *The Two Cultures and the Scientific Revolution* (Cambridge: The University Press, 1959).
7 Ruth Benedict, *Patterns of Culture* (London: Routledge and Kegan Paul, 1935).
8 A. L. Kroeber and Clyde Kluckhohn, *Culture: A Critical Review of Concepts and Definitions* (New York: Random House, n.d.), p. 291. (Originally published as vol. XLVII, no. 1, of the *Papers of the Peabody Museum of American Archaeology and Ethnology* [Cambridge: Harvard University, 1952].)
9 Hans Bak, ed., *Multiculturalism and the Canon of American Culture* (Amsterdam: VU University Press, 1993), p. 107.

10 W. C Sellar and R. J. Yeatman, *1066 And All That* (London: E. P. Dutton, 1931), a̲
   And Now All This (London: Methuen, 1936).
11 Steven C. Rockefeller, "Comments," in *Multiculturalism and the "Politics of
   Recognition,"* p. 97.
12 Taylor, "The Politics of Recognition," p. 33. [See p. 79 in this volume — ed.]
13 Ibid., pp. 33–4. [See p. 80 in this volume — ed.]
14 Frederick Douglass, *Narrative of the Life of Frederick Douglass, An American
   Slave. Written by Himself* (Cambridge: Harvard University Press, 1960 [original
   edition 1845]).
15 I have argued the point about the convergence and the objectivity of science against
   the skeptical and relativist views of people like Feyerabend, Toulmin, Rorty, Laudan,
   etc., at length in several places; see my *Yorick's World: Science and the Knowing
   Subject* (Berkeley and Los Angeles: University of California Press, 1993), ch. 18
   and passim.
16 The culture in question was that of a closed and tightly-knit religious group known
   as the Exclusive Brethren.
17 Walt Whitman, "Song of Myself," in *Leaves of Grass*.
18 "Fanatic" is from Latin *fanum*, "temple," and means anyone so single-mindedly
   committed to what the temple represents as to be blinded to alternatives, or to reason
   itself (compare "profane," meaning one who is before, i.e., outside, the temple).
19 Jean-Paul Sartre, *Being and Nothingness*, tr. Hazel Barnes (New York: Philosophical
   Library, 1956), passim.
20 Jean-Paul Sartre, *The Condemned of Altona*, tr. Sylvia and George Leeson (New
   York: Alfred A. Knopf, 1964), p. 11.
21 I borrow this formulation from my recent article "What World Philosophy Might Do
   for World Culture," in *Philosophy and Cultural Development*, eds Ioanna Kucuradi
   and Evandro Agazzi (Ankara: Turkey, Editions of the Philosophical Society of
   Turkey for the International Federation of Philosophic Societies, 1993), p. 105.
22 "The Last Testament of Bertrand Russell," *The Independent* (London), 2,215
   (November 24, 1993), p. 21.
23 Renford Bambrough, "The Scope of Reason: An Epistle to the Persians," in
   Objectivity and Cultural Divergence, ed. S. C. Brown (Cambridge: Cambridge
   University Press, 1984), p. 205.

18

Ota Benga's Flight Through Geronimo's Eyes: Tales of Science and Multiculturalism

Cedric J. Robinson

... all men who differ from others as much as the body differs from the soul ... are by nature slaves, and it is better for them ... to be ruled by a master. A man is thus by nature a slave if he is capable of becoming ... the property of another, and if he participates in reason to the extent of apprehending it in another, though destitute of it himself.

Aristotle[1]

Notwithstanding many of the premising assumptions of the current debate, multiculturalism has been an aspect of the Western social sciences since their inceptions as research disciplines in the eighteenth, nineteenth, and twentieth centuries. The modern era, too, had its progenitors since we can discern the specter of multiculturalism in the classical Greek social and moral sciences from which the modernists claimed descent. Isocrates, the fourth-century pan-Hellenic fanatic, employed a multiculturalism of difference to inspire Greeks to renounce democracy for a crusade of world domination. His contemporary Aristotle, the natural scientist, rhetorician, and political philosopher, pursued justifications of slavery, the subordination of women, and a hierarchy of distinctive constitutional orders by insinuating natural laws of multiculturalism. And his mentor Plato implicated a multiculturalist discourse in moral therapeutics ranging from cultural quarantine to eugenics.[2] In the Christian era, the examples of the perceived terrors of multiculturalism are far too numerous to detail. Any one of them would suffice: in the mid-seventeenth century, John Hare, the English "Teuton," recapitulated his diverse progenitors and anticipated their successors when he suggested that Englishmen claiming descent from the Normans reimagine themselves as Norwegians, and English laws, "devested of their French rags be restored into the English or Latine tongues."[3]

For millennia, as these instances suggest, premodernist multiculturalism, the preemption of multiculturalism as a construction of contamination, has preoccupied the intellectual imagination of agents of civilizations and regimes familiar with slavery, colonialism, and imperialism. Discourses in alterity thrived long before the appearance of the West as an episteme and insinuated themselves into the latter. Indeed, these premodernist discourses were the enabling practices which legislated the modernist narrative of multiculturalism which posited the West as *the* civilization, and the European white as *the* conscious agency of humanity's historical development. Consequently, the multiculturalism at the center of the current controversy, that is, anti(post)modernist multiculturalism, is a third variant, one which contests the epistemic claims of modernist multiculturalism and its progenitor, premodernist multiculturalism. And though they crudely can be arranged historically, chronology attests to their respective hegemonic moments rather than to their actual historicity. By analytic indirection, it can be surmised that Aristotle's porous defense of slavery is addressed to antecedent representatives of postmodernist multiculturalists skeptical of the naturalness of slavery and the incontestability of Greek superiority over the Other;[4] just as Hare's futile strategy of "ethnic cleansing" was a response to the historical processes of cross-cultural pollination of "English" culture to which he took offense. Whether the context was ancient, medieval or more recent world-systems, premodernist and modernist multiculturalism are discourses intended to conceal: to conceal the prerogatives of power, conceal the humanity of the Other, conceal the awful policing devices of subordination.

Indeed, as the more recent history of science literature has attested, research protocols such as anthropology and its derivatives, eugenics, psychometry, etc., were inspired by a desire to achieve epistemic orderings and to rationalize binaries of domination and subordination in multicultural social formations. And as Donna Haraway has demonstrated in her work on the development of biology, the natural sciences embedded identical ambitions in the pursuit of empirical discursive practices.

> Not just anything can emerge as a fact; not just anything can be seen or done, and so told. Scientific practice may be considered a kind of storytelling practice — a rule-governed, constrained, historically changing craft of narrating the history of nature. Scientific practice and scientific theories produce and are embedded in particular kinds of stories....

The primate body, as part of the body of nature, may be read as a map of power. Biology, and primatology, are inherently political discourses, whose chief objects of knowledge ... are icons (condensations) of the whole of the history and politics of the culture that constructed them for contemplation and manipulation....

[In the natural sciences] Nature is only the raw material of culture, appropriated, preserved, enslaved, exalted, or otherwise made flexible for disposal by culture in the logic of capitalist colonialism.[5]

The question, then, is not what consequences multiculturalism might obtain for the social sciences, but rather what alternative significations of multiculturalism might presently be embraced by the social sciences and why.

For more than two hundred years, the objective of the ensemble of race sciences and their subdisciplinary adjutants (for example, comparative politics) was to secure fixed taxonomies, stable racial-historical and gender identities which, in turn, could be composed into a natural sociology of hierarchy. The primary colors of race — white, black, yellow, red, brown — coordinated with an Aristotelian construction of sex differences, were to be arranged in a descending order of humanity thus justifying social privileges at home and abroad. This paradigm of multiculturalism, a concomitant to the domestic sites of Western slave economies and female subordination, and imperialism and colonialism in the outlands, pursued the appearance of a natural history. This weave of scientific difference was reprised in every furnishing of culture. The certain exactness of science was embroidered in popular culture, transmitted by lyric, limerick, and letters. And there it remains today, a haunted, majestic presence of an enduring construction of plurality and difference. Haunted, I insist, because it is no longer uncontested.

The Right Multiculturalism

Louis Agassiz, the Harvard-domiciled Swiss naturalist who was one of the nineteenth century's most authorial artisans of the modernist multiculturalism's scientism,[6] was also one of the first and few of his numbers to acknowledge the audacious deceit of the project and admit defeat. Hidden away in his private notes, his secret confessional recorded his physical repulsion and fear of the dark, simian creature which inspired his professional enterprise: "he just 'knew' [blacks] were barely higher than apes."[7] Publicly more generous at least, Agassiz first rejected civil comity with blacks ("No man has a right to what he is unfit to use."), and then, after hearing the testaments of black military heroism and sacrifice during the American Civil War, conceded the rights of American citizenry to this lower order.[8]

Stephen Jay Gould informs us that "For Agassiz, nothing inspired more fear than the prospect of amalgamation by intermarriage."[9] But we are no more obliged to pause and explore the admixture of circuitous subjectivity and curious logic in Agassiz's mind than we would a member of the frequent lynch mobs of the late nineteenth century. Our concern is historical. Agassiz and his coconspirators, both those performing before the public gaze of the academy and later mobbed in local secrecy among the trees, organized race-hate and practiced race-death. One conduct decoratively civil and learned, the other nakedly hysterical and compulsive, they coalesced into what Fanon would term "a mode of domination."

Intelligence, Reason, and Rationality, imagined to be superior *and* inferior, were the premodernist multiculturalist coda around which the modern social sciences grouped. The terrain, however, was inhospitable because of two features: the unstable and shifting construction of intelligence and the absence of categorical research material. Lacking any universal or culturally-neutral concept of intelligence, the modernists fabricated one. Lacking the required research or experimental subjects, that is, pure-race specimens, they invented them.[10] The technical provenance of the present intelligence tests were the paraphernalia of early anthropometry: the calipers and craniometers of Victorian anthropology and their equivalents in France, Germany, Switzerland, and elsewhere. Data were characteristically inconclusive but that could be managed by fraud and finagling.[11] The psychometric provenance of the present white, black, Hispanic/Latino, Asian, etc., experimental/tested races were the imagined Europeans, Africans, Orientals, etc., of yesteryear.[12] Undaunted by the necessity for scientistic shell games, and distracted by them from any profound investigation of the mind, the proponents of the modernist multiculturalism constructed a forgery of the mind as a predisposition towards civilization.

A counterfeit architectonic of civilization — the linear progression from hunting and gathering to urban commerce — was sutured to the forgery of the mind and encrusted with a fabricated inheritance: the birth of the West in Ancient Greece and Rome. And from the seventeenth or eighteenth centuries until now, these scrubbed-white mantras — the natural history of humankind; rationality; and the Ancient Mediterranean — were the means to drown the humanity of the Other. In Europe, George Mosse observes:

> Greek beauty provided the ideal type, which set the aesthetic criteria to which man must relate himself ... Classical beauty symbolized the perfect human form within which a true soul would be bound to reside ... From the eighteenth century onwards ... the ideal type and countertype would not vary much for the next century and a half, nor would it matter fundamentally whether the inferior race was black or Jewish. The ideal type symbolized by a classical beauty and proper morals determined attitudes toward all men.[13]

And in American colleges and universities, well into the late nineteenth century, the classical curriculum of Greek, Latin, mathematics, natural philosophy, moral philosophy and logic concretized the premodernist multiculturalist frame in the minds of the educated. As the Yale Report of 1828 substantiated, no worthy alternative presented itself: "the single consideration that divine truth was communicated to man in the ancient languages, ought to ... give to them perpetuity."[14]

In American science in the 1820s and 1830s, phrenology and ethnology brought up the rear. Legislated by the appropriation of classical aesthetics and racial resignifications in the statistical means of craniology/craniometry and facial angles, a modernist phrenology determined the racial limits of intelligence, civilization, and moral achievement from the size of the skull and the mass of cerebral organization.[15] Championed by Charles Caldwell (*Thoughts on the Original Unity of the Human Race*, 1830) and Samuel Morton (*Crania Americana*, 1839; *Crania Ægyptica*, 1844), both American physicians and professors of anatomy, this variant of phrenology with its scientific demonstration of superior and inferior races was employed in the defense of slavery and conquest.[16] In the public debate on emancipation and abolition fueled by the Nat Turner rebellion and Native American resistance, modernist phrenology was the master-race science.[17] And under its subsequent guise as ethnology, the new American anthropology, race science confirmed the historical singularity of the white race: "Among the more important conclusions in Morton's books, noted in many journal articles in the latter half of the century, was his claim that the ancient Egyptians were not Negroes, merely dark-skinned Caucasians."[18] And with the arrival of Agassiz at Harvard in 1848, race science extended its hegemony from the modest environs of Transylvania University (Caldwell's regime in Kentucky) to the best endowed academic institutions in America.[19]

Anointed by some of the most eminent scientists and most prestigious institutions in the nation, race science hailed the inferior races, greeting the newest arrivals, the immigrant Irish, Slavs, Italians, Chinese, and Japanese, with fabulous narratives of natural baseness; and treating the already-domiciled Other, the Africans, and the Native Americans, to slavery, reservations, and segregation. So ineluctable was the march of [white] civilization that it was common and scientific knowledge that neither the blacks nor the Indians would survive into the twentieth century, and the most benevolent fate for the lesser whites was crossbreeding with the Anglo-Saxons, the Aryans, the Nordics, or whichever "blood" group was nominated as the most superior Caucasians. As one of Morton's students, Dr. Josiah Nott declared in 1854: "No two distinctly-marked races can dwell together on equal terms. Some races, moreover, appear destined to live and prosper for a time, until the destroying race comes, which is to exterminate and supplant them."[20] And with a suddenness which appears to confirm Haraway's construction of Western science's political nature, following the abolition of slavery American ethnologists transferred their attentions almost exclusively to the Native American. St Clair Drake reports:

The Bureau of American Ethnology and the Smithsonian Institution did not concern themselves with Afro-Americans. Their role was to assist in forming and carrying out an Indian policy while the Native Americans were being swept off the plains and prairies and herded onto reservations ... in collaboration with a government that was intent on stamping out the last vestiges of rebellion, abolishing treaty relations, and turning the land over to settlers, railroad and mining corporations. Blacks ... were left to the home missionary societies....[21]

At the beginning of the nineteenth century, Thomas Jefferson had betrayed his "all men are created equal" dictum, publicizing his nightmarish vision of a land cohabited by blacks and white.[22] And well through his century and much of our own, Americans substantiated his dreadful anticipation through slave rebellions, Indian wars, immigration riots, Civil War, the lynchings of lesser whites, blacks, Indians, and Asians, race-inspired vigilantism, segregation, race riots, anti-immigration and antimiscegenation laws, and the like.[23] In each instance, when the canons of race science and racism came under challenge, the modernist discourse on multiculturalism was revived. Audrey Smedley has observed of these "cycles in history" that the parallel between Samuel Morton and Arthur Jensen is instructive: "Both men published scholarly works promoting the idea of black inferiority. In both cases, their major publications came in the wake of dramatic events that tended to advance the cause of racial equality: Morton in the wake of the abolitionist movement; Jensen following the civil rights movement of the 1950s and 1960s."[24]

In the late nineteenth and early twentieth centuries, natural and social scientists at Harvard (President Charles W. Eliot, Ernest Hooton, Edwin Katzenellenbogen — the latter convicted of war crimes at Buchenwald), Stanford (Lewis Terman) and Yale, frequently subsidized by private research foundations like the Rockefeller Foundation (for example, The China Medical Board) and the Kellogg Foundation (the Eugenics Records Office), espoused a modernist multiculturalist public policy in the forms of intelligence tests, eugenics, and sterilization. Terman testified that "... 1,000 Harvard graduates will at the end of 200 years have but 50 descendants, while in the same period, 1,000 south Italians will have multiplied to 100,000...." In 1937, Hooton, the pioneer of physical anthropology in America (and president of the American Association of Physical Anthropologists) informed the *New York Times*, "I think that a biological purge is the essential prerequisite for a social and spiritual salvation." And at his trial at Dachau, Katzenellenbogen, the former Harvard Medical School faculty member, defended his participation in Nazi sterilization programs by reminding his Allied accusers that he had drafted sterilization legislation for the governor of Indiana.[25]

American anthropologists at the turn of the century, however, did not entirely confine themselves to the hallways of academia, the boardrooms of industrial capital and government. They were not above the lure of providing the public spectacles of multiculturalism. In their forays into mass opinion, they most often chose the sedate environs of museums and zoological gardens to impress their modernist constructions of multiculturalism on school children and the middling representatives of the educated. But on occasion, they employed sensationalism, the chosen discursive practice of their well-heeled sponsors. Here, the intended consumers were the mass audience. Haraway reminds us that "The relation of hoax and popular natural history is unnervingly close."[26]

One such occasion was the St Louis World Fair of 1904 where the Fair's Anthropology Department (the first in the history of such expositions) displayed the human loot of colonialism and conquest: Igorots, Negritos, and Moros from the Philippines; Ainus from Japan; Zulus from South Africa; a Batatele prince and Batwa "Pygmies" from Leopold's Congo (including Ota Benga, the lone "Chirichiri" pygmy who was destined to be housed in the Bronx Zoo's Primate House in 1906); Geronimo, the aging (70-plus years) Chiricahua prisoner of war; Kwakiutl Indians from the Northwest; the Cocopas of the lower Colorado; Kiowas; Nez Perce; Seri, etc. And after a summer as public exhibits — over 18,000,000 visitors according to the *New York Times* (December 2, 1904) — they were subjected to the "touch of the dynamometer, the pulse controller, the cephalometer, aesthesiometer, pantograph, sphygmograph, and tape measure."

> Anthropology Days were understood to buttress, "complement and on the whole fully conform with" the anthropometrical data "of function and structure" arrived at in the lab. The fair was built with the assumption that Caucasians were superior. Now the builders had compiled the numbers to prove it.[27]

Although the numbers were far from perfect statistical sets, they were appreciated by psychologists like Marion Mayo who acknowledged in his 1913 dissertation *The Mental Capacity of the American Negro* that his own "negro" subjects were "a mixed and not a pure type." Mayo conceded that the scientific literature had yet to demonstrate convincingly racial inequality and that his own findings on racial "variability" were inconclusive. Nevertheless, he was persuaded that this construction of intelligence centered around the incidents of genius among race groups and, originating in Francis Galton's claims of superior mental inheritance among the English upper classes,[28] would likely settle the controversy:

> Though very little is as yet definitely known about the variability of races, there is some evidence that the European white is more variable than the negro, and that civilized peoples are more variable than primitive peoples. Also, as between the sexes, that man is more variable than woman.[29]

Within one year of Mayo's publication, "Henry Goddard's famous book *The Kallikak Family* (1914) indicted the poor for being mentally deficient and conjured up lurid scenes from the netherworld of the slums."

Once the theory of differential intelligence was accepted its implicit political applications became operational. Subjectively, psychologists were unaware of the ideological constraints upon their scientific endeavors, but their political perspective is easily discerned. Those social scientists involved in intelligence testing tended to view the propertied classes as the more naturally gifted of society whose social position was directly attributable to superior innate intellectual qualities.[30]

The Aristotelian conceits were restored in their entirety.

Race science, initially the cloistered terrain of academics and gentlemen of leisure and adventure, by the nineteenth century had transmuted into a specular entertainment in circuses, burlesque, vaudeville, and minstrelsy complementing the specular performances presented to the participants in slavery, colonialism, and wars of conquest. And now, at the beginnings of the twentieth century, with the advent of mass entertainment forms like the cinema and radio, the spectacle and incantations of modernist multiculturalism were everywhere. Still they were not sufficient to extinguish fugitive, oppositional impulses.

How It All Went Wrong

The discerning spectator at the "Olympic games" competition, organized for the savages by the anthropologists at the St Louis Fair, might have been alerted by the deportments of Geronimo and the pygmies. As the sport of exhibited inferiors was now transformed (converted) to the exhibition of sport and the numerics of comparative cerebral and physiognomic structures linked with their counterparts in athleticism, movement was required. And in the regulated space of athletic performance, the inferiors located unexpected sites of dominion.

According to the sports page of the *St Louis Post-Dispatch*, August 13, 1904, Geronimo "... leaned silently against the track-rail looking on but gave no other sign that he was at all interested;" and the pygmies, Bradford and Blume recount, "... backpedaled and did woozy figure eights on the hundred yard dash."[31] If, as Haraway assures us, "*Both* the scientist and the organism are actors in a storytelling practice," then we must surmise that the specular actors (Geronimo/the anthropologists/the exposition's visitors) and the performers (the pygmies/the starter with his gun) were occupying alternative yarns. Something was recognizably amiss since, in the sports-page account, the two sentences devoted to Geronimo are the only reference to someone who did not run, jump, throw, or organize the competition. He ruptures the joviality, the athleticism of the performative narrative; he disrupts the report/er. For Ota Benga, the pygmy, however, Geronimo's presence was entirely benevolent. Ota remembered Geronimo smiling to him that day; he also recalled that a few days earlier, Geronimo had given him an arrowhead, had then chanted and danced around him.

And when Ota looked into Geronimo's eyes, Ota "had the impression for a moment that he was flying. Below him was a dry red landscape of rocks, gorges, and animals he had never seen before."[32] Thankfully, the *Post-Dispatch's* reporter had been spared the full brunt of Ota's knowledge.

Ota conceived of America as the land of the dead. And until his arrival in New Orleans where he joined with some black street musicians in an impromptu stroll and dance, he found particularly dreadful the fact that musicians read from sheets. Ota was convinced they had forgotten how to play. He had determined to remain in this metaphysical realm until he could fathom its order. And when, after twelve years, he realized "he had stopped" but could not return to Africa — the World War, its devastation of the Congo, the price of a steamship ticket — he put a bullet in his heart.[33]

Among Ota's antecedents, the other Africans in America, an identical quest, the attempt to return in the nineteenth century had presaged an anthropology distinctly subversive of the hegemonic physical anthropology. While the modernists were patrolling medical schools and graveyards for black bodies and skulls and furtively confiscating skeletons buried in Egyptian tombs to add to their congregation of race evidence, an oppositional signification for Africa was being assembled.[34] In 1859, as St Clair Drake reports, Martin Delaney headed the Niger Valley Exploring Party on behalf of the National Emigration Convention of Colored Men. The extraordinary impulse in Delaney, the link between he and Ota Benga, is apparent in Delaney's call seven years earlier:

> Every people should be the originators of their own designs, the projector of their own schemes, and creators of the events that lead to their destiny — the consummation of their desires....
>
> We have native hearts and virtues, just as other nations; which in their pristine purity are noble, potent, and worthy of example. We are a nation within a nation....[35]

An anthropology premised on the dominion of the Other, an alternative space to that of the West, would necessarily transcend the delimitations of anthropometry. An anthropology postulated on the dignity and agency of the other as "originators" would generate an interrogation of alternative histories, alternative cultures, and alternative social orders. The beginnings of such an anthropology could be found in Delaney's and Robert Campbell's *Search for a Place: Black Separatism and Africa* (1860) when they negotiated their alternative aesthetics, describing the physical beauty of their Yoruba hosts, the complexity of their language, and the intricacies of their economic institutions.[36]

The anthropology of Delaney and Campbell, of official black envoys like George Washington Williams (Leopold's Congo and Haiti), John Henry Smyth (Liberia), George Washington Ellis (Liberia) and Frederick Douglas (Haiti), and of black missionaries like Henry McNeal Turner, Alexander Crummell, Edward

Wilmot Blyden and William Henry Sheppard belied the inferiorization of Africans and Africans-in-the-Americas through cultural studies.[37] In the late nineteenth century, published accounts of religious life, linguistics (for example, Ellis' study of the Vai-speaking peoples; Sheppard's studies of Tshiluba and Tshikuba), and economics shadowed the rhetoric of skulls which sought to evacuate the workings of any creative intelligence among the Other. And following the abolition of slavery in the United States, scholars like Williams and Sheppard turned their attention to the black sites of the world-system cemented into the most exploitative apparatus.

In 1889, George Washington Williams, the author of the two-volume *A History of the Negro Race in America from 1619 to 1880* (1883),[38] was commissioned by the American government to investigate the conditions in Leopold's Congo. On July 18, 1890, Williams wrote an open letter to his "Good and Great Friend," King Leopold of Belgium. In his conclusion, Williams exposed the counterfeits of the West's claims to superior moral and ethical development:

> Against the deceit, fraud, robberies, arson, murder, slave raiding, and general policy of cruelty of your Majesty's Government to the natives, stands their record of unexampled patience, long-suffering and forgiving spirit, which put the boasted civilization and professed religion of your Majesty's Government to the blush.[39]

Among the twelve detailed charges Williams brought against Leopold were slavery, the prostitution of African women, forced labor, violations of international law and sovereignty, "waging unjust and cruel wars against natives," gratuitous homicide, and the encouragement of cannibalism. Each indictment destructed the pillars of the epistemic hierarchy imagined for the West. But Williams also recognized the discursive restraints insinuated into any attempt to communicate between his anthropology and the system of knowledge barricading white consciousness. Despite his reputation for eloquence, Williams repeatedly capitulated before the horrors he witnessed: "I have no adequate terms with which to depict...."

In that same year, 1890, William Sheppard and Samuel Lapsley met with Leopold before proceeding to the Congo to cofound the American Presbyterian Congo Mission. They were together because the Presbyterian Society could not imagine a black man heading a civilizing mission. Two years later, Lapsley, Sheppard's "white permission slip," was dead, and Sheppard began the odyssey which would lead him into the "space of death" that Leopold had commissioned around rubber extraction in his private state. And in the ninth year of his Mission, far from the racial violence at home he had sought to escape, his African communicants implored him to go and witness Leopold's culture of terror. Sheppard knew what awaited him: "It is just as if I were to take a rope and go out behind the house and hang myself to that tree"; but he went. And in the village of the Zappo-Zap, Sheppard's anthropology was transformed into a politics of outrage:

> He made note of three hundred human skeletons, the flesh of many of them having been prepared as food. He saw a spear sticking out of the blackened heart of a man who had once been a friend. He counted 81 right hands — hacked from the living and dead — from the arms of adults and children, which were to be put in a basket and delivered to Bula Mutadi [Leopold's military and civil functionaries].
>
> The Zappo-Zaps were unashamed. They held back nothing. Were they not the Force Publique, trained and corrupted first by the slave trade and now selling their skills to Leopold, who demanded they bring back either tribute or proof of corporal punishment?[40]

Sheppard's testimony joined that of Williams, bonding with the anthropological narratives woven by Delaney, Crummell, Blyden, Smyth, Turner, Ellis, and all the other Africans who dreamed of home. Williams and Sheppard had given the most exacting accounts of the human costs of the Congo rubber trade and, eventually, when those officials and their publics who could not qualify a black anthropology, read the redacted versions published by Edmund Morel, Roger Casement, Arthur Conan Doyle, and Joseph Conrad, the crusade to rid the Congo of Leopold's rule was on. Not surprisingly, given the space dominated by *real* anthropology, when the historians reconstructed the humanitarian campaign, the contributions of Williams and Sheppard vanished.[41]

Similarly, the erasure of this alternative anthropology occurs in the dominant narratives of the rehabilitation of American anthropology. In the central space of this narrative appears, instead, the figure of Franz Boas. It is Boas who "made short work of the fabled cranial index,"[42] Boas who develops "a systematic critique of the racial, psychological, and cultural assumptions of nineteenth-century evolutionary anthropology,"[43] Boas who battled the hereditarian racists and invented cultural anthropology,[44] Boas who raised American anthropology to a science.[45] And there is much credit to be accorded to Boas for rescuing American anthropology from the likes of Daniel Brinton and William McGee. (We have already encountered McGee, the first president of the American Anthropological Association, in one of the several guises he would assume throughout his career: he was the chief of the Anthropology Department at the St Louis Fair. And if it wasn't already obvious, as Marvin Harris ventures: "McGee was an inexhaustible mine of every error of substance and theory that it was possible to commit on the basis of the most vulgar prejudices masquerading as scientific expertise."[46]) In short, Boas is the "culture-hero" of twentieth-century American anthropology; a sort of remedial potion or antidote for the poisonous Agassiz.

Baldly put, Boas has been made to occupy the great man theory of (intellectual) history; here pinioned on Boas' training as a physicist, and substantiated by the testimony of his students (who included Alfred Kroeber, Margaret Mead, Benedict, Robert Lowie, Edward Sapir, Melville Herskovits, Clark Wissler, Ashley Montagu, Jules Henry, and Leslie Spier).[47] No Hegel/Kuhn (*The Structure of Scientific Revolutions*, 1962) paradigmatic shifts are required. Even Marvin Harris, who reconstructs the Boasian shift as a reaction to historical materialism, attributes Boas' profound recasting of anthropology to his "natural gifts, superior education," and his "puritan" devotion to facts.[48]

Notwithstanding, Boas' sustained challenge to the modernist construction of anthropology, he and those of his students who resituated "primitive" cultures within the embrace of human development obtained no clear victory. Until the present, academic anthropology and its kindred sciences (for example, sociobiology, intelligence studies, population genetics) have accommodated the discourses of human unity and racial hierarchy. As Stephen Jay Gould warns, the biological determinists inhabit both the ephemeral and deep structures of Western culture:

> Who even remembers the hot topics of ten years ago: Shockley's proposals for reimbursing voluntarily sterilized individuals according to the number of IQ points below 100, the great XYY debate, or the attempt to explain urban riots by diseased neurology of rioters ... But I was inspired to write this book because biological determinism is rising in popularity again, as it always does in times of political retrenchment. The cocktail party circuit has been buzzing with its usual profundity about innate aggression, sex roles, and the naked ape.[49]

Undaunted by the miserable errors and chicaneries of their predecessors, the reincarnations of Agassiz and McGee are concomitants of the cultural seasons occasioned by historical, economic, and political crises. Neither the Boasians nor Gould or Noam Chomsky and his colleagues are sufficient to nullify the credibility immediately extended to determinists like Phillippe Rushton or Frederick Goodwin, to name two of the most recently celebrated.[50] Each, for a brief moment, constitutes the immediate justification for the chain-of-practices which result, for an example, in the campaigns of sterilization which still target black and brown women in particular.[51]

No rapprochement, no real proximity occurred between Boas' destabilizing cultural anthropology and the anthropology imagined by the Other. The strategic negotiations around scientific practices between the epistemes of Boas and McGee concerned the definition of the Other as a contested site for discovery but not a locale of subjectivity. For an instance, between 1928–1933, Wissler, one of Boas' students and eventually director of the Committee for Research in Problems of Sex (Rockefeller Foundation funding), sought to interrogate the "natural" sex behaviors of the "uncivilized" (Native Americans, Solomon Islanders). Not until 1933 did Wissler acknowledge the existence of culture among his subjects, forcing him to transfer his attention to anthropoids.[52] Herskovits, on the other hand, stood fast on the original turf, pushing "the disproof of the superiority of Euro-American culture in the realm of religion, social organization, and family life ... [to the point] that the very word 'primitive' came to be regarded as inadmissibly invidious and pejorative."[53]

Caroline Bond Day, probably the first black Ph.D. in anthropology (trained by Hooton), and Zora Neale Hurston (Boas) aided the Boasians in their rupture of the fixed identities required by anthropometry. Day's *A Study of Some Negro-White Families in the United States* documented the vitality of mulattoes thus raising them above Hooton's sterilization threshold, while Boas sent Hurston into Harlem to collect cephalic indexes.[54] Eventually, "Papa Franz" sent Hurston off to study black folklore, a journey from which Hurston never really returned, and further distanced his work from the subjectivity of the Other.[55] It was not as if such opportunities were frequent. Including Day and Hurston, St Clair Drake reports, "Up to 1945 when World War II ended, only ten Afro-Americans had secured professional training in anthropology...."[56] And until the black studies movement, generally located from the late 1960s, most black social scientists adhered rather closely to their disciplinary mainstreams with occasional forays into the hereditary genetics and IQ controversies. The bolder intellects, the heirs of Williams and Sheppard like Hurston, Dunham, W. E. B. Du Bois, Carter G. Woodson, Oliver C. Cox, Horace Cayton, and Drake, remained in semiquarantine in mission- and business-funded black colleges and educational organizations.[57]

In light of the profound failures of American scientific practices and canon to achieve some internal legislative discipline over the hegemon of race, the black studies movement began the retrieval of the antimodernist multiculturalism deposited in the anticolonialist studies of Williams, Sheppard, Blyden, George Padmore, C. L. R. James, Frantz Fanon, Aimé Césaire, Amilcar Cabral, Jean-Price Mars, and others. Accompanied by similar initiatives in feminist and ethnic studies, the rupture of academia's modernist discourse on multiculturalism now appears permanent. No amount of exposure, however, dissuades the conceits of fabulists.[58] They remain eminent, powerful, and committed to the Aristotelian construction of the Other. But now they are haunted by students who have encountered the antimodernist anthropology, by colleagues whose research and publications (and classrooms) have obtained prodigious volume.

The eclipse of the racial fabulists, however, is momentary. They will continue to preserve their systems of knowledge for as long as the social order which they "legitimate" endures. And at present, not content merely to exist, drifting from one conceit to another, from one counterfeit to another, the racial fabulists and their sponsors have staked the future of higher education in their attempts to restore modernism. For the fabulists and their economic and state sponsors, the assault against antimodernist multiculturalism is an assault against the democratization of knowledge. For them, either this Other multiculturalism or higher education must be vanquished. This is the form assumed by antidemocracy for the moment.

Notes

1 Aristotle, *The Politics*, Book 1, 1254b19–25.

2 Alexander Fuks, "Isocrates and the Socioeconomic Situation in Greece," *Ancient Society*, 3 (1972); Gregory Vlastos, "Slavery in Plato's Thought," in *Slavery in Classical Antiquity*, ed. M. I. Finley (New York: Barnes & Noble, 1960); Mavis Campbell, "Aristotle and Black Slavery," *Race*, XV, 3 (1974); and Cedric J. Robinson, "Slavery and the Platonic Origins of Anti-Democracy," in press.

3 John Hare, *St Edward's Ghost: or, Anti-Normanisme. Being a Patheticall Complaint and Motion in the Behalfe of our English Nation Against her Grand (yet neglected) Grievance, Normanisme* (1647), quoted in Hugh A. MacDougall, *Racial Myth in English History* (Montreal: Harvest House, 1982), p. 61.

4 Frank Snowden instances Ephorus, the fourth-century historian and contemporary of Isocrates and Aristotle, as one of those who "admired non-Greek peoples," *Blacks in Antiquity* (Cambridge: Harvard University, 1971), pp. 170 ff. and 318, n.12. Notwithstanding Aristotle's direct appeal to nature, David Theo Goldberg still insists that Greek notions of inferiority were generally based on political and cultural rather than biological notions, Goldberg, *Racist Culture* (Oxford: Blackwell, 1993), pp. 21–2.

5 Donna Haraway, *Primate Visions* (New York: Routledge, 1989), pp. 4, 10 and 13.

6 Audrey Smedley, *Race in North America* (Boulder: Westview Press, 1993), p. 240 ff.; Stephen Jay Gould, *The Mismeasure of Man* (New York: W. W. Norton, 1981), p. 45.

7 John Trumpbour, "Introducing Harvard: A Social, Philosophical, and Political Profile," in *How Harvard Rules*, ed. John Trumpbour (Boston: South End Press, 1989), p. 20. Stephen Jay Gould restored and translated sections of Agassiz's correspondence which had been expurgated by Agassiz's wife and largely ignored by historians. One passage from a letter to his mother in December 1846, the year beginning his sojourn in the United States, reads: "It was in Philadelphia that I first found myself in prolonged contact with negroes ... the feeling that they inspired in me is contrary to all our ideas about the confraternity of the human type ... In seeing their black faces with their thick lips and grimacing teeth, the wool on their head, their bent knees, their elongated hands, their large curved nails, and especially the livid color of the palm of their hands, I could not take my eyes off their face in order to tell them to stay far away." Gould, *The Mismeasure of Man* (New York: W. W. Norton, 1981), pp. 44–5. Agassiz was the principal scientific authority for polygeny — the thesis that the races had distinctive origins. Cf. Gould, p. 43; and George Frederickson, *The Black Image in the White Mind: The Debate on Afro-American Character and Destiny, 1817–1914* (New York: Harper, 1971), pp. 75, 137.

8 Stephen Bonsal, "The Negro Soldier in War and Peace," *The North American Review*, CLXXXVI (June 1907), pp. 321–2. In 1863, Agassiz, responding to questions from Dr Samuel Gridley Howe, the radical abolitionist appointed by Lincoln to the Freedmen's Inquiry Commission authorized to recommend policy on the freed slaves, Agassiz responded: "the colored people in whom the negro nature

prevails will tend toward the South, while the weaker and lighter ones will remain and die out among us." Frederickson, *The Black Image in the White Mind,* p. 161.

9 Gould, *The Mismeasure of Man,* p. 48.

10 George Stocking Jr, *Victorian Anthropology* (New York: Free Press, 1987), p. 233 ff.

11 Gould, *The Mismeasure of Man,* reports on the craniometric frauds perpetrated by Morton (p. 54 ff.); in 1906 by Robert Bennett Bean, the Virginian physician (p. 80); the IQ fakery of Cyril Burt (ch. 6); and Arthur Jensen (p. 317 ff.).

12 Jane Mercer and Wayne Curtis Brown, "Racial Differences in IQ: Fact or Artifact?," in *The Fallacy of IQ,* ed. Carl Senna (New York: The Third Press, 1973), p. 66 ff.; and Mallory Wober, "Race and Intelligence," *Transition,* 40 (December 1971), p. 24.

13 George Mosse, *Toward The Final Solution: A History of European Racism* (London: J. M. Dent & Sons, 1978), pp. 11–12.

14 Quoted in Lawrence Levine, "Clio, Canons, and Culture," *The Journal of American History,* 80, 3 (December 1993), p. 854.

15 At its site of origin, Edinburgh (Scotland), phrenology was identified with a populist reform movement which "lobbied for changes in the provision of education, for penal reform, the more effective treatment of the insane, 'enlightened' colonial policies, and a more humane system of factory production...." Stephen Shapin, "The Politics of Observation: Cerebral Anatomy and the Social Interests in the Edinburgh Phrenology Disputes," in *On the Margins of Science: The Social Construction of Rejected Knowledge,* ed. Roy Wallis (Staffordshire: Keele University, March 1979), p. 146.

16 Reginald Horsman, *Race and Manifest Destiny* (Cambridge: Harvard University Press, 1981), chs 7 and 8.

17 Horsman, ibid., pp. 56–9; Smedley, *Race in North America,* p. 237 ff.

18 Smedley, ibid., p. 238.

19 Trumpbour, "Blinding Them with Science: Scientific Ideologies in the Ruling of the Modern World," in *How Harvard Rules,* ed. John Trumpbour; Smedley, *Race in North America,* pp. 241–2.

20 Nott and his coauthor, George Gliddon, from *Types of Mankind* (1854) as quoted by Horsman, *Race and Manifest Destiny,* p. 137.

21 St Clair Drake, "Anthropology and the Black Experience," *The Black Scholar,* 11, 7 (September/October 1980), p. 9.

22 John Miller, *The Wolf by the Ears: Jefferson and Slavery* (Charlottesville: University Press of Virginia, 1991); Winthrop Jordan, *White over Black* (Chapel Hill: University of North Carolina Press, 1969).

23 For the role of intelligence testing in the formulation of anti-immigration laws, see Gould, *The Mismeasure of Man,* pp. 226–33.

24 Smedley, *Race in North America,* p. 253, n. 7. See also Noam Chomsky, "IQ Tests: Building Blocks or the New Class System," in *Shaping the American Educational State,* ed. Clarence Karier (New York: Free Press, 1975).

25 The quotes from Terman and Hooton, and the summary of Katzenellenbogen's testimony, are from Trumpbour, "Blinding Them with Science," pp. 224–5.

26 Haraway, *Primate Visions,* p. 279.

27 Phillips Verner Bradford and Harvey Blume, *Ota Benga, the Pygmy in the Zoo* (New York: Delta, 1992), pp. 121–3.

28 "In 1869 he published *Hereditary Genius*, a landmark volume designed to convince all but the most irascible skeptics of the superior hereditary endowment of certain eminent British families." Smedley, *Race in North America*, p. 266.

29 Marion Mayo, *The Mental Capacity of the American Negro*, reprinted from the Archives of Psychology (New York, 1913), pp. 58 and 69. Further on gender, Mayo quotes Dr. C. S. Myers in "Papers on Inter-Racial Problems" to the effect that: "Certainly there is not an instance of first-class musical genius ... among European women, despite centuries of opportunity." Mayo summarized the preliminary findings of R. S. Woodworth's St Louis Fair study of "Indians, Filipinos, Africans and Ainu." R. S. Woodworth, "Racial Differences and Mental Traits," *Science* (February 1910) cited in Mayo, pp. 64–6.

30 Gilbert Gonzalez, "The Historical Development of the Concept of Intelligence," *The Review of Radical Political Economics*, 11, 2 (Summer 1979), p. 46. Goddard, in the furtherance of restrictive immigration laws and sterilization, faked data and altered photographs in his "studies" of morons. Cf. Gould, *The Mismeasure of Man*, pp. 164–71.

31 Bradford and Blume, *Ota Benga, the Pygmy in the Zoo*, pp. 253 and 122.

32 Ibid., p. 212.

33 Ibid., p. 216 ff.

34 Even more macabre was the predilection among anthropometrists for weighing each other's brains. Gould reports "The dissection of dead colleagues became something of a cottage industry among nineteenth-century craniometricians." Gould describes the crisis of "small-brained men of eminence," e.g., Walt Whitman, Franz Josef Gall, Anatole France, K. F. Gauss, etc., in Gould, *The Mismeasure of Man*, 92 ff.

35 Martin Robison Delaney, "A Project for an Expedition of Adventure, to the Eastern Coast of Africa," the appendix to *The Condition, Elevation, Emigration and Destiny of the Colored People of the United States, Politically Considered* (1852), reprinted in *Apropos of Africa*, eds Adelaide Cromwell Hill and Martin Kilson (London: Frank Cass, 1969), p. 22.

36 Drake, "Anthropology and the Black Experience," pp. 12–13.

37 For pithy biographies of Crummell, Delaney, Douglas, Turner, Smyth, and Williams, as well as excerpts of their writings on Africa, see Hill and Kilson, eds, *Apropos of Africa*, passim.

38 Subtitled *Negroes as Slaves, as Soldiers, and as Citizens; Together with a Preliminary Consideration of the Unity of the Human Family, an Historical Sketch of Africa, and an Account of the Negro Governments of Sierra Leone and Liberia*, the work cited more than 1,000 of the 12,000 volumes Williams consulted, and dismissed the polygenist argument. In 1888, Williams published his *A History of the Negro Troops in the War of the Rebellion, 1861–1865, Preceded by a Review of the Military Services of Negroes in Ancient and Modern Times*. Cf. Earl Thorpe, *Black Historians* (New York: William Morrow, 1971), pp. 46–55.

39 Reprinted in Hill and Kilson, eds, *Apropos of Africa*, p. 106.

40 Bradford and Blume, *Ota Benga, the Pygmy in the Zoo*, pp. 38–52.

41 Michael Taussig, one of the more recent scholars to rehearse the holocaust of Leopold's Congo, and from whom I have borrowed the phrases "culture of terror"

and "space of death," does not mention Williams or Sheppard in his otherwise extraordinary work *Shamanism, Colonialism and the Wild Man* (Chicago: University of Chicago, 1987).

42 Gould, *The Mismeasure of Man,* p. 108.

43 Stocking, *Victorian Anthropology,* p. 287.

44 Frederickson, *The Black Image in the White Mind,* pp. 330, 315.

45 Ruth Benedict, "Obituary of Franz Boas," *Science,* 97 (1943), p. 61. Benedict was one of Boas' students.

46 Marvin Harris, *The Rise of Anthropological Theory* (New York: Thomas Crowell, 1968), p. 255.

47 Cf. ibid., p. 251 for a more complete but still partial listing.

48 Ibid., pp. 257 and 248–9.

49 Gould, *The Mismeasure of Man,* p. 28.

50 For Rushton's claims for craniometry, see his "Cranial Capacity Related to Sex, Rank, and Race in a Stratified Random Sample of 6,325 US Military Personnel," *Intelligence,* 16, 3–4 (July–December 1992); "Evolutionary Biology and Heritable Traits," *Psychological Reports,* 71, 3 (December 1992); "Race and Crime," *Canadian Journal of Criminology,* 32, 2 (April 1990); and Edward Reed and Arthur Jensen, "Cranial Capacity: New Caucasian Data and Comments on Rushton's Claimed Mongoloid–Caucasoid Brain-Size Differences," *Intelligence,* 17, 3 (July–September 1993). Critiques of Rushton include Zack Cernovsky and Larry Litman, "Reanalyses of J. P. Rushton's Crime Data," *Canadian Journal of Criminology,* 35, 1 (January 1993); and John Maddox, "How to Publish the Unpalatable?" *Nature,* 358 (July 16, 1992). For Goodwin, the former Director of the National Institute of Mental Health and the Alcohol, Drug Abuse and Mental Health Administration, who compared inner-city black youths to monkeys in the jungle, see the articles in the *Washington Post* (February 22, 1992), p. A5; (February 27, 1992), p. A4; (February 28, 1992), p. A4. For his defenders, see the *Washington Post* (March 1, 1992), p. C3; and (March 21, 1992), p. A22; and the editorial, "The Speech Police," *Wall Street Journal* (March 9, 1992), p. A14.

51 Loretta Ross, "Sterilization and 'de facto' Sterilization," *Amicus Journal,* 15, 4 (Winter 1994) p. 29; and Lynora Williams, "Violence Against Women," *Black Scholar* (January–February 1981), p. 19.

52 Haraway, *Primate Visions,* pp. 93–4.

53 Harris, *The Rise of Anthropological Theory,* p. 431.

54 Drake, "Anthropology and the Black Experience," pp. 16–17.

55 Zora Hurston, *Dust Tracks on a Road* (Philadelphia: J. P. Lipincott, 1971), pp. 170–4.

56 Drake, "Anthropology and the Black Experience," p. 5. Drake identifies Katherine Dunham, Mark Hanna Watkins, Arthur Huff Fauset, Irene Diggs, Allison Davis, Montague Cobb, Lorenzo Turner, and himself among the others.

57 For the influence of commerce on black higher education in the United States and Africa, see James D. Anderson, "Philanthropic Control over Private Black Higher Education," and Edward H. Bernman, "Educational Colonialism in Africa: The Role of American Foundations, 1910–1945," in *Philanthropy and Cultural Imperialism,* ed. Robert F. Arnove (Bloomington: Indiana University Press, 1982).

58 Fabulists like Arthur Schlesinger Jr, C. Vann Woodward, George Will, Lynne Cheney, and Eugene Genovese, have declared that antimodernist multiculturalism is "an

attack on the common American identity" (Schlesinger); "a war of aggression against the Western political tradition and the ideas that animate it" (Will); a terrorist campaign which can only be defeated "by unleashing counterterrorism against cowardly administrators and their complicit faculty" (Genovese). This mantra, Levine asserts, constitutes "a small growth industry, this jeremiad against the universities and the professoriat, this series of claims that something has suddenly turned sour in the academe, that the Pure Aims and Honest Values and True Worth of the past have been sullied and fouled by politics, by radicals disguised as professors." Levine, "Clio, Canons, and Culture," pp. 851–3.

19

Anthropology and Multiculturalism: What Is Anthropology that Multiculturalists Should Be Mindful of It?

TERENCE TURNER[1]

Anthropologists have been doing a lot of complaining that they are being ignored by the new academic specializations in "culture," such as cultural studies, and by academic and extra-academic manifestations of "multiculturalism." Few anthropologists, however, appear to have made the effort to comprehend the reasons for that indifference from the standpoint of what multiculturalists are trying to do and fewer still have taken an active part in the discussions surrounding multiculturalism. Most of us have been sitting around like so many disconsolate intellectual wallflowers waiting to be asked to impart our higher wisdom and more than a little resentful that the invitations never come.

Culture as Anthropological Theory versus *Culture* as Identity Politics: A Dialogue of the Deaf?

The term *multiculturalism* has come to be used primarily in connection with demands on behalf of black and other minority groups for separate and equal representation in college curricula and extra-academic cultural programs and events. It also has assumed more general connotations as an ideological stance towards participation by such minorities in national "cultures" and societies and the changing nature of national and transnational cultures themselves. As a code word for minority demands for separate recognition in academic and other cultural institutions, *multiculturalism* tends to become a form of identity politics in which the concept of *culture* becomes merged with that of ethnic identity. From an anthropological standpoint, this move, at least in its more simplistic ideological forms, is fraught with theoretical and practical dangers. It risks essentializing the idea of culture as the property of an ethnic group or race; it risks reifying cultures as separate entities by overemphasizing their boundedness and mutual distinctness; it risks overemphasizing the internal homogeneity of cultures in terms that potentially legitimize repressive demands for communal conformity; and by treating cultures as badges of group identity, it tends to fetishize them in ways that put them beyond the reach of critical analysis—and thus of anthropology.

With these risks, however, go important theoretical and political possibilities. Multiculturalists may claim to stand for a liberating recognition of the de facto heterogeneity of the cultural and ethnic makeup of contemporary metropolitan societies, and to call for a critical retheorizing of the relation of culture and political society that would accommodate rather than ignore or repress the multiplicity of identities and social groups comprised by such societies. Multiculturalism, in this form, becomes a vantage point for unique critical insights into the nature of contemporary national cultures as well as current developments and transformations of culture associated with transnational developments in media technology, commodity consumption, and other political and economic changes. Multiculturalist thinking of all kinds has been importantly associated with intra- and extra-academic social activism aimed at reversing the prevailing cultural devaluation of ethnic and other minorities. This activism, in turn, has taken its place as an important mode of contemporary struggle against the continuing social and political oppression of such groups.

There are a number of ways that anthropologists could contribute constructively and critically to multiculturalist thinking and practice, and a number of ways also that they might expand their own theoretical and practical horizons by doing so. Any useful intervention by anthropologists in multiculturalist discourse, however, must begin with the realization that multiculturalists use the term *culture* in different ways and for different purposes than anthropologists. *Multiculturalism*, unlike anthropology, is primarily a movement for change. To the extent that it has developed a theoretical analysis, it is primarily a conceptual framework for challenging the cultural hegemony of the dominant ethnic group (or the dominant class constituted almost exclusively by that ethnic group) in the United States and the United Kingdom[2] by calling for equal recognition of the cultural expressions of nonhegemonic groups within the educational system. *Culture* for multiculturalists, then, refers primarily to collective social identities engaged in struggles for social equality. For multiculturalism, *culture* is thus not an end in itself (whether as an object of theoretical research or teaching) but a means to an end and not all aspects of culture as conceived by anthropologists are relevant to the achievement of that end.

Much of the misunderstanding, mutual indifference, and resentment between multiculturalists and anthropologists springs from this basic difference. Anthropology and its various concepts of culture are not oriented principally toward programs of social change, political mobilization, or cultural transformation. As anthropologists protest that they are being ignored by multiculturalists, therefore, they should first ask themselves the hard question of precisely what they and their theories of culture have to contribute to the multiculturalist project of educational reform and, more broadly, to social, political and cultural transformation. What use are our notions of culture (say, Tylor's encyclopedic inventory, Benedict's configurations, Lévi-Strauss' structures, Chicago's erstwhile neo-Parsonian systems of symbols and meanings, or Harris' reduction to protein) to socially and culturally marginalized minorities struggling to redefine and revalorize their collective identities? Certain aspects of the concept of culture originally developed by the anthropologists (such as the distinction of culture and race) are unquestionably relevant to multiculturalist positions but, for the most part, these by now have been assimilated into the common sense of Anglo-American culture in the form of vulgar cultural relativism, according to which all cultural traditions are regarded in principle as equally valuable. Apart from making ideological use of this broadly "anthropological" notion of cultural relativism as an ideological weapon against Eurocentrism, however, multiculturalism remains essentially unconcerned with culture in any of its usual anthropological senses.

Contradictory Multiculturalisms, Contradictory Anthropologies: *Critical* and *Difference* Approaches to Culture

The question is, *should* it be so conceived? This translates into the question of what anthropological notions of culture might contribute to a political movement for cultural empowerment like multiculturalism. Before this question can even be addressed, one must specify *which* multiculturalism an anthropologist might want to contribute to. As already noted, there are contradictory tendencies within contemporary Anglo-American multiculturalism which may be grouped for convenience under two headings that we may call *critical multiculturalism* and *difference multiculturalism*.[3]

Critical multiculturalism seeks to use cultural diversity as a basis for challenging, revising, and relativizing basic notions and principles common to dominant and minority cultures alike, so as to construct a more vital, open, and democratic common culture. Critical multiculturalism, in this sense, is well represented by the Statement of Principles of Teachers for a Democratic Culture:

Whereas a few short years ago institutions of higher education were exclusive citadels often closed to women, minorities, and the disadvantaged, today efforts are being made to give a far richer diversity of Americans access to a college education. Reforms in the content of the curriculum have also begun to make our classrooms more representative of our nation's diverse peoples and beliefs and to provide a more truthful account of our history and cultural heritage ... It is our view that recent curricular reforms influenced by multiculturalism and feminism have greatly enriched education rather than corrupted it. It is our view as well that the controversies that have been provoked over admissions and hiring practices, the social functions of teaching and scholarship, and the status of such concepts as objectivity and ideology are signs of educational health, not decline....

What does the notion of a "democratic culture" mean and how does it relate to education? In our view, a democratic culture is one that acknowledges that criteria of value in art are not permanently fixed by tradition and authority, but are subject to constant revision. It is a culture in which terms like canon, literature, tradition, artistic value, common culture,and even truth are seen as disputed rather than given. This means not that standards for judging art and scholarship must be discarded, but that such standards should evolve out of democratic processes in which they can be thoughtfully challenged.[4]

In sharp contrast to critical multiculturalism is that of cultural nationalists and fetishists of *difference* for whom *culture* reduces to a tag for ethnic identity and a license for political and intellectual separatism. This is the stereotype of multiculturalism that has been touted by neoconservative critics of "political correctness" in academia who, apart from their other distortions, have described multiculturalism as if it were a homogeneous set of ideas and attitudes. There is no denying, however, that some participants in the multiculturalist debates have adopted positions approximating this stereotype of difference multiculturalism; these positions have aroused more honest concern and more trenchant criticism on the Left than on the Right. Todd Gitlin, for example, sees difference multiculturalism as a symptom of the disarray of the Left:

The academic left has degenerated into a loose aggregation of margins — often cannibalistic, romancing the varieties of otherness, speaking in tongues.

In this new interest-group pluralism, the shopping center of identity politics makes a fetish of the virtues of the minority, which, in the end, is not only intellectually stultifying but also politically suicidal. It creates a kind of parochialism in which one is justified in having every interest in difference and no interest in commonality. One's identification with an interest group comes to be the first and final word that opens and terminates one's intellectual curiosity. As soon as I declare I am a Jew, a black, a Hispanic, a woman, a gay, I have no more need to define my point of view....

If America's multiculturalism means respect for actual difference, we should uphold and encourage this reality against the white-bread, golden-arch version of Disneyland America.

On the other hand, if multiculturalism means there is nothing but difference, then we must do everything we can to disavow it. We cannot condone the creation by the Left of separate cultural reservations on which to frolic.[5]

Katha Pollitt criticizes feminist approaches predicated on inherent biological, psychological, or cultural differences between women and men which she lumps under the term *difference feminism* in terms that she suggests are equally applicable to *difference multiculturalism*:

For its academic proponents ... difference feminism is a way to carve out a safe space in the face of academia's resistance to female advancement. It works much like multiculturalism, making an end run around a static and discriminatory employment structure by creating an intellectual niche that can be filled only by members of the discriminated-against group. And like other forms of multiculturalism, it looks everywhere for its explanatory force — biology, psychology, sociology, cultural identity — *except* economics. The difference feminists cannot say that the differences between men and women are the result of their relative economic positions because to say that would be to move the whole discussion out of the realm of psychology and feel-good cultural pride and into the realm of a tough political struggle over the distribution of resources and justice and money.[6]

What Gitlin calls the "romancing of otherness" — essentially the reification of semiotic contrasts at the level of cultural (or anthropological) texts into social/political oppositions involving inequalities of power — is a besetting vice of much of what passes for "theory" in the trendier and less critical contemporary forms of cultural and multicultural studies. As a form of reification or romantic essentialism, it presupposes the abstraction of cultural phenomena from their real social and political economic contests (as Pollitt trenchantly observes), leaving the social and political significance of the "difference" as a vacuum to be filled by the cultural theorist. This exercise yields an intellectual pseudopolitics that implicitly empowers the theorist while explicitly disempowering real cultural subjects. It also renders invisible the common grounds of cultural continuity and identity which alone render cultural and social differences meaningful in real cultural and political practice. Surely this is a point to which anthropology should be able to contribute, substantively and critically, to a demystified "respect for actual difference," in Gitlin's terms. To do so, however, anthropology must come to terms with some of its own internal differences, old and recent.

Anthropology, like multiculturalism, of course, is far from homogeneous in its approach to culture. Much anthropological thinking about culture has been uncritical in ways analogous to difference multiculturalism. One might include under this head the chronic anthropological tendency, born as much from the practice of intensive fieldwork as from theory, to focus on cultures as discrete units in isolation. Also deserving mention are the tendencies (particularly strong in the United States) to treat culture as an autonomous domain, for example, as "systems of symbols and meanings" essentially unconditioned by material and social and political processes, and the concomitant abstraction of cultural change from political or social relations, particularly relations of inequality, domination, and exploitation. Most of the paradigmatic anthropological approaches to history and change have shared this shortcoming, from *evolution* through *acculturation* to *drift* and *diffusion*. One might also add the paradoxical failure of those anthropologists most concerned with cultures as symbolic structures or *systems of meanings* to produce adequate analyses of such structures or meaningful constructs much above the level of individual symbols and tropes. (More interesting results in this area might at least have given textually-oriented multiculturalists more reason to pay attention to anthropological writings.)

The multiculturalists' critique of Eurocentrism has attempted to confront the implicit cultural assumptions embedded in the institutional structures of education and political power in our society and to integrate a critical exposure of the social and political meanings encoded in literary texts into its educational program. Given the *aporias* of anthropological thinking on these points, multiculturalists can hardly be blamed for looking elsewhere rather than to anthropology for theoretical models for these aspects of their program.

Historically, anthropology has made important contributions to the critical decentering of Eurocentric biases both in the academic disciplines of social thought and in popular consciousness: anthropological *cultural relativism* is a direct ancestor of critical multiculturalism. Notions like cultural relativism and the anthropological notion of cultures themselves as systems of shared forms of consciousness, values, and patterns of conduct possessed in fundamentally similar form by all human groups, are no longer, however, the exclusive possession of anthropology. Other fundamental anthropological contributions to a more critical cultural awareness such as the rejection of the essentialist identification of culture and race and the overthrow of evolutionist notions of cultural difference that held other cultures to be "lower" or inferior in proportion to their degree of difference from the hegemonic Western culture, have passed by now into the common culture of our own society and have been incorporated into most, if not all, multiculturalist perspectives.

Anthropology's greatest shortcoming has been its failure to develop these foundational insights into a socially- and historically-grounded critical understanding of cultural phenomena. By this I mean a theoretically articulated awareness that cultural forms are neither constructed in abstraction from the social existence of their bearers nor do they merely express, encode, or transparently embody their real social life-world or historical experience. Rather such forms may *mis*represent and conceal crucial aspects of that world, particularly those involving relations of domination and exploitation.

What might such a critical anthropological perspective have to offer to multiculturalist thinking? Multiculturalism, as an academic position, proceeds from a critical view of the received curriculum as an instrument for reproducing the hegemony of the dominant social group. This view is specifically grounded in contentions that the canonical humanities curriculum and conventional history-teaching approaches embody notions of "high culture" and social relevance that inculcate and reproduce relations of social and political inequality by representing the cultural tradition of the dominant social group as being naturally central and preeminent. Those of marginal or subordinate minorities, meanwhile, are unrepresented and thus rendered invisible. The focus of the multiculturalist challenge to these aspects of the traditional curriculum, however, has ironically led many academic multiculturalists, even as they call for a decentering of the dominant Eurocentric notion of high culture, to adopt much of its schematic content as the form of their own oppositional conception of minority "cultures." The result is that the ideological forms and values of established hegemonic notions of culture and history have tended to be carried over into multiculturalist challenges to these forms. Thus, multiculturalist alternative curricula often continue to emphasize the elite aesthetic forms central to the received humanistic canon, like "art," music, and texts of a "literary" character, as well as historical claims to outstanding achievement, discoveries, invention, and so on. While challenging the evaluative distinction between *high* and *low* or *popular* culture as it has functioned in the traditional canon to marginalize the cultural productions of minority groups, multiculturalists, nonetheless, have formulated these challenges by revaluing minority cultural productions in terms of the sorts of aesthetic criteria employed to define the value of canonical "high cultural" forms of art, literature, or music. The hegemonic Eurocentric categories (literature, art) in which the canonical notion of *culture* as *high culture* is framed thus go unchallenged.

By contrast, a critical socioanthropological view of culture as collective forms of social consciousness arising in the context of historical social processes, the humanistic notion of *culture* in terms of a canon of elite aesthetic products itself becomes a cultural form in need of critical analysis — analysis that would point to its function in legitimizing the sorts of inequalities that multiculturalists purport to challenge. A major point of divergence between the critical perspective of many social anthropologists on *culture* and much of the multiculturalist discourse on culture is that the latter continues to accept conventional humanistic conceptions of culture in terms of elite aesthetic criteria of evaluation and canonical works rather than critically confronting the way such elite forms of culture serve as the foundation of the hegemony of social, political, ethnic, and class elites. The result, in anthropological terms, can only be rebellion rather than revolution: specifically, the replication of the hegemonic pattern of cultural elitism through the creation of new hegemonic elites comprised of academic specialists in the revalorized products of minority cultures.

Or again: to the extent that multiculturalists reduce their program to a mere demand for a pluralization of canons, with separate curricula for each recognized ethnic group based on its own culture conceived in such uncritical terms, they only end by ratifying the divisions and inequalities imposed by the social system they aspire to change. Indeed, they fixate on the nature of those social and political divisions as *cultural* differences, thus obscuring their political and economic roots, as Pollitt charges. This amounts to the inverse mystification of that represented by an uncritical liberal pluralism which would see equal cultural representation in a multicultural educational program as a cultural "solution" to social and political inequities. All of this bears little resemblance to what thoughtful multiculturalist spokespersons have been saying (as we will see immediately below), but it has an undeniable relevance to the implicit pretensions of what I have characterized as difference multiculturalism.

There are, then, valid grounds on which anthropologists might argue the critical relevance of their own approach to culture to at least some varieties of multiculturalist thinking. That they have not done so is due largely to the fact that relatively few anthropologists actually seem to operate with such a critical view of culture. In the absence of such anthropological input, multiculturalist scholars and thinkers have been supplying their own critical formulations. Take, for example, Gates' reply to the charge (summarized in the preceding paragraph) that multiculturalism threatens to balkanize the nation:

> Those who fear that "Balkanization" and social fragmentation lie this way [for example, Roger Kimball, Dinesh D'Souza, George Will] have got it exactly backward. Ours is a world that already is fissured by nationality, ethnicity, race and gender. And the only way to transcend those divisions — to forge, for once, a civic culture that respects both differences and commonalities — is through education that seeks to comprehend the diversity of human culture.[7]

Shohat and Stam further develop the same point:

> Multiculturalists are accused of pulling people apart, of balkanizing the nation, of emphasizing what divides people rather than what brings them together. Multiculturalism is seen by conservative writers, educators, and politicians as a threat because it seems to summon "ethnic" communities to form hermetically sealed enclaves.... That the current system of power relations within and outside the United States itself generates divisiveness goes unacknowledged; that multiculturalism offers a more egalitarian vision of representation is ignored.[8]

As Shohat and Stam go on to argue, the "egalitarian vision of representation" presented by multiculturalism does not imply an uncritical "pluralism" but presupposes a critical decentering of hegemonic ideological notions of culture:

[M]ulticulturalism and the critique of Eurocentrism are inseparable concepts....
[M]ulticulturalism without anti-Eurocentrism runs the risk of being merely accretive
— a shopping mall ... of the world's cultures — without any interrogation of
Euro-American hegemony.[9]

Nor is this critically decentered multicultural approach a mere theoretically inert,
ideological construct, lacking implications for the conceptualization of culture:
"Polycentric multiculturalism, in our view, calls for a profound
reconceptualization of the relations between cultural communities both within and
between nations," which, the authors argue, implies an equally profound
reconceptualization of the internal nature of cultural communities — in short, of
culture itself:

> Critical multiculturalism refuses a ghettoizing discourse that would consider groups
> [i.e., "cultures"] in isolation. It is precisely this emphasis on relationality that
> differentiates [it from] liberal pluralism. [In contrast to pluralism, a critical,
> anti-Eurocentric multiculturalism substitutes for [a] discourse of tolerance [one
> which] sees all utterance and discourse in relation to the deforming effects of social
> power.... [It] rejects a unified, essentialist concept of identity, taken as the referential
> sign of a static set of practices, meanings and experiences. Rather, it sees the self as
> polycentric, multiple, unstable, historically situated, the product of ongoing
> differentiation and polymorphous identifications.... [It therefore views] all acts of
> verbal or cultural exchange [as taking] place not between essential bounded
> individuals but rather between permeable, changeable subjects. Each act of cultural
> interlocution, within an ongoing struggle of hegemony and resistance, leaves both
> interlocutors changed.[10]

Gates makes essentially the same point: "[Multiculturalism] sees cultures as
porous, dynamic, and interactive, rather than the fixed property of particular ethnic
groups. Thus the idea of a monolithic, homogeneous 'West' itself comes into
question."[11]

Anthropology's Contribution: Complexity or Theoretical Critique?

A pervasive ground of suspicion and even disdain for multiculturalist notions
of culture on the part of anthropologists is that most multiculturalists are literary
scholars with no background in social science, let alone anthropology, and no
personal experience of different cultural or social groups. Little wonder, then, that
many anthropologists dismiss their ideas of culture as overly textual,
underanalyzed, and naively unaware of the various dimensions and complexities
of cultural systems, such as kinship, that anthropologists have had to learn through
arduous and prolonged bouts of fieldwork. I quote from a representative
anthropological complaint:

As well-meaning as the multiculturalists may be, their naivete has unfortunate consequences. [Their] concept of culture is often simplistic…. This often shows up in assumptions that one can sample other cultures through brief encounters…. [T]hey often rely on a … visceral approach … and go straight for what it "feels like" to be one of them.

A perception seems to exist that this empathetic grasp is attainable through short, vivid descriptions and insightful anecdotes depicting slices of life in exotic locales….

They commonly confuse cultural relativism with moral relativism … [and] tend to view non-Western cultures as stable, tradition-bound, timeless entities, [which] shifts us dangerously back toward viewing the others as beings who are profoundly and inherently different from ourselves…. The sense of the "timeless heritage" of traditional peoples, albeit respectful, is just a short step from ethnic essentialism…. At its worst, this romanticism tends to blur the distinction between culture and race — a distinction that we anthropologists thought we had established several generations ago.[12]

The author is referring specifically to multiculturalist colleagues at his own campus, but he clearly intends his remarks in a more general sense. I do not question the accuracy of his characterization of the views of his own multiculturalist colleagues, or its applicability to some others. I do question its applicability to the more sophisticated varieties of multiculturalist thinking, such as those represented by many of the passages I have quoted. As Perry himself indicates elsewhere in the same passage, noting the preference of his "viscerally" oriented multiculturalist colleagues for certain articles by Clifford Geertz, an impressionistic approach to culture that emphasizes subjective experience and evocation is hardly alien to contemporary anthropology. Against this facile approach, Perry suggests that anthropology's essential contribution is a realization of the complexity of cultures, evidenced by the amount of time, effort, and discomfort — in short, the fieldwork — it takes to understand them. It is disturbing, but perhaps indicative of the current crisis of theoretical confidence in the field, that this assertion of complexity (fair enough as far as it goes) lacks any specific theoretical content. Are anthropologists prepared to say precisely what, other than complexity itself, their discipline has to offer multiculturalism at the level of ideas?

Anthropology and Cultural Studies

The development of multiculturalism followed the revolt against the canon in English and American literary studies and the Eurocentric canon in history (manifested, for example, by the influence of subaltern studies and the concern with colonial and postcolonial resistance to capitalist exploitation and Western hegemony). The development of *cultural studies*, strongly influenced by the work of the Center for Cultural Studies in the United Kingdom, also formed part of this intellectual landscape and directly influenced the rise of multiculturalism. Cultural studies similarly is concerned with the subcultures, media, and genres of representation of groups of the margins of the hegemonic classes and status groups of British and American society. Like multiculturalism, it represents a decentering move in the study and teaching of culture, and the working concepts of culture it has developed have had a direct influence on multiculturalism. The two movements have involved essentially the same academic constituencies (mostly English and other modern literatures) and have been similarly indifferent toward anthropology as they developed their own approaches to culture.

Bearing in mind that cultural studies and multiculturalism are concerned with cultural aspects of the historical present in the United States and United Kingdom, one may ask what precisely they have missed by neglecting us. Let me quote from a proposal for a specialization in cultural studies at Cornell University drafted by a group of graduate students in English literature, with no anthropologists participating:

> "Cultural studies" as an interdisciplinary genre of cultural analysis and criticism ... comprehends work on what has been described as the "social circulation of symbolic forms," that is, the institutional and political relations and practices through which cultural production acquires and constructs social meanings. Situated at the intersection of social theory, cultural analysis, and literary criticism, it puts pressure on each of these elements in light of the others.... [W]ork in cultural studies has been interested in examining processes of cultural change and reproduction and the sociopolitical relationships within which such processes occur.... [It] involves both a recognition of the role of "culture," in the sense of "symbolic constructions," in a broad range of social practices and identities ... and a corresponding recognition that the analytical tools developed in the study of literature can be useful in (and perhaps revised by) examining radically different, but related, kind of material....

> Alongside more traditional areas of literary and historical study, [cultural studies is concerned with] cultural forms such as movies, television, video, popular music, magazines and newspapers, and the media industries and other institutions which produce and regulate them.... Often, indeed, the focus of study is precisely the systematic social relations between or among different kinds of cultural production, whether within a single social or historical context or across differing contexts.[13]

Note that in this statement *culture* is nowhere treated as a reified entity or a bounded internally-consistent domain in abstraction from social and historical reality. Rather, specific cultural forms are taken as the focus with their degree of relatedness as components of a single system left open as an empirical question. The emphasis is consistently on the social contextualization of cultural forms (defined as *symbolic constructs*) as mediators of social processes. Among the types of processes prominently mentioned are production and reproduction with a specific emphasis on new forms of cultural production, like new media, as sites of social transformation. There is a focus on historical change and an interest in comparison across historical periods and spatial boundaries. At the same time, the statement emphasizes the continuing relevance of techniques of close textual analysis carried over from traditional literary studies.

Theoretically, this is no superficial touchy-feely formulation of culture as *visceral* experience directly accessible through the reading of a few anecdotal texts. I venture to say that many anthropologists would be hard-pressed to come up with as theoretically sophisticated a formulation of the nature of culture in contemporary US and British society, one as powerfully contextualized in social and historical terms and as fruitful in pointing to productive lines of research. Let us not fool ourselves with dismissive caricatures: a lot of the competition is very good and is doing quite well without us. If anthropology is going to make a contribution to the new academic approaches to culture emerging out of cultural studies and multiculturalist curricula, it will not be simply by sitting still and waiting to be consulted because we had culture first. Anthropologists will have to engage actively and critically with multiculturalist formulations to demonstrate that they have valuable theoretical points and relevant critical perspectives to contribute.

Let me give an example of the kind of constructive critical contribution I have in mind; a critique by an anthropologist of several anti-Eurocentric works that have played a foundational role in multiculturalist thinking, especially difference multiculturalism. The article is Fernando Coronil's "Beyond Occidentalism."[14] In the portion from which I shall quote, the works in question are Said's *Orientalism* (1978) and Todorov's *The Conquest of America* (1984). Coronil argues that the nature of the Eurocentric ("Occidentalist") point of view is at least as problematic as the distortions in Western representations of the non-Western "Other" (that is, Orientalism) that have thus far been the focus of multiculturalist critiques and, from an anthropological point of view, should form part of the same analysis. I quote at length from the passage in which he develops these ideas. A critical approach to the understanding of Western representations of Oriental cultures, Coronil suggests, should proceed by

> directing our attention to the relational nature of representations of human collectivities, [and thus bringing into] focus their genesis in asymmetrical relations of power, including the power to obscure their genesis in inequality, to sever their historical connections, and thus to present as the internal and separate attributes of bounded entities what are in fact historical outcomes of connected peoples.... Perhaps one could take a step in this direction by shifting our perspective from the problematic of "Orientalism" to that of "Occidentalism." ... Occidentalism, as I define it here, is thus not the reverse of Orientalism but its condition of possibility, its dark side (as in a mirror). A simple reversal would only be possible in the context

of symmetrical relations between "Self" and "Other" — but then who would be the "Other"? In the context of equal relations, difference would not be cast as "Otherness"....

Challenging Orientalism entails disrupting Occidentalism as an ensemble of representational strategies and practices whose effect is to produce "Selfhood" as well as "Otherness." In other words, by Occidentalism I refer to the complex ensemble of representational strategies engaged in the production of conceptions of the world that a) separates its components into bounded units; b) disaggregates their relational histories; c) turns difference into hierarchy; d) naturalizes these representations; and therefore e) intervenes, however unwittingly, in the reproduction of existing asymmetrical power relations.[15]

This passage is framed in an anthropological perspective on the nature of culture formulated in terms specifically relevant to issues with which multiculturalists are concerned (for example, the relations between different cultures and ethnicities and the critique of Eurocentrism) and makes a characteristically anthropological contribution to the understanding of those issues. It is a piece of anthropological writing with specific critical relevance to the conceptualization and educational presentation of intercultural relations which constructively challenges and deepens theoretical formulations central to multiculturalism (and cultural studies as well).

Like the programmatic Cornell statement on cultural studies cited above, but unlike in many more familiar and consensual anthropological notions of culture, Coronil insists that cultural formations must be understood in the context of their role in the mediation of social relations, particularly "asymmetrical power relations." He defines culture as constituted by processes of production of the self and the other and calls for a critical understanding of the way these processes produce representations that conceal the interdependence of the entities involved, reifying difference as otherness and masking the nature of the entities thus represented as historical products. Coronil thus demonstrates how a more powerfully conceived anthropological analysis can further decenter works that have served multiculturalists as models of decentered understanding, altering their interpretation in ways that potentially deepen the critical perspective of multiculturalism itself.

Coronil's is a textual analysis but the same principles apply to anthropological analyses of field data and the presentation of cultural materials in an educational curriculum. When anthropologists contextualize their ideas about culture by focusing on the ways cultural constructs mediate the social processes and political struggles through which people produce themselves and resist and/or accommodate asymmetrical power relations, and when they combine the critical decentering of cultural representations with the decentering of their own theoretical perspectives on those representations, then they will not merely have a base from which to complain about being ignored by multiculturalists, but a basis for making constructive critical contributions to the critical multiculturalist program for a democratic culture.

Multiculturalism as Cultural and Political-Economic Phenomenon: Toward an Anthropological Analysis of the Meaning of *Culture*

Multiculturalism has appeared under specific social and political conditions and forms part of the response of its creators to those conditions. The cultural and political significance of multiculturalism must be understood in relation to these conditions.

Multiculturalism is one manifestation of the postmodernist reaction to the delegitimization of the state and the erosion of the hegemony of the dominant culture in advanced capitalist countries. This weakening of "centers" is part of a material *decentering* process grounded in the organization of capital on a global scale, manifested in the development of transnational labor, commodity and capital markets, and corporate structures which have reduced the power of traditional political and social structures to control or protect social groups within the state. As state structures have lost much of their power to control social and economic conditions within their boundaries, and the transnational centralization of political and economic power and exploitation has intensified, people all over the world have turned to ethnic and cultural identity as a means of mobilizing themselves for the defense of their social and political/economic interests. The increasing political importance of culture as an ideological vehicle for the new forms of ethnic nationalism and identity politics that have accompanied the weakening or collapse of colonial empires and multiethnic states has made it a favored idiom of political mobilization for resistance against central political authorities and hegemonic national cultures. In this respect, the intensification of ethnocultural nationalism has overlapped with the rise of identity politics and subcultures of symbolic resistance among nonethnic (feminist, youth, and alternative sexual) groups in the metropolitan societies of the First World.

Coinciding with, and paradoxically reinforcing, the development of the new cultural politics of resistance to social inequality has been the florescence of capitalist commodity production and consumption on an unprecedented scale. This has led to the accompanying growth of consumerist forms of identity-production denoted by such terms as *lifestyle, life politics,* etc. These are essentially cultural forms of self-construction which employ commodities as their symbolic medium. *Culture* here appears as the *jouissance* of the late-capitalist consumerist subject, playing with the heady new opportunities for self-creation that the ever-growing world of commodities appears to provide. This aspect of contemporary capitalist reality has also reinforced the historically emergent sense of *culture* as a domain of self-creation on a collective scale seemingly liberated from the constraints of normative social and political structures. This postmodern sense of culture, in turn, has contributed to the formulation of the notions of culture employed in multiculturalist discourse.

In all of these respects, culture has come to serve as the basis of *imagined communities* and individual *identities* deemed to be "authentic" in contrast to repressive, alien, or otherwise "inauthentic" normative codes, social institutions, and political structures. This historical unwedging of *culture* and *society* as politico-economic structures has converged with, and greatly reinforced, the idealistic culturalism (that is, their abstraction from, or avoidance or rejection of, sociological, politico-economic, or other forms of materialistic analysis) of the disciplines and thinkers primarily involved with multiculturalism.

The meaning of *culture*, in other words, currently is undergoing yet another of its historical transformations. The contemporary conjuncture of the global organization of capital and the concomitant surpassing of the nation-state, the rise of ethnic and identity politics, the explosive growth of new informational technologies and media, and the florescence of late-capitalist consumerism has created a context in which culture has taken on new meanings and connotations. Among the most significant of these is the idea that culture, as distinct from nationality, is a source or locus of collective rights to self-determination. Culture, as such, becomes a source of values that can be converted into political assets, internally as bases of group solidarity and mobilization and externally as claims on the support of other social groups, governments, and public opinion all over the globe. Culture in these new senses, as a universal category distinct from, but subsuming, specific cultures can be understood as the cultural form of the new global historical conjuncture: in effect, metaculture, or "culture of cultures."[16]

This social/political/economic/cultural conjuncture is the material context for multiculturalism as a cultural phenomenon and intellectual movement. It is a conjuncture significantly different from previous colonial, neocolonial, and precolonial moments which provided the context for most anthropological theorizing about culture. This is why so much anthropological thinking about culture no longer seems adequate or relevant to what culture has come to mean, especially for many self-conscious "cultural" groups and movements which have defined their cultural identities in ways that exploit the possibilities and implications of the new conjuncture. New ideological and theoretical positions like multiculturalism and cultural studies are attempting to express these new meanings, often, it seems to me, with more success and relevance than anthropology.

Toward a Convergence of Critical Anthropology and Critical Multiculturalism: *Culture* as Capacity and Empowerment

A critical anthropology could contribute a deeper understanding of the relation of multiculturalism and the new meanings and political significance of *culture* from which it arises, to the social and material conditions of the contemporary world-historical conjuncture. Here, the way is being shown by a number of anthropologists working with politically- and socially-implicated cultural forms such as ethnicity, gender, sexual identity, the politics of reproductive choice, postcolonial consciousness, the resistance of peasant and other peripheral groups to domination by centralized political or economic regimes, human rights and indigenous advocacy work, to name some (but by no means all) of the substantive areas in which work fraught with critical implication for multiculturalist thinking is currently being done by anthropologists. By and large, however, these anthropologists have not yet taken time out from their specific projects to address the theoretical implication of their work for multiculturalist positions and programs. The present essay is essentially an attempt to formulate in relatively abstract and general terms the import of such current work.

The critical understanding of the cultural dimensions of contemporary political issues and struggles that anthropologists can provide — and, in fact, are providing in many specific areas of research — is important, not only theoretical but politically, for thinkers and groups attempting to theorize about, or organize around, the fissive and integrative roles of "culture" and "identities" in contemporary societies. It specifically is essential to a realization of the implicitly revolutionary nature of multiculturalism as a program of cultural, social and political transformation.

In calling for the formal equality of all cultures within the purview of the state and its educational system, multiculturalism represents a demand for the dissociation (decentering) of the political community and its common social institutions from identification with any one cultural tradition. (This denial of a privileged role as the unique idiom of social consensus to the hegemonic Eurocentric subculture is the point of the multiculturalist program that most outrages its conservative critics.) The implications of this demand for the decentering of culture(s) from the political system and social community go beyond a mere celebration of cultural differences or of individual cultures for their own sakes, and even beyond an emphasis on the interdependence, overlapping, and hybridization of cultures with one another. To replace the Burkean vision of conservative proponents of a unitary hegemonic culture as the indispensable consensual basis of national political institutions with the principle that the political institutions of the state should derive their legitimation from promoting and coordinating the coexistence of diverse cultural groups, traditions, and identities, in turn implies the repudiation of the idea that national political viability depends on *any* common culture or even confederation of different cultures as such. Implicitly, it asserts in its place the principle that the promotion and protection of the universal right to cultural self-definition and self-production in general is the ultimate ground of political legitimacy. It implies, by the same token, the elevation of "culture" as a new category of collective human rights, and defines it, as such, as a legitimate goal of political struggle for equal representation in the public domain. Such unprecedented claims imply a recognition of some common property or properties of "cultures" that make them worthy of equal protection and support by the state and give them a legitimate claim on such support. The specification of the essential properties of culture in general has thus ceased to be a purely academic concern of anthropological theory and has begun to emerge as a fundamental political issue. At this point, multiculturalism as a political movement opens back into anthropology, the one discipline that has concerned itself with such questions. It is here that anthropology should be able to make a unique and valuable contribution, not only to multiculturalist theory and practice but to the more general issues in the emerging pattern of transnational politics of which multiculturalism is but one manifestation.

Even though such general theoretical questions have been out of fashion in anthropology of late, raising them again in the politicized context of the current debates over multiculturalism and identity politics should give them new practical relevance and cogency as well as new theoretical direction. As in the case of multiculturalist notions of *culture*, anthropological approaches to the question have been divided, on the one hand, between *encyclopedic* conceptions of cultures as more or less practico-inert arrays of traits and, on the other, praxis-oriented notions of culture as the realization of a collective human potential for self-production and transformation.

Thinking of the latter sort is represented by earlier anthropological concerns with such themes as "man's capacity for culture" or "man makes himself." In this type of anthropological perspective, the multiplicity and historical mutability of human cultures is significant above all as an indication of the generality of human powers of collective self-creation; that is, the human "capacity for culture." Cultures are the way specific social groups, acting under specific historical and material conditions, have "made themselves." The theoretical contribution of the anthropological approach to culture, in sum, has been the focus on the capacity for culture as a collective power emergent in human social interaction, and the decentering awareness of specific cultures as historically contingent products of such collective activity. This anthropological emphasis on the capacity for culture as a level of human potential immanent in but also transcending specific cultures implicitly decenters the focus of culturalism in all its forms (mono-, bi-, and multi-) from a fixation on particular cultures and cultural identities for their own sakes, to the appropriation of the historical achievements of all cultures for the sake of promoting collective empowerment and ongoing cultural self-production in the present.

Two features of the anthropological concept of the capacity for culture are particularly relevant in this context: its inherently social character and its virtually infinite plasticity. The capacity for culture does not inhere in individuals as such but arises as an aspect of collective social life with its concomitants of cooperative human and social reproduction. Its almost infinite malleability, however, means that there are virtually no limits to the kinds of social groups, networks, or relations that can generate a cultural identity of their own. The group can be a "natural" one, for example, a tribe engaged in subsistence activity, or it can be a self-consciously formed voluntary grouping like the generation-, gender-, occupational-, or class-based subcultures of contemporary society. Ethnic groups with self-consciously cultivated cultural identities of the types that enter into multiculturalist programs in contemporary schools and universities approximate the latter type more closely than the former, but even small, recently contacted tribal societies are rapidly learning to reconceptualize themselves as "cultures" for purposes of political interaction with the current world-system, in ways that resemble the identity politics of subcultural groupings in First-World societies.[17] The point here is that multiculturalism in this larger theoretical and historical context implicitly becomes a program not merely for the equalization of relations among existing cultural groups and identities but for the liberation and encouragement of the process of creating new ones.

As the conjunctural forces in the late-capitalist world favoring the development, political recognition, and social valuation of cultural and subcultural identities gather momentum, the prospect is for the steady proliferation of new cultural identities along with the increasing assertion of established ones. What I have called the *conjuncture* thus increasingly takes on the character of a metacultural framework bringing into being a metacultural network of forces, institutions, values, and policies which fosters and reinforces the proliferation of cultural groups, identities, and issues in the public domain.

Insofar as the new conjuncture favors the self-definition, production, and assertion of cultural groups and identities, in general, as distinct from any particular cultural, ethnic-group, or subcultural identity per se, it acts as a material vector for the *capacity for culture* as a general principle or power. The conjuncture becomes, in other words, a historical vehicle and catalyst not only for the political assertion and ideological valuation of particular cultures but of the generic human ability and right to create them.

There is, thus, a convergence of sorts between certain material forces in the present conjuncture and the relatively abstruse and elusive anthropological notion of the human capacity for culture which underlies but implicitly transcends the various forms of multiculturalism that have recently developed. It is a convergence, however, that can only be realized if anthropologists reconceive their theoretical formulation of the capacity for culture in the more concretely social and political terms of collective empowerment for self-production rather than as an abstract array of evolutionary cognitive, physical, and social traits. Doing so would lead anthropologists to confront the ways the social and political context of collective empowerment and, by extension, the present historical conjuncture of politico-economic forces may also involve contradictory forces which constrain, combat, and mystify the capacity for self-production which, in other ways, it promotes. *Multiculturalism*, as a movement in support of the collective empowerment of all relatively disempowered culturally-identified groups, would thus entail struggle against such forces, including those of an overtly noncultural character such as economic exploitation and political repression.

In such an anthropological perspective, then, the ultimate aim of any general policy of *multiculturalism* would be explicitly envisioned as the empowerment of the basic human capacity for self-creation (that is, for culture, in the active sense of collective self-production) for all members and groups of society. Respecting and fostering the collective forms in which this capacity historically has realized itself (for example, as existing cultures and ethnic groups) becomes, within this more general perspective, not an end in itself but a means to this more general end. The multiculturalist movement within this historical perspective assumes the role of a moment in the historical struggle for a freer and more flexible formation of groups and identities based on self-consciously shared values, orientations, activities, and politico-economic positions.

In other words, from the critical vantage point of a conception of culture as empowerment for collective action, self-production, and struggle, the presently constituted forms of *multiculturalism* may be seen as embryonic expressions of the revolutionary principle that the protection and fostering of the human capacity for culture is a general human right and, as such, a legitimate goal of politically-organized society. Anthropology should have a lot to say about the nature of this goal and what its promotion, under specific circumstances, might concretely involve. Meanwhile, much as St Paul revealed to the Athenians the identity of the unknown god they had been worshipping, anthropologists might play a useful role in helping multiculturalists realize the revolutionary implications of the course upon which they have embarked.

Notes

1 *Acknowledgements.* Reproduced by the permission of the American Anthropological Association from *Cultural Anthropology,* 8, 4 (November 1993). Not for further production. This paper was originally presented in the Presidential Session "Anthropology and Multiculturalism" at the American Anthropological Association Meetings in San Francisco in 1992. James Peacock provided an insightful and constructive commentary on the paper at that session. I am extremely indebted to numerous friends and colleagues who took that time and trouble to orient me to the issues and literature of multiculturalism. Kathleen Hall, John Comaroff, Robert Stam, Ella Shohat, Steve Sangren, and Fred Myers are not responsible for the specific views expressed in this paper, but it could not have been written without their knowledgeable discussion and extensive bibliographical and critical suggestions. Jane Fajans gave the manuscript a careful critical reading which resulted in many changes.

2 I am indebted to Kathleen Hall (*"Education for All": The Rhetoric of Incorporation in British Educational Policy Debates.* Manuscript, n.d. and personal

communication) for a history and overview of the multicultural debate in the United Kingdom, particularly as it effects education and South Asian minorities in Britain.

3 In a lecture at the University of Chicago, my colleague John Comaroff made a similar distinction between *encyclopedic* and *critical* multiculturalism which has become part of the local oral tradition without as yet having been reduced to written form. Pollitt has used the term *difference feminism* to denote feminist positions based on the thesis that the received social, politico-economic, and cultural differences in the status of men and women are the result of inherent differences that become manifested in a distinct women's "culture" (passage quoted below). Gitlin's distinction between multiculturalism based on "the romance of the other" and that based on respect for "real" social and cultural differences (also quoted below) is basically identical.

4 Teachers for a Democratic Culture, "Statement of Principles" in *Beyond PC: Toward a Politics of Understanding,* ed. Patricia Aufderheide (St Paul, MN: Greywolf Press, 1992), pp. 67–70.

5 Todd Gitlin, "On the Virtues of a Loose Canon" in *Beyond PC: Toward a Politics of Understanding,* ed. Patricia Aufderheide (St Paul, MN: Greywolf Press, 1992), pp. 188–9.

6 Katha Pollitt, "Marooned on Gilligan's Island: Are Women Morally Superior to Men?" *The Nation,* (December 28, 1992), p. 806.

7 Henry Louis Gates Jr, "The Debate Has Been Miscast from the Start," *Boston Globe Magazine* (October 1991), p. 36.

8 Robert Stam and Ella Shohat, *Unthinking Eurocentrism: Multiculturalism, Film and the Media.* Manuscript. n.d., pp. 14–15. [This has since been published by Routledge, 1994 — ed.]

9 Ibid., pp. 13–14.

10 Ibid., pp. 15–17.

11 Henry Louis Gates Jr, "The Debate Has Been Miscast from the Start," p. 37.

12 Richard J. Perry, "Why Do Multiculturalists Ignore Anthropologists?" *Chronicle of Higher Education* (March 1992), p. 52.

13 Cornell University Cultural Studies Discussion Group, *Proposal for a Cultural Studies Concentration* (Ithaca, NY: Cornell University, 1991).

14 Fernando Coronil, "Beyond Occidentalism: Towards Post-Imperial Geohistorical Categories" *Critical Inquiry* (in press).

15 Ibid., pp. 5–6.

16 Marshall Sahlins, "Goodbye to Tristes Tropes: Ethnography in the Context of Modern World History," *The University of Chicago Record,* 27, 3 (1993), p. 5.

17 Terence S. Turner, "Representing, Resisting, Rethinking: Historical Transformations of Kayapo Culture and Anthropological Consciousness" in *Colonial Situations: History of Anthropology,* Vol. 7, ed. George W. Stocking Jr, (Madison: University of Wisconsin Press, 1991) pp. 285–313.

LIST OF CONTRIBUTORS

Anita Allen is currently Professor of Law, Georgetown University Law Center. She has a Ph.D. in Philosophy from the University of Michigan and a J.D. from Harvard University. She is the author of numerous books and articles concerning the right to privacy, women's rights, racial diversity, and free speech.

Lauren Berlant teaches English at the University of Chicago. She is the author of *The Anatomy of National Fantasy: Hawthorne, Utopia, and Everyday Life*, and of various essays on citizenship, sexuality, identity, and the public sphere. She is a coeditor of *Critical Inquiry* and *Public Culture*.

Peter Caws is University Professor of Philosophy at The George Washington University. His books include *Yorick's World: Science and the Knowing Subject*; *Structuralism: The Art of the Intelligible*; and *Sartre*.

Barbara Christian is Professor of African-American Studies at the University of California, Berkeley, where she is also active in the Ethnic Studies Ph.D. program. Her books include *Black Feminist Criticism: Perspectives on Black Women Writers* and *Black Women Novelists: The Development of a Tradition 1892–1976*, and she has just edited a volume of critical essays on Alice Walker's *Everyday Use*.

Angie Chabram Dernersesian currently teaches in the Department of Chicana/Chicano Studies at the University of California, Davis, and is a member of The Chicana Institute. She has written on feminism, ethnography, and criticism, and recently coedited a special volume of *Cultural Studies* on Chicana/o cultural representations.

Michael Eric Dyson is presently Professor of Communication Studies at the University of North Carolina, Chapel Hill. The author of *Reflecting Black: African-American Cultural Criticism* and coeditor of *Rethinking Malcolm X* (with Wahneema Lubiano), he is presently at work on a major reinterpretation of black males entitled *Boys to Men: Black Males in America* (Random House, 1997), and is editing an anthology of black nationalist writings, entitled *"It's Nation Time": A Black Nationalism Reader*.

Henry Louis Gates Jr, is W. E. B. Du Bois Professor of the Humanities and Director of the W. E. B. Du Bois Institute for Afro-American Research at Harvard University. He chairs the Department of Afro-American Studies and is a member of the English Department at Harvard University. His many books include *Colored People*; *Loose Canons: Notes on the Cultural Wars*; *Figures in Black: Words, Signs and the "Racial Self*; and *The Signifying Monkey: A Theory of Afro-American Literary Criticism*. He is general editor of the Schomburg Library of Nineteenth-Century Black Women Writers and of *Transition* magazine (With K. Anthony Appiah), and Director of the Black Periodical Literature Project.

Henry A. Giroux is the Waterbury Chair Professor in Secondary Education at Pennsylvania State University. His many books include *Disturbing Pleasures: Learning Popular Culture*; *Border Crossings*; *Between Borders* (with Peter McLaren); and *Postmodern Education* (with Stanley Aronowitz).

David Theo Goldberg is Professor of Justice Studies and the Graduate Committee on Law and Social Science at Arizona State University. He is the author of *Racist Culture: Philosophy and the Politics of Meaning* and *Ethical Theory and Social Issues* (2nd. ed.). He is the editor of *Anatomy of Racism*, and coeditor of *Jewish Identity* (with Michael Krausz) and of *Social Identities: A Journal for the Study of Race, Nation and Culture* (with Abebe Zegeye).

Ramon A. Gutierrez is Professor of History, founding Chair of the Ethnic Studies Department, and Director of the Center for the Study of Race and Ethnicity at the University of California, San Diego. He is the author of *When Jesus Came, the Corn Mothers Went Away: Marriage, Sexuality, and Power in New Mexico, 1500–1846*, winner of the Frederick Jackson Turner Prize, The John Hope Franklin Prize, and the Hubert E. Bolton Prize. He is a coeditor of the multivolume *Encyclopedia of the North American Colonies*, *Recovering the US Hispanic Literary Heritage*, and *Festivals and Celebrations in American Ethnic Communities*.

Sandra Harding is Professor of Philosophy at the University of Delaware and at the University of California, Los Angeles. She is the author and editor of several books on issues in science and epistemology, including The Science Issue in Feminism; *Whose Science? Whose Knowledge?*; and most recently *The "Racial" Economy of Science: Toward a Democratic Future*.

Tommy L. Lott is Professor of Philosophy at San José State University. His research interests include published articles on early modern philosophy and on a variety of topics in African-American social philosophy. He is editor of a volume on *Slavery and Social Philosophy*.

Peter McLaren is Associate Professor in the Graduate School of Education and Information Studies, University of California, Los Angeles. His recent books include *Life in Schools*; *Schooling as a Ritual Performance;* and *Critical Pedagogy and Predatory Culture: Oppositional Politics in a Postmodern Era*. He has coedited *Critical Literacy: Politics, Praxis, and the Postmodern* and *Politics of Liberation: Paths from Freire* (both with Colin Lankshear); and *Between Borders* (with Henry Giroux).

Cedric Robinson is Professor of Political Science, Chair of Black Studies, and former Chair of Political Science at the University of California, Santa Barbara. His books include *Black Marxism* and *Terms of Order*.

Ella Shohat is Associate Professor of Women's Studies and Cultural Studies at the CUNY Graduate Center, and of Cinema Studies at CUNY, Staten Island. She is the author of *Israeli Cinema: East/West and the Politics of Representation*, and coauthor (with Robert Stam) of *Unthinking Eurocentrism: Multiculturalism and the Media.* She is a coeditor of *Social Text,* and she has curated numerous film, video, and cultural events including a "Multicultural Feminism" conference at the New Museum, New York City.

Robert Stam is a Professor of Cinema Studies at New York University. He has published extensively on issues of multicultural representation. His books include *Brazilian Cinema* (with Randall Johnson); *Subversive Pleasures: Bakhtin, Cultural Criticism and Film*; and *New Vocabularies in Film Semiotics,* and is coauthor (with Ella Shohat) of *Unthinking Eurocentrism: Multiculturalism and the Media.*

Judith Hicks Stiehm is a Professor of Political Science at Florida International University. She served as Provost there, and as Vice-Provost and Director of the Program for the Study of Women and Men in Society at the University of Southern California. She is the author of Nonviolent Power; *Bring Me Men and Women: Mandated Change at the US Air Force Academy*; and *Arms and the Enlisted Women.* She is now working on a book on higher education.

Charles Taylor is Professor of Philosophy and Political Science at McGill University. His many books include *The Explanation of Behavior*; *Hegel*; *Human Agency and Language*; *The Ethics of Authenticity*; *Philosophy and the Human Sciences*; and *Sources of the Self.* He has run for Canadian Federal Parliament on behalf of the New Democratic Party, and was recently appointed to the Conseil de la Langue in Quebec.

Terence Turner is Professor of Anthropology at the University of Chicago. He is known for many publications and films on the Kayapo Indians of Brazil, and has worked for pro-indigenous and human rights advocacy.

Michele Wallace is Associate Professor of English and Women's Studies at City College of New York and City University of New York Graduate Center. She is the author of *Black Macho and the Myth of the Superwoman* and *Invisibility Blues: From Pop to Theory,* and Project Director of *Black Popular Culture* (edited by Gina Dent).

Michael Warner teaches English at Rutgers University. He is the author of *Letters of the Republic,* and editor of *Fear of a Queer Planet: Queer Politics and Social Theory.*

Selected Bibliography

Ahmad, Aijaz (1987) "Jameson's Rhetoric of Otherness and the 'National Allegory',"
Social Text, 17 (Fall).

Ahmad, Aijaz (1992) *In Theory* (London: Verso).

Alexander, Edward (1990) "Race Fever," *Commentary*, 90, 5 (November).

Amin, Samir (1985) *Delinking: Towards a Polycentric World* (London: Zed).

Ansley, Frances Lee (1991) "Race and the Core Curriculum in Legal Education,"
California Law Review, 79, 6 (December).

Anthony, Kathryn H. and Bradford C. Grant (1993) "Gender and Multiculturalism in
Architectural Education," *Journal of Architectural Education* (September).

Anzaldúa, Gloria (1987) *Borderlands/La Frontera: The New Mestiza* (San Francisco:
Spinsters/Aunt Lute Book Company).

Anzaldúa, Gloria, ed. (1990) *Making Face, Making Soul* (San Francisco: Aunt Lute).

Appadurai, Arjun (1990) "Disjuncture and Difference in the Global Cultural Economy,"
Public Culture, 2, 2.

Appadurai, Arjun (1993) "Consumption, Duration, and History," *Stanford Literature
Review*, 10.

Appadurai, Arjun (1993) "The Heart of Whiteness," *Callaloo*, 16, 4.

Appleton, Nicholas (1978) *Multiculturalism and the Courts* (Los Angeles: National
Dissemination and Assessment Center, California State University).

Arnold, Matthew (1937) *Culture and Anarchy* (Cambridge: The University Press, [1932;
original publication 1869]).

Arnove, Robert F., ed. (1982) *Philanthropy and Cultural Imperialism* (Bloomington:
Indiana University Press).

Asad, Talal (1990) "Multiculturalism and British Identity in the Wake of the Rushdie
Affair," *Politics & Society* (December).

Asad, Talal (1993) "A Comment on Aijaz Ahmad's *In Theory*," *Public Culture*, 6, 1 (Fall).

Asante, Molefi (1988) *Afrocentricity* (Trenton, NJ: Africa World Press).

Asante, Molefi (1988) *The Afrocentricity Idea* (Philadelphia: Temple University Press).

Asante, Molefi Kete (1991) "Multiculturalism: An Exchange," *The American Scholar*
(Spring).

Astin, Alexander W. (1993) "Diversity and Multiculturalism on the Campus: How Are
Students Affected," *Change* (March).

Aufderheide, Patricia, ed. (1992) *Beyond PC: Toward a Politics of Understanding* (St
Paul, MN: Greywolf Press).

Axtell, James (1981) *The European and the Indian: Essays in the Ethnohistory of
Colonial North America* (New York: Oxford University Press).

Bak, Hans, ed. (1993) *Multiculturalism and the Canon of American Culture* (Amsterdam:
VU University Press).

Baker, Houston A. Jr (1993) *Black Studies, Rap, and the Academy* (Chicago: University
of Chicago Press)

Baldwin, James (1988) "A Talk to Teachers," in *Multicultural Literacy: Opening the American Mind,* eds Rick Simonson and Scott Waler (St Paul, MN: Greywolf Press).

Baraka, Ras (1991) "Mo' Dialogue," *The Source,* 24 (September).

Barnard, James (1990) "The Rise of Rap: Reflections on the Growth of the Hip Hop Nation," *African Commentary* (June).

Bass, Jack (1978) *Widening the Mainstream of American Culture: A Ford Foundation Report on Ethnic Studies* (New York: Ford Foundation).

Bell, Derrick (1986) "Strangers in Academic Paradise: Law Teachers of Color in Still White Schools," 20 *USF L* 385.

Bell, Derrick (1986) "The Price and Pain of Racial Perspectives," *Stanford Law School Journal,* 5 (May 9).

Bell, Derrick (1992) *Faces at the Bottom of the Well: The Permanence of Racism* (New York: BasicBooks).

Benedict, Ruth (1935) *Patterns of Culture* (London: Routledge and Kegan Paul).

Benhabib, Seyla (1992) *Situating the Self: Gender, Community and Postmodernism in Contemporary Ethics* (London: Routledge).

Benjamin, Jessica (1988) *Bonds of Love: Psychoanalysis, Feminism and the Problem of Domination* (New York: Pantheon).

Bennett, William J. (1984) *To Reclaim a Legacy: Report on the Humanities in Higher Education* (Washington, DC: National Endowment for the Humanities)

Bennett, William J., ed. (1993) *The Book of Virtues* (New York: Simon and Schuster).

Berger, Bridgitte (1993) "Multiculturalism and the Modern University," *Partisan Review* (Fall).

Berman, Paul, ed. (1992) *Debating P.C.: The Controversy over Political Correctness on College Campuses* (New York: Laurel Paperbacks).

Bernal, Martin (1987) *Black Athena* (New Brunswick, NJ: Rutgers University Press).

Berube, Michael and Cary Nelson, eds (1994) *Higher Education Under Fire* (New York: Routledge).

Bhabha, Homi and Bhikhu Parekh (1989) "Identities on Parade: A Conversation," *Marxism Today* (June).

Bigelow, Bill (1991) "Discovering Columbus, Re-reading the Past," in "Rethinking Columbus," a special quincentenary issue of *Rethinking Schools*.

Blaut, J. M. (1992) "The Theory of Cultural Racism," *Antipode,* 24, 4.

Blaut, J. M. (1993) *The Colonizer's Model of the World: Geographical Diffusionism and Eurocentrism* (New York: Guilford Press).

Bloom, Allan (1987) *The Closing of the American Mind* (New York: Simon & Schuster).

Blum, Lawrence (1991) "Philosophy and the Values of a Multicultural Community," *Teaching Philosophy,* 14 (June).

Bly, Y. N. (1989) *The Anti-Social Contract* (Atlanta: Clarity Press).

Boskin, Joseph (1986) *Sambo* (New York: Oxford University Press).

Boskin, Joseph (n.d.) "The Life and Death of Sambo: Overview of an Historical Hang-Up," in *Remus, Rastas, Revolution,* ed. Marshall Fishwick (Bowling Green, OH: Bowling Green Popular Press).

Bourdieu, Pierre and Jean-Claude Passeron (1977) *Reproduction in Education, Society and Culture,* tr. Richard Nice (London: Sage).

Bowser, Benjamin P. (1993) *Confronting Diversity Issues on Campus* (Newbury Park, CA: Sage Publications).

Boxill, Bernard (1984) *Blacks and Social Justice* (Totowa, NJ: Rowman and Allanheld).

Boyer, Ernest (1987) *College: The Undergraduate Experience in America* (New York: Harper and Row).

Bozeman, Adda Bruemmer (1971) *The Future of Law in a Multicultural World* (Princeton: Princeton University Press).

Bradford, Phillips Verner and Harvey Blume (1992) *Ota Benga: The Pygmy in the Zoo* (New York: St Martin's Press).

Bristow, Joseph (1991) *Empire Boys: Adventures in a Man's World* (London: Harper Collins).

Brown, Darryl (1990) "Racism and Race Relations in the University," *Virginia Law Review,* 79.

Butler, Johnella E. (1991) "Ethnic Studies: A Matrix Model for the Major," *Liberal Education,* 77.

Butler, Johnella E. and Betty Schmitz (1992) "Ethnic Studies, Women's Studies, and Multiculturalism," *Change* (January/February).

Butler, Johnella E. and John C. Walter (1991) *Transforming the Curriculum: Ethnic Studies and Women's Studies* (Albany, NY: SUNY Press).

Butler, Judith and Joan Scott, eds (1992) *Feminists Theorize the Political* (New York: Routledge).

Carby, Hazel (1980) "Multi-Culture," *Screen Education,* 34 (Spring).

Carby, Hazel (1992) "The Multicultural Wars" in *Black Popular Culture,* ed. Gina Dent (Seattle: Bay Press).

Castles, Stephen (1992) "The Australian Model of Immigration and Multiculturalism: Is It Applicable to Europe," *International Migration Review* (Summer).

Cheney, Lynne V. (1988) *Humanities in America: A Report to the President, the Congress, and the American People* (Washington, DC: National Endowment for the Humanities).

Cheney, Lynne V. (1989) *50 Hours: A Core Curriculum for College Students* (Washington, DC: National Endowment for the Humanities).

Cheney, Lynne V. (1990) *Tyrannical Machines: A Report on Educational Practices Gone Wrong and Our Best Hopes for Setting Them Right* (Washington, DC: National Endowment for the Humanities).

Cheney, Lynne V. (1993) "Forum: Multiculturalism Done Right: Taking Steps to Build Support for Change," *Change* (January).

Childs, John Brown (1981) *Leadership, Conflict, and Cooperation in Afro-American Social Thought* (Philadelphia: Temple University Press).

Chinweizu (1975) *The West and the Rest of Us: White Predators, Black Slaves and the African Elite* (New York: Random House).

Chused, Richard H. (1988) "The Hiring and Retention of Minorities and Women on American Law School Faculties," 137 *University of Pennsylvania Law Review,* 537.

Clifford, James and George E. Marcus (1986) *Writing Culture: The Poetics and Politics of Ethnography* (Berkeley: University of California Press).

Cohen, Marshall, Thomas Nagel, and Thomas Scanlon, eds (1977) *Equality and Preferential Treatment* (Princeton: Princeton University Press).

Considine, J. D. (1992) "Fear of a Rap Planet," *Musician* (February).

Copjec, Joan (1991) "The *Unvermogender* Other: Hysteria and Democracy in America," *New Formations,* 14 (Summer).

Coronil, Fernando (In press) "Beyond Occidentalism: Towards Post-Imperial Geohistorical Categories," *Critical Inquiry.*

Cottrol, Robert J. (1990) "America the Multicultural," *American Educator* (Winter).

Cripps, Thomas (1983) "Amos 'n Andy and the Debate Over American Racial Integration," in *American History/American Television,* ed. John E. O'Connor (New York: Frederick Ungar Publishing Co.).

Culp, Jerome McCristal Jr (1992) "Diversity, Multiculturalism, and Affirmative Action: Duke, the NAS, and Apartheid," *De Paul Law Review* (Summer).

Cultural Conservatism: Toward a New Agenda (1987) (Washington, DC: Institute for Cultural Conservatism/Free Congress Research and Education Foundation).

D'Souza, Dinesh (1991) *Illiberal Education: The Politics of Race and Sex on Campus* (New York: The Free Press).

D'Souza, Dinesh (1991) "Multiculturalism 101: Great Books of the Non-Western World," *Policy Review,* 56 (Spring).

D'Souza, Dinesh (1991) "The New Segregation on Campus," *American Scholar,* 60, 1 (Winter).

Dance, Daryl Cumber (1978) *Shuckin' and Jivin'* (Bloomington: Indiana University Press).

David Schoem, ed. (1993) *Multicultural Teaching in the University* (New York: Praeger).

David, Charles T. and Henry Louis Gates Jr, eds (1985) *The Slave's Narrative* (New York: Oxford University Press).

Davis, Regina (1993) "Writing Multiculturalism into Architectural Curricula," *Journal of Architectural Education* (September).

Decker, Jeff (1993) "The State of Rap," *Social Text,* 34.

Decter, Midge (1991) "E Pluribus Nihil: Multiculturalism and Black Children," *Commentary,* 92, 3 (September).

Delgado, Richard (1987) "The Ethereal Scholar: Does Critical Legal Studies Have What Minorities Want?" *Harvard Civil Rights-Civil Liberties Law Review,* 22.

Dent, Gina, ed. (1992) *Black Popular Culture* (Seattle: Bay Press).

Diamond, Sara (1991) "Readin', Writin' and Repressin'," *Z Magazine* (February).

Diawara, Manthia (1992) "Black Studies, Cultural Studies: Performative Acts," *Afterimage,* 20, 3 (October).

Dillard, J. L. (1977) *Lexicon of Black English* (Seabury Press).

Donald, James and Ali Rattansi, eds (1992) *"Race," Culture and Difference* (London: Sage Publications in association with the Open University).

Douglass, Frederick (1960) *Narrative of the Life of Frederick Douglass, An American Slave. Written by Himself* (Cambridge: Harvard University Press, [original edition 1845]).

Drake, St Clair (1980) "Anthropology and the Black Experience," *The Black Scholar,* 11, 7 (September/October).

Dumm, Thomas (1994) "Strangers and Liberals," *Political Theory,* 22, 1 (February).

Duster, Troy (1992) *The Diversity Project: Final Report* (Berkeley: University of California).

Dyer, Richard (1988) "White," *Screen,* 29, 4.

Dyson, Michael E. (1993) *Reflecting Black: African-American Cultural Criticism* (Minneapolis: University of Minnesota Press).

Ellis, John M. (1989) *Against Deconstruction* (Princeton: Princeton University Press).

Ely, Melvil Patrick (1991) *The Adventures of Amos 'n Andy* (New York: The Free Press).

Erickson, Peter (1992) "Multiculturalism and the Problem of Liberalism," *Reconstruction.*

Erickson, Peter (1992) "What Multiculturalism Means," *Transition*, 55.

Escoffier, Jeffrey (1991) "The Limits of Multiculturalism," *Socialist Review* (July).

Estrada, Kelly and Peter McLaren (1993) "A Dialogue on Multiculturalism and Democracy," *Educational Researcher* (April).

Fabian, Johannes (1990) "Presence and Representation: The Other and Anthropological Writing," *Critical Inquiry*, 16 (Summer).

Fanon, Frantz (1967) *Black Skin, White Masks* (New York: Grove Press).

Ferguson, Russell Martha Gever, Trinh T. Minh-ha, and Cornel West (1990) *Out There: Marginalization and Contemporary Cultures* (Cambridge: The MIT Press and The New Museum of Contemporary Art, New York).

Feuer, Lewis S. (1991) "From Pluralism to Multiculturalism," *Society* (November).

Fish, Stanley (1992) "Bad Company," *Transition*, 56.

Foster, Hal, ed. (1983) *The Anti-Aesthetic: Essays on Postmodern Culture* (Seattle: Bay Press).

Frederickson, George (1971) *The Black Image in the White Mind: The Debate on Afro-American Character and Destiny, 1817–1914* (New York: Harper).

Fregoso, Rosa Linda and Angie Chabram, eds (1990) "Chicana/o Cultural Representations: Reframing Alternative Critical Discourses," special issue of *Cultural Studies*, 4, 3.

Friedman, Lester and Diane Carson, eds (1992) *Multicultural Media in the Classroom* (Urbana: University of Illinois Press).

Fullinwider, Robert K. (1980) *The Reverse Discrimination Controversy: A Moral and Legal Analysis* (Totowa, NJ: Rowman and Littlefield).

Gamson, Zelda (1991) "The View from Student Affairs," *Change* (September/October).

Gates, Henry Louis Jr, ed. (1985) *"Race," Writing and Difference* (Chicago: The University of Chicago Press).

Gates, Henry Louis Jr (1987) *Figures in Black* (New York: Oxford University Press).

Gates, Henry Louis Jr (1988) *The Signifying Monkey* (New York: Oxford University Press).

Gates, Henry Louis Jr (1992) *Loose Canons: Notes on the Culture Wars* (Oxford: Oxford University Press).

Gates, Henry Louis Jr (1992) "The Black Man's Burden," in *Black Popular Culture*, ed. Gina Dent (Seattle: Bay Press).

Geyer, Michael (1993) "Multiculturalism and the Politics of General Education," *Critical Inquiry* (Spring).

Gilligan, Carol (1982) *In a Different Voice* (Cambridge: Harvard University Press).

Gilroy, Paul (1987) *There Ain't No Black in the Union Jack* (London: Hutchinson).

Gilroy, Paul (1991) "It Ain't Where You're From ... It's Where You're At ...: The Dialectics of Diasporic Identification," *Third Text*, 13.

Gilroy, Paul (1993) *The Black Atlantic: Modernity and Double Consciousness* (Cambridge: Harvard University Press).

Giroux, Henry A. (1992) *Border Crossings* (London: Routledge).

Giroux, Henry A. (1994) *Disturbing Pleasures: Learning Popular Culture* (New York: Routledge).

Giroux, Henry A. and Peter McLaren (1991) "Leon Golub's Radical Pessimism: Toward a Pedagogy of Representation," *Exposure*, 28, 12.

Glazer, Nathan (1991) "In Defense of Multiculturalism," *New Republic* (September 2).

Glazer, Nathan (1993) "School Wars: A Brief History of Multiculturalism in America," *The Brookings Review* (Fall).

Goldberg, David Theo (1993) *Racist Culture: Philosophy and the Politics of Meaning* (Oxford: Blackwell).

Gordon, Milton (1964) *Assimilation in American Life* (New York: Oxford University Press).

Gould, Stephen Jay (1981) *The Mismeasure of Man* (New York: W. W. Norton).

Graff, Gerald (1988) "Teach the Conflicts: An Alternative to Educational Fundamentalism," in *Literature, Language, and Politics*, ed. Betty Jean Craige (Athens: The University of Georgia Press).

Graff, Gerald and Bruce Robbins (1992) "Cultural Criticism," in *Redrawing the Boundaries*, eds Stephen Greenblat and Giles Gunn (New York: MLA).

Greenawalt, Kent (1983) *Discrimination and Reverse Discrimination* (New York: Alfred A. Knopf).

Greene, Linda S. (1992) "Multiculturalism as Metaphor," *De Paul Law Review* (Summer).

Grinde, Donald A. Jr and Bruce E. Johansen (1991) *Exemplar of Liberty: Native America and the Evolution of Democracy* (Los Angeles: American Indian Studies Center).

Grossberg, Lawrence, Cary Nelson, and Paula Treichler, eds (1992) *Cultural Studies* (London: Routledge).

Guillory, John (1991) "Canon, Syllabus, List: A Note on the Pedagogic Imaginary," *Transition*, 52.

Guillory, John (1993) *Cultural Capital* (Chicago: University of Chicago Press).

Gutmann, Amy (1993) "The Challenge of Multiculturalism in Political Ethics," *Philosophy & Public Affairs* (Summer).

Gutmann, Amy, Steven C. Rockefeller, Michael Walzer, and Susan Wolf, eds (1992) *Multiculturalism and "The Politics of Recognition"* (Princeton: Princeton University Press).

Hacker, Andrew (1992) *Two Nations: Black and White, Separate, Hostile, Unequal* (New York: Charles Scribner).

Hacker, Andrew (1992) "Why the Shortage of Black Professors?" *The Journal of Blacks in Higher Education*, 1 (Autumn).

Hall, Stuart (1987) "Minimal Selves," in *Identity: The Real Me*, ed. Lisa Appignanesi (London: ICA).

Hall, Stuart (1990) "The Emergence of Cultural Studies and the Crisis of the Humanities," *October*, 53 (Summer).

Hall, Stuart (1991) "Ethnicity: Identity and Difference," *Radical America*, 23, 4.

Hall, Stuart and Bram Gieben, eds (1992) *Formations of Modernity* (Cambridge: Polity Press).

Hammer, Rhonda and Peter McLaren (1992) "The Spectacularization of Subjectivity: Media Knowledges, Global Citizenry and the New World Order," *Polygraph*, 5.

Handlin, Oscar (1941) *Boston's Immigrants* (Cambridge: Harvard University Press).

Haraway, Donna (1990) *Simians, Cyborgs and Women* (London: Free Association Books).

Harvey, David (1989) *The Condition of Postmodernity* (Oxford: Basil Blackwell).

Hecht, Brian (1991) "Dr. Uncool J: The Sun-Man Cometh to Harvard," *New Republic* (March 2).

Hickling-Hudson, Ann (1993) "Curricular Responses to Multiculturalism: An Overview of Teacher Education Courses in Australia," *Teaching and Teacher Education*

Hicks, D. Emily (1992) *Border Writing* (Minneapolis: University of Minnesota Press).

Hill, Herbert, ed. (1968) *Anger, and Beyond* (New York: Harper and Row).

Himmelstein, Jerome L. (1990) *To the Right: The Transformation of American Conservativism* (Berkeley: University of California Press).

Hirsch, E. D. Jr (1987) *Cultural Literacy: What Every American Needs to Know* (Boston: Houghton Mifflin).

Hoeveler, J. David Jr (1991) *Watch on the Right: Conservative Intellectuals in the Reagan Era* (Madison: University of Wisconsin Press).

Holland, Eugene W. and Vassilis Lambropoulos (1990) "The Humanities as Social Technology — An Introduction," *October,* 53 (Summer).

hooks, bell (1982) *Ain't I A Woman: Black Women and Feminism* (Boston: South End Press).

hooks, bell (1990) *Yearning: Race, Gender, and Cultural Politics* (Boston: South End Press).

hooks, bell (1992) *Black Looks: Race and Representation* (Boston: South End Press).

Horsman, Reginald (1981) *Race and Manifest Destiny* (Cambridge: Harvard University Press).

Hunt, John A. (1992) "Monoculturalism to Multiculturalism: Lessons for Three Public Universities," *New Directions for Teaching and Learning* (Winter).

Hunter, Ian (1988) *Culture and Government: The Emergence of Literary Education* (Houndmills, Basingstoke: Macmillan).

Hymowitz, Kay S. (1992) "Multiculturalism in the Public Schools," *Dissent* (Winter).

Iannone, Carol (1985) "Feminism and Literature," *New Criterion,* 4, 3 (November).

James, Joy and Ruth Farmer, eds (1993) *Spirit, Space and Survival: African American Women in (White) Academe* (New York: Routledge).

Jarvis, Sonia R. (1992) "Brown and the Afrocentric Curriculum,"*Yale Law Journal,* 101, 6 (April).

Kelley, Robin D. G. (1992) "Notes on Deconstructing 'The Folk'," *American Historical Review* (December).

Kelly, Robin D. G. (1994) "Kickin' Reality, Kickin' Ballistics: The Cultural Politics of Gangsta Rap in Postindustrial Los Angeles," in *Dropin' Science: Critical Essays on Rap Music and Hip Hop Culture,* ed. Eric Perkins (Philadelphia: Temple University Press).

Kessler-Harris, Alice (1992) "Cultural Locations: Positioning American Studies in the Great Debate," *American Quarterly,* 44, 3.

Kimball, Roger (1990) *Tenured Radicals: How Politics Has Corrupted Higher Education* (New York: Harper Collins).

Kimball, Roger (1991) "Multiculturalism and the American University," *Quadrant* (July).

Koning, Hans (1976) *Columbus, His Enterprise: Exploding the Myth* (New York: Monthly Review Press).

Kristeva, Julia, (1991) *Strangers to Ourselves* (New York: Columbia University Press).

Kroeber, A. L. and Clyde Kluckhohn, (n.d.) *Culture: A Critical Review of Concepts and Definitions* (New York, Random House), (originally published as vol. XLVII, no. 1, of the *Papers of the Peabody Museum of American Archaeology and Ethnology* [Cambridge: Harvard University, 1952]).

Krupnick, Mark (1986) *Lionel Trilling and the Fate of Cultural Criticism* (Evanston: Northwestern University Press).

Kulik, Gary (1993) "Special Issue on Multiculturalism: Editor's Introduction," *American Quarterly* (June 1).

Kymlicka, Will (1989) *Liberalism, Community and Culture* (Oxford: Clarendon Press).

LaCapra, Dominick, ed. (1992) *The Bounds of Race* (Ithaca, NY: Cornell University Press).

Laszlo, Ervin, ed. (1993) *The Multicultural Planet: The Report of a UNESCO Expert Group* (Oxford: One World).

Lehman, David (1991) *Signs of the Times: Deconstruction and the Fall of Paul de Man* (New York: Poseiden).

Lerner, Gerda, ed. (1972) *Black Women in White America: A Documentary History* (New York: Vintage).

Levin, Margarita, "Caring New World: Feminism and Science," *American Scholar,* 54, 1 (Winter).

Levine, George, Peter Brooks, Jonathan Culler, Marjorie Garber, E. Ann Kaplan, and Catharine R. Simpson (1989) *Speaking for the Humanities* (New York: American Council of Learned Societies).

Levine, Lawrence (1993) "Clio, Canons, and Culture," *The Journal of American History,* 80, 3 (December).

Lind, William S. (1986) "What Is Cultural Conservatism?" *Essays in Our Times,* 2, 1 (March).

Lind, William S. and William H. Marshner, eds (1991) *Cultural Conservatism: Theory and Practice* (Washington, DC: Free Congress Foundation).

Lippard, Lucy R. (1990) *Mixed Blessings: New Art in a Multicultural America* (New York: Pantheon Books).

Littlejohn, Edward J. (1985) "Black Law Professors: A Past ... A Future?" *Michigan Bar Journal,* 539 (June).

Locke, Alain and Bernard J. Stern, eds (1942) *When Peoples Meet* (New York: Progressive Education Association).

Locke, Alain LeRoy (1992) *Race Contacts and Interracial Relations,* ed. J. Stewart (Washington, DC: Howard University Press).

Locke, Don C. (1992) *Increasing Multicultural Understanding: A Comprehensive Model* (Newbury Park, CA: Sage Publications).

Lubiano, Wahneema (1992) "Multiculturalism: Negotiating Politics and Knowledge," *Concerns,* 2, 3.

Lusane, Clarence (1993) "Rap, race and politics," *Race and Class,* 35, 1 (July–September).

Lynch, James (1989) *Multicultural Education in a Global Society* (London: Falmer Press).

MacCannell, Dean (1992) *Empty Meeting Grounds: The Tourist Papers* (London: Routledge).

Macedo, Donald (In press) "Literacy for Stupidification: The Pedagogy of Big Lies," *Harvard Educational Review.*

Marable, Manning (1992) *Black America: Multicultural Democracy* (Westfield, NJ: Open Media).

Marable, Manning (1992) "Blueprint for Black Studies and Multiculturalism," *The Black Scholar* (Summer).

McCarthy, Cameron (1988) "Rethinking Liberal and Radical Perspectives on Racial Inequality in Schooling: Making the Case for Nonsynchrony," *Harvard Educational Review,* 58, 3.

McClintock, Anne (1992) "The Angel of Progress: Pitfalls of the Term 'Post-Colonialism'," *Social Text,* 31, 2.

McGary, Howard and Bill E. Lawson, (1992) *Between Slavery and Freedom* (Bloomington: Indiana University Press).

McLaren, Peter (1990) "Schooling the Postmodern Body," in *Postmodernism, Feminism, and Cultural Politics,* ed. Henry A. Giroux (Albany, NY: SUNY Press).

McLaren, Peter (In press) "Border Disputes: Multicultural Narrative, Critical Pedagogy and Identity Formation in Postmodern America," in *Naming Silenced Lives,* eds J. McLaughlin and William G. Tierney (New York: Routledge).

McLaren, Peter and Rhonda Hammer (1992) "Media Knowledges, Warrior Citizenry, and Postmodern Literacies," *Journal of Urban and Cultural Studies,* 2, 2.

Mercer, Kobena (1987) "Black Hair/Style Politics," *New Formations,* 3 (Winter).

Mercer, Kobena (1990) "Welcome to the Jungle: Identity and Diversity in Postmodern Politics," in *Identity: Community, Culture, Difference,* ed. Jonathan Rutherford (London: Lawrence and Wishart).

Mercer, Kobena (1992) "1968: Periodizing Politics and Identity," in *Cultural Studies,* eds Lawrence Grossberg, Cary Nelson, and Paula Treichler (London: Routledge).

Mercer, Kobena (1992) "Back to my Routes: A Postscript on the 80s," *Ten.8,* 2, 3.

Messer-Davidow, Ellen (1993) "Manufacturing the Attack on Liberalized Higher Education," *Social Text,* 36.

Meyerowitz, Joshua and John Maguire (1993) "Media, Place, and Multiculturalism," *Society* (July).

Minority Critiques of the Critical Legal Studies Movement (1987) Special issue of *Harvard Civil Rights-Civil Liberties Law Review,* 22.

Mohanty, Chandra Talpade (1990) "On Race and Voice: Challenges for Liberal Education in the 1990s," *Cultural Critique* (Winter).

Mohanty, Chandra Talpade, Ann Russo, and Lourdes Torres, eds (1991) *Third World Women and the Politics of Feminism* (Bloomington: Indiana University Press).

Moràga, Cherríe and Gloria Anzaldúa, eds (1981) *This Bridge Called My Back: Writings by Radical Women of Color* (Watertown, MA: South End Press).

Morrison, Toni, ed. (1992) *Race-ing Justice, Engendering Power: Essays on Anita Hill, Clarence Thomas, and the Construction of Social Reality* (New York: Pantheon).

Morton, Patricia (1991) *Disfigured Images: The Historical Assault on Afro-American Women* (Westport, CT: Greenwood Press).

Mosse, George (1978) *Toward The Final Solution: A History of European Racism* (London: J. M. Dent & Sons).

Munoz, Carlos (1989) *Youth, Identity, Power* (London: Verso).

Nelson, Cary (1993) "Multiculturalism Without Guarantees: From Anthologies to Social Text," *The Journal of the Midwest Modern Language Association* (Spring).

Nelson, David, George Gheverghese Joseph and Julian Williams (1993) *Multicultural Mathematics* (Oxford, New York: Oxford University Press).

Newfield, Christopher (1993) "What Was Political Correctness?" *Critical Inquiry* (Winter).

Nicholson, Linda J., ed. (1990) *Feminism/Postmodernism* (New York: Routledge).

Nieto, Sonia (1992) *Affirming Diversity: The Sociopolitical Context of Multicultural Education* (White Plains, NY: Longman).

Nordquist, Joan, comp. (1992) *The Multicultural Education Debate in the University: A Bibliography* (Santa Cruz, CA: Reference and Research Services).

Null, Gary (1975) *Black Hollywood* (Secaucus, NJ: Citadel Press).

Park, Robert E. (1950) *Race and Culture* (Glencoe, IL: The Free Press).

Peele, Gillian (1984) *Revival and Reaction: The Right in Contemporary America* (Oxford: Clarendon).

Perry, Richard J. (1992) "Why Do Multiculturalists Ignore Anthropologists?" *Chronicle of Higher Education* (March).

Piersen, William D. (1993) *Black Legacy: America's Hidden Heritage* (Amherst: University of Massachusetts Press).

Pieterse, Jan Nederveen (1992) *White on Black: Images of Africa and Blacks in Western Popular Culture* (New Haven: Yale University Press).

Pinkney, Tony, ed. (1989) *The Politics of Modernism: Against the New Conformists* (London: Verso).

Poster, Mark (1992) "Postmodernity and the Politics of Multiculturalism: The Lyotard-Habermas Debate Over Social Theory," *Modern Fiction Studies* (Fall).

Ravitch, Diane (1990) "Diversity and Democracy: Multicultural Education in America," *American Educator* (Spring).

Ravitch, Diane (1990) "Multiculturalism; E. Pluribus Plures," *The American Scholar* (Summer).

Raz, Joseph (1994) "Multiculturalism: A Liberal Perspective," *Dissent* (Winter).

Redlawsk, David P. (1993) "An Attempt to Find Middle Ground: The Controversy over Multiculturalism at Duke University." Paper presented at the Law and Society Association Meeting, Chicago.

Rendon, Armando (1972) *The Chicano Manifesto* (New York: MacMillan).

Robbins, Bruce (1991) "Othering the Academy: Professionalism and Multiculturalism," *Social Research* (Summer).

Roberts, John W. (1989) *From Trickster to Badman* (Philadelphia: University of Pennsylvania Press).

Rooney, Ellen (1990) "Discipline and Vanish: Feminism, the Resistance to Theory, and the Politics of Cultural Studies," *differences: A Journal of Feminist Cultural Studies*, 2.

Rorty, Amelie Oksenberg (1994) "The Hidden Politics of Cultural Identification," *Political Theory*, 22, 1 (February).

Rosaldo, Renato (1989) *Culture and Truth: The Remaking of Social Analysis* (Boston: Beacon).

Rose, Tricia (1994) *Black Noise: Rap Music and Black Culture in Contemporary American Popular Culture* (Middletown, CT: Wesleyan University Press).

Roseberry, William (1992) "Multiculturalism and the Challenge of Anthropology," *Social Research* (Winter).

Ross, Andrew, ed. (1988) *Universal Abandon? The Politics of Postmodernism* (Minneapolis: University of Minnesota Press, 1988),

Rutherford, Jonathan, ed. (1990) *Identity: Community, Culture, Difference* (London: Lawrence and Wishart).

Ryan, John Paul (1975) *Cultural Diversity and the American Experience: Political Participation Among Blacks, Appalachians, and Indians* (Beverly Hills, CA: Sage Publications).

Sahlins, Marshall (1993) "Goodbye to Tristes Tropes: Ethnography in the Context of Modern World History," *The University of Chicago Record,* 27, 3.

Said, Edward (1993) *Culture and Imperialism* (London: Chatto and Windus).

Samuels, David (1991) "The Rap on Rap," *The New Republic* (November 11).

San Juan, E. Jr (1991) "Multiculturalism vs. Hegemony: Ethnic Studies, Asian Americans, and US Racial Politics," *The Massachusetts Review* (Fall).

San Juan, E. Jr (1992) *Racial Formations/Critical Transformations: Articulations of Power in Ethnic and Racial Studies in the United States* (Atlantic Highlands, NJ: Humanities Press).

Sawchuck, Mariette T., ed. (1993) *Infusing Multicultural Perspectives Across the Curriculum* (Los Angeles, CA: Prism Publishing of Mount St Mary's College).

Schlesinger, Arthur Jr (1992) *The Disuniting of America* (Knoxville, TN: Whittle District Books).

Scott, Joan (1992) "Experience," in *Feminists Theorize the Political,* eds Judith Butler and Joan W. Scott (New York: Routledge).

Scott, Joan (1992) "Multiculturalism and the Politics of Identity," *October,* 61 (Summer).

Searle, John (1990) "The Storm over the University," *New York Review of Books* (December 6).

Shaw, Peter (1986) "Decloning Discourse," *Society,* 23, 3 (March–April).

Shohat, Ella (1992) "Notes on the 'Post-Colonial'," *Social Text,* 31.

Short, Thomas (1988) "A 'New Racism' on Campus?" *Commentary,* 86, 2 (August).

Siegel, Fred (1991) "The Cult of Multiculturalism," *New Republic* (February 18).

Siegel, Fred (1992) "Multiculturalism and Other Mistakes," *De Paul Law Review* (Summer).

Sierra, Judy and Roger Kaminski with selected translations by Adela Artola Allen (1991) *Multicultural Folktales: Stories to Tell Young Children* (Phoenix, AZ: Oryx Press).

Simon, Roger I. (1992) *Teaching Against the Grain* (New York: Bergin and Garvey Press).

Simone, Timothy Maliqualim (1989) *About Face: Race in Postmodern America* (Brooklyn, NY: Autonomedia).

Smedley, Audrey (1993) *Race in North America* (Boulder: Westview Press).

Smith, Page (1990) *Killing the Spirit: Higher Education in America* (New York: Viking).

Snow, C. P. (1959) *The Two Cultures and the Scientific Revolution* (Cambridge: The University Press).

Snowden, Frank (1971) *Blacks in Antiquity* (Cambridge: Harvard University).

Social Text (1993) "A Symposium on Popular Culture and Political Correctness," *Social Text,* 36.

Solomon, Robert and Jon Solomon (1993) *Up the University: Re-Creating Higher Education in America* (Reading, MA: Addison Wesley).

Spencer, Michael (1993) "Trends of Opposition to Multiculturalism," *The Black Scholar* (Winter).

Spivak, Gayatri Chakravorty (1988) "Subaltern Studies: Deconstructing Historiography," in *Selected Subaltern Studies,* eds Ranajit Guha and Gayatri Chakravorty Spivak (New York: Oxford University Press).

Spivak, Gayatri Chakravorty (1992) "Acting Bits/Identity Talk," *Critical Inquiry* (Summer).

Spivak, Gayatri Chakravorty and Sneja Gunew (1993), "Questions of Multiculturalism," in *The Cultural Studies Reader,* ed. Simon During (London: Routledge).

Stam, Robert and Ella Shohat (1994) *Unthinking Eurocentrism: Multiculturalism and the Media* (Routledge).

Sullivan, Andrew (1990) "Racism 101," *New Republic,* 18 (November 26).

Sykes, Charles (1988) *Profscam: Professors and the Demise of Higher Education* (Washington, DC: Regnery Gateway).

Sykes, Charles (1990) *The Hollow Men: Politics and Corruption in Higher Education* (Washington, DC: Regnery Gateway).

Takaki, Ronald, ed. (1989) *From Different Shores* (Oxford: Oxford University Press)

Takaki, Ronald (1991) "The Value of Multiculturalism," *Liberal Education* (May).

Takaki, Ronald (1993) "Multiculturalism: Battleground or Meeting Ground?" *Annals of the American Academy of Political and Social Science* (November).

Takaki, Ronald T. (1993) *A Different Mirror: A History of Multicultural America* (Boston: Little, Brown & Co.).

Taussig, Michael (1987) *Shamanism, Colonialism and the Wild Man* (Chicago: University of Chicago Press).

Taylor, Charles (1989) *Sources of the Self* (Cambridge: Harvard University Press).

Todorov, Tzvetan (1984) *The Conquest of America* (New York: Harper Colophon).

Todorov, Tzvetan (1992) *On Human Diversity* (Cambridge: Harvard University Press).

Trager, Oliver, ed. (1992) *America's Minorities and the Multicultural Debate* (New York: Facts on File).

Trilling, Lionel (1969) *Sincerity and Authenticity* (New York: W. W. Norton).

Trinh T. Minh-Ha (1989) *Woman Native Other* (Bloomington: Indiana University Press).

University of Illinois (1992) *Symposium on Race Consciousness and Legal Scholarship: Hate Speech and Political Correctness* (Urbana: University of Illinois Law).

Walker, Samuel (1994) *Hate Speech: The History of an American Controversy* (Lincoln: University of Nebraska Press).

Wallace, Michele (1991) "Multiculturalism and Oppositionality," *Afterimage* (October).

Wallerstein, Immanuel (1991) *Geopolitics and Geoculture: Essays on the Changing World-System* (Cambridge: Cambridge University Press).

Walzer, Michael (1992) *What It Means To Be an American* (New York: Marsilio).

Walzer, Michael (1994) "Multiculturalism and Individualism," *Dissent* (Spring).

West, Cornel (1988) "Colloquy: CLS and a Liberal Critic," *Yale Law Journal,* 97.

West, Cornel (1992) "On Afro-American Popular Music: From Bebop to Rap," *Black Sacred Music,* 6, 1 (Spring).

West, Cornel (1993) *Beyond Eurocentrism and Multiculturalism* (Monroe, ME: Common Courage Press).

West, Cornel (1993) *Prophetic Reflections: Notes on Race and Power in America* (Monroe, ME: Common Courage Press).

West, Cornel (1993) *Race Matters* (Boston: Beacon Press).

Williams, Patricia J. (1991) *The Alchemy of Race and Rights* (Cambridge: Harvard University Press).

Williams, Walter E. (1989) "Race, Scholarship, and Affirmative Action," *National Review* (May 5).

Yates, Steven (1992) "Multiculturalism and Epistemology," *Public Affairs Quarterly*, 6, 4 (October).

Young, Iris (1990) *Justice and the Politics of Difference* (Princeton: Princeton University Press).

Yúdice, George, Jean Franco, and Juan Flores, eds (1992) *On Edge* (Minneapolis: University of Minnesota Press).

Index